VARIORUM COLLECTED STUDIES SERIES

Papal Reform and Canon Law in the 11th and 12th Centuries

Professor Uta-Renate Blumenthal

Uta-Renate Blumenthal

———

Papal Reform and
Canon Law in the
11th and 12th Centuries

———

Ashgate

VARIORUM

Aldershot · Brookfield USA · Singapore · Sydney

Published in the Variorum Collected Studies Series by

Ashgate Publishing Limited
Gower House, Croft Road,
Aldershot, Hampshire GU11 3HR
Great Britain

Ashgate Publishing Company
Old Post Road,
Brookfield, Vermont 05036–9704
USA

ISBN 0–86078–695–1

British Library CIP Data
Blumenthal, Uta-Renate
    Papal Reform and Canon Law in the 11th and 12th Centuries.
    (Variorum Collected Studies Series: CS618).
    1. Catholic Church – Government. 2. Canon Law – History. 3. Church History –
    11th Century. 4. Church History – 12th Century. I. Title.
    262.9'22

US Library of Congress CIP Data
Blumenthal, Uta-Renate
    Papal Reform and Canon Law in the 11th and 12th Centuries / Uta-Renate Blumenthal
        p.   cm. – (Variorum Collected Studies Series CS618)
    1. Papacy – History – to 1309. 2. Canon Law – History. 3. Europe – Church History –
    600–1500. I. Title II. Series: Variorum Colected Studies Series.
    BX1178.B58   1998   98–24267
    262'.13'09021 – dc21   CIP

The paper used in this publication meets the minimum requirements of the American National
    Standard for Information Sciences – Permanence of Paper for Printed Library Materials,
    ANSI Z39.48–1984. ∞   ™

Printed by Galliard (Printers) Ltd, Great Yarmouth, Norfolk, Great Britain

VARIORUM COLLECTED STUDIES SERIES CS618

CONTENTS

This volume contains xii + 334 pages

ACKNOWLEDGEMENTS

Grateful acknowledgment is made to the following persons, journals, institutions and publishers for their permission to reproduce the articles included in this volume: Professor Dr Rudolf Schieffer on behalf of *Monumenta Germaniae Historica*, Munich (I, IV); Professor Dr Peter Landau on behalf of the Leopold Wenger Institut, Munich (II, VII, XV, XVI); Rev. Professor Charles J. Ermatinger, S.J. on behalf of the Vatican Film Library, St Louis (III); Jan Thorbecke Verlag GmbH & Co, Sigmaringen (V); Rev. Msgr. Robert Trisco on behalf of *The Catholic Historical Review*, Washington DC (VI); FR Guiseppe Zuchelli on behalf of *Libreria Ateneo Salesiano*, Rome (VIII, XVIII); Professor Robert Somerville, New York (IX); Dr Johannes Grohe on behalf of *Annuarium Historicae Conciliorum*, Augsburg (X); the Rev. Professor Paulius Rabikauskas, S.J. on behalf of Archivum Historiae Pontificiae, Rome (XI, XVII); Professor Dr Arnold Esch on behalf of the Istituto Storico Germanico, Rome (XIII); and the Center of Medieval and Early Renaissance Studies, Binghamton, NY (XIV).

PREFACE

In memoriam Gérard Fransen

Colleagues, friends and students have asked me repeatedly to collect my papers to make them more accessible, and in particular, so as to keep them all together. I have always felt very flattered, of course, but have only now, when I find myself still trying to understand the institutional and intellectual history of the eleventh and twelfth centuries, come to see that a volume of my papers would make a lot of sense. The articles which I assembled reflect that side of my research which is best described as 'work in progress', for they are indeed stepping stones to a larger whole. They deepen the perspectives which I laid out in my books, *The Early Councils of Pope Paschal II: 1100–1110* and *The Investiture Controversy: Church and Monarchy from the Ninth to the Twelfth Century* (1988, first published in German in 1982).

I dedicate the collection to the Rev. Gérard Fransen whose kindness and generosity to a beginner I will always remember with deep gratitude.

Washington DC,   UTA-RENATE BLUMENTHAL
February 2 1998

PUBLISHER'S NOTE

Ein neuer Text für das Reimser Konzil Leos IX. (1049)?

Die engen Beziehungen zwischen Leo IX. und der Kirchenreform des 11. Jahrhunderts sind oft hervorgehoben und zuweilen bezweifelt worden[1]). Eine Handschrift der Biblioteca Apostolica Vaticana, der Codex Reginensis lat. 711/II[2]), enthält einen bisher unbekannten Text, der mit hoher Wahrscheinlichkeit Leo IX. zugeschrieben werden kann und die spärliche Überlieferung für die Konzilien dieses Papstes bereichert.

Reg. lat. 711/II ist eine Sammelhandschrift, in der Teile von acht Manuskripten zusammengebunden worden sind, die wahrscheinlich alle aus

---

[1]) Über Leo IX. vgl. die Literaturangaben im Lex. f. Theol. u. Kirche 6 [2](1961) S. 949 f. (B. S u t t e r) und R. B l o c h, Die Klosterpolitik Leos IX. in Deutschland, Burgund und Italien, AUF 11 (1930) S. 176 ff.; für ältere Literatur ist immer noch wichtig C. J. H e f e l e — H. L e c l e r c q, Histoire des Conciles 4,2 (1911) S. 995 ff. In der Sekundärliteratur wurde der Einfluß Leos IX. besonders von A. F l i c h e, La réforme grégorienne 1 (1924) S. 129 ff. hervorgehoben. Dieses Bild, das sich einige Abstriche hat gefallen lassen müssen, hat grundsätzlich auch heute noch Gültigkeit. Kritischer über den Pontifikat Leos IX. äußerten sich P. S c h m i d, Der Begriff der kanonischen Wahl in den Anfängen des Investiturstreits (1926) S. 68 ff. und J. H a l l e r, Das Papsttum. Idee und Wirklichkeit 2 [2](1951) S. 581 ff. Vgl. dazu H. H o f f m a n n, Von Cluny zum Investiturstreit, Archiv für Kulturgeschichte 45 (1963) S. 187 ff. und O. C a p i t a n i, Immunità vescovili ed ecclesiologia in età ‚pregregoriana‘ e ‚gregoriana‘. L'avvio alla ‚restaurazione‘, Biblioteca degli Studi Medievali 3 (1966) S. 149 ff. — Herrn Dr. M. Bertram und Herrn Professor Dr. H. Hoffmann sei für ihre freundliche Hilfe gedankt. Das Manuskript ist von Herrn Dr. D. Jasper für den Druck ergänzt und eingerichtet worden.

[2]) Der Codex wurde zusammen mit Reg. lat. 711/I kurz von Montfaucon unter der Nummer 173 beschrieben. (Les manuscrits de la Reine de Suède au Vatican, Réédition du Catalogue de Montfaucon et côtes actuelles [Studi e Testi 238, 1964] S. 14.) Zu Reg. lat. 711/I. vgl. ferner L. D e l i s l e, Le Chroniqueur Girard d'Auvergne ou d'Anvers, Journal des Savants (Mai 1900) S. 285—294. Reg. lat. 711/II wurde beschrieben von L. A u v r a y, Documents Parisiens (wie Anm. 11) S. 17 Anm. 1. Irrtümlicherweise spricht Auvray dort von 711 A anstelle von 711/II.

Frankreich stammen[3]). Das fünfte Fragment, fol. 63[r]—66[v] [4]), ist hier
von Interesse. Es gehörte einst der 1618 aufgehobenen Pariser Benedik-
tinerabtei von Saint-Magloire[5]). Das Schicksal ihrer Bibliothek ist in
Dunkel gehüllt. Abgesehen von den Kartularien[6]) sind nur zwei Handschriften bekannt, die früher der Abtei gehörten[7]). Eine dieser beiden
Handschriften war zeitweilig im Besitz von Paul Petau[8]), wurde dann
von Königin Christina von Schweden erworben und gelangte so in den
Fondo Reginense des Vatikans[9]). Es ist anzunehmen — obwohl es sich
nicht beweisen läßt — daß Reg. lat. 711/II auf dem gleichen Wege nach
Rom gekommen ist, denn sowohl auf fol. 1[r] als auch auf fol. 61[r] finden
sich Eintragungen von der Hand Paul Petaus[10]). Die Provenienz aus

---

[3]) Das Institut de Recherche et d'Histoire des Textes, Paris, hat entsprechendes
Material über den Codex gesammelt, das mir liebenswürdigerweise zur Ver-
fügung gestellt worden ist.

[4]) Die Blätter in Reg. lat. 711/II sind zweimal numeriert. Die Zahlen oben
rechts stammen aus der Zeit, als 711/I und 711/II noch zusammengebunden
waren und laufen für 711/II von 28—114 = fol. 1—87 der neuen Zählung.
Die von mir benutzte Numerierung steht am unteren Rand rechts.

[5]) Zur Geschichte der Abtei vgl. R. M e r l e t, Les origines du monastère de
Saint Magloire, BECh 56 (1895) S. 237—273; H. C o t t i n e a u, Répertoire
topo-bibliographique des abbayes et prieurés 2 (1939) Sp. 2214; Gallia Christiana 7 (1744) Sp. 306—328.

[6]) H. S t e i n, Bibliographie générale des cartulaires français ou relatifs à
l'histoire de France (1907) S. 395—396, nos. 2883—2886: Das große Kartular
(Paris, B. N. lat. 5413) gehörte zeitweilig Paul Petau.

[7]) L. D e l i s l e, Le Cabinet des Manuscrits de la Bibliothèque Nationale 2
(1874) S. 258 Anm. 1 und S. 407. Die Handschriften befinden sich beide in
Paris, B. N. lat. 9768 und 13 701.

[8]) Vgl. Petaus Notiz auf fol. 1[r], B. N. lat. 9768, dem berühmten Nithard-
Codex.

[9]) Vgl. K. A. d e M e y i e r, Paul en Alexandre Petau en de geschiedenis
van hun Handschriften (Dissertationen inaugurales Batavae ad res antiquas
pertinentes 5, 1947) S. 5 f. Anm. 21. Der Codex, der 1650 mit den Sammlungen
Paul und Alexander Petaus von Isaak Vossius († 1689) für Königin Christina
erworben wurde, in der Vaticana die Signatur Reg. lat. 1964 trug, wurde 1797
nach Paris gebracht und hat heute die Hss.-Nr. 9768 der B. N.; vgl. Ph. L a u e r,
Les Annales de Flodoard (Collection de textes 39, 1907) S. XXXVI ff. und
E. M ü l l e r in seiner Nithard-Ausgabe (MGH Scr. rer. Germ. [44], ³1907)
S. XI f. — Zur Bibliothek der Königin Christina vgl. die Übersicht von J. B i g -
n a m i - O d i e r, Le Fonds de la Reine à la Bibliothèque Vaticane, in: Collectanea Vaticana in honorem Anselmi M. Card. Albareda (Studi e Testi 219,
1962) S. 159 ff.

[10]) Es ließ sich nicht feststellen, auf welche Weise Paul Petau in den Besitz
der verschiedenen Handschriften von Saint-Magloire gekommen ist. Einige
Fragmente in Reg. lat. 711/II stammen aus Saint-Benoît-sur-Loire und enthalten
Notizen von der Hand des Juristen und Philologen Pierre Daniel († 1604).
L. D e l i s l e, Le Cabinet des Manuscrits de la Bibliothèque Impériale 1 (1868)
S. 287 erwähnt, daß zumindest einige von Daniels Handschriften aus dem Klo-

I

Saint-Magloire für fol. 63ʳ—66ᵛ, dem fünften Teil der Handschrift, steht jedoch fest. Nicht nur ein Ex-libris auf fol. 63ʳ bestätigen dies, sondern auch die Texte, die von verschiedenen Händen auf diesen Seiten eingetragen worden sind. Sie wurden mit einer Ausnahme von Lucien Auvray veröffentlicht[11]). Diese Ausnahme bilden zwei Kolumnen auf fol. 65ᵛ, deren Inhalt Auvray auch nicht identifizierte[12]). Der Text, von einer einzigen Hand des ausgehenden 11. oder beginnenden 12. Jahrhunderts geschrieben[13]), beginnt: *Hec est sanctorum patrum auctoritas a Leone papa corroborata.* Wie in der Textanalyse unten gezeigt werden wird, muß es sich wohl um Papst Leo IX. handeln sowie — auch das ist klar — um Sätze, die eines seiner Konzilien betreffen.

In der folgenden Edition werden aus Gründen, auf die später zurückzukommen sein wird, in parallelen Kolumnen Texte des Konzils von Reims angegeben. Diese Synode, die Papst Leo IX. vom 3.–5. Oktober 1049 gehalten hat, ist verhältnismäßig gut dokumentiert[14]). Sie wurde

ster Fleury später von Petau erworben wurden. Vgl. dazu A. V i d i e r , L'historiographie à Saint-Benoît-sur-Loire et les miracles de Saint-Benoît (1965) S. 27 ff.; E. P e l l e g r i n , Membra disiecta, BECh 107 (1947) S. 74 ff.; d i e s., Membra disiecta Floriacensia, ebenda 117 (1959) S. 5 ff.; d i e s., Essai d'identification de fragments dispersées dans des manuscrits des Bibliothèques de Berne et de Paris, Bull. d'information de l'Institut de Recherche et d'Histoire des Textes 9 (1960) S. 7 ff.; J. L a p ô t r e , Fleury, Dictionnaire d'histoire et de géographie ecclésiastiques 17 (1971) S. 473 f. — Zu P. Daniel vgl. H. H a g e n , Der Jurist und Philolog Pierre Daniel (1873) und R. d ' A m a t, Daniel, Pierre, Dictionnaire de biographie française 10 (1965) S. 115 f. Eine Vermittlerrolle Daniels bei dem Erwerb von Hss. aus Saint-Magloire durch P. Petau muß eine bloße Vermutung bleiben.

[11]) L. A u v r a y , Documents Parisiens tirés de la Bibliothèque du Vatican: VIIᵉ—XIIIᵉ siècle, Extrait des Mémoires de la Société de l'Histoire de Paris et de l'Île-de-France 19 (1892) S. 17–35.

[12]) Ebenda S. 33: „Préceptes tirés des canons de l'Église.". In der dazugehörigen Anmerkung schreibt er: „Il me parait inutile d'entrer dans le détail de cette partie du ms."

[13]) Eine zweite, etwas spätere Hand fügte am Ende von Kolumne b hinzu: *In nomine sanctae et individuae trinitatis in Monte Celio ubi requiescunt sancti septem dormientes, id est Malcus, Maximianus, Martinianus, Dionisius, Johannes, Serapion et Constantinus quorum meritis et precibus requiescat et dormiat iste dei famulus vel famula.* Die beiden letzten Worte wurden über der Zeile nachgetragen. Die Geschichte der Sieben Schläfer von Ephesus war nicht nur in Byzanz, sondern auch in Frankreich durch Gregor von Tours weit verbreitet, vgl. H. L e c l e r c q , Dictionnaire d'archéologie chrétienne et de liturgie 15,1 (1950) Sp. 1254.

[14]) Die Quellen sind zusammengestellt bei G. D. M a n s i , Sacrorum conciliorum nova et amplissima collectio 19 (1774) Sp. 727—750. Die bekannten Daten über das Konzil wurden zuletzt kurz zusammengefaßt von S. G i e t , Le concile de Reims de 1049, Mémoires de la Société d'agriculture, commerce, sciences et arts du département de la Marne 85 (1960) S. 31—36.

26

in Verbindung mit Leos Weihe der neuen Basilika von Saint-Rémi abgehalten, und als der Reimser Abt einige Jahre später [15]) einen seiner Mönche beauftragte, die Historia dedicationis S. Remigii [16]) zu schreiben, wurde auch das Konzil nicht vergessen. Der Autor wird seit 1679, dem Erscheinungsjahr des zweiten Bandes von Guillaume Marlots Metropolis Remensis historia, mit einem gewissen Anselm identifiziert, der in Sigeberts Liber de viris illustribus einen Platz gefunden hat [17]). Es gibt Gründe, die gegen diese Annahme sprechen [18]), und vielleicht hatte

---

15) Wie der Prolog der Historia dedicationis zeigt, entstand das Werk nach dem Tode Leos IX. (1054): ... *ex imperio domini abbatis Herimari seriem dedicationis hujus sanctissimi patris ecclesiae silentio non patiar oblitterari. Sed quoniam a beatae recordationis Papa nono Leone, Deo auctore, facta est, eo magis dignam litteris tradam pro modulo ingenioli mei* ... (Historia dedicationis [wie Anm. 16] S. 713) sowie nach dem Amtsantritt von Erzbischof Gervasius von Reims (1055—1067), S. 724.

16) C. B a r o n i o, Annales Ecclesiastici 11 (1605) S. 806—818, veröffentlichte als erster ausführliche Auszüge aus der Historia dedicationis als Itinerarium papae Leonis IX a. 1049 in Galliam. Unabhängig von Baronio publizierte G. M a r l o t Auszüge in seiner Metropolis Remensis historia sive supplementum Frodoardi 2 (1679) S. 88—104. Die einzige vollständige Ausgabe ist die J. M a b i l l o n s, die hier zitiert wird: Historia dedicationis ecclesiae S. Remigii apud Remos, Acta Sanctorum O. S. B. 6,1 (1701) S. 711—727. Die folgenden späteren Teileditionen beruhen auf Mabillons Ausgabe, vgl. Repertorium Fontium Historiae Medii Aevi 2 (1967) S. 369 s. v. Anselmus monachus S. Remigii Remensis, wo jedoch keine Handschriften angegeben werden. Zwei Handschriften sind bekannt, beide in der Bibliothèque municipale von Reims: Hs. 1417 (K. 790), s. XII ex. aus der Abtei Saint Nicaise (Reims) und Hs. 1418 (K. 791) s. XV aus der Kapitelbücherei der Kathedrale und wahrscheinlich eine Abschrift von Nr. 1417. (Catalogue Général des Manuscrits des Bibliothèques Publiques de France, Départements 39, 1904 S. 656 ff. und S. 659 ff.). Die Histoire Littéraire de France 7 (1746) S. 477 ff. erwähnt ein Manuskript in Tours. Es wird jedoch im Catalogue Général 37 (1900) nicht verzeichnet und war auch L. D e l i s l e nicht bekannt (Notice sur les manuscrits disparus de la Bibliothèque de Tours pendant la première moitié du XIXe siècle, in: Notices et Extraits des Manuscrits 31 [1884] S. 157 ff.). Die Behauptung J. L o s e r t h s, Zu Pseudo-Udalricus' ‚De Continentia Clericorum' und zu Bruno's von Segni ‚De Symoniacis', NA 20 (1895) S. 449, daß sich der Text der Reimser Synode (M i g n e, PL 142, 1403 = M a b i l l o n cap. 14, S. 720) unter den Eintragungen auf fol. 131r—136r im Codex Universitätsbibliothek Graz 1242 (s. XII in.) findet, beruht auf einem Irrtum.

17) R. W i t t e, Catalogus Sigeberti Gemblacensis monachi de viris illustribus. Kritische Ausgabe (Lateinische Sprache und Literatur des MA 1, 1974) § 153 S. 95 f. und S. 144.

18) Sigeberts Notiz hat inhaltlich sehr wenig mit der Historia dedicationis gemeinsam: *Anselmus Remensis monachus scripsit itinerarium noni Leonis pape a Roma in Gallias ob hoc maxime, ut notificaret, quanta auctoritate Remis vel in aliis urbibus synodum celebraverit, quanta iustitia et subtilitate examinaverit causas ecclesiasticas, qua discretione peccantes correxerit, quomodo ei virtus Dei cooperata sit. Quod satis patuit in una causa Remensis synodi ubi dum epis-*

Cesare Baronio recht, wenn er meinte, daß außer der dann anonymen Historia dedicationis ein Traktat dieses Anselm existierte, der Itinerarium genannt war[19]. Die Historia dedicationis, ob nun von Anselm oder einem anderen Reimser Mönch geschrieben, vermittelt wertvolle und zum Teil sogar sehr ausführliche Nachrichten über Leos Konzil. Insbesondere enthält der Bericht eine Zusammenfassung von 12 oder 13 Canones[20]. Nur weniges ist über päpstliche Konziliengesetzgebung dieser Zeit bekannt, aber aufgrund von Robert Somervilles Untersuchungen[21] läßt sich immerhin sagen, daß es sich bei den Canones der Historia wohl

---

copus Frisigensis contumaciter ageret contra apostolicam auctoritatem, repente in oculis omnium obmutuit. Bischof Nizo von Freising, der mit dieser Bemerkung gemeint sein muß, wird nirgends als Teilnehmer an der Reimser Synode erwähnt. Die Historia berichtet zwar ein solches Wunder, aber bezieht es auf Erzbischof Hugo von Besançon (Historia S. 722); vgl. in diesem Zusammenhang G. D r i o u x , Un diocèse de France à la veille de la réforme Grégorienne, Studi Gregoriani 2 (1947) S. 31—41. Außerdem ist es bemerkenswert, daß Sigebert das Hauptanliegen der Historia, die Weihe der neuen Basilika, überhaupt nicht erwähnt. Über Anselm vgl. Repertorium (wie oben Anm. 16) S. 369 und P. F o u r n i e r , Dictionnaire d'histoire et de géographie ecclésiastiques 3 (1924) S. 454—455. Johannes T r i t h e m i u s , De scriptoribus ecclesiasticis (hg. von F a b r i c i u s , Bibliotheca Ecclesiastica, cap. 333, S. 85) schmückte Sigeberts Notiz weiter aus: *Anselmus ... vir in scripturis divinis exercitatum habens ingenium, scripsit quaedam ... opuscula, quae ad manus nostras adhuc minime venerunt.* Diese Bemerkung des Abtes von Sponheim veranlaßte die Herausgeber der Histoire Littéraire de France nach weiteren Werken zu suchen, die Anselm zugeschrieben werden könnten, so zum Beispiel ein anonymer Brief an die Mönche von Montecassino über die Reliquien des Hl. Benedikt (Histoire Littéraire de France 7 [1746] S. 478). Sie hat aber, wie K. A r n o l d zeigt, nur rhetorischen Wert. (Johannes Trithemius: 1462—1516 [Quellen und Forschungen zur Geschichte des Bistums und Hochstifts Würzburg 23, 1971] S. 125).

[19] C. B a r o n i o , Annales 11, S. 806; vgl. auch A. P a g i , Annales ecclesiastici auctore Caesare Baronio ... una cum critica historico-chronologica 17 (1745) S. 27 ff. Anm.

[20] Der zweite Canon von Reims wurde von G. M a r l o t , (wie Anm. 16) S. 101 f. unterteilt, so daß sich in seiner Ausgabe die Gesamtzahl der Canones auf 13 erhöht. Alle anderen Ausgaben zählen 12 Canones in Übereinstimmung mit der Ausgabe von Mabillon. Wenn weiter unten in der Edition des Textes der Hs. Reg. lat. 711/II als c. 13 und c. 14 zwei Sätze herangezogen werden, die in Mabillons Ausgabe den Canones von Reims direkt folgen, aber verständlicherweise nicht als Canones abgesetzt wurden, so geschieht das nur, um den Vergleich zu erleichtern.

[21] R. S o m e r v i l l e , The Councils of Urban II, 1: Decreta Claromontensia (Annuarium Historiae Conciliorum, Supplementum Nr. 1, 1972) S. 20—40. Sehr wichtig sind die Untersuchungen von Ch. R. C h e n e y , obwohl sie sich nicht mit päpstlichen Konzilien befassen: Textual Problems of the English Provincial Canons, in: La Critica del Testo 1 (Atti del 2° Congresso internazionale della Società Italiana di Storia del Diritto [1971], S. 165—188) (Nachdruck in dessen Medieval Texts and Studies [1973] S. 111—137).

I

28

um breviaria handeln dürfte, die von einem Augenzeugen des Konzils gemacht wurden. Die Ähnlichkeit zwischen den Canones und den Tagesordnungsvorschlägen des päpstlichen Sprechers in Reims, dem römischen Diakon Peter, die auch in der Historia dedicationis überliefert sind, ist Bürge für ihre Authentizität [22]).

Die Sigle für Reg. lat. 711/II ist im folgenden V, die für die Canones der Historia dedicationis H und für die Tagesordnungsvorschläge des Diakons Peter P. Die Reihenfolge des Materials H und P wurde V angepaßt, doch wird die ursprüngliche Anordnung, wie sie in Mabillons Ausgabe vorliegt, am Ende eines jeden Canons in Klammern angegeben [23]). Die Canones in V sind nicht numeriert. Da die Handschrift jedoch Absatzzeichen und große Anfangsbuchstaben aufweist, folgt die Unterteilung des Textes weitgehend der Handschrift. Auch die Schreibweise von V wurde mit Ausnahme von offensichtlichen orthographischen Fehlern beibehalten. Die selten auftretende littera e-caudata wird als ae übertragen. Fol. 65ᵛ ist am unteren linken Rand leicht beschädigt.

Die Verifizierung der Vorlagen hatte ihre Schwierigkeiten. Da wir in V offensichtlich nicht den präzisen offiziellen Text vor uns haben, war es nicht möglich, durch das Aufspüren von wörtlichen Übereinstimmungen direkte Vorlagen zu bestimmen. Es mußte genügen, auf einige Beispiele thematischer Übereinstimmung hinzuweisen. Mit Ausnahme der alten ökumenischen Konzilien, denen Papst Leo IX. sowohl auf dem römischen als auch auf dem Reimser Konzil von 1049 besondere Beachtung schenkte [24]), werden in den Anmerkungen im allgemeinen nur Konzilien aus dem späten 10. und der ersten Hälfte des 11. Jahrhunderts zitiert. Die Canones in V zeigen mit diesen Konzilien weitaus mehr Ähnlichkeit als mit kanonistischen Texten, die hauptsächlich durch die Libri duo de synodalibus causis des Regino von Prüm und das Dekret Burchards von Worms vertreten sind [25]).

---

[22]) O. Capitani, (wie Anm. 1) S. 164 ff., spricht von „cosidetti canones" und meint, daß sie dem Autor der Historia zuzuschreiben seien, weil sie auffallende Ähnlichkeit mit den Vorschlägen des Diakons Peter hätten. Diese Annahme ist ungerechtfertigt (vgl. Somerville, Decreta Claromontensia S. 20 ff.), obwohl kein Zweifel besteht, daß die Historia nicht die offizielle Fassung der Canones enthält. Vgl. Giet (wie Anm. 14) S. 36. — Zum Diakon Peter vgl. Wattenbach-Holtzmann, S. 189.
[23]) S. o. Anm. 20.
[24]) S. u. Anm. 52.
[25]) Regino, hg. von F. G. A. Wasserschleben (1840), und Burchard von Worms in Migne, PL 140, 537 ff.

V	H	P
Hec est sanctorum patrum auctoritas a Leone papa corroborata.	… multa quae in Gallicana ecclesia exercebantur illicita ne fierent ulterius sub anathemate prohibuit, videlicet	Quibus ita residentibus imperato silentio ex praecepto domini papae surrexit Petrus S. Romanae ecclesiae diaconus expedito sermone proponens de quibus in eadem synodo sermo esset habendus, de multis scilicet inlicitis quae contra canonum statuta in Gallicis finibus exercebantur, id est …
1) Primum ut episcopi et alii ordines, qui per simoniacam eresim intraverunt in aecclesiam, se emendent et amodo non faciant[26].	Ne quis sacros ordines aut ministeria ecclesiastica, vel altaria emeret aut venderet; et si quis clericorum quidlibet eorum emisset, id cum digna satisfactione suo episcopo redderet. (c. 2)	de simoniaca heresi; (c. 1)
2) Clerici arma non ferant[27].	Ne quis clericorum arma gestaret aut mundanae militiae deserviret. (c. 6)	item de clericis mundiali militiae studentibus; (c. 6)

---

[26]) Vgl. Chalcedon, c. 2 (Conciliorum Oecumenicorum Decreta, ed. J. A l b e r i g o u. a. [³1973] S. 87 f.) und die Canones Apostolorum c. 30 (C.H. T u r n e r , Ecclesiae Occidentalis Monumenta Iuris Antiquissima 1,1 [1899] S. 20). Beide wurden zitiert bei Regino 1.236 f.; Chalcedon, c. 2 bei Burchard 1.112. Vgl. auch das Konzil von Ravenna, 997, c. 3 (M a n s i 19, 220—221) und das römische Konzil von 983 (M a n s i 19, 77—79) sowie Burchard 1.21 und 3.110.

[27]) Vgl. Regino 1.176 und Burchard 2.212 mit 8.4 und dazu F. P r i n z , Klerus und Krieg im früheren Mittelalter (Monographien zur Geschichte des Mittelalters 2, 1971) S. 29 Anm. 93 sowie das erste Gottesfriedenskonzil, Le Puy, 994 (M a n s i 19, 271) vgl. H. H o f f m a n n , Gottesfriede und Treuga Dei (Schriften der MGH 20, 1964) S. 16 ff.

3) Ut clerici ad clericatum et monachi ad monachicam vitam redeant[28]).	Ne quis monachus vel clericus a suo gradu apostataret. (c. 8)	de monachis et clericis a sancto proposito et habitu recedentibus; (c. 5)
4) Laici altaria et queque ad altaria pertinent dimittant; hoc est: tertiam partem annonae[29]), oblationes, sepulturam, atrium[30]) et censum, nec ullam consuetudinem in atrio accipiant propter hoc quod difinitum est[31]).	Vgl. c. 5	de pravis consuetudinibus, quae ab eis in atriis ecclesiarum accipiebantur; (c. 3)
5) Ministerium aecclesiae vel atrii laici non habeant[32]).	Ne quis laicorum ecclesiasticum ministerium vel altaria teneret nec episcoporum quilibet consentirent. (c. 3)	de ministeriis ecclesiasticis et altaribus quae a laicis tenebantur; (c. 2)

---

[28]) Vgl. Nicaea, c. 12 und Chalcedon, c. 7 (A l b e r i g o , Decreta, S. 11 f. und S. 90); Arles II, c. 25 (Concilia Galliae, ed. C. M u n i e r [Corpus Christianorum, Series Latina 148, 1963] S. 119); Angers, c. 7 (ebenda S. 138); Burchard 19.67; vgl. ferner Regino 1.318 und Burchard 19.66; Bourges, c. 23 und 24 (M a n s i 19, 505—506 und H o f f m a n n , Gottesfriede, S. 35—36 sowie u. S. 40 ff.).

[29]) Zur Dreiteilung des Zehnten in Spanien und im südlichen Gallien vgl. U. S t u t z , Geschichte des kirchlichen Benefizialwesens, 1,1 (1893) S. 241 und G. C o n s t a b l e , Monastic Tithes from their Origins to the Twelfth Century (1964) S. 54 ff.

[30]) Zur Bedeutung von *atrium* vgl. J. B a l o n , Grand Dictionnaire de Droit du Moyen Age 5 (1973) S. 848.

[31]) Zu dem Canon im ganzen vgl. U. S t u t z (wie Anm. 29) S. 267 Anm. 23 und G. C o n s t a b l e (wie Anm. 29) S. 63 ff.

[32]) Vgl. Regino 1.121; 200; Burchard 3.214; 5.30; 8.87; 15.12 und 43.

6) Clericum nec monachum nec monacham nec laicam feminam seu eos qui cum eis erunt non accipiant nec ea que sua sunt tollant[33]).

Ne quis pauperes homines rapinis vel captionibus vexaret. (c. 10)

de rapinis pauperumque iniustis captionibus; (c. 7)

7) Corpus domini non venundetur.

Vgl. den folgenden Kanon

8) Sacerdotes pro visitatione infirmi ac pro sepultura mortui sive pro confessione peccatoris nichil nisi ad voluntatem hominis requirant[34]).

Ne quis pro sepultura vel baptismo sive pro eucharistia aut infirmorum visitatione quidquam exigeret. (c. 5)

9) Laici uxores suas non dimittant nec alias accipiant neque iuxta suas adulterium faciant; quod si fecerint ad primitivas redeant et de facto peniteant[35]).

Ne quis legitima uxore derelicta aliam duceret. (c. 12)

de incestis coniugiis et eis, qui legitimas relinquentes uxores adulterinis iterum nuptiis implicabantur; (c. 4)

10) Consanguinei consanguineas aut uxores consanguineorum non acci-

Ne quis incestuosae conjunctioni se copularet. (c. 11)

Vgl. c. 9

---

[33]) Vgl. c. 21.
[34]) Vgl. neben Regino 1.75; 122—124; Burchard 4.77; 110. die Konzilien von Le Puy (994) (M a n s i 19, 272), Poitiers (ca. 1000—1014) c. 2 (M a n s i 19, 267), und Tribur (1036) c. 4 und 5 (MGH Const. 1, S. 89).
[35]) Vgl. Regino 2.75; 99 f.; 103; Burchard 9.15; 17; 72 und das Gottesfriedenskonzil von Elne, 1027 (M a n s i 19, 483).

piant et, qui in
consanguinitate
iacent, resipiscant
et peniteant [36]).

11) Sodomitica luxu-   Pari modo (d. h. mit   de sodomitico vitio;
ria remaneat om-   der   Exkommunika-   (c. 8)
nino [37]).   tion) damnavit et so-
   domitas.
   (c. 14)

12) Praedam penitus
non faciant; qui
vero fecerint et
non resipuerint,
a communione to-
tius christianitatis
in vita et morte
alieni fiant [38]).

13) Si autem [39]) prae-
dator ad eccle-
siam confugerit
ubi consecutus
fuerit, presbiter si
adfuerit [39]) eum
cum praeda red-
dat. Si [39]) vero
abfuerit presbiter
ipse consecutor
eum et quod se-
cum habuerit ac-
cipiat (s. u. S. 46).

14) Terras sanctuarii
laicus invadere

---

[36]) Vgl. Regino 2.263; Burchard 7.2 und Elne, 1027 (M a n s i 19, 483).
[37]) Vgl. Regino 2.255.
[38]) Vgl. Le Puy, 994 (M a n s i 19, 272) und das Konzil von Bourges, 1031
(M a n s i 19, 549).
[39]) Das Wort ist wegen Beschädigung des unteren linken Randes von fol. 65[v]
nur teilweise zu lesen.

non praesumat nec novas consuetudines adcrescat [40]).

15) Heretici nullam communionem cum christianis habeant [41]).

Et quia novi haeretici in Gallicanis partibus emerserant, eos excommunicavit, illis additis qui ab eis aliquod munus vel servitium acciperent, aut quodlibet defensionis patrocinium illis impenderent. (c. 13)

et [de] quibusdam haeresibus quae in eisdem pullulaverant partibus. (c. 9)

16) Si aliqua querimonia inter homines exhorta fuerit, ante episcopum veniant et capitale si fuerit aut fundum terrae reddant; sin autem ante archiepiscopum, quod si noluerint itidem sicut alii, ab omni christianitate priventur, et episcopi litteras suas papae mittant [42]).

---

[40]) Vgl. Le Puy, 994 (M a n s i 19, 271 f.).
[41]) Vgl. Regino 2.397 und App. III, 66; Burchard 11.31.
[42]) S. u. S. 45.

17) Usuram nemo clericus vel laicus accipiat [43]).

Ne quis clericus vel laicus usuras exerceret.
(c. 7)

18) Qui vuadimonia tenent, tam diu teneant quousque capitalia habeant et capitalibus acceptis vuadimonia dimittant et amplius non accipiant. Si autem ex hoc neglegens aliquis extiterit, in excommunicatione erit [44]).

19) Christiane femine iudeorum in-

---

[43]) Vgl. Nicaea, c. 17 (A l b e r i g o , Decreta, S. 14) und die Canones Apostolorum c. 44 (ed. T u r n e r , S. 29 f.) sowie Burchard 2.125 und Atto von Vercelli, Collectio Canonum, c. 49 (M a n s i 18, 253). F. S c h a u b , Der Kampf gegen den Zinswucher, ungerechten Preis und unlauteren Handel im Mittelalter (1905) S. 27—28. Anm. 4 erläutert die Textgeschichte dieses Canons und seine Aufnahme in verschiedene Canonessammlungen.

[44]) Vgl. S c h a u b , Zinswucher, S. 45. Der Liber Tarraconensis enthält eine Serie von Bestimmungen, die der Gregorianischen Reform zugeordnet werden können und nach Fournier aus dem Zentrum oder dem Südwesten Frankreichs stammen (P. F o u r n i e r , Le Liber Tarraconensis, in: Mélanges Julien Havet [1895] S. 259 ff., 275 ff. und besonders S. 276). Einer der Canones, die in der Handschrift des Liber Tarraconensis, Vat. lat. 6093 (12. Jh., fol. 49ᵛ—51ʳ) Papst Gregor VII. zugeschrieben werden, beschäftigt sich mit Wucher in einer Weise, die an Leos Dekret erinnert: *Usurarii et qui tenent pignus, postquam inde habent, quod praestaverunt, excommunicentur.* Die Canones wurden zuerst von W. G i e s e b r e c h t , Die Gesetzgebung der römischen Kirche zur Zeit Gregors VII, Münchner Historisches Jahrbuch 1866,S. 188 ff. und später von J. v o n P f l u g k - H a r t t u n g , Acta Pontificum Romanorum Inedita 2 (1884) S. 126 aus einer Abschrift der Correctores Romani im Codex der Biblioteca Vallicelliana C. 24 veröffentlicht. Fournier zeigte, daß die Zuweisung der Canones an Gregor VII. abzulehnen ist. (Liber Tarraconensis, S. 276 f.). Über die Hs. Vall. C. 24 zuletzt L. G a s p a r r i , Osservazioni sul codice Vallicelliano C. 24, Studi Gregoriani 9 (1972) S. 469 ff.

fantes non ablac-
tent [45]).

20) Pedalia novel-
la [46]) non accipi-
ant nisi ubi pon-
tes et necessarius
transitus est sicut
antiquitus.

21) Mercatores et pe-　　Ne quis cum aliqui-
regrinos non as-　　bus sacri ordinis iter
salliant nec suum　　agentibus violentiam
habere eis tol-　　ullam inferre audeat.
lant [47]).　　(c. 9) Vgl. o. c. 6

22) Pax de homici-
diis patrum, filio-
rum, nepotum vel
consanguineorum
omnino fiat [48]).

23) Corpus et sangui-
nem domini, mor-
tem eius aut pas-
sionem seu ali-
quod membrum
eius non iurent.

24) De tonsura bar-
barum et ornatu
vestium se pro
dei amore emen-
dent [49]).

---

[45]) Vgl. das 4. Konzil von Toledo c. 60; 63; ed. J. V i v e s , Concilios visi-
góticos e hispano-romanos (España Cristiana 1, 1963) S. 212 f.

[46]) Vgl. D u C a n g e , Glossarium medii et infimae latinitatis 6 (1886) S. 242:
Pedale, Tributum quod penditur, idem quod pedagium.

[47]) Vgl. Le Puy, 994 (M a n s i 19, 271) und das Konzil von Narbonne (1054)
c. 25 (Mansi 19, 831).

[48]) Vgl. Regino 2.80.

[49]) Vgl. den Brief Siegfrieds von Gorze an Poppo von Stablo (1043), hg. von
W. v o n G i e s e b r e c h t , Geschichte der deutschen Kaiserzeit 2 [5](1885)

25) Electio episcopa-   Ne quis sine electione
    lis sit in commu-   cleri et populi ad re-
    ni assensu cleri et   gimen ecclesiasticum
    populi viduate   proveheretur.
    diocesis[50]).   (c. 1)

26) Praepositorum et
    archidiaconorum
    electio et aliorum
    ordinum sit in
    consensu clerico-
    rum.

Die Inskription der obigen Canones in der Hs. Reg. lat. 711/II spricht von *auctoritas*, die von einem Papst Leo bestätigt wurde. *Auctoritas sanctorum patrum* erscheint hier gleichbedeutend mit *sententiae patrum*, mit anderen Worten: den Dekreten und Aussprüchen der heiligen Väter, die in Canonessammlungen überliefert worden sind[51]). Es ist bekannt, daß Reformer des 11. Jahrhunderts in erster Linie die renovatio der

---

S. 718: *ignominiosa Franciscarum ineptiarum consuetudo introducitur, scilicet in tonsione barbarum, in turpissima et pudicis obtutibus execranda decurtatione ac deformitate vestium multisque aliis novitatibus, quas enumerare longum est quasque temporibus Ottonum ac Heinricorum introdocere nulli fuit licitum,* und G. Z i m m e r m a n n, Ordensleben und Lebensstandard. Die Cura corporis in den Ordensvorschriften des abendländischen Hochmittelalters (Beiträge zur Geschichte des alten Mönchtums und des Benediktinerordens 32, 1973) S. 90, 126 ff.

[50]) Vgl. Nicaea, c. 4 (A l b e r i g o , Decreta, S. 7) und c. 31 der Canones Apostolorum (ed. T u r n e r , S. 20 f.), die beide 787 auf dem zweiten Konzil von Nicaea zitiert wurden (c. 3; A l b e r i g o , Decreta, S. 140). Vgl. auch Burchard 1.11 f.

[51]) Zur Einführung in die vorgratianischen Sammlungen vgl. P. F o u r n i e r und G. L e B r a s , Histoire des Collections Canoniques en Occident, 2 Bde. (1931—32). Ein gutes Beispiel für den Gebrauch des Ausdrucks *sententiae patrum* ist die 74-Titel-Sammlung aus der zweiten Hälfte des 11. Jahrhunderts, die seinerzeit hauptsächlich als *Diversorum patrum sententie* bekannt war. Sie wurde kürzlich von J. T. G i l c h r i s t herausgegeben (Monumenta Iuris Canonici, Series B: Corpus Collectionum 1, 1973). Zu Sentenzen vgl. M. G r a b m a n n , Die Geschichte der scholastischen Methode 2 (1911) S. 21 ff. Zur Bedeutung von *auctoritas* als Konzilskanon vgl. Mittellateinisches Wörterbuch 1 S. 1181; zur Sache A. M i c h e l , Die Sentenzen des Kardinals Humbert, das erste Rechtsbuch der päpstlichen Reform (Schriften der MGH 7, 1943) im Register unter „patres" und H. M o r d e k , Kirchenrecht und Reform im Frankenreich (Beiträge zur Geschichte und Quellenkunde des Mittelalters 1, 1975) im Register unter „Autoritäten auf kirchenrechtlichem Gebiet".

decreta patrum vor Augen hatten, als sie für die libertas der Kirche stritten. Ein Papst dieser Zeit, der dieses Ziel betonte, ist Papst Leo IX [52]). Aber handelt es sich denn in der Inskription wirklich um diesen Papst? Sowohl Inhalt als auch Datierung der Handschrift Reg. lat. 711/II ergeben, daß Leo IX. der jüngste Papst dieses Namens ist, der mit dem Text in Verbindung gebracht werden kann. Von den Päpsten Leo I. bis Leo VIII. kommt nur Papst Leo IV. (847—855) ganz entfernt als Autor der Canones in Frage, falls man den sogenannten Sermo Synodalis wirklich diesem Papst zuschreiben will, was vom Herausgeber R. Amiet abgelehnt wird [53]). Die Admonitio berührt erstaunlich oft die gleichen Probleme, die auch das Reimser Konzil beschäftigen: ... *feminas non habeatis ... nullus vestrum pro baptizandis infantibus, aut infirmis reconciliandis, aut mortuis sepeliendis praemium vel munus exigat ... nullus arma ferat in seditione, quia arma nostra spiritualia debent esse ... nullus vestrum usuras exigat et conductor sui foenoris existat ... nullus per potestatem saecularium ecclesiam obtineat ... cum excommunicatis nolite communicare ... raptum omnimodo prohibete, et ut nullus ad proximam sanguinis sui accedat et ut alterius sponsam nullus ducat ...* [54]). Dies ist jedoch lediglich ein Beweis für die Zusammenhänge zwischen karolingischen Kapitularien einerseits und den Gottesfriedenskonzilien, beziehungsweise einem Teil der Reimser Beschlüsse,

---

[52]) Vgl. zum Beispiel die Vita Leonis (wie Anm. 59) zum Konzil von Rom 1049 (S. 154): *Quantam autem solertiam in catholica lege conservanda adhibuerit in primo Romano concilio ... demonstravit, ubi statuta quatuor synodorum principalium viva voce corroboravit, decretaque omnium antecessorum suorum pontificum tenenda confirmavit.* Zu Reims 1049 vgl. die folgenden Sätze der Historia (ed. M a b i l l o n , wie Anm. 16): *... lectis sententiis super hac re olim promulgatis ab orthodoxis patribus, declaratum est quod solus Romanae sedis pontifex universalis ecclesia primas esset et apostolicus* (S. 721); *quod in canonibus de sacrorum ordinum venditoribus sit decretum, iussit tantum modo recitari ...* (S. 723); *lectae sunt sententiae super huiuscemodi re promulgatae ab orthodoxis patribus ...* (S. 723).
[53]) An älterer Literatur vgl. G. F l a d e , Die Erziehung des Klerus durch die Visitationen bis zum 10. Jahrhundert (1933), besonders S. 39 Anm. 20 und G. M o r i n , L'auteur de l'Admonition synodale sur les devoirs du clergé, Revue Bénédictine 9 (1892) S. 99—108; bis jetzt R. A m i e t , Une 'Admonitio synodalis' de l'époque carolingienne: Étude critique et édition, Mediaeval Studies 26 (1964) S. 12—82. Amiet schreibt den Sermo einem Provinzialkonzil aus dem frühen 9. Jahrhundert zu. Eine neue Ausgabe bereitet Dr. P. Brommer (Koblenz) vor, zur handschriftlichen Überlieferung vgl. d e r s., Die bischöfliche Gesetzgebung Theodulfs von Orléans, ZRG Kan. 60 (1974) S. 35 Anm. 221 und S. 119 f.
[54]) Vgl. A m i e t , S. 50, 54 f., 62 f.

andrerseits[55]), denn wenn man die obigen Auszüge in dem dazugehörigen Zusammenhang liest, kann nicht bezweifelt werden, daß das Fragment aus Saint-Magloire weit eher mit der Historia dedicationis verwandt ist als mit dem Sermo Synodalis.

Es wäre erfreulich, wenn sich mit einem ähnlichen Grad von Wahrscheinlichkeit nun zeigen ließe, mit welcher der vielen Synoden, die Leo IX. zwischen 1049 und 1053 gehalten hat[56]), der neue Text in Beziehung zu bringen ist. Bedauerlicherweise weiß man aber über die große Mehrzahl der Kirchenversammlungen seines Pontifikats wenig mehr als daß sie stattfanden. Dies gilt insbesondere für die Synode von Pavia 1049, die süditalienischen Konzilien von 1050, die Synode von Mantua von 1052 oder 1053 und die römischen Versammlungen von 1051 und 1053. Über einige andere Konzilien wie das von Vercelli, September 1050, ist etwas mehr bekannt, aber noch immer fehlen in den Quellen direkte Aussagen über Canones, die wiederholt oder neu erlassen worden sind. Erst von den Synoden von Mainz (1049) und Rom (1050) kann man mit einiger Sicherheit sagen, daß dort Dekrete gegen Simonie und/oder Priesterehen beschlossen wurden[57]).

---

[55]) H o f f m a n n (wie Anm. 27) S. 71, hält es für fraglich, „ob die Treuga Dei bei ihrer Entstehung einen dünnen Faden weiterspann, der seit der karolingischen Epoche nicht abgerissen war." Eine thematische Ähnlichkeit zwischen Kapitularien und der Pax und Treuga läßt sich jedoch nicht leugnen, vgl. G. D u b y , Les laics et la paix de Dieu, in: I laici nella 'societas christiana' dei secoli XI e XII (Pubblicazioni dell'Università Cattolica del Sacro Cuore, Ser. 3, Varia 5, 1968) S. 451; Nachdruck in dessen Hommes et structures du moyen âge (1973) S. 230.

[56]) Obwohl M a n s i s Sacrorum conciliorum amplissima collectio nur mit großer Vorsicht gebraucht werden kann, bieten die Bände nach wie vor die am besten zugängliche Zusammenstellung der Quellen für Leos Konzilien. Für die römische Synode vom April 1049 vgl. M a n s i 19, 721—726; für Pavia (Juni 1049) S. 725—726; für Reims S. 727—750; für Mainz (Oktober 1049) S. 749—750; für Rom (April 1050) S. 759—772; für Vercelli (1050) S. 773—782; für Rom (Frühjahr 1051) S. 795—798; für Mantua (Frühjahr 1052 oder 1053) S. 799—800; für Rom (Frühjahr 1053) S. 809—812. Zu den eben genannten kommen noch drei Synoden, die wahrscheinlich 1050 in Süditalien stattfanden (vgl. vor JL 4212), so daß sich die Gesamtzahl der bekannten Konzilien Leos auf mindestens 12 erhöht; vgl. auch den Überblick bei M. B o y e , Quellenkatalog der Synoden Deutschlands und Reichsitaliens von 922—1059, NA 48 (1930) S. 84 ff.

[57]) Zur Synode von Mainz vgl. bes. JL 4188 (MGH Const. 1, S. 97 n. 51) und Adam von Bremen, Gesta Hammaburgensis Ecclesiae Pontificum III, 30, ed. B. S c h m e i d l e r (MGH Scr. rer. Germ. [2], ³1917) S. 172: *Praeterea multa ibidem sanctita sunt ad utilitatem ecclesiae, pre quibus symoniaca heresis et nefanda sacerdotum coniugia olographa synodi manu perpetuo dampnata sunt.* Zu Rom (1050) vgl. Bonizo, Liber ad amicum, MGH Libelli de lite 1, S. 589: *Sequenti vero anno prefatus pontifex sinodum congregavit, in qua omnibus tam clericis quam laicis auctoritate sancti Petri et romanae ecclesiae pre-*

Die großen Ausnahmen, was die Überlieferung von Canones Leos IX. anbelangt, sind die Konzilien von 1049, die der Papst in Rom und Reims gehalten hat. Die Hauptquelle für das Konzil von Reims ist die Historia dedicationis [58]), deren kanonistische Texte in der obigen Edition mit angegeben worden sind. Über die römische Synode von 1049 berichtet am ausführlichsten die Vita Leonis [59]), aber auch Petrus Damiani [60]) und Bonizo [61]) erwähnen gefaßte Beschlüsse. Aus der Vita erfährt man, daß Leo ... *simoniacam etiam haeresim damnavit ... Decimas quoque a cunctis dandas Christianis, quarum nec mentio erat apud Apuliam, et per quosdam orbis fines ecclesiis restituit; venditiones altarium sub anathemate prohibuit, sed constituit ut partes decimarium ad episcopum pertinentes, aut quisque praesul sibi teneret aut cuicumque vellet tri-*

---

ceptum est, ut abstinerent se a fornicatorum sacerdotum et levitarum communione. JL 4225 wird gewöhnlich zitiert, um zu zeigen, daß Leo auf dem gleichen Konzil auch ein Dekret gegen die Simonie erlassen hat. Obwohl diese Annahme viel für sich hat, bildet der Brief jedoch keinen Beweis. Er besagt lediglich, daß der praesul von Dol mit seinen Parteigängern wegen Simonie exkommuniziert wurde, vgl. J. J. R y a n , Saint Peter Damiani and His Canonical Sources (Pontifical Institute of Mediaeval Studies, Studies and Texts 2, 1956) no. 182. J. H a r t z h e i m , Concilia Germaniae 3 (1760) S. 113, dem C. J. v o n H e f e l e , Conciliengeschichte 4 ²(1879) S. 735 gefolgt ist, gibt weitere Einzelheiten über die Mainzer Gesetzgebung an, die er der Chronica de prinicipibus terrae Bavarorum des Andreas von Regensburg entnommen haben will. Die von G. L e i d i n g e r , Andreas von Regensburg, Sämtliche Werke (Quellen und Erörterungen zur bayerischen und deutschen Geschichte N. F. 1, 1903) besorgte kritische Ausgabe der Schriften des Andreas von Regensburg enthält die von Hartzheim zitierten Canones nicht, so daß man sie zumindest als dubia ansehen muß.

[58]) S. Anm. 16.
[59]) Die Vita Leonis wurde kurz nach dem Tode Leos (1054) geschrieben, vielleicht von einem Touler Kleriker, aber die Autorschaft ist umstritten; vgl. H. T r i t z , Die hagiographischen Quellen zur Geschichte Papst Leos IX., Studi Gregoriani 4 (1952) S. 191—353; H. H o f f m a n n (wie Anm. 1), Exkurs S. 203—209; H. H o e s c h , Die kanonischen Quellen im Werk von Humbert von Moyenmoutier (Forschungen zur kirchlichen Rechtsgeschichte und zum Kirchenrecht 10, 1970) und H.-G. K r a u s e , unten S. 49 ff.
[60]) Opusc. XVIII: Contra clericorum intemperantiam (M i g n e , PL 145, S. 411 B): *In plenaria plane synodo sanctae memoriae Leo papa constituit, ut quaecunque damnabiles feminae intra Romana moenia reperirentur presbyteris prostitutae, extunc et deinceps Lateranensis palatio adjudicarentur ancillae;* vgl. R y a n (wie Anm. 57) no. 197.
[61]) Liber ad amicum, S. 588, 10 ff.: *... synodum mox congregavit, ... in qua etiam sub anathemate interdictum est non licere alicui episcopo archidiaconatus et preposituras vel abbacias seu beneficia aecclesiarum vel prebendas vel ecclesiarum vel altarium commendationes vendere, et ut sacerdotes et levitae vel subdiaconi cum uxoribus non coeant ...* Zu der Stelle vgl. W. B e r s c h i n , Bonizo von Sutri. Leben und Werk (Beiträge zur Geschichte und Quellenkunde des Mittelalters 2, 1972) S. 43 Anm. 221.

bueret; partem autem ad altare pertinentem, proprio pastori ecclesiae gratis concederet. Incestas consanguineorum nuptias, in multis orbis partibus indiscrete habitas, discidit pluresque nobilium hoc turpi devinctos nexu separavit [62]). Vergleicht man die Überlieferungen für die Synoden von Rom und Reims, so ergeben sich keine großen Unterschiede. Simonie, der Verkauf von Altären und Verwandtschaftsehen wurden auf beiden Konzilien verboten [63]). Der Zehnt stand ebenfalls an beiden Orten zur Debatte [64]).

Nicht die Vita Leonis [65]), sondern Bonizo von Sutri überliefert einen römischen Canon gegen Nikolaitismus [66]). Da der Kampf gegen Simonie und Nikolaitismus von Leo betont wurde [67]), nahm man an, daß Klerikerehen nicht nur in Rom und auf anderen italienischen Konzilen, sondern auch in Reims verboten wurden [68]). Zwei voneinander abhängige Viten des Abtes Hugo von Cluny († 1109), die beide wohl nicht sehr

---

[62]) Vita Leonis, ed. J. W a t t e r i c h , S. 154 f.

[63]) Für das Konzil von Reims vgl. can. 2 und 11 der Historia und can. 1 und 10 der Hs. Reg. lat. 711/II (s. oben S. 29, 31 f.).

[64]) Vgl. obiges Zitat aus der Vita Leonis mit dem can. 4 des Reg. lat. 711/II (s. oben S. 30) Über den Zehnten und Papst Leo IX. vgl. G. C o n s t a b l e , (wie Anm. 29) S. 85 ff. und im Index unter dem Stichwort „Leo IX." A. M i c h e l , Die Anfänge des Kardinals Humbert, Studi Gregoriani 3 (1948), S. 301, Anm. 10, nahm irrtümlicherweise an, daß sich der aus der Vita Leonis, S. 154 f. zitierte Text „wohl" auf das Konzil von Reims beziehen müßte.

[65]) Der Autor der Vita Leonis bricht den Bericht über das Konzil von Rom (1049) mit folgender Bemerkung ab: *Alia quoque perplura canonum capitula studuit renovare, quae ne fastidium gignant, hic supersedimus recitare* (ed. W a t t e r i c h , S. 155).

[66]) S. Anm. 61.

[67]) Vgl. z. B. J. H a l l e r , (wie Anm. 1) S. 291; J. D r e h m a n n , Papst Leo IX. und die Simonie. Ein Beitrag zur Untersuchung der Vorgeschichte des Investiturstreites (Beiträge zur Kulturgeschichte des Mittelalters und der Renaissance 2, 1908) S. 1—21. Drehmann ist in bezug auf ein Simonieverbot in Rom im April 1049 erstaunlich unsicher. Die Vita Leonis schreibt klar und deutlich, *decretaque omnium antecessorum suorum pontificum tenenda confirmavit: simoniacam etiam haeresim damnavit, quae iam nonnullas mundi partes invaserat* (ed. W a t t e r i c h , S. 154). Vgl. ferner N.-N. H u y g h e b a e r t , Saint Léon IX et la lutte contre la simonie dans le diocèse de Verdun, Studi Gregoriani 1 (1947) S. 417—432, bes. S. 426; A. M i c h e l , Die folgenschweren Ideen des Kardinals Humbert und ihr Einfluß auf Gregor VII., ebenda S. 79 ff.; J. L e c l e r c q , „Simoniaca heresis", ebenda S. 523 ff.; G. M i c c o l i , Il problema delle ordinazioni simoniache e le sinodi Lateranensi del 1060 e 1061, ebenda 5 (1956) S. 47 Anm. 27 und H. M e i e r - W e l c k e r , Die Simonie im frühen Mittelalter, ZKG 64 (1952/53) S. 84 ff.

[68]) Vgl. bes. P.-P. B r u c k e r , L'Alsace et l'Église au temps du pape saint Léon IX, 2 (1889) S. 20 ff.

zuverlässig sind [69]), und eine kurze Bemerkung von Ordericus Vitalis über das Konzil von Reims, *ibidem generale concilium tenuit et inter reliqua aecclesiae commoda quae constituit presbiteris arma ferre et coniuges habere omnino prohibuit* [70]), schienen den gewünschten Beweis zu liefern. Da jedoch alle drei Quellen verhältnismäßig jungen Datums sind (sie stammen aus der ersten und zweiten Hälfte des zwölften Jahrhunderts) und schon aus diesem Grunde weniger überzeugten als die sehr viel ausführlichere Historia dedicationis, die kurz nach dem Tode Leos 1054 von einem Augenzeugen der Reimser Synode verfaßt worden war, suchte man verständlicherweise in der Historia selbst nach Hinweisen, daß in Reims ein Verbot gegen Priesterehen erlassen wurde. Man glaubte, dies Verbot in Mabillons c. 8 der Historia (c. 3 des Reginensis s. oben S. 30) sehen zu können [71]). Werner Bröcking betonte schon, daß dies eine gewaltsame und rein willkürliche Auslegung des Canons sei. [72]). Abtrünnige Priester und Mönche waren 1049 kein neues Problem. Schon c. 12 des Konzils non Nicaea und c. 7 des Konzils von Chalcedon befaßten sich mit ihnen [73]). Aus diesen und zahlreichen ähnlichen Texten geht hervor, daß unter der Abkehr von Gelübde und geistlichem Stand nicht Heirat oder Priesterkonkubinat verstanden wurde. Daß diese Interpretation auch für das Reimser Konzil zutrifft, scheint ein Canon des Dekrets Burchards von Worms zu zeigen, in dem die beiden Formulierungen der Historia, *a suo gradu apostataret* (H) und *a sancto proposito et habitu suo recedentibus* (P) sowie die Formulierung in V: *ad clericatum et ... ad monachicam vitam redeant,* anklingen (s. oben S. 30): *Hi qui post sanctae religionis propositum apostatant, et ad saeculum redeunt, et postmodum poenitentiae remedia non requirunt, communionem non accipiant sine poenitentia: quos etiam jubemus ad clericatus officium non admitti, et quicunque ille est post poenitentiam habitum saecularem non praesumat. Quod si praesumpserit, ab Ecclesia*

---

[69]) Es handelt sich um die Viten von Hildebert von Lavardin (M i g n e , PL 159, 866) und von Rainald (M i g n e , PL 159, 903). Vgl. dazu W a t t e n - b a c h - H o l t z m a n n S. 794—796, und zu Hildebert von Lavardin P. v o n M o o s , Consolatio 1—4 (Münstersche Mittelalter-Schriften 3, 1—4, 1971/72) im Register unter Hildebert von Lavardin.

[70]) The Ecclesiastical History of Orderic Vitalis, hg. von M. C h i b n a l l , 3 (1972) S. 120 (V, c. 12).

[71]) B r u c k e r , L'Alsace 2, 5.22.

[72]) W. B r ö c k i n g , Die französische Politik Papst Leos IX. (1891) S. 21, u. d e r s., in: Deutsche Zs. für Geschichtswissenschaft 9 (1893) S. 290 ff.

[73]) A l b e r i g o , Decreta S. 11 f. und S. 90.

alienus habeatur[74]). Es geht hier darum, daß jemand den monastischen Stand aufgibt und in die Welt zurückkehrt; er soll nicht Weltgeistlicher werden. Eheverbote für Priester sahen anders aus, wie zum Beispiel c. 3 des Konzils von Nicaea[75]) und Burchards Dekret 2.108[76]) zeigen. Auch Leo ließ es an Direktheit nicht fehlen[77]). Man kann nicht umhin, aus allem zu schließen, daß sich unter den erhaltenen Reimser Dekreten Leos keines ausdrücklich gegen verheiratete Kleriker richtet[78]).

Was läßt sich über den Text im Fragment von Saint-Magloire und über seine Beziehung zu den übrigen Konzilien Leos IX. sagen? Zunächst muß festgehalten werden, daß wir aufgrund der Quellenlage für Leos Konzilien nur die Möglichkeit haben, V mit den Überlieferungen für Rom und Reims 1049 zu vergleichen. Das heißt selbstverständlich nicht, daß V unbedingt zu einer der beiden Synoden gehört. Das Schweigen der Chronisten läßt viele Möglichkeiten offen[79]), und solange konziliare Texte nicht in offizieller Überlieferung erhalten geblieben sind[80]), bestehen selbst vorhandene Nachrichten über Kirchenversammlungen stets aus einer Auswahl behandelter Themen, die aufgrund der Neigung und des Interesses des Berichterstatters getroffen wurde[81]). Immerhin ergibt sich als Fazit aus dem eben angestellten Vergleich zwischen den Überlieferungen von Rom und Reims, daß — wenn man die Frage nach einem möglichen Reimser Canon gegen verheiratete Priester einmal offen läßt — die Anweisungen über den Zehnten sowohl in der Canonesreihe von V als auch in der Historia dedicationis den Berichten in der Vita Leonis widersprechen. Infolgedessen möchte man meinen, daß V

[74]) Burchard 19.67 = Regino 1.319; vgl. dazu J. L e c l e r c q , Documents sur les „fugitifs", in: Analecta monastica 7 (Studia Anselmiana 54, 1965) S. 87 ff. und R. B. C. H u y g e n s , in: Studi medievali, 3. ser. 13, 1 (1972) S. 404 Anm. mit weiterer Literatur.

[75]) *Interdixit per omnia magna synodus, nec episcopo nec presbytero nec alicui prorsus, qui est in clero, licere subintroductam habere mulierem, nisi forte matrem aut sororem aut amitam vel eas tantum personas quae suspicionem effugiunt* (A l b e r g i o , Decreta S. 7).

[76]) *Presbyter si uxorem acceperit, ab ordine deponatur*; vgl. Regino 1.85.

[77]) S. Anm. 60.

[78]) Vgl. C. N. L. B r o o k e , Gregorian Reform in Action, Cambridge Historical Journal 12 (1956) S. 2 Anm. 3 und F. K e m p f , in: Handbuch der Kirchengeschichte, hg. von H. Jedin, 3: Die mittelalterliche Kirche 1 (1966) S. 407 f.

[79]) S. Anm. 65.

[80]) JL 4185 zeigt, daß Leo eine offizielle Fassung der Reimser Canones anfertigen ließ, die er auf späteren Konzilien wiederholte. Der Brief kann übrigens nicht in das Jahr 1049 gehören, da Leo nicht nur von seiner Reise nach Frankreich im Perfekt spricht, sondern auch bereits von weiteren Konzilien, *quas habuimus*.

[81]) S. die Anm. 21 zitierte Literatur.

eher zur Reimser Tradition als zur römischen gehört. Dieses freilich
magere Ergebnis wird in mancher Hinsicht auch durch einen Vergleich
der drei in der Edition angeführten Textreihen unterstützt, obwohl die
Unterschiede, die sich besonders zwischen H und P einerseits und V
andrerseits bemerkbar machen, nicht übersehen werden dürfen. Übereinstimmungen und Differenzen seien kurz zusammengestellt:

1. Alle Canones der Historia dedicationis sowie die Tagesordnungsvorschläge des Diakons Peter finden ihr Gegenstück in Hs. Reg. lat. 711/II.

2. Die Zahl der überlieferten Texte ist verschieden; sie beträgt für P 9,
für H 12, für V 26 Canones.

Die Unterschiede sind zum Teil dadurch entstanden, daß ein gleiches
Thema, welches in der einen Überlieferung nur angedeutet ist, in einer
anderen ausführlicher behandelt wird[82]. Weitere Unterschiede zwischen P, H und V scheinen mit dem Konzilsverfahren zusammenzuhän-
gen, das wenigstens zum Teil durch die Historia dedicationis bekannt
ist. Die Tagesordnungsvorschläge wurden auf Wunsch des Papstes ver-
lesen und dann zur Diskussion gestellt[83]. Aber auch andere Probleme
wurden verhandelt, wie die Historia einmal zeigt: Gegen Schluß des
ersten Tages wurde anscheinend ganz unvermittelt die Frage aufgewor-
fen, wem das Recht zustünde, den Titel *universalis primas* und *apostolicus* zu gebrauchen, eine Frage, die mit einem Erlaß zugunsten Roms
entschieden wurde[84]. Auf ähnliche Weise, so darf man wohl annehmen,
sind jene Probleme zur Sprache gekommen, die zwar in den Canones
in H ihren Niederschlag gefunden haben, aber in der Eröffnungsansprache nicht erwähnt sind. Dies sind c. 17 (= H c. 7 s. oben S. 34)
und vor allen Dingen c. 25 (= H c. 1 s. oben S. 36).

C. 17, *Ne quis clericus vel laicus usuras exerceret*, der sich in der
Hs. Reg. lat. 711/II auch im sehr viel weiterreichenden c. 18 widerspie-
gelt, gehört zu einer Reihe von Bestimmungen, die sich hauptsächlich mit
der Regelung des täglichen Lebens befassen. Es sind gerade die Canones 12—23, die in erster Linie für den zahlenmäßigen Unterschied zwischen der Überlieferung in H und V verantwortlich sind. Einige der
Canones 12—23 erinnern an Bestimmungen der Pax- und Treuga-Dei-

---

[82] Wie auch im Fall von H und P entstehen einige Unterschiede zwischen H
und V dadurch, daß V Canones der Historia unter mehreren Rubriken behandelt. Besonders deutlich wird dies im Fall von cc. 4—5, cc. 7—8 und cc. 25—26.

[83] Historia, ed. M a b i l l o n (wie Anm. 16) S. 721: *Quibus propositis, admo-
nuit omnes qui aderant ut inde secum prudenti deliberatione tractarent consilium quae cum opportuno adjutorio domno papae praeberent, quomodo haec
zizania divinae segetis semen suffocantia exstirpari valerent.*

[84] Historia S. 721: vgl. F. K e m p f , (wie Anm. 78) S. 408.

Bewegung des späten 10. und 11. Jahrhunderts in Frankreich und im nördlichen Spanien. In seinem Buch über den Gottesfrieden faßt Hoffmann die anfänglichen Merkmale des Gottesfriedens zusammen als „die Kombination des dreifachen, allgemeinen Schutzes zugunsten der Geistlichen, des Kirchenguts und der pauperes; die Teilnahme der Laien an den Beschlüssen; der Appell an die Reliquien" [85]). All das trifft für das Konzil von Reims zu, und Hoffmann entschied sich schon aufgrund des in der Historia dedicationis enthaltenen Materials dafür, in Leo IX. den ersten Papst zu sehen, der diese Bewegung unterstützte, wenn auch, wie Hoffmann es ausdrückte, auf recht konservative Art und Weise [86]). Einige der Canones über den Gottesfrieden in V sind traditionell, zum Beispiel die Bestimmung über den Schutz der pauperes, wozu auch die Kaufleute gehören [87]). C. 14 ist ebenfalls ein gutes Beispiel für die Beziehungen zwischen den Dekreten Leos und den ältesten Bestimmungen des Gottesfriedens. Schon 936 waren *malae consuetudines* und der Angriff auf kirchliche Ländereien von einer Assoziation zum Schutz der Kirche von Brioude verboten [88]), Leo ging jedoch einen Schritt weiter, wenn er in c. 12 Laienbesitz unter ähnlichen Schutz stellte [89]). Aber Leo IX. war auch ein Neuerer, wie das Fehdeverbot in c. 22 zeigt. Fehdeverbote finden sich im allgemeinen nicht unter den bekannten Treuga-Dekreten [90]) und haben auch mit der allgemeinen Waffenruhe unter der Pax Dei kaum etwas gemeinsam. Trotzdem gibt es auch für c. 22 einen interessanten Präzedenzfall. Um das Jahr 1035 bemühten sich nordfranzösische Bischöfe, die Fehde unmöglich zu machen oder zumindest zu beschränken. Unter Androhung des Anathem verlangten sie, *arma quisquam non ferret; direpta non repeteret; sui sanguinis vel cuiuslibet proximi ultor minime existens percussoribus cogeretur indulgere* [91]). Bischof Gerhard I. von Cambrai (1013—1047) erhob Einwände,

---

[85]) H. Hoffmann, (wie Anm. 27) S. 47.

[86]) Ebenda, S. 218: „Die Formulierungen waren, gemessen an französischen Verhältnissen, alles andere als revolutionär. Ein Sonderfriede für Geistliche und pauperes — das hat es schon in den Canones der ältesten Gottesfriedenskonzilien gegeben." Hoffmanns Bemerkungen beziehen sich auf c. 9 und 10 der Historia (s. o. c. 6 und 21 des Reginensis S. 31, 35).

[87]) S. oben S. 31, 35, c. 6 und 21 des Reginensis und K. Bosl, Potens und pauper, in: Alteuropa und die moderne Gesellschaft. Festschrift für O. Brunner (1963) S. 86.

[88]) Hoffmann (wie Anm. 27) S. 15 f.

[89]) S. oben S. 32 den Text des Canon.

[90]) Vgl. dazu Hoffman (wie Anm. 27) S. 71 f. und im Register unter Fehde(verbot).

[91]) Gesta Pontificum Cameracensium, MGH SS 7, S. 485 f.

weil er der Ansicht war, daß es nicht gut sei, die Trennung zwischen den
Aufgaben der Bischöfe und der Könige aufzuheben; Bischöfe hätten zu
beten, und Könige für die Wahrung des Friedens zu sorgen[92]). Im
Gegensatz zu Gerhard zögerte Leo jedoch nicht damit, die Kirche mit
dieser königlichen Aufgabe zu betrauen, sicherlich weil Heinrich I. von
Frankreich keine Anstalten machte, den Gottesfrieden zu unterstützen[93]).
Anders handelte Kaiser Heinrich III., der 1043, 1044 und 1047 eine
generelle Amnestie verkündigte, die mit den Bemühungen um die Treuga
und Pax verglichen wird[94]) und Leo möglicherweise beeinflußte. Hoffmann belegte die nordfranzösischen Bemühungen um einen generellen
Frieden mit dem Adjektiv „radikal"[95]), und obwohl Leos Forderungen
bescheidener sind — er verlangte in c. 2 nur, daß Kleriker keine Waffen
tragen sollten und sprach, soviel wir wissen, nicht von einem Verzicht
auf die Rückgabe geraubten Gutes —, beweist c. 22 im Codex Reg.
lat. 711/II doch, daß der Papst nicht zögerte, neue Wege zu beschreiten.

Dies zeigen auch die Canones 16, 17 und 18 in V, die ebenfalls mit
dem Gottesfrieden verwandt sind. C. 16 verlangt, daß *querimonia* vor
dem Bischof oder Erzbischof entschieden werden sollen. Die *capitula de
treuga et de pace* einer Gottesfriedenssynode in Narbonne 1054 nehmen
dies alte Thema wieder auf — das, bevor Leo ihm neue Geltung ver-
lieh nicht mehr aktuell erschien[96]) —, jedoch mit einem bemerkens-
werten Unterschied zu Leos Dekret: Streitigkeiten sollen sowohl von
dem zuständigen Bischof als auch dem jeweiligen Fürsten geschlichtet
werden[97]).

Leo sprach zumindest nach Hs. Reg. lat. 711/II nur vom Bischof oder
Erzbischof. Aber wie dem auch sei, Leo IX. war seit langem der erste
Papst, der ein Konzil zum Anlaß nahm, um alten Kirchengesetzen über
Zinswucher neue Geltung zu verschaffen. Franz Schaub, der natürlich
nur mit der Historia dedicationis c. 7 (V c. 17; s. oben S. 34) vertraut
war, stellte schon fest, daß der Papst damit für seine Nachfolger bis zu

---

[92]) Gesta Pontificum Cameracensium S. 485 f.; vgl. dazu Th. S c h i e f f e r,
Ein deutscher Bischof des 11. Jahrhunderts: Gerhard I. von Cambrai (1012—
1051), DA 1 (1937) S. 344 ff. und H o f f m a n n (wie Anm. 27) S. 57 ff.
[93]) H o f f m a n n (wie Anm. 27) S. 66 f. und D u b y (wie Anm. 55) S. 229
und 231.
[94]) H o f f m a n n (wie Anm. 27) S. 63 mit Anm. 59. G. L a d n e r, Theologie und Politik vor dem Investiturstreit (1936) S. 70 ff.
[95]) H o f f m a n n (wie Anm. 27) S. 64.
[96]) Vgl. H o f f m a n n (wie Anm. 27) S. 70 und den Index s. v. Besitzstrei-
tigkeiten.
[97]) C. 18, M a n s i, 19, 830—831.

Alexander III. zum Vorbild wurde[98]). Durch V wissen wir jetzt, daß Leo Zinswucher nicht nur verboten hat, sondern auch anordnete, daß Wucherer unter das Anathem fallen würden.

Leo übernahm aber die Gottesfriedens-Bestimmungen, die in Frankreich zur Tradition gehörten, nicht unbesehen. Wie V zeigt, unternahm er anscheinend auch Schritte, die dazu dienen sollten, einen Mißbrauch dieser Anordnungen zu vermeiden. Der Gottesfrieden hatte das alte Asylrecht wieder stark betont. C. 13, das wahrscheinlich mit c. 12 zusammenhängt, verwehrt Dieben und Räubern diesen Schutz[99]). Vor 1036, dem Konzil von Tribur, auf dem Räuber mit Exkommunikation bedroht wurden[100]), wurde Asyl nur Mördern, Ehebrechern, öffentlichen Schuldnern und einigen anderen Verbrechern verweigert[101]). Leo, genauer als die Versammlung von Tribur, wollte wohl dafür sorgen, daß die Kirche ihren Schutz nicht auf Unwürdige ausdehnt[102]). Außerdem konnte der Schutz von Dieben leicht zum Schutz von Diebesgut führen und Laien würden dadurch verleitet werden, Kirchen anzugreifen[103]). Dieses Problem wurde schon einmal im Zusammenhang mit der Pax und Treuga Dei auf einem Konzil in Katalonien im Jahr 1033 behandelt, auf dem beschlossen wurde, daß Kirchenimmunität auf solche geweihten Stätten nicht voll anwendbar sein sollte, wo Räuber und Diebe ihre Beute angesammelt hatten[104]).

3. Die Reihenfolge der überlieferten Texte ist verschieden. Am auffälligsten ist wohl die Stellung von c. 25 über die Bischofswahl in V, das in H als c. 1 erscheint[105]). Sowohl in V wie in der Eröffnungsansprache des Diakons Peter (P) erscheint das Verbot der Simonie an

---

[98]) S c h a u b (wie Anm. 43) S. 126—132. J. T. N o o n a n , J r., The Scholastic Analysis of Usury (1957) übernahm Schaubs Ansichten. Vgl. ferner G. G ö t z , Das kanonische Zinsverbot und die moderne Wirtschaft (Diss. iur. Tübingen 1948, masch.).

[99]) S. oben S. 32.

[100]) C. 8: *Raptores et fures si in rapto ipso comprehendantur vel publice rei esse convincantur, sub anathemate sint, et quicumque eos quacumque poena affecerint vel certe occiderint, nullius iudicio subiaceant;* MGH Const. 1, 89.

[101]) Vgl. H. E. F e i n e , Kirchliche Rechtsgeschichte ⁴1964, S. 72 und den Artikel von G. L e B r a s , in: Dictionnaire d'histoire et de géographie ecclésiastiques 4 (1930) col. 1035—1047 sowie H o f f m a n n (wie Anm. 27) S. 55 und S. 151.

[102]) Vgl. P. T i m b a l D u c l a u x d e M a r t i n , Le Droit d'Asile (1939) S. 210 ff.

[103]) Vgl. L e B r a s (wie Anm. 101) Sp. 1038 und besonders H o f f m a n n (wie Anm. 27) S. 151, der auf ein Beispiel von ca. 1100 aus Arras verweist.

[104]) Ebenda S. 260 ff.

[105]) S. oben S. 36.

erster Stelle. Es wurde außerdem zuerst diskutiert[106]). Die Frage nach
der Ursache der veränderten Abfolge läßt sich nicht beantworten, aber
es ist bekannt, daß selbst authentische Berichte sehr große Variationen
zeigen, solange es sich nicht um eine offizielle Veröffentlichung handelt[107]). Es muß offen gelassen werden, ob das berühmte Kapitel über
die Bischofswahl von Leo später selbst an die Spitze der Reimser
Dekrete gerückt worden ist oder etwa vom Autor der Historia dedicationis, obwohl dieser nichts über eine Diskussion zu diesem Punkt
berichtet. Dieser Canon über die Wahl ist insofern von besonderer
Bedeutung, als auf seiner Interpretation die Einstufung Leos als konser-
vativ oder reformfreundlich beruht[108]). Es handelt sich darum, ob es
möglich ist, den zitierten Canon als einen Vorgänger der Dekrete gegen
die Laieninvestitur zu sehen. G. B. Borino lehnte diese Interpretation
als letzter ausdrücklich ab[109]). Hoffmann hingegen stellte fest, daß nur
die Methode, aber nicht der Zweck gewechselt hätte, als das Verbot der
Laieninvestitur zum wichtigsten Programmpunkt der Neuerer geworden war. „Wahl und Investitur waren zwei verschiedene Momente innerhalb ein und desselben Vorgangs"[110]). Paul Schmid hat die Bedeutung
des Wortes „Wahl" zur Zeit Leos IX. ausführlich untersucht, wobei er
zu einem Ergebnis kommt, das Hoffmann widerspricht. Leo IX., so
meinte er, war weit davon entfernt, dem Begriff Wahl einen neuen
Inhalt zu geben. Das Reimser Wahldekret sei lediglich gegen die
Pseudo-Wahl, die *obtrusio* oder *electio timore extorta*, gerichtet gewesen.
Leo habe königliche Nominierung erlaubt, solange diese Bischöfe in
ihren Diözesen willig akzeptiert wurden. Von freier Wahl im Sinn der
gregorianischen Reform könne daher nicht die Rede sein[111]). C. 25 des
Codex Reg. lat. 711/II unterstützt auf den ersten Blick Schmids Interpretation: *Electio episcopalis sit in communi assensu cleri et populi
viduate diocesis.* Er ist eindeutig formuliert: die Zustimmung der Kleriker und Laien der verwaisten Diözese ist konstitutiv für die bischöfliche Wahl. Nominierung, gleich von welcher Seite, wird nicht ausgeschlossen. Warum dann aber einen Canon über Bischofswahlen, dem
sogleich ein weiterer Canon über die Besetzung niedrigerer kirchlicher
Ämter folgt? Leos eigene Nominierung und die Bedingungen, die er

---

[106]) Historia, ed. M a b i l l o n (wie Anm. 16) S. 721.
[107]) Vgl. die Übersichtstafeln bei S o m e r v i l l e (wie Anm. 21) S. 143 ff.
[108]) S. oben Anm. 1.
[109]) G. B. B o r i n o , L'investitura laica dal decreto di Nicolo II al decreto
di Gregorio VII, Studi Gregoriani 5 (1956) S. 345 ff., bes. S. 345 mit Anm. 2.
[110]) H o f f m a n n (wie Anm. 1) S. 193.
[111]) S c h m i d (wie Anm. 1) S. 19—23; 83—89 und S. 97.

stellte, bevor er sie annahm, zeigt am besten, wie falsch es wäre, Konsens mit Scheinwahl oder Akklamation gleichzusetzen. Damit war der Papst weder für sich noch für andere Diener der Kirche zufrieden[112]. Laut Schmid stellt der Ausschluß von Laien das neue, revolutionäre Element der gregorianischen Reform dar[113]. C. 25 muß als erster Schritt in diese Richtung verstanden werden, wie c. 26 beweist, der Laieneinfluß jeglicher Art für niedrigere Kirchenämter ausschließt.

Besteht die Möglichkeit, den Text in Reg. lat. 711/II dem Reimser Konzil von 1049 zuzuordnen? Zumindest kann man eine solche Zugehörigkeit nicht ausschließen. Der Schreiber im Kloster von Saint-Magloire mag Notizen eines Teilnehmers, vielleicht seines Abtes, zur Erinnerung an die einzige französische Synode des Papstes in die letzten Folien einer Handschrift der Abtei eingetragen haben, wo sie noch heute neben anderen für die Abtei wichtigen Eintragungen erscheint. Derlei Überlegungen werden besonders durch den Zusammenhang zwischen den Canones in V und französischer Friedensgesetzgebung nahegelegt. Es sollte jedoch beachtet werden, daß selbst dieser unleugbare Zusammenhang keinen Beweis bildet. Theoretisch zumindest wäre es möglich, daß Leo versucht haben könnte, die Friedensbewegung in Italien heimisch zu machen, wie es zum Beispiel Reimbald von Arles, Benedikt von Avignon und Nithard von Nizza sowie Odilo von Cluny taten[114].

---

[112] Vgl. H o f f m a n n (wie Anm. 1) S. 190 ff., wo auch Leos Verhalten bei den einzelnen Bischofswahlen in Deutschland und Frankreich diskutiert wird.
[113] S c h m i d (wie Anm. 1) S. 40 f. und S. 201 f.
[114] H o f f m a n n (wie Anm. 27) S. 81 ff.

II

Codex Guarnerius 203

A manuscript of the Collection in 74 Titles at San Daniele del Friuli*

MS 203 of the Biblioteca Civica Guarneriana, San Daniele del Friuli,[1] was among the treasures left to his home town by Giusto Fontanini (1666-1736), titular archbishop of Ancyra.[2] Below his *ex libris* on the first paper fly leaf, '1730, Justi Fontanini, Archiepiscopi Ancyrani 48',[3] the archbishop listed briefly the contents of the manuscript he had acquired. This incomplete and unsatisfactory listing was eventually reproduced by Mazzatinti with a few variations that did not improve matters. The misleading date 's. XIV', for example, is an addition, and while Fontanini had identified the first item of the codex as 'Collectio canonum', Mazzatinti wrote 'Lucii I Canones apostolorum'.[4] Although the manuscript was seen by Wilhelm Levison in 1907,[5] no complete

Editor's Note. — We had hoped to pair this paper with one by Hubert Mordek, describing another previously overlooked manuscript of the Collection in 74 Titles, which he identified in Berlin (West), Stiftung preussischer Kulturbesitz MS theol. lat. fol. 281 (s. xii). He first called this text to the Editor's attention in an oral communication, October 1973, referring to V. Rose's concise and, on the whole, competent description in the *Verzeichniss der lateinischen Handschriften der königlichen Bibliothek zu Berlin* 2.1 (1901) No. 322, pp. 107-12. Other commitments have prevented Dr. Mordek from completing his contribution for the present issue of the *Bulletin*; we hope to publish it next year. (S. K.)

* The author would like to thank Direttore Gian Paolo Beinat of San Daniele and Dottoressa Lelia Serena, Bibl. Com. di Udine, for their kindness during her visits to the Biblioteca Guarneriana. I am also very grateful to Professor Stephan Kuttner for his generous help and for the acquisition of a microfilm of the manuscript. A grant from the Research Council of Vanderbilt University was a very welcome aid.

[1] G. Mazzatinti, *Inventari dei manoscritti delle biblioteche d'Italia*, 3 (Forlì 1893) 144-5. A brief discussion of the history of the Biblioteca Civica Guarneriana is found *ibid.* 100-09, but most helpful is L. Narducci, *Notizie storiche della Biblioteca Comunale di Sandaniele del Friuli per le nozze Narducci-Bonin* (Venice 1875). See also G. P. Beinat, *San Daniele del Friuli* (San Daniele del Friuli 1967) 11-38.

[2] A good bibliography for the archbishop has been given by G. Marchetti, *Il Friuli: Uomini e Tempi* (Udine 1959) 354-66. Particularly valuable contributions are: C. G. Mor, *Giusto Fontanini* (San Daniele del Friuli 1938-9) and the article in the *Dizionario enciclopedico della letteratura italiana* 2 (Bari and Rome 1966) 502-4.

[3] According to Mr. Beinat the date 1730 refers to the rebinding of the codex. The back of the binding reads: Varia MSS; To: XXXXVIII.

[4] See above n. 1.

[5] To the best of my knowledge Levison did not himself publish a description of the manuscript. He passed the notes he had gathered on to A. Hofmeister who used the codex in his critical edition of the Concordat of Worms. (A. Hofmeister, 'Das Wormser Konkordat:

description exists as yet. The codex Guarnerianus contains three major medieval works: the *Liber Beati Augustini de fide ad Petrum* (see below no. 12), Cardinal Deusdedit's *Libellus contra invasores et symoniacos et reliquos scismaticos* (see below no. 13), identified by Professor Levison, and the canonical collection known as *Diversorum patrum sententie* or *Collection in 74 Titles* (subsequently cited 74T; see below, no. 6).

The last two items are comparatively rare. A critical edition of the *Libellus* was published by Ernst Sackur[6] on the basis of manuscripts all younger than San Daniele MS 203 (siglum Sd).[7] A full collation shows that Sd is an early representative of Sackur's class B, offering occasionally better and more complete readings. Most of the variants, however, do not greatly alter the published text and only more significant departures will be briefly noted below. It seems useful to make a full collation of 74T available, omitting only insignificant variants, since the text found in Sd exhibits extensive rearrangements of the final third of the collection, and, moreover, it furnishes numerous additions[8] to the text established in John T. Gilchrist's critical edition.[9] Chapters 1-222 of 74T were transcribed as a block, interrupted only by three isolated canons that were inserted to strengthen points made in the collection. The first major interruption occurs after c.222. Eight canons, strongly emphasizing the readmission of penitent heretics to the Catholic community with full rights, obviously serve as counterargument to c.223 of 74T which follows, and the chapters have blunted the impact of this canon which stipulates that heretical clergy could only be readmitted 'adempta sibi omni spe promotionis'. The second large insertion of chapters is found after c.225. Expanding the theme of 74T (tit.68 and c.309) the additions urge strict observance of the rules governing excommunication. It incorporates two canons from the Swabian Appendix, ancient conciliar decisions as well as patristic texts which are usually found in a very similar form in other late eleventh- and early twelfth-century canonical collections. This discussion of excommunication can be seen as a logical continuation of the first block of additions, but it is difficult to unravel the logical thread that could have served as a guide to the rearrangement of the remainder of the collection that deals with various other aspects of church discipline from simony and nicolaitism to penitence, marriage and consanguinity. But in spite

---

Zum Streit um seine Bedeutung', *Forschungen und Versuche zur Geschichte des Mittelalters und der Neuzeit: Festschrift Dietrich Schäfer* (Jena 1915; repr. Darmstadt 1962) 64-148. Notes on the Guarnerius are found especially *ibid.* 127-8, n. 5).

[6] MGH *Libelli* 2 (1892, repr. 1956) 292-365.

[7] Hofmeister, 'Konkordat' 127, referred to the manuscript as Nr. 220. He employed the siglum SD.

[8] See Appendix I.

[9] MIC, series B: Corpus Collectionum, 1 (Città del Vaticano 1973). Sigla, title and chapter numbers throughout this article refer to the edition by Professor Gilchrist.

of the seeming confusion only three canons of 74T[10] were actually omitted, even though the scribe of Sd did not work very carefully. Individual words are rather frequently omitted, abbreviations misread and somewhat unusual Latin words misspelled. A corrector emended some of these mistakes. It should also be noted that the structural changes are all reflected in the *capitulatio* directly preceding 74T which begins with the last two lines of the final folio of the chapter listing. It is reasonable to conclude that Sd was transcribed from an exemplar that had probably been compiled in order to adapt 74T to early twelfth-century requirements.

The exemplar of Sd was evidently a manuscript of the Cassino K recension, belonging to the sub-group VsFa of the stemma of manuscripts established by Professor Gilchrist. The preponderance in Sd of Vs variants in the first place, and Fa variants in the second, is obvious.[11] Numerical evidence and the importance of the variants indicate that Sd is closer to Vs than Fa. Nonetheless, the relationship between Sd and Vs was not a direct one. 74T c.253, for example, is longer in Sd than in the critical edition following the original source with the exception of the last sentence that could not be traced.[12]

One further preliminary remark is perhaps necessary with regard to c.321 and c.323 of the Swabian recension (Σ) that are not found in K, but are represented in Sd. One of them, c.323, was transcribed from a source other than Σ leaving only a single canon that could be derived from recension Σ. Such a derivation, however, contradicts all other available evidence, and it is perhaps not rash to conclude that Sd is not directly connected to Σ, particularly because c.321 was very familiar to canonists of the period as indicated by the *apparatus fontium* in Gilchrist's edition.

The San Daniele MS 203 consists of 159 parchment folios,[13] 13×19 cm. It is usually written in long lines,[14] with red titles, inscriptions and initial letters.[15] Two main hands, Italian, first half s. XII, can be distinguished. A¹ from the

---

[10] Apart from the Swabian Appendix.

[11] Variants in Sd coincide as follows with the variants listed in Gilchrist's apparatus for the different manuscripts: C = 10 times; Fl = 28 times; Lc = 54 times; N = 55 times; Y = 53 times; Vs = 110 times; Fa = 101 times; B = 54 times; Rc = 56 times; Lz = 69 times; Rv = 68 times; V1 = 56 times; W = 58 times; G = 52 times; E = 51 times; S = 54 times; Vh = 50 times; M = 49 times.

[12] See the analysis below.

[13] Although the manuscript has in general been well preserved, the first 12 fols. are damaged in the upper right hand corner and fol. 159v has been so darkened by age that the text has become illegible, at least without ultraviolet light.

[14] Exceptions are the *capitulatio* of 74T in 3 columns (fols. 9r-15r) and the papal and imperial catalogues in 2 columns (fols. 77v-87r).

[15] The last section of the manuscript was less carefully executed, and initials and inscriptions are in black or brown ink. Occasionally, blank spaces have been left, especially in the marginal entries.

late 1120's or early 1130's[16] is responsible for writing fols. 1r-83r; A[2] for fols. 90r-154r. The folios in between these two sections and the final five folios have been filled with canonical and patristic excerpts written by many different hands, mostly from the later twelfth and early thirteenth century, with the exception of fol. 158r that has again been written by A[1]. Fol. 84r is blank. A[1] ordinarily omits the aspirant 'h',[17] but sometimes adds the 'h' incorrectly by overcompensating.[18] 'D' and 't' as well as 'p' and 'b' have been interchanged rather frequently.[19] The syllable 'in' is usually changed to 'im' when combined with the following word (e.g. fol. 19v *imposterum* for *in posterum*), 'mn' is spelled 'mpn' (e.g. *dampnetur*), and the use of 'i' instead of a possible 'y' predominates (e.g. *martir*). An interlinear gloss on fol. 18r, *id est ammoue*, accompanies *auelle* in c.19, 7.

The dating of the manuscript on the basis of the script is confirmed by the papal catalogue (below no. 8) where a new hand added the name of Pope Calixtus II (1119-1124) and then continued the list down to Pope Innocent III (1198-1216). The years of Innocent's pontificate have not been entered. Further evidence is perhaps provided by a transcription, imitating the appearance of official documents, of both the papal and the imperial declarations of the so-called Concordat of Worms (below no. 15) and last but not least by a letter of Pope Honorius II, dated 1125 (below no. 20).

While the approximate date of codex Guarnerius 203 can thus be established with relative ease, the same cannot be said for its provenance or origin. It is certain that the Guarneriana received the manuscript as a legacy from Giusto Fontanini,[20] but unfortunately he did not keep a record of the provenance of his acquisitions or if he did, it has not been preserved. Most of his manuscripts were obtained by him in Venice and Rome where Fontanini was tutor and librarian of the Moro family and librarian of Cardinal Imperiali. After Fontanini's death in 1736, the many claims raised to parts of his collection[21] show that his methods of acquisition were not always very scrupulous, but nobody claimed Guarnerius 203. It passed apparently without contention to the library at San Daniele and thus no light is shed on its provenance on this occasion either. Adolf Hofmeister who used Sd in the critical edition of the Concordat of Worms, concluded that Sd was a 'sister manuscript' of Vat. lat. 1984.[22] This

---

[16] The author is much indebted to Professor Horst Fuhrmann for his help in dating the script.

[17] e.g. odierna (fol. 28v), ueementer (fol. 34r), eresim (fol. 49v), actenus (fol. 54v).

[18] e.g. hac = ac (fol. 20r, 22v, 30v etc.), hostiarius = ostiarius (fol. 25r), his = is (fol. 30v, 32r etc.), horta = orta (fol. 31v).

[19] e.g. aput (fol. 55v, 57r), adque (fol. 57v), babtismus (fol. 49r)

[20] See above.

[21] Narducci, *Nozze* 18-26.

[22] Hofmeister, 'Konkordat' 132-3.

is probably correct,[23] but, unfortunately, nothing is known about the origin or provenance of Vat. lat. 1984 beyond the fact that the codex is Italian.[24]

Some of the entries in Sd provide certain clues, although these tend to remain ambiguous and contradictory.[25] First, there is the letter *Calamitates et miserias* entrusted by Honorius II to his legate Comes whom he sent to Pisa and Genoa on a mission of peace.[26] The letter in Sd is a copy of the missive addressed to the Pisans, and whoever transcribed the letter, which is not otherwise preserved, must have been an interested party to the truce negotiations at the time. Not only the Pisans and Genoese, but also the Corsicans or possibly somebody at the Roman curia might have wanted a copy of the letter. Secondly, there is the entry at the bottom of fol. 158v in a thirteenth-century (?) hand: 'ducati .ii.' This note seems to indicate that the codex was sold at this time in an area of Italy under Byzantine influence. *Ducat*, according to Du-Cange, refers (a) to a silver coin issued in 1140 by Roger II of Sicily; (b) to a Venetian silver coin issued in 1202 and usually known as 'grosso'; (c) to the first Venetian gold coins minted in 1284.[27]

These very tenuous links to Greek Italy are somewhat strengthened by the composition of the list of emperors found in Sd. It contains the names of Roman emperors and their Byzantine successors as far as Basil I (867-886), the founder of the Macedonian dynasty who restored several areas of southern Italy to Byzantine rule.[28] No Carolingian ruler is included. The twelfth-century copyist thus betrays an anti-Frankish bias that, while he may not have shared it, must have been present in the exemplar of the regnal list he copied. The problem is that neither Pisa nor Genoa were under Byzantine influence, for pride of place among these clues to provenance and origin belongs clearly to the Honorius letter whose date approximates rather closely that of the estimated date of origin of Sd and whose content is not of general interest.

The subsequent brief identification of the contents of Sd will be followed by a collation and partial edition of 74T prepared in accordance with the principles of the Institute of Medieval Canon Law.[29] Additional chapters are briefly

---

[23] It is perhaps worth pointing out that both manuscripts contain excerpts from the rarely preserved works of Cardinal Deusdedit. Spelling characteristics also seem to coincide.

[24] For a bibliography of MS Vat. lat. 1984, see Hofmeister, 'Konkordat' 124 n. 2.

[25] Two entries by the previous owner or owners on fol. 1r: 'XIII liber de decretorum' (in a hand from the 15th/16th century) and 'in isto libro continetur decreta apostolorum et liber Augustini de fide' (in a different and earlier hand) do not provide a lead.

[26] Published in BMCL 4 (1974) 64-66.

[27] In addition to DuCange, *s.v. ducat*, see E. Fournial, *Histoire monétaire de l'occident médiéval* (Paris 1970) 81.

[28] In general see A. A. Vasiliev, *History of the Byzantine empire* 1 (2nd ed. Madison 1958) 303f. and especially the article by L. Bréhier, DHGE 6 (1932) 1082ff. on Emperor Basil I.

[29] See S. Kuttner, 'Notes on the presentation of text and apparatus . . .', *Traditio* 15 (1959) 452-64.

identified wherever possible. Insignificant variants are omitted. *E caudata* is transcribed 'ae'. Canons entered into the margins of the manuscript can be found in Appendix III. Appendix II lists the incipits of chapters added to 74T.[30]

Description of San Daniele 203

1] fol. 1r-4r: Incipiunt canones apostolorum . . . spiritus sancti amen.
Canones Apostolorum (ed. C. H. Turner, *Ecclesiae Occidentalis Monumenta Iuris Antiquissima*, I, 1 [Oxford 1899] 1.2-32). Of the usual 50 canons, c.18 was accidentally omitted at the bottom of fol. 1v. The inscription of c.10 was omitted as well, and the inscriptions of cc.7-9 are placed after the appropriate canons. Most canons show slight variants compared to Turner's text.

2] fol. 4r-6r: *De canonum auctoribus et numero et tempore.* Apostolorum canones . . . uinculo conligauit. Anonymous canonical treatise, the so-called three *Adnotationes*, unedited (see Seckel-Fuhrmann, 'Die erste Zeile Pseudoisidors . . .', *Sb. Akad. Berlin* 1959, Nr. 4, p. 26 Maassen, *Geschichte* 403, no. 529: 'Stücke unbekannter Verfasser; Mixta'; *ibid.* 958, Beilage XVII); H. Mordek, ZRG Kan. Abt. 55 (1969) 49ff. Identified by textual comparison with MS Paris, B.N. lat. 1453.

3] fol. 6r-6v: *Augustinus ex libro de utilitate credendi.* Hereticus est . . . blasphemare dediscant. Brief patristic excerpts, especially from the writings of Augustine concluding with an excerpt from JK 1032 (P. M. Gassó and C. M. Batlle, *Pelagii I Papae epistulae quae supersunt: 556-561* [Montserrat 1956] ep. 74, p. 187, lines 1-2).

4] fol. 6v-7r: *De penitentia Salomonis.* Hieronimus in septimo . . . semen eius di . . . Anonymous penitential treatise, incomplete in Sd ending abruptly at the bottom of fol. 7r, but apparently complete in Fulda, Landesbibliothek, MS Aa Theologie 36, 4° (E. 43), fol. 74v (pencil numbering; fol. 71v in red ink) — fol. 75v: *De penitentia regis Salmonis.* Quid sanctus Augustinus . . . est depositus. A different recension was published by H. Boehmer, *De paenitentia regum*, MGH Libelli 3.609f.

5] fol. 7v-8v: *[Isi]dorus super Exod. cap. xxxvi.* Incipit illegible . . . sunt peccata aliena. Patristic excerpts from Isidore and Augustine, including In gestis . . . commisse restituit = excerpt from *Dicta cuiusdam de discordia papae et regis* (ed. K. Francke, MGH Libelli 1.454-60) corresponding to redaction 3 edited from Brussels, B.R. MS 5576-5604 (*ibid.* 456-8 No. 24)

6] fol. 9r-64v: Diversorvm patrvm sententiae. *De primatu Romanae aecclesiae.* In libro Deuteronomi . . . pena de legibus feriendi. *Diversorum*

---

[30] The following abbreviations will be used: Ans. ded. = Anselmo dedicata (Besse, excerpts); Ans. = Anselm of Lucca, *Collectio canonum*; for books 10-13 a microfilm of MS Naples, Bibl. Naz. AXII-39 was used; capitula not included by Thaner or the Naples codex are not referred to even although they might be indicated in Friedberg's edition of Gratian; Burch. = Burchard, *Decretum*; Coll. Mil. = *Collezioni canoniche milanesi* ed. Picasso; Deusd. = Deusdedit, *Kanonessammlung*; H = Pseudo-Isidore Hinschius; Ivo Decr. = *Decretum*; Ivo Pan. = *Panormia*; Poly. = *Polycarpus*, MS Paris, B.N. lat. 3881; Reg. = Regino, *Libri duo de synodalibus causis.*

patrum sententie siue Collectio in LXXIV titulos digesta, ed. J. T. Gilchrist (MIC, Corpus Collectionum 1; Città del Vaticano 1973). The text of 74T is preceded by a *capitulatio* (fol. 9r-15r) which includes the additions and omissions from the text as published by Gilchrist. Sd will be collated with Gilchrist's edition below.

7] fol. 65r-77v: *Augustinus contra Faustum*. Panis et . . . posse seruare. Ivo Decr. 2, 1-8 with several inserts. Ivo Decr. 2, 3 is found in the margin of fol. 66v.

8] fol. 77v-83v: Beatus Petrus . . . Innocentius sedit annos.   Papal catalogue, Peter to Innocent III (1198-1216). The years of the latter's pontificate are not indicated. Preceded by a brief theological excerpt (Tria genera sacrificiorum . . . deuictos esse recognoscebant), the catalogue was begun by A¹; a second hand continued the catalogue from Calixtus II (1119-1124), written over an erasure to Innocent III. After Innocent II a name was erased. As usual in old recensions the catalogue is prefaced by the apocryphal letters exchanged between Jerome and Pope Damasus. (See Duchesne, *Le Liber Pontificalis* 2, xxxiii ff. The text of the letters is found *ibid*. 1 part 4.48 and 1 part 5.117. Sd exhibits slight variants.) Since, with the exception of the Carolingian period, the catalogue lists only names and dates, it cannot be assigned to any particular tradition (see *ibid*. 2.xx).

    fol. 84r: blank

9] fol. 84v-87r: Catalogue of emperors, Augustus to Basil I (867-886). The list does not include Frankish rulers. Eleven persecutions, some of the early councils, and the death of the Visigothic Prince Hermenegild (ca. 584), who was converted from Arianism to Catholicism, are mentioned.

10] fol. 87r: Si qua mulier . . . singulos gradus.   3 canons on marriage subsequently added by A¹:
1. Si qua mulier . . . mariti coniungi.   Poly. 6.4.6   cf. Ans. 10.65 Grat. C.35 q.10 c.5 palea;
2. Et hoc quoque . . . non separentur.   cf. Ans. 10.66   Grat. C.35 q.2 et 3 c.12;
3. Si quis desponsauit . . . singulos gradus.   JK †199   cf. Poly. 6.4. 34   Grat. C.27 q.2 c.15.

11] fol. 87v-89v: Manus Dei patri . . . graduum deficit nomen.   Miscellaneous fragments added at various times by several mostly later hands, including an excerpt from a letter of Ivo of Chartres (ep. 161; PL 162, 165) and excerpts from the *Etymologies* of Isidore of Seville (PL 82.73ff).

12] fol. 90r-108r: *Liber Beati Augustini de fide ad Petrum*. Epistolam fili Petre tuae . . . quoque illic Deus reuelauit. Ps. Augustine (PL 40.753ff). The author is Fulgentius of Ruspe (Clavis no. 826).

13] fol. 108r-142v: Opitulante Domini Dei nostri . . . non erat fiat. Deusdedit Presbyteri Cardinalis *Libellus contra invasores et symoniacos et reliquos scismaticos*, ed. E. Sackur (MGH Libelli 2 [1892, repr. 1956] 292-365). The text begins with a large red initial, but without inscription for which room was left. Chapters are mostly unnumbered, and divisions of text were rarely indicated. Inscriptions are usually omitted. Sd is a representative of Sackur's class B. Only important variations from the critical edition are indicated here. Page and line references are to the *Monumenta*'s edition.

300.23 aliud est officium regum.] Sacerdotis enim officium est principaliter aecclesiae et clero et maximo religioni prouidere et regi contra iustitiam resistentes communione priuare *add.*

320.20 panis luctus] panis pollutus

327.1 uidetur] Item Stephanus iunior Damasum sequens ordinatos a Constantino inuasore et neophyto alios penitus abicit, alios in pristinum gradum reuocat, aliis electionem et consecrationem iterat. Similiter duodecimus Iohannes papa de promot:s a Leone curiali neophyto periurio et inuasore *add.* *Cf.* Duchesne, *Liber Pontificalis* 1.476

327.10 Anastasius] Anastasius ordinatos *sine lac.*

328.2 sacerdos non est] sed sacerdos non est *add.*

328.27-330.29 Quae omnia—priora redeamus (= *cap. xi. et xii.*) *om.*

346.1 episcopo] Larisseo *praem.*

347.22 et caetera, usque tunc veniens] munus tuum ante altarem et uade prius reconciliari fratri tuo et tunc veniens offeres munus tuum

348.5 oculi mei] et qui uos spernit me spernit, et qui uos audit me audit *add.*

358.14 qui appellatur] diurnus *add.*

361.23-29 Sub magno—non erat fiat] Sancti uiri cum maledictionis sententiam proferunt non ad hanc ex uoto ultionis sed ex iustitia examinis erumpunt. Intus enim subtile Dei iudicium aspiciunt et male foris ex urgentia quae a maledicto non peccant eo quod ab interno iudicio non discordant

364.34-35 Nihil—superbia *om.*

365.1-8 Odit Deus—infidelis] *om. sed add.* Sub magno . . . non erat fiat (= 361.23-29)

14] fol. 142v: *Leo papa regi uel exercitui francorum.* Omni timore ac . . . minime negabuntur.   JE 2642 (MGH *Epp.* 5.601)   Ivo Decr. 10.87 Grat. C.23 q.8 c.9.

15] fol. 143r-143v: In nomine sanctae . . . huius discordiae.   The privileges exchanged in 1122 between Emperor Henry V and Pope Calixtus II (the so-called Concordat of Worms). This text was used in Hofmeister's edition (MS A3*, siglum SD) of the documents (see above, note 6).

16] fol. 143v-144r: DEFINITIONES SANCTORVM PATRVM DE NOMINE QVOD DICITVR HERETICVS VEL HERESIS. *Ysidorus ait.* Heresis grece . . . facilis adruendum.   Excerpts from the writings of Augustine, Cicero, Isidore and Jerome.

17] fol. 144r-153v: Sufficere quidem fidei . . . qualescumque socii deberemus.*   Ps. Jerome, ep. 12 de septem ordinibus (Clavis 764).

18] fol. 153v-154r: DE IMPERATORIBVS AC REGIBVS AB EPISCOPIS DEPOSITIS. *Ex epistola Gelasii papae contra Acacium ad episcopos Dardaniae.* Nathan propheta palam . . . portauit iniquitatem.   Collection of precedents for the deposition of kings by ecclesiastics, followed however by 2 fragments attributed to Augustine stressing the sanctity of oaths rendered to secular rulers. The first excerpt is from JK 664 c. 7 (Quesn.), ed. Guenther, *Coll. Avellana* 95 (CSEL 35.786.3-6 [cf. 369]; PL 56.649).

---

* This section of the codex will be discussed by Professor Roger Reynolds. Cf. his article 'The Pseudo-Hieronymiam "De septem ordinibus ecclesiae",' RB 80 (1970) 238-52.

19] fol. 154v: [*Nico*]*laus papa in concilio episcoporum xiii.* Si quis apostolicae . . . integre reseruentur.   Nicholas II, *Conc. Rom.* 1059, c.1 and 2
(MGH Const. 1.547)   Ans. 6.12   Deusd. 1.168   Poly. 1.4.4
cf. Grat. D.79 c.1 (c.1 only).

[Si] quis pecunia . . . inthronizatus sit.   Nicholas II, *Conc. Rom.* 1060
c.4 (MGH Const. 1.551)   Ans. 6.13   Deusd. 1.169   Poly. 1.4.5
cf. Grat. D.79 c.9.

Oportet ut hec sacrosancta . . . diaconibus ordinaretur.   Stephen III,
Conc. Rom. 769   Poly. 1.4.6   cf. Deusd. 2.161   Grat. D.79 c.3.

20] fol. 154v: Calamitates et miserias . . . tutiare curauimus.   Honorius II   JL— ; Kehr, *It. pont.* 3.323 no. *19; ed. BMCL 4 (1974) 64-66.

21] fol. 155r-158r: Queris Dardana . . . alterum caritatis est.   Jerome,
ep. 129   (CSEL 56.162-75; PL 22,1099-1107).

22] fol. 158r: Gregorivs papa ad Petrvm Diaconem. [*Δ* ianem Sd]. *Gregorius
seruus Dei presbitero et abbati monasterii Sancti Theodori in Sicilia prouincia,
panormitano territorio constituti.* Insinuauit nobis . . . sopire festinauimus.
JE 1076 (Gregorii I Reg.1.9).
Item. Silvester Papa.   [S]ingularum (*corr. ex.* 'ingulis') aecclesiarum . . .
mouere certamen.   *Conc. Chalced.,* c.17 vers. Dion.   Burch. 3.148
cf. Grat. C.16 q.3 c.1 vers. Hisp. 'Per singulas ecclesias'.

23] fol. 158r-159r: [B]*eatissimo pape Damaso Ieronimus presbiter in Domino
salutem.* Inter alia . . . et bibunt.   Ps. Jerome (Clavis no. 633) ed. S.
Kuttner, BMCL 1 (1971) 26-28.

24] fol. 159r-159v: Dum medium silentium teneret . . . (ending is illegible).
Meditations on Sap. 18.14 (not the Vulgate version: cf. Ps. Hugo of St. Victor,
PL 177.315 and also the *Missale Romanum,* introit for the Sunday in the Octave
of Christmas which are based on the same version as the text in Sd).

Collation of San Daniele 203

Collation of the *Diuersorum patrum sententiae* in Sd with J. T. Gilchrist's
edition (see no. 6 above). All references are to Gilchrist's text and apparatus.
Insignificant variants in Sd are omitted.

1-61   fol. 15r-24r

 1   5 iudicium *cum* Vs BLz S   7-8 et (ad *om.* Sd) iudices qui fuerint *cum* Vs *Λ*
 2   3-4 apostolis] aliis
 4   2 Calixtus *cum cett. praeter* B CRc Vh   9 habere] erit (haberi *corr. manu
     recenti* s. xviii)
 6   6 sententias *cum* Vs
 7   2 Sixtus *cum* FIVsFa B ESVh
 8   3 temperare *cum Λ* (*praeter* B) *Σ*
10   3 fas de omnibus habeat Sd, de omnibus fas habeat VsFa
11   4 reseruaberit
13   1 *rubr.* Item de eadem re cap. x.   9 uestram rogantes karitatem] vestrae
     caritati   15 cleri] suo   16 subintrarunt *cum cett. praeter* CFl E
14   1 *rubr.* Item de eadem re cap. eodem
15   1 *rubr.* Item cap. eodem *cum* LcVs   6 quisquam] quisquis   10 aliis *cum*
     orig. *et* N LzRv *Σ* (*absque* Vl)

16 1 *rubr.* Item cap. eodem *cum* LcY   5 decertent

18 1 *rubr.* Item de eodem cap. i. Ex epistola Cecilii Cypriani contra Nouatianum de unitate aecclesiae cap. vii. *corr. marg.*
5 et quamuis] ante quamvis *corr.*   16 tenere] firmiter *add.*

19 1 *rubr.* eodem²] *om. cum* FlN   4 solis] *om. cum* VsFa   5 tenaci radice fundatum] tenax radice fundamentum Sd, tenacem radice fundamentum Vs
7 auelle] id est ammoue *interlin. gl.*   9 et] *om.*   10 per orbem totum *cum orig. et cett. praeter* C E Rc   15 cubilis *cum* Vs Rv

20 1 *rubr.* Item de eodem cap. *cum* FlNVs
tit. 2 1 *rubr.* et¹ *om. cum* Fa

21 2 *inscr.* Christi *om.*   a Domino constitutus *tr.*   10 ambo sanctam] et pariter supradictam   11 aliisque] aliis *cum orig. et cett. praeter* CFl *Λ* (*absque* B)

22 2 *inscr.* omnibus *om.*   10 ambo sanctam] pariter supradictam

23 15 morarentur *cum* W E

24 5 temporibus] *supra scr.* omnibus *cum* Rc

25 4 fideliter] *om.*

26 2 meretur] uidetur   sibi] si

27 1 *rubr.* cap. *add.*

28 1 *rubr.* cap. cxxvii. *add.*   4 seruarı] firmari   7 sacerdotibus (*homoiotel.*)

29 1 *rubr.* cap. *add.*   6 hoc *om. cum* VlW

30 6-7 oportuit] optinuit

33 1 *rubr.* Item de eadem re cap. eodem, *corr. marg.* Ex epistola Hincmari archiepiscopi ad Karolum imperatorem cap. i.   5 obligauit *cum* Cᵃᶜ RcLzRvᵃᶜ

35 2 *inscr.* decreuerunt *corr. marg.*   quos] quosque *cum* VsFa   2-3 constituerit   4-5 decreuimus

36 3 diuersi

39 8 de futura quiete eorum *tr. cum orig. et cett. praeter* C   12 curauimus
24 cuiusque   35 et] ad *add.*   36 iudicium   abbate *supra lin.*
corr. ex apte   39 omnino   47 nostrorum *om.*   54 de his *om.*
56 Angellus *cum* VsFa   57-58 a nobis promulgato *om.*   59 a nobis promulgato *om.*

40 1 *rubr.* re *add.*   ccxv] ccxc *cum* Vs

41 1 *rubr.* re *add.*   4 sint] sunt *cum* VsFa LzRv VlW   7 monachina *cum* VsFa

42 3 peruenerat *supra lin. corr.*   10 hec] audiens *add. cum* Vs   14 tantummodo causa accedendi *om.*   19 ne *om.*, nec *supra lin. corr.*

43 5 prouehantur] promoueantur (*cum* Lz) officiis uel

44 8 autem] enim *cum* Fl *et orig.*

45 2 esse *post* accusatores *tr. cum* VsFa

46 2 *inscr.* Rome] Romane urbis *cum cett.* (*praeter* CFl B)   3-4 et infamationibus *om.* (*homoiotel.*)

48 3 persone enucleatim *tr.*   16 hebetant] habent, *corr. marg.*

49 3 clerici reliqui *tr. cum* VsFa   a saecularium] *cancell. et supra scr.* ecclesiarum

50 1 *rubr.* idem de eadem re *praem.*

54 1 *rubr.* Item de eadem re *om.*   2 priusquam] prius qui (*male legitur*)
3 est *om.*

58 2 *inscr.* Gidius papa

60 2 *inscr.* synodo *om.*

61 1 *rubr.* Item de eadem re *om.*   3 cinctum] uinctum (cintum *corr. marg.*) *cum*
Vs (*lect. incerta*)   3-4 quoniam] quia

61a ITEM DE EADEM RE CAP.   fol. 24r
Sinodus Cartaginensis. Querendum est ... Dei estis.
Ps. Conc. Carthag. IV (*Statuta eccl. antiqua*) c.96 (ed. H. T. Bruns, *Canones
Apostolorum et conciliorum* [Berlin 1839; repr. Turin 1959] 1.150; ed. C. Munier,
Concilia Galliae A. 314 - A. 506 [CCL 148; Turnhout 1963] 174 c.52).

62-164   fol. 24r-38r
62 7 inibi *corr. mar. ex* nisi
63 1 *rubr.* item *om.*
64 1 *rubr.* eodem   cap. vii. *om.*
65 2 *inscr.* episcopis omnibus *tr. cum cett. praeter* CFl ES   6 cause *om. sed
lacuna per lineam indicatur*
tit. 7 ordines *cum* Fa *Λ*
67 1 *rubr.* cap. ii. *cum* LcYVs   4-5 iudicium *om.* (*corr. manu recenti* [*s. xiii?*]
marg.)
68 4 effectus *om. cum* VsFa LzRv
69 2 *inscr.* dixit synodo *tr.*   4 acolitus aduersus subdiaconum *om. cum* VsFa
(*homoiotel.*)
70 6 ad eos recurrat *tr. cum cett.* (*praeter* CFl)   8 cognouerint *cum* W
71 3 actores] lectores   7 secus] aliter *marg.*
72 2 *inscr.* Syxtus *cum* LcY B Vl   6 deducuntur *cum* FlLcFaVsΛN
73 3-4 ipse ab eis caritatiue *tr. cum orig. et cett. praeter* CFlYFa   8 inibi *corr.
supra lin. ex* finibus   [9 quo] quod
tit. 9 possint *cum K* (*praeter* CFl)
74 8 doctores] rectores *cum orig. et cett. praeter* CFl
78 7 a] *om.*   8 aut] et
79 5 ab] *om. cum cett. praeter* CFl
80 4 perpauci nimis] per paucissime *cum Λ*
82 3 propriis *om.*   7 tenent] *corr. marg. ex* temptant   9 aliquis *om.*
83 5 iterato] in tanto   7 comprouincialibus episcopis *tr. cum cett. praeter* CFl
8 permissum]   praesumendum
84 7 elegit *om.*
86 4-5 in synodo suo tempore] in suo tempore in synodo   9 Christo *om.*
87 2 metropolitano eorum *tr.*   4 licet] liceat *cum* VsFa   9 in terra *om.*
88 1 *rubr.* de eadem re *om.*   6 expoposcerint *cum* Lz
90 4 omnes] omnibus   5 concordentur   6 episcopos] omnes *praem.*
sancte] *om. cum* Vh
91 2 *inscr.* ecclesie *om.*   uniuersis] omnibus *cum* VsFa   5 et *om.*
9 causa] causam *cum Σ*
93 1 *rubr.* Eadem re cap. i. *tantum*   2 *inscr.* Sixtus *cum* FlVs *Σ*   3 aut
om. cum Vs
94 7 substantiam suam   12 uocentur *cum* G
95 1 *rubr.* i.] ii. *cum* YVs   2 *inscr.* Anatholio   6 canonice *om. cum* Lz
96 3-4 propria pellere sede *tr. cum orig. et cett.* (*praeter* CFlLc LzRv ESVh)
100 1 *rubr.* cap. iii. *tantum cum* N
101 5 talionem] talionere
tit. 13 et de iniustis iudiciis *om. cum* Lz *K* (*praeter* Y)
104 1 *rubr.* cap. ii.] cap. eodem *cum* LcVs

105   1 *rubr.* De iniustis iudiciis (cap. i. *add.* FlLcVs) *cum K* (praeter Y)
106   1 *rubr.* ii.] iii.   2 *inscr.* omnibus episcopis tr. cum *Λ* (*absque* B) ES
107   2 *inscr.* omnibus episcopis *tr. cum* Fl LzRv ESVh
tit. 14 et de synodica uocatione] *om. cum K* (praeter FlY)
108   2 *inscr.* ceterisque] cunctisque
109   2 aut] uel
110   *tit.* De uocatione synodica *praem. cum K* (*praeter* Y)   3 nisi] si *cum* VsFa B
111   5 fuit discipulus *tr.*   eumque *om.*   sacerdotum   summum fieri *tr.*
    6 ullo] nullo *cum* FlLcVsFa Rv
114   1 *rubr.* ii.] i. *cum* Vs   3 futuri] pro *praem.* (prefuturi *orig.*)
115   2 tolerabilius   3 excusatio (*homoiotel.*)
116   1 *rubr.* Item cap.
117   1 *rubr.* Cap. i. *tantum*
118   1 *rubr.* re *om.*   iii.] ii. *cum* Y   5 non] nec   6 copulauit   7 electio
    est] electione
119   8 quod] quem *cum orig. et* Fl
120   6 prouidenterque (*homoiotel.*)
121   4 personam *cum* FlLcFa
123   4 desiderat episcopatum *tr.*
124   4 enim *om.*   5 suam *om.*   11 inseruiat] ut seruiat
126   6 honoris   23 locis illis est *tr. cum cett. praeter* N VlE   27 inane
    29 est tacere *tr.*
127   2 nos] uos *cum cett. praeter* FlN LzRv   4 meroris *corr. ex* roris   6 da-
    tione] actione   8 nulla de actu probatio *om.*   26 patenter] pa-
    teunt
128   5 quasi *om.*   7-8 sed que—impenditur *om. cum* VsFa (*homoiotel.*)
    12 commodatio *cum* VsFa   20-22 Nam aliud—committere *om.*
129   6 sint] sunt *cum* LcVs LzRv
130   1 *rubr.* cap. eodem *om.*   8 imponenda   12 et[1] *om.*
131   5 aliquod *corr. ex* aliquid   8 he] ea *cum* Fa, *supra lin. corr.* h
132   1 *rubr.* cap. eodem
133   1 *rubr.* cap. *om. cum* Fa   9 aliud *om. cum* VsFa   11 indebite] debite
    (indebite *interlin.*)
134   3 quoniam] quando
135   5 ex *om.*
136   1 *rubr. om.*   2 *inscr.* cap. i. *add.*   Voluimus   6 lirnei *cum* LcN[ac]
    VsFa VlG   10 culmen *om. cum* Vs   13 frequenter maiorum *tr.*
    adhuc *om.*
137   3 personam   7 experientia] ex merito (*homoiotel.*)   11 consecrauerint-
    qualem *om. cum* Fa (*homoiotel.*)   12 aliquomodo] aliquando
138   12 qui *om.*
139   3 secundam] certe *praem. cum cett. praeter* CFl G   uxorem] uel coniugem
    add.
141   4 cepisse   qui] in *add.*   8 qui] quia
147   6-7 cauendum est ab his *tr. cum* Y *Σ*
148   3 sint] sunt cum N[ac] *Λ* (*praeter* Lz)
149   4 in quo] quoque
150   2 *inscr.* omnibus episcopis *tr. cum* FlFaVs RcLzRv WS
154   2 *inscr.* omnibus episcopis *tr. cum* YΛ (*praeter* B) *Σ*
156   4 ignorantes   5-6 ad sacros ordines *om.*

158 3 et] aut *cum cett. praeter* CF1   4 designatis
160 14 hierosolimitanorum
161 2 *inscr.* Anitius   3 diem *om. cum* E   8 archiepiscopi] episcopi
    est *om. cum* W   13 ab omnibus episcopis quibus preest *om.* (*homoiotel.*)
162 2 *inscr.* Rotomagentium
163 1 *rubr.* iii.] i. *cum* Vs   6 perficiendus *cum* LzRv
164 1 *rubr.* re *om.*

164a ITEM DE EADEM RE   fol. 38r
In Niceno concilio cap. vi. Nullum absolute . . . ordinantis iniuriam.
Conc. Chalcedon. c.6 vers. Dion (COD ed. 3 [1973] p. 90)   cf. Ans. ded. 2.37,
4.24, Reg. 1.397, Burch. 2.6   Ans. 7.88   Ivo Decr. 6.26   Coll.
Mil. 1.143   Grat. D.70 c.1 vers. Hisp.

165-210   fol. 38r-46r
165 10 paschka   pertinere *om.*
166 4 ieiunium
167 6 uestimentis *cum cett. praeter* CF1 G
168 2 episcopis omnibus *tr. cum* Σ
tit. 21 et continentia clericorum *om. cum* Y
170 6 honore privari *tr.*
171 5 licere exponere cum Fa, *lect. incerta* Vs   9 sancta—possunt *om.*
173 2 qui] quis
174 3 generali] uenerabili
175 7 prebere] probare
177 3 pertulerunt *cum* Fa, *lect. incerta* Vs
178 3 *rubr. om. cum* YFa RcRv
179 1 *rubr. om., sed* de obseruatione decretorum pontificum romanorum cap. iii.
    (= *tit.* 23 *et* 178 1 *rubr.*) *repet.*
180 4 etatum] estatum   4-5 condicione] consideratione
182 3 clericorum *om.*   9 totius] cleritius (*homoiotel.*)
184 5 hoc absit *tr.*
185 6 uerbis] nobis *interlin.* uobis   8 meus namque est honor uniuersalis honor
    11 negat] se *add. cum cett. praeter* CF1
186 19 eius] cuius
187 2 *inscr.* Kalixtus *cum* Fa Rc   5 aut]uel *cum cett. praeter* CF1   13 fuerit
    ecclesia *tr. cum cett. praeter* CF1
188 13 cogente] coactus *cum cett. praeter* CF1   14 et inthronizatus *om. cum*
    VsFa   15 ordinare regulariter *tr. cum cett. praeter* CF1   18 etenim]
    est enim   19 est *om.*
189 2 *inscr.* omnibus episcopis *tr. cum cett. praeter* CF1Lc
190 6 auaritiam concupiuit] superbiam spreuit   6-7 superbiam spreuit] auaritiam
    concupiuit   7 contentus] contemptus *cum* CF1LcVs^ac FaΛ (*praeter* B)
tit. 26 contemptus *cum* VsFa Λ (*absque* Rc)
191 6 aut] uel   8-9 ad apostolicam hanc sedem *tr.*   9 episcoporum—sunt] iu-
    dicia episcoporum commissa sunt terminare *cum* VsFa
192 2 *inscr.* Calixtus cum F1YVsFa Λ (*absque* B)   3 parrochiam pertinet *tr.*
194 1 *rubr.* eodem] ii. *cum* NVs B
195 2 *inscr.* Xystus] Calixtus   5 sui *om.*   6 nullatenus *cum* NVh
196 1 *rubr.* cap.] cxcvi. *add.*
197 13 patet] omnibus *praem.*

198   9 quidem] quicquam
199   2 *rubr.* ii.] cxcviiii.   3 *inscr.* Calixtus *cum* FlYVs LzRv
200   1 *rubr.* cap.] cc. *add.*   2 et] etiam
201   8 discordamur   16 qui] quia   17 ingemuerit saluus erit   20 separaretur] proiceretur *cum cett. praeter* CFl   23-24 Deo dignam *tr.* 26 perspexit peccata sua *tr. cum* VsFa
202   7 inquisitionis vice *tr.*   10 est *om.*   11 Aquiritano   18 studiosa] superstitiosa *cum cett. praeter* CFl   22-23 emendationem penitentie *tr. cum cett. praeter* C   23 magis *om.*   32 dignitatem (*homoiotel.*) 36 ecclesia *om.* tua *om. cum* VsFa LzRv   39 angelo] euangelio 42 ergo *om. cum* VzFa   47-48 sacerdotali dignitate *tr.*   55 sequatur 59 electione] lectione *cum* LcVsFa B[ac] LzRv   60 patres sancti *tr.* 76 maios] magis *cum* LzRv *Σ* (*absque* Vh)   77 auctoritas *om.*
    tit. 29 debeant missas celebrare (missa celebrare VsFa)
204   12 oblationem celebrare (oblationes celebrare Vh)
205   5 sacrificium cum VsFa
207   1 *rubr.* xvii.] xvi.   2 Sic] sicut
208   1 *rubr.* Item eodem capitulo *tantum*
210   7 sacrandas cum *K* (absque CFl) BRc *Σ* (absque SVh)

210a Item de eadem re cap.   fol. 46r
Vigilius papa romanus Eleutherio episcopo. De fabrica . . . sanctificationis accipiet.
JK †907   H 711 no. 4   Burch. 3.62   Ivo Decr. 3.25   Poly. 3.6.3   cf. Ivo Pan. 2.14   Grat. de cons. D.1 c.24

211-221   fol. 46r-47r
212   7 omnes] homines
214   4 episcoporum *om.*
215   2 *inscr.* episcopis] presbiteris *cum* VsFa
216   1 *rubr.* Item in eodem capitulo   2-3 transiturus   8 non potest peccare *tr. cum cett. praeter* CFl *Σ*
217   7 sed *om.*   8 oleo] loco
218   3 pentecostes *cum* E
219   3 inesse] in homine (inomine MS)
221   1 *rubr.* cap. vi. *cum* Y B

221a Item de eadem re   fol. 47r-47v
Gregorius episcopus Ianuario episcopo Caralutino. Peruenit ad nos . . . debeant concedimus.
JE 1298 (Gregorii I *Regist.* 4.26)   cf. Grat. D.95 c.1 (Pervenit quoque)
222   fol. 47v

222a Item de eadem re   fol. 47v
Petrus Deo amabilis presbiter et locum retinens sanctissimi Adriani papae Romani dixit. Ut aiunt ystoriographi . . . est repudiata.
Ex *Conc. Nicaeni II* actione 1 (vers. Anastasii biblioth. ed. Mansi 12.1037B).
222b Qvod sacramenta per iniqvvm tradita non ledvntvr.   fol. 47v-48r
Gloriosissimo et clementissimo filio Anastasio Augusto. Secundum ecclesie . . . divina uideantur.
JK †744   cf. H 656 no. 7-8 (8 in part)   Ans. ded. 2.25   Reg. App. 3.16   Ivo Decr. 1.151 (Sacratissimum serenitatis)   Poly. 3.10.11 (Nam secundum)   Grat. D.19 c.8

222c Item de eadem re   fol. 48r
Quia corporis ... honoribus receperunt.
August. ep. 185 (*De correctione Donatistarum liber*, CSEL 57.40f.), excerpts
compiled from cc. 46 and 47. The same compilation in Vat. lat. 1346 (Collection
in Seven Books) fol. 192r.

222d Item de eadem re   fol. 48v
*Domino dilecto et amantissimo comministro Rufiniano Athanasius in Domino
salutem.* Quoniam amore ... indulgentia tributa consistit.

222e De receptione Donatistarvm   fol. 48v-49r
Ex ipsis Donatistis quicumque correpto ... unitati consuletur.
Codex Ecclesiae Africanae c.68 (ed. Bruns, *Canones* 1.173, Lines 3-21; ed. C.
Munier, *Concilia Africae A. 325 - A. 535* [CCL 149; Turnhout 1974] 200, lines
608-26 [*Registri eccl. Carthag. excerpta*])

222f De ordinatione non iteranda   fol. 49r
Gregorius Iohanni Rauennati. Sicut baptizatus ... ordo seruari.
JE 1198 (Gregorii I *Regist.* 2.45)   cf. Ivo Decr. 6.82 (Illud quod)   Ivo
Pan. 3.76   Poly. 2.35.3   Grat. D.68 c.1 (Sicut semel)

222g Item de eadem re cap.   fol. 49r
Honoratus et Urbanus episcopi dixerunt. Illud autem suggerimus ... est,
placet.
Conc. Carth. III c.38 (ed. Bruns, *Canones* 1.128-129, lines 1-4, 18-19; ed. Munier,
Conc. Afr 335-6, lines 220-22, 237-8.

222h Item de eadem re   fol. 49r
Trinitatis sacramenta ... dari oportet.

222i Item de eadem re   fol. 49r-49v
Babtismus et ordinatio ... fiat iniuria.

223   fol. 49v
    4 miscuerunt

223a Item de eadem re   fol. 49v
Quicumque a peruerso ... hostis ore piatis.

224-225   fol. 49v
    224 2 rubr. *om. cum* NFa LzRv *Λ*   3 *inscr.* christianis] episcopis *cum* VsFa *Σ*
         (*praeter* B)   3 episcoporum in *tr.*   4 excelse] in *praem. cum* LzRv V1

225a Vt excommvnicatis non commvnicetur   fol. 50r
Gregorius in homelia paschalis. Siue iuste ... erat fiat.
Greg. M. *Hom. in Evangelia* 2.26. cf. PL 76.1201 (Sed utrum juste)

309   fol. 50r
    tit. 68 Item ut excommunicatis non communicetur

309a Item de eadem re cap. ii.   fol. 50r
Antiocenum concilium cap. ii. Si quilibet ex ... confundit aecclesiae.
Conc. Ant. c.2 vers. Hisp. (cf. PL 84.123; vers. Dion. PL 67.60)

309b Item   fol. 50r
Cartaginense cap. xxviiii. Qui tempore excommunicationis ... protulisse sen-
tentiam.
Codex Ecclesiae Africanae c.29 (lines 3-5 ed. Bruns, *Canones* 1.165; Munier
Conc. Afr. 110, lines 294-6 [*Canones in causa Apiarii*])   cf. Reg. 2.408,
Burch. 1.200, Ans. 12.26, Ivo Decr. 5.314 etc.   cf. Grat. C11 q.3 c.9

309c Item · fol. 50r
Ex concilio Antioceno. Si quis episcopus dampnatus ... habere satisfactionis.
Conc. Ant. c. 4 vers. Dion. (cf. PL 67.62; vers. Hisp. PL 84.124) · cf. Ans.
ded. 2.42 · Reg. 2.407 · Burch. 1.199 · Ans. 12.25 · Ivo Decr.
5.362 · Grat. C.11 q.3 c.6

321 · fol. 50r-50v
tit. 80 *om. scrip. tantum* Item de eadem re cap. · 3 *inscr.* Calixtus · 5 iustam
om. · 6 quia *om.* · in¹] uero *praem.* · in²] *om. cum* G scienter]
eis *praem.* · 6-7 excommunicatis *om.* · 7 institutiones · 8 excommunicatione subiaceant

321a Item de eadem re · fol. 50v
Gelasius. Quicumque igitur ... non possumus (= 74T c.**323**). Sane qui
ante audientiam ... mortis interuentu *add.* Sd
JK 693

321b Item de eadem re · fol. 50v
Leo uniuersis episcopis per Italiam. Misimus ad uos ... coniunctionem lo-
quantur.

321c Item de eadem · fol. 50v
Si quis a proprio ... penitus aperiri.

321d Qvomodo ivngatvr qvis excommvnicatis. · fol. 50v-51r
Augustinus in epistola concilii ad Donatistas. Quisquis a catholica. .. non
habet criminis.

321e Item de eadem re · fol. 51r
Nemo ante tempus ... insultanter arguatis.

321f Item de eadem re · fol. 51r-51v
Ecce, inquiunt quidam ... ore non parcere.
Augustine, *Sermo* 88 no. 23-24 (PL 38.551-552) · cf. Ans. 12.64 (Illud in-
quiunt) · Poly. 7.9.9 · Grat. C.23 q.4 c.4

321g Item de eadem re · fol. 51v
Certe manifeste ... ne tangatis.
Augustine, *Sermo* 88 no. 25 (PL 38.553) · Ans. 12.64 · cf. Poly. 7.9.9
Grat. C.23 q.4 c.4

314-315 · fol. 51v-52r
314 13 denuo non praesumas *tr. cum cett. praeter* CFl
315 tit. 74 *deest* · 2 *rubr.* Item de eadem re cap. x. *tantum* · 9 exercenda

315a Qvod omnis qvi donvm Dei vendiderit deponatvr · fol. 52r
Omnis ergo episcopus ... disciplinis eruditi.
Conc. Nic. II, ex epistola Tarasii ad Iohannem presbyterum, vers. Anastas.
(Mansi 13.476) · Ans. 6.76 · cf. Ivo Decr. 5.121 (Omnis episcopus)

315b Item de eadem re · fol. 52r-52v
Gregorius Nazanzenus. Qui donum Dei ... communicet iudicamus.
Ex eadem epistola Tarasii · cf. Deusd. 4.151 · Grat. C.1 q.1 c.11 (Qui
studet)

226-232 · fol. 52v-53v
226 3 aliter *om.*
227 4 pondus *om.* · 8 causam

228 5 celebrans
229 3 *rubr.* cap. iii
230 1 *rubr.* item cap. i. *cum* N   5 esse immunis *tr. cum cett. praeter* CFl
232 4 monasterio *cum* LcY Lz   6 seruitium omnipotentis *tr.*   Dei *om. cum* VsFa
     10-11 ferunt] fuerunt   16 proueatur *cum cett. praeter* CFl   17 mul-
     tantur morte *tr.*

232a ITEM DE EADEM RE   fol. 53v
Gelasius papa Romanus episcopis omnibus. Quisquis propriae ... sunt re-
seruanda.

233   fol. 53v
     8 misterium (*corr. interlin.* ni = ministerium)

233a QVOD EADEM LEX CONTINENTIE SIT MINISTRIS ALTARIS   fol. 53v
Leo urbis Romae episcopus Rustico Narbonensi episcopo. Lex continentie
aedem . . . opera nuptiarum.
JK 544   H 616 c.3   Ans. ded. 4.88   Burch. 2.114   Ans. 6.201
Ivo Decr. 6.68   Ivo Pan. 3.106   Poly. 4.32.23

236   fol. 53v-54r
     3-4 *inscr.* cunctisque fidelibus *om.*   4 illo] ullo est *om. cum* VsFa VlW

249-250   fol. 54r
     249 3 culpe ordinum *tr.*
     250 4 plectatur] spectatur

246   fol. 54r
     tit. 52 *deest*   2 *rubr.* cap. ii.] Item de eadem re cap.

237-240   fol. 54r-54v
     237 tit. 47 Ne] quod   sint] non *praem.*   6 sancta] sacra   enim] etiam
          cum cett. praeter CFl Σ
     239 9 missam

313   fol. 54v
          4 nata est *tr. cum* Σ

312   fol. 54v

241-245   fol. 54v-55r
     241 9 predicare *om.*
     243 3 *inscr.*   ierosolimorum *cum* K (*praeter* C)
     245 2 sacra] sacrata *cum* Fa

248   fol. 55v

251-253   fol. 55v-56r
     251 3 *inscr.* Berentio   9 desperationem] seperationem
     252 2-3 nubunt Domino *tr.*   6 uiuente *om.*   7 ante *om.*
     253 7 ingemuerit *cum* Fa   8 erit *cum* Fa Rc   14 consequantur] *add.* Se-
          ruata tamen regula . . . communicare non possumus = JK 485 (H 625-6 *fine
          excepta; cf.* Grat. de poen. D.1 c.49)

253a ITEM DE EADEM RE   fol. 56r
Is qui penitentiam . . . dedit probauerit.
Ps.-Conc. Cart. IV (*Statuta eccl. antiqua*) c.76   (ed. Bruns *Canones* 1.148;
ed. Munier, *Conc. Galliae* 170 c.20)   Ivo Decr. 15.8   Grat. C.26 q.6 c.8
cf. Ans. ded. 7.90   Burch. 18.10   Ans. 11.18   Poly. 8.1.13

253b ITEM DE EADEM RE   fol. 56r
Egrogantes si . . . dixerint baptizentur.
Conc. Cart. III c.34 (ed. Bruns, *Canones* 1.128; ed. Munier *Conc. Afr.* 335)
cf. Burch. 4.36   Ivo Decr. 1.123 and 230   Ivo Pan. 1.14   Grat.
de cons. D.4 c.75

254-266   fol. 56r-57v
  254 3 incesta] incerta
  255 7 enim] ergo *cum cett. praeter* CFl Vh
  256 7 qui licet] quilibet *cf.* Vs^(ac) Fa Rc
  tit. 59 2 personis comittantur *tr.*
  258 3 *rubr. om. cum* CFlFa Rv Σ 13 distribuat *cum* Vs^(ac) Fa
  259 1 *rubr.* cap. lx. *tantum*   2 *inscr.* Arthemio   5 prospici (s *interlin.*)
  tit. 60 facultatem commitatur aecclesiae *cum* Fa
  261 6 officii (*homoiotel.*)   7 conueniat] conciliet
  263 4 *inscr.* christianis] orthodoxis *cum cett. praeter* CFl
  264 1 *rubr.* Item cap. i. *tantum*   6 explendum Domino *tr. cum cett. praeter* CFl
      14 ceciderunt
  265 3 matris] sanctae *praem. cum cett. praeter* CFlFa   6 iudicantur] iudicandi
      sunt
  266 2 *inscr.* Simmachus cum FINYFa B EVl   4 Domino *om.*

266a ITEM DE EADEM RE CAP.   fol. 57v-58r
Simmachus papa R. dilectissimo fratri Cesario. Possessiones quas . . . tem-
poraliter perfruantur.
JK 764   H 657.1   Ans. 5.43   Deusd. 3.46   Poly. 3.12.12
(Possessiones igitur quas)

267-270   fol. 58r
  267 1 *rubr.* Item] de eadem re *add.*   6 dictum *cum cett. praeter* CNY
      7 secundi] seculi
  268 3 se citissime *tr. cum cett. praeter* CVs   5 ecclesie res *tr.*   7 uel *om.*
      cum VsFa
  269 1 *rubr.* de eadem re *om. cum* Vs
  270 1 *rubr. om. cum* Σ 2 sacrilegium *cum* $\Lambda\Sigma$

270a ITEM DE EADEM RE   fol. 58v
Si qua de rebus . . . pretio reddidisse.
Conc. Ancyr. c.15 vers. Hisp. (cf. PL 84.107)   cf. H 262   Ans. 6.155
Deusd. 3.13   Grat. C.12 q.2 c.42

247   fol. 58v
  2 *rubr. om.*   6 deliquerunt *cum* Fa, *lect. incerta* Vs

247a DE STIPENDIIS VEL OBLATIONIBVS   fol. 58v-59r
Gregorius papa R. Augustino Canturiorum episcopo ecclesie. Mos apostolicae
. . . munda sunt uobis.
JE 1843 (Gregorii I *Regist.* 11.56a)   cf. Ans. 5.60   Ivo Pan. 2.8
Grat. C.12 q.2 c.30

247b ITEM DE EADEM RE   fol. 59r
Nicolaus episcopus omnibus episcopis. De redditibus primitiarum . . . reddi-
derit anathematizetur.
cf. Ivo Pan. 2.9

271   fol. 59r
tit. 62 De legitimo coniugio   15 suffrata fuerit

271a ITEM DE EADEM RE   fol. 59r
Desponsatas puellas . . . ammississe constiterit.
Conc. Ancyr. c.11 vers. Hisp. (PL 84.106)   cf. vers. Dion. in: Ans. ded.
7.276   Reg. 2.154   Burch. 9.38   Ivo Decr. 8.176   Ivo Pan.
6.19   Grat. C.27 q.2 c.46

271b ITEM DE EADEM RE   fol. 59v
Ex responsis Nicholai papae ad consulta bulgarorum. Sufficiat secundum . . .
sed uoluntas.
JE 2812 (PL 119.978)   Ivo Pan. 6.107   Cf. Grat. C.27 q.2 c.2 and c.4

271c ITEM DE EADEM RE   fol. 59v
Siricius papa Ymerio Terraconensi episcopo. De coniugali . . . transgressione
uioletur.
JK 255   Reg. 2.154   Burch. 9.31   Ans. 10.7   Ivo Decr.
8.169   Grat. C.27 q.2 c.50

272-274
272   3 *inscr.* Aquileiensi *cum* FINYVs VlWGS
273   3 *inscr.* Theotiste *cum* VsFa   6 qui] quod (*homoiotel.*)   7 excepto *cum*
      Fa *Λ* (absque Rc)   9 dimittet *cum* VlW
274   8 quoddam] quondam *cum* NYVs*Λ*   9 ne] nec   15 copulationem *cum* S

274a ITEM DE EADEM RE   fol. 60r-60v
Usque adeo manent . . . fidei non ammittit.
Augustine, *De nuptiis et concupiscentia* (CSEL 42.223, lines 14-24)   cf.
Ivo Decr. 8.12-13   Ivo Pan. 6.74   Grat. C.32 q.7 c.28

274b ITEM DE EADEM RE   fol. 60v
Hieronimus super Mathaeum. Dominus ait phariseis . . . secundum accipiat
uirum.
Jerome, *In Matheum* III 19.8-9 (CCL 77.166-7, lines 749-51, 759-60, 771-2,
775-7)

274c ITEM DE EADEM RE   fol. 60v-61r
Dominus praecipit mulierem . . . moritur Deus.

274d QVOD POST PENITENTIAM NON EST TEMPORIS RECONCILIATIO   fol. 61r
Cum non iubeat . . . remissio peccatorum.
Augustine, *De adulterinis coniugiis* 2.9 (CSEL 41.401 ff; PL 40.431ff.)

274e DE HIS QVI VXORES SVAS SACRO [*sic*] IN ADVLTERIO DEPRE-
HENDVNT   fol. 61r-61v
Hi uero qui . . . mitius praelibauimus.

274f DE HIS QVI COMISCERI NEQVEVNT   fol. 61v
De his requisitis . . . nuptias expetunt.
cf. Burch. 9.44   Ans. 10.23   Ivo Decr. 8.182   Ivo Pan. 6.116
Poly. 6.4.17   Grat. C.33 q.1 c.2

274g DE SEPTIMO GRADV COGNATIONIS   fol. 61v-62r
De gradibus . . . ultionibus separentur.
cf. Poly. 6.4.57   Grat. C.35 q.8 c.1

274h DE HIS QVOS REGENERATIO IVNGIT [*scr.* uincit *vel* iuncit]   fol. 62r
Ex responsis Nicholai papae ad consulta bulgarorum. Inter eos non ... se cernimur.
JE 2812   cf. C.30 q.3 c.1

274i DE HIS QVI FILIOS DE FONTE SVSCIPIVNT   fol. 62r-62v
Deusdedit sanctae R. ecclesie episcopus Gordiano yspaniensis aecclesiae episcopo.
Peruenit ad nos ... et uir uxorem.
JE †2003   Burch. 17.44 cf. Ans. 10.29   Grat. C.30 q.1 c.1

274j DE BAPTISMO FIDELIBVS LAICIS CONCESSO   fol. 62v-63r
Iohannes episcopus Anselmo episcopo lementinae aecclesiae. Ad limina ...
separare deberet.
JE 3258   Ans. 10.30   Ivo Decr. 1.306   cf. Grat. C.30 q.1 c.7

274k DE PRESBITERIS NEGLEGENTIBVS   fol. 63r
Xystus papa sacerdotibus uniuersis. Perpendant presbiteri ... euenerit neglectum.
JK †33   Ivo Decr. 1.240   cf. Burch. 4.46

274l   fol. 63r
Martinus papa omnibus Christi sacerdotibus. Quicumque presbiter ... moritur deponatur.
Burch. 4.47   Ans. 9.58   Ivo Decr. 1.241   Grat. de cons. D.4
c.22 palea

274m DE NVMERO PATRINORVM   fol. 63r
Leo papa. Ut non plures ... quoque id ipsum fiat.
Burch. 4.25   Ans. 9.16   Ivo Decr. 1.219   cf. Ivo Pan. 1.78
Grat. de cons. D.4 c.101 (Non plures)

274n ITEM DE EADEM RE   fol. 63r
[*H*]*iginus papa.* In catecumino ... singuli suscipiant.
Burch. 4.24   cf. Ivo Decr. 1.218   Ivo Pan. 1.77   Grat. de cons.
D.4 c.100

275-307   fol. 63r-64r
   275 1 *rubr. om.*   5 aut] eum
   278 1 *rubr. om.*   2 sit *om.*
   280 2 fratris uxorem] sororem
   284-289 *rubr. omnes om., saepe etiam om.* anathema sit.
   284 2 cognatione] sua *add.*
   288 3 locis] de *praem.*
   289 2 comam] communia
   tit. 66 2 beato *om.*   3-4 pro sua causa ibi agebatur
   290 7 se *om. cum* B
   291 1 *rubr. om.*
   293-307 *rubr. omnes om.*
   299 3 fine
   302 2-3 reddiderint   3 excommunicentur *cum* Vs Rc

234-235   fol. 64r
   234 2 *rubr. om. cum* Fa LzRv EVh
   235 3 *inscr.* agnorum

308   fol. 64r

310-311   fol. 64r-64v

   310 2 *rubr.* xlvi. *cum* C LzRv   5 que concessa sunt eis *tr.*

   311 5 inueniuntur eos *tr.*

311a DE HIS QVI DE SERVITIO IVDEORVM CONVERTI VOLVNT   fol. 64v
Gregorius Fortunato Neapolitano episcopo. Fraternitatem uestram oportet ...
omnibus uendicetur.

JE 1409 (Gregorii I *Regist.* 6.29)   cf. Ivo Decr. 13.106   Poly. 7.13.3
Grat. D.54 c.15

311b ITEM DE EADEM RE   fol. 64v
Gregorius Ianuario Caralitano episcopo. Peruenit ad nos seruos ... modis
omnibus defendatur.

JE 1281 (Gregorii I *Regist.* 4.9)   Ivo Decr. 13.102

311c ITEM DE EADEM RE   fol. 64v
Gregorius Leoni Cathenensi episcopo. Comperimus quod iudei ... legibus feriendi.

JE 1410 (Gregorii I *Regist.* 6.30)

APPENDIX 1

Sequence of 74T canons in Sd,
with the number of inserted canons indicated in parentheses

1-61 (+1)	251-253 (+2)
62-164 (+1)	254-266 (+1)
165-210 (+1)	267-270 (+1)
211-221 (+1)	247 (+2)
222 (+9)	271 (+3)
223 (+1)	272-274 (+14)
224-225 (+1)	275-307
309 (+3)	234-235
321 (+7)	308
314-315 (+2)	310-311 (+3)
226-232 (+1)	
233 (+1)	*74T canons omitted in Sd:*
236	246
249-250	249
246	250
237-240	316-320
313	322
312	[323: cf. Sd 321a]
241-245	324-330
248	

APPENDIX 2

Initia of canons added to 74T

Ad limina 274j	Comperimus quod 311c
Babtismus et 222i	Cum non iubeat 274d
Certe manifeste 321g	De coniugali 271c

De fabrica 210a

De gradibus 274g

De his requisitis 274f

De redditibus 247b

Desponsatas puellas 271a

Dominus ait phariseis 274b

*Dominus praecipit 274c

Ecce inquiunt 321f

Egrogantes si 253b

Ex ipsis Donatistis 222e

Fraternitatem uestram 311a

*Hi uero 274e

Illud autem 222g

In catecumino 274n

Is qui penitentiam 253a

Inter eos 274h

Lex continentie 233a

*Misimus ad uos 321b

Mos apostolicae 247a

*Nemo ante 321e

Nullum absolute 164a

Omnis ergo episcopus 315a

Perpendant presbiteri 274k

Peruenit ad nos 221a

Peruenit ad nos 274i

Peruenit ad nos 311b

Possessiones quas 266a

Querendum est 61a

*Quicumque a peruerso 223a

Quicumque igitur 321a

Quicumque presbiter 274e

Qui donum 315b

*Quisquis a catholica 321d

Quisquis propriae 232a

Qui tempore 309b

*Quoniam amore 222d

Quia corporis 222c

Secundum ecclesie 222b

Si qua de rebus 270a

Si quilibet 309a

*Si quis a 321c

Si quis episcopus 309c

Sicut baptizatus 222f

Siue iuste 225a

Sufficiat secundum 271b

*Trinitatis sacramenta 222h

Usque adeo 274a

Ut aiunt ystoriographi 222a

Ut non plures 274m

APPENDIX 3

Canonical marginalia in Sd (s. xii)

fol. 4v (margin is badly damaged)] excerpt from JK 286 = 74T c.252

fol. 22v] *Telesophorus in prima.* Decet in talibus . . . illaesi liberentur. (H. 112 c.5)

fol. 25r] 2 canons, only in part preserved because of trimming of the margin.

fol. 32v] DE MISERICORDIA. *Ambrosius super psalmum Beati immaculati* (Ps. 118) *Lege tua mis[erere] mei* (v. 29). Lege miseretur qui cum iustitia . . . miseremur iniuste.

Ambr. Expos. in Ps. 118, serm. 4 c.28 ad v.29 (PL 15.1248 C)

fol. 55v] *De uirginibus non uelatis si deuiauerint. cap. xx.* Hae uero quae . . . saeculorum amen.

JK 286 *ex* H 531 c.13 to end of letter (PL 56.526-7). The canon was begun in the margin, but the complete text is found on an inserted small parchment folio.

cf. Burch. 8.12 Ivo Decr. 7.18 Poly. 4.36.2 Grat. C.27 q.1 c.9

* unidentified canons

fol. 59r]   In qvo ramvscvlo consangvinitatis legitima conivgia fieri possint. *Ex dictis Isidori.* Beatus Isidorus de consanguinitate . . . gradibus terminetur.

Burch. 7.10   cf. Grat. C.35 q.4 c.un. (Consanguinitas dum) and C.35 q.5 c.1 (Series consanguinitatis)

De eodem. *Ex epistola Gregorii papae.* Progeniem suam . . . fecerint separentur.

JE 2239   Burch. 7.11   Grat. C.35 q.2 et 3 c.16

fol. 59v]   *Fabianus papa in suo decreto.* [C]onsanguineos extraneorum . . . fuerit separentur.

JK 284   Burch. 7.21   Ivo Decr. 9.57   Ivo Pan. 7.85   Grat. C.35 q.6 c.1

<Sacramentvm> de parentela qvomodo sit inqvirenda. *Ex concilio Romano Gregorii II.* [De] illa parentela . . . sanctorum reliquiae.

Reg. 2.232   Burch. 7.25 (De ista parentela)   Ivo Decr. 9.61
Ivo Pan. 7.87   Grat. C.35 q.6 c.5   cf. Poly. 6.4.67

Ivramentvm testivm. [I]stud sacramentum . . . sanctorum reliquiae.

Poly. 6.4.68   cf. Reg. 2.233   Burch. 7.26   Ivo Decr. 9.62
Ivo Pan. 7.88   Grat. C.35 q.6 c.6

fol. 60r]   De incestuorum discidio. [A]b isto die . . . sanctorum reliquiae.

Reg. 2.234   Burch. 7.27   Ivo Decr. 9.63   cf. Ivo Pan. 7.40
Poly. 6.4.69   Grat. C.35 q.6 c.11

fol. 66v]   In libro de unico baptismo. An uero . . . penas luant.

Ivo, Decr. 2.3

III

Canossa and Royal Ideology in 1077: Two Unknown Manuscripts of *De penitentia regis Salomonis*

Few developments in the course of the Middle Ages so agitated Europe as the Gregorian reform of the second half of the eleventh and the early twelfth century, also known as the investiture controversy.[1] Contemporary manuscripts in European libraries still witness to that struggle between *regnum* and *sacerdotium*, since the protagonists, mainly the German court of Henry IV and Henry V, and the papal reformers, respectively, undertook to justify their claims in treatises compiled by their supporters.[2] The present note contains the edition of such a treatise. Dating probably from 1077, it deals with royal penance. Heinrich Boehmer partially published the brief tract, *De paenitentia regum*, from a single manuscript known to him: Bamberg, Staatsbibliothek, codex Can. 9 (P.I.9.64).[3] As it turns out, the Bamberg manuscript is badly corrupted and incomplete.

Boehmer already linked the anonymous little work by an imperialist sympathizer to Henry IV's penance at Canossa in January 1077. It would be surprising if this event had not caused a stir.[4] The

---

[1] Some basic works among the voluminous literature for this phase of history are Hubert Jedin and John Dolan, eds., *Handbook of Chruch History*, vol. 3: *The Church in the Age of Feudalism*, ed. by Friedrich Kempf et al., translated by A. Biggs (New York, 1969); Gerd Tellenbach, *Church, State and Christian Society at the Time of the Investiture Contest*, translated by R. F. Bennett (Oxford, 1940); Geoffrey Barraclough, *The Origins of Modern Germany*, 2nd ed. (New York, 1963), especially pp. 101-134; Augustin Fliche, *La réforme grégorienne et la réconquête chrétienne*, Histoire de l'église 8 (Paris, 1946); Gerold Meyer von Knonau, *Jahrbücher des Deutschen Reiches unter Heinrich IV. and Heinrich V.*, Jahrbücher der Deutschen Geschichte 17.2 (Munich, 1894; repr. Berlin 1964) especially pp. 694-764 and Excurs 7, pp. 894- 903.
[2] See Carl Mirbt, *Die Publizistik im Zeitalter Gregors VII.* (Leipzig, 1894); Monumenta Germaniae Historica, *Libelli de lite*, 3 vols. (Hanover 1891-1897; repr., Hanover 1956).
[3] Heinrich Boehmer, "De paenitentia regum et de investitura regali collectanea," *Libelli de lite* 3:608-614; for a description of the manuscript see *ibid.*, pp. 608-9 with further references, and in particular Friedrich Leitschuh and Hans Fischer, *Katalog der Handschriften der königlichen Bibliothek zu Bamberg*, vol. 1, erste Abtheilung, 5. Lieferung (Bamberg, 1903), pp. 866-868.
[4] In addition to the general references given above in n. 1 see in particular the essays edited by Hellmut Kämpf in: *Canossa als Wende; ausgewählte Aufsätze zur neueren Forschung*, Wege der Forschung 12 (Darmstadt, 1969); Helmut

opposition to Henry IV united at Tribur in October 1076, and forced the king to submit his case to adjudication by Pope Gregory VII, who was to celebrate a council at Augsburg in Germany in February 1077. If Gregory should not absolve Henry from the excommunication the pope had pronounced at the Roman Lenten synod of 1076,[5] the German princes and bishops would elect another king. In other words, they would give effect to the deposition of Henry IV which Gregory had promulgated in February 1076 together with the excommunication. Late in 1076, therefore, everything looked as if the pontiff would truimph over his adversary. King Henry IV, however, outwitted his opponents. He intercepted Pope Gregory VII, who was on his way to Germany, in the Alps and appeared as a penitent at the gates of the fortress of Canossa, where Gregory had sought protection. The pope could not but readmit Henry to communion with the Church, whatever his attitude towards this particular sinner, and whatever the political implications of this pastoral act.[6] Through the reconciliation Henry gained time to rally his forces and to eventually defeat the German opposition.

It can be seen, therefore, why the royal submission is often regarded as a victory for the king.[7] Johannes Haller is one of the few historians who recognize Canossa for what it really was: a severe defeat.[8] Even outwardly, Henry's humiliation was profound. As a barefoot penitent the king waited for three days in the snow for papal forgiveness.[9] Through this action Henry admitted the right of the pope to judge and even to depose kings, abandoning the vision of a kingship by the grace of God. What Canossa meant for royal ideology is strikingly revealed by a glance at tract four of the Norman Anonymous, presenting the most extreme claims for kingship. In the well-known tract the king is seen as both king and priest; through grace god and *christus Domini*, whose official ac-

---

Beumann, "Tribur, Rom und Canossa," *"Investiturstreit und Reichsverfassung,* Vorträge und Forschungen 17 (Sigmaringen, 1973), 33-60, and in conjunction with Beumann now Eduard Hlawitschka, "Zwischen Tribur und Canossa," *Historisches Jahrbuch* 94 (1974), 25-45.

[5] *Das Register Gregors VII.,* ed. Erich Caspar, MGH Epistolae selectae 2.1-2. (Berlin, 1920-23), pp. 268-271 = register 3.10a.

[6] *Ibid.,* pp. 311-315 = register 4.12.

[7] E.g. Fliche, *La réforme grégorienne,* pp. 142-144.

[8] Johannes Haller, *Das Papsttum. Idee und Wirklichkeit,* 2nd rev. ed., 2 (Basel, 1951), pp. 399-400.

[9] *Das Register Gregors VII.* pp. 312-313 = register 4.12.

tions are not of human character but divine.[10] More usual was the image of a king as a new David and Salomon. Either in 751 or 754, the reference to David and Salomon became part of the Carolingian coronation liturgy and remained a cornerstone of Christian royal ideology.[11]

The treatise De paenitentia regis Salomonis shows that imperial supporters were fully aware of the damaging consequences of the events at Canossa. The anonymous author turned to the Christian tradition of kingship to save as much as possible of royal ideology. After all, Salomon, the wisest of kings had sinned, and so had David. Excerpts from the Scriptures and patristic commentaries are skilfully linked into a rejection of Gregorian claims and the activity of the Lenten council of 1076. According to the testimony of the Scriptures as excerpted here, a king is judged by God alone and cannot be deposed except by his own action. God has mercy on a penitent king and does not withdraw his grace either from the wayward king or his dynasty.

The propagandistic character of the little treatise, only vaguely adumbrated in the Bamberg codex, is made clear in two additional manuscripts of the tract. The codices, at the Biblioteca Comunale Guarneriana at San Daniele del Friuli[12] and at the Landesbibliothek Fulda, indicate that De paenitentia regis Salomonis was popular

---

[10] Si ergo sacerdos et rex uterque per gratiam deus est et christus Domini, quicquid agit et operatur secundum hanc gratiam, iam non homo agit et operatur, sed deus et christus Domini . . . Tractatus Eboracenses 4, ed. Heinrich Boehmer, MGH Libelli de lite 3:665, lines 31-33. The edition by Karl Pellens, Die Texte des Normannischen Anonymus unter Konsultation der Teilausgaben von H. Böhmer, H. Scherrinsky und G. H. Williams neu aus der Handschrift 415 des Corpus Christi College Cambridge herausgegeben, Veröffentlichungen des Instituts für Europäische Geschichte Mainz 42 (Mainz, 1966), and Karl Pellens, Das Kirchendenken des Normannischen Anonymus, Veröffentlichungen des Instituts für Europäische Geschichte Mainz 69 (Mainz, 1973) should be consulted with the critical article by Wilfried Hartmann, "Beziehungen des Normannischen Anonymus zu frühscholastischen Bildungszentren," Deutsches Archiv zur Erforschung mittelalterlicher Geschichte 31 (1975)108-143.

[11] See in particular Eugen Ewig, "Zum christlichen Königsgedanken im Frühmittelalter," Das Königtum, seine geistigen und rechtlichen Grundlagen, Vorträge und Forschungen 3 (Lindau, 1956), pp. 7-73, here especially pp. 45-46. For the use of the images of David and Salomon at the time of the investiture controversy J. Funkenstein, Das Alte Testament im Kampf von regnum und sacerdotium zur Zeit des Investiturstreits (Dortmund, 1938) can be consulted.

[12] As a consequence of the recent earthquakes in northern Italy, the manuscript has now probably been moved. Cf. the article in the New York Times, May 12, 1976, p. 4.

beyond the narrow confines of the royalist-inclined cathedral of Bamberg, the origin of Boehmer's manuscript. They are also both better and more complete. As the apparatus criticus of the following edition shows,[13] pride of place belongs to the manuscript from San Daniele, Guarnerius 203 (hereafter Sd), fully described elsewhere.[14] It is therefore chosen as basic MS, even though it lacks, like codex Bamberg, Staatsbibliothek, Can. 9 (hereafter B), the introduction which is provided by the third codex used in this edition, MS Landesbibliothek Fulda, Aa Theologie 36, 4° (E.43), a florilegium of patristic and canonical excerpts from the twelfth century (hereafter F).[15] It should be noted that in both B and F *De paenitentia regis Salomonis* is followed by the inedited tract *De Antichristo,* which is lacking in the Italian manuscript. The fragmentary, garbled conclusion in B is proof that the long quotation from the *Liber Ecclesiastes* was fully cited in the archetype of the tract.

DE PENITENTIA REGIS SALOMONIS[a]

[Quid sanctus Augustinus, doctor egregius, senserit, quid interpres et expositor diuinae legis, Hieronimus, de paenitentia regis Salomonis scripserit, uel ubi illum catholicae fidei defensor Ambrosius sanctum appellauerit pauens intimabo. In expositione libri genesis ad litteram Augustinus[1] de eo, *Salomon,* inquit, *uir tantae sapientiae, nunquidnam credendum est, quod in simulacrorum cultu credidit aliquid esse de utilitate, sed mulierum amori ad hoc malum trahenti resistere non ualuit, faciens quod sciebat non esse faciendum, ne suas quibus deperibat atque defluebat delicias contristaret.*][b] Hieronimus in septimo decimo

---

[13] The edition was prepared in accordance with the principles of the Institute of Medieval Canon Law, Berkeley. See Stephan Kuttner, "Notes on the Presentation of Text and Apparatus in Editing Works of the Decretists and Decretalists," *Traditio* 15 (1959), 452-464.

[14] Uta-Renate Blumenthal, "Codex Guarnerius 203: A Manuscript of the Collection in 74 Titles at San Daniele del Friuli," *Bulletin of Medieval Canon Law,* n.s. 5 (1975) 11-34. The tract, *De paenitentia regis Salomonis,* is found on fols. 6v-7v.

[15] MS Fulda Aa Theologie 36, 4° (E.43), s. 12, parchment, 76 fols., 2 cols., rubrics and red initials, fols. 74v-75v (pencil ennumeration).

[a] *rubr.* regis *om.* Sd   De paenitentia regum. Testimonia de penitencia Salomonis B
[b] Quid-contristaret *om.* F Sd

[1] Liber 11.42 = *CSEL* 28.1, pp. 377-378 (*PL* 34:453 = Liber 12.59); Dekkers ns. 266-268.

libro^c super Ezechielem de^d extrema uisione eius, que facta est ei^e de edificatione^f in monte constituto, facit mentionem de Salomone dicens[2]: *Quamuis peccasset tamen egit penitentiam*^g *scribens prouerbia,*^h *ubi dicit*[3]: Nouissime egi *penitentiam et respexi ut eligerem disciplinam.* Item Hieronimusⁱ super Ecclesiasten[4]: *Aiunt*^j *Hebrei hunc librum esse Salomonis penitentiam agentis.*^k Ambrosius^l in apologia Dauid[5]: Quid de Dauid dicam et *quid*^m *de sancto Salomone,*ⁿ qui quamquam^o *Iudaicum uulgus*^p estimabat eum *uenisse pro Christo,* ne uideretur esse^q *super hominem,* nutu^r diuino corruit. Et^s Dauid non dicitur sanctus,^t qui ab omnibus esse sanctus scitur,^u et Salomonem sanctum nominat ut nobis de penitentia eius dubietatem^v tollat.^w Item^x Ambrosius de Satiro, fratre suo,^y hoc ait:[6] *sanctus Salomon.* Aiunt^z libri Ebrei[7] Salomonem quinquies tractum fuisse per plateas Hierusalem cause penitentiae. Item aiunt^a eum^b uenisse in

^c in-libro *om.* B
^d de] loquens *praem.* F
^e de-ei] ubi scripsit B
^f aedificio B F
^g tamen egit penitentiam] paenitentiam egit F
^h *corr. ex* propheta F
ⁱ Hieronimus *om.* F
^j inquit *add.* B
^k penitentiam agentis] paenitentis F
^l Ambrosius *supplevi ex* B *et* F; Sd *illegibilis est*
^m quid *om.* F
ⁿ Salomone sancto *tr.* F
^o quamquam] *emendavi ex* quam (haplography)   quamuis B   quoniam F
^p Iudaicus populus B
^q esse *om.* F
^r nutu] idem Christum *praem.* B
^s Et *om.* F
^t esse *add.* F
^u qui scitur] qui ab hominibus sanctus esse scitur F   qui sanctus ab omnibus esse scitur B
^v nobis-dubietatem] nobis dubietatem de paenitentia eius F
^w tollat] sicut Dauid in psalmo: *Irritauerunt Moysen in castris, Aaron sanctum Domini add.* B (Ps. 105.16).
^x item *om.* F
^y de fratre suo Satyro F   inquit *add.* B
^z aiunt] asserunt F   aiunt-penitentiae *om.* B
^a Item aiunt] item dicit F   item Ambrosius, aiunt, inquit B; *cf. editio Boehmeri b. m.* pag. 609, n. 11.
^b eum]illum F   Salemonem B

[2] Comment. in Ezechielem, Liber 13.43 = *PL* 25.419; Dekkers no. 587.
[3] Prov. 24.32.
[4] Comment. in Ecclesiasten, Liber 1.12 = *CC* 72, p. 258 = *PL* 23.1021; Dekkers no. 583.
[5] Liber 1.13 = *CSEL* 32.2, p. 308 = *PL* 14.851; Dekkers no. 135.
[6] Liber 2.30 = *CSEL* 73, p. 265.
[7] *Non inveni; de libris hebraeicis in expositione sacrae scripturae cf.* B. Smalley, *The Study of the Bible in the Middle Ages,* 2d ed. (Notre Dame, 1964), pag. 43, 103, 126.

templum, quod ipse edificauerat[c] cum quinque uirgis de quibus dedit[d] quatuor legis peritis ut uerberaretur ab illis.[e] Qui communi accepto[f] consilio dixerunt,[g] quod in unctum Domini non manum[h] mitterent.[i] Inde frustratus ab illis[j] a se ipso depositus est[k] [de regno. Verba Solomonis de se ipso postquam sponte ammiserat regnum, scribens Ecclesiasten[8]: Christus *purgauit peccata ipsius et exaltauit in eternum cornu ipsius. Et dedit illi testamentum regum et sedem glorie in* Ierusalem. *Post ipsum surrexit filius sensatus et propter illum deiecit omnem potentiam inimicorum. Salomon imperauit in diebus* suis, *cui subiecit Deus omnes hostes, ut conderet domum in nomine suo, et pararet sanctitatem in sempiternum; quemadmodum eruditus est in iuventute* sua, *et impletus* est, *quasi flumen sapientia, et terra retexuit anima* sua. *Et replesti in comparationibus enigmata: ad insulas longe diuulgatum est nomen tuum, et dilectus es in pace tua. In cantilenis, et prouerbiis, et comparationibus, et interpretationibus mirate sunt terre, et in nomini Domini cuius est cognomen Deus Israel. Collegisti quasi auricalcum aurum, et inclinasti foemora tua mulieribus, potestatem habuisti in tempore* tuo. *Dedisti maculam in gloria tua, et profanasti semen tuum.* inducere[l] *iracundiam ad liberos tuos et* in terris *stultitiam tuam,*[m] *ut faceres imperium bipertitum et ex Effreym imperium*[n] [imperare durum. Deus autem non derelinquet misericordiam suam, et non corrumpet neque dolebit opera sua neque perdet ab stirpe nepotes electi sui, et semen eius di‹ligit Dominus.›[o]

---

[c] aedificauerit ipse *tr.* F   [d] dedicauerat B
[d] dedit *om.* F
[e] pro penitentia *add.* B
[f] accepto *om.* F B
[g] dixerunt consilio *tr.* B
[h] manum non *tr.* F B
[i] testante Dauid: *Nolite tangere christos meos add.* B (Ps. 104.15).
[j] Inde-illis *om.* B; ab illis *om.* F
[k] est depositus *tr.* F
[l] inducere *scripsi cum orig.* inducem Sd
[m] de regno-stultitiam tuam *om. F B*
[n] ut-imperium] *om.* F; *et retinuit tantummodo tribum Ephraym et fecit sibi bipertitum imperium* B; *post-ponit* B: Item aiunt Salemonem quinquies tractum fuisse per plateas Iherusalem causa paenitentiae.
[o] imperare-Dominus *om.* F B; diligit Dominus *suppleui ex orig. Codex Sd illegibilis est.*

[8] Liber Eccl. 47.13-24.

IV

Fälschungen bei Kanonisten der Kirchenreform des 11. Jahrhunderts

Das *veri et falsi discrimen* ist nicht immer leicht; besondere Schwierigkeiten bieten aber Sammlungen, gleich ob rechtlicher oder literarischer Art, die ihrer Natur nach aus Auszügen bestehen und daher schon vom Prinzip her Quellen verändern, indem sie Texte in einen ihnen ursprünglich fremden Zusammenhang bringen. Man hat den Verdacht, daß die vielen Distinktionen und Graduierungen zwischen Wahrheit oder Authentizität, Halbwahrheit, Interpolation, Verfälschung und Fälschung[1] zuweilen ein Dilemma verdecken, da mit der Entscheidung wahr oder nicht, echt oder nicht, auch im Zeitalter des Computers meist eine moralische Wertung verbunden bleibt. Seit den Untersuchungen Fourniers zu Kirchenrechtssammlungen zwischen Pseudo-Isidor und Gratian weiß man von der Abkehr von Apokryphen in gregorianischen Kanonessammlungen, einschließlich der Sammlung des Kardinals Deusdedit, der diese Bemerkungen in der Hauptsache gelten[2]. Bei einem Vergleich der Samm-

---

1) Zu Fälschung als mittelalterlichem Begriff siehe besonders Horst FUHRMANN, Einfluß und Verbreitung der pseudoisidorischen Fälschungen. Von ihrem Auftauchen bis in die neuere Zeit 1 (Schriften der MGH 24,1, 1972) S. 64–136; Peter HERDE, Römisches und kanonisches Recht bei der Verfolgung des Fälschungsdelikts im Mittelalter, Traditio 21 (1965) S. 291–362 und Giles CONSTABLE, Forgery and Plagiarism in the Middle Ages, AfD 29 (1983) S. 1–41. Besonderen Dank schulde ich für Hilfe bei der Beschaffung von schwer erreichbarem Material Ann Freeman und Paul Meyvaert, Martin Bertram, dem Institute of Medieval Canon Law sowie Robert Somerville und Barbara Motyka, die das Manuskript gelesen haben. Der Catholic University of America danke ich für finanzielle Hilfe bei der Beschaffung von Mikrofilmen und meinem Kollegen Nelson Minnich für Hinweise auf den Konziliarismus.
2) Die Kanonessammlung des Kardinals Deusdedit, hg. von Victor WOLF VON GLANVELL (1905; zitiert als Deusdedit). Siehe dazu mit Literatur FUHRMANN, Pseudoisidorische Fälschungen 2, S. 522–533; Paul FOURNIER, Un tournant de l'histoire du droit: 1060–1140, Nouvelle revue historique de droit français et étranger 41 (1917) S. 129–180, hier S. 138 f.; DERS., Les Collections canoniques romaines de l'Epoque de Grégoire VII, Mémoires de l'Académie des Inscriptions et Belles-Lettres 41 (1920) S. 271–396, besonders S. 328 ff.; Stephan KUTTNER, Urban II and the Doctrine of Inter-

lungen Deusdedits und Anselms von Lucca wies Fournier zwar darauf hin, daß er trotz Vorbehalten geneigt sei, Deusdedit selbst für einige Textveränderungen verantwortlich zu halten, doch nur um anschließend zu verneinen, daß Deusdedit „se laissait guider par le machiavélique dessein de tromper ses contemporains et la postérité …" und allgemein zu schließen: „Les canonistes grégoriens rajeunissent les textes, mais ne les démarquent pas"[3].

Um es gleich vorweg zu sagen, was bei Kirchenrechtssammlungen des 11. Jahrhunderts überrascht, ist im allgemeinen die Texttreue, wie das für die Falschen Dekretalen sowohl bei Anselm als auch bei Deusdedit gezeigt worden ist[4]. Wenn ich mich heute trotzdem der Sammlung Deusdedits im Zusammenhang mit dem heiklen Thema Fälschung zuwende, so einmal deswegen, weil Deusdedit ein eifriger Kritiker von Fälschungen war[5], und zum anderen, weil er von ehemaligen Kardinalskollegen der Fälschung bezichtigt wurde[6], Kritik, die sich schon aus chronologischen Gründen auf seine Kanonessammlung von 1087 beziehen muß. Deusdedit stand inmitten der Polemik einer Zeit, wo der Übergang zwischen Streitschrift, *libellus,* und Kanonessammlung manchmal fließend war, und in der das Recht, in dem wir gewohnt sind, objektive Normen zu sehen, im Dienst der Reform stand und sich mit ihr zusammen entwickelte[7]. Eine Überprüfung seiner Sammlung im Hinblick auf die Frage nach der Textbehandlung scheint aus allen diesen Gründen angebracht.

---

pretation, a Turning Point? in: Studia Gratiana 15 (= Post Scripta: Essays on Medieval Law and the Emergence of the European State in Honor of Gaines Post, 1972) S. 55–86, jetzt zu benutzen als Neudruck mit Retractiones in: DERS., The history of ideas and doctrines of canon law in the Middle Ages (Variorum Reprints CS 113, 1980).

3) FOURNIER, Collections canoniques romaines, S. 358 und S. 360.

4) FUHRMANN, Pseudoisidorische Fälschungen (wie Anm. 1) 2, S. 521 f. zu Anselm und S. 532 f. zu Deusdedit. Siehe auch FOURNIER, Collections canoniques romaines (wie Anm. 2) S. 322 und S. 358 ff., in der Bewertung zu kontrastieren mit Ian Stuart ROBINSON, Authority and Resistance in the Investiture Contest (1978) S. 42: „Deusdedit's collection contains numerous examples of modifications in canonical texts intended to support a Gregorian thesis" und S. 48 f.

5) Deusdedit, Libellus contra invasores et symoniacos et reliquos schismaticos, ed. Ernst SACKUR, MGH Ldl 2 (1892) S. 310, Z. 8–11: *Preterea autem prefatus Guibertus … quaedam in eodem decreto addendo, quaedam mutando, ita illud reddiderunt a se dissidens, ut aut pauca aut nulla exemplaria sibi concordantia valeant inveniri …* Zur römischen Synode von 1059 siehe auch unten Anm. 67–70.

6) Benonis aliorumque cardinalium schismaticorum … scripta, ed. Kuno FRANCKE, MGH Ldl 2 (1892) S. 366–422, hier Traktat III, S. 399, cap. 14 und S. 400, cap. 15.

7) ROBINSON, Authority and Resistance (wie Anm. 4) S. 43 f.

Deusdedit, wahrscheinlich Südfranzose, Mönch, Dichter und Gelehrter, wurde vor 1078 in jungen Jahren Kardinalpriester des Titels Apostolorum in Eudoxia, heute S. Pietro in Vincoli. Er widmete seine vierteilige Kirchenrechtssammlung 1087 Papst Viktor III. und allen Klerikern der heiligen römischen Kirche, denen sie in Zukunft wohl als eine Art Handbuch dienen sollte[8]. Sie gibt noch manches Rätsel auf, obwohl sie in einer guten kritischen Ausgabe vorliegt. Einmal enthält sie sonst nirgends überlieferte Texte, und außerdem geht sie zum Teil auf mehrere heute wohl nicht mehr vorhandene Zwischensammlungen zurück, zu denen auch andere Sammler Zugang hatten, mit deren Texten Deusdedits Text, der handschriftlich allerdings schlecht überliefert ist, aber selten völlig übereinstimmt[9]. Wie hat Deusdedit gearbeitet? Wie andere seiner Zeitgenossen verkörperte auch er sowohl kritischen Sinn als auch unkritische Haltung[10]. Und obwohl durchaus Andeutungen für eine kritische Textbehandlung vorliegen, zögerte der Kardinal andererseits nicht, Kritik an den

---

8) Zu den Lebensdaten siehe außer der Einleitung GLANVELLS, Deusdedit (wie Anm. 2) besonders Walther HOLTZMANN, Kardinal Deusdedit als Dichter, HJb 57 (1937) S. 217–232.

9) Deusdedit S. XXIV. Zu den Zwischensammlungen siehe besonders FUHRMANN, Pseudoisidorische Fälschungen (wie Anm. 1) 2, S. 517–519, S. 522–533 mit Anm. 268 und 271 sowie S. 539, Anm. 309. Eigene Kollationen führten stets zu den gleichen Ergebnissen. Zu den zuerst bei Deusdedit greifbaren Texten gehören z. B. 1.306, 327; 4.179, 180, 181, 428–431.

10) Horst FUHRMANN, Kritischer Sinn und unkritische Haltung. Vorgratianische Einwände zu Pseudo-Clemens-Briefen, in: Aus Kirche und Reich. Studien zu Theologie, Politik und Recht im Mittelalter. Festschrift für Friedrich Kempf, hg. von Hubert MORDEK (1983) S. 81–95. Zur Arbeitsmethode Deusdedits siehe FUHRMANN (wie Anm. 2) und FOURNIER, Collections canoniques romaines (wie Anm. 2). Der Kardinal ging mit der erklärten Absicht an Quellen heran, dort auszusuchen, was ihm für seine Zwecke passend schien: ... et de reliquis conciliis Orientalibus non abreputaui, quę congrua mihi uisa sunt, mutuare ... (Deusdedit S. 3, Z. 21 f.) Die Methode gilt sicherlich für das gesamte Werk. Er war sich der Bedeutung unterschiedlicher Überlieferungen bewußt. Texte aus dem Constitutum Silvestri schöpfte er aus vier verschiedenen Quellen (S. KUTTNER, Cardinalis: The History of a Canonical Concept, Traditio 3 [1945] S. 129–214, hier S. 208 α und S. 214), und die Falschen Dekretalen benutzte er wohl außer durch Zwischensammlungen in mehreren Handschriften (FUHRMANN, Pseudoisidorische Fälschungen 2, S. 527). Mit wenigen Ausnahmen (4.420 oder 3.106) lassen seine Rubriken die Leser über solche Details im Dunkeln, wenn die „Privilegiensammlung" im 3. Buch nicht berücksichtigt wird (dazu Rudolf SCHIEFFER, Tomus Gregorii papae, AfD 17 [1971] S. 169 ff.); trotzdem forderte Deusdedit die curiosi in seinem Vorwort dazu auf, seine Auszüge in den Quellen nachzulesen, dem Text aber nichts hinzuzufügen (S. 5, Z. 9–12).

Clemensbriefen zum Beispiel einfach mit einem Hinweis darauf zurückzuweisen, daß sie von verschiedenen Päpsten benutzt worden und daher authentisch seien[11]. Häufiger als Atto, Anselm oder der unbekannte Verfasser der 74-Titel-Sammlung hat Deusdedit rein formale Änderungen an Texten vorgenommen, um den Inhalt für seine Zeitgenossen zu verdeutlichen; in die gleiche Kategorie von rein formalen redaktionellen Eingriffen gehören auch Textkürzungen, die häufig vorkommen und bei denen Deusdedit mit eigenen Worten oft sehr geschickt kurz den Zusammenhang andeutet[12]. Er liebt es auch, Texte zu erweitern, indem er anonyme Zitate seiner Vorlagen durch Einschübe identifiziert, oft in der Form *ut ait beatus Gregorius* (4.176) oder *ut ait primus papa Stephanus* (4.54)[13]. Einer dieser charakteristischen Einschübe, *sicut ait primus Nicholaus* (4.184), steht zusammen mit einer zweiten Parallelerweiterung in einem Auszug aus dem 2. Brief Gregors VII. an Hermann von Metz[14], der weit verbreitet war und sicher leicht überprüft werden konnte[15]. Man darf daraus mit Four-

---

11) Deusdedit S. 4, Z. 19 ff. und FUHRMANN, Kritischer Sinn (wie Anm. 10) S. 91.

12) Z. B. 1.30, 194, 217, 324; 2.11 (die von Glanvell kursiv gedruckten Worte entsprechen dem Inhalt von c.15 des zweiten Konzils von Nicaea [787]), 40, 152. Knappe Zusammenfassungen liegen vor in 1.4. und 5, wie bei FOURNIER, Collections canoniques romaines (wie Anm. 2) S. 339, vermerkt. Beispiele für einfache Textkürzungen sind 1.59, 197, 218, 229 und 280. Textsprünge, manchmal bei Deusdedit an der gleichen Stelle wie bei Anselm von Lucca und deswegen wohl aus ihrer gemeinsamen Vorlage übernommen, werden oft, aber durchaus nicht immer, mit *et infra*, *et paulo post* oder *et post pauca* angedeutet, wie z. B. bei 1.24, 32, 33, 61, 65, 153, 277. Vgl. dazu FOURNIER, Collections canoniques romaines, S. 352. Beispiele für Deusdedits Angewohnheit, mehrere Stücke eines Autors aus verschiedenen Schriften zu einem Thema oder mehrere Kanones eines Konzils ohne Hinweis zusammenzufassen, sind 2.65 und 4.224.

13) Anders geartete Zusätze erklärender Art, die ebenfalls nur als redaktionelle Eingriffe zu betrachten sind, finden sich z. B. in 1.43, 45, 51, 146, 194, 215, 251; 2.106, 141; 3.62, 88; 4.29, 46, 242. FOURNIER, Collections canoniques romaines, S. 353: „Il est permis de laisser de côté les très nombreuses interpolations purement explicatives du texte".

14) Deusdedit 4.184 (S. 490) und Gregor VII., Register, hg. von Erich CASPAR (MGH Epp. sel. 2. 1–2, 1920–1932) 8.21 (JL 5201) S. 544 ff., hier S. 554 und S. 551 zur zweiten Erweiterung *Set Anacletus*. Beide Einschübe sind verhältnismäßig lang. Zur Nikolaus-Stelle siehe besonders Ernst PERELS, Die Briefe Papst Nikolaus' I., NA 39 (1914) S. 45–153, hier S. 77 f., Anm. 8. Allgemein zu JL 5201 Rudolf SCHIEFFER, Von Mailand nach Canossa, DA 28 (1972) S. 333 ff., hier besonders S. 362 ff.

15) Zur Verbreitung des Briefes siehe außer Caspars Angaben (S. 544–546) John GILCHRIST, The Reception of Pope Gregory VII into the Canon Law (1073–1141), ZRG Kan. 59 (1973) S. 35–82, hier S. 70 und die Tafel unter der Registernummer 8.21.

nier wohl schließen, daß zusätzliche Parallel-Zitate nicht als textentstellend empfunden wurden[16]. Auch Ivo von Chartres stützte Gegors Aussagen in diesem traktat-ähnlichen Brief mit einem Parallelhinweis, in diesem Fall auf einen Brief Gregors I.[17]. Auch bei Zusammenfassungen verschiedener Texte eines Autors und erkennbaren Glossen wird man zögern, von absichtlichen Textveränderungen zu sprechen, obwohl es hier natürlich Grenzfälle gibt, wie 1.1, wo zu *suburbicaria loca,* die dem römischen Bischof unterstehen sollen, gesetzt wird, *idest regna, que tunc erant sub urbe*[18]. Hier handelt es sich weniger um Ergänzung oder Erklärung — die suburbikarischen Bistümer waren ja gut bekannt und entsprachen keineswegs dem Römischen Reich — als um Interpretation, wahrscheinlich angeregt durch die Konstantinische Schenkung, die in ihrer romgünstig bearbeiteten Fassung[19] Deusdedits viertes Buch eröffnet.

Neben diesen und ähnlichen Änderungen formaler Art bleiben aber doch Texte mit geringfügigen, aber soweit es sich beurteilen läßt, absichtlichen, sachlichen Veränderungen, die es erlauben, Besonderheiten in Deusdedits Sammlung zu deuten und ihn so von anderen Kanonisten der Zeit Gregors VII., Viktors III. und Urbans II. zu unterscheiden. Diesen Text möchte ich mich nunmehr zuwenden. Bekanntlich hat Deusdedit zweimal den Namen seiner Titelkirche, Apostolorum in Eudoxia, eingeschoben, um ihre Weihe durch Sixtus III. (432-440) zu belegen und ihr im liturgischen Zeremoniell der römischen Kirche erhöhte Bedeutung zu geben[20]. Weniger beachtet wurde, daß

16) FOURNIER, Collections canoniques romaines (wie Anm. 2) S. 358 f. sowie S. 353, Anm. 2, Schluß, mit Fourniers Hinweis auf Anselm von Lucca 1.80, wo die Erweiterungen fehlen.

17) Ivo von Chartres, Decretum 5.378 (MIGNE PL 161.437–438) und CASPAR, Register (wie Anm. 14) S. 555, Z. 19–25.

18) Deusdedit 1.1, S. 30. Nur hier findet sich c.6 des Konzils von Nicaea im gleichen Kapitel sowohl in der Versio Prisca als auch in der Versio Hispana. Der zitierte Zusatz fehlt nach Glanvell in der Hs. Vat. lat. 1984. Zur Versio Prisca bei Anselm und Deusdedit siehe FOURNIER, Collections canoniques romaines (wie Anm. 2) S. 307, 339 und 348. Zu Anaclet siehe das Stellenverzeichnis bei FUHRMANN, Pseudoisidorische Fälschungen (wie Anm. 1) 3, S. 850, Nr. 148, Anm. 431. Die Anselmo dedicata, Hs. Vercelli, Capitolo Metropolitano XV, fol. 18v (1.117) enthält den Text in der Vers. Hispana mit einigen Abweichungen: *Antiqua consuetudo seruetur per Aegyptum ... seruentur ecclesiis.*

19) FUHRMANN, Pseudoisidorische Fälschungen 2, S. 377, 382–385 und 519.

20) Deusdedit 2.103 und 108. FOURNIER, Collections canoniques romaines (wie Anm. 2) S. 354 f. Zur Geschichte von S. Pietro a vinculis siehe Christian C. F. HUELSEN, Le Chiese di Roma nel medio evo (1927), S. LXVIII und S. 418 f., Nr. 16.

Deusdedit auch die Rolle des Apostels Paulus sehr betonte. Mehrfach hat er den Namen des *coapostolus* hinzugefügt, wenn die mutmaßliche Vorlage nur von Petrus sprach[21]. So in auffälliger Weise in zwei Formeln des Liber Diurnus, insbesondere der päpstlichen Profeß vor der Weihe (2.110; 2.111)[22]. Im Anschluß an Matth. 16.19 wird hier der wahre Glaube von Christus an den zukünftigen Papst nicht nur durch Petrus weitergegeben, sondern *per te et beatissimum coapostolum tuum Paulum*[23]; weiter verspricht der Papst nach Deusdedit, die heiligen Kanones und die kanonischen Dekrete zu achten und Verstöße gegen kanonische Regeln auf den Rat seiner Söhne entweder zu bessern oder zu tolerieren, und zwar *tua et beatissimi coapostoli tui Pauli patrocinante intercessione*[24]. Obwohl der Zusammenhang bei Deusdedit ungewöhnlich ist, besteht an sich kein Grund, sich über die besondere Nennung des Apostels Paulus zu wundern, denn die gemeinsame Verehrung von Petrus und Paulus ist ja seit frühesten Zeiten für die römische Kirche charakteristisch. Aber im allgemeinen[25] entsprach der Erstarkung des Papsttums und der Weiterentwick-

---

21) Deusdedit 2.110 (S. 235 und 236), 2.111 und 3.58.

22) Zu den Liber Diurnus-Formeln bei Deusdedit siehe Liber Diurnus Romanorum pontificum, Gesamtausgabe von Hans FOERSTER (1958), besonders S. 68 (Aufstellung mit Konkordanz für die erhaltenen Hss.) und S. 69–72 zur „zeitgemäßen Umformung" und der Deusdedit vorliegenden Hs. Foerster berichtet, daß Peitz zu 2.111 in seinen hinterlassenen Notizen betone, daß „die Unterschiede in den Formularen bei Deusdedit keineswegs auf willkürlichen Änderungen des Kardinals beruhen" (S. 71), doch kommt Foerster selbst wie Santifaller zu dem Schluß, daß Deusdedits Vorlage „wohl ein in der Kanzlei wirklich gebrauchtes, inzwischen aber außer Verwendung gestelltes Exemplar des Liber Diurnus gewesen" sei (S. 71 f.): Leo SANTIFALLER, Liber Diurnus. Studien und Forschungen, hg. von H. ZIMMERMANN, (Päpste und Papsttum 10, 1976) S. 81 ff. und S. 226 ff. Die Praefatio in der Ausgabe des Liber Diurnus von Theodor VON SICKEL (1889) S.L–LVI zu Deusdedit bleibt wichtig. Siehe auch KUTTNER, Cardinalis (wie Anm. 10) S. 176 mit Anm. 110.

23) Deusdedit S. 236, Z. 22 f.

24) S. 236, Z. 22 f. Siehe KUTTNER (wie Anm. 22).

25) Eine bemerkenswerte und im Register Gregors VII. auffällige Ausnahme ist die zweite Absetzung und Exkommunikation Heinrichs IV. 1080 in einer feierlichen Anrufung Peters und Pauls (Register 7.14a, S. 483 ff.), zu vergleichen mit Register 3.10a = S. 270 f. Leo MEULENBERG, Der Primat der römischen Kirche im Denken und Handeln Gregors VII (1965) S. 20, weist auch auf einige andere Stellen des Registers hin, in welchen auf beide Apostel verwiesen wird, aber auch Meulenberg betont, daß bei „Gregor ... am stärksten die Person Petri in den Vordergrund" tritt. Das Namenregister in CASPARS Ausgabe des Registers (S. 666 f.) illustriert den sehr wesentlichen Unterschied auf das deutlichste.

lung der römischen Primatsidee seit der Mitte des 11. Jahrhunderts eine bemerkenswert exklusive Betonung der Rolle des Petrus, dem *princeps apostolorum*[26]. Die Petrusmystik Gregors VII. ist zurecht oft betont worden[27]. Die vielleicht älteste Sammlung der Kirchenreform des 11. Jahrhunderts, die Sammlung in 74 Titeln, zeigt deutlich die Spannung, die damals zwischen der Petrus-Idee einerseits und dem traditionellen Doppel-Aposteltum Peters und Pauls andererseits entstand. Das Argument des Papstes Vigilius, *licet omnium apostolorum par esset electio, beato tamen Petro concessum est ut ceteris premineret*[28], war nicht ohne weiteres auf Paulus anwendbar. Es galt, einen Ausgleich zu finden zwischen der Feststellung Pseudo-Anaklets, daß die *prima sedes* das himmlische Lehen der römischen Kirche sei, die durch das gemeinsame Martyrium Peters und Pauls geweiht worden wäre[29], und der Gelasius zu-

---

26) Im einzelnen läßt sich die Verschiebung leicht übersehen, wie z. B. im Auszug aus einem Brief Nikolaus' I. in der Sammlung Diuersorum patrum sententie siue Collectio in LXXIV titulos digesta, ed. J. GILCHRIST (Monumenta iuris canonici, series B, 1, 1973) cap. 17 (S. 28). Ernst PERELS, Die Briefe Papst Nikolaus' I. (wie Anm. 14) zeigt, wie der Kompilator der 74-Titel Sammlung (unten zitiert 74 T) oder dessen Vorlage „durch eine bemerkenswerte Umstellung der Satzteile" und „ein paar Veränderungen" (S. 72) den Primat nicht mehr auf die römische Kirche, sondern auf Petrus bezieht. Vergleiche auch Hans Martin KLINKENBERG, Der römische Primat im 10. Jahrhundert, ZRG Kan. 41 (1955) S. 1-57, hier S. 43 f. mit Anm. 86. Siehe allgemein zu Klinkenberg die Rezensionen des Aufsatzes von H. FUHRMANN, DA 13 (1957) S. 280 f. und H. KELLER, DA 20 (1964) S. 354, Anm. 134. Auf die starke Betonung der Figur des Petrus in der Sammlung Anselms von Lucca verweist FUHRMANN, Pseudoisidorische Fälschungen (wie Anm. 1) 2, S. 519.
27) August NITSCHKE, Die Wirksamkeit Gottes in der Welt Gregors VII., Studi Gregoriani 5 (1956) S. 115–219, hier S. 155 ff.; MEULENBERG, Primat (wie Anm. 25), besonders S. 25 ff. „Öfters fällt jede Distanz zwischen Petrus und Gregor weg. Der Papst identifiziert sich dann in mystischem Glauben ohne weiteres mit dem Apostelfürsten ..." (S. 28); Yves M.-J. CONGAR, Der Platz des Papsttums in der Kirchenfrömmigkeit der Reformer des 11. Jahrhunderts, in: Sentire ecclesiam, Festschrift Hugo Rahner, hg. von J. DANIÉLOU und H. VORGRIMLER (1961), hier S. 214 mit der Literatur in Anm. 63.
28) JK 907, Paul HINSCHIUS (Hg.), Decretales Pseudo-Isidorianae (1863) S. 712; 74 T (wie Anm. 26) c.12, S. 25; weitere Stellen sind vermerkt bei FUHRMANN, Pseudoisidorische Fälschungen (wie Anm. 1) 3, S. 896, Stellenverzeichnis Nr. 245.
29) 74 T c.21 (S. 30 f.); cf. Deusdedit 1.61 (S. 63 f.) = cap. L in Deusdedits Zählung, siehe dazu seine capitulatio auf S. 6. Für andere Sammlungen mit diesem Text und deren Varianten siehe FUHRMANN, Pseudoisidorische Fälschungen 3, S. 850, Nr. 148. Sowohl Deusdedit 1.61 als auch Anselm von Lucca, Collectio canonum ..., ed. F. THANER (1906–1915) 1.66 enthalten einen auf Paulus bezüglichen Satz, der bei 74 T c.21 fehlt:

geschriebenen Erklärung: *Est ergo prima Petri apostoli sedes Romana ecclesia*[30]. In der 74-Titel-Sammlung zeigt schon die Rubrik des entsprechenden Titels, daß Paulus neben Petrus eine untergeordnete Rolle eingeräumt wird[31]. Deusdedit dagegen betont schon in seinem Vorwort, und zwar im Präsens, daß sowohl Petrus als auch Paulus der römischen Kirche vorstehen und in ihr lebendig sind[32]. In der Sammlung zitiert er unter anderem eine Predigt Leos d. Gr., in der auf Christus als das Haupt der Kirche verwiesen wird, mit Petrus und Paulus als Zwillingslicht der Augen im Körper der Kirche (1.290)[33]. Noch pro-

---

... *Et licet pro omnibus assidua apud deum omnium sanctorum fundatur oratio, his tamen urbis* [lies *uerbis*] *Paulus beatissimus apostolus Romanis primo cirographo pollicetur dicens: ... quod sine intermissione memoriam uestri facio semper in orationibus meis* (vgl. HINSCHIUS S. 83, Z. 14–17). Zur besonderen Verbindung zwischen Paulus und der römischen Gemeinde vergleiche auch KLINKENBERG, Römischer Primat (wie Anm. 26) S. 12 ff.

30) 74 T (wie Anm. 26) c.22, S. 31 f.

31) 2: *Item de eadem re et quod Petrus et Paulus passi sunt una die. De eadem re* bezieht sich auf Titel 1: *De primatu romane ecclesie.*

32) Deusdedit, Vorwort (S. 2, Z. 15 ff.), nach einem Hinweis auf Cyprians Briefwechsel mit den Priestern und Diakonen der römischen Kirche *dum careret pontifice: Arbitrati quippe sunt patres spiritu dei pleni, beatos apostolos Petrum et Paulum in ea magnificis meritis iuiuere et preesse fidemque, quam ab eisdem suscepit, que in toto mundo eodem beato Paulo attestante annuntiata est et laudata, in eadem usque in secula non deficere, set, ut eidem beato Petro imperatum fuerat, usquequaque positos fratres in eadem fide confirmare. Haec et si ... opprimitur, meritis tamen principum apostolorum, qui in ea et uiuunt et president, non obruitur.* Ernst HIRSCH, Die rechtliche Stellung der römischen Kirche und des Papstes nach Kardinal Deusdedit, Archiv für katholisches Kirchenrecht 88 (1908) S. 595–624, hier S. 595, Anm. 4, benutzte diese Stelle hier anders als auf S. 598 zusammen mit einem kurzen Vermerk in Deusdedits Libellus contra invasores et symoniacos (ed. E. SACKUR, MGH Ldl 2, 1892, S. 292 ff., hier S. 303, Z. 18) als Beleg für die Feststellung: „Wiederholt spricht Deusdedit den Gedanken aus, daß Petrus selbst in und mit dem Papste als seinem Rechtsnachfolger zu Rom fortlebe und fortregiere". Ähnlich und undifferenziert in diesem Fall auch ROBINSON, Authority (wie Anm. 4) S. 172 mit Anm. 128, der die Erwähnung von Cyprians Korrespondenz im Zusammenhang mit den Kardinalpriestern und Diakonen Roms sowie dem Doppelaposteltum Petrus und Paulus mißverstanden zu haben scheint:" ... Cardinal Deusdedit and Bonizo of Sutri transformed Cyprian's *unitas ecclesiae catholicae* into an *unitas Petri* ...". Siehe aber KUTTNER, Cardinalis (wie Anm. 10) S. 176 f. Anm. 10.

33) Zu Leo I. in den Schriften der schismatischen Kardinäle vgl. ebenfalls ROBINSON, Authority, S. 48 und Anm. 210. Weitere wichtige Texte zum gleichen Thema bei Deusdedit sind außer den Indexthesen auf S. 6, Z. 13–20; 1.291 (Gregor I.), 1.292 (Augustin), 1.61 (siehe auch Anm. 29), 1.78 (dazu FUHRMANN, Pseudoisidorische Fälschungen [wie Anm. 1] 3, Stellenverzeichnis Nr. 21 und Nr. 146), 1.285 (Anselm Luc. 1.69), 1.288 (vgl.

minenter ist in der Sammlung ein Thema, das für den spätmittelalterlichen Konziliarismus von großer Bedeutung werden sollte, von Zeitgenossen Deusdedits aber äußerst selten berührt wurde: der Streit zwischen Petrus und Paulus in Jerusalem, das sogenannte Apostelkonzil[34]. Ausgewählte Stellen aus Act. 15, 1-35, eröffnen in ein Kapitel zusammengefaßt Buch 2 der Sammlung Deusdedits[35]. Ein weiterer Text aus einem Brief Gregors I. (2.85) hat die Demut *(humilitas)* des Petrus zum Inhalt, der durchaus willens ist, sich von seinen Brüdern korrigieren zu lassen, ihnen Rede zu stehen, sowie diese als Zeugen anzuführen. Im Zusammenhang mit dem Primat Petri zitiert Deusdedit schon vorher in einer Augustin-Passage Cyprian mit einem Verweis auf die Demut des

---

74 T c.23; Anselm Luc. 1.69, pars 2), 1.295; auch 1.277 spricht von *potestas,* die für alle gleich sei (Z. 18 f.). 1.125 zeigt am Beispiel der Glaubensfestigkeit, die von Christus an Petrus und von Petrus auf alle Apostel übertragen wurde, wie man sich auch die Übertragung anderer Vorrechte an die römische Kirche vorzustellen hat. Von Zeitgenossen Deusdedits hat Gottfried von Vendôme mit besonderer Betonung auf den gemeinsamen Apostolat von Petrus und Paulus hingewiesen, allerdings mit einem anderen Petrus-Verständnis (Libellus I, ed. E. SACKUR, MGH Ldl 2, 1892, S. 680 ff., hier S. 680, Z. 31 ff.; Carl MIRBT, Die Publizistik im Zeitalter Gregors VII., 1894, S. 553, Anm. 2).

34) Deusdedit 2.1; auch hier findet sich der Zusatz *et presbiteris . . . idest presbiteri* zu *senioribus* bzw. *seniores fratres,* allerdings nur in der Pariser Hs. der Sammlung (B. N. lat. 1458) und als Nachtrag. Act. 15,2 spricht von *presbyteros,* die ab Act. 15,4 *seniores* genannt werden. Siehe FUHRMANN, Pseudoisidorische Fälschungen 2, S. 519 zu *presbyteros, id est seniores* bei Deusdedit 2.35 und Anselm Luc. 7.84, die den Einfluß von Burchards Decretum (2.5) zu zeigen scheinen. Vgl. auch Bernold, Apologeticus, c. 23 (ed. F. THANER, MGH Ldl 2, S. 58 ff.) S. 87, Z. 6f.: *Unde idem apostolus et a senioribus sui temporis, id est presbiteris sive episcopis . . . obedientiam generaliter exegit . . .* und schon vorher, c.15, S. 75, Z. 32 f. Zur Gleichung *presbyter, episcopus* bei Deusdedit siehe außerdem unten Anm. 41. Zu möglichen Beziehungen zwischen Bernold und Deusdedit FUHRMANN, Pseudoisidorische Fälschungen 2, S. 523 f.

35) Auf den Streit zwischen Petrus und Paulus im Zusammenhang mit dem päpstlichen Primat kamen zur Zeit Deusdedits auch Adalbert und Bernold in einer Epistel an Bernhard von Hildesheim/Konstanz zu sprechen. Sie stimmten Bernhard zu, daß, obwohl der Heilige Stuhl zuweilen von unwürdigen Päpsten eingenommen würde, er doch stets den Vorrang vor anderen Kirchen besäße. Die Päpste dürften dann von ihren Untergebenen *(subditis)* ermahnt werden, wie der erste Inhaber seinerzeit von Paulus *caritativa liberalitate.* (Libellus II Bernaldi presbyteri monachi, De damnatione scismaticorum, ed. F. THANER, MGH Ldl 2, 1892, S. 47 f., Z. 37 ff.). In ähnlichem Zusammenhang bezieht sich Hugo von Fleury auf das Treffen von Antiochia (Gal. 2, 11–16) (Tractatus de regia potestate et sacerdotali dignitate, ed. E. SACKUR, MGH Ldl 2, S. 465 ff., hier S. 491). Zum gleichen Thema bei Odo von Cluny KLINKENBERG, Primat (wie Anm. 26) S. 44, Anm. 87.

Petrus (1.295), der in seinem Streit mit Paulus niemals so unverschämt und ar-
rogant sei, etwa zu behaupten, er hätte den Primat inne: *Nam nec Petrus ... uen-
dicauit sibi aliquid insolenter aut arroganter assumpsit, ut diceret se primatum tenere ...* oder etwa Paulus wegen seiner alten Rolle als Saul zu verachten. Das
von Deusdedit aufgenommene Exzerpt schließt mit Augustins Hinweis, daß
Cyprian und Petrus als gleichrangig zu betrachten seien, zumindest was ihr
Martyrium anbelange, obwohl Rom als Bischofssitz natürlich mit Karthago
nicht vergleichbar sei. Bei Ivo findet sich nur der zweite Teil dieses ungewöhn-
lichen Kanons, der für sich allein genommen unklar ist[36].

Sicherlich geht diese Betonung der Rolle des Paulus neben der des Petrus —
auch für ihn gibt es interpolierte Texte[37] — genauso wie der Bezug auf den Titel
Eudoxia auf Deusdedits Wunsch zurück, die Heiligen seines Titels zu verherrli-
chen. Nach einer sonst nicht nachweisbaren Tradition waren es die Ketten des
Petrus und des Paulus, die in S. Pietro in Vincoli als Reliquien verehrt wurden,
wie Deusdedit in seinen Versen erwähnt. In der Capitulatio zur Kanonessammlung schreibt er ohne Kapitelverweis: *Quod uincula beati Petri tituli
Eudoxię, sint etiam beati Pauli* (S. 24)[38]. Aber es war wohl nur zum Teil dieser
Grund, der Deusdedit bewog, als er seine besondere Verehrung für Paulus zum
Ausdruck brachte. Der zu seiner Zeit bereits ausschließlich übliche Name für
seine Kirche war S. Pietro a vinculis, und Deusdedits Rückgriff auf die Tradition des 5. Jahrhunderts muß gewiß unter anderem durch eine persönliche
Vorliebe des Kardinals für diesen sonst vergessenen Namen erklärt werden[39],
in dem die Rom-Verbundenheit beider Apostel so deutlich zum Ausdruck
kam.

Im allgemeinen macht sich in den Paulus-Texten eine kollegiale Tendenz bemerkbar, die einem weiteren Anliegen Deusdedits entgegenkommt, das zu-

---

36) Ivo, Decretum 5.24 (MIGNE PL 161. 330).

37) Zum Beispiel Deusdedit 1.185 und 186. S. KUTTNER, Universal Pope or Servant
of God's Servants: The Canonists, Papal Titles, and Innocent III, Revue de Droit Cano-
nique 32 (1981) S. 109–149, hier S. 113 f., weist nach, daß Deusdedit ganz im Geist Gregors VII. dem Papst den Titel *universalis* zuerkennt, indem er, wieder durch eine geringfügige Änderung, den Sinn der Originaltexte in ihr Gegenteil verkehrt.

38) HOLTZMANN, Deusdedit als Dichter (wie Anm. 8) S. 221, Z. 40–45. Siehe außerdem Deusdedit 3.108 (= Anselm Luc. 1.70) und 3.109.

39) HUELSEN, Chiese di Roma (wie Anm. 20) S. 418 f. Vgl. ebenda S. 3 Nr. 11; 5 Nr.
64 und 6 Nr. 17: Die Einträge in den frühen Katalogen sprechen alle nur von den Ketten
des Petrus. Zu beachten sind die Konzilsunterschriften von Ephesus sowie der römischen Synoden von 499 und 595, in denen jeweils beide Apostel für den Titel von Eudoxia genannt werden und an denen Deusdedit besonders viel gelegen haben dürfte.

nächst ebenfalls durch Textverfälschungen Aufmerksamkeit erregt: die Betonung der Sancta Romana Ecclesia als Körperschaft, die von den Kardinalpres-
bytern und Kardinaldiakonen zusammen mit dem aus ihren Reihen hervorge-
gangenen und von ihnen gewählten Papst repräsentiert wird. In eine ähnliche
Richtung verweist wohl auch die Akribie, mit der Deusdedit bei päpstlichen
Briefen an Bischöfe die Anrede *frater* oder *fraternitas* beachtet oder eingeschoben hat[40]. Dabei ist zu bedenken, daß Deusdedit, selbst Kardinalpresbyter, zwischen Bischöfen und Priestern kaum Unterschiede gelten ließ: *Eosdem esse presbiteros, quos episcopos,* und: *Quod episcopi magis consuetudine quam dominica dispensatione presbiteris sint maiores,* schrieb er in den Indexsätzen, ebenso, konse-
quenterweise, *Quod Romani pontifices presbiteros suos fratres et compresbiteros
appellant* (S. 16). Die Rolle der römischen Kardinalpriester und Diakone als
ständiger Rat des Papstes (2.110) sieht Deusdedit in Analogie zur Rolle der Priester und Diakone an Bischofssitzen, und wenn er schreibt: *Ut sententia episcopi
presbiterorum et diaconorum subsciptione firmetur* (S. 17), dann darf man schließen, daß Deusdedit bereits in den achtziger Jahren und nicht erst mehr als zehn
Jahre später mit dem schismatischen Kardinal Hugo einer Meinung war, der
behauptete, es sei ... ein Privileg des Römischen Stuhls durch die Kardinalpresbyter und die Diakone dem Papst ... immer zu assistieren, ohne deren Unterschriften päpstliche Verlautbarungen keine Gültigkeit besäßen[41].

Die Rolle der römischen Priester hebt Deusdedit innerhalb der Sammlung
auf gleiche Art hervor wie die des Paulus[42], so daß aus Petrus, dem *princeps apo-*

---

40) Beispiele für Zusätze sind Deusdedit 1.208, 246, 297; 2.46; 3.109. Vergleiche
Hans-Friedrich CASPERS, Was bedeutet im Zeitalter Gregors VII. die Bezeichnung
„coepiscopus"?, ZRG Kan. 22 (1933) S. 336-346.
41) Benonis aliorumque cardinalium scripta, ed. K. FRANCKE, MGH Ldl 2(1892) S.
418, Z. 14 ff. Zu Deusdedit siehe die Kanonessammlung S. 16 f., 2.22, 36, 140 (Z. 10:
Nam cum apostolus perspicue doceat eosdem esse presbiteros quos episcopos . . .), 141 und
2.143 (*communi presbiterorum consilio ecclesie gubernabantur* . . . Z. 8) sowie HIRSCH,
Rechtliche Stellung (wie Anm. 32) S. 622 mit Anm. 5. Zu Unterschriften römischer
Priester und Diakone zusammen mit dem Papst Deusdedit 2.80 sowie, weniger deutlich, 2.69.
42) Deusdedit 2.108, 109 (S. 234, Z. 6) 110 (der erwählte Papst ist ein *presbiter*, nicht
ein Diakon wie im Original). Bei diesen liturgischen Texten kann man mit FOURNIER
von „rajeunir" (siehe oben S. 242) oder mit FOERSTER (wie Anm. 22) von „zeitgemäßer
Umformung" sprechen, was den Texten und Änderungen aber nichts von ihrer Bedeutung nimmt. Das Gegenteil ist der Fall, denn auch wie Deusdedits Vorwort und seine
Indexthesen, so müssen auch die „Umformungen" als persönliche Meinungsäußerun-
gen bewertet werden. Dies trifft zu, selbst wenn Deusdedit selber nicht ihr Autor gewe-

stolorum, ein Petrus wird, dem Christus, das Haupt der Kirche, *principaliter*
und *specialiter* Vorrechte verliehen hat, die besonders Paulus mit diesem teilt,
die aber auch an den römischen Klerus weitergegeben werden. So betrachtet,
gewinnt man eine Perspektive, aus der heraus die Rolle des Papstes in dem bekannten Bonifacius-Text *De Sancta Romana Ecclesia* (1.306), dessen Häresieklausel ... *nisi a fide devius* ... durch Gratians D. 40 c. 6 besonders berühmt ist,
nicht als Gegensatz gegenüber der Sammlung als ganzem erscheint, sondern als
keineswegs unabsichtliche Folgerung bestimmter Gedankengänge Deusdedits.
Der Text trägt deutliche Züge der cyprianischen Ideologie der Ecclesia, die
man eigentlich mit dem 10. Jahrhundert und der vorgregorianischen Zeit
verbindet[43]. Deusdedits Bild von der Kirche unter den verschiedenen Aspekten
des kirchlichen Lebens erschöpft sich durchaus nicht mit wiederholten Hinweisen auf den päpstlichen Primat. Man braucht den Libellus contra invasores
nicht heranzuziehen, um bestätigen zu können: Der Akzent bei Deusdedit
liegt anders, als man bisher angenommen hat, selbst wenn Deusdedit auch nirgends wie Kardinal Hugo geschrieben hat: *Petri privilegium potius Romanae
sedis esse quam solius Romani pontificis*[44].

---

sen sein sollte (vergleiche FOERSTER, wie Anm. 22). Siehe weiter Deusdedit 2.1 und
2.41, wo das Wort *cardinalis* in der falschen Inskription mit *presbiteri* im Text des Kapi-
tels gleichgesetzt wird. Siehe KUTTNER, Cardinalis (wie Anm. 10) S. 193, Anm. 71 zu
Deusdedit 2.113 und S. 176 f. mit Anm. 110 zu „Kardinal" in der Sammlung insgesamt.
Zum Gebrauch dieses Begriffs in Rom zur Zeit Deusdedits besonders H. E. J. COW-
DREY, The Age of Abbot Desiderius. Montecassino, the Papacy and the Normans in
the Eleventh and Early Twelfth Centuries (1983) S. 48–55 und Detlev JASPER, Das
Papstwahldekret von 1059. Überlieferung und Textgestalt (Beiträge zur Geschichte und
Quellenkunde des Mittelalters 12, 1986) S. 72–76. Sehr wichtig, aber im allgemeinen
übersehen, ist der scharfe Kontrast zwischen Papst Leo IX. und Deusdedit (KUTTNER,
Cardinalis, S. 176, Anm. 109 mit Literatur; darunter besonders klar GRAUERT). Beinahe ebenso aufschlußreich wie 2.160 für Deusdedits Standpunkt ist 2.33, wo *docens* zu
docentes verändert und auf *sacerdotes* bezogen wird, wohingegen bei Anselm Luc. 7.58
das auf Petrus bezogene *docens* des Originals erhalten geblieben ist. Siehe allgemein zu
diesem Text FUHRMANN, Pseudoisidorische Fälschungen (wie Anm. 1) 2, S. 518 Anm.
252 und 3, S. 992, Nr. 434.

43) CONGAR, Der Platz des Papsttums (wie Anm. 27) S. 198, S. 197 sowie S. 205 f.;
KLINKENBERG, Primat (wie Anm. 26). Zu Deusdedit 1.306 und 1.327 besonders J. Joseph RYAN, Kardinal Humbert, *De s. Romana ecclesia*. Relics of Roman-Byzantine Relations 1053–1054, Mediaeval Studies 20 (1958) S. 206–238, besonders S. 228 zusammenfassend zu 1.306. Siehe aber auch Ryan's Hinweis, S. 229, daß unter Umständen Leo IX.
der Autor des Textes gewesen sein könnte.

44) Benonis aliorumque cardinalium scripta (wie Anm. 41) S. 419, Z. 22. MIRBT, Publizistik (wie Anm. 33) S. 552 Anm. 3 und S. 561 f. Ein sehr deutliches Beispiel für Deus-

Um Mißverständnissen vorzubeugen, möchte ich kurz auch auf die Gestalt des Petrus in Deusdedits Sammlung eingehen. Bekanntlich hat man im Text und besonders in den vorausgehenden Indexthesen Parallelen gesucht und gefunden zu den 27 Sätzen des *dictatus papae* im Register Gregors VII., einem Dokument, das recht extrem wirkende Thesen über päpstliche Vorrechte aufstellt[45]. Deusdedit war ein Anhänger dieses Papstes, der der Sache des Reformpapsttums auch nach 1084 treu blieb. Es ist selbstverständlich, daß bei Deusdedit, wie auch in anderen Sammlungen und Streitschriften dieser Zeit mit Ausnahme der Schriften der schismatischen Kardinäle, der päpstliche Primat eine große Rolle spielt. Unbestreitbar gebührt in der Sammlung Deusdedits Petrus der erste Platz unter den beiden Aposteln von Eudoxia. Der Kardinal betonte den einzigartigen Vorrang des Petrus im Zusammenhang mit der Einberufung, dem Vorsitz und der Bestätigung von Synoden sowie dem Jurisdiktionsprimat[46]. Petrus seien *specialiter claues regni cęlorum et iudicii principatum* verliehen worden, um, wie der entsprechende Text Bedas erklärt, die Einheit des Glaubens zu versinnbildlichen (1.305). Kein Schreiben sei authentisch ohne päpstliche Bestätigung[47]. Ennodius' Plädoyer für Papst Symmachus aus dem Jahre 501 wird bei Deusdedit wie bei Gregor VII. und Anselm zitiert.

---

dedit findet sich in 1.95, Z. 10 ff.: *Beati Petri uice hodie gratia dei legatione pro christo fungimur et omnes huius sanctę sedis presules eius uicem gesserunt, gerunt et gerent . . .*

45) Register (wie Anm. 14) 2.55 a, S. 201 ff.; Ernst SACKUR, Der Dictatus papae und die Canonsammlung des Deusdedit, NA 18 (1892) S. 135-53; Karl HOFMANN, Der „Dictatus Papae" Gregors VII. Eine rechtsgeschichtliche Erklärung (1933); Manuel RÍOS FERNÁNDEZ, La „Collectio Canonum" del Cardenal Deusdedit y el „Dictatus papae",Compostellanum, Sección de ciencias eclesiasticas 5 (1960) S. 181–212 und dazu FUHRMANN, Pseudoisidorische Fälschungen (wie Anm. 1) 2, S. 524 Anm. 262; Hubert MORDEK, Proprie auctoritates apostolice sedis. Ein zweiter Dictatus papae Gregors VII.?, DA 28 (1972) S. 105–132.

46) Beispiele unter den Indexsätzen finden sich auf S. 6, Z. 4, Z. 8 (mit Bezug auf 1.10: *. . . Canonibus quippe in Nicena synodo iubentibus non debere preter sententiam Romani pontificis ullo modo concilia celebrari nec episcopos damnari*); S. 7, Z. 36 ff.: *Quare beatus Petrus specialiter claues et principatum iudicii accepit*, eine These, die den Text von 1.305 (S. 176 f.) aufnimmt; S. 8, Z. 29 und S. 10, Z. 3. Allgemein wird der Platz Petri besonders unterstrichen durch 1.57, 58, 60, 69, 79, 87, 88, 138, 139, 145, 147, 152; 4.159, 164.

47) Deusdedit, S. 10, Z. 28 f., mit den dazugehörigen Texten: 1.7, 1.95–96, 1.110 und 1.295; Kapitel 106, das auch angegeben ist, fehlt wohl in den Hss., siehe 1.129 in Glanvells Zählung (= 105 in Deusdedits Zählung) und 1.130 (= 107 in Deusdedits Zählung). 1.130 ist ein Exzerpt aus der Epistola decretalis de recipiendis et non recipiendis libris und würde zum Indexsatz passen. Gar nicht paßt dagegen 1.295 (= 222 in Deusdedits Zählung). Die anderen Texte betreffen alle die Bestätigung von Konzilsentscheidungen.

Danach genügen die Verdienste des Petrus zur Heiligung des Papstes, selbst wenn dieser persönlich unwürdig sei[48]. Der Papst darf von niemandem gerichtet werden, denn *non est discipulus super magistrum* (1.89). Und wie der Autor der 74-Titel-Sammlung (c. 291) übernimmt Deusdedit auch einen im römischen Sinn veränderten Satz der Capitula Angilramni, der den Dekreten der Päpste den Vorrang vor anderen Gesetzen einräumt[49].

Auf sehr charakteristische Weise treten bei Deusdedit aber neben die *sancta decreta* der Päpste die Gebote der heiligen Kanones, die von niemandem übertreten werden dürfen[50]. Mehr noch, in seinem Vorwort vertritt Deusdedit die Ansicht, daß nicht nur die Canones Apostolorum, sondern auch alle Kanones und Einrichtungen der ehrwürdigen Väter und Konzilien gültig wären, die weder dem rechten Glauben, den guten Sitten, noch den Dekreten Roms Abbruch täten (S. 4). Bewußt oder unbewußt hat er dadurch die tendenziöse Umarbeitung Angilrams wieder aufgehoben, die er wie 74-Titel übernommen hatte (1.147). Die scheinbar so eindeutigen Thesen über die Vorrechte des Apostels Petrus, die auf Clemens und seine Nachfolger übertragen wurden, besitzen also innerhalb der Sammlung nicht immer ausschließliche und unbedingte Gültigkeit. Es sei nur nebenbei bemerkt, daß der hier besprochene Satz: *Constitutiones contra sancta decreta Romanorum presulum nullius sint momenti* bei Deusdedit ein zweischneidiges Schwert ist. In seinem Libellus benutzt er ihn nämlich, um zu beweisen, daß das Decretum der Synode von 1059 unter Nikolaus II. keine Gültigkeit hätte — ein Decretum, das doch unseres Erachtens ganz gewiß zu den *decreta Romanorum presulum* gehört[51]!

---

48) Deusdedit 1.132 und S. 8, Z. 8 f. Anselm Luc. 6.2. Gregor VII., Register 2.55 a, Nr. 23, S. 207. Dazu zuletzt Horst FUHRMANN, Über die Heiligkeit des Papstes, Jb. der Akademie der Wissenschaften Göttingen (1980) S. 28–43, besonders S. 33 ff. mit Literatur.

49) Deusdedit 1.147 zu vergleichen mit 74 T. c.291. Dazu Horst FUHRMANN, Über den Reformgeist der 74-Titel-Sammlung, in: Festschrift Hermann Heimpel zum 70. Geburtstag (Veröffentlichung des Max-Planck-Instituts für Geschichte 36, 1972) 2, S. 1101–1120, hier S. 1117; DERS., Schlußwort, HZ 197 (1963) S. 590; DERS., Pseudoisidorische Fälschungen (wie Anm. 1) 1, S. 89 f.

50) Deusdedit 1.16 mit den Bemerkungen von FUHRMANN, Pseudoisidorische Fälschungen 2, S. 527. Die Stelle lautet in den Falschen Dekretalen: . . . *apostolicae sedis iussionibus inobedientem* . . . wie bei Deusdedit 1.66 und Anselm Luc. 2.15. Zu *canones* siehe weiter besonders Deusdedit 1.98, 99 und 4.168 (Z. 21), sowie die Betonung der kanonischen Konsekration für den Papst, S. 8, Z. 8. HOFMANN, Dictatus Papae (wie Anm. 45) S. 70 ff.; HIRSCH, Rechtliche Stellung (wie Anm. 41) S. 618 f.

51) Deusdedit, Libellus contra invasores (wie Anm. 5) S. 311, Z. 8 f. mit der Einleitung zu cap. 12, S. 310, Z. 26 ff.

Wesentlich wichtiger aber als die Relativierung einzelner Aussagen ist in der
Sicht Deusdedits die Übertragung der Vorrechte des Petrus und Paulus, die beide den Prinzipat unter den Aposteln innehaben (1.61, 78, 125 mit S. 6, Z. 13,
285, 295), auf die Sancta Romana Ecclesia. Petrus und Paulus machten die von
Gott gegründete römische Kirche zur Mutter aller Kirchen und die römische
Kirche selbst zum ersten aller Bischofssitze (1.61). Das Gebet Christi für den
Glauben des Apostelfürsten gilt ebenfalls für die heilige römische Kirche (1.78,
87), und diese besitzt durch Petrus die Prima sedes als himmlisches Lehen
(1.61). Der Primat aber wurde ihr durch Christus verliehen[52]. Unter den pro-
grammatischen Indexthesen zum ersten Buch in Deusdedits Sammlung, das
vom Priuilegium auctritatis der römischen Kirche handelt (S. 2), beziehen sich
ungefähr 8 auf Petrus und Paulus, ungefähr 51 auf den Papst und Papstwahlen
und ungefähr 61 auf Vorrechte der Sancta Romana Ecclesia (SRE). Oft sind
Formulierungen so ineinander verschachtelt, ebenso wie die dazu aufgeführten
Kapitel, daß sich die Texte nicht einordnen lassen und Beziehungen unscharf
bleiben. Doch deuten selbst die ungefähren Zahlenverhältnisse das Ungewöhnliche an Deusdedits Betonung der SRE wenigstens an. Bei näherem Zusehen
zeigt sich, daß die Vorrechte der römischen Kirche durchaus nicht immer mit
päpstlichen Vorrechten auf einer Ebene stehen, so daß sie ohne weiteres ausge-
tauscht werden könnten[53]. Die römische Kirche — der Ausdruck nähert sich
inhaltlich dem der Universalkirche[54] — hat zwar Anspruch auf päpstliche Privilegien, sie ist aber außerdem eine vom Papst unabhängige Institution; sie ist
eine Herrengründung, Christus war ihr erste Hirte, Petrus nur ihr zweiter (S.
7, Z. 35). Im dictatus papae Gregors VII. gelten bekanntlich ebenfalls drei der
bedeutendsten Thesen für die römische Kirche und wenigstens dem Wortlaut
nach nicht für den Papst, den Petrus-Nachfolger[55], dessen Verhältnis zu dieser

---

52) Deusdedit 1.76 und dazu das Stellenverzeichnis bei FUHRMANN, Pseudoisidorische Fälschungen 3, Nr. 138 und Nr. 171. Deusdedit 1.23, 1.139 und die Indexthesen S.
6, Z. 2 sowie S. 7, Z. 35. FUHRMANN, Pseudoisidorische Fälschungen 2, S. 525: „Was
Deusdedit stets neu belegt, ist das *Privilegium sanctae Romanae ecclesiae* . . .". Die Capitulatio, die an Deusdedits Vorwort anschließt, wird also eröffnet mit: *Quod Romana
ecclesia a Christo primatum optinuit* (S. 6, Z. 2). Vergleiche auch 1.61, wo der Text des
betreffenden Satzes (Z. 12) aber nicht gesichert ist.
53) So HIRSCH, Rechtliche Stellung (wie Anm. 41) S. 595 f.
54) Vergleiche CONGAR, Der Platz des Papsttums (wie Anm. 27) S. 199 f.
55) Register 2.55 a, Nr. 1 (S. 202), Nr. 22 und 26 (S. 207). Zu Nr. 1 MEULENBERG,
Primat (wie Anm. 25) S. 21 f.

ein wichtiges noch nicht geklärtes Problem darstellt[56], besonders wenn man, wie dies geschieht, das Wesen der Ekklesiologie der Reformer darin sieht, daß einem monarchischen Papst die Ecclesia untergeordnet wird[57]. Bei Deusdedit zeigt sich die, verglichen mit dem Papst, höhere Autorität der SRE vor allen Dingen darin, daß sie durch die kanonischen *decreta sanctorum patrum* (1.124), einschließlich der kanonischen Papstdekretalen (1.147) verkörpert wird, die den Päpsten als Richtschnur dienen müssen[58]. Den Erlassen der Universal- oder Plenar-Konzilien gebührt unter diesen kanonischen Autoritäten ein ganz besonderer Platz. In seinem Vorwort (S. 3) beschreibt Deusdedit diese Konzilien als von den fünf Patriarchen oder gegebenenfalls ihren Vikaren abgehalten. Kanones dieser Konzilien können nur von Konzilien gleicher Art wieder aufgehoben werden[59]. Nur unter besonderen Umständen und nur auf beschränkte Zeit dürfen die Päpste von der Beachtung der heiligen Kanones dispensieren und ihre Strenge mildern[60]. In einem nur bei Deusdedit anzutreffenden Text wird nicht jegliches Abweichen von den Befehlen des heiligen Stuhls absolut verboten, sondern jegliches Abweichen von den Anordnungen der heiligen Kanones (1.16)[61].

Daß es Deusdedit ernst war mit der Gebundenheit der Päpste an kanonische Tradition und daß er sonst seltene Texte nicht nur zufällig und gedankenlos beim Abschreiben aus einer Vorlage übernommen hat, zeigen nicht nur der Libellus contra invasores von 1097, sondern auch in der Sammlung selbst Textänderungen in der Liber Diurnus-formula für die Papstweihe[62]. Hier interes-

---

56) Zur Frage der Identifizierung Gregors VII. mit der SRE siehe MEULENBERG, Primat, S. 41 f. mit Literatur und John GILCHRIST, Gregory VII and the Primacy of the Roman Church, Tijdschrift voor Rechtsgeschiedenis 36 (1968) S. 123–135, hier S. 129 f. mit Literatur; Walter ULLMANN, Cardinal Humbert and the ecclesia romana, Studi Gregoriani 4 (1952) S. 111–127.

57) CONGAR, Der Platz des Papsttums (wie Anm. 27) S. 205 f. und S. 208 f.

58) HIRSCH, Rechtliche Stellung (wie Anm. 41) S. 614–616.

59) Deusdedit 1.296 und Indexsatz S. 7, Z. 32: *Quod priora uniuersalia interdum emendantur a posterioribus uniuersalibus.* 1.296 spricht von *plenaria concilia*, für Deusdedit also ein Synonym für *uniuersalia concilia.* HIRSCH, Rechtliche Stellung, S. 616 f. bereits mit Hinweis auf Deusdedit, Libellus contra invasores (vgl. dort [wie Anm. 5] S. 316, Z. 24 ff.).

60) Siehe den Indexsatz S. 10, Z. 26 (*Quod causa exigente sanctorum patrum temperet instituta*) mit den dazugehörigen Kapiteln 1.101 (= 124 Glanvell), 105 = (129 Glanvell), 176 (= 222 Glanvell), 4.94 (= 4.167 Glanvell) und 95 (= 168 Glanvell). Siehe auch 4.434, bemerkenswerterweise in der Capitulatio nicht angeführt.

61) Siehe oben Anm. 50.

62) Deusdedit 2.110. Zum Liber Diurnus siehe oben (Anm. 22 und 42). Keine der

siert besonders der Zusatz des Adjektivs *canonicus* in der *Professio futuris pontificis*. Viermal schränkt der Kardinal die Tradition der Kirche durch das Wort *canonicus* ein. Der zukünftige Papst, bei Deusdedit ein Kardinalpriester, in den bekannten Vorlagen des Liber Diurnus ein Diakon, verspricht, alle *decreta canonica* seiner Vorgänger, *disciplinam et ritum ... canonicę traditum,* und allgemein die kanonische Tradition sowie die *canonica constituta pontificum* zu halten[63]. Die Formel enthält außerdem unter weiteren Versprechen eins, das Deusdedit besonders willkommen gewesen sein muß, nämlich die Bestimmungen der ökumenischen Konzilien *usque ad unum apicem inmutilata* zu bewahren[64].

Deusdedit war offensichtlich der Ansicht, daß die kanonische Autorität der römischen Kirche nur ungenügend beachtet wurde. In seiner Widmung an Papst Viktor III., die er seiner Sammlung vorausschickt, erklärt er, daß er seinem Werk auch den *antiquum ordinem electionis seu consecrationis Romani pontificis et cleri eius* beigefügt habe, da sich ,einst' gewisse Leute in Verachtung der Beschlüsse Gottes und der heiligen Väter in vermessener Eitelkeit die leere Autorität zulegten, was von keinem der Kanones erlaubt sei, eine neue Papstwahlordnung zu schreiben. Ihm schaudere davor, niederzuschreiben, was Unrechtes und Gott-Feindliches darin beschlossen worden sei; *qui legit intellegat,* schließt der Absatz sybillinisch[65]. Daß hiermit das Papstwahldekret von 1059 und speziell die Zurücksetzung der Kardinalpriester und Diakone gemeint ist

---

drei heute bekannten Hss. — sie stammen alle aus Nordost-Italien — kann die Vorlage Deusdedits gewesen sein, so daß sich nicht zeigen läßt, ob Textabweichungen auf Deusdedit oder seine, nach FOERSTER auf jeden Fall gleichzeitige, Vorlage zurückgehen.

63) Deusdedit 2.110, S. 236, Z. 9, Z. 14, Z. 19 und Z. 24. Dazu auch HIRSCH, Rechtliche Stellung (wie Anm. 41) S. 616 ff.

64) S. 236, Z. 3 ff.: *Sancta quoque VII uniuersalia concilia* (dazu HIRSCH, S. 617, Anm. 1), *idest ... usque ad unum apicem inmutilata seruare et pari honore et ueneratione digna habere et que predicauerunt et statuerunt, omnimodis sequi et predicare ...*

65) Deusdedit, S. 4 f., Z. 30 ff.: *Preterea antiquum ordinem electionis seu consecrationis Romani pontificis et cleri eius huic operi inserere libuit. Nam quidam olim in dei et sanctorum patrum sanctionibus contemptum ad sui scilicet ostentationem et adscribendam sibi uentosam auctoritatem, quę nullis canonicis legibus stare potest, scripserunt sibi nouam ordinationem eiusdem Romani pontificis, in qua quam nefanda quam deo inimica statuerunt, horreo scribere; qui legit intellegat.* Zu Deusdedits Widmung und seinem Verhältnis zu Viktor III. und Montecassino COWDREY, Abbot Desiderius (wie Anm. 42) S. 99–102 und S. 158–160, hier besonders Anm. 173. Hans-Georg KRAUSE, Das Papstwahldekret von 1059 und seine Rolle im Investiturstreit (Studi Gregoriani 7, 1960) erwähnt die Widmung nicht.

und nicht der ‚Königsparagraph' wie im Libellus contra invasores, dem bisher die Aufmerksamkeit von Historikern im Zusammenhang mit 1059 so gut wie ausschließlich gegolten hat, beweisen die von Deusdedit der Sammlung beigefügte Papstwahlordnung von 769 und verwandte Dekrete[66]. Das *qui legit intellegat* scheint besonders auf Viktor III. gemünzt zu sein, denn er hatte als Kardinalpriester von S. Cecilia als einer der wenigen nicht-bischöflichen Kardinäle das Papstwahldekret unterschrieben[67]. Sowohl Anselms (6.12) als auch Deusdedits (1.168) Sammlungen enthalten einen Auszug aus dem Synodalschreiben *Vigilantia universalis*, das unter anderem das Wahldekret von 1059 resümiert, sowie ein Exzerpt aus dem Simonieverbot (JL 4431a) der gleichen Synode (Ans. Luc. 6.13; Deusd. 1.169)[68], aber im Gegensatz zum Original wird in den Sammlungen das Wort Kardinalbischöfe durch das Wort Kardinäle ersetzt[69]. Deusde-

---

66) 2.161–163 mit 1.255 (Liber pontificalis-Eintrag über die Synode) sowie 1.149 (JE 2692 von 862) und 4.434, S. 614, Z. 12–15 (JE 3271 von 879). Siehe KUTTNER, Cardinalis (wie Anm. 10) S. 163 f. sowie S. 192. FOURNIER, Collections canoniques romaines (wie Anm. 2) S. 343 f., hielt 2.161-163 für Nachträge, doch widerspricht dem bereits der aus dem Vorwort in Anm. 65 zitierte Text. Siehe auch WOLF VON GLANVELLS Einleitung, Deusdedit, S. XVf. Ausgabe der Texte zu 769: MGH Conc. 2, 1, Nr. 14, S. 74 ff., besonders S. 86 ff. Die Sigle für Deusdedit ist D. Zu Holstes Ausgabe, die für Anselm benutzt wurde, siehe Anm. 71 unten. Allgemein zur Synode von 769 Harald ZIMMERMANN, Papstabsetzungen des Mittelalters (1968) S. 13 ff.; Ottorino BERTOLINI, La caduta del primicerio Cristoforo (771), Storia della Chiesa in Italia 1 (1947) S. 227–289 und jetzt Thomas F. X. NOBLE, The Republic of St. Peter (1984) S. 112 ff. Zur Synode und den Kardinälen, außer Kuttner, Hans-Walter KLEWITZ, Die Entstehung des Kardinalkollegiums, ZRG Kan. 25 (1936) S. 115–221, hier zitiert nach dem Neudruck in: DERS., Reformpapsttum und Kardinalkolleg (1957) S. 11–134, besonders S. 60 und S. 67 f.

67) JASPER, Papstwahldekret (wie Anm. 42) S. 111, Z. 193 f. Siehe auch KRAUSE, Papstwahldekret (wie Anm. 65) S. 70 f.; Rudolf HÜLS, Kardinäle, Klerus und Kirchen Roms 1049–1130 (Bibliothek des Deutschen Historischen Instituts Rom 48, 1977) S. 154 ff.; COWDREY, Abbot Desiderius (wie Anm. 42) S. 117.

68) Zum Schreiben *Vigilantia universalis* (JL 4405/JL 4406) Rudolf SCHIEFFER, Die Entstehung des päpstlichen Investiturverbots für den deutschen König (MGH Schriften 28, 1981) Anhang 1, S. 208 ff. und JASPER, Papstwahldekret, besonders S. 62 ff. Jasper kann zeigen, daß auch JL 4431 a (Simonieverbot; Deusdedit 1.169 und Anselm Luc. 6.13) dem Konzil von 1059 angehört: „Es ist die protokollartige Aufzeichnung einer Ansprache Nikolaus II. an die Konzilsväter . . ." (S. 67).

69) JASPER, Papstwahldekret, S. 76–78. Bei der damals fließenden Bedeutung des Wortes *cardinalis* (JASPER, S. 72-76 und COWDREY, Abbot Desiderius [wie Anm. 42] S. 48–55, jeweils mit Literatur) erscheint Jaspers These (S. 78: „Wir können hier lediglich die zufällige Verwendung desselben Wortes cardinales in der Verfälschung und in den Reformsammlungen konstatieren.") sehr einleuchtend, doch ließe sich dann Deusde-

IV

Fälschungen bei Kanonisten der Kirchenreform   259

dit wußte, daß es sich dabei um eine Fälschung handeln mußte, denn nur der echte Text von 1059, der die Kardinalbischöfe als Hauptinstanz mit der Papstwahl betraute und den Kreis der *papabiles* ausdehnte, widersprach durch diese Begrenzung des Wählerkreises und vor allem durch die Erweiterung des Kreises der Kandidaten für die Papstwahl dem alten Papstwahlordo, den Deusdedit zur Belehrung des Papstes und zum Nutzen des römischen Klerus, das heißt der Kardinalpriester und Diakone, in die Sammlung aufnahm[70].

Es handelt sich dabei in erster Linie um drei Texte der römischen Synode Papst Stephans III. von 769, auf die sich vor Deusdedit zuletzt Papst Johannes VIII. in einem Brief bezog und die erst der Kardinal wieder in Umlauf brachte, und zwar mit Erfolg[71]. Das Konzil Stephans III. stand im Zeichen der Vorgänge des Jahres 768, als Papst Constantin II. nach der unangefochtenen Regierungszeit eines Jahres durch grausame Verstümmelungen ums Leben kam, und ein zweiter Papst nach vollzogener Weihe am gleichen Tag noch wieder in sein

---

dits heftige Reaktion auf das Papstwahldekret (Pwd) von 1059 nicht erklären. In der Diskussion von Deusdedits Stellungnahme zum Pwd von 1059 im Libellus contra invasores von ca. 1097 weist Jasper darauf hin, daß Deusdedit „nähere Kenntnis verschiedener Texte des Pwd" besessen haben muß (S. 55).

70) Vgl. die Widmung bei Deusdedit, S. 1. Der Text des Dekrets bei JASPER, Papstwahldekret, besonders S. 101, Z. 40 ff., ist zu vergleichen mit Deusdedit 2.161: . . . *Oportebat, ut . . . Romana ęcclesia . . . rite ordinaretur et in apostolatus culmen unus de cardinalibus presbiteris aut diaconibus consecraretur* (S. 268); Deusdedit 2.163, S. 269, Z. 21–26. Zum Wählerkreis Deusdedit 2.162, Z. 17–20: *Set et hoc sub anathematis interdictionibus decernimus, ut nulli umquam laicorum siue ex manu armata uel ex aliis ordinibus presumant inueniri in electione pontificis. Set a cunctis sacerdotibus atque proceribus ęcclesię et cuncto clero ipsa pontificalis electio proueniat* . . . Siehe auch den Libellus contra invasores (wie Anm.1) S. 310, Z. 4 ff.

71) Lucas HOLSTENIUS (1596–1661), Collectio Romana bipartita veterum aliquot historiae ecclesiasticae monumentorum (1662), veröffentlichte in Band 1, S. 257–267, aus „Anselmo lib. VI. cap. 24 et seqq." einen Text, der Deusdedit 1.255 und 2.161–163 entspricht. Wie aus Thaners Ausgabe ersichtlich, fehlten diese Texte jedoch in Anselms ursprünglicher Sammlung. Zwei Hss. der Klasse A, Cambridge, Corpus Christi College 269 und Vat. lat. 1363, bestätigen dies. Hs. Vat. lat. 1364 (Anselm B), fol. 123v–124r, enthält als VI.25.1–3 die aus Gratians Decretum bekannten Texte, D. 79, c.4, c.3 und c.5 in dieser Reihenfolge. Das gleiche gilt für Hs. Vat. lat. 4983 (Anselm C, nicht foliiert) VI.25, 26, 27. Holstes Hs. ist nach wie vor unbekannt. Zur Klassifizierung der Anselm-Hss. S. KUTTNER, Some Roman Manuscripts of Canonical Collections, Bulletin of Medieval Canon Law, n. s. 1 (1971) S. 7–29, S. 13 ff. — Zum Polycarpus siehe Uwe HORST, Die Kanonessammlung Polycarpus des Gregor von S. Grisogono. Quellen und Tendenzen. (MGH Hilfsmittel 5, 1980) S. 59 mit Anm. 200. Hs. Vat. lat. 1346 der 7-Bücher-Sammlung enthält die Texte zum Teil als Nachträge auf fol. 2r. Siehe auch oben Anm. 66.

Kloster zurückgeschickt wurde, um dem Kandidaten des militärischen Siegers, eben Stephan III., Platz zu machen[72]. Zwei Bestimmungen von damals dürften Deusdedit besonders interessiert haben: 1. (nur) ein Kardinalpriester oder Diakon darf für das hohe apostolische Amt gewählt werden (2.161; 2.163; 1.255) und 2. keiner bewaffneten Macht soll ein Eingreifen in die Papstwahl gestattet sein ..., sondern die Papstwahl habe von allen Priestern und Magnaten der Kirche sowie dem gesamten Klerus auszugehen (2.162 und 2.163).

Wer unter dem gesamten Klerus zu verstehen ist, ergibt sich aus einem anderen, sehr langen Kapitel (2.57), das auf den ersten Blick nur aus der Subskriptionsliste von Titelpriestern und Diakonen des synodale decretum vom Jahre 499 des Papstes Symmachus zu bestehen scheint. Doch enthält das Kapitel Deusdedits einen kurzen rätselhaften Satz mit dem Hinweis, daß man einstimmige Beschlüsse über die Papstwahl gefaßt hätte. Den Inhalt der Beschlüsse, die mit seinen Ansichten über die Papstwahl nicht übereinstimmen, verschweigt er[73]. Die Unterschriften vom Jahre 499 dienten ihm sicherlich in erster Linie dazu, einen Zusammenhang zwischen Kardinalpriestern sowie Diakonen und den Papstwahlen herzustellen und damit die Beschlüsse von 769 durch eine weitere *auctoritas* zu stützen. Einen ähnlichen Zweck erfüllt auch 2.104. Deusdedit erwähnt hier unter seinen zahlreichen Auszügen aus dem Liber pontificalis unter Papst Simplicius ein *constitutum de omni ęcclesia*, das nach dem Tod Felix' III. von Kardinalpriestern und Diakonen verabschiedet wurde.

Diese Texte zur Papstwahl und insbesondere 2.109, ein Formular des Liber diurnus, in der die Kardinalprieser und Diakone über die von ihnen nach dem Tode eines Papstes vorgenommene Neuwahl berichten, dienen gleichzeitig dazu, den Vorrang der Kardinalpriester und Diakone und damit ihre führende Stellung als „unterstützender Beirat des Papstes"[74] und bei Sedisvakanz als dessen Stellvertreter zu betonen, ein Wunsch Deusdedits, der im ersten und noch mehr im zweiten Buch seiner Sammlung oft zum Ausdruck kommt, nicht selten durch Textänderungen, besonders zugunsten der Kardinalpriester[75]. Doch

72) Siehe oben Anm. 66.
73) Hg. von Theodor MOMMSEN, MGH Auct. ant. 12 (1894) S. 399 ff. Es werden päpstliche Designation (c.4, S. 403 f.) und ein erwählter Bischof (c.5, S. 404) erwähnt. Zu beachten ist aber auch Deusdedits Indexthese, S. 14, Z. 30. Die Designation eines Nachfolgers durch einen sterbenden Papst hat Deusdedit also nicht grundsätzlich abgelehnt.
74) HIRSCH, Rechtliche Stellung (wie Anm. 41) S. 621.
75) Siehe oben Anm. 42. Besonders wichtige Kapitel zur Rolle des römischen Klerus, dem ja das zweite Buch ganz gewidmet ist, sind, abgesehen vom Vorwort mit einem betonten Hinweis auf die Korrespondenz Cyprians mit dem römischen Kardinalklerus (S.

ist Deusdedits lebhaftes Interesse am römischen Klerus gut bekannt, ganz im Gegensatz zu seiner Ekklesiologie, die bisher kaum zur Kenntnis genommen worden ist[76]. Es schien ausgemacht, daß Deusdedit ein strenger Gregorianer war, der zusammen mit Hildebrandus, Turbanus und Anshelmus Lucensis episcopus „gleichsam in der Teufelsküche (stand), in der sie allerlei Verderben für die Welt zusammenbrauten", wie Ernst Sackur einmal sehr anschaulich die Anklagen der schismatischen Kardinäle interpretierte[77]. Leichte und scheinbar geringfügige Textverfälschungen, vor allem durch Einschübe und Erweiterungen sowie Auslassungen, haben für uns aber über eine Distanz von fast tausend Jahren hinweg die Sonderstellung angedeutet, die der Kardinalpriester von S. Apostolorum in Eudoxia unter den römischen Reformern im 11. Jahrhundert einnahm. Deusdedit als Anwalt der Sancta Romana Ecclesia und damit der Kardinalpriester und Diakone war damit zweifellos auch gleichzeitig ein Anwalt der römischen Familien, in deren Hände diese Ämter traditionsgemäß gelegen haben müssen, genauso wie bis zum Eingreifen Heinrichs III. in 1046 das Papsttum selbst. Deusdedits Unwillen über das ‚unkanonische‘ Papstwahldekret von 1059, der in seiner Kanonessammlung zum Ausdruck kommt, ist verständlich und darf auch in den betroffenen römischen Kreisen vorausgesetzt werden. Durch Deusdedit hat vielleicht die einheimisch-römische Kirchenreform seinerzeit ihre Stimme gefunden.

Die hier gezeigten Einblicke in das Werk Deusdedits sind einer strengen Analyse der sehr verschiedenartigen, eigenwilligen Textänderungen in seiner Kanonessammlung zu verdanken. War Deusdedit ein Fälscher? Oder besser, hätte

---

2), 2.69, 80, 84, 88, 100, 107, 108, 110, 121–123, 126–132 und 152 sowie 2.160, die bekannte Erweiterung eines veränderten Satzes aus Isidors Etymologiae zu *cardo* (lib. 15, c.7). Daneben sind zu beachten 1.191, 192, 205, 255, 257, 261 (besonders S. 153, Z. 26), 2.41, 43, 44, 57, 60, 75, 4.434. Siehe Kuttner, Cardinalis (wie Anm. 10) S. 176 f., Anm. 110.

76) Andeutungen bei Robinson, Authority and Resistance (wie Anm. 4) S. 47 ff. sind Ausnahmen: „Clearly, the *Collectio canonum* of Deusdedit, even though it shows the influence of the Gregorian blueprint, *Dictatus papae*, cannot be classified simply as a „Gregorian collection" (S. 49). Das von Congar, Der Platz des Papsttums (wie Anm. 27) als Ideologie der Reformer herausgestellte Prinzip, einem monarchischen Papst die Ekklesia unterzuordnen (S. 205 f., S. 208 f.), trifft zumindest für Deusdedit nicht zu. Es ist bezeichnend, daß sich Congars einziges Textbeispiel aus der Sammlung Deusdedits (Vorwort, S. 2: *Itaque ego auctoritatis ipsius [Romanae Eccl.] privilegium, quo omni Christiano orbi preminent, ignorantibus patefacere cupiens . . .*) nicht auf den Papst, wie Congars Text nach anzunehmen wäre, sondern auf die Sancta Romana Ecclesia bezieht.

77) Sackur, Dictatus papae (wie Anm. 45) S. 141 und Anm. 5.

er einen solchen Vorwurf für berechtigt gehalten? Sowohl Deusdedit als auch seine Kritiker, die schismatischen Kardinäle, wandten im Zitatenkampf des Investiturstreits strenge Maßstäbe an, um Authentizität und Entfernung vom Original zu messen[78]. Um Kritik, mit der er schon von vornherein rechnete[79], zu entwaffnen, arbeitete Deusdedit häufig mit Auslassungen[80], anders als die schismatischen Kardinäle, denen es zwar auch nicht um Buchstabentreue, aber doch um ein wissenschaftlich authentisches Gesamtbild ging[81]. Doch selbst wenn die Gegenpartei Deusdedits Spielregeln akzeptiert hätte, wäre es ihr durchaus möglich gewesen, ihn für Verfälschung einzelner Texte verantwortlich zu halten, natürlich vorausgesetzt, sie hätte Zugang zu den Quellen des Kardinals gehabt. Er „änderte und setzte hinzu", um Texten wie denjenigen der Synode von 769 zum Durchbruch zu verhelfen. Zusätze und Veränderungen entsprechen einem bewußten Abweichen vom Original. Hielt Deusdedit dieses Abweichen ohne weiteres für legitim? Sicherlich nicht. Bedenkt man die strengen Vorschriften zur Beachtung alten Rechts, die er den Päpsten zur Pflicht machte, dann muß man davon ausgehen, daß er auch für sich selbst keinesfalls ein persönliches Recht zu beliebigen Textänderungen in Anspruch genommen haben kann. Die angetroffenen Änderungen stellen also Textverfälschungen dar und damit zugleich eine außerordentlich aufschlußreiche Verständnishilfe für Historiker, die schon aus diesem Grund allein auf den Ausdruck Fälschung nicht verzichten sollten. Fehl gehen Historiker erst dann, wenn Fälschungen nicht nur festgestellt, sondern dem Autor zum Vorwurf gemacht werden. Die mittelalterliche Lücke zwischen Theorie und Verhaltensweise ist heute unüberbrückbar[82].

---

78) Ein anderes Beispiel bei Horst FUHRMANN, Pseudoisidor, Otto von Ostia (Urban II.) und der Zitatenkampf von Gerstungen (1085), ZRG Kan. 68 (1982) S. 52–69, besonders S. 56 f., Anm. 11.

79) Deusdedit, Vorwort S. 3, Z. 29 ff., S. 4, Z. 27 ff.

80) Deusdedit S. 5, Z. 9 ff.: *Et quoniam dum breuitati studeo, plurima utilia me preterire doleo, moneo curiosum lectorem, ut cum uacat, his, a quibus hęc deflorata sunt, studium adhibeat, non ut defloratis aliquid adiungat, set ut suo desiderio satisfaciat.*

81) Benonis aliorumque cardinalium scripta (wie Anm. 41) Traktat III, cap. 9, S. 391 f.

82) FUHRMANN, Kritischer Sinn (wie Anm. 10) und DERS., Pseudoisidorische Fälschungen (wie Anm. 1) 1, S. 85: „Mit Augustin verwirft die Theologie des Mittelalters die Lüge und den Betrug in einer erstaunlichen Unbedingtheit — offenbar im Gegensatz zur Alltagspraxis". Zitate zum Wahrheitsbegriff in der Sammlung Deusdedits gehören deutlich einem anderen Zusammenhang an, der priesterlichen Mahnungspflicht, und sagen deswegen zur Textkritik bei Deusdedit nichts aus. Siehe Deusdedit 4.374, 4.65 und vor allem 4.61.

V

Rom in der Kanonistik

Die Kirchenreform des elften Jahrhunderts kam in vielfältigen Formen zum Ausdruck[1]. Nachdem seit dem Pontifikat Leos IX. (1049–1054) das Papsttum die Führung übernommen hatte, rückten mit dem Papst auch Rom und die römische Kirche in den Mittelpunkt der Bewegung. Dabei wurde die Reform zu dem nach Papst Gregor VII. (1073–1085) benannten Gregorianismus: so könnte man die Entwicklung vielleicht kurz skizzieren, denn die sogenannten Gregorianer werden allgemein kurz und knapp mit den Reformern gleichgesetzt[2]. Doch schon vor Jahren zeigte J. J. Ryan, daß es unter den Reformern zumindest zwei verschiedene Richtungen gab, für die Humbert von Silva Candida und Petrus Damiani als beispielhaft gelten[3]. Hier soll auf eine weitere Strömung unter den römischen – aus Rom gebürtig waren sie sehr selten – Reformern hingewiesen werden, die Wesentliches zum Verständnis des Rombilds in der Kanonistik des späten elften und frühen zwölften Jahrhunderts beiträgt. Der Einfachheit halber und zur Unterscheidung sei sie hier als stadtrömisch bezeichnet, obwohl die Vertreter dieser Strömung die *sancta romana ecclesia* genauso für universal hielten wie die Gregorianer allgemein[4].

Die wichtigste Quelle für stadtrömische Tendenzen unter den Reformern ist die Kanonessammlung des Kardinals Deusdedit[5], die 1087 beendet wurde. Bevor ich mich Deusdedit zuwende, sei kurz an die Umstände erinnert, unter denen sich die Reform zum ersten Mal in der römischen Kirche durchsetzte. Bruno von Toul, wie Leo IX. vor der Papstwahl hieß, soll die Annahme des päpstlichen Amtes von der freien Wahl durch die Römer abhängig gemacht und Rom zum ersten Mal in Pilgerkleidung betreten haben. Er sah sich also deutlich als Bischof von Rom und hatte nicht die Absicht, die Römer zu brüskieren. Dem entspricht es, daß die ersten

Darunter verstehe ich eine starke Wiederbelebung des christlichen Glaubens allgemein sowie ein verändertes Selbstverständnis des Papsttums. – Bei Quellenzitaten ist e caudata durch einfaches »e« ersetzt.

Zur berechtigten Kritik am unreflektierten Gebrauch des Wortes Reform kürzlich Gerd TELLENBACH, Die westliche Kirche vom 10. bis zum frühen 12. Jahrhundert (Die Kirche in ihrer Geschichte 2), 1988, S. 133.

Saint Peter Damiani and His Canonical Sources (Pontifical Institute of Mediaeval Studies, Studies and Texts 2), 1956, S. 172–175.

Vgl. Yves M.-J. CONGAR, Der Platz des Papsttums in der Kirchenfrömmigkeit der Reformer des 11. Jahrhunderts, in: Sentire Ecclesiam. Das Bewußtsein von der Kirche als gestaltende Kraft der Frömmigkeit, hg. von J. DANIELOU und H. VORGRIMLER, 1961, S. 196–217, S. 200f.

Die Kanonessammlung des Kardinals Deusdedit, hg. von Victor WOLF VON GLANVELL, 1905, Neudruck 1967. Angaben zur Bibliographie bei Horst FUHRMANN, Einfluß und Verbreitung der pseudoisidorischen Fälschungen (Schriften der MGH 24,2), 1973, S. 522ff., bes. S. 522 Anm. 258. Vgl. auch Wilhelm KURZE, Notizen zu den Päpsten Johannes VII., Gregor III. und Benedikt III. in der Kanonessammlung des Kardinals Deusdedit, QFIAB 70, 1990, S. 23–45.

Jahrzehnte des 11. Jahrhunderts die Zeit der Neuansätze in der päpstlichen Verwaltung, der sacrum palatium Lateranense mit seinen Verbindungen zum römischen Adel, waren und nich die Zeit der Reform, obwohl Leo sich nicht scheute, neue Formen für päpstliche Privilegie einzuführen[6]. Man konnte in Rom also durchaus annehmen, daß selbst unter einem fremde Papst mit landfremden Beratern römischer Einfluß kaum gemindert werden würde. Doch de Schein täuschte, wie vor allem Benedikt IX. und Benedikt X. mit ihren Anhängern schnel lernten.

Unter Papst Nikolaus II. (1058–1061) kamen die gespannten Verhältnisse in Rom, über di wir sonst schlecht unterrichtet sind, deutlich in der Neuordnung der Papstwahl zum Ausdruck Das auf der Synode von 1059 verkündete Papstwahldekret schloß die Römer und den größte Teil des Klerus, darunter auch die Kardinalpriester und Kardinaldiakone, von der eigentliche Wahl aus, die in Zukunft von den Kardinalbischöfen vorgenommen werden sollte, denen da Vorschlagsrecht zugesprochen wurde[7]. Unruhen, wie sie sich nach dem Tod Stephans IX (1057–1058) ereigneten, und der Wahl von den Reformern nicht genehmen Päpsten sollte ein fü allemal der Riegel vorgeschoben werden[8].

Die Gegensätze unter den Römern, die sich hinter dem Papstwahldekret verbergen kommen sehr wahrscheinlich in den Unterschriften des Dokuments zum Ausdruck. Obwol damals eine genaue Unterschriften-Regelung erst im Entstehen war[9], würde man erwarten, da der stadtrömische Klerus unter den Unterzeichnern stark vertreten gewesen wäre. Bei de Kardinalbischöfen war das auch der Fall, denn von sieben Kardinälen dieses Ranges unter schrieben fünf, also alle, abgesehen von Johannes II. von Velletri, der vom römischen Adel zu »Gegen«papst erhoben worden war, und von Abt Rainer von SS. Cosmae et Damiani in Mic aurea (S. Cosimato), der gleichzeitig Kardinalbischof von Palestrina war und zu den Parteigär gern Johannes' gehörte[10]. Aber sucht man nach den Namen der Kardinalpresbyter un Kardinaldiakone unter den Unterzeichnern, ergibt sich ein wesentlich anderes Bild. Von de

---

6 Reinhard ELZE, Das »Sacrum Palatium Lateranense« im 10. und 11. Jahrhundert, Studi Gregoriani 1952, S. 27–54 mit weiterer Literatur und zu Leo IX. besonders Leo SANTIFALLER, Über die Neugestaltun der äußeren Form der Papstprivilegien unter Leo IX., in: Festschrift Hermann Wiesflecker zum sechzigste Geburtstag, hg. von A. NOVOTNY und O. PICKL, 1973, S. 29–38 sowie Joachim DAHLHAUS, Aufkomme und Bedeutung der Rota in den Urkunden des Papstes Leo IX., Archivum Historiae Pontificiae 27, 198 S. 7–84.
7 Detlev JASPER, Das Papstwahldekret von 1059. Überlieferung und Textgestalt (Beiträge zur Geschich und Quellenkunde des Mittelalters 12), 1986, Text auf S. 101 f., Z. 40–57 in der echten Fassung: . decernimus atque statuimus, ut obeunte huius Romane universalis ecclesie pontifice inprimis cardinal episcopi diligentissima simul consideratione tractantes, mox sibi clericos cardinales adhibeant, sicque reliqu clerus et populus ad consensum nove electionis accedant ...
8 Dazu allgemein Hans-Georg KRAUSE, Das Papstwahldekret von 1059 und seine Rolle im Investiturstre (Studi Gregoriani 7), 1960, S. 62 ff., 76 ff. Eine Diskussion der neueren Literatur findet man in JASPER (w Anm. 7), S. 1, Anm. 2.
9 B. KATTERBACH und W. M. PEITZ, Die Unterschriften der Päpste und Kardinäle in den ›Bullae Maiore vom 11. bis 14. Jahrhundert, in: Miscellanea Francesco Ehrle 4 (Studi e testi 40), 1924, S. 177–274, hier 17
10 Hans-Walter KLEWITZ, Die Entstehung des Kardinalkollegiums, ZRG Kan. 25, 1936, S. 115–221, hi zitiert nach dem Wiederabdruck in: DERS., Reformpapsttum und Kardinalkolleg, 1957, S. 11–134, S. 34 und Rudolf HUELS, Kardinäle, Klerus und Kirchen Roms 1049–1130 (Bibl. des Deutschen Historische Instituts in Rom 48), 1977, S. 108 f., Nr. 2 und S. 144, Nr. 4. Für die Unterschriften selbst s. JASPER (w Anm. 7), S. 110 ...

damals 28 Kardinalpriestern unterschrieben 1059 nur vier[11] und von den damals vielleicht schon 18 Kardinaldiakonen nur drei[12]. Wir kennen die Gründe für diese immerhin auffällige Zurückhaltung der Mehrheit des römischen Klerus gegenüber Nikolaus II. im allgemeinen nicht. Indizien sind weniger die Wahlen Benedikts IX. und Benedikts X. als vielmehr die Opposition gegen Papst Gregor VII., besonders 1082[13] und 1084, als ein großer Teil der beiden unteren Kardinalsränge zu Wibert überging[14]. Wie diese Ereignisse zeigen, bedeutete ein Reformer zu sein nicht ohne weiteres, mit dem päpstlichen Reformkreis übereinzustimmen.

In der Kanonessammlung des Kardinalpresbyters Deusdedit von SS. Apostolorum in Eudoxia (S. Pietro in Vincoli) erkennt man deutlicher, warum es dem reformierten Papsttum schwerfiel, sich in vielen der stadtrömischen Kirchen durchzusetzen. Im Gegensatz zur Haupttendenz unter den Reformern, einem monarchischen Papst die Ecclesia unterzuordnen[15], vertritt Deusdedit in seiner Kanonessammlung einen Standpunkt, der den Primat nicht den Päpsten, sondern der *sancta Romana ecclesia* zuspricht. Der Papst, als Nachfolger Petri, hat lediglich eine bedingte und begrenzte Führungsrolle. Deusdedits Ansichten entsprechen also nicht in jeder Hinsicht den vom Papsttum verfochtenen Zielen. Die Stellung der *sancta Romana ecclesia* und damit des christlichen Roms im Denken Deusdedits soll im Folgenden an zwei Einzelbeispielen kurz erläutert werden: einmal in Deusdedits Haltung zu den Konzilien, insbesondere dem Laterankonzil von 1059, und zweitens in seinen Aussagen zur *sancta Romana ecclesia*. Deusdedits Rolle als Vertreter der Rechte der beiden unteren Kardinalsränge, die bekannt ist, wird dabei nur im Vorübergehen gestreift. Ein weiterer, sehr wesentlicher Punkt, die für die Frömmigkeit der Römer sehr bezeichnende Betonung der besonderen Stellung des Apostels Paulus, von Hans Martin Klinkenberg besonders belegt, ist anderenorts behandelt worden[16].

1. Konzilien

In der Widmungsepistel seiner Sammlung an Papst Viktor III. unterzog Deusdedit das Laterankonzil und das Papstwahldekret von 1059 einer beißenden Kritik. Er schrieb, daß es sich in »Verachtung der Beschlüsse Gottes und der heiligen Väter in vermessener Eitelkeit die leere Autorität« zugelegt hätte, eine neue Papstwahlordnung zu schreiben, was von keinem der Kanones erlaubt sei, *in qua quam nefanda quam deo inimica statuerunt, horreo scribere*. Der

[11] Ebd., S. 110 f. In Anm. 56 weist Jasper darauf hin, daß alle Unterzeichner cardinales S. Petri waren.
[12] Ebd., S. 111 mit Anm. 60–62; HUELS (wie Anm. 10), S. 17–19 für die Zahl von 18 Diakoniekirchen sowie KUTTNER, Cardinalis: The History of a Canonical Concept, Traditio 3, 1945, S. 129–214, S. 178–198.
[13] Zur Versammlung vom 4. Mai 1082, die »zweifellos gegen Gregor VII. gerichtet« die Verpfändung von Kirchenbesitz zum Kampf gegen Wibert verbot, s. die Angaben bei KRAUSE (wie Anm. 8), S. 248, Anm. 44; Celina ZAFARANA, Sul ›conventus‹ del clero romano nel maggio 1082, Studi Medievali, ser. terza, 7, 1966, 399–403 und mit neuer Literatur JASPER (wie Anm. 7), S. 73, Anm. 286.
[14] Unter der Kardinälen, die 1084 offen zur Obödienz Wiberts von Ravenna übergingen, war nur ein Kardinalbischof, Johannes von Porto: HUELS (wie Anm. 10), S. 118 ff., Nr. 3. Ansonsten war die Empörung gegen Gregor VII. ganz von Kardinalpriestern und Kardinaldiakonen getragen: KRAUSE (wie Anm. 8), 248 f. Anm. 44. S. besonders Jürgen ZIESE, Wibert von Ravenna. Der Gegenpapst Clemens III. (1084–1100), (Päpste und Papsttum 20), 1982, S. 99–102 mit vollständigen Literaturangaben.
[15] CONGAR (wie Anm. 4), S. 205 f. und S. 208 f.
[16] Hans Martin KLINKENBERG, Der römische Primat im 10. Jahrhundert, ZRG Kan. Abt. 41, 1955, 1–57; BLUMENTHAL (wie Anm. 17).

Leser, so schließt er, wüßte wohl, wovon er spräche[17]. Der Leser, das war besonders Pa[
Viktor III., der als Kardinalpriester von S. Cecilia das Papstwahldekret unterschrieben hat
Zur Belehrung Viktors und des »gesamten Klerus der heiligen römischen Kirche«, d(
Deusdedit die Sammlung neben dem Papst gewidmet hatte, fügte Deusdedit unter anderem (
Papstwahlordnung von 769 bei: ... *Oportebat, ut hec sacrosancta domina nostra Roma*
ecclesia iuxta quod a beato Petro et eius successoribus institutum est, rite ordinaretur et
apostolatus culmen unus de cardinalibus presbiteris aut diaconibus consecraretur[18].

Es sind zwei eng verwandte Aspekte, gegen die Deusdedit rebelliert. Einmal handelt es si
um die Autorität des Konzils und zum anderen um den Inhalt der neuen Wahlregelung, vor c
Deusdedit so schauderte, daß er sie nicht beschreiben kann. Im rund zehn Jahre spä
entstandenen *Libellus contra invasores et symoniacos* (1097) klingt die Entrüstung des Kardin
priesters noch sehr deutlich nach. Nikolaus, ein einziger der Patriarchen, könne doch nicht r
dem Rat einiger Bischöfe die mit dem Glauben übereinstimmenden Beschlüsse der heiligen fü
Patriarchen umwerfen[19]! Das Dekret Nikolaus' II. entbehre jeglicher Rechtskraft: *prefat(
decretum nullius momenti esse nec umquam aliquid virium habuisse.* Es handele sich bei d(
Papstwahldekret um eine menschliche Verfehlung des Papstes[20]. Diese Überzeugung Deus(
dits war in seiner Kanonessammlung sehr viel gründlicher ausgeführt worden. Zur höchs(
irdischen Autorität in der Kirche erklärte Deusdedit in seinem Vorwort die Kanones (
Universal- oder Plenar-Konzilien, das heißt der ökumenischen Konzilien, die von den f(
Patriarchen oder gegebenenfalls ihren Vikaren abgehalten wurden. Ihre Erlasse könnten (
von Konzilien gleicher Art wieder aufgehoben werden und binden selbst die Päpste: *Q(
priora uniuersalia interdum emendantur a posterioribus universalibus*[21]. Es ist die *san
Romana ecclesia,* die Generalsynoden einberuft, und ohne ihre Erlaubnis dürfen noch ni(
einmal reguläre Synoden abgehalten werden. Üblicherweise sind die Päpste nur durch i(
Legaten – sprich Kardinäle – die Vorsitzer der Universalkonzilien[22]. Das Konzil von Nic
habe den Papst ernannt[23]. Man wundert sich nicht mehr, daß Deusdedit Auszüge (
Photianischen Synode von 861 in sein Werk aufnahm (IV.428–31), die von Papst Nikolau(
verworfen worden war[24].

---

17 GLANVELL (wie Anm. 5), S. 4 f. Zeile 31 ff. Uta-Renate BLUMENTHAL, Fälschungen bei Kanonisten
Kirchenreform des 11. Jahrhunderts, in: Fälschungen im Mittelalter 2: Gefälschte Rechtstexte. Der bestr.
Fälscher (Schriften der MGH 33.2), 1988, S. 241–262, S. 257 f.
18 Deusdedit II.161, Glanvell (wie Anm. 5), S. 268. Dieses Dekret findet sich nicht in der Samml(
Anselms von Lucca, wie Glanvell aufgrund von Theiners Angaben vermutet hatte (Glanvell, S. LII
sondern erst wieder im Polycarpus des Kardinalpresbyters Gregor von S. Grisogono (um 1111) I 4,6. (
dann im Decretum Gratians als D. 79 c. 3. Zum Polycarpus s. Uwe HORST, Die Kanonessamml(
Polycarpus des Gregor von S. Grisogono (Hilfsmittel der MGH 5), 1980, hier S. 5 und 59. Vgl. fer
KLEWITZ (wie Anm. 10), S. 67 f. und BLUMENTHAL (wie Anm. 17), S. 259 f. zu weiteren Texten Deusdec
19 Deusdedit, Libellus contra invasores et symoniacos, c. 11, Z. 12 ff., ed. E. Sackur, MGH Ldl 2, 1(
S. 310.
20 Ebd., S. 311 f., Z. 21–2.
21 Deusdedit (wie Anm. 5), Indexthese S. 7, Z. 32 f.
22 Ebd., S. 7, Z. 12 ff. und 15 ff.
23 Ebd., S. 8, Z. 10.
24 Stephan KUTTNER, Liber canonicus: A Note on »Dictatus papae« c. 17, Studi Gregoriani 2, 1(
S. 387–401, hier S. 395 mit Anm. 35.

V

In diesem Zusammenhang ist es sehr charakteristisch, daß man nur bei Deusdedit einen Text
det, in dem nicht jegliches Abweichen von den Befehlen des Heiligen Stuhls absolut verboten
rd, wie in mehreren anderen Reformsammlungen, sondern jegliches Abweichen von den
ordnungen der heiligen Kanones (I.16)[25]. Das Ausmaß dieser Verpflichtung wird durch
usdedits Gebrauch des Adjektivs »canonicus« innerhalb der Sammlung verdeutlicht, so
onders in der *Professio futuri pontificis*, einer der Formeln des *Liber Diurnus*. Viermal
schreibt Deusdedit in seiner Sammlung – in Abweichung von der sonst überlieferten Formel
lie Tradition der Kirche, die der zukünftige Papst zu halten verspricht, durch das Wort
onicus: alle *decreta canonica* seiner Vorgänger, *disciplinam et ritum* ... *canonice traditum*, die
ionische Tradition allgemein sowie die *canonica constituta pontificum*. Außerdem enthält die
rmel, wie sie bei Deusdedit verzeichnet ist, das weitere Versprechen des Papstes, die Bestim-
ingen der ökumenischen Konzilien *usque ad unum apicem inmutilata* zu bewahren[26].
Zeit seines Lebens blieb Deusdedit dieser Einstellung treu, wie der *Libellus* contra
asores et symoniacos zeigt. Aber anders als in seiner Kanonessammlung, wo es ihm bei den
r interessierenden Texten in erster Linie um das Papstwahldekret von 1059 ging, richtete
1, wie er selbst angibt, seine Polemik im *Libellus* gegen die Beteiligung von unberufenen
en, insbesondere Königen, an der Papstwahl[27]. Deshalb ist es äußerst bemerkenswert, daß
ost unter diesen Umständen von allen Kanones, die Deusdedit in den einleitenden Kapiteln
Libellus zur Untermauerung seiner These anführt, nur c. 7 speziell mit Laieneinmischung
tun hat[28]. Die anderen in c. 2–9 aufgereihten decreta betonen vielmehr zum einen, daß der
amte Klerus und das Volk für Bischofs- oder Papstwahlen verantwortlich sind, und zum
leren, daß kein Ortsfremder als Bischof gewählt werden dürfte, es sei denn, am Ort sei
ne geeignete Persönlichkeit vorhanden, ein Fall, der allerdings schlechterdings unvorstell-
sei[29]. Alles in allem zeigt sich deutlich, daß Deusdedit auch den *Libellus* zum Anlaß nahm,
sehr konzentrierter Form wieder die alte, im Kirchenrecht verankerte Regelung der
ostwahlen zu betonen, wie sie unter anderem im Kanon von 769 zu lesen war: *Oportebat, ut
in apostolatus culmen unus de cardinalibus presbyteris aut diaconibus consecraretur*[30].
mit widerlegt er noch Ende des 11. Jahrhunderts die Bestimmungen von 1059[31], und zwar
ohl was den Kreis der Wähler als auch was den Kreis der *papabiles* anlangte. Die Wähler,
waren für ihn der römische Klerus und das römische Volk[32], die *papabiles* die römischen
dinalpriester und -diakone. Das christliche Rom mit seinen Märtyrerstätten war der Hüter

Einzelnachweise und weitere Angaben bei BLUMENTHAL (wie Anm. 17), besonders S. 256 f.
Deusdedit (wie Anm. 5), 2.110, S. 236, Z. 9, Z. 14, Z. 19 und Z. 24 sowie Z. 3 ff. Siehe dazu auch Ernst
SCH, Die rechtliche Stellung der römischen Kirche und des Papstes nach Kardinal Deusdedit, Archiv
katholisches Kirchenrecht 88, 1908, S. 595–624, hier S. 616 f. sowie BLUMENTHAL (wie Anm. 17),
6 f.
E. g. Libellus (wie Anm. 19), S. 300, Z. 14, 20 f., S. 307, Z. 18 ff.
Ebd., S. 305 f. Die Beteiligung einer *turba* lehnt er aber ab: S. 307, Z. 13–16.
Ebd., S. 302, Z. 3–5 und S. 304, Z. 15–25, S. 305, Z. 2–4.
Ebd., S. 306 f., Z. 24 ff. und die Collectio canonum 2,161.
Wie JASPER (wie Anm. 7), S. 34–46, zeigen konnte, hat übrigens auch der spätere Gregor VII., der
iidiakon Hildebrand, das Papstwahldekret wahrscheinlich nicht unterschrieben. Dies ist umso
erkenswerter, als Hildebrands Beteiligung an der Lateransynode von 1059 in anderer Beziehung gut
gt ist: JASPER (wie Anm. 7), S. 39, Anm. 145. Deusdedit verdankte Gregor VII. seine Stellung als
dinalpresbyter.
Libellus (wie Anm. 19), S. 310, Z. 5.

und Erbe Petri und Pauli, verkörpert in der *sancta Romana ecclesia*, der Wächterin über ⟨
kanonische Tradition. Deshalb schrieb er auch in seinen Indexthesen: *Quod heretici sint, ⟨
Romane ecclesiae non concordent et qui eius priuilegia nituntur auferre*[33].

2. Deusdedit und die sancta Romana ecclesia

In einem einflußreichen Aufsatz beschrieb Yves Congar Quelle und Richtschnur der neu⟨
Phase des Kirchenrechts der gregorianischen Reform als die wahrhaft monarchische Gewalt ⟨
römischen Stuhles. »Der Papst ist der, ›a quo omnis ecclesiastica potestas procedit‹«
Deusdedit wird neben dem anonymen Autor der »Sammlung in 74 Titeln«, neben Atto u⟨
Anselm von Lucca als führender Kopf dieser neuen Phase des Kirchenrechts angeführt. Di⟨
Ansicht wird heute allgemein vertreten[35], stellten doch schon die schismatischen Kardin⟨
Deusdedit neben Gregor VII. und Anselm von Lucca, und mit ihnen wird er seitdem zu d
»rigoristischen Gregorianern« gezählt[36]. Es mag daher verwegen erscheinen, ausgerechnet ⟨
als einen frühen Vertreter des Konziliarismus und insofern als Gegner einer uneingeschränkt⟨
päpstlichen *plenitudo potestatis* zu bezeichnen. Man sieht inzwischen zwar in Deusdedit d
unermüdlichen Vorkämpfer für die Rechte der Kardinalpriester und Kardinaldiakone[37], al⟨
unterschätzt bisher zu Unrecht die viel weiter gehende Ausnahmestellung, die er durch sei
Verteidigung der angestammten Vorrechte der Kardinalpresbyter und Kardinaldiakone – u⟨
damit des christlichen Roms zu Lasten des monarchischen Papsttums – einnimmt[38].

Als einer der gelehrtesten Männer seiner Zeit, auch wenn er in seinem Vorwort d
Mönchsvater Benedikt mit Papst Benedikt verwechselte[39], bereicherte er die kanonistisc⟨
Überlieferung in ungewöhnlichem Umfang durch neue, fremde Texte. Dabei spielt es ke⟨
Rolle, ob er, um ein Beispiel zu nennen, die berühmte Serie III.49 selbst zusammengestellt od⟨
was wahrscheinlicher ist, aus einer in Vergessenheit geratenen älteren Zusammenstellu⟨
abgeschrieben hat[40]. Zu den von Deusdedit zuerst überlieferten Texten gehören auch c. 306 u⟨
327 im ersten Buch seiner Kanonessammlung, beide unter der Rubrik *Ex gestis sancti Bonif⟨
martyris et archiepiscopi, legati Romanae ecclesiae*[41]. Percy E. Schramm, der Michel folgend
als Auszüge aus dem Werk Humberts von Silva Candida bezeichnete, meinte: »Es ist wohl ni⟨

---

33 Deusdedit, S. 8, Z. 22 ff.
34 CONGAR (wie Anm. 4), S. 208 f.
35 Ebd., S. 206–208.
36 Ernst SACKUR, NA 18, 1892, S. 141, Anm. 5.
37 S. KUTTNER, Cardinalis: The History of a Canonical Concept, Traditio 3, 1945, S. 129–214, ⟨
besonders S. 176 f., Anm. 110. Zu den gefälschten 1059-Texten, in denen das Wort »Kardinalbischö⟨
durch das Wort »Kardinäle« ersetzt wurde, vgl. BLUMENTHAL (wie Anm. 17), S. 258 f. mit Anm. 68 und
38 Zur unterschiedlichen Bedeutung des Wortes *cardinalis* bei Leo IX. und Deusdedit KUTTNER (⟨
Anm. 37), S. 176 mit Anm. 109.
39 Deusdedit (wie Anm. 5), S. 4, Z. 19–23 und dazu Horst FUHRMANN, Kritischer Sinn und unkritis⟨
Haltung. Vorgratianische Einwände zu Pseudo-Clemens-Briefen, in: Aus Kirche und Reich, Festschrift⟨
Friedrich Kempf, hg. von Hubert MORDEK, 1983, S. 81–95. Zum Werdegang Deusdedits besond⟨
HOLTZMANN (wie Anm. 54).
40 Rudolf SCHIEFFER, Tomus Gregorii papae, AfD 17, 1971, S. 169 ff.
41 Deusdedit (wie Anm. 5), S. 177 f. (Text A) und S. 189–192 (Text B). Dazu zuletzt mit ausführlic⟨
Literatur Angaben J. Joseph RYAN, Cardinal Humbert *De s. Romana ecclesia*: Relics of Roman-Byzan⟨
Relations 1053–1054, Mediaeval Studies 20 (1958) S. 206–238.

u viel gesagt, wenn man [sie] in eine Reihe mit dem ›Dictatus papae‹ Gregors VII. stellt, der für
as Reformpapsttum auf der Höhe der Machtansprüche das bedeutet, was unser Text für die
rste Phase darstellt. Ja vielleicht darf man ihm [= dem Traktat] noch den Vorzug vor dem
)ictatus geben, weil er nicht nur die päpstlichen Rechte erläutert, sondern auch in großartiger
prache eine Rechtfertigung von durchschlagender Wucht für die Forderungen der Päpste
efert«[42]. In der bisherigen Literatur erscheint es als ein reiner Zufall, daß es Deusdedit war, der
ie beiden Bonifacius-Texte überlieferte, die hier nicht im einzelnen besprochen werden sollen.
ie feiern das christliche Rom, die Märtyrerstätte der Apostel Petrus und Paulus, und die Würde
es Papsttums auf einmalige Weise[43]. Aber Deusdedit hat seine Texte im allgemeinen sehr
orgfältig ausgewählt und beide Abschnitte tragen deutliche Züge einer Ekklesiologie, die
urchaus mit dem Ton der Sammlung als ganzer harmonisiert und Deusdedits Einstellung voll
nd ganz entspricht, wie noch zu zeigen ist. Walter Ullmann war sich der Schwierigkeiten wohl
ewußt, die sich ihm in den Weg stellten, als er De s. Romana ecclesia, den berühmteren der
eiden Texte, Humbert zuschrieb, auch er unter dem Einfluß der Argumente Anton Michels:
Nevertheless, the Humbertine fixation of papal immunity is an astonishing piece: does it not
row out of gear the whole papalist-hierocratic machinery?[44]« Er konnte nicht umhin
uzugeben, daß der Text (Text A; Deusd. I.306) sich auf die Römische Kirche bezieht und daß
ie Betonung auf der Römischen Kirche liegt, dem Stuhle Petri, und zwar zu Lasten des Papstes.
m übrigen seien die Römische Kirche und die Römische Kurie identisch[45]. Es muß noch
inzugefügt werden, daß die später so wichtige Häresieklausel, die in Text A enthalten ist, und
on Gratian als D. 40 c. 6 übernommen wurde[46], ohne besondere Betonung lediglich einen
.spekt des Verhältnisses zwischen Papst und sancta Romana ecclesia ausdrückte, das Text A
anz allgemein zugrunde liegt[47].

Noch viel deutlicher wird die Rolle Roms im Text B, dem zweiten der sogenannten
Bonifacius-Fragmente (Deusd. I.327). Das Rom des Romulus und Remus wird hier vom Rom
es Petrus und Paulus abgelöst[48], ein Rom, das gleichgesetzt wird mit der sancta Romana
cclesia: Sancta Romana ecclesia et reuerenda et amanda est, non quia Roma fundata est super
renam per Romulum et Remum, profana sacerdote et quo nescitur sacrilego editos, set quia

---

2 Percy Ernst SCHRAMM, Kaiser, Rom und Renovatio. Studien und Texte zur Geschichte des römischen
rneuerungsgedankens vom Ende des karolingischen Reiches bis zum Investiturstreit (Studien der
ibliothek Warburg, Teil 1 und 2), 1929, S. 238–246; Zitat auf S. 238. Die Texte sind in Band 2 ediert,
. 120–133. Die Annahme, daß Humbert der Autor der Texte war, ist eine unbeweisbare Vermutung. RYAN,
)e s. Romana ecclesia, S. 215 ff. bringt eine englische Übersetzung des Textes A mit korrigierten und
rweiterten Anmerkungen; S. 214 und 221 ff. knappe Hinweise auf die Quellen und Interpretation der
Iäresieklausel, D. 40, c. 6. Er berichtigt ULLMANN (wie Anm. 44). Zur Einschätzung s. a. RYAN, S. 207.
3 Zur Stellung des Apostels Paulus in der Kanonessammlung vgl. BLUMENTHAL (wie Anm. 17), besonders
. 247–250.
4 Walter ULLMANN, Cardinal Humbert and the ecclesia Romana, Studi Gregoriani 4, 1952, S. 111–127,
Zitat auf S. 118.
5 Ebd., S. 122. RYAN De s. Romana ecclesia hat diese Gedankengänge akzeptiert (S. 220).
6 Zu D. 40 c. 6 siehe Brian TIERNEY, Foundations of the Conciliar Theory (1955, Nachdruck 1968),
. 7–10.
7 Zum Ursprung der Häresieklausel RYAN (wie Anm. 42), S. 221–223; zur Interpretation des Textes in
erschiedenen Sammlungen s. S. 213 f.
8 Zum Vergleich Romulus/Remus-Petrus/Paulus SCHRAMM, Kaiser, Rom und Renovatio I (wie
\nm. 42), S. 33 ff.

hedificata est super Christum per Petrum et Paulum[49]. Die sieben Hügel Roms, so stellt der Tex unter anderem fest, sind jetzt mit dem Kreuz Jesu geschmückt und den Basiliken der Heiliger Ikonen und Titelkirchen. Rom sollte man nicht so sehr als Stadt der Menschen bezeichner sondern vielmehr als den Friedhof der Märtyrer, deren Blut sich alles zu eigen gemacht habe von den Bädern über das Forum zu den Kloaken. Allen Heiligen voran gehen Petrus un Paulus[50]. Man könnte so weit gehen, in diesem Text eine Zusammenfassung der Ansichten de Kardinals Deusdedit zu sehen, wie sie in den Haupttendenzen seiner Sammlung zum Ausdruc kommen. Für einen unvoreingenommenen Leser der Sammlung wäre es unmöglich, mit Erns Hirsch zu schließen, »daß Petrus selbst in und mit dem Papste als seinem Rechtsnachfolger z Rom fortlebe und fortregiere«, wenn Deusdedit selbst bei dieser Feststellung ausdrücklich vo Petrus und Paulus und nicht vom Papst, sondern von der *sancta Romana ecclesia* spricht[51], als von der Stadt Rom, geführt und repräsentiert von der *sancta Romana ecclesia*, der nacl Deusdedit Christus den Primat verliehen hat: *Quod Romana ecclesia a Christo primatur optinuit*[52].

Im Unterschied zu anderen kanonistischen Sammlungen aus der zweiten Hälfte des elfter Jahrhunderts hat Deusdedit sehr genaue Vorstellungen von den Privilegien der *sancta Roman ecclesia* und trennt diese auch klar von päpstlichen Vorrechten[53]. Deusdedits Inhaltsangabe z seiner Kanonessammlung wie auch diejenige zu seinem kleinen poetischen Werk[54] habe besonderes Gewicht. Hirsch hat seinerzeit schon hervorgehoben, daß Deusdedit durch di thesenartige Inhaltsangabe einen Mittelweg zwischen einer chronologischen und einer systema tischen Sammlung fand[55]. Sie geht insofern über die gewöhnliche *capitulatio* hinaus, als de Thesen oder Titeln von Deusdedit die Texte der Sammlung zugeordnet werden. Damit weiß de Leser, wie Deusdedit einen bestimmten Text verstanden haben will. Zum Vergleich bietet sicl vor allem die berühmte, fast gleichzeitige Sammlung Anselms von Lucca an (circa 1083). Di wohldurchdachte Struktur der in 13 Bücher unterteilten Sammlung wird gepriesen. Dabei is aufgefallen, daß Anselms Rubriken, die als *capitulatio* jedem Buch vorangehen und dann nocl einmal vor den einzelnen Kapiteln stehen, sich engstens an den Text anlehnen. »Das konnte be ihm zu solcher Manie ausarten, daß im Titel geradezu wortgleich dasselbe stand wie in den anschließenden Kapitel«[56]. Obwohl Deusdedits und Anselms Rubriken verschiedenes Gewich zukommt – Deusdedit gibt Angaben zu Themen, Anselm eine Inhaltsangabe in der Reihenfolg der Texte –, ist schon ein probeweiser Vergleich der ersten Titel für das erste Buch Deusdedit über das *priuilegium auctoritatis* der Römischen Kirche mit dem entsprechenden Buch un Titeln Anselms, *De potestate et primatu apostolicae sedis*, aufschlußreich. Dabei ist z bedenken, daß beide Autoren unabhängig voneinander beinahe gleichzeitig zu einem nich

---

49 Deusdedit (wie Anm. 5), I.327, S. 189 f.
50 Ebd., S. 190.
51 Ernst HIRSCH (wie Anm. 26), S. 595 mit den Texten in Anm. 4.
52 Deusdedit (wie Anm. 5), Indexthese 1, S. 6, Z. 1.
53 Vgl. HIRSCH (wie Anm. 26), S. 595–597, der für das Gegenteil plädiert.
54 Libellus theopoesos, veröffentlicht von Walther HOLTZMANN, Kardinal Deusdedit als Dichter, HJb 5? 1937, S. 217–232, hier S. 220 f. Auf S. 221 zum Schluß des Gedichts bezeichnet Deusdedit sich als Priester *qu tibi militat in cardine Romuleo*.
55 Ernst HIRSCH, Leben und Werke des Kardinals Deusdedit, AkathKR. 85, 1905, S. 706 ff.
56 FUHRMANN (wie Anm. 5), S. 520. Zu sachlichen Redaktionen, die ihn als Gregorianer ausweiser S. 520 f., und zur Sammlung selbst und weiterer Literatur, S. 509 ff.

eringen Teil die gleichen Quellen benutzten[57]. Die Unterschiede in Auswahl und Sequenz müssen also auf unterschiedliche Ansichten zurückgeführt werden. Von den ersten fünfzig Titeln Anselms nennen 16 den Papst (*papa* oder *Apostolicus*) direkt[58]. Darunter befinden sich bemerkenswerte Aussagen wie: *Quod Christum non recipit qui papam contristaverit* (5), *Quod nec loqui debemus, cui papa non loquitur* (6), *Quod papa a nullo nisi a Deo erit iudicandus* (24), *Quod papa pro universis ecclesiis principaliter curare debet* (28); *Ut nullus decreta sedis postolicae temerare presumat, quia hoc ad potentissimum sacerdotem papam corrigendum pertinet* (45); *Ut irritum sit quicquid in apostolica sede absque Apostolico decernitur* (50)[59], aber auch: *Quod nullus magis debeat observare canones quam Apostolicus* (49)[60].

Wie anders lesen sich dagegen die ersten 50 Indexthesen zum ersten Buch Deusdedits. Das trifft zu, obwohl die letzten dieser Thesen eine Fünfergruppe (Nr. 45–49) mit Aussagen über päpstliche Vorrechte enthalten, die dazu geführt haben, in Deusdedit den Verfasser des *Dictatus papae* zu vermuten[61]. Die Gruppe darf hier außer Betracht bleiben, da allein schon Indexthese 50: *Quod a Nicena synodo nominatus sit papa* (S. 8, Z. 10), die Thesen 45 bis 49 relativiert, wie das auch die jeweils zu den Indexthesen 45 bis 49 angegebenen Kapitel inhaltlich tun. Unter den Thesen 1 bis 44 wird der Papst nur zweimal genannt (Nr. 31 und 35)[62], und zwar ohne Betonung irgendwelcher aktiver, päpstlicher Vorrechte: *Quod non sit consuetudo pape preesse uniuersalibus sinodis nisi per legatos suos* (Nr. 31) und *Qualiter Orientales sinodis subscribunt, quas mittunt pape* (Nr. 35). Alle anderen verkünden die Größe der *Romana ecclesia* oder – seltener – der *sedes apostolica*, wie man schnell feststellt, wenn man die Substantive der Pronomina nachschlägt. Sicher hätte man die äußerst ungewöhnliche Betonung der *sancta Romana ecclesia* schon längst bemerkt, wenn man nicht stets ganz automatisch von der Annahme ausgegangen wäre, daß die *ecclesia Romana* mit dem Papst identisch sei, also eine historisch etwas spätere Entwicklung vorausgenommen hätte[63]. Nur drei seien hier angegeben, um das Ausmaß der Vorrechte der *sancta Romana ecclesia* nach Deusdedit wenigstens etwas anzudeuten: *Quod ab eodem omnium ecclesiarum caput sit instituta* (Nr. 2); *Quod eius singulare priuilegium sit aperire et claudere cœlum* (Nr. 6); *Quod generales synodos ipsa conuocare debeat* (Nr. 28).

Nimmt man Deusdedit, den Kardinalpriester des Titulus Apostolorum in Eudoxia, wie er sich immer nennt, beim Wort, gibt es für ihn nur einen Primat der Römischen Kirche. Ein Blick auf die erste Indexthese seines ersten Buches: *Quod Romana ecclesia a Christo primatum optinuit. Cap. XVIIII, L, LXXVI; et in IIIIo libro XCII*, soll hier sowohl die Schwierigkeiten der Interpretation der Indexthesen als auch die Berechtigung der vorgeschlagenen Revision der

57 Ebd. 2, S. 518f. mit kritischen Bemerkungen zur bisherigen Literatur.

58 Anselm von Lucca, Collectio canonum, hg. von Friedrich THANER, 1906–15, Neudruck 1965, S. 3–4, Nr. 5, 6, 14, 24, 25, 26, 28, 32, 33, 38, 39, 40, 43, 45, 49, 50.

59 Vgl. HIRSCH (wie Anm. 26), S. 597.

60 Zum Thema auch Ovidio CAPITANI, La figura del vescovo in alcune collezioni canoniche della seconda metà del secolo XI, in: Vescovi e diocesi in Italia nel medioevo (sec. IX–XIII). Atti del II Convegno di Storia della Chiesa in Italia (Roma, 5–9 Sett. 1961), 1964, S. 161–191, hier S. 185. Zum Einfluß der 74-Titel-Sammlung auf die Collectio canonum Anselms jetzt FUHRMANN (wie Anm. 5) 2, S. 512ff. und S. 521.

61 Deusdedit (wie Anm. 5), S. 8, Z. 1–9 und darunter besonders Nr. 48 (*Quod illius pedes a fidelibus osculari debent*) und 49 (*Quod ipse indubitanter sanctus sit, si canonice consecratus est*). Literatur über Deusdedit und den *Dictatus papae* bei FUHRMANN (wie Anm. 5), S. 524 mit Anm. 262.

62 Deusdedit (wie Anm. 5), S. 7, Z. 15 und Z. 23.

63 Besonders HIRSCH (wie Anm. 26), S. 595–597.

V

38

Einschätzung Deusdedits verdeutlichen. In der Numerierung Victor Wolf von Glanvell handelt es sich bei Deusdedits Beweismaterial zu seiner ersten These um folgende Texte: I.2 (S. 37) I.61 (S. 63) I.90 (S. 75) und IV.165 (S. 477). Alle Auszüge im ersten Buch sind Stücke au den pseudoisidorischen Fälschungen: I.22 vgl. Fuhrmann Nr. 284[64]; I.61 vgl. Fuhrman Nr. 148; I.90 vgl. Fuhrmann Nr. 330. Der Auszug IV.165 ist ein Absatz aus dem berühmte Brief Nikolaus I. an Kaiser Michael[65]. Sowohl Deusd.I.22 als auch I.90 behandeln Berufunge von Konzilien an den Heiligen Stuhl, also den Jurisdiktionsprimat. Nun enthalten beid Kanones einen auf den Papst bezogenen Satz, nämlich daß es nicht erlaubt sei, ohne *Romar pontificis sententiam concilia celebrari nec episcopos damnari,* wie es in I.22 heißt. Könnte ma bei c. 22 über das Verhältnis *sancta sedes* und Papst im Zweifel sein und sich daher fragen, wa der Kanon mit der Indexthese zu tun habe, so zeigt sich bereits bei I.90, daß Deusdedit M 16,18[66] direkt auf die *prima sedes* bezieht. Aufgrund der Erklärung Christi an Petrus hätte si die *prima sedes,* nämlich den Primat erhalten. Der Kanon IV.165, durch Deusdedit von de übrigen Auszügen aus dem gleichen Brief Nikolaus' als gesondertes Kapitel abgehoben, ist ei einziger Hymnus auf die Privilegien und Rechte der Römischen Kirche, die ihr durch den Mun Christi in Petrus zugesichert wurden: *Presertim cum ecclesie Romane priuilegia Christi ore i beato Petro firmata, in ecclesia ipsa disposita, antiquitus obseruata et a sanctis uniuersalibu synodis celebrata atque a cuncta ecclesia iugiter uenerate nullatenus possint minui ...*[67]. In de Kanonessammlung des Anselm von Lucca, in der die päpstlichen Vorrechte stark hervorgeho ben werden, findet sich dieser Text zwar auch, aber nur als Teil eines selbst in gedruckter For fast zehn Seiten langen Auszugs (I.72). Er geht bei Anselm also praktisch unter, denn entgege Anselms sonstiger Gewohnheit hat die Rubrik bemerkenswerterweise ein völlig andere Thema: *Quod sacerdotibus imperatores obedire debent non iubere*[68]. Alles in allem wird au diesen drei Belegen ganz klar, daß für Kardinal Deusdedit die *Ecclesia Romana* die grundle gende Wirklichkeit ist und keineswegs der Papst, dem lediglich – zusammen mit dem Apost Paulus – ein Ehrenplatz innerhalb der römischen Kirche zugewiesen wird[69].

Es ist schwieriger, den vierten Beleg (I.61), den Deusdedit zur ersten Indexthese angibt[70], i den vielen Sammlungen zu verfolgen, die den Text Pseudo-Anaclets aufgenommen haben[7] Man fühlt sich fast in einen Irrgarten versetzt. Das hat aber den Vorteil, daß wieder einmal kla wird, wie sorgfältig Deusdedit seine Auszüge zusammengestellt hat[72]. Noch wichtiger schein aber, daß dieser viel zitierte Text zum päpstlichen Primat Unterschiede zwischen Deusded:

64 Die Fuhrmann-Nummern beziehen sich auf die laufende Nummer im Stellenverzeichnis bei Hor: FUHRMANN (wie Anm. 5) 3, S. 770ff. Das wertvolle Register ermöglicht es ohne weiteres, Parallelstellen i anderen, von Fuhrmann untersuchten Sammlungen zu überprüfen.
65 Epistolae Karolini aevi 4, ed. E. PERELS, MGH Epp. 6 (1902–1925) no. 88, S. 454–487. Siehe dazu Ern: PERELS, Die Briefe Papst Nikolaus' I., NA 39, 1914, S. 45–153, besonders S. 78–86.
66 Das *et reliqua* schließt wahrscheinlich Vers 19 mit ein.
67 Deusdedit (wie Anm. 5), IV.165, S. 477, Z. 19ff.
68 Anselm von Lucca (wie Anm. 58), S. 39–48. Der mit Deusdedit IV.165 übereinstimmende Absatz stel auf S. 43f.
69 Vgl. CONGAR (wie Anm. 4), S. 197.
70 Sie ist zu vergleichen mit dem ersten Satz des *Dictatus papae: Quod Romana ecclesia a solo Domino s fundata,* Das Register Gregors VII. II, 55a (I), ed. Erich CASPAR, MGH Epp. sel. 2,1, 1920, Nachdruc 1967, S. 202.
71 Fuhrmann Nr. 148.
72 Zur Benutzung Pseudo-Isidors bei Deusdedit FUHRMANN (wie Anm. 5) 2, S. 525–527.

erseits und Anselm von Lucca und der »Sammlung in 74 Titeln« andererseits beleuchtet, um
r nicht noch auf andere, ältere Kanonessammlungen wie die *Anselmo dedicata* und das
cretum Burchards einzugehen[73]. Deusd. I.61 beschreibt in größerer Ausführlichkeit und mit
onderer Betonung der Rolle des Paulus – verglichen mit den anderen drei Belegstellen zu
1er ersten Indexthese – die Übergabe des Primats an die Römische Kirche durch Christus.
e Exzerpte aus mehreren Kapiteln des dritten Brief Pseudo-Anaclets stehen wortgleich bei
selm von Lucca (I.66). In anderer Gestaltung stehen Auszüge aus dem gleichen Brief auch in
1 der »Sammlung in 74 Titeln« sowie im berühmten c. 2 dieser Sammlung[74], wobei die
ssagen zu Paulus von den Aussagen zum Primat getrennt werden[75]. Kapitel 2 der »Sammlung
74 Titeln« steht an genauso prominenter Stelle wie c. 2 des ersten Buchs in der Sammlung des
selm von Lucca. Auch hier fehlt also ein Hinweis auf Paulus, dem bei Deusdedit (I.61) der
at in erster Linie gilt. Das trifft auch für Ans. Luc. I.66 zu, das aber in seiner Bedeutung von
s. Luc. I.2 völlig überschattet wird. Deusdedit aber hat den Text I.2 der »Sammlung in 74
eln« = Ans. Luc. I.2 in seine Sammlung nirgends aufgenommen. Dazu kommt noch ein
iterer Unterschied. Im Eröffnungskapitel I.1, einem Dekret des Konzils von Nicaea, weist
usdedit indirekt mit der Bemerkung ... *de qua scribit Anacletus in tertia epistola sua* auf den
eudo-Anaclet Text in I.61 hin, um den Primat des römischen Bischofs weiter zu klären. In
usdedit I.1 erscheint der Primat nämlich kommentarlos neben den Privilegien der Patriar-
ensitze von Alexandrien und Antiochien mit der Anweisung: *sua privilegia unicuique*
uentur ecclesie. Auch Deusdedit I.61 beschreibt die Hierarchie der Patriarchate, aber mit
em wesentlichen ekklesiologischen Unterschied: Petrus wurde von Christus eingesetzt,
m aber von Petrus und Paulus: *Et ambo sanctam Romanam ecclesiam consecrauerunt aliisque*
nibus urbibus in uniuerso mundo eam sua presentia atque uenerando triumpho pretulerunt[76].
ist das gemeinsame Martyrium der beiden Apostel, das Roms Sonderstellung in der Kirche
hert. Der Kreis schließt sich. An Deusdedits Feststellungen über den Vorrang der ökumeni-
ien Konzilien schließen sich beinahe nahtlos die Autoritäten über die hervorragende Rolle
r *sancta Romana ecclesia* an.

Zu den hier erwähnten Kanonessammlungen siehe generell Paul FOURNIER und Gabriel LE BRAS,
stoire des collections canoniques en occident, 2 Bände, 1931 und 1932, Nachdruck 1972. Einzelnachweise
d moderne Literatur finden sich bei FUHRMANN (wie Anm. 5).
Diuersorum patrum sentenie siue Collectio in LXXIV titulos digesta, ed. Joannes T. GILCHRIST,
onumenta Iuris Canonici, Ser. B,1), 1973, S. 20 und S. 30.
Zum päpstlichen Primat in 74T vgl. PERELS, Briefe (wie Anm. 65), S. 72.
Deusdedit, S. 63, Z. 16 ff.

VI

HISTORY AND TRADITION
IN ELEVENTH-CENTURY ROME

What shall I say about the people? They are the Roman people. I cannot express my feelings about the people of your diocese more briefly or more forcefully. What has been so well known to the ages as the arrogance and the obstinacy of the Romans? They are a people unaccustomed to peace, given to tumult; people rough and intractable even today and unable to be subdued except when they no longer have the means to resist.

Thus wrote Bernard of Clairvaux around 1152 to Pope Eugene III, a Cistercian monk who once had been a novice at Clairvaux.[1] The Romans had a very bad press during much of the Middle Ages; examples could easily be multiplied. Yet historians have long been content to assume that foreign reformers from Germany and France, who appeared with startling suddenness in eleventh-century Rome, just as suddenly converted these very Romans to their new-old vision of the Church.[2] According to the eminent

*Dr. Blumenthal is a professor of history and director of the Medieval and Byzantine Studies Program in the Catholic University of America. She presented a version of this paper at the annual meeting of the American Catholic Historical Association in Chicago on December 28, 1991, and an expanded form at the University of Würzburg in July, 1992. She wishes to thank particularly Professors Dale Kinney, Thomas Connolly, and Thomas F. X. Noble, as well as her colleague, Dr. Linda Safran, for their lively discussion and valuable assistance.

[1] Bernard of Clairvaux, *De consideratione,* 4.2.2 edd. J. Leclercq and H. M. Rochais, *Sancti Bernardi Opera,* Vol. III (Rome, 1963), pp. 394–493, here pp. 449f. I am quoting from the English translation by John D. Anderson and Elizabeth T. Kennan, *Five Books on Consideration* (Cistercian Fathers series 37: The Works of Bernard of Clairvaux 13 [Kalamazoo, Michigan, 1976]), p. 111.

[2] An excellent brief history of the 'Gregorian reform' is found in the chapters of Friedrich Kempf in *Handbook of Church History,* edd. Hubert Jedin and John Dolan, Vol. III: *The Church in the Age of Feudalism,* trans. Anselm Biggs (New York, 1969). See also this author's *The*

theologian and church historian Yves Congar, this vision was of a church
under the monarchical leadership of the pope: "the men of the Gregorian
Reform saw the church as dependent on and as if derived from the papal
power."[3] To be sure, there were some initial difficulties as the elections of
several (anti-)popes go to show, and in particular the conciliar decree of
1059 which practically excluded the Romans and most of the Roman clergy
from the papal elections.[4] However, in general 'the papacy,' 'Rome,' and
'Gregorian reformers' are used by historians loosely as interchangeable
terms. This is a pity, for such assumptions can easily cloud historical fact. J.
Joseph Ryan showed many years ago that at least two different factions
have to be distinguished among the reformers, represented by the works of
Cardinal Humbert of Silva Candida and Peter Damian respectively.[5] More
recently, Rudolf Huels was able to document the geographical distribution
of the noble Roman opposition to the reformed, i.e., transalpine, papacy in
the Eternal City.[6] This paper will discuss one of the factions among the
reformers themselves, ecclesiastics whose ideas were firmly based upon the
religious traditions of the city of Rome.

The most explicit extant source for peculiarly Roman sentiments in the
late eleventh century among the men in the entourage of Pope Gregory VII
is the writings of Cardinal Deusdedit, in particular his canonical collection.[7]
Deusdedit has always been described as a 'strict Gregorian' by contemporaries as well as by historians. Together with "Hildebrandus, Turbanus, and

---

Investiture Controversy (Philadelphia, 1988), particularly chaper 3 with its bibliography. An
important account of northern influence is the article of Hartmut Hoffmann, "Von Cluny zum
Investiturstreit," *Archiv für Kulturgeschichte,* 45 (1963), 165-203, reprinted with additions in:
Cluny, ed. Helmut Richter (Darmstadt, 1975), pp. 319–370. Recent accounts are found in Colin
Morris, *The Papal Monarchy: The Western Church from 1050 to 1250* ("Oxford History of the
Christian Church" [Oxford and New York, 1989]) and in I. S. Robinson, *The Papacy 1073–1198:
Continuity and Innovation* ("Cambridge Medieval Textbooks" [Cambridge, 1990]).

[3] Yves J.-M. Congar, "Der Platz des Papsttums in der Kirchenfrömmigkeit der Reformer des 11.
Jahrhunderts", in: *Sentire Ecclesiam, Festschrift Hugo Rahner,* edd. Jean Daniélou and Herbert
Vorgrimler (Freiburg, 1961), pp. 196–217. The quotation is found on p. 197: "Die Männer der
gregorianischen Reform sehen die Kirche in Abhängigkeit und gleichsam abgeleitet von der
päpstlichen Gewalt."

[4] The decree has been critically edited and extensively annotated by Detlev Jasper, *Das Papstwahldekret von 1059: Überlieferung und Textgestalt* ("Beiträge zur Geschichte und Quellenkunde des Mittelalters," Band 12 [Sigmaringen, 1986]).

[5] J. Joseph Ryan, *Saint Peter Damiani and his Canonical Sources* ("Studies and Texts," Vol. 2
[Toronto, 1956]), pp. 172–175.

[6] Rudolf Huels, *Kardinäle, Klerus und Kirchen Roms 1049–1130* ("Bibliothek des Deutschen
Historischen Instituts in Rom," Band 48 [Tübingen, 1977]), especially pp. 260–272.

[7] *Die Kanonessammlung des Kardinals Deusdedit,* ed. V. W. von Glanvell (1905).

Anshelmus Lucensis episcopus," Deusdedit stood at the witches' cauldron, brewing misfortune for the world, as Ernst Sackur unforgettably translated equivalent statements by the schismatic cardinals, who also were contemporaries of Gregory VII.[8] Facts, however, do not easily fit this picture. Deusdedit, the devoted partisan of the papacy, was not a Roman by birth, it seems.[9] Moreover, it is well known that Deusdedit defended the prerogatives of the lower ranks of the cardinals, although the logical consequences of such a position when the College of Cardinals was still in its infancy have yet to be taken into account.[10] This defense would suffice all by itself as an indication of Deusdedit's unusual position among the supporters of the eleventh-century renewal of the Church. Other pointers in the same direction are a strong emphasis on the dignity of the city of Rome, of the Roman clergy, not to mention the Roman Church, on the special place of the Apostle Paul, and on the powers of the ecumenical council, as will be shown.[11]

The canonical collections of the eleventh and early twelfth century were private compilations by individuals who most often excerpted from older collections whatever they found most suitable for their particular purpose: conciliar canons, papal decretals, patristic sentences, and penitential texts. Even over the distance of nearly a thousand years, therefore, small changes made by the authors of these collections in their presentation of traditional texts may reveal the intentions of the compiler. A study of the differences between the original source and Deusdedit's canonical collection reveals the great care which he used in the selection of excerpts. It also indicates a few but significant changes. These provide a new emphasis in an old context. Among such changes is the noteworthy stress on the role of the Apostle Paul. On several occasions Deusdedit added the name of the *coapostolus,* when the source only referred to Peter.[12] Two formulae of

[8]Ernst Sackur, "Der Dictatus papae und die Canonsammlung des Deusdedit," *Neues Archiv,* 18 (1892), 135–153; the quotation is found on p. 141.

[9]For the biography of Cardinal Deusdedit see in addition to the introduction found in Glanvell's introduction to the edition of the *Collectio canonum* (as in n. 7) especially Walther Holtzmann, "Kardinal Deusdedit als Dichter," *Historisches Jahrbuch,* 57 (1937), 217–232, and Horst Fuhrmann. *Einfluss und Verbreitung der pseudoisidorischen Fälschungen* ("Monumenta Germaniae Historica," *Schriften,* 24/1–3 [Stuttgart, 1972, 1973, 1974]), Vol. 2, pp. 522–533.

[10]See Stephan Kuttner, "Cardinalis: The History of a Canonical Concept," *Traditio,* 3 (1945), 129–214, pp. 176f., note 110.

[11]See this author's "Fälschungen bei Kanonisten der Kirchenreform des 11. Jahrhunderts," in: *Fälschungen im Mittelalter: Internationaler Kongress der Monumenta Germaniae Historica* ("Monumenta Germaniae Historica," *Schriften* 33/1–6 [Hanover, 1988–1990]), Vol. 2, pp. 241–262.

[12]Deusdedit 2.110 (pp. 235 and 236), 2.111 and 3.58.

the *Liber diurnus,* especially the papal profession of faith before the consecration, are striking examples of this procedure. In connection with Matt.
16:19 the true faith is passed on by Christ to the future pope not by Peter, as
in the original formula, but *per te et beatissimum coapostolum tuum
Paulum*[13]; the future pontiff promises, furthermore, not only to observe
the sacred canons and the canonical decrees, but also either to emend or to
tolerate any contravention by the intercession of Peter *and* Paul. Deusdedit's preface had emphasized already, using the present tense, that both
Peter and Paul are the living head of the Roman Church,[14] as if intending to
counterbalance the famous sermons of Pope Leo the Great referring to
Peter alone.[15] Leo is quoted frequently in the collection, but a brief excerpt
(1.290), typical for Deusdedit's use of Leo the Great, emphasized instead of
the Petrine primacy the equality of Peter and Paul, describing the apostles
as the two eyes of the body of the Church whose head is Christ.[16] Another
excerpt, opening the second book of Deusdedit's collection dedicated to
the clergy of Rome, is formed by a text which was also highly unusual at
the time, as far as we know. It is a reference to the quarrel between the
apostles, including Peter, at Jerusalem and Paul, the so-called council of the
Apostles (2.1)[17]; in chapter 85 of the same book an excerpt from a letter of
Pope Gregory I discusses the humility of Peter; the Apostle is ready to
respond to the charges of the believers and to provide witnesses regarding
his behavior. Let me add one final example for Deusdedit's emphasis on St.
Paul and with it on the collegiality among the Roman clergy, echoing the
communal organization of the first Christians at Jerusalem. Book 1, chapter
295, consists of a passage from Augustine. In the text Augustine quotes
Cyprian's contention that Peter had never once arrogantly claimed that he
held a primacy among the apostles: "For Peter . . . never claimed anything
insolently or presumed to utter arrogantly that he held the primacy, let

---

[13]Deusdedit, *Kanonessammlung* 2.110, here p. 236, line 22f. See also *Liber Diurnus
Romanorum pontificum,* ed. Hans Förster (Freiburg, 1958), pp. 69–72, and Leo Santifaller, *Liber
Diurnus: Studien und Forschungen,* ed. Harald Zimmermann ("Päpste und Papsttum," Band 10
[Stuttgart, 1976]), pp. 81ff. and 226ff.

[14]Deusdedit, *Kanonessammlung,* preface, p. 2, lines 15ff.

[15]Leo, Serm. 3.3 (Migne, *PL,* Vol. 54, cols. 146f.); Hans Martin Klinkenberg, "Papsttum und
Reichskirche bei Leo d. Gr.," *Zeitschrift der Savigny-Stiftung für Rechtsgeschichte,* Kanonistische
Abteilung 38 (1952), 37–112, esp. pp. 43f. with further references.

[16]Klinkenberg, "Der römische Primat" (as in n.25), pp. 41ff., compares sermon 4 of Leo the
Great with its interpretation in the tenth century by Abbot Odo of Cluny. Deusdedit's attitude
toward the Leonine sermons is very close to that of St. Odo.

[17]But see Odo of Cluny, Collatio III,10 (*PL,* Vol. 133, col. 598 A) with Klinkenberg, "Der
römische Primat," p. 44.

alone despised Paul because of the latter's former activity as Saul." Augustine concluded that Peter and Paul were of the same rank, certainly with regard to their martyrdom. Four chapters earlier (1.291), Deusdedit altered an excerpt from the Dialogues of Gregory the Great to state that "Paul is the brother in the apostolic principate of Peter, the first of the apostles, and in heaven their merits are equal."

Both Peter and Paul are the great patron saints of the Roman Church, and provided all else is equal, references to the special sanctity of Paul, and conceivably even to the equality of Paul with Peter, are not at all surprising. Among the popes, it was especially Nicholas I (d. 867) who emphasized the role of both Peter and Paul.[18] He relied on an ancient tradition, and can hardly be called an innovator, as Michele Maccarrone pointed out.[19] Eloquent witnesses are the famous Roman apse mosaics of, for instance, SS. Cosma e Damiano, S. Prassede, and S. Cecilia and, last not least, Old St. Peter's as preserved in the Tableau Mariotti. The Apostle Paul is always depicted at the right of Christ, or to the right of the first of the titular saints, i.e., to the right of S. Cosma in the case of SS. Cosma e Damiano.[20] However, by the end of the eleventh century the renewed strength of the papacy and developments in the concept of the papal primacy corresponded to an almost exclusive reliance[21] and emphasis on the merits and the prerogatives of the Apostle Peter and, of course, on Peter as the only prince of the Apostles. The mystical identification of Gregory VII with

[18]Yves M.-J. Congar, "S. Nicholas Ier (†867): ses positions ecclésiologiques," *Rivista di Storia della Chiesa in Italia,* 21 (1967), 393–410, here especially p. 396.

[19]Michele Maccarrone, "I Fondamenti 'Petrini' del primato romano in Gregorio VII," *Studi Gregoriani,* 13 (1989), 55–122, here p. 57, n. 4: . . .: "Non si può dire, per altro, che Niccolò I abbia 'inaugurato' quel riferimento anche all'autorità di Paolo, perchè e ben più antico nella tradizione romana." Cf. also Victor Saxer, "Le culte des apôtres Pierre et Paul dans les plus vieux formulaires romains de la Messe du 29 juin; Recherches sur la thématique des sections XV–XVI du sacramentaire Léonien," *Saecularia Petri et Pauli* (Vatican City, 1969), pp. 201–240, and in general William R. Farmer and Roch Kereszty, *Peter and Paul in the Church of Rome* (New York, 1990).

[20]See Guglielmo Matthiae, *Mosaici medioevali delle chiese di Roma* (2 vols.; Rome, 1967), Vol. 2, tav. 16 and 17 for SS. Cosma e Damiano; tav. 31 and 32 for S. Prassede with tav. 198 for the Zeno Chapel; tav. 39 and 40 for S. Cecilia. For S. Prassede R. Wisskirchen, "Zur Zenokapelle in S. Prassede, Rom," *Frühmittelalterliche Studien,* 25 (1991), 96–108, should also be consulted. For the ninth-century apse of S. Cecilia·in Trastevere see also Walter F. Oakeshott, *The Mosaics of Rome from the Third to the Fourteenth Century* (London, 1967), #129 with p. 212. Illustration #138 (p. 240) shows the famous Christ with Peter and Paul from the tomb of Emperor Otto II.

[21]Cf. Maccarrone, "Fondamenti 'Petrini,'" p. 93, n. 169, with an arenga of Pope Eugene III (1145–1153), emphasizing their equality.

VI

The Tableau Mariotti, showing the apsidal mosaic of Old Saint Peter's Basilica, Rome. (Courtesy of the Prefecture of the

Peter is often and justly highlighted.[22] The tendencies of Gregory's collaborator Deusdedit, cardinal-priest of S. Pietro in Vincoli, were more conservative. Even more than his older contemporary, Peter Damian, he continued the Roman tradition of assigning Paul a special place of honor.[23] The cardinal called himself without exception cardinal-priest of Apostolorum in Eudoxia, an ancient name which had been long forgotten even then. In his poem and his canonistic writings, he claimed that his church, Apostolorum in Eudoxia, preserved as relics not only the chains of St. Peter but also the chains of St. Paul, a claim which is not supported by any other earlier source.[24] How is this stress on the presence of two apostles to be understood? A preliminary, partial answer is provided by Roman traditions, as we have just seen. Popular piety in Rome encompassed both Peter and Paul, in the tenth century most likely with special emphasis on St. Paul. A poem from tenth-century Rome, *Carmen in assumptione sanctae Mariae*, describes Paul as the shepherd of her Christians. Paul had pastured them and led them to the water of belief; all that is said of Peter is that he had baptized there.[25] The epitaph of Pope John XIII (d. 972) declared in a very similar vein that the *summus pontifex* had gained heaven through the merits of St. Paul. It is easy to see how Hans Martin Klinkenberg could conclude that claims to a Petrine primacy, first fully formulated by Leo the

---

[22]Striking proof is provided by the index of Caspar's edition of the register of Pope Gregory VII, *Das Register Gregors VII.,* ed. Erich Caspar ("Monumenta Germaniae Historica," *Epistolae selectae* 2.1–2 [Berlin, Dublin, Zurich, 1920 and 1923]), pp. 666f. *s.v. Petrus* compared with the few entries found *ibid., s.v. Paulus.* An example for secondary literature is Leo Meulenberg, *Der Primat der römischen Kirche im Denken und Handeln Gregors VII.* (The Hague, 1965), pp. 25ff.

[23]See Peter Damian, Opusculum 35, in Migne, *PL*, Vol. 145, cols. 589ff. The treatise, discussing the place of honor of the Apostle Paul to the right of Christ, will appear in part 4 of the MGH edition (*Briefe der deutschen Kaiserzeit* IV) of the letters of St. Peter Damian, by Kurt Reindel, who assigned the Opusculum no. 159. See *idem,* "Neue Literatur zu Petrus Damiani," *Deutsches Archiv*, 32 (1976), 405–443, here p. 436, with a reference to G. Cacciamani, "I Ss. Apostoli Pietro e Paolo negli scritti di S. Pierdamiano," in: *Atti dei Convegni di Cesena e Ravenna del Centro Studi e Ricerche sull'antica provincia ecclesiastica Ravennate*, 1 (1969), 595–614 (not seen).

[24]Cf. Christian C. F. Huelsen, *Le Chiese di Roma nel medio evo* (1927), esp. p. LXVIII and 418f. It is intriguing that a reference to the chains of both Peter and Paul at S. Pietro in Vincoli appears in the *Mirabilia urbis Romae* of Benedict, a canon of St. Peter, datable to 1140–1143. See Herbert Bloch, "Der Autor der 'Graphia aureae urbis Romae,'" *Deutsches Archiv*, 40 (1984), 55–175, p. 59, and his discussion of the critical editions of the *Mirabilia, ibid.,* p. 46, n. 1, and p. 58, n. 12. An English translation of the relevant text is found in *The Marvels of Rome*, trans. Francis Morgan Nichols, 2nd ed. by Eileen Gardiner (New York, 1986), pp. 26–28, esp. p. 28.

[25]For this and the following reference see Hans Martin Klinkenberg, "Der römische Primat im 10. Jahrhundert," *Zeitschrift der Savigny-Stiftung für Rechtsgeschichte*, Kanonistische Abteilung 41 (1955), pp. 1–57, here pp. 13f.

Great centuries earlier, were in abeyance in the tenth century though not entirely forgotten. Deusdedit's reaction a hundred years later to some of the principles of the reform papacy as expressed, for instance, in the election decree of 1059, was therefore well in keeping with Roman traditions. But only in part.

Rome, her martyrs and saints evoked his fervent devotion, a devotion that was nourished both by piety and great learning. I know of no other Italian who combined knowledge of the past with the astuteness and concern for reform of a Deusdedit. His canonical collection has preserved several unique and valuable texts which the cardinal unearthed in Roman and northern archives. Among them are two excerpts under the rubric: *Ex gestis sancti Bonifatii martyris et archiepiscopi, legati Romanae ecclesiae* (1.306 and 1.327), perhaps dating from the conflicts between Rome and Constantinople in 1053/54, but long forgotten by the end of the century, when Deusdedit included them in his collection. Percy E. Schramm, who followed Anton Michel in attributing these texts to the radical reformer Humbert of Silva Candida, judged them to be of at least equal significance to the *Dictatus papae* of Gregory VII.[26] The first of the two texts (I.306), given by editors for very good reasons the title *De s. Romana ecclesia,* celebrates in solemn language the greatness of the Roman Church, who by divine and human authority has been made the head of all churches after Christ. Using Paul's second letter to the Corinthians as a basis (II Cor. 1:12, 14), it highlights the tremendous responsibility of the pope whose 'health' or 'illness' is reflected in the entire body of the Church. The pope, therefore [the Latin used is *dispensator*], has to do his utmost to be found unblemished both in deeds and words. If he should be remiss in any respect he would drag the innumerable multitude down with him to hell (*gehennae*). But no mortal is to reproach this leader for his faults, for he who can judge everybody is to be judged by no one, unless he digresses from the faith. The Church justly holds the reins in heaven and on earth *specialius in Petro;* anyone divided from her cannot prosper.

The focus of canonists, especially beginning with Gratian's *Decretum* of c. 1140, which included the relevant excerpt from Deusdedit's text (D.40

---

[26]P. E. Schramm, *Kaiser, Rom und Renovatio. Studien und Texte zur Geschichte des römischen Erneuerungsgedankens vom Ende des karolingischen Reiches bis zum Investiturstreit* ("Studien der Bibliothek Warburg," parts 1 and 2 [1929]), pp. 238–246, esp. p. 238. The texts have been edited in Vol. 2, pp. 120–133. It is impossible to prove that Humbert was the author of the texts. See J. Joseph Ryan, "Cardinal Humbert *De s. Romana ecclesia:* Relics of Roman-Byzantine Relations 1053–54, *Mediaeval Studies,* 20 (1958), 206–238. The *dictatus papae* is found in Erich Caspar's edition of the register of Gregory VII (see n. 22) on pp. 201–208.

c.6), lay on the heresy clause, to be made famous later by the conciliarists, but Deusdedit stressed papal responsibility to and for the Church in a much more comprehensive, moral sense. At the same time, however, it is the Church who is "the special mother of all the faithful in Christ" and has to instruct and censure, who is to be obeyed—who is the source nourishing the stream[27]—and who is the head of all the churches after Christ. Walter Ullmann clearly realized the contradiction between this text and the theories of its presumptive author, Humbert of Silva Candida, who like some other reformers was a radical supporter of the papal primacy. ". . . The Humbertine fixation of papal immunity [as found in Deusdedit's text] is an astonishing piece: does it not throw out of gear the whole papalist-hierocratic machinery?"[28]

The second of the Boniface texts in the canonical collection of Cardinal Deusdedit (1.327), finally, closes the circle. The passage equates the city of Rome with the *sancta Romana ecclesia,* the Rome of Romulus and Remus having been replaced by that of Peter and Paul: *Sancta Romana ecclesia et reuerenda et amanda est, non quia Roma fundata est super arenam per Romulum et Remum, . . . set quia hedificata est super Christum per Petrum et Paulum.*[29] Now, the text eventually concludes, the seven hills of Rome are decorated with the cross of Jesus, and the basilicas of the saints, icons and titular churches. All the saints are preceded by Peter and Paul. Rome ought not to be described as a city with human inhabitants, but rather as the cemetery of the martyrs whose blood made everything their own property, be it the baths, temples, theaters, towers, arches, bridges, the forum, houses, stables, and sewers. The city of Rome is equated with the *sancta Romana ecclesia,* who was given the primacy by Christ, as Deusdedit points out in the prefatory index theses: *Quod Romana ecclesia a Christo primatum optinuit.*[30]

It has always been assumed that Deusdedit included both pieces by pure chance. However, the themes touched upon in both Boniface excerpts very clearly express the tendency of the entire canonical collection compiled by Deusdedit. The cardinal is a fervent, even fanatical defender of the preroga-

---

[27]For the metaphor see the references provided by Ryan, "Cardinal Humbert," pp. 216f.

[28]W. Ullmann, "Cardinal Humbert and the ecclesia Romana," *Studi Gregoriani,* 4 (1952), 111–127. The quotation is found on p. 118.

[29]The holy Roman Church is to be revered and to be loved, not because Rome has been founded on the sand by Romulus and Remus . . . but because she has been built upon Christ by Peter and Paul." The comparison Romulus/Remus-Peter/Paul is discussed by Schramm, *Kaiser, Rom und Renovatio,* pt. 1, pp. 33ff.

[30]Cf. Blumenthal, "Fälschungen," p. 247, n. 29.

tives of the Roman Church, often at the expense of a monarchical papacy and in contrast with other canonical collections, for example, that of Bishop Anselm II of Lucca.[31] Deusdedit's concern for the *sancta Romana ecclesia,* unusual in the context of the reform, could escape the notice of historians only because mistaken hindsight equated the papacy, that is, the popes, with the holy Roman Church, an identification that began to evolve only very gradually in the course of the twelfth century.[32] Deusdedit, however, leaves no doubt that the corporate entity *Sancta Romana Ecclesia* is represented by the cardinal-priests and cardinal-deacons together with the popes who are to be elected by them from among their number.

A development intimately connected with the reform and beginning with the accession of Leo IX (1049–1054) shifted, during the eleventh century, the main functions of the old Roman cardinal priests, deacons, and bishops "from liturgical duties and prerogatives to prominent participation in the government of the Church universal."[33] To begin with, the most noteworthy changes concerned the cardinal bishops. The Lateran synod of 1059, held under Pope Nicholas II, reserved the primary right to elect a pope to the cardinal bishops, who were to consult with the rest of the cardinals and the Roman clergy and people.[34] The candidate may be selected from the Roman Church or from any other if no Roman cleric should be suitable or fitting.[35] Much has been written about this decree, nearly always with an emphasis on references to royal participation in the papal election. The significance of a forged version circulated almost immediately by even the most faithful adherents of the legitimate papacy has

[31]Anselm's collection has been partially edited by Friedrich Thaner, *Collectio Canonum una cum collectione minore* (Innsbruck, 1906–1915). For the detailed comparison see Blumenthal, "Rom in der Kanonistik," in: *Rom im hohen Mittelalter: Studien zu den Romvorstellungen und zur Rompolitik vom 10. bis zum 12. Jahrhundert,* edd. Bernhard Schimmelpfennig and Ludwig Schmugge (Sigmaringen, 1992), pp. 29–39, here pp. 36f.

[32]But see H. Fuhrmann, *Pseudoisidorische Fälschungen,* Vol. 2, pp. 533: "Sein [Deusdedit's] Werk ist mehr eine Ansammlung von Vorrechten der römischen Kirche als eine Sammlung von Rechten." See also *idem,* "Ecclesia Romana—Ecclesia Universalis," in *Rom im hohen Mittelalter* (as in n. 31 *supra*), pp. 41–45, for a subtle discussion of the evolution of the meaning of *universalis* during the reform period.

[33]S. Kuttner, "Cardinalis: The History of a Canonical Concept," *Traditio,* 3 (1945), 129–214; for the quotation see p. 172. Kuttner's bibliography is still very relevant. For the council of 1059 see Jasper, *Das Papstwahldekret* (as in n. 5 *supra*).

[34]Jasper, *ibid.,* authentic version, pp. 101f., lines 37ff: "Quapropter . . . decernimus atque statuimus ut obeunte huius Romane universalis ecclesie pontifice inprimis cardinales episcopi diligentissima simul consideratione tractantes//mox sibi clericos cardinales adhibeant, sicque reliquus clerus et populus ad consensum nove electionis accedant. . . ."

[35]*Ibid.,* p. 104, authentic version, lines 80ff.

been overlooked. Deusdedit was one of these adherents who replaced the term cardinal bishops by the term cardinals. The uproar caused among the Romans by the election decree of 1059 cannot be overstated, it seems. It is very likely that the differences of opinion were reflected immediately in the signatures of the synodal document. As customary, the Roman clergy should have been prominent among the signatories, especially considering that the reform papacy was very much in need of local support. And, in fact, of seven cardinal bishops five signed the decree. The only missing signatures are those of the antipope and his supporter, Abbot Rainer of S. Cosimato, who was also cardinal bishop of Palestrina (Preneste). The results are very different with regard to the cardinal priests and cardinal deacons. Only four of twenty-eight cardinal priests are among the signatories, and of the likely number of eighteen cardinal deacons only three. The opposition to Pope Gregory VII, especially in 1082 and 1084, seems to be adumbrated in 1059. In the forgery the Roman opposition divested the cardinal bishops, almost exclusively foreigners appointed by the reform popes, of the unheard-of prerogatives granted to them in 1059.

Deusdedit's collection is the most eloquent document for the claims of the lower-ranking cardinals, most of them Romans. It is dedicated to Pope Victor III (1087). Deusdedit addresses the pontiff in his preface, stating that his work also included the ancient election and consecration ordo for the Roman bishop and his clergy, because certain people some time ago had dared to presume to write an utterly abominable new papal election decree, thus violating every single one of the decrees of God and the holy fathers. "Let him who reads understand" (*Qui legit intellegat*), Deusdedit concludes.[36] It seems clear that this is a thinly veiled reference to the election ordo of 1059, in particular the exclusion of the cardinal priests and deacons, and the expansion of the circle of *papabiles*. Pope Victor III himself, the person to whom the preface was addressed, as cardinal priest of S. Cecilia before his election to the papacy, had been one of the four non-episcopal cardinals to sign the election decree in 1059. Deusdedit included in his compilation the papal election ordo of 769, highlighting its significance by numerous additional references to it in his canonical collection. Two of the items of 769 had been flatly contradicted in 1059: (1) only a cardinal priest or deacon can be elected to the Holy See; (2) priests, magnates, and the entire clergy of the Roman Church are to carry out the election.[37] Deusdedit never ceased to rail against the 1059 decree; in his

---

[36]Deusdedit, *Kanonessammlung*, pp. 4ff., lines 30ff.
[37]Deusdedit, *Kanonessammlung* 2.161; 2.162; 2.163; 1.255. See also 2.57 for the meaning of "entire Roman clergy." See, furthermore, the formulary in 2.109 and Blumenthal, "Fälschungen," pp. 260 f., n. 75.

Libellus contra invasores et simoniacos, dating from shortly before his death in 1098 or 1099, he used an interpolated reform decree to show that the 1059 decree had no validity; explaining that Nicholas II had succumbed to human weakness, Deusdedit excused the papal action while upholding the illegality of the 1059 election ordo: Nicholas, only one of the patriarchs, could not overthrow the joint decisions of the holy five patriarchs that agreed with the catholic faith.[38]

By his outspoken opposition to the 1059 decree Deusdedit, cardinal priest of SS. Apostolorum in Eudoxia, clearly associated himself with the claims of the Roman Church in general, with the claims of all the cardinal priests and deacons, and thus with the claims of the Roman families who traditionally influenced and held these offices. Whereas the opposition to the foreign popes—the papal office, too, had been in the hands of the Roman nobility before the intervention of Emperor Henry III in 1046—was only fitfully successful and died down, the development of the cardinalate took account of Roman claims. The differentiation between cardinal bishops and the other ranks of cardinals disappeared entirely in the course of the twelfth century. All the prerogatives claimed by Deusdedit for Roman priests and deacons in his canonical collection became the prerogatives of the later College of Cardinals.[39] There is, however, one very striking difference: largely under the influence of the new jurisprudence the papal primacy came to supersede the claims of the *sancta romana ecclesia* to be the only guardian of the canonical authority and tradition as defined by the five patriarchs in the ecumenical councils of old and as upheld by the Romans in the eleventh century.

[38]Deusdedit, *Libellus contra invasores et symoniacos,* ed. Ernst Sackur ("Monumenta Germaniae Historica," *Libelli de lite* 2 [Hanover, 1892]), p. 310 and pp. 311ff., lines 21–22.

[39]See the bibliographic references in Kuttner's article "Cardinalis" as in n. 30 *supra.*

VII

Conciliar Canons and Manuscripts:
the Implications of Their Transmission in the Eleventh Century[*]

The investigation of conciliar sources in the post-Carolingian/ pre-Gratian period long has been most successful when focused on canonistic writings, especially collections of canon law. Contemporary interest in such collections surged during the second half of the 11th and the early 12th century, creating the material basis for Gratian's *Concordia discordantium canonum*. Important papal councils have been elucidated with the aid of such manuscripts recently, for instance the Lateran synod of 1059 and the council of Clermont, held by Pope Urban II in 1095[1]. Not to be forgotten are the extensive analyses of Professor *Gilchrist* for Pope Gregory VII, also concentrating practically exclusively on manuscripts of this type and period[2]. At the same time, however, some scholars tend onesiddly to emphasize papal authority over councils and canons, assuming explicitly or implicitly that the councils rapidly declined into insignificance under the popes of the Gregorian reform[3]. This twen-

---

[*] The author would like to thank the Catholic University of America for a travel grant and Martin Brett, John Gilchrist, Wilfried Hartmann, Linda Fowler-Magerl, Lotte Kéry as well as especially Robert Somerville, wo read a draft of the present paper, for their very helpful suggestions and comments.

[1] Detlev Jasper, *Das Papstwahldekret von 1059: Überlieferung und Textgestalt*, Sigmaringen 1986 (Beiträge zur Geschichte und Quellenkunde des Mittelalters 12); see the description of MS Bergamo, Biblioteca Civica MA 244 on 19-25 as well as the edition in general. Robert Somerville, *The Councils of Urban II*, vol.1: Decreta Claromontensia, Amsterdam 1972 (Annuarium Historiae Conciliorum, Supplementum 1); the manuscript index is found on 165 f.

[2] John Gilchrist, *Was There a Gregorian Reform Movement in the Eleventh Century?* in: *Canadian Catholic Historical Association, Study Session 1970*, 1-10; idem, *The Reception of Pope Gregory VII into the Canon Law (1073-1141)*, ZRG Kan. Abt. 59 (1973), 35-81 [cited below 'Reception 1']; idem, *The Reception of Pope Gregory VII into the Canon Law (1073-1141) Part II*, ZRG Kan. Abt. 66 (1980), 192-229 [cited below: 'Reception 2'].

[3] Franz-Josef Schmale, *Synodus - synodale concilium - concilium*, AHC 8 (1976), 80-102, see 94 and 101 f. "Das 'concilium' des 12. Jahrhunderts, ob mit oder ohne den Zusatz *generalis*, ist nicht mehr die Versammlung der Bischöfe, die rechtfindend und rechtweisend einen gemeinsamen Weg gehen, sondern nur mehr eine Versammlung, die zusammengerufen wird, um dem vom Papst gesetzten Recht ihr Placet zu geben" (quote on 102). I. S. Robinson, *The Papacy 1073-1198*, Cambridge/Engl. 1990, accepts Schmale's contention that "*ca.* 1100 the papal synod disappeared, to be replaced by the new institutions of the 'general council' and the consistory" (quote on 108), although

358

tieth-century view is very much at odds with the medieval evaluation of the councils of the reform as reflected in the numerous manuscripts which preserve conciliar canons. The dichotomy raises many questions in my mind and in the following pages three of them will be tentatively outlined: 1) the transmission of councils up to the pontificate of Paschal II; 2) the implications of this textual transmission; and 3) the position of councils in papal thought and within the framework of the traditional corpus of canon law.

1) Transmission

"...die Periode der regsten synodalen Tätigkeit, welche die Geschichte des Papstthums aufzuweisen hat" as Hinschius described the time around 1100, is often said to have come to a conclusion with the Lateran council of 1123[4]. The period opened with the pontificate of Leo IX (1049-1054), a pontiff famous among contemporaries and historians alike for the many councils (at

---

it has been shown that until the time of Innocent III the consistory, a solemn public judicial assembly, has to be distinguished from papal meetings with his advisors. See Werner Maleczek, *Papst und Kardinalskolleg von 1191 bis 1216*, Wien 1984, especially 300f. For the meaning of 'generalis' and 'universalis' see in addition to Horst Fuhrmann, *Das Oekumenische Konzil und seine historischen Grundlagen*, Geschichte in Wissenschaft und Unterricht 12 (1961), 672-695, esp. 680-685. Gérard Fransen, *Papes, Conciles Généraux et Oecuméniques*, in: *Atti Mendola 1971*, Milan 1974, 203-228 (Miscellanea del Centro di studi medioevali 7). The expressions council and synod are used as equivalent in this paper in accordance with the contemporary sources (e.g. Schmale, *Synodus*, 87f.; for Bernold of Constance cf. Hermann-Josef Sieben, *Konzilien in der Sicht des Gregorianers Bernold von Konstanz [d.1100]*, AHC 11 (1979), 104-141, 117f.:"...die Termini *synodus* und *concilium* sind zwar grundsätzlich austauschbar...deutlich ist aber die Tendenz, mit dem Terminus *synodus* die Versammlung als solche zu bezeichnen, während das Wort *concilium* eher auf die Konzilsakten, vor allem die Kanones, abhebt"; see *ibid.*, 133, for *concilium generale*. Bernold is not familiar with it). Cf. Brigitte Basdevant-Gaudemet, *Les évêques, les papes et les princes dans la vie conciliaire en France du IVe au XIIe siècle*, RHD 69 (1991), 1-16, 10: "La réforme elle-même s'éffectua largement, on le sait, par le biais des conciles réunis à Rome par Nicolas II, puis par ses successeurs...le concile apparaissait comme un moyen de gouvernement...".
Paul Hinschius, *Das Kirchenrecht der Katholiken und Protestanten in Deutschland*, Berlin 1883, 3.525; see *ibid.*, 728, for the reference to the Lateran council of 1123 as the point in time when "das alleinige oberste Recht des Papstes zur kirchlichen Gesetzgebung...ein für alle Mal sicher gestellt [war]". Fransen, *Papes, Conciles Généraux et Oecuméniques* (see the preceding note), 205, sees the watershed in the Third and Fourth Lateran Councils. Schmale, *Synodus*, agrees that councils under the reformed papacy greatly increased in frequency (88) and idem, *Systematisches zu den Konzilien des Reformpapsttums im 12. Jahrhundert*, AHC 6 (1974), 21-39, 21.

least twelve), which he celebrated both north and south of the Alps[5]. The manuscript transmission for these synods is still meagre, despite the great significance Leo himself attached to them[6]. So far, hardly any evidence - one exception will be discussed - has come to light which would indicate how the decrees from his synods were disseminated other than through repetition at other councils and through accounts of participants. Nonetheless, Leo's statements indicate that traditional papal councils had not been forgotten, although they had fallen into desuetude after the pontificates of Nicholas I and John VIII[7]. According to the near-contemporary *Vita Leonis*, at his very first council (Rome, April 1049), Leo IX confirmed aloud the statutes of the first four ecumenical councils and the decrees of all his predecessors[8]. The formula of the *Vita* recalls the profession of faith at papal consecrations preserved in the ancient *Liber diurnus* (albeit there with a reference to five oecumenical councils)[9]. And it might, therefore, be considered purely cere-

---

[5]   See, for instance, the letter Abbot John of Fécamp addressed to Leo: "...Denique quis pastor in Romana Ecclesia post aurea illa saecula in quibus Leo, Gregorius claruerunt, vitro puriora spiritalis doctrinae lumina, surrexit tam diligens et vigilans, ut tu, praesulum sanctissime, qui pascis gregem Dominicum super vividos. Nam ut fidem dictis faciam, quis non miretur, et in laudis jubilum prorumpat, pro inaudita nostris saeculis oculati pastoris providentia? qui non eo contentus in propria sede urbis Romae uni populo consulere, aut solam frugum fertilem Italiam imbre coelestis verbi irrigare, verum etiam Cisalpinas Ecclesias synodali scrutinio circuit et lustrat...emendat et corrigit" (PL 143.797 = Edmond Martène and Ursin Durand, *Thesaurus Novus anecdotorum*, Paris 1717, 1.207), first noted by Hauck, *Kirchengeschichte* 3.603.

[6]   See the references assembled in Uta-Renate Blumenthal, *Ein neuer Text für das Reimser Konzil Leos IX. (1049)?*, DA 32 (1976), 23-48, 38f. and notes 56 and 57 and idem, 'Quellen', TRE 20.743.

[7]   See the remarks of Joachim Dahlhaus, *Aufkommen und Bedeutung der Rota in den Urkunden des Papstes Leo IX.*, AHP 27 (1989), 7-84, here 47 n.200.

[8]   The Vita Leonis was composed shortly after the death of the pope, perhaps by a cleric from Toul, but scholars are far from unanimous regarding the question of authorship. A critical edition is planned by the MGH, Munich; see Hans-Georg Krause, *Über den Verfasser der Vita Leonis IX papae*, DA 32 (1976), 49-85 with further bibliography. See Heinrich Tritz, *Die hagiographischen Quellen zur Geschichte Papst Leos IX.*, in: *Studi Gregoriani* 4, Roma 1952, 191-364, 214-219 for printed editions. I.M. Watterich, *Pontificum Romanorum vitae*, Leipzig 1862, 1.127-170, 154 f.

[9]   Theodor E. von Sickel (Ed.), *Liber diurnus romanorum pontificum*, Wien 1889; repr. Aalen 1966, no. 83, 90-93 and ed. Hans Foerster, Bern 1958, 334-338. The formula is also found in Deusdedit's canonical collection, ed. Victor Wolf von Glanvell, Paderborn 1905; repr. Aalen 1967, 2.110, 235 f. with a reference to 7 oecumenical councils. For the differences between the *Liber Diurnus* and the canonical collection of Deusdedit see Leo Santifaller, *Liber Diurnus*, ed. Harald Zimmermann, Cologne 1976, 81ff.

monial in nature. This is unlikely, however, given the preeminent position of this Roman council. It may have served as a forum for a presentation of Leo's papal program. In a detailed analysis of Leo's still extant original privileges, *Joachim Dahlhaus* concluded that Leo IX very likely introduced the new rota at this point[10]. The rota symbolized world-wide papal responsibilities:

> "Die Figur des Kreuzes im Ring und die Umschrift *Misericordia Domini plena est terra* erläutern sich wechselseitig: Der Doppelkreis ist als Bild der vom Ozean umgürteten Erdscheibe zu verstehen und das Innenkreuz als Zeichen der die Erde erfüllenden Barmherzigkeit des Herrn"[11].

The introduction of the rota as solemn papal signature, then, was a change heavy with significance. In the light of further evidence in Leo's letters, it would appear that the declaration of adherence to the councils and decrees of his predecessors also was a programmatic statement of principle.

Anselm, the probable author of the *Historia dedicationis ecclesiae S. Remigii apud Remos*, to whom we owe an extensive account of the council of Reims of October 1049, closed this section of his narrative with the transcription of a letter of Leo IX (JL 4185), enjoining the clergy and the faithful of the entire realm of France (*universum regnum Francorum*) to celebrate the feast day of St. Remi annually on October 1[12]. More important in the present context, however, is the first part of the letter, a declaration that he, the pontiff, had ordered that the recension of the decrees of the council of Reims,

---

and 226 ff. (Päpste und Papsttum 10) and in particular Stephan Kuttner, *Cardinalis: The History of a Canonical Concept*, Traditio 3 (1945), 129-214, 176 with n.110 as well as the comments by Foerster, *Liber diurnus*, 68-73.

[10] Joachim Dahlhaus, *Aufkommen und Bedeutung der Rota in den Urkunden des Papstes Leo IX.* (as in n.7), especially 48 and 62:"Der Papst beansprucht für sein Amt weltweite Zuständigkeit..."; see 30-39 for the significance of Leo's rota, cross and inscription. Leo's claims already were noted by Albert Hauck, *Kirchengeschichte* 3.614 with a reference to JL 4197. In general, see the considerations by Othmar Hageneder, *Weltherrschaft im Mittelalter*, MIÖG 93 (1985), 257-278. For Leo IX see also n.22 below.

[11] Ibid., 30.

[12] The edition of the *Historia* used here is that of Jean Mabillon, *Acta Sanctorum O.S.B. in saeculorum classes distributa. Saeculum sextum pars prima*, Venice 1733?, 8.624-38; the letter *Compertum* is found *ibid.*, 637 f. and has been frequently reprinted; see PL 143.616 f. The recent edition of the *Historia* by J. Hourlier, *Anselme de Saint-Rémy: Histoire de la dédicace de Saint-Rémy*, in: *La Champagne bénédictine*, Reims 1981, 179-285 (Travaux de l'Académie nationale de Reims 160) was unavailable.

VII

which he had celebrated in connection with the dedication of the basilica of
St. Remi, was to be added to the decrees of the ancient councils:

> "...post consecrationem ecclesiae in eadem synodum celebrantes, plurima
> ad utilitatem Christianae religionis necessaria, consilio coepiscoporum
> nostrorum,...statuendo confirmavimus: quae omnia capitulis digesta inter
> canones haberi praecepimus"[13].

Leo's emphasis on continuity is remarkable, no less so than his emphasis on
councils and canonical collections. It is also clear that the pontiff was very
much in charge of the councils which he convoked and which he inspired, not
excluding the council of Mainz (Oct. 1049), where Leo shared the presidency
with Emperor Henry III[14]. The document concluding the Mainz proceedings
has been preserved (JL 4188). In it the emperor's signature precedes a long
row of signatures by archbishops, bishops and abbots in keeping with the
traditional imperial position in the church. At the same time, however, considering the symbolism of the rota, there can be no doubt whatsoever that
Henry's signature ranked far lower than the papal rota, monogram and comma which solemnized the synodal document instead of a simple papal signature[15].

The most familiar of Leo's references to councils occurs in two letters
addressed to African bishops[16]. The pope prohibits them from holding a
'universal' synod:

---

[13] J.D. Mansi 19, coll.744 f., reprints JL 4185 without address, but he included Anselm's
introduction which seems to be his, Anselm's, summary of the papal letter; unfortunately, his Latin is not always very clear: "Plurima etiam ad ecclesiasticam utilitatem
pertinentia, quae in praefata synodo in eius basilica habita tractaverat, iussit apud eos
capitulatim digeri et inter orthodoxos canones numerari..." is a puzzling passage in the
context of Leo's letter, which must be dated later than 1049, since the pontiff refers in
it to several councils, "quas habuimus", where he repeated the Reims canons (Blumenthal, *Neuer Text* as in n.6, 42, n.80). It is not clear to me what Anselm meant by "iussit
apud eos capitulatim digeri" with reference to the Reims decrees and whether any
significance should or could be attached to these words, given the generally poor
Latinity of Anselm's account, in the light of Leo's own words cited in the text above.
[14] "...innotescimus...quae gessimus in synodo Moguntina, in qua nobis consedit pruden-
tissima filii nostri Henrici II Romanorum imperatoris majestas..." (PL 143.622); see
also the following note.
[15] Dahlhaus, *Aufkommen*, 24 with n.94. JL 4188 has been edited in MGH Const. 1, 97,
no.51.
[16] JL 4304 and JL 4305 = PL 143.728-730. I would like to thank Professor Somerville
for reminding me of the importance of these letters.

"...Hoc autem nolo vos lateat, non debere praeter sententiam Romani pontificis universale concilium celebrari, *aut* episcopos damnari vel deponi; quia, etsi licet vobis aliquos episcopos examinare, diffinitivam tamen sententiam absque consultu Romani pontificis, ut dictum est, non licet dare..." (JL 4304).

Scholars appear to agree that *universalis* can be equated with *generalis*; moreover, c.8 of the preface of Pseudo-Isidore in the recension found in the *Decretum* of Burchard of Worms (1.42) is commonly accepted as source[17]. What is still debated is the force of the *aut* in the above quote, the link between a universal council and the adjudication of bishops and thus, in the final analysis, the definition of a papal synod during the 11th-century reform period[18]. In the letters Leo replied to inquiries sent by Archbishop Thomas of Carthage and jointly by Bishops Peter and John in support of Thomas, challenging the right of the bishop of Gummi, probably located in the ancient province Africa Byzacena and known today as Mahdia on the Tunisian coast[19], to "consecrate or depose bishops or to convoke a provincial council without the consent of the bishop of Carthage"[20]. Leo confirmed their position regarding the primacy of the bishop of Carthage, adding, however, as one might say on a cautionary note, the reference to the exclusive papal prerogatives cited above. Quoting the False Decretals at length, the pope insisted that not only adjudication of bishops but all *maiores et difficiliores causae* of whatever church were reserved to the successor of Peter in accordance with the canons. In the response to the bishops Peter and John, Leo implied that

---

[17] A detailed analysis is given by Horst Fuhrmann, *Das ökumenische Konzil* (as in n.3), 682-685.

[18] Fuhrmann, *Das Ökumenische Konzil*, emphasized the first half of Leo's statement, interpreting *universale concilium* as an assembly "deren innere Übereinstimmung mit der Glaubens- und Sittenlehre der Gesamtkirche vom Papst bestätigt worden ist" (685). Fransen, *Papes, Conciles Généraux et Oecuméniques* argues that in the context of the letters *universale concilium* is defined as an assembly judging bishops (see esp. 208f.). Schmale, *Synodus*, 86, n.28, takes the same position.

[19] See S. Lancel in DHGE 22, 1988, col.1157-58 with a specific reference to Leo's letter. Since Carthage was the metropolitan city of Africa Proconsularis, the unknown bishop of Gummi would have been within his rights to consider himself an archbishop, provided the geographic identification is indeed accurate.

[20] JL 4304, PL 143.728: "Noveris ergo procul dubio quia, post Romanum pontificem, primus archiepiscopus et totius Africae maximus metropolitanus est Carthaginensis episcopus: nec quicumque sit, ille Gummitanus episcopus aliquam licentiam consecrandi episcopos, vel deponendi, seu provinciale concilium convocandi habet, sine consensu Carthaginensis archiepiscopi...".

they had held a council as commanded by the pope: "Bene equidem fecistis, quod jussi a nobis concilium de rebus ecclesiasticis habuistis: quod etiam omni anno vel semel agere debetis..."[21]. Even a council dealing with *res ecclesiasticae*, therefore, from the papal perspective, should be sanctioned by the pope, although Leo did not go so far as to deny expressly the right of the archbishop of Carthage to convoke a pronvincial synod as we have just seen[22]. It should be noted that Leo's letter to the suffragan bishops Peter and John does include a further vague allusion to the type of council they had held at "the command of the pope": it is a council to be held once every year, presumably in accordance with c.5 of the Breviarium Hipponense, relating to the Hippo council of 393 or c.73 and c.76 of the council of Carthage of 401[23], illustrating the African tradition which would correspond to the bi-annual councils elsewhere mentioned in c.5 of the council of Nicaea of 325[24]. With hindsight it is clear how impractical, not to say impossible, it would have been to require papal permission for regular provincial synods, but the conclusion seems inescapable that Leo considered papal approval for all kinds of synods essential, and reserved for the pope alone universal councils with their *causae maiores et difficiliores*, including final decisions in the cases of bishops[25]. His approval of all synods was not a meaningless formality either, at least from the papal perspective. "Et procul dubio constat, quod infirmum et invalidum est omne quod in ecclesia geritur, nisi huius auctoritate sedis corroboretur", the pontiff declared in a privilege of 1049, confirming a donation to the abbey of Notre-Dame at Bréteuil in the diocese of Beau-

---

[21] JL 4305, PL 143.729.
[22] See the quote from JL 4304 in the text above.
[23] See Somerville, *Gregory VII* (as in n.48), 36 and Gregory VII, Reg.I.43, 66 n.14. For the text of the canons see Charles Munier, *Concilia Africae A.345-A.525*, 32, 34 (CCL 149) 34 and the commentary on xxf. for the Breviarium and 202f. with commentary on xxiv for 401, in each case with bibliography.
[24] J.Alberigo etc., COD, 8.
[25] Papal councils were by no means limited to such issues; *e.g.* the council of Reims (1049) in Mansi 19, coll.727-750, or the canons of Urban's council of Clermont (1095) in Somerville's edition (as in n.1).

vais[26]. Leo's primary means of executing his universal sollicitude were the councils, his own as well as those assembled by others.

Among the thinly scattered references to Leo's councils the transmission for the canons of Reims stands out. They were preserved incidentally in an account of the dedication of the basilica of St. Remi. Their manner of preservation, therefore, was not very different from that of conciliar canons in the late- and post-Carolingian period in general. An overwhelming majority of Carolingian synodal canons has been transmitted among and as capitularies, thus benefitting from the Carolingian emphasis on written documentation[27]. However, with the decline of the capitulary mode of legislation, the survival of canons became fortuitous and linked to the interests and the influence of individuals. An early instance is the council of Mainz, held in October 847. The texts pertaining to this assembly have been preserved as an independent dossier in a manuscript at the Stiftsbibliothek of St. Gall. The explanation for this is simple. The abbot of St. Gall, Grimald, was a friend of Hrabanus Maurus (†856), in 847 archbishop of Mainz and personally responsible both for the synod and for the redaction of at least some of its decrees[28].

Professor *Hartmann* noted that the absence of ecclesiastical capitularies, in fact of capitularies altogether, is typical for the east Frankish kingdom, where the transmission of conciliar decrees was left entirely in the hands of the bishops[29]. This is clearly illustrated for Germany and Italy from 916 to 960. Only three of the councils held there at the time found more than merely passing acceptance in later canonical collections: Hohenaltheim 916, Koblenz 922, and Erfurt 932. In every case the respective texts were included by the

---

[26] Dietrich Lohrmann, *Papsturkunden in Frankreich*, Neue Folge VII: *Nördliche Ile-de-France und Vermandois*, Göttingen 1976, 33-35 no.9. The arenga opens with another statement on world-wide papal responsibility: "Quia nos propitia diuinitas uniuersalem papam et esse uoluit et appellari, uniuersalem omnibus per orbem ecclesiis sollicitudinem exhibere debemus...". See also Hauck, *Kirchengeschichte* (as in n.9).

[27] An instructive example is the synod of Meaux-Paris. See Wilfried Hartmann, *Die Konzilien der Karolingischen Teilreiche 843-859*, Hannover 1984, 72-80 (MGH, Conc, 3) (Nachwirkung) and idem, *Zu einigen Problemen der karolingischen Konzilsgeschichte*, AHC 9 (1977), 6-28, here 18. See in general Rosamond McKitterick, *The Carolingians and the Written Word*, Cambridge/Engl. 1989.

[28] Hartmann, *Konzilien*, 152ff. For the reception of texts in the canonical tradition see 155 f. For Grimald see also Dieter Geuenich, *Beobachtungen zu Grimald von St. Gallen, Erzkapellan und Oberkanzler Ludwigs des Deutschen*, in: Michael Borgolte and Herrad Spilling (Edd.), *Litterae Medii Aevi. FS Johanne Autenrieth zu ihrem 65. Geburtstag*, Sigmaringen 1988, 55-68.

[29] Hartmann, *Karolingische Konzilsgeschichte*, 20 f.

Decretum of Bishop Burchard of Worms and the *Collectio XII partium*. The only complete manuscript for the decrees from Hohenaltheim originated at Freising, as the editor of the critical edition, *Horst Fuhrmann*, noted[30]. After the synod of Pîtres in 862, the conditions in the West-Frankish kingdom became very similar. Even Reims is no exception, for the great Hincmar, after all, was archbishop of Reims (845-882) and thus takes his place in the line of bishops who helped almost single-handedly to preserve Carolingian traditions, however poorly. Archbishop Radbot of Trier (†915) also is a member of this group of churchmen. It was he who inspired the handbook of Abbot Regino of Prüm, compiled ca. 906 at the request of Radbot and dedicated to Hatto of Mainz (†913), who had presided at the council of Tribur (895)[31]. Regino considered his collection an abridgement (*codicillum*) for emergencies, for it seemed to him that Hatto might find it a bother to lug the many volumes of councils (*plurima conciliorum volumina*) about the countryside, when he engaged in public administration, that is, presided at the *Sendgericht*[32]. Regino's *Libri duo de synodalibus causis et disciplinis ecclesiasticis* made extensive use of the *Dionysio-Hadriana*, of Frankish capitularies and of penitentials among other sources. Particularly impressive, however, is his use of conciliar canons from the council of Nicaea to the recent council of Tribur. The 455 chapters of book 1, dealing with the clergy, include 187 conciliar canons identified as such in the inscriptions; the 454 chapters of book 2, dealing with the laity, 196 such canons.

Regino's compilation was part of the *nucleus canonum* that formed the basis for the very influential *Decretum* of Burchard of Worms (†1025) and

---

[30]   Ernst-Dieter Hehl (Ed.), *Die Konzilien Deutschlands und Reichsitaliens, 916-1001, 1: 916-960*, Hannover 1987, 1-40 (MGH Conc 6/1) for Hohenaltheim with the reference to Freising see 2.57-74 for Koblenz 922 (see here esp. 65 f.) and 97-114 for Erfurt 932 (see here esp. 104 f.). Recently, Jörg Müller has argued persuasively that bishops of Freising may have been especially active in the collection of canonical material; see *Untersuchungen* (as in n.33), 360-363.

[31]   Regino, *Libri duo de synodalibus causis et disciplinis ecclesiasticis*, ed. F.G.A. Wasserschleben, Leipzig 1840 (repr.Graz 1964). See the preface, 1. A general introduction to the collection is given in: Paul Fournier and Gabriel Le Bras, *Histoire*, Paris 1931, repr. Aalen 1972, 1.244-268. The most recent bibliography is found in Horst Fuhrmann, *Einfluß und Verbreitung der pseudoisidorischen Fälschungen*, Stuttgart 1973, 2.435-441 (MGH, Schriften 24,1-3).

[32]   Regino, preface, 1.

the *Collectio duodecim partium*[33]. Regino feared that he might be criticized for including very frequently canons from councils held in Gaul and Germany, but concluded that such texts would be most useful for their perilous times; moreover, he wrote, the multitude of crimes never heard of before his day required contemporary penitential legislation[34]. What such canons would have lacked was papal sanction. In a similar context Agobard of Lyons (†840) argued against persons who rejected Gallican or other local canons, because they had not been promulgated in the presence of Roman or imperial legates[35]. Later, in the 1070's, Cardinal-priest Atto of San Marco compiled a canonical collection for the canons of his church specifically in order to alert them to apocryphal texts and texts which were not approved by the papacy, referring in particular to the so-called Roman penitential and to councils:

"secundum Iulium papam nullum ratum est concilium quod huius sedis non est fultum auctoritate, nec sine huius sedis auctoritate rata sunt scripta quibus fieri solent concilia"[36];

however, Atto may have thought the same as Regino in his time, for he made an exception for Burchard, Regino's heir:

"Transalpina uero concilia que in Bruchardo leguntur, si non sunt contra rationem aut contra instituta romane ecclesie, in locis suis ubi facta sunt

---

[33] See Jörg Müller, *Untersuchungen zur Collectio Duodecim Partium*, Ebelsbach 1989 (Abhandlungen zur Rechtswissenschaftlichen Grundlagenforschung 73) with Hartmut Hoffmann and Rudolf Pokorny, *Das Dekret des Bischofs Burchard von Worms*, Munich 1991 (MGH Hilfsmittel 12). A succinct introduction to Burchard is given by Max Kerner, 'Burchard', LMA 2.946-951. See also Fuhrmann, *Einfluß*, 2.463 ff.

[34] Regino, preface, 2.

[35] Agobard of Lyons, *De dispensatione ecclesiasticarum rerum*, c.20, in: L. van Ackers (Ed.), *Agobardi Lugdunensis opera omnia*, Turnhout 1981, 134 (CCM 52). The text is quoted by Wilfried Hartmann, *Autoritäten im Kirchenrecht und Autorität des Kirchenrechts in der Salierzeit*, in: Stefan Weinfurter (Ed.) with the assistance of Hubertus Seibert, *Die Salier und das Reich, Gesellschaftlicher und ideengeschichtlicher Wandel im Reich der Salier*, Sigmaringen 1991, 3.425-446, 428 n.15; there and on 427, n.13, references to Hubert Mordek, *Kanonistik und gregorianische Reform; Marginalien zu einem nicht-marginalen Thema*, in: Karl Schmid (Ed.), *Reich und Kirche vor dem Investiturstreit*, Sigmaringen 1985, 65-82; relevant here are especially 71 f. of Mordek's article.

[36] For the reference to Pope Julius I see *Historia tripartita* 4, 9 (CSEL 71, 165); cf. Fuhrmann, *Ökumenisches Konzil* (as in n.3), 680 with n.25.

obtinent firmitatem. Alias autem si non sint hac confirmata non ualent nisi ex partis utriusque consensu"[37].

In general, however, and in particular with the most influential collections of Burchard of Worms and Ivo of Chartres, the content rather than the derivation of a particular text, whether of conciliar origin or not, came to matter once it had been absorbed by a systematic collection[38].

2.Implications of the textual transmission.

Noteworthy in the present context is first of all the link between canonical collections and councils, and secondly the episcopal impetus which often inspired the non-monastic collections and, naturally, the councils. Both aspects remained predominant features of the transmission of conciliar canons, including canons from papal councils, until the new jurisprudence and the growing papal dominance in ecclesiastical administration everywhere brought decretals and their collectors to the forefront in the course of the twelfth century. It is not surprising, then, that Professor *Capitani* could differentiate earlier from later eleventh-century reform collections by focusing on the respective degree of emphasis on 'la figura del vescovo'[39].

The influence of the pontificate of Gregory VII on canonical collections has been studied with particular intensity. Already in a first study, Professor *Gilchrist* concluded that the unequal and scant distribution of *capitula* from Gregory VII - the collection of Deusdedit is the exception - "meant one thing: Gregory's influence was not generally expressed in canonical collections"[40]. More detailed and greatly expanded studies covering additional collections

---

[37] See MS Vat.lat.586, fol.91v, for both excerpts. Atto's *Breviarium* has been edited by Angelo Mai, *Scriptorum veterum nova collectio e Vaticanis codicibus edita* 6,2, Rome 1832, 60 ff., but this edition (unavailable to me) has been judged unreliable by Franz Pelster S.J., *Das Dekret Burkhards von Worms in einer Redaktion aus dem Beginn der Gregorianischen Reform*, in: *Studi Gregoriani* 1, Roma 1947, 321-351, here 323 and especially by Fuhrmann, *Einfluß*, 529-532, here 529 f. n.282. (I have transcribed e caudata as e.)

[38] Hartmann, *Karolingische Konzilsgeschichte*, 25: "Durch die Systematik, in die alle Sätze ohne Unterschied eingepaßt wurden, war nicht mehr der Ursprung, sondern fast ausschließlich der Inhalt für den Benutzer interessant: ein Exzerpt aus einer Papstdekretale ebenso wie ein Kanon eines partikularen Konzils empfing seine Geltung aus dem Ansehen der Rechtssammlung, in die er aufgenommen worden war...".

[39] Ovidio Capitani, *Immunità vescovili ed ecclesiologia in età "pregregoriana" e "Gregoriana": L'Avvio alla "Restaurazione"*, Spoleto 1966.

[40] Gilchrist, *Gregorian Reform Movement* (as in n.2), 9.

appeared in 1973 and 1980[41]. They confirmed *Gilchrist*'s original view: 386 *capitula* attributed to Gregory VII occurred in approximately 46 collections, a comparatively insignificant number. Moreover, a single item, the decrees of the autumn synod of 1078 (Reg. 6.5b) constituted the bulk of these chapters, 198 out of a total of 284 conciliar items[42]. The autumn synod of 1078 is followed distantly by the Lenten council of the same year (Reg.5.14a), represented by 42 chapters. Today, the manuscripts containing these texts can be found all over Latin Europe, including England[43]. They originated at locations as distant from each other as Passau (Clm 16085)[44] and Reims/Thérouanne (*e.g.* Wolfenbüttel, Gud. 212; Paris, BN lat. 10743)[45], southern France and from the Pyrenées region, areas represented by manuscripts of the *Liber Tarraconensis*, the *Caesaraugustana*, and the *Collection of Sémur (Reims)* (*e.g.* MS Madrid, BN Nac. 428). Last not least, the texts occur in manuscripts from all regions of Italy, including Rome[46]. In the sixteenth century, Antonio Agustìn (1517-1586) included Gregory's October 1078 synod on his list of general, oecumenical councils, without giving a reason. That the Spanish scholar could have been swayed by the abundance of manuscript evidence for this particular council of Gregory VII is hypothetically suggested by another synod, also on Agustìn's preliminary list of oecumenical councils and also widely represented in the manuscripts: Urban's council of November 1095 at

---

[41] John Gilchrist, *Reception 1*, and *Reception 2* (as in n.2).

[42] Gilchrist, *Reception 2*, 223; my figures are additions of the 1973 and 1980 columns. The relationships between individual MSS as given by Gilchrist, *Reception 2*, 221f. and n.53 have to be taken into consideration.

[43] For English MSS see H.E.J. Cowdrey, *Pope Gregory VII and the Anglo-Norman Church and Kingdom*, in: *Studi Gregoriani* 9, Roma 1972, 79-114, 105, n.102 regarding Oxford, Bodleian Library, MS Bodley 718 (2632) and Martin Brett, *The Collectio Lanfranci and its Competitors*, in: *Intellectual Life* (as in n.75 below), 170 n.48 for Cambridge, Corpus Christi College, MS 442; in addition, see *idem* in these *Proceedings*, note 78.

[44] St. Nikolaus at Passau, a chapter of canons, was a foundation of Bishop Altmann, a fervent partisan of Gregory VII. Cf. Max Sdralek, *Die Streitschriften Altmanns von Passau und Wezilos von Mainz*, Paderborn 1890, 17-28. See now Wilfried Hartmann, *Das Bistum Passau im Investiturstreit*, in: Ostbairische Grenzmarken, *Passauer Jahrbuch* 31, 1989, 46-60 with further literature. I am grateful to Dr. Detlev Jasper for originally alerting me to the publication and Professor Hartmann for an offprint.

[45] For the probable origin of the *Collection in Ten Parts* see n.53 below.

[46] See Table II in Gilchrist, *Reception 1*, and Table I, *Reception 2*, 226 f. Cf. the references in the two preceding notes.

Clermont[47]. And it is to this council that I shall turn briefly to illustrate the continuous influence of the Carolingian-episcopal tradition, a point that must be in doubt for Gregory VII insofar as the original impetus for the dissemination of canons from his councils is concerned. The near-uniformity of the texts which survived for his councils indicates that the measures which he took to promulgate the decrees were highly successful. Referring to the canons of the Lenten synod of 1075 (Reg.2,52a), Gregory wrote to Bishop Burchard of Halberstadt, that they were "promulgated far and wide by letters and legates" (Reg.2,66)[48]. The result of such an enterprise would have to be fairly uniform texts in canonical collections and their appendices as well as in chronicles, and this is precisely what we find, certain exceptions notwithstanding (e.g. the late 12th-century MS Vienna, Österr.NB lat. 2153). It is of interest to note that in the case of c.5 of the decrees of the Roman synod of November 1078 (Reg.6,5b), which might be considered an exception, the canonistic reception represented by the *Decretum* of Ivo of Chartres and the *Tripartita* preserved the uncorrected text from Gregory's register as *Robert Somerville* has shown[49].

Thanks to the critical edition of the decrees of Clermont by *Somerville* it is evident that for present purposes they may be divided into three basic sets of transmission: 1) the Northern French and Anglo/Norman group, 2) the Cencius-*Polycarpus* or Roman group, and 3) the *Caesaraugustana* group. As for the third group of texts, the Clermont canons preserved in the manuscripts of the first and second recension of the *Caesaraugustana*, it so happens that under the inscription *Urbanus II papa in concilio Clarimontis* we find exclusively decrees known from Urban councils other than Clermont: Piacenza cc.1-7 and 12-13 as well as c.8 of Melfi[50]. Presumably, therefore, their derivation could only be unravelled in connection with a critical edition of Urban's councils of Piacenza and Melfi, although sources, including in particular the *Polycarpus*, agree that the pontiff indeed repeated canons from his earlier councils at Clermont[51]. In the present context, however, the intriguing set of Clermont decrees in the *Caesaraugustana* may be set aside.

[47] Fransen, *Papes, Conciles Généraux* (as in n.3), 204 f. with further references.
[48] The most recent discussion of the councils of Gregory VII is Robert Somerville, The Councils of Gregory VII, in: *Studi Gregoriani* 13, Roma 1989, 33-53. See also the following note.
[49] Somerville, *ibid.*, 46-48 and Caspar, Reg.6,5b, 404 n.t with further references.
[50] Somerville (as in n.1), 126.
[51] *Ibid.*, 123 for c.5 of the *Polycarpus* tradition.

In a very general sense, the remaining sets of Clermont decrees[52] are clearly differentiated by a) great variety in expression and direct, simple language and b) uniformity and sophistication of language. As for the first set, the Northern French/Norman tradition, all are traceable to northern France. Moreover, the majority of extant manuscripts probably can be linked to Arras, Ghent and Thérouanne, and the activities of bishops Lambert of Arras (†1115), Aimon de Bazoches of Châlons (†1153) and very probably also of John de Warneton of Thérouanne (†1130), the latter a pupil of Ivo of Chartres and conceivably responsible for a redaction of the Collection in 9 Books or of St. Germain-des-Prés, as *Fournier* called it, preserved in manuscripts now at Wolfenbüttel and at Ghent[53]. That collection was revised to the *Collection in Ten Parts* shortly after 1123, very likely by Archdeacon Walter of Thérouanne[54]. *Ten Parts* in turn was incorporated in the *Summa Haimonis* and the First and Second Collections of Châlons[55]. The diocese of Arras had been recently separated from Cambrai and thanks to Pope Urban II regained its independence in 1093. Bishop Lambert had participated in the council of Clermont in 1095 and included John de Warneton in his entourage, at that time his archdeacon. John's election to the bishopric of Thérouanne was confirmed by Urban at the Roman council of 1099[56]. Professor *Somerville* argued persuasively that a single source, the Arras delegation at Cler-

---

[52] Individual canons or liturgical and pastoral texts will not be considered.

[53] See Laurent Waelkens and Dirk van den Auweele, *La collection de Thérouanne en IX livres à l'abbaye de Saint-Pierre-au-Mont-Blandine. Le codex Gandavensis 235*, Sacris Eruditi 24 (1980), 115-153, with a critical discussion of the older bibliography, including the unpublished studies of J. M. De Smet, *De heilige Jan van Waasten en de Gregoriaansche hervorming in het bisdom Terwaan*, Leuven 1943 (mémoire de licence dactylographie; not seen). Despite Waelkens' and van den Auweele's re-evaluation of de Smet's and Sdralek's occasionally weak arguments (they were unaware of the codex Gent, Universiteitsbibliotheek, 235, from ca.1100), they agree that the preponderance of the evidence available at the moment seems to point to the involvement of Jean de Warneton. See especially 136-39. My remarks in this paper dilute their argument on 136 regarding the textual differences between the *Liber Lamberti* and the Collection in 9 Books.

[54] For the *Collection in Ten Parts* see in addition to the article by Waelkens and van den Auweele quoted in the preceding note, Peter Landau, *Officium und Libertas christiana*, Abh. Akad. Munich 1991, Heft 3, 23, with the suggestion that the *Collection in Ten Parts* should be considered an "archidiakonale Rechtssammlung".

[55] Fournier-Le Bras, *Histoire* 2.285-313.

[56] See now Lotte Kéry, *Die Verhandlungen über die Errichtung des Bistums Arras auf der Provinzialsynode in Reims (20. März 1093)*, in these *Proceedings* with further bibliography.

mont headed by Bishop Lambert, has to be behind this extraordinarily far-flung distribution, variants and different order of the decrees in some manuscripts notwithstanding. At Arras, Somerville concluded, "'*notae Claromontenses*' were copied in various combinations"[57].

Aside from isolated decrees as in codex Paris, BN lat. 18219, and from the independent sets in Paris MS, BN lat. 9631 and Oxford, Bodleian Selden Supra 90, whose origin is still unknown[58], a distinct second set of canons for Clermont, therefore, emerges only in an appendix to the first recension of the Roman collection *Polycarpus* (ca.1109-1113). The same set of decrees as in this early twelfth-century collection had been discovered by *Gabriel Cossart* in a now lost manuscript of the *Liber Censuum*. As *Somerville* noted, Urban's successors Paschal II, Calixtus II, Innocent II, and Eugene III all cited from a similar source[59]. Documentary form and diction alike set these decrees clearly apart from the Arras transmission discussed earlier. To the best of my knowledge they seem to be indeed "fragments of the official decrees"[60]. Given the narrative passages which are included in the *Polycarpus* text as well as the reference preceding the canon from Urban's council of Troia in the collections of Ivo of Chartres, *Ex registro Urbani secundi*[61], it is not impossible to argue that the set may be derived from Urban's register[62]. The diplomatic form of the *Notitia* of Clermont corresponds closely to the account

---

[57] Somerville, *Decreta Claromontensia*, 58 ff. The quote is found on 59. There are only minor differences between these 'Arras' texts and the Clermont decrees found in Anglo-Norman chronicles like that of Ordericus Vitalis and William of Malmesbury, see *ibid.*, chapter IV, especially 83-88 and 100-106 for the chronicles of Bernold of Constance and Fulcher of Chartres.

[58] Somerville, *Decreta Claromontensia*, 118 and 110 and 18, 35-37 as well as 112 for the Oxford codex. The latter is probably not of English origin, as Dr. M. Brett kindly mentioned in conversation.

[59] *Ibid.*, 119; for the text and the manuscripts see 120-24.

[60] *Ibid.*, 119. Uwe Horst, *Die Kanonessammlung Polycarpus des Gregor von S. Grisogono*, Munich 1980 (MGH Hilfsmittel 5) does not include appendices in his discussion.

[61] See Robert Somerville's forthcoming edition of Urban's council of Melfi for further references.

[62] Uta-Renate Blumenthal, *Bemerkungen zum Register Papst Paschalis II.*, QF 66 (1986), 1-19, here 8 and idem, *Papal Registers in the twelfth century*, in: *Proceedings 7Cong-MCL Cambridge 1984*, Città del Vaticano 1988, 135-151, here 140 and 144 (MIC, C, 8). The reference to the register of Urban II is also found in the second recension of the *Tripartita B* in connection with c.1 from the council of Troia. See Somerville, *Decreta Claromontensia*, 121 n.10, and the discussion below.

of Paschal's 1112 Lateran synod[63] and is still the formula used to introduce the decrees of the council of Tours of 1163 in Boso's Life of Pope Alexander III[64].

This rapid comparison of the Northern French and *Polycarpus*-Cencius sets of the Clermont decrees posits once again the dilemma debated more than half a century ago by *Victor Krause* and *Emil Seckel* regarding the decrees of the 895 synod of Tribur[65]. What is the meaning of authentic? How might notes be taken at a council in this period? The notary Galbert of Bruges, writing in 1127, left a vivid and detailed description of how he "set down on tablets a summary of events", but "had to wait for moments of peace during the night or day to set in order the present account"[66]. The siege of the castle of Bruges after the murder of Count Charles the Good of Flanders is, of course, not precisely the same as a papal council that took place thirty years earlier. But Clermont also could not have provided much leisure, as the council was attended by large crowds and had a very busy agenda[67]. The notes and eventual summaries made by participants after the event thus would naturally differ from individual to individual. As in the case of the council of Tribur and the *Libri* of Regino of Prüm, therefore, official and 'authoritative', semi-official, decrees should be differentiated, but with few exceptions - invented decrees - both are authentic[68]. The legal validity of the texts found

---

[63] MGH Const.1, 570-574, no.399 and no.400. For Boso's Life of Paschal II see Duchesne (Ed.), *Liber Pontificalis* 2.369-371.

[64] Robert Somerville, *Pope Alexander III And the Council of Tours (1163)*, Berkeley, Los Angeles, London, 1977, 40 f. for Boso's Vita of Alexander III and of other popes. The relevant text is found in Duchesne's edition of the *Liber Pontificalis*, 1892, 2.397-446, here 408.

[65] Victor Krause, *Die Acten der Triburer Synode 895*, NA 17 (1892), 51-82 and 283-326; Emil Seckel, *Zu den Acten der Triburer Synode 895*, NA 18 (1893), 365-409 with Krause's response, *Die Triburer Acten in der Chalons'er Handschrift, ibid.*, 413-427. - After my paper went to press, Rudolf Pokorny re-examined the textual transmission of the Tribur material, suggesting that the brief versions of the texts preceded the 'vulgate' recension. The interesting results go beyond Seckel's acceptance of the brief texts as 'authoritative', endowing them with greater 'authenticity' (DA 48 (1992), 429-491).

[66] Galbert of Bruges, *The Murder of Charles the Good, Count of Flanders*, transl. and ed. J.B. Ross, New York 1967, 164, c.35, whose English translation I cite.

[67] Paschal II recalled the council at Clermont as "populosissim[us]"; see Robert Somerville, *The French Councils of Pope Urban II: Some basic Considerations*, AHC 2 (1970), 56-65, here 58.

[68] See Seckel, *Zu den Acten*, here 370-372 and 371 n.2.

in canonical collections was usually not an issue, apart from the exceptions mentioned earlier, at a time when textual criticism was extremely rare. The hierarchy of canonical sources and contradictions among them were novel problems as well at the time of the Gregorian reform as will be seen. First, however, let us turn to the third of the pontiffs whose councils have been recently examined, Paschal II.

Francis Gossman concluded in his study of Urban II that without the letters preserved in the collection known as *Britannica*, the majority of texts of Urban II in canonical collections were conciliar canons[69]. For Urban, the preponderance of conciliar texts, to be sure, is not nearly so overwhelming as in the case of Gregory VII, but all the same the contrast between Urban II and Paschal II is striking. It illustrates that by the early twelfth century the revival of jurisprudence and the emphasis on contemporary papal decretals was well underway. If sets of conciliar canons from a particular synod are counted as single items of transmission, then six conciliar items of Paschal have to be contrasted with 30 decretals in the broad sense of the term from this pontiff[70]. Moreover, one of the conciliar items, the decree from Paschal's Lateran council of 1102, is preserved as excerpt from Paschal's letter to Anselm of Canterbury (JL 5908), and its status is therefore ambiguous. But this is not all. Today at least seven from among the 30 decretals of Paschal II are preserved exclusively in early decretal collections. It is difficult to evaluate this fact although it indicates in any event that the influence of Paschal's decretals lasted well into the second half of the twelfth century[71]. The most frequently found item, divided into several sections, is a letter *de illicitis coniugiis*, addressing also questions of spiritual affinities. It occurs in canonical as well as decretal collections, and three segments are found in

---

[69] *Pope Urban II and Canon Law*, Washington D.C. 1960, 103.

[70] Uta-Renate Blumenthal, *Decrees and decretals of Pope Paschal II in twelfth-century canonical collections*, BMCL 10 (1980), 15-30, here 16 with n.3 for the definition of decretal which I use in the present paper as well.

[71] Regarding the legislation of Urban II, Martin Brett has argued persuasively that "At least the *Decretum* and the *Panormia* were written later [than 1095], and the legislation of Urban II was incorporated in French collections a good deal more slowly and incompletely than we have commonly supposed" (*Urban II and the collections attributed to Ivo of Chartres*, in: *Proceedings 8CongMCL San Diego 1988*, Città del Vaticano 1992, 27-46, here 46 (MIC, C, 9). For the little studied use of pre-Gratian canonical collections by decretists, see Peter Landau, *Vorgratianische Kanonessammlungen bei den Dekretisten und in frühen Dekretalensammlungen*, ibid., 93-116.

Gratian's *Decretum* as 30.4.5, 30.3.5 and 35.2 et 3.22[72]. In Europe north of the Alps, the *Collection in Ten Parts* and its derivatives are once again noteworthy for their attention to texts of Paschal II. However, the most extensive excerpts from Paschal's councils, Guastalla (1106) and the Lateran synod of 1110, are found in Italian collections[73], more precisely, in appendices to Italian collections compiled during the reform period. One example is the canonical collection of *Anselm of Lucca*. Recension A' included addenda at the end of several of the thirteen books into which the collection had been divided. A sequence of decrees from Guastalla (1106) is appended appropriately to book 6 dealing with bishops in manuscripts of recension A' or related to it. The provenance of the recension is very likely northern Italy[74]. Twelfth-century manuscripts of canonical collections often show a new look: large blank spaces at the end of subdivisions and even several blank folios interspersed with the text[75]. These were intended to accommodate future additions to keep collections up to date. There is nothing new about the intention, however. The *Decretum* of Burchard of Worms was completed a decade

---

[72] JL 6436; IP 5.367 no.7. See Blumenthal, *Decrees*, 19 f. The thematic differences between the texts of Gregory VII and Paschal II are very revealing and worth pursuing.

[73] Uta-Renate Blumenthal, *The Early Councils of Pope Paschal II: 1100-1110*, Toronto 1978, chapters 2 and 4. 104, n.13, should be corrected. According to Linda Fowler-Magerl, *Vier französische und spanische vorgratianische Kanonessammlungen*, in: *Aspekte europäischer Rechtsgeschichte. FS Helmut Coing zum 70. Geburtstag*, Frankfurt 1982, 145, the first of the two canons from Paschal's council of Benevento of 1108, *Et diuine legis*, is found in MS Barcelona, Archivio de la Corona de Aragon, San Cugat 63 (a redistributed *Coll. Caesaraugustana?*) on fol.84r. As for Paschal's letter JL 66ll, I erroneously described it as an 'integral part' of the Coll. of Santa Maria Novella (*Decrees*, 26, n.55); the letter is an addition. See Giuseppe Motta, *Liber canonum diuersorum sanctorum patrum siue Collectio in CLXXXIII titulos digesta*, Vatican City 1988, xxvii (MIC, B, 7). However, the Lateran decrees of 1110 were always described as addition.

[74] Peter Landau, *Erweiterte Fassungen der Kanonessammlung des Anselm von Lucca aus dem 12. Jahrhundert*, in: P. Golinelli (Ed.), *Sant'Anselmo, Mantova e la lotta per le investiture*, Bologna 1987, 323-338 (Atti del convegno internazionale di studi 1986), followed by an Italian translation of the paper. See here 327 f.

[75] A striking example is MS Paris, Bibliothèque de l'Arsenal 713. See the papers of Robert Somerville, *Papal Excerpts in Arsenal MS 713B: Alexander II and Urban II*, and of Martin Brett, *The sources and influence of MS Paris, Bibl. Arsenal, 713*, in these *Proceedings*; see also Martin Brett, *The Collectio Lanfranci and its Competitors* for the case of Oxford, Bodleian Library, MS Bodley 561, in: L. Smith and B. Ward (Edd.), *Intellectual Life in the Middle Ages; Essays presented to Margaret Gibson*, London 1992, 157-74.

or so before the council of Seligenstadt of 1023 whose decrees originally, therefore, were not included. Almost immediately, however, the *Decretum* was augmented with the decisions of this very synod. So rapidly did this process occur that Burchard's collection is responsible for a considerable part of the reception of the texts of Seligenstadt[76]. Late eleventh- and early twelfth-century manuscripts with their blank folios, therefore, merely made systematic provision for what had been customary earlier. A procedure was rationalized. My intention here is to highlight the give and take between conciliar collections and the councils themselves, quite apart from the frequently discussed use of canonical collections at these assemblies in accordance with conciliar ordines. Exceptions, such as the contemporary *Collection in Seventy-Four Titles*, consisting almost exclusively of papal decretals, merely add confirmation, for the *Collection in Four Books*, "improved the structure of 74T" almost immediately, in particular by adding a new section, a fourth book - composed entirely of conciliar canons[77].

3.The position of councils in papal thought.

It is well known that Gregory VII strongly emphasized the place and use of councils, to be held either by himself in Rome - the council proposed for Augsburg in 1077 was the exception - or by his legates elsewhere, at times simply to repromulgate locally what had been ratified earlier in Rome[78].

---

[76] Fuhrmann, *Einfluß*, 2.452.
[77] See Fournier-Le Bras, *Histoire*, 2.235-240, here 236 f., and especially the most recent study by John Gilchrist, *Changing the Structure of a Canonical Collection: The Collection in Seventy-four Titles, Four Books, and the Pseudo-Isidorian Decretals*, in: Steven B. Bowman and Blanche E. Cody (Edd.), *In Iure Veritas: Studies in Canon Law in Memory of Schafer Williams*, Cincinnati 1991, 93-117 with further bibliography.
[78] In the case of the synod of Autun (September 1077) and the synod of Poitiers (January 15, 1078), the decrees promulgated by Gregory's legate, Hugh of Die, preceded the decisions of Gregory's Roman synods of 1078. Hugh, however, had been carefully instructed by Gregory VII. See most recently Rudolf Schieffer, *Die Entstehung des päpstlichen Investiturverbots für den deutschen König*, Stuttgart 1981, 162 ff.(MGH Schriften 28), who points out that: "Die Kanones von Poitiers sind zwar ebenso wie ihre Vorläufer in Autun letztlich von Gregor VII. angeregt und kraft seiner Autorität von dem Legaten verkündet worden, stellen aber doch nach der Form ihres Zustandekommens nur partikulares Kirchenrecht dar, das nicht überall unmittelbare Geltung beanspruchen konnte" (166). - For the general activity of Gregory's legates in France see Theodor Schieffer, *Die päpstlichen Legaten in Frankreich vom Vertrage von Meersen (870) bis zum Schisma von 1130*, Berlin 1935, repr. Vaduz 1965, 88-139;

VII

This is true although his *dictatus papae* includes the claim that the pope can depose bishops without a synod and that he, the pope, can also depose those who are absent (Reg.2,55a c.3 and c.5, 202f.). One is allowed to infer, however, that these drastic steps - in the case of c.5 in contradiction to the generally received canon law - were not to be the rule. The oath of obedience for bishops consecrated by the pope and for archbishops was just coming into use. Gregory's register preserves the formula used by Udalric of Aquileia at the Lenten synod of February 1079, including the telling phrase:"...ad synodum, ad quam me vocabunt vel per se vel per suos nuntios vel per suas litteras, veniam et canonice oboediam, aut, si non potero, legatos meos mittam...." (Reg.6,17a, 4, 428f.). The first such oath was recorded under Pope Alexander II for Archbishop Wibert of Ravenna[79]. The attendance at papal councils had evidently become an essential feature of the episcopal office. Caspar has shown convincingly that the structure of the original register of Gregory VII is closely intertwined with the papal councils beginning with book III. The number of entries peaked when synods met, certain of them were precisely contemporary with the conciliar events they recorded, as shown by the oath of Berengar of Tours in 1079, and other entries appear to date from either shortly before or after a synod. The records of the councils themselves progress from a bare reference in 1074 to extensive excerpts in 1080 (Reg.7,14a). "Die Synode vom Februar 1081 hat dann das seit Monaten

Alfons Becker, *Studien zum Investiturproblem in Frankreich*, Saarbrücken 1955, 51-80. Fransen, *Papes, Conciles Généraux et Oecuméniques* (as in n.3), listed in an appendix on 225-228 selected excerpts concerning councils from the register of Gregory VII. Gregory's attitude towards councils is well illustrated by a letter the pope sent to Bishop Hugh of Die in May 1077 (Reg.IV, 22, ed. Caspar, 330-334). Gérard, bishop-elect of Cambrai, is to swear a solemn oath that before his investiture with the bishopric by King Henry IV he had not heard of the king's excommunication and of the pope's "decretum nostrum de prohibitione huiuscemodi investiendi et accipiendi ecclesias neque per legatum nostrum neque ab aliqua persona, que se his statutis interfuisse et ea audisse fateretur, significatum et indubitanter notificatum fuerit" (Reg.IV,22, here 331, lines 24-28). As the editor, Erich Caspar, already pointed out, these lines indicate how conciliar decrees were promulgated: by legates and by those who were present. What is missing in this particular case is the reference to letters (see Reg.II.66), presumably leading Caspar to conclude that the investiture prohibition had not yet been officially publicized. It is not possible to discuss Gregory's synods fully in the present context. See Somerville, *Gregory VII*, as in n.46.

[79] Deusdedit, *Kanonessammlung*, ed. Victor Wolf von Glanvell, Paderborn 1905, repr. Aalen 1967, 4.423 (599f.). For Gregory and the use of the oath see Leo Meulenberg, *Der Primat der römischen Kirche im Denken und Handeln Gregors VII*, The Hague 1965, here 66 and n.150.

stockende Registriergeschäft noch einmal in Gang gebracht, die vom November 1083 an dem schon seit zwei Jahren erstorbenen einen Wiederbelebungs-
versuch, allerdings ohne dauernden Erfolg, gemacht," noted Caspar[80]. Whatever the intended purpose of the register may have been, the ever increasing
significance of councils in the pontificate of Gregory VII cannot be doubted.
This is also supported by the manuscript evidence for the October 1078
decrees mentioned earlier. Their textual uniformity as well as the frequency
with which they are encountered in contemporary canonical collections shows
that the papal attempts to disseminate them "far and wide by letters and
legates" (Reg. 2,66), was very successful as well as realistic and in keeping
with contemporary practices.

Much less can be known about the place of synods in the politics of
Gregory's successors, Urban II (1088-1099) and Paschal II (1099-1118), but
they certainly continued to be very important[81]. The settlement of contemporary problems touching the church at large such as the investiture controversy,
the treatment of schismatics and schismatic ordinations, all of the *causae
maiores* continued to be reserved for councils, but as we have seen, by the
time of Paschal II the interest among canonists probably began to shift to
decretals, i.e. specific papal decisions, perhaps in part because of the repetiti-
ve nature of some of the conciliar canons.

Despite the danger of great oversimplification I would like to turn in
conclusion briefly to the question of papal authority over conciliar canons in
the period around 1100. The reminder that all collections were private, and
that any compiler could choose among the traditional components of canon
law whatever appealed to him most, is hardly necessary here. Moreover, the
jurisperiti were fully conscious of their power to assemble strings of canons
to support either defendants or plaintiffs - except that not everybody would
have had a command of the field even remotely comparable to that of an Ivo
of Chartres. The great freedom to pick and choose among the *decreta sanctorum patrum* could and did entail serious difficulties. One reminder is an open
letter, *libellus*, which Peter Damian dedicated to Pope Leo IX shortly after his

---

[80]   Erich Caspar, *Studien zum Register Gregors VII.*, NA 38 (1913), 145-226, here 212.
      Especially relevant for the present article are 155-160, 181f. and 206-213. The most
      recent full-length study of Gregory's register is Hartmut Hoffmann, *Zum Register und
      zu den Briefen Papst Gregors VII.*, DA 32 (1976), 86-130 with older bibliography. See
      also Hans-Eberhard Hilpert, *Zu den Rubriken im Register Gregors VII. (Reg. Vat. 2)*,
      DA 40 (1984), 606-611.

[81]   E.g. Somerville, *Decreta Claromontensia*.

accession in 1049[82]. The letter intervenes in the debate over clerical marriage and concubinage. Damian argued against what he considered overly lenient punishments prescribed in the *sententiae patrum* in the case of sexual offences. In the preface and the conclusion, two sections which are specifically addressed to Leo, Damian requested the pontiff to examine the canons which in his opinion should be rejected,"quia et rationi contrarium et canonicis patrum sanctionibus probatur adversum"; but his, Damian's, decision should not be considered final[83], for no individual had the privilege to make such a decision, except for the successor of St. Peter. What was true for individuals, however, was not true for councils. Councils as well as popes issued authentic texts in Damian's view:"quod omnes autentici canones aut in venerandis synodalibus conciliis sunt inventi aut a sanctis patribus sedis apostolicae pontificibus promulgati"[84]. In his conclusion, Damian entreated the pontiff to examine the sacred canons together with "spiritual and wise advisors", although, he hastened to add, he knew full well that Leo by the grace of God was able to do so alone. But the consensus of many would lay the opposition to rest, whereas a decision pronounced by a single individual as equitable might be described by others as *praeiudicium*[85]. Compared to declarations by Bernold of Constance, for example, Damian's ambivalence is obvious[86].

In a letter to the archbishop of Magdeburg dated March 1075, Gregory VII confirmed the decrees of the Lenten synod he had just celebrated, emphasizing that he is not submitting "nostra decreta, quamquam licenter, si opus esset, possemus...sed a sanctis patribus statuta renovamus..."[87]. Considering the *dictatus papae* c.7 (Reg.2,55a, 203) it is apparent that Gregory himself shared Damian's sentiments. In texts from these years of the reform, it is still possible to distinguish between theories with new applications, and customary interpretations or approaches. It is possible as well to discern in the texts the requirements of the moral and institutional reform, which is at times negated by the multi-facetted canonistic inheritance. Not much later the fluctuations

---

[82] Kurt Reindel (Ed.), *Die Briefe des Petrus Damiani*, Munich 1983, n.31, 1.284-330 (MGH Briefe der deutschen Kaiserzeit 4.1). Cf. J. J. Ryan, *Saint Peter Damiani and His Canonical Sources*, Toronto 1956, 29f. and Wilfried Hartmann, *Autoritäten im Kirchenrecht* (as in n.35).

[83] 289, lines 3-6.

[84] *Ibid.*, 304, lines 5-8.

[85] *Ibid.*, 329, lines 8-19.

[86] Hartmann, *Autoritäten*, 434 f.

[87] JL 4950; Reg.2,68, here 226.

were resolved in favor of papal approbation and the exclusion of texts contradicting papal decisions[88]. Nonetheless, given the freedom of interpretation of this approval principle, the traditional place of conciliar legislation was effectively left unchanged until the mid-twelfth century. It was the growth of jurisprudence based on Gratian's *Decretum* and papal decretals that was to end the independent approach to the corpus of canon law and to its interpretation that had characterized the centuries before the Gregorian reform[89].

---

[88]   See the discussion by Hartmann, *Autoritäten*, esp. 428-438 with further bibliography.

[89]   See Horst Fuhrmann, *Das Reformpapsttum und die Rechtswissenschaft*, in: J. Flekkenstein (Ed.), *Investiturstreit und Reichsverfassung*, Sigmaringen 1973, 175-203; here esp. 203 (VuF Konstanzer Arbeitskreis 17).

VIII

SOME NOTES ON PAPAL POLICIES AT GUASTALLA, 1106

The least known of the popes of the Gregorian reform is perhaps Paschal II (1099–1118) (1) even although he was responsible for the settlement of the conflict over investitures in the case of England and France (2). The agreements of Santa Maria in Turri on February 4 and of Sutri of February 9, 1111 (3), constitute an unsuccessful attempt to reconcile also papacy and empire (4). Nevertheless, as Ernst Bernheim has shown, the Concordat of Worms that effected this reconciliation in 1122 under Pope Calixtus II is based to a large extent on the precedents established in 1111 (5). Evidently, Paschal's pontificate is significant, but he has nonetheless remained a shadowy figure, having 'partisans' as well as 'enemies' among historians. Both sides present little evidence to support their opinions. Fliche defended

---

(1) The most carefully compiled biography of Paschal II is that by J.M. MARCH, *Liber Pontificalis prout exstat in codice manuscripto Dertusensi* (Barcelona 1925) 154-61. Detailed bibliographical notes are found in *Realenzyklopädie für Protestantische Theologie und Kirch·* 14 (1904) 717-24 (C. MIRBT), and in C.-J. HEFELE and H. LECLERCQ, *Histoire des Conciles* (Paris 1912) V/1.465 n. 3; more recent are the bibliographies given by T. SCHIEFFER, *LThK.* 8 (1963) 128-9 and in the *Handbook of Church History*, ed. H. JEDIN and J. DOLAN, 3 (tr. A. BIGGS, New York and London 1969) 542. Mr. Carlo Servatius, Saarbrücken, is preparing a biographical monograph.

(2) For England see below 68. Less than about the English agreement is known about the negotiations led by the pontiff himself with King Philip I and Louis VI at St. Denis before the 1107 council of Troyes. *Cf.* A. BECKER, *Studien zum Investiturproblem in Frankreich* (Saarbrücken 1955) 121-3.

(3) *MGH, Const.* 1.137-139 and 139-140 (nos. 83-88).

(4) *Ibid.* 140-2 (no. 90); see also M.J. WILKS, *Ecclesiastica and Regalia: Papal Investiture Policy from the Council of Guastalla to the First Lateran Council, 1106-23* in *Studies in Church History* 7 (1971) 69-85.

(5) E. BERNHEIM, *Das Wormser Konkordat und seine Vorurkunden* (Breslau 1906).

Paschal because of saintliness and simplemindedness (6); Hauck admitted Paschal's intellectual brilliance but added that nothing could be more dangerous than a combination of high intelligence and weakness of character (7); more recently it has been argued by Professor Zerbi that Paschal proposed a rigid separation of church and world advocating 'apostolic poverty' for the church (8); a thesis which is similar to that of Cantor who referred to Paschal as 'a dour old monk' and 'representative of the most radical group among the reformers... second in importance only to Hildebrand himself' (9).

This diversity of opinion regarding Paschal II is more likely than not the result of conscious or unconscious attempts to interpret Paschal's pontificate in the light of the decisions he made in the spring of 1111 (10). It is inevitable that this dramatic period should have excited much interest, but, when considered alone, it is an insufficient basis on which to evaluate Paschal's attitudes. The key to his policies has to be sought primarily in the first ten years of his pontificate, since the remainder is dominated by the events of 1111 (11). Of particular significance for the period between the pontiff's accession in August 1099 and his capture by King Henry V of Germany in February 1111 is the council of Guastalla held in October 1106. The policies which Paschal pursued during most of his long pontificate are those laid down in connection with this synod.

It was not by accident that the pontiff journeyed north in the fall of 1106. Events in Germany, reaching back as far as December 1104, when Henry V (1104–1125) secretly left the

---

(6) A. FLICHE and V. MARTIN, *Histoire de l'Eglise* 8 (Paris 1944) 339.

(7) A. HAUCK, *Kirchengeschichte Deutschlands* 3 (Leipzig 1896) 893 n. 2.

(8) P. ZERBI, *Pasquale II e l'ideale della povertà della chiesa* in *Annuario dell'Università Cattolica del Sacro Cuore* (Milan 1964-65) 207-29. *Cf.* WILKS, *Ecclesiastica* 73-5. Valuable in this context is the study by W. KRATZ, *Der Armutsgedanke im Entäusserungsplan des Papstes Paschalis II.* (Freiburg 1933).

(9) N.F. CANTOR, *Church, Kingship and Lay Investiture in England: 1089-1135* (Princeton 1958) 124 and 122.

(10) See G. MEYER VON KNONAU, *Jahrbücher des Deutschen Reiches unter Heinrich IV. und Heinrich V* (*Jahrbücher der Deutschen Geschichte* 17, 7 vols.) 6.138-205 with bibliography; HAUCK, *Kirchengeschichte* 3.890-9; FLICHE-MARTIN, *Histoire* 8.356-71; *Handbook*, 395-8.

(11) *e.g.* the Lateran council of 1116 (MANSI, *Sacrorum conciliorum nova et amplissima collectio* 21, 145 ff.).

camp of his father, Emperor Henry IV (1054-1106) (12), seemed to have made peace between Germany and the papacy a real possibility. The revolt of the younger Henry against his father, the antagonist of Gregory VII and Urban II, once again created a strong papal party in Germany (13). Henry V made the papal fight against simony and uncanonical elections to a large extent his own—investitures were the notable exception (14). Together with the papal legate Gebhard of Constance and Archbishop Rothard of Mainz the new king suspended or deposed schismatic bishops, that is bishops appointed and invested by the emperor and therefore not in communion with Rome. He then proceeded to replace them with members of the royal–papal 'coalition' (15). Henry's uprising met with the approval of Paschal who welcomed the re–organization of the German church. In a letter to Archbishop Rothard of November 1105 (JL 6050) the pontiff laid down guidelines for this re–organization: *De ordinationibus clericorum qui in nostri temporis schismate ordinati sunt, non aliud scribendum duximus quam in Placentina synodo per sanctae memoriae Urbanum predecessorem nostrum deliberatum est* (16). At the same time he specified that bishops who had been schismatically consecrated were to be judged at a general council: *Porro episcopos qui sub excommunicatione in eodem schismate manus impositionem susceperunt, ad concilii sententiam deferendos arbitramur. Tantum enim tantarum personarum malum generaliter deliberatione aut curandum est aut detruncandum.* (JL 6050)

    This general synod was the council of Guastalla. Invitations were sent out in March 1106. One of them, a letter to the Archbishop of Mainz, has been preserved, one of the rare examples of papal conciliar practice in the eleventh and early twelfth

---

(12) See Knonau, *Jahrbücher* 5.203 and Fliche-Martin, *Histoire* 8.345.

(13) For the relationship between Urban II and the empire see A. Becker, *Papst Urban II. (1088-1099)*, *(MGH, Schriften* 19¹; Stuttgart 1964) 139-64 as well as G. Henking, *Gebhard III., Bischof von Constanz: 1084-1110* (Stuttgart 1880) *passim.*

(14) It has often been noted that Henry V, even at this stage of his career, continued to invest bishops. See especially H. Guleke, *Deutschlands innere Kirchenpolitik von 1105-1111* (Dorpat 1882) esp. 49 and Appendix.

(15) For a narrative of the events in Germany in 1105 see especially Knonau, *Jahrbücher* 5.203-73.

(16) The best available edition of the canons of Piacenza is that by L. Weiland, *MGH, Const.* 1.560-63.

centuries (17). Piacenza in the north of Italy was originally to be the place of assembly, a free commune in the territories of the Countess Mathilda of Tuscany (18). But at the last minute, for reasons unknown, the meeting place was changed to Guastalla, a small town not far from Piacenza that was part of the patrimony of Mathilda, Paschal's hostess (19). Participants were apparently numerous (20), and even today relatively many can be named with the help of 'acta', letters and chronicles, a clear reflection of the interest the synod aroused among contemporaries. Archbishop Hugh of Lyons (21) and Bishop Rupert of Würzburg (22) died on the way to Italy. Present were archbishops Bruno of Trier, who led an official delegation sent by Henry V composed of other high ecclesiastics and nobles (23), and Konrad of Salzburg (24). Bishops Gebehard of Trent (25), Otto of Bamberg (26), Wido of Chur (27), and Hermann of Augs-

---

(17) ...duximus et magna consultatione deliberavimus: ut in proximis Octobribus Idibus synodalem vobiscum debeamus celebrare conventum. Idcirco tam te, karissime frater, quam omnes Moguntinae ecclesiae suffraganeos litteris praesentibus praemonemus: ut, convocatis dyocesium vestrarum qui digniores videntur abbatibus, convocatis etiam clericorum personis quibus concilii tractatus necessarius est, praenominato in tempore citra Alpes nobiscum convenire omni occasione seposita procuretis; quatinus, largiente Domino, ablatis de medio scismatum causis, ecclesiae ac regno pacis reformetur integritas (JL 6076).

(18) Seherus, Primordia Calmosiacensis monasterii ord. S. Aug. libri duo ed. P. JAFFÉ (MGH, SS 12; 1856) 324-47, 336.

(19) ibid. For Mathilda of Tuscany see the entry under Donizo, Vita Mathildis in the Repertorium Fontium Historiae Medii Aevi 4 (forthcoming) 241-2, and the bibliographical references given by L. SIMEONI, Il contributo della contessa Matilde al papato nella lotta per le investiture, in Studi Gregoriani 1 (1947) 352-72.

(20) A contemporary chronicler from the monastery of Helmarshausen in Saxony included in the account of the translation of St. Modoald a lively description of the journey to Guastalla and the meeting of other delegates, especially the embassy of Henry V, along the way. (Translatio S. Modoaldi, ed. P. JAFFÉ [MGH, SS 12; 1856] 284-310, 295.

(21) W. LÜHE, Hugo von Die und Lyon, Legat von Gallien (Breslau 1898) 118-9 with bibliography.

(22) Chronica Regia Coloniensis, ed. G. WAITZ (MGH, SS in usum scholarum; 1880) 45.

(23) See n. 20 above.

(24) Gesta archiepiscoporum Salisburgensium, ed. W. WATTENBACH (MGH, SS 11; 1854) 41.

(25) Ekkehardi Uraugiensis Chronica, ed. G. WAITZ (MGH, SS 6; 1844) 1-297, 240.

(26) See G. JURITSCH, Geschichte des Bischofs Otto I. von Bamberg, des Pommern-Apostels (1102-1139) (Gotha 1889) esp. 84-7. JL 6143.

(27) JL 6143.

burg (28) did not mind the burden of the journey. Italian bishops at Guastalla whose names are known are Aldo of Piacenza (29) and probably Bruno of Segni (30). Among the invited abbots were Tietmar of Helmarshausen (31), Abbot Hartmann of the famous Benedictine abbey of Göttweig in lower Austria (32), Gonter of the monastery of S. Lambert at Liesse (Dép. Aisne) (33), Seherus from the Lotharingian monastery of Chaumouzey in the diocese of Toul (34), Gerbert of the monastery St. Vannes at Verdun (35), and Abbess Berta of the ancient monastery of S. Maria Teodatae (or della Pusterla) that is said to have been founded by Pope Gregory I (36). Chronicles and the 'acta' of the council are evidence that in addition bishops, cathedral chapters and monasteries sent delegations to Guastalla; the city of Parma, for instance, was represented by a group of citizens. Paschal himself was accompanied by several Roman cardinals and his chancellor, John of Gaeta. All in all, a distinguished assembly gathered at Guastalla (37).

The activities at the synod were many, and the pontiff was busy: *monasteriis privilegia concesserit, presentes ovium Christi pastores mellifluis alloquiis, absentes paternis commonitoriorum litteris instruxerit*, wrote Ekkehard of Aura (38). A less amiable

---

(28) Udalschalk, *De Eginone et Herimanno*, ed. P. Jaffé (*MGH, SS* 12; 1856) 429-48, 438.

(29) The bishop of Piacenza accompanied Paschal to France together with Roman clergy. See JL 6125 and the report given by Suger, *Vie de Louis VI le Gros*, ed. H. Waquet (Paris 1929), 56 about Aldo's activity as Paschal's official spokesman at the meeting held in 1107 at Châlons-sur-Marne with a German delegation.

(30) See JL 6098, a privilege for Abbot Hugh of St. Gilles in Nîmes. It is dated Parma, November 2, 1106, and was signed by Paschal, Bruno of Segni and Cardinal Landulf. It is likely that Bruno had joined Paschal already at Guastalla.

(31) *Translatio S. Modoaldi* 295.

(32) Udalschalk, *De Eginone* 438.

(33) JL 6093.

(34) *Primordia Calmosiacensis* 336-7.

(35) *Laurentii de Leodio gesta episcoporum Virdunensium*, ed. G. Waitz (*MGH, SS* 10; 1852) 486-525, 498.

(36) The monastery was located near Pavia. See P.F. Kehr, *Italia Pontificia* VI/1 (Berlin 1913) 180 n. 30 and *ibid.* 212 n. 1.

(37) Only some of the more prominent participants have been named here. For a fuller discussion of the participants at Guastalla see the author's *The Councils of Pope Paschal II, 1100-1110: a Text-Critical Study* (Columbia University dissertation 1973) chapter 2.

(38) *MGH, SS* 6,240. JL 6093, 6095-6098 illustrate Ekkehard's description.

pontiff and a more militant synod is reflected in a passage from the *Annales Patherbrunenses*:

> Plures ibi episcopi Italiae damnantur, quidam anathematizantur. Patriarcha Aquileiae anathematizatur; Fridericus Halverstatensis, accusantibus eum ecclesiae canonicis, honore episcopali privatur. Similis sententia de Widelone Mindensi habetur. Leodicensis et Cameracensis anathematizantur (39).

The only Italian bishop known to have been censured is Peter of Padua (1096–1106, d. 1119), who was deposed at Guastalla (40). The excommunication of Udalric, patriarch of Aquileia and abbot of St. Gall (41), and of the bishops of Halberstadt, Minden, Liège, and Cambrai (42) shows that the policy laid down in Paschal's letter of November 1105 to Archbishop Rothard of Mainz was adhered to (43). Schismatic bishops, or in other words bishops who had been invested by Emperor Henry IV, were deposed at Guastalla—if they were absent and thus refused to be reconciled to the Roman church (44). The patriarch of Aquileia, a loyal follower of Henry IV, not only fell under anathema but also had to see the dismemberment of the archdiocese of Ravenna: the towns Parma, Piacenza, Reggio, Modena and Bologna, or rather their bishops, were now to be directly subject to the pontiff (45).

On the other hand it is perhaps more significant that bish-

---

(39) *Annales Patherbrunnenses* ed. P. SCHEFFER-BOICHORST (Innsbruck 1870) 116.

(40) P.F. KEHR, *Italia Pontificia* VII/1.159 no. 7.

(41) *ibid.* 34, no. 74; KNONAU, *Jahrbücher* 5.211 n. 4.

(42) Frederic of Halberstadt and Widelo of Minden had been suspended by the papal legates early in 1105. Their sentences were now confirmed. See *ibid.* 223 and 227 as well as *ibid.* 6.45n.

(43) See above 63 (JL 6050).

(44) This is illustrated by the case of Otbert of Liège with striking clarity. In a letter of November 1106, only a few weeks after the synod, Paschal asked Bruno of Trier to reconcile Otbert, his clergy and his city with the Roman church. Otbert had sent a delegation that reached Paschal shortly after the council and *suppliciter consortium nostrae communionis expeciit*, (JL 6099) as the pontiff explained to Bruno, and therefore the sentence of excommunication the synod had proclaimed should be lifted.

(45) See *MGH, Const.* 1.565 c.2; P.F. KEHR, *Italia Pontificia* 5 (Berlin 1911) 57 no. 188 with bibliography. This decision of the council of Guastalla has also been independently transmitted. This transmission has been discussed in *The Councils of Pope Paschal II.*

ops who were present, and thus expressed their willingness to end the schism, were treated with great leniency. One example, the case of the archbishop of Trier, may suffice as an illustration (46). According to the *Gesta Treverorum* Bruno of Trier who led the royal embassy at Guastalla, was deposed at the beginning of the council because he had been invested by the emperor with ring and staff. Not only that, he had also assumed his duties without having received the pallium which he would have had to obtain from the hands of the pope (47). The reproaches were serious, but nevertheless Bruno's deposition lasted only three days. He was almost immediately reinstated by the synod and received the pallium from Paschal. A penalty so light that it had only symbolical value was enjoined for the next three years: whenever the archbishop of Trier would celebrate mass, he was not to use the dalmatic (48).

The dominant aspect of the synod was a determined effort to overcome the problems that disturbed the relationship between the papacy and the secular European powers. The oldest life of Paschal reports: *In Langobardia apud Guardastallum celebravit concilium, in quo quidem de investituris, de hominiis et sacramentis episcoporum laicis exhibitis exhibendisque certis capitulis statutum est* (49). These *capitula* have not survived even although they were part of the official legislation (50), but the *Liber Pontificalis* text just quoted implies that Paschal's negotiations with Henry I of England had been on the agenda and were confirmed. In a letter to Archbishop Anselm of Canterbury Paschal transmitted details about his agreement with Henry I that bring the *Liber Pontificalis capitula* immediately to mind: *...Si qui vero deinceps praeter investituram ecclesiarum praelationes assumpserint, etiam si regi hominia fecerint, nequaquam ob hoc a benedictionis munere arceantur, donec per omnipotentis dei gratiam ad hoc omittendum cor regium tuae praedictionis imbribus*

---

(46) See also n. 44 above.

(47) The significance of the pallium, and the importance it assumed under Pope Paschal II has been discussed by R.L. BENSON, *The Bishop-Elect* (Princeton 1968), 169-73.

(48) *Gesta Treverorum* ed. G.H. WAITZ (*MGH, SS* 8; 1848) 111-260, 122.

(49) L. DUCHESNE, *Le Liber Pontificalis. Texte, Introduction et Commentaire* (*Bibliothèque des Écoles francaises d'Athènes et de Rome*; repr. Paris 1955-57) (vol. 3 C. VOGEL) 2.299.

(50) They were probably part of Paschal's register. *Cf.* below 70.

molliatur (51). Paschal and the assembly at Guastalla were ready to compromise — but not with regard to investiture with ring and staff (52). King Kálmán of Hungary (1095-1116) renounced investiture at some point of Paschal's pontificate (53) and some scholars conclude that this renunciation was received by the assembly at Guastalla (54).

The conciliatory character of the synod with regard to any difficulty except investiture is well reflected in its legislation as known today. One canon in particular demonstrates this clearly:

> Per multos iam annos regni Teutonici latitudo ab apostolice sedis unitate divisa est. In quo nimirum scismate tantum periculum factum est ut, quod cum dolore dicimus, vix pauci sacerdotes aut clerici catholici in tanta terrarum latitudine reperiantur. Tot igitur filiis in hac strage iacentibus, christiane pacis necessitas exigit, ut super hos materna Ecclesie viscera aperiantur. Patrum itaque nostrorum exemplis et scriptis instructi, qui diversis temporibus Novatianos, Donatistas et alios hereticos in suis ordinibus susceperunt, prefati regni episcopos in scismate ordinatos, nisi aut invasores aut symoniaci aut criminosi comprobentur, in officio episcopali suscipimus; id ipsum de clericis cuiuscumque ordinis constituimus, quos vita scientiaque commendat (55).

This canon is part of a series of Guastalla legislation that has long been known and was published by Baronius in the twelfth volume of his *Annales Ecclesiastici* appearing in 1607. The learned cardinal had discovered the canons in '*Vaticano codice, qui liber Censum inscribitur, a Cencio Camerali collecto*' (56). The reference

---

(51) S. *Anselmi Cantuariensis Archiepiscopi Opera Omnia* ed. F.S. SCHMITT, 6 vols. (Edinburgh 1949) 5.340-42, ep. 397.

(52) See below.

(53) See *Martini Oppaviensis Chronicon Pontificum et Imperatorum* ed. L. WEILAND (*MGH, SS* 22) 435. The manuscript evidence is very difficult to evaluate. I would like to thank Professor James Sweeney for his kind help.

(54) e.g. G. PRAY, *Annales Regum Hungariae*, Pars I (Vienna 1764) 110; LASZLO MEZEY, *Ungarn und Europa im 12. Jahrhundert*, in *Konstanzer Arbeitskreis für Mittelalterliche Geschichte. Vorträge und Forschungen* 1 (1968) 255-6; see also *Handbook* 3.402.

(55) *Liber Pontificalis* 2.371-2 = *MGH, Const.* 1.565 no.4.

(56) *Annales Ecclesiastici* 12.53.

is to the *Liber Censuum*, compiled by Cencio Savelli, papal camerarius at the close of the twelfth century and later himself Pope Honorius III (57). His work, however, does not contain the Guastalla canons printed by Baronius. Nevertheless the problem of the origin of these canons can be solved with relative ease. The French scholar Duchesne already concluded that what Baronius had used was not the original *Liber Censuum* but a Vatican copy of the work of Nicolas Roselli (also called Cardinal of Aragon) (58) who had compiled a new redaction of the *Liber Censuum* in the first half of the fourteenth century. Roselli had used for this new redaction, as Duchesne could show, a particular copy of the original *Liber Censuum*: MS 228 at the Biblioteca Riccardiana in Florence (59). This codex differed from other *Liber Censuum* transcriptions because it included an insert: the continuation of the *Liber Pontificalis* by Cardinal Boso, possibly an Englishman who came to Rome at the time of Pope Hadrian IV (Nicholas Breakspear, 1154–1159), but more likely an Italian ecclesiastic prominent at this time (60). Boso included in his life of Paschal the text of several canons from Guastalla. As a textual comparison will show, Roselli copied Boso's canons and made some additions of his own (61). The Roselli version of the *Liber Censuum* was used by the conciliar editors from Binius to Mansi in the eighteenth century (62). They fol-

---

(57) The *Liber Censuum* has been edited by P. Fabre and L. Duchesne (*Bibl. des Écoles francaises d'Athènes et de Rome*, 2 vols.; Paris 1889-1910) an index volume has been published by G. Mollat (Paris 1962).

(58) For a bibliography of Cardinal Nicolas Roselli see J. Quétif and J. Échard, *Scriptores ordinis praedicatorum recensiti*, 2 vols. in 4 (Paris 1719-23) I/2, 649-51 and now L. Gasparri, *Osservazioni sul codice Vallicelliano C.24* in *Studi Gregoriani* 9 (1972) 467-513, 507 n.1.

(59) *Liber Pontificalis* l.xxxviii no.29.

(60) See F. Geisthardt, *Der Kämmerer Boso* (*Historische Studien* 293; Berlin 1936) esp. 37-40. *Cf. Liber Pontificalis* l.xxxix and xxxvii-xliv.

(61) See *Vitae nonnullorum pontificum Romanorum a Nicolao Aragonii S.R.E. cardinali conscriptae*, ed. N. Aloisia (*Rerum Italicarum Scriptores* III/1 [ed. L. Muratori]; Milan 1733) 274-587, 364. Roselli listed JL 5971, in reality unconnected to the council, as 'aliud capitulum concilii.' Baronius did not use the same inscription but the very fact that he connected the letter with Paschal's council of 1106 shows that he must have had a copy of the Roselli redaction in front of him.

(62) The various collections of conciliar material have been discussed by A.M. Stickler, *Historia iuris canonici latini* (Turin 1950) 294-8 and A. van Hove, *Prolegomena ad codicem iuris canonici* (2nd ed., Mechlin and Rome 1945) 391-3.

lowed Baronius' lead in the description of the council of Guastalla, thus using a secondary source Roselli, for the series of canons that had originally been transcribed by Cardinal Boso.

Cardinal Boso's sources for the life of Paschal have been discussed by Duchesne in his edition of the *Liber Pontificalis*. [Boso's] *notice de Pascal II n'est guère qu'une collection de pièces d'archives, dont plusieurs se sont conservées en dehors du texte de Boson... Les autres pièces reproduites par lui viennent... d'une autre source, et cette source, je pense, est le registre lui–même. Mais s'il en est ainsi on doit s'étonner que, disposant d'une série ordonnée chronologiquement comme étaient les registres pontificaux, Boson n'ait pas mis plus d'ordre dans ses extraits. On trouve consecutivement des pièces de 1111, 1109, 1112, 1106, 1104, 1112* (63). With regard to the Guastalla canons at least Duchesne's estimate is partially confirmed. Boso's text seems to fall into two distinct sections: 1) *Aliud quoque concilium...* explicit: *vita scientiaque commendat*, and 2) *Aliud capitulum. Iamdiu...* explicit: *periculum patiatur* (64). The first part of the text was copied by Boso from Paschal's register. A letter sent by Cardinal Pietro Diani to his fellow citizens of Piacenza indicates this much for the first two canons. He wrote: *Nos vero... registra summorum pontificum diligente indagatione perquisivimus, et in registro beatissimi Paschalis II decretum exemptionis civitatis nostrae a jugo Ravennae invenimus... In hoc concilio constitutum est...*(65) The second part of the Guastalla canons might well be characterized as part of the miscellaneous '*pièces d'archives*' which Boso included.

It is unfortunately impossible to determine their origin more precisely. The transmission of conciliar legislation during the late eleventh– und early twelfth centuries raises numerous questions that cannot be answered because of lack of evidence (66).

---

(63) *Liber Pontificalis* 2.xli. *Cf. The Councils*, ch. 2.

(64) For the text of the canons is found *ibid.* 371-2 and also readily available in *MGH, Const.* 1.565-6. The distinct second part consists of Weiland's canons 5 and 6.

(65) See P.M. Campi, *Dell'Historia ecclesiastica di Piacenza*, vol. 2 (Piacenza 1651) Document XXXVIII, 369-70; *cf. Liber Censuum*, 115 n.2 col. a.

(66) See the reconstruction of conciliar procedures in R. Somerville, *The Councils of Urban II*, I: *Decreta Claromontensia* (*Annuarium Historiae Conciliorum*, Supplementum Nr. 1; Amsterdam 1972) chapter 2 and C.R. Cheney, *Textual problems of the English provincial canons*, first published in *La Critica del Testo* (*Atti del 2° Congresso internazionale della Società Italiana di Storia del Diritto*; Florence 1971), i.165-88 and now reprinted in *Medieval Texts and Studies* (Oxford 1973) 111-37.

It is clear, however, that Boso only transcribed a few canons selected at random from several accounts, including the pontifical register of Paschal II (67). It is now possible to supplement Boso's excerpts. Conciliar material is quite often found as addition to canonical manuscripts. A visit to the University Library of Graz proved rewarding through the discovery of a second set of Guastalla decrees in a twelfth–century manuscript of the *Collectio Canonum* of Anselm of Lucca (68), MS 351 (69). The collection of Anselm of Lucca itself, compiled in the early 1080's, does generally not contain Paschal II material (70). In the Graz codex, however, at the end of book VI of the collection, entitled *'De electione et ordinatione ac de omni potestate sive statu episcoporum'*, the same hand that had written the main text included a set of 6 canons with the inscription *Ex concilio Pascalis pape*. The same set of canons, with slightly varying inscriptions, sometimes no inscription at all, and not once with an inscription indicating the date and location of the council of Paschal referred to, was subsequently found in five additional Anselm of Lucca manuscripts in libraries at Parma, Naples and Florence as well as in MS Vat. lat. 1361 (71).

The tentative identification of the canons was made possible with the help of two manuscripts at the Biblioteca Apostolica Vaticana. One of them, Vat. lat. 4891, in particular provided the key which solved as far as possible the problems connected with the Anselm of Lucca canons. The sixteenth–century paper manuscript contains notes of the *Correctores Romani* (72), the

---

(67) Cc.1-3 seem to serve as introduction to c.4 (quoted above 12-3), but it should be noted that c.4 has frequently been transmitted independently in manuscripts preserved in German libraries or those of neighboring regions at the time still part of the empire. Two redactions exist, but both are close to the *Liber Pontificalis* text. A special effort must have been undertaken in order to bring c.4 of Guastalla to the attention of German ecclesiastics. See *The Councils of Pope Paschal II*, ch. 2.

(68) For a brief introduction to this important canonical collection see STICKLER, *Historia* 170-2 and VAN HOVE, *Prolegomena* 323-4. The collection has been partially edited by F. THANER, *Anselmi Lucensis collectio canonica una cum collectione minore* (Innsbruck 1906-15).

(69) See A. KERN, *Die Handschriften der Universitätsbibliothek Graz* (*Verzeichnis der Handschriften im Deutschen Reich* 2; 1, 1939-42) 208.

(70) *Cf.* THANER's edition.

(71) The manuscripts have been described in *The Councils of Pope Paschal II*.

(72) On the *Correctores Romani* see FRIEDBERG's introduction lxxvi ff; most recently SOMERVILLE, *Decreta Claromontensia* 22.

mid–siteenth–century papal commission that was entrusted with
the task of emending the *Decretum* of Gratian. Their notes in
Vat. lat. 4891 comment on the canons included in the *Decretum*. The majority of the Paschal canons in the addition to book
VI of Anselm of Lucca's *Collectio* has been incorporated by Gratian (73), and for 2 of them (C.16 q.7 c.16 and c.18) the *Correc-
ores* provided a commentary with the following introduction:
in concilio generale apud Guardastalum habito anno Domini 1116
(sic) *quod habetur in Bibliotheca Vaticana et R. D. Episcopus Signin.*
fragmentum adduxit in quo haec capita habeantur. (fol. 169v)
MS Vat. lat. 4891 makes it clear that the *Correctores Romani*
possessed at the time two manuscripts showing that C.16 q.7
c.16 (*Si quis clericus*) and c.18 (*Nullus laicorum*) (74) were part
of the legislation promulgated by Paschal at Guastalla: a codex
in the Vatican library and a fragment given to them by the bishop
of Segni (75). The *Editio Romana* of Gratian's *Concordia Discordantium Canonum* included the Guastalla note in MS Vat. lat.
4891 at least in garbled form, in contrast to many of the other
notes of the *Correctores* that are not found at all in the printed
editions (76). It accompanies C.16 q.7 c.16 and confirms the reference to the fragment from Segni: *Capitis huius et sequentis
sensus est in fragmento manuscripto concilii apud Guardastallum,
a Paschali habiti A.D. 1116, quod in bibliotheca Vaticana serva-
tur* (77). The original *Correctores* note in MS Vat. lat. 4891 is
recognizable, but was disregarded by FRIEDBERG in his edition.

---

(73) The Graz Guastalla canons are distributed in Gratian's *Decretum* as follows: c.1
Episcopi lectioni = C.2 q.7 c.60; c.2 *Nullus episcopus* = not incorporated; c.3 *Nullius laicorum* = C.16 q.7 c.18 (an abbreviation of the longer canon found in MS Graz 351); c.4 *Sicut
Domini* = C.16 q.7 c.19; c.5 *Abbatibus qui* = C.18 q.6 c.18; c.6 *Si quis clericus* = C.16 q.7
c.16; See *The Councils of Pope Paschal II*, Appendix II.

(74) The manuscripts of the *Correctores* also contained C.16 q.7 c.17 (*Constitutiones*)
and described it as a canon promulgated at Guastalla. Since this canon is, however, not among
the canons found in the Graz codex its discussion is here omitted.

(75) The name of the bishop of Segni who provided the *Correctores* with the manuscript
is not indicated. He must have been a contemporary of the *Correctores* (active under the
pontificates of Pius IV, Pius V, and Gregory XIII) who cooperated with the commission
at some point between 1559 and 1572 when the notes in MS Vat. lat. 4891 were written. Two
bishops are possible choices: Ambrosius Monticelli (1551-69) and Joseph Pamfili, O.S.A.
(1570-81).

(76) SOMERVILLE, *Decreta Claromontensia* 48-50.

(77) See n.72 above; *sequentis* refers to C.16 q.7 c.17.

The *Correctores* were a group of famous scholars, and there is no reason why their statement in MS Vat. lat. 4891 should not be accepted at face value even although both their Guastalla manuscripts have to be considered lost. The Vatican codex probably had the old shelf mark 1882 in 4⁰ (78), and it has proven impossible to discover its present where-abouts (79). As far as the fragment from Segni is concerned, which was perhaps just a leaf from a codex, it should be kept in mind that the donor's predecessor of many centuries ago, the famous Bruno (80), probably participated in the council of Guastalla (81). A letter Bruno sent to Paschal during the crisis of 1111 (82) shows that the bishop of Segni was very familiar with the synod's legislation. Historians owe a good deal of conciliar material to the habit of scribes to enter small items that were of particular interest to their respective houses on manuscript fly leaves. Perhaps this is what had occurred at the chapter library of Segni. At any rate it would be unreasonable to doubt the existence of a manuscript fragment at Segni with canons from Paschal's council of Guastalla at the time of the *Correctores* which they could consult. To conclude, it is probable that several canons from C.16 q.7 were taken by Gratian from Paschal's Guastalla legislation.

Two among these items, C.16 q.7 c.16 (*Si quis clericus*) and c.18 (*Nullus laicorum*) (83) are also found in MS Graz 351 and

---

(78) This could be established by the author with the help of another Vaticana manuscript, MS Barb. lat. 860.

(79) The author would like to thank Msgr. Ruysschaert and Professor Stephan Kuttner for their kind help.

(80) See the entry in the *Dizionario Biografico degli Italiani* 14 (1972) 644-7 (H. HOFF-MANN).

(81) See above n.30.

(82) *Ep.* 2 *MGH, LL* 2 (1893) 564.

(83) The text in the *Decretum* (*Nullus laicorum ecclesias vel ecclesiarum bona occupet vel disponat. Qui vero secus egerit, iuxta B. Alexandri capitulum ab ecclesiae liminibus arceatur'*) is an abbreviation of the longer Anselm of Lucca decree (*Nullus laicorum ecclesias vel ecclesiarum bona occupet vel disponat. Sicut enim beatus Stephanus papa martyr scribit, laici quamvis religiosi sint, nulli tamen de ecclesiasticis facultatibus aliquid disponendi legitur umquam attributa facultas. Qui vero secus egerit iuxta beati Alexandri primi capitulum ab ecclesie liminibus arceatur*). Nevertheless, their identity seems certain because the connection between the prohibition of lay investiture and the reference to a capitulum of Pope Alexander II occurs only at Guastalla.

at least with regard to them the location of Paschal's council could now be added to the inscription. Could the same be said for the remaining four items? It seems certain that they were not copied from Gratian (84) since one decree is not found in the *Decretum* at all (85). Conceivably, a writer might have assembled Paschal II decrees from various sources in an appendix, but the inscription *'Ex concilio Pascalis pape'* precludes this possibility. No canon in the Anselm set appears among material definitely known to have been issued at any one of the other councils held by this pontiff. Regrettably, no stemma codicum of the *Collectio Canonum* of Anselm of Lucca has as yet evolved from the studies of this collection (86). Nothing can be said, therefore, about the time or manner of adoption of the Paschal canons into the body of the canonical collection, but even without this help the other evidence assembled leads to the conclusion that the set of decrees found in 5 of the manuscripts of Anselm's canonical collection has been derived from Paschal's council at Guastalla.

A comparison between the Boso and Anselm of Lucca canons shows that they have very little in common. The first section of the Boso text culminating in c.4 (87) is not at all reflected in the Anselm series, where also c.6 of Boso, prohibiting sale and mortgage of ecclesiastical property (88), is missing. But c.5, the solemn prohibition of lay investiture, is common to both series although in each case worded differently. C.5 in Boso's *Liber Pontificalis* appears to be the most polished version:

> *Aliud capitulum.* Iamdiu a pravis hominibus tam clericis quam laicis catholica est ecclesia conculcata; unde plura temporibus nostris schismata et hereses emerserunt. Nunc autem, per Dei gratiam huius nequitie deficientibus auctoribus, in ingenuam libertatem resurgit

---

(84) This is a theoretical possibility because of the date of the codices.

(85) See above n.71.

(86) See S. KUTTNER, *Some Roman manuscripts of canonical collections* in *Bulletin of Medieval Canon Law* N.S. 1 (1971) 1-29.

(87) Above 68.

(88) *Aliud capitulum. Nullus abbas, nullus archipresbiter, nullus prepositus ecclesie audeat possessiones ecclesie sue vendere, commutare, locare vel in feudum dare sine communi fratrum consensu vel episcopi proprie civitatis; alioquin ordinis sui periculum patiatur.*

Ecclesia. Unde providendum est, ut horum schismatum cause penitus abscidantur. Patrum ergo nostrorum constitutionibus consentientes, ecclesiarum investituras a laicis fieri omni modo prohibemus. Si quis autem decreti huius temerator extiterit, tamquam materne iniurie reus, clericus quidem ab eiusdem dignitatis consortio repellatur, laycus vero ab ecclesie liminibus arceatur.

In the Anselm of Lucca series, the prohibition of lay investiture is expressed differently and has been divided into 2 canons, one dealing with laymen, and the other dealing with ecclesiastics (89).

Nullus laicorum ecclesias vel ecclesiarum bona occupet vel disponat. Sicut enim beatus Stephanus papa martyr scribit, laici, quamvis religiosi sint, nulli tamen de ecclesiasticis facultatibus aliquid disponendi legitur umquam attributa facultas. Qui vero secus egerit iuxta beati Alexandri primi capitulum ab ecclesie liminibus arceatur.

The second 'anti–investiture' canon reads:

Si quis clericus, abbas vel monachus per laicos ecclesias obtinuerit, secundum sanctorum apostolorum canones et Antioceni concilii capitulum excommunicationi subiaceat.

Keeping in mind what little is known about conciliar procedures during this period (90) it can be said that the canons *Nullus* and *Si quis clericus* represent perhaps an earlier stage in the drafting of the legislation. The decree *Iamdiu* only alludes to more ancient conciliar legislation on the same subject: *patrum ergo nostrorum constitutionibus consentientes...* both other canons directly name the precedents presumably found in the canonical collections used at the council of Guastalla (91). The ornate *Iamdiu* seems to be the later and final redaction made at the papal curia. If this hypothesis is correct it should be noted that the c. *Si quis clericus* is reflected hardly at all in *Iamdiu*. *Iamdiu* refers only once to clerics, pointing out that in contrast to laymen clerics

---

(89) For the edition of these texts see *The Councils of Pope Paschal II.*

(90) See above n.64.

(91) See *The Councils of Pope Paschal II.*

would not be excommunicated but would only lose their ecclesiastical rank. This contradicts and softens *Si quis clericus* considerably. It should be remembered, though, that conceivably the source used by Boso contained in addition to *Iamdiu* a decree just as ornately phrased but based on *Si quis clericus* instead of on *Nullus laicorum* (92). The investiture problem was evidently hotly debated at Guastalla. C.16 q.7 c.17, identified in the Segni fragment as Guastalla legislation (93) provides yet a third expression of the same principle:

> Constitutiones sanctorum canonum sequentes statuimus ut quicumque clericorum ab hac hora in antea investituram ecclesiae vel ecclesiasticae dignitatis de manu laica acceperit, et qui ei manum imposuerit, gradus sui periculo subiaceat, et communione privetur.

Here the stress lies again on the receiving cleric rather than the lay donor.

While several different versions of the investiture prohibition have come down to us, also canons dealing with other subjects must have circulated among the participants. Boso's c.6 indicates as much, the Anselm series provides fuller evidence. Paschal tried to insure at Guastalla that each diocese would be administered according to ancient canon law. One canon confirms to a large extent the subjection of abbots to the bishops of their diocese (94) and last not least the unity between the bishop and his church was strongly emphasized:

> Sicut domini vestimentum scissum non est sed de eo sortiti sunt ita nec ecclesia scindi debet quia in unitate tota consistit. In potestate ergo proprii episcopi ecclesie reducantur et ab ipso sicut in sacris canonibus cautum est ordinentur alioquin et ecclesie ipse et clerici earundem divinis destituantur officiis.

---

(92) The subject of the c. *Nullus laicorum* is much closer to the c. *Iamdiu* than the subject of *Si quis clericus*.

(93) See above n.72.

(94) Abbatibus qui neque sub episcopo neque sub metropolitano neque sub primate neque sub patriarcha sunt nullus prorsus episcoporum episcopalia quelibet amministret. Cum enim se nulli omnino subesse profiteantur episcopo, consequens est ut nullus ipsorum que sua sunt eis tamquam exteris largiatur.

The rightful bishop was to be reinstated in his diocese and his leadership accepted. Factional strife was to be laid to rest in other words, and the church was to become once again a harmonious whole. Even here, therefore, in legislation not dealing directly with investitures, Paschal and the ecclesiastics assembled at Guastalla did not lose sight of their aim: the healing of the schism (95). The revolt of Henry V seemed to provide the means for the reconciliation so greatly desired as the council of Guastalla shows. Paschal was willing to compromise in the spirit of the council of Piacenza, but with regard to one issue, investiture, compromise was impossible. The pontiff, together with many of his contemporaries attributed to the symbols used: ring and staff, sacramental character. Priests would be completely superfluous if they should be bestowed by laymen (96). Paschal's attitude is forcefully expressed in the Guastalla canons prohibiting investiture. It never wavered until physical violence forced his hand in April 1111.

---

(95) See above 67.

(96) See JL 5928 sent to St. Anselm of Canterbury.

IX

Patrimonia and *Regalia* in 1111

The spring of the year 1111 is usually seen as the nadir of the pontificate of Paschal II (1099–1118).[1] King Henry V of Germany had celebrated Christmas at Florence and soon afterwards advanced steadily and threateningly towards Rome. He came at the head of a large army to claim the imperial coronation. Under these circumstances Pope Paschal II entered once again into negotiations with his adversary. Basic agreement was reached by royal and papal legates in Rome on 4 February 1111 at S. Maria in Turri, a church of the St. Peter's complex, and Henry confirmed this agreement on 9 February, at Sutri. It stipulated that Henry would renounce on the day of his coronation (12 February 1111) investiture with ring and staff and return the territorial possessions of St. Peter to the pope. Since the time of Constantine the Great (d. 337), emperors as well as the nobility in general had enriched the church with large landholdings, from the sixth century onwards often called *patrimonium* or *patrimonia Petri*, but the donations usually remained a dead letter. The lands were hardly ever in the actual possession of the popes,[2] and Henry's promise to rectify this state of affairs was therefore very welcome indeed. Paschal, in turn, would order all bishops and abbots of the empire to return the *regalia* they held.[3] The coronation and the exchange of public declarations never took place as planned, however, and Paschal and his entourage were captured by Henry on the evening of 12 February. After two months of captivity the pope submitted to Henry, who had by then resurrected his old demand for investiture and homage. In the treaty of Ponte Mammolo (11 April 1111), the pontiff conceded investiture with ring and staff, and promised to abstain from any future excommunication of the king and to crown him in St. Peter's.[4] After the coronation on 13 April, Henry withdrew with his forces, and the Romans celebrated the return of the pope. The Latin church, however, was torn by dissent, and Paschal may have planned to abdicate.

Historians have frequently discussed and analyzed these dramatic events, and especial attention is paid to Paschal's concessions at S. Maria in Turri, in other words, the pontiff's plan to have *regalia* returned to the king. In the agreement of S. Maria it was said that:

domnus papa precipiet aepiscopis presentibus in die coronationis eius, ut dimittant regalia regi, et regno quae ad regnum pertinebant tempore Karoli, Lodoici, Heinrici et aliorum praedecessorum . . . id est civitates, ducatus, marchias, comitatus, monetas, teloneum, mercatum, advocatias regni, iura centurionum et curtes quae . . . regni erant, cum pertinentiis suis, militiam et castra [regni].[5]

It is generally assumed that Paschal advocated on this occasion apostolic poverty for a church that was overburdened by secular cares. A very thoughtful essay by Piero Zerbi is the most recent statement in this connection.[6] Zerbi translated Paschal's decision to return the *regalia* of the empire into Tellenbach's terminology, suggesting that the pontiff's promised privilege represented a "flight from the world," that is, the motif of ascetic withdrawal. At the same time, Zerbi insisted that this ascetic and rigorous demand upon bishops and abbots is a perfect continuation of the policies of Gregory VII, since it was the only means available under the given circumstances to realize the prohibition of investiture.

The present study will be concerned, once again, with the events of February 1111. It will be shown (1) that from Paschal's point of view the negotiations in Rome and Sutri were a highly successful culmination of previous papal policies concerning investiture and the papal states; and (2) that manuscript evidence eliminates arguments against the objectivity of Paschal's account in his register. This register, now fully acceptable as evidence, shows that the pontiff and King Henry V differed greatly on the meaning of the term *regalia*. Paschal had no intention to impoverish the church.

The gains made by Paschal during the February negotiations are usually regarded as limited to Henry's proffered renunciation of investiture. It is barely mentioned that the German king also promised to return the *patrimonia* of the Holy See, that is, territories, provinces, towns and islands which had been granted in previous imperial donations to St. Peter.[7] This forgotten aspect of the negotiations deserves emphasis. Papal politics, at least since the period of Leo IX (1048–54) had not only centered on reform of the church, but also on the vindication of papal temporal possessions, in other words, the vindication of the patrimony of St. Peter.

Paschal was capable of belligerence. Even when he was dying in the Castello S. Angelo in January 1118, he had war engines mounted to bombard rebels in St. Peter's.[8] At the very beginning of his pontificate he conquered Benevento to reduce the city once again to the status of a papal vassal.[9] When Ninfa was forced to submit to Paschal, the men of Ninfa had to agree to swear fealty, come to the feudal host, attend court, observe the ban, give hospitality dues, tolls and relief as well as cartage services.[10] Henry's promise of February 1111, fully to restore the papal states, would have meant that Paschal's successes at Benevento and Ninfa, for example, would be repeated throughout Italy—and not by means of hard campaigns but simply by a stroke of the pen. Paschal could have marshalled feudal service of the type required from Ninfa on a large scale. The days of political weakness and of abject poverty of the papacy would have been over.[11]

Since Paschal was greatly concerned about the restitution of papal territories, it is probably not without significance that the first discussions between papal and royal representatives in 1111 took place in the church of

S. Maria in Turri. Adjacent to the church were three bronze portals, leading to the atrium of the basilica of St. Peter, inscribed with the names of the possessions or *patrimonia* of the Holy See granted by previous emperors. The doors graphically illustrated the meaning of the promise made by Henry V at every stage of the negotiations, that is, "to grant and return the patrimony and possessions to St. Peter as had been done by Charles, Louis, Henry and other emperors, and aid the papacy to retain them as far as was in his power."[12] This declaration, part of the agreement of 4 February from S. Maria in Turri, was confirmed by an oath taken at Sutri on 9 February on behalf of Henry V by Duke Frederic of Swabia, Chancellor Adalbert and other German nobles.[13] On 12 February, Henry again swore to preserve the patrimony of St. Peter and signed a corresponding declaration at the Silver Gate leading into Saint Peter's basilica.[14] How important these promises were to Paschal is made particularly clear in April 1111 at Ponte Mammolo. Although the pontiff surrendered at that time almost everything for which he and his predecessors had fought, he insisted once again on the restitution of the patrimony. Henry swore "faithfully to aid Paschal to hold the papacy quietly and securely, . . . to make restitution of the patrimony and possessions of the Roman church and to aid in the recovery and keeping of everything else which belonged to the church by right according to the custom of his ancestors."[15] As a result of the oath to return the patrimony, Henry V abstained from an attack, already planned, on the southern Italian Normans who held parts of the patrimony of St. Peter as vassals of the papacy.[16]

For the moment,[17] Paschal must have believed that even if he had not gained a renunciation of investiture, then at least he had saved the temporal possessions of St. Peter, which was one of the objectives he had achieved during the February negotiations. In this respect, he was continuing the policies of his predecessors. Paul Fabre traced a new system of registration for papal property back to the pontificate of Gregory VII,[18] and various contributions from this period eventually flowed into the *Liber censuum*. These included the main precedents for the privileges of Henry V concerning the restitution of the *patrimonia* in 1111: Charlemagne's confirmation of Pepin's grant of the papal states of 754, the grant of Emperor Louis the Pious of 817, and the confirmation of these earlier privileges by Emperor Henry II.[19] The source for Cencio Savelli, the papal *camerarius* who compiled the *Liber censuum* towards the end of the twelfth century and later became Pope Honorius III, was, in this instance, the late eleventh-century *Collectio canonum* of Cardinal Deusdedit of the title church Apostolorum in Eudoxia (today S. Pietro in Vincoli).[20] It is easy to exaggerate connections between theory and practice, but a link between Deusdedit's *Collectio* and Roman curial activities during the pontificate of Paschal II can be postulated. Paschal prominently quoted the work, dedicated in 1086–87 to Pope Victor III, in three letters sent from the synod of Troyes (1107) to the German bishops Gebhard of Constance, Reinhard of Halberstadt, and Rothard of Mainz.[21] Canons from Deusdedit

12

were used both at Troyes and at the Lateran council of 1110 for the prohibition of investiture.[22]

The emphasis of the reform papacy on papal territorial possessions and related rights had caused a reaction in imperialist circles embodied in the so-called *Cessio donationum*.[23] The *Cessio* formed part of the collection of forgeries originating in the 1080s at Ravenna. The forgeries were accepted as authentic by both papalists and imperialists as shown by the negotiations of Châlons in 1107 and the *Tractatus de investitura episcoporum* used for the first time in 1109.[24] In the *Cessio* Pope Leo VIII purportedly returned to Emperor Otto I all "regales res huius regni Italie" that were given to earlier popes by the emperors beginning with Charles' father Pepin. A long list of towns, duchies, islands, mountains and their towns, monasteries, fortified places and other territories follows.[25] What Paschal achieved in 1111 was in effect a cancellation of the *Cessio donationum*, and a reconfirmation of the previous imperial grants which were the basis for the papal states. These donations until then had frequently remained a dead letter, and it might be wondered that Paschal could assume that Henry V would concede to him such extensive sovereign rights and lands in Italy. It would, nonetheless, be wrong to dismiss Henry's promises as a conventional formula used on the occasion of imperial coronations. Paschal very clearly believed Henry's oath that the patrimony of St. Peter would be returned, and must have had reasons for doing so even if these are difficult to grasp in retrospect.[26]

The promise of a restitution of the *patrimonia* had, in February 1111, been combined with Henry's promise no longer to demand investiture and homage of ecclesiastics. Yet the coronation ceremony, where Henry was formally to make these declarations, was interrupted by an uproar, and the pope and his supporters were taken into custody. Although these events were described in papal and imperial official reports, it has been unclear what really happened because the two versions are contradictory. The imperial report is an encyclical of Henry V which is preserved in several chronicles, sometimes slightly altered and re-arranged, and in the *Codex Udalrici*.[27] It gives the following account:

> The king enters Rome. Although some Germans are attacked and killed, Henry pronounces and signs, at the portals of S. Peter, a promise to preserve the ancient possessions of the church. He then immediately requests the pontiff to fulfill his written promises. When the king continues to insist, all ecclesiastics and sons of the church, both on the papal and imperial side, resist the pontiff, proclaiming his decree evident heresy. If he (Paschal) had been able, he would have read the document requiring the return of the *regalia*. The document (MGH LL IV, I: 141–42) is attached.[28]

Henry is thus claiming that all those present at the coronation regarded Paschal's proposal to return the *regalia* as heretical. *Regalia* were indeed the issue which was discussed at the occasion of Henry's interrupted coronation on 12 February, but these discussions did not lead to an uproar among the assembled ecclesiastics nor to accusations that the pope's privilege was heretical. These facts emerge from the papal account, which was preserved in Paschal's register, as will be shown below. This version is much more explicit than Henry's encyclical:

> After the solemn reception of Henry in Rome on Saturday, he swears on the day of the coronation [12 February] two oaths to the Roman people and is led to the steps of St. Peter's. At the top of the stairs he is received by the pope and ecclesiastical dignitaries and taken to the Silver Gate, the main entrance to the basilica. Henry reads the imperial profession and is designated emperor by Paschal. When everybody has entered the basilica, Henry and Paschal take seats at the rota porphyretica. Paschal demands from Henry the reading of the privileges to which the king had consented at S. Maria in Turri and Sutri. Henry, however, withdraws with his bishops and princes to negotiate with them. The discussions become protracted; Paschal sends emissaries to ask again for the investiture renunciation. Transalpine bishops join the pope, but soon friends of the king claim that the concluded agreement [concerning the return of the *regalia*] cannot be confirmed if authority and justice are to be maintained. Although they are answered with Scriptural and canonical citations, among them prominently 'reddenda sunt cesari quae sunt cesaris' and 'nemo militans Deo implicat se negotiis saecularibus,' they persist in their refusal to ratify the agreement. Towards evening some ecclesiastics suggest, as a compromise, that the king should be crowned that day and the other negotiations postponed to the following week, but the imperial party rejects this solution. Meanwhile the pope, the prefect, and the papal entourage are guarded by armed soldiers; Paschal is barely able to celebrate mass, and he and his companions are taken from the church. Few escape; Rome revolts.[29]

A comparison between the earlier text from Henry's encyclical and this selection reveals two basic contradictions:

> (1) instead of Paschal's demand that Henry should read the privileges which he had promised to grant, the imperial encyclical claims that the ceremony began with a request by Henry that Paschal should read the document announcing the return of the *regalia*. This distinction is significant because it implies that Henry pretended that he fulfilled his own obligations when he read and signed his declaration before the Silver Gate. But the agreements of S. Maria and Sutri differed greatly from Henry's coronation grant as will be seen;

> (2) according to the imperial encyclical, everybody revolts against the pope; according to Paschal's register, Henry secedes with his adherents. In the course of the day, imperial supporters begin to declare that the *regalia* decree is unjust. They also reject a compromise offered by a group of clergy. The importance here lies in the fact that (a) Paschal's proposal was by no means universally rejected and (b) that it needed Henry's persuasion to convince even his own supporters that the papal promise to return the *regalia* was unjust.

Before it is possible to draw any conclusions from these distinctions it is necessary to discuss the manuscript tradition for the papal account of the events of February 1111. Until now the papal account was thought to be biased, since—it is said, but incorrectly as will be discussed below—it omitted all documents concerning the return of the *regalia* which supposedly would have damaged Paschal's cause.[30] As a consequence, the report has been hitherto disparaged as a piece of propaganda.

The following manuscripts contain the papal account for the events of 1111:

(1) Biblioteca Apostolica Vaticana, MS Vat. lat. 1984—*Annales Romani*[31]

(2) Biblioteca Apostolica Vaticana, MS Ottob. lat. 3057—*Digesta Pauperis Scholaris Albini*[32]

14

(3) Biblioteca Apostolica Vaticana, MS Vat. lat. 8486—*Liber censuum*[33]

(4) Venice, Biblioteca Naz. Marciana, MS lat. XIV. 102 (2805)[34]

Most of the relevant documents are also found in the *Vita Paschalis* by Boso,[35] and the *Chronicon* of Montecassino. Boso, however, is very likely dependent on MS Vat. lat. 1984,[36] and the chronicle interpolates and distorts the documents.[37] Both traditions possess no independent value and will, therefore, not be discussed. The papal account for the events of February and April 1111 was edited by Ludwig Weiland, but at the time the manuscripts were not examined carefully. Weiland relied, instead, to a large extent on partial editions from the manuscripts which were already available in print: Augustin Theiner's *Codex diplomaticus* served instead of MS Vat. lat. 8486,[38] and Duchesne's edition of the *Liber pontificalis* was used for MS Vat. lat. 1984. A closer look at the manuscripts yields surprises.

All of the codices listed above for the 1111 account are closely related. Independently from each other, they relied upon the same source. P. Fabre showed this for the *Liber censuum* and the *Digesta* of Albinus,[39] and E. Stevenson demonstrated the same for the *Liber censuum*, Albinus and Vat. lat. 1984.[40] The common source, as will be shown, was Paschal's register, now lost.[41] Two among these manuscripts, Ottob. lat. 3057 and Marciana, lat. XIV. 102 (2805) are unfortunately incomplete. The codices just mentioned do not include the section for 12 February 1111, and, therefore, do not contain information that would be useful in the present context. Only MSS Vat. lat. 1984 and Vat. lat. 8486 with the complete series of documents for February and April 1111 are relevant here. The latter, the *Liber censuum* codex, presents the material, however, in a reorganized version, omitting the narratives that connect the documents. Thus only MS Vat. lat. 1984 remains for a closer analysis.

Duchesne reproduced various parts of this codex, just as Pertz had done before,[42] but "not in the disorder in which they are found in the manuscript but chronologically arranged."[43] Furthermore, he only edited what seemed particularly interesting. Both Duchesne and Pertz added to this "smoothed out" account the title *Annales Romani*, an identification not found in the codex. Completely unintentionally,[44] these scholars thus created the myth of a unified narrative, coining the expression *Relatio papalis*, also nowhere found in the manuscripts, for entries actually excerpted from Paschal's register for the spring of 1111, as will be shown.[45] This would not matter, however, if historians had not assumed, as a consequence, that MS Vat. lat. 1984 contains a composition analogous to the encyclical of Henry V, but written from the papal point of view.

Pertz and Duchesne had combined as *Annales Romani* different texts, which betray very eclectic interests, made during the 1120's by several hands.[46] The entries were scattered throughout Vat. lat. 1984 wherever a blank space was available. It is difficult to distinguish the hands of the scribes,[47] but Bethmann was probably correct when he claimed that a single hand was responsible for the Paschalian texts published by Duchesne as well as for some other historical material omitted in the so-called *Annales*.[48] Among these omissions are three documents from the spring of 1111, and the report about the Lateran council of 1112. They are all found on fol. 193v. Written in the tiny script of fol. 194r, they follow each other closely:

(1) Privilegium Paschalis II. pape prime conventionis inter se et H[enricum] r[egem]. Paschalis episcopus H[enrico] eiusque successoribus in perpetuum. Et divine legis . . . duos menses.[49]

(2) Conventio secunda vi extorta. Domnus P[aschalis] papa concedet . . . et imperium.[50]

(3) P[aschalis] episcopus servus servorum dei karissimo in Christo filio H[enrico] glorioso teutonicorum regi et per dei omnipotentis gratiam romanorum imperatori augusto salutem et apostolicam benedictionem. Regnum vestrum . . . et Portuensi.[51]

(4) Actio concilii contra heresim de investituris.[52]

These privileges of Paschal for Henry are the very documents the papal account was accused of having omitted. The first item, the *Privilegium prime conventionis,* is Paschal's concession of S. Maria in Turri promising the return of the *regalia*.[53] It is fortunate that the scribe even indicated that not only the documents on fol. 194r, which are included in the so-called *Annales*, but also the additional items on fol. 193v (omitted by Duchesne and Pertz) are derived from Paschal's register. The scribe added at the end of the second privilege: "Et hoc sacramentum ex parte pontificis sicut in registro residet. Eiusdem pape privilegium secundo etiam." These lines escaped the attention of all editors, Weiland included. They show that the excerpts from Paschal's register printed as part of the *Annales* were selected arbitrarily, and it can no longer be maintained that the papacy felt any need to hide the fact that Paschal promised Henry a return of *regalia* held by ecclesiastics in the empire. The register did include the corresponding privilege. The entries for 1111 in MS Vat. lat. 1984 are, it appears, reasonably complete.

As a result of this observation, the way is open for a reinterpretation of the events of 12 February 1111. The objectivity of the papal account appears vindicated, and the conclusion emerges that opposition to the return of the *regalia* was raised at first by Henry and eventually by royal supporters, but never by the adherents of Paschal II. The reason for the disagreement between the two parties is a different understanding of the concept *regalia* at the German court, on the one hand, and at the papal curia on the other. In a recent article, Johannes Fried argued convincingly that the meaning of the term *regalia* north of the Alps corresponded to the expressions found in the *Tractatus de investituris*.[54] According to this anonymous imperialist treatise, all property and fiscal rights which secular rulers had granted to the church were *regalia*.[55] Furthermore, as Fried pointed out, the empire did not distinguish royal gifts of any type from other temporal, ecclesiastical possessions.[56] The declaration which Henry signed at the Silver Gate on 12 February reflects this interpretation found at the German court. He promised to

16

preserve for monasteries and churches "omnia quae antecessores mei reges vel imperatores eis concesserunt vel tradiderunt."[57]

The German attitude also explains the misinterpretation of Paschal's intentions in Henry's encyclical: "ecclesie decimis et oblationibus suis contentae sint, rex vero omnia praedia et regalia . . . detineat."[58] If such had been the pope's request an uproar among ecclesiastics, assembled in St. Peter's basilica, could indeed have been expected. A wealthy and powerful section of the German nobility, the ecclesiastical princes, would suddenly be forced to live on tithes and occasional gifts. There is no need to attribute cynicism to the king when he writes in the encyclical that his emissaries at S. Maria knew that it would be impossible for the pope to keep his promise.[59]

In contrast to Henry, however, Paschal distinguished between *regalia* and other temporal possessions of the church that belonged to her by hereditary rights. Henry's privilege for the papacy, as it was hammered out by royal and papal emissaries in S. Maria in Turri, reflected Paschal's views: "[Rex] dimittet ecclesias liberas cum oblationibus et possessionibus quae ad regnum manifeste non pertinebant."[60] These properties might originally have been royal gifts, but they were not inalienable prerogatives of the *regnum* and thus in the papal opinion not *regalia*.[61] Once they had been given to churches they fell under the concept of "ecclesias cum oblationibus et hereditariis possessionibus que ad regnum manifeste non pertinebant,"[62] and would forever remain in the outright ownership of the church. Paschal only agreed to request bishops to return "regalia regi et regno quae ad regnum pertinebant."[63] Public rights, duties and lands were to be given up to eliminate royal need for investiture and homage. Certainly, imperial ecclesiastics would tend to lose, in addition to regalian income, some of their influence at the Salian court;[64] but it is not certain by any means that overburdened churchmen would not have been grateful for a partial release from public service,[65] particularly if, in exchange for the return of the *regalia*, Henry would have renounced investiture and returned the patrimony of St. Peter. A precondition for such an arrangement would, of course, have been Henry's acceptance of the Paschalian definition of *regalia*. This acceptance was not forthcoming, and before the controversy over investiture could be terminated a different solution had to be found.

Notes

1. Bibliographical references in the footnotes have been restricted to a minimum. For the general history of the period see Gerold Meyer von Knonau, *Jahrbücher des Deutschen Reiches unter Heinrich IV, und Heinrich V.,* Jahrbücher der Deutschen Geschichte XVII.6 (Leipzig, 1907), pp. 138–230 and Exkurs 1, pp. 370–90; *Handbook of Church History,* ed. Hubert Jedin, III (tr. Anselm Biggs): *The Church in the Age of Feudalism* (New York, 1969), pp.395–97; Wilhelm Schum, "Kaiser Heinrich V. und Papst Paschalis II. im Jahr 1112: Ein Beitrag zur Geschichte des Investitur-Streites auf Grund ungedruckten Materiales," *Jahrbücher der*

Königlichen Akademie gemeinnütziger Wissenschaften zu Erfurt, N. F. VIII (1877), 189–318; Adolf Waas, *Heinrich V., Gestalt und Verhängnis des letzten salischen Kaisers* (Munich, 1967). Research for this paper was done in Rome with the aid of summer grants from the National Endowment of the Humanities, the American Philosophical Society and the American Council of Learned Societies, for which I am very grateful.

2. In general, see *Quellen zur Entstehung des Kirchenstaates*, ed. Horst Fuhrmann, Historische Texte, Mittelalter VII (Göttingen, 1968) and Peter Partner, *The Lands of St. Peter* (Berkeley-Los Angeles, 1972).

3. MGH LL IV, I: 138–39, 140–42.

4. Ibid.: 142–45.

5. Ibid.: 138–39.

6. "Pasquale II e l' Ideale della Povertà della Chiesa," *Annuario dell 'Università Cattolica del Sacro Cuore* (Milan, 1965), pp. 203–29.

7. See the references given above, n. 2.

8. For Paschal's campaigns see especially the *Vita Paschalis II* by Pandulf, ed. Louis Duchesne, *Liber pontificalis*, Bibliothèque des Écoles françaises d'Athènes et de Rome III (repr., Paris, 1955), pp. 296–310, here p. 305: "Iamque bonus pontifex ad perficiendum quod inceperat machinas et tormenta et quaeque necessaria bello incredibili agilitate per biduum per suos parari fecerat."

9. See particularly Otto Vehse, "Benevent als Territorium des Kirchenstaates bis zum Beginn der avignonesischen Epoche. I. Teil," *Quellen und Forschungen aus italienischen Archiven und Bibliotheken* XXII (1930–31), 87–160.

10. See the corresponding document from Paschal's register preserved in the *Liber censuum*, Bibliothèque des Écoles françaises d'Athènes et de Rome, 3 vols., ed. Paul Fabre, Louis Duchesne and Guy Mollat (Paris, 1910–52), I: 407–8 and n. 2.

11. See, for example, the references given in the edition of *Goffridi Abbatis Vindocinensis Libelli*, MGH Lib. de lite II: 676–700, 677 and n. 2.

12. MGH LL IV, I: 137: "Patrimonia et possessiones beati Petri restituet et concedet, sicut a Karolo, Lodoico, Heinrico et aliis inperatoribus factum est, et tenere adiuvabit secundum suum posse."

13. Ibid.: 140.

14. Ibid.: 140. See the remarks p. 15, concerning the distinctive features of this declaration.

15. Ibid., p. 144: "Domnum papam Paschalem fideliter adiuvabo, ut papatum quiete et secure teneat; patrimonia et possessiones Romane ecclesiae que abstuli restituam, et cetera que iure habere debet more antecessorum meorum recuperare et tenere adiuvabo."

16. Walther Holtzmann, "England, Unteritalien und der Vertrag von Ponte Mammolo," *Neues Archiv* L (1935), 282–301.

17. Paschal soon had occasion to complain to Henry about non-fulfillment of the agreement. See JL 6295 (PL CLXIII: 288): "Siquidem nos per Dei gratiam boni sumus, licet quidam iussioni vestrae in his, quae B. Petro restitui praecepistis, adhuc noluerint obedire, incolae videlicet civitatis Castellanae, Castri Corcoli, Monti Alti, Montis Acuti et Narnienses; nos tamen ea et comitatus Peruginum, Eugubrinum, Tubertinum, Balneum Regis, castellum Felicitatis, ducatum Spoletanum, marchiam Ferraniam, et alias beati Petri possessiones per mandati vestri praeceptionem confidimus obtinere."

18. Paul Fabre, *Étude sur le Liber censuum* (Paris, 1892), p. 9.

19. *Liber censuum*, nos. 77–79; cf. Deusdedit, *Collectio canonum*, ed. Victor Wolf von Glanvell (Paderborn, 1905), bk. 3, cc. 184, 280, 282.

20. Deusdedit, *Collectio canonum*, p. xix; *Liber censuum*, I: 9; E. Stevenson, "Osservazioni sulla Collectio Canonum di Deusdedit," *Archivio della R. Società Romana di Storia Patria* VIII (1885), 305–98, esp. 332; cf. Ibid., 333. For the relationship between Deusdedit's works and those of Anselm of Lucca see the remarks by Horst Fuhrmann, *Einfluss und Verbreitung der pseudoisidorischen Fälschungen*, MGH Schriften XXIV.2 (Stuttgart, 1973), p. 528.

21. JL 6143–JL 6145; the citations are discussed in my *The Early Councils of Pope Paschal II*, Pontifical Institute of Mediaeval Studies, Toronto (forthcoming).

18

22. It cannot be assumed that this was Paschal's only use of the work of Deusdedit. It is usually very difficult, though, to distinguish in new conciliar canons the use of various reform collections.

23. MGH LL IV, i: 660–78.

24. See Suger, *Vita Ludovici grossi regis*, chap. 10, ed. H. Waquet, *Les Classiques de l'Histoire de France au Moyen* âge xi (Paris, 1929), pp. 56–58, and the discussions by Robert Benson, *The Bishop-Elect: A Study in Medieval Ecclesiastical Office* (Princeton, 1968), pp. 242–44 (esp. nn. 52–53) as well as those by Alfons Becker, *Studien zum Investiturproblem in Frankreich* (Saarbrücken, 1955), esp. pp. 99ff. *Tractatus de investitura episcoporum*, ed. Ernst Bernheim, MGH Lib. de lite ii: 495–504, 498: "Adrianus papa . . . Karolo magno eiusque successoribus, futuris imperatoribus, sub anathemate concessit patriciatum Romanum, et per se vel per nuncios suos confirmationem in electione vel in consecratione Romani pontificis concessit; et investituras episcoporum eis determinavit, ut non consecretur episcopus, qui per regem vel imperatorem non introierit pure et integre, exceptis quos papas Romanus investire et consecrare debet ex antiquo dono regum et imperatorum cum aliis que vocantur regalia, id est a regibus et imperatoribus pontificibus Romanis data in fundis et reditibus."

25. Cf. Johannes Fried, "Der Regalienbegriff im 11. und 12. Jahrhundert," *Deutsches Archiv* xxix (1973), 450–528, here pp. 505–6.

26. See above n. 17.

27. The controversies surrounding the authenticity of individual letters in the *Codex Udalrici* hardly touch the encyclical because the chronicle tradition uniformly supports the readings of the *Codex*. Cf. W. Wattenbach and R. Holtzmann, *Deutschlands Geschichtsquellen* (Tübingen, 1948), i.3: 439–42, with earlier bibliography; Peter Classen, "Heinrich IV. Briefe im Codex Udalrici," *Deutsches Archiv* xx (1964), 115–29 and Robert Somerville, "Honorius II, Conrad and Lothar III," *Archivum Historiae Pontificiae* x (1972), 341–46 are two recent contributions that partially invalidate some of the findings of Franz-Josef Schmale, "Fiktionen im Codex Udalrici," *Zeitschrift für bayerische Landesgeschichte* xx (1957), 437–74.

28. MGH LL IV, i: 150–51, "De traditione vero in nos et in nostros sic se res habet. Vix portas civitatis ingressi sumus, cum ex nostris infra menia secure vagantibus quidam vulnerati, alii interfecti sunt, omnes vero spoliati aut capti sunt. Ego tamen quasi pro levi causa non motus, bona et tranquilla mente usque ad ecclesiae beati Petri ianuas cum processione perveni . . . :Ego Heinricus Dei . . . subtrahere recuso [ibid.: 140]. Hoc decreto a me lecto et subscripto, petii ab eo, ut sicut in carta conventionis eius scriptum est, mihi adimpleret. Haec est carta conventionis eius ad me: Domnus papa precipiet . . . eum habere potuero. [ibid.: 138–39]. . . . Cum ergo supradictae postulationi insisterem, scilicet ut cum iustitia et auctoritate promissam mihi conventionem firmaret, universis in faciem eius resistentibus et decreto suo planam heresim inclamantibus, scilicet episcopis, abbatibus, tam suis quam nostris, et omnibus ecclesiae filiis, hoc, si salva pace ecclesiae dici potest, privilegium proferre voluit. Paschalis episcopus servus . . . reddituri pro animabus eorum." [ibid.: 140–41]

29. Ibid.: 147–50: "Post haec idem rex Romam accessit terito Idus, id est XI. die Februarias, in sabbato videlicet ante quinquagesima. Altero die oviam ei domnus papa misit in Montem Gaudii, qui et Mons Malus dicitur, signiferos cum bandis, scriniarii, iudices et stratores. Maxima etiam populi multitudo ei cum ramis occurrit. Duo iusta priorum imperatorum consuetudinem iuramenta, unum ante ponticellum, alterum ante portam porticus Romanorum populo fecit. Ante portam a Iudeis, in porta a Grecis cantando exsceptus est. Illic omnis Romanae urbis clerus convenerat ex precepto pontificis. Et eum ex equo descendentem usque ad Sancti Petri gradus cum laudibus deduxerunt. Cum vero ad superiora graduum ascendisset, illic domnus papa cum episcopis pluribus, cum cardinalibus presbiteris et diaconibus, cum subdiaconibus et ceteris scole cantorum ministris affuit. Ad cuius vestigia cum rex corruisset, post pedum oscula ad oris oscula elevatus est. Ter se invicem complexi, ter se invicem osculati sunt. Mox dexteram pontificis tenens cum magno populorum gaudio et clamore ad portam pervenit argenteam. Ibi ex libro professionem imperatoriam fecit, et a pontifice imperator designatus est; . . . Post ingressum basilicae cum in Rotam porfireticam pervenisset, positis utrimque sedibus consederunt. Pontifex refutationem investiturae et

cetera, quae in conventionis carta scripta fuerant, requisivit, paratus et ipse que in alia conventionis carta scripta fuerant adimplere. Ille cum episcopis suis et principibus secessit in partem iusta secretarium; ibi diutius quod eis placuit tractaverunt. In quo tractatu interfuerunt Longobardi episcopi tres. . . . Cum autem longior se hora protraeret, missis nuntiis pontifex conventionis supradicte tenorem repetiit adinpleri. Tunc episcopi transalpini ad pontificis vestigia corruerunt et ad oris oscula surrexerunt. Set post paululum familiares regi dolos suos paulatim aperire coeperunt, dicentes: scriptum illut, quod condictum fuerat, non posse firmari auctoritate et iustitia. Quibus cum euangelica et apostolica obiceretur auctoritas, quia et 'reddenda sunt cesari quae sunt cesaris' et 'nemo militans Deo implicat se negotiis saecularibus', cum armorum usus, secundum beatum Ambrosium, ab episcopali officio alienus sit. Cum hec et alia illis apostolica et canonica capitula obicerentur, illi tamen in dolositate sua et pertinacia permanebant. Cum iam dies declinaret in vespera, consultum a fratribus, ut rex eodem die coronaretur, ceterorum tractatus in sequentem ebdomadam differretur. Illi etiam hoc adversati sunt. Inter haec tam pontifex quamque et prefectus et omnes, qui cum eo erant, a militibus armatis custodiebantur. Vix tandem ad altare beati Petri pro audiendis missae officiis conscenderunt, vix ad sacramenta divina conficienda panem, vinum et aquam invenire potuerunt. Post missam ex cathedra descendere compulsus pontifex deorsum ante confessionem beati Petri cum fratribus sedit. Ibi usque ad noctis tenebras ab armatis militibus custoditus. Inde ad ospitium extra aecclesiae atrium cum fratribus deductus est . . . Factus est igitur in Urbe tota repentinus tumultus, dolor et gemitus."

30. Knonau, *Jahrbücher*, VI: 183.

31. Duchesne, *Liber pontificalis*, II: 329–50, here particularly pp. 338–43; the manuscript is described pp. xxii–xxiii. The codex is now divided into two parts, MSS Vat. lat. 1984 and Vat. lat. 1984 A. For descriptions see also B. Nogara, *Codices Vaticani Latini* (Rome, 1912), III: 387–90; V. W. von Glanvell, ed., *Die Kanonessammlung des Kardinals Deusdedit* (Paderborn, 1905), pp. xxxi–xxxiii; still useful is the old description by Ludwig von Bethmann, "Die ältesten Streitschriften über die Papstwahl," *Archiv* XI (1858), 841–49. See also *Repertorium fontium historiae medii aevi* (Rome, 1967), II: 324.

32. For Albinus see *Dizionario Biografico degli Italiani* (1960), II: 11–12 (V. Fenicchia) and most recently *Repertorium fontium*, II: 324. The *Digesta* were partially edited in the *Liber censuum*, II: 87–137, here especially pp. 135–37, no. 54. For the *Liber censuum*, see above, n. 10.

33. Edited from this manuscript by P. Fabre and L. Duchesne, 2 vols., and G. Mollat, vol. 3. See above, n. 10.

34. The text ends after the first lines of MGH LL IV, I: 139: "id est Petrus Leonis." The volume consists of old parchment folios from Aquileia, collected by G. Fontanini in 1713 and mounted on paper. The 1111 text is found on p. 352, on a mounted parchment folio written in the first half of the twelfth century. Cf. Wilhelm Schum, "Beiträge zur deutschen Kaiserdiplomatik aus italienischen Archiven," *Neues Archiv* I (1876), 121–58, 130–31.

35. Duchesne, *Liber Pontificalis* II: 369.

36. Fritz Geisthardt, *Der Kämmerer Boso*. Historische Studien Ebering CCXCIII (Berlin, 1936), p. 9.

37. For the *Chronicon* see now Hartmut Hoffmann, "Studien zur Chronik von Montecassino," *Deutsches Archiv* XXIX (1973), 59–162. A detailed analysis of the numerous pertinent chronicle accounts satisfied the present author that they also are irrelevant in the present context. The analysis is here omitted because of lack of space.

38. *Codex diplomaticus dominii temporalis s. sedis* (Rome, 1861), I: 10–11.

39. *Liber censuum*, I, esp. pp. 6–7.

40. Stevenson, "Osservazioni," p. 375.

41. For traces of the register in the *Liber censuum*, Albinus and Vat. lat. 1984, see Stevenson, "Osservazioni," p. 373 n. 2.

42. MGH SS V: 468–89.

43. Duchesne, *Liber pontificalis*, II: 329.

44. See G. H. Pertz, "Bemerkungen über einzelne Handschriften und Urkundenn," *Archiv* V (1824), 80–86, and Duchesne, *Liber Pontificalis*, II: xxiii, no. 18, and p. 229.

45. Duchesne, *Liber Pontificalis*, II: 338–43 = MGH LL IV, I: 147–50.

46. See Pertz, "Bemerkungen," pp. 80–86, and Duchesne, *Liber Pontificalis*, II: xxiii: "On a puisé aux chroniques, aux registres pontificaux, aux collections de pièces mises en circulation par les défenseurs du pape et par les tenants des revendications impériales, et on l'a fait avec un tel éclectisme qu'il serait difficile de déterminer la cause que l'on a entendu servir. Peut-être tenait-on surtout à se renseigner." For the date see now Dieter Hägermann, "Untersuchungen zum Papstwahldekret 1059," *Zeitschrift der Savigny-Stiftung für Rechtsgeschichte*, Kan. Abt. LVI (1970), 163 n. 19.

47. The hand which Bethmann designated as no. 4 ("Streitschriften," esp. p. 842, and pp. 847–49), wrote the curial *a*. Cf. Reinhard Elze, "Der Liber Censuum des Cencius (Cod. Vat. lat. 8486) von 1192 bis 1228," *Bullettino dell' "Archivio paleografico Italiano,"* n. s. II–III (1956–57), 251–70, esp. p. 263, where the letter is discussed in a different context.

48. Bethmann, "Streitschriften," pp. 447–48. It is impossible to be more definite because of the poor condition of the manuscript. On some of the folios portions of the tiny script were redrawn. The conclusions drawn by Nogara, *Codices Latini*, p. 390, are very similar.

49. MGH LL IV, I: 140–42. The narrative of MS Vat. lat. 1984 at the end of the privilege is included in small print on p. 142.

50. Cf. MGH LL IV, I: 142.

51. MGH LL IV, I: 144–45 ("apostolica" MS). Again the Vat. lat. 1984 text was added in small print.

52. Ibid.: 570–74.

53. Ibid.: 140–42.

54. For the *Tractatus* see above n. 24. For the development of the concept *regalia* see Fried, "Regalienbegriff," esp. pp. 467–81, and Benson, *The Bishop-Elect*, pp. 203–50, esp. pp. 218ff.

55. See the excerpt cited above in n. 24.

56. Fried, "Regalienbegriff," p. 470, and esp. n. 64.

57. MGH LL IV, I: 140.

58. Ibid.: 150. See also Fried, "Regalienbegriff," p. 478.

59. MGH LL IV, I: 150: "nostris itidem firmantibus, si hoc . . . complesset—quod tamen nullo modo posse fieri sciebant—me quoque investituras . . . refutaturum."

60. Ibid.: 137.

61. See Gerhoch von Reichersberg, *De edificio Dei*, chap. 17 (MGH Lib. de lite III: 149, ll. 19–22): "sic et modo inter multas aecclesiarum villas, quas partim a regibus, partim ab aliis Deum timentibus accepit aecclesia, non apparet aliquas eam villas regalis pertinentiae habere, pro quibus debeat aut fiscum regalem implere aut milites ad procinctum stipendiare." Cf. Fried, "Regalienbegriff," p. 473, n. 72.

62. MGH LL IV, I: 141.

63. Ibid.: 138–39; see also Ibid.: 141: "Tibi . . . et regno regalia illa dimittenda precipimus que ad regnum manifeste pertinebant."

64. The king could still bestow *regalia* on ecclesiastics, but not as a matter of course: "nec se deinceps nisi per gratiam regis de ipsis regalibus intromittant." (Ibid.: 141. See the discussion by Benson, *The Bishop Elect*, pp. 245–47.) See also the careful wording of Paschal's privilege (MGH LL IV, I: 140–42). Absences from the diocese are allowed for several reasons, but they ought not to be excessive.

65. For the demanding life of an ambitious archbishop see for example the recent study by Georg Jenal, *Erzbischof Anno II. von Köln (1056–75) und sein politisches Wirken*, Monographien zur Geschichte des Mittelalters VIII. 1–2 (Stuttgart, 1974–75).

X

Opposition to Pope Paschal II:
Some Comments on the Lateran Council of 1112*

The pontificate of Paschal II (1099—1118) was beset by not a few external and internal difficulties. Historians generally tend to assume that opposition to Paschal within the church was at its height in connection with his well-known proposal of February 1111 to return r e g a l i a of the church to the German ruler[1]. This was, however, not the case[2]. Hostility to Paschal II on the part of the Italian clergy[3] and the curia was not in evidence until after the pope concluded the agreement of Ponte Mammolo with King Henry V of Germany in April 1111[4]. At the time, Paschal and most members of the Roman clergy were Henry's prisoners, and the privilege was granted in return for their liberty. It will not

* Research for this paper was done with the aid of a Fellowship for Independent Study and Research from the American Council of Learned Societies during my appointment as Fellow of the Radcliffe Institute. I am most grateful to Professor R. Somerville who kindly read a first draft of this article.

[1] For the text of the grant see MGH Const. 1, 138—142, especially nos. 85 and 90: Paschalis II. privilegium primae conventionis. Secondary literature is voluminous, e.g. F. KEMPF et al., The Church in the Age of Feudalism, trans. A. Biggs (= Handbook of Church History, eds. H. Jedin and J. Dolan, 3) New York 1969, 392—398 and p. 542; A. FLICHE, La Réforme grégorienne et la Reconquête chrétienne (1057—1123) (= Histoire de l'Eglise, 8) Paris 1950, 359—361; G. MEYER von KNONAU, Jahrbücher des Deutschen Reiches unter Heinrich IV. und Heinrich V. (= Jahrbücher der Deutschen Geschichte 17/6) Leipzig 1907, 138—230; R. BENSON, The Bishop-Elect, A Study in Medieval Ecclesiastical Office, Princeton 1968, 203—250; M. J. WILKS, Ecclesiastica and Regalia: Papal Investiture Policy from the Council of Guastalla to the First Lateran Council, 1106—23, in: Studies in Church History 7, Cambridge 1971, 69—85; S. CHODOROW, Ideology and Canon Law in the Crisis of 1111, in: Proceedings of the Fourth International Congress of Medieval Canon Law (Toronto 1972), (= Monumenta iuris canonici, ser. C., subsidia 5) Vatican City 1976, 55—80; F. FRIED, Der Regalienbegriff im 11. und 12. Jahrhundert, in: DA 29 (1973) 450—528; U.-R. BLUMENTHAL, Patrimonia and Regalia in 1111, in: Law, Church, and Society: Essays in Honor of Stephan Kuttner, Philadelphia 1977, 9—20.

[2] See FRIED, Regalienbegriff, and BLUMENTHAL, Patrimonia, cited in the preceding note.

[3] Bishops from northern Italy acted as mediators between German and other Italian ecclesiastics in St. Peter's basilica on February 12, 1111 (MGH Const. 1, no. 99, p. 148).

[4] MGH Const. 1, 142—147, nos. 91—95, especially no. 96, pp. 144—145; Privilegium Paschalis II. de investituris.

come as a surprise, therefore, that it contained far reaching concessions to the king. Henry was granted the imperial crown and the right to invest ecclesiastics of the Empire with their offices through ring and staff. The prelates were to be elected in the imperial presence and, it was stated, they could not be consecrated unless they had first bound themselves to the ruler through homage. The agreement of Ponte Mammolo thus guaranteed Henry practically free disposal of the offices of the German church and of all its wealth. German ecclesiastics would henceforth be primarily subjects of the German ruler and their dependence on the papacy could be expected to be nominal at best[5]. The church was stunned once the privilege of Ponte Mammolo became known and the question arose whether it was legal[6]. With a stroke of the pen Paschal had signed away almost all of the tenets for which the reform papacy and Paschal himself had fought for decades: lay investiture, prohibited directly for the first time by Pope Gregory VII[7]; lay homage, outlawed since the council of Clermont held by Urban II[8]; and indirectly free elections as well, a key demand since the time of Pope Leo IX and the sine qua non for the liberty of the church[9]. All that remained after Ponte Mammolo of the gains won during the investiture struggle was the prohibition of simony, but even this one could doubt, for lay investiture, lay homage, and simony were closely related in the eyes of most reformers[10]. Paschal, it is true, had repeatedly obtained solemn promises from Henry V that he, Henry, would restore the *patrimonia* of the Holy See, that is, territories, provinces, towns and islands which had been granted in previous imperial donations to St. Peter, but these promises remained a dead letter.

The synod of 1112, which is the subject of this paper, met in response to these events[11]. It represents the most concentrated expression of ecclesiastical oppo-

---

[5] In addition to the bibliography indicated in n. 1 above see W. SCHUM, Kaiser Heinrich V. und Papst Paschalis II. im Jahre 1112, in: Jahrbücher der Königlichen Akademie gemeinnütziger Wissenschaften zu Erfurt, n. s. 8 (1877) 189—318.

[6] See CHODOROW, 'Ideology and Canon Law.'

[7] Das Register Gregors VII., ed. E. CASPAR, MGH Epistolae selectae 2/1—2 (Berlin 1920 bis 1923), no. 6.5b, c. 3, p. 403 with G. B. BORINO, Il decreto di Gregorio VII contro le investiture fu "promulgato" nel 1075, in: Studi Gregoriani 6 (1959—1961) 329—348; cf. idem, L'Investitura laica dal decreto di Nicolò II al decreto di Gregorio VII, ibid. 5 (1956) 345—359.

[8] R. SOMERVILLE, The Councils of Urban II, 1: Decreta Claromontensia, Annuarium Historiae Conciliorum Supplementum 1, Amsterdam 1972, 78, c. 15 and the other references given under no. 19, p. 145.

[9] See in general P. SCHMID, Der Begriff der kanonischen Wahl in den Anfängen des Investiturstreits, Stuttgart 1926.

[10] J. Gilchrist, "Simoniaca Haeresis" and the Problem of Orders from Leo IX to Gratian, in: Proceedings of the Second International Congress of Medieval Canon Law (Boston 1963), (= Monumenta iuris canonici, ser. C, subsidia 1), Vatican City 1965, 209—235, 215.

[11] The records of the synod are published partially by L. WEILAND, MGH Const. 1, 570—574, nos. 399 and 400 and partially by L. DUCHESNE, Le Liber Pontificalis, (= Biblio-

sition to Pope Paschal II. An analysis of this council's events is, therefore, a prerequisite, if hostility to Paschal and his alleged inadequacy as Roman pontiff is to be explained. This paper will show that hostility to Paschal in 1112 ran very deep indeed and was more powerful than hitherto assumed. At the same time, however, it will be seen that this hostility revolved around a single issue, the investiture privilege for Henry V granted at Ponte Mammolo and the supposedly heretical character of this document.

The council's most obvious activity was the revocation of the privilege of Ponte Mammolo [12]. The implications of this action for the idea of papal primacy deserve to be noted [13], but it is perhaps more remarkable yet that the synod appears to have made an attempt either to depose Paschal II or to obtain his abdication. The evidence in the fragmentary records of the council [14] for the proceedings against the pope is indirect, but if only the wish to revoke the privilege of Ponte Mammolo had animated the synod its very striking hostility to Paschal, which will become evident in the course of this paper, could not be explained. At least since June 1111 Paschal had declared himself willing to make amends for his concessions to the German emperor, granted 'for the sake of his brethren and sons, [to avoid] the destruction of the city and the whole province,' as the pontiff wrote in a letter to Cardinals John of Tusculum and Leo of Ostia

thèque des Ecoles Françaises d'Athènes et de Rome, 2) Paris 1892, reprinted 1955, 369—371 (abbreviated below LP 2); see also G. D. MANSI, Amplissima ... conciliorum collectio, 20, Venice 1776, 1212—1214; 21, Venice 1776, 49—53 and 68—70 (abbreviated below Mansi). Narrative accounts of the synod are most detailed in C. J. HEFELE - H. LECLERCQ, Histoire des conciles, 5/1, Paris 1912, 532—534; MEYER VON KNONAU, Jahrbücher 17/6, 231—236; see also the secondary literature indicated above nn. 1 and 5 as well as P. R. MCKEON, The Lateran Council of 1112, the "Heresy" of Lay Investiture, and the Excommunication of Henry V, in: Medievalia et Humanistica, 17 (1966) 3—12.

[12] The privilege was formally condemned at the final session, see MGH Const. 1.572 and LP 2.370—371: *Privilegium illud, quod non est privilegium set vere debet dici pravilegium, pro liberatione captivorum et Ecclesie a domno papa Paschali per violentiam Henrici regis extortum, nos omnes, in hoc sancto concilio cum eodem domno papa congregato, canonica censura et ecclesiastica auctoritate, iudicio sancti Spiritus dampnatum et irritum esse iudicamus atque omnino cassamus, et ne quit auctoritatis et efficacitatis habeat penitus excommunicamus. Ideo autem dampnatum est quia in eo privilegio continetur quod electus canonice a clero et populo a nemine consecretur, nisi prius a rege investiatur, quod est contra Spiritum sanctum et canonicam institutionem.*

[13] MCKEON, The Lateran Council of 1112, noted in passing that the polemics of 1111 — 1112 "furnished in prototype many ideas which would later find a place in the arguments of advocates of Conciliarism." (p. 3) The study of B. TIERNEY, Foundations of the Conciliar Theory, Cambridge/Engl. 1955, begins with the analysis of relevant Decretist texts and does not refer to the synod of 1112.

[14] Both recensions of the conciliar acta (recension 1 = MGH Const. 1, 571—572; recension 2 = LP 2, 370—371) contain no information for the first three days of the meeting. Recension 1 records only the final session, recension 2 includes in addition brief references to the two preceding sessions.

who acted as spokesmen for a dissatisfied group of cardinals who had gathered in Rome to protest against the privilege[15]. The pontiff wrote in a similar vein to his French legate, Girard of Angoulême, to Ivo of Chartres, and perhaps others[16], but delayed decisive action against the privilege, in part probably because some papal advisors feared that such a step might bring with it yet greater evils[17]. The only demands Paschal resisted on account of his oath at Ponte Mammolo were calls for the excommunication of Henry V and for the official designation of lay investiture as heresy, but these demands were of secondary importance to Paschal's critics and subsumed under a request for a revocation of Paschal's grant[18]. The pontiff seemed willing, although not enthusiastic, to accommodate his opponents on this point. More must have been at stake, therefore. It is sometimes thought that Paschal abdicated in the fall of 1111 when he withdrew to the island of Pontin or that he offered to resign at the 1112 synod[19]. The evidence for this is very ambiguous. Everything, however, points to the fact that rumors of abdication and/or deposition were rife in Rome in 1111 and 1112. Emperor Henry V was informed by one of his supporters that 'a synod was to be held in Rome at which Pope Paschal was to be deposed and another elected ... because the Lord Paschal does not dare to excommunicate you ...'[20]

---

[15] JL 6301, dated Terracina, July 5 [1111]: ... *nos tamen confisi de misericordia divina, pro animae nostrae salute cogitamus, et commissum, quod pro fratribus atque filiis, pro excidio urbis et universae provinciae fecimus, emendare curabimus.*

[16] The letter to Girard of Angoulême was published by SCHUM, Kaiser Heinrich V., 278—279; Paschal's letter to Ivo of Chartres did not survive, but the canonist quoted from it in two of his epistles, no. 233 = Migne PL 162, 236 (... *Nec ista contra domnum papam dico, quia quibusdam litteris mihi scripsit se coactum fecisse quod fecit, et adhuc se prohibere quod prohibuit, quamvis quaedam nefanda quibusdam nefandis scripta permiserit* ...) and in ep. no. 236 to Josceran of Lyons = ed. E. Sackur, MGH Libelli de lite 2, 647—654, p. 650, lines 19—23; this same letter refers ibid., line 21, to letters Paschal had sent *quibusdam nostris*, but without naming addressees.

[17] Ibid., 651, lines 16—18: ... *Quodsi papa adhuc in Teutonicum regem debitam severitatem non exercet, credimus, quia consulte differt secundum consilium quorundam doctorum, qui consulunt quedam admittenda pericula, ut possint vitari maiora* ...

[18] See Bruno of Segni's letter to Pope Paschal II, ed. E. Sackur, MGH Libelli de lite 2, 564—565; Placidus of Nonantola, Liber de honore ecclesiae, eds. L. von Heinemann and E. Sackur, MGH Libelli de lite 2.566—639, c. 118, especially pp. 625—626 and cc. 133 and 134 (p. 629).

[19] The sources: Historia pontificum et comitum Engolismensium, ed. Bouquet, in: Recueil des historiens des Gaules et de la France 12, Paris 1877, 394; Suger of St. Denis, Vita Ludovici Grossi, ed. H. Waquet, Paris 1929, and the Epistola de Paschali papa, ed. E. Sackur, MGH Libelli de lite 2.671, lines 5—18, are quoted extensively by SCHUM, 'Kaiser Heinrich V.,' 220—222; see also HEFELE - LECLERCQ, Histoire des Conciles 5/1.532 and n. 2 and MCKEON, Lateran Council, p. 6. The Epistola de Paschali papa can no longer be attributed to Hildebert of Lavardin, see P. VON MOOS, Hildebert von Lavardin: 1056—1133, Stuttgart 1965, 337—340.

[20] Codex Udalricus, no. 161, ed. P. Jaffé, Monumenta Bambergensia, Bibliotheca rerum germanicarum 5, Berlin 1869, 288: *Notum igitur vobis facio, quod audivi: synodum videlicet*

The information conveyed to the emperor by Bishop Azo was correct. As the following analysis of the surviving records will show the council met in order to judge the pope, canonical prohibitions notwithstanding. The principle, 'the pope is to be judged by no one'[21], was appealed to for the first time during the schism between Symmachus (498—514) and Laurentius (498 — c. 505), when the supporters of the former referred to the protocol of a synod of Sinuessa held allegedly in 303 near Capua where, it was said, Pope Marcellinus was obliged to judge himself because the assembly refused to do so although it had found Marcellinus guilty of an error in faith[22]. The Symmachian party further strengthened their claim that the pope could not be judged by anyone with a reference to a pseudo-constitution of Sylvester I, who was said to have decreed at a synod in the presence of Emperor Constantine the Great that nobody could judge the pope, 'nobody shall judge the Holy See'[23]. Pope Nicholas I quoted both instances in the letter he sent in 865 to the Byzantine Emperor Michael III in defense of the Patriarch Ignatius[24], and subsequently the decree of Sylvester I and/or the letter of Nicholas the Great were quoted frequently, last not least in the numerous canon law collections from the late eleventh- and early twelfth century, including the collections of Anselm of Lucca[25], Cardinal Deusdedit[26], and Ivo of Chartres[27]. The D i c t a t u s p a p a e of Gregory VII, c. 19, stated simply:

Romae fieri, in qua asserunt domnum papam P(aschalem) deponi et alterum debere eligi, qui omne consilium pacis, quod cum domno P(aschali) firmastis, dissolvat; pro eo quod domnus P(aschalis) non audet vos propter factas inter vos et ipsum securitates excommunicare.

[21] Codex iuris canonici c. 1556.

[22] Migne PL 6, 9—20; GRATIAN, Decretum D.21 c. 7; for details and a bibliography see H. ZIMMERMANN, Papstabsetzungen des Mittelalters, Graz 1968, 2.

[23] Ibid. and Mansi 2.632, c. 20.

[24] JE 2796 = MGH Epistolae Karolini aevi 4, Berlin 1925, 454—487.

[25] Collectio canonum 1.19, ed. F. Thaner, Innsbruck 1906—15; reprinted Aalen 1965, 15. For Anselm see Dizionario biografico degli Italiani 3 (1961) 399 ff. (C. Violante); A. VAN HOVE, Prolegomena ad codicem iuris canonici, 2nd rev. ed., Mechlin and Rome 1945, 323—324; A. STICKLER, Historia iuris canonici latini, Turin 1950, 1.170—171; P. FOURNIER — G. LE BRAS, Histoire des collections canoniques en occident 2, Paris 1932, reprinted Aalen 1972, 25—37; a detailed and recent bibliography can be found in H. FUHRMANN, Einfluß und Verbreitung der pseudoisidorischen Fälschungen, (= MGH Schriften 24/2) Stuttgart 1973, 509—522.

[26] Die Kanonessammlung des Kardinals Deusdedit 1.89, ed. V. W. von Glanvell, Paderborn 1905; reprinted Aalen 1967, 74; for Deusdedit see VAN HOVE, Prolegomena, 324—325; STICKLER, Historia 1.172; FOURNIER - LE BRAS, Histoire 2.37—53; FUHRMANN, Fälschungen 2.522—533.

[27] Ivo of Chartres, Decretum 5.8 = Migne PL 161.324; Panormia 4.5 = Migne PL 161.1183; for Ivo see VAN HOVE, Prolegomena, 331—332; STICKLER, Historia 1.180 f.; FOURNIER - LE BRAS, Histoire 2.55—114; FUHRMANN, Fälschungen 2.542—562; see also GRATIAN, D. 21 c. 7 and C. 9 q. 3 c. 13 for further quotations of the decree.

'That he [the pope] is not to be judged by anyone'[28]. The so-called D i c t a t u s of Avranches was more precise: 'The pope cannot be judged by anyone, even although he denies the faith as shown by [the case of] Marcellinus'[29]. It is the case of Marcellinus that is referred to by Ivo of Chartres together with the threefold denial of Christ by the Apostle Peter in his letter to Josceran of Lyons in order to prove that the council called by Josceran to meet at Anse was useless and illegal because it was directed against a person who could not be judged[30].

In Italy, however, feelings ran so high that the familiar prohibition against subjecting the pontiff to human judgment was overlooked, as for example by Placidus of Nonantola, one of the best known polemicists of late 1111[31]. Placidus' influence can perhaps be debated[32], but it is certain that his omission of the customary references to papal judicial immunity and his unusual statement on the corporate nature of the church[33] corresponded to the sentiments of many, for neither Paschal nor his supporters could prevent the gathering of the Lateran

---

[28] Das Register Gregors VII., 2.55a, 206: Quod a nemine ipse iudicari debeat. Recent discussions of the nature of the Dictatus papae are found in G. B. BORINO, Un' ipotesi sul "Dictatus papae" di Gregorio VII, in: Archivio della R. Deputazione Romana di Storia Patria 67 (1944) 237—252; K. HOFMANN, Der "Dictatus Papae" Gregors VII. als Index einer Kanonessammlung? in: Studi Gregoriani 1 (1947) 531—537; S. KUTTNER, Liber canonicus. A Note on "Dictatus papae" c. 17, in: Studi Gregoriani 2 (1947) 387—401; H. MORDEK, Proprie auctoritates apostolice sedis: Ein zweiter Dictatus papae Gregors VII.? in: DA 28 (1972) 105—132; F. KEMPF, S. I., Ein zweiter Dictatus Papae? Ein Beitrag zum Depositionsanspruch Gregors VII, in: Archivum Historiae Pontificiae 13 (1975) 119—139.

[29] MORDEK, Proprie auctoritates, 115, c. 7: A nemine papa iudicari potest, etiamsi fidem negaverit ut de Marcellino constat.

[30] Ep. 236 = MGH Libelli de lite 2, 650, lines 23—26 and p. 652, lines 3—7: Ad hoc non videtur nobis utile consilium ad illa concilia convenire, in quibus non possumus eas personas, contra quas agitur, condempnare vel iudicare, quia nec nostro nec ullius hominum probantur subiacere iudicio. Cf. above n. 16. On the position of Ivo of Chartres during the investiture controversy see especially H. HOFMANN, Ivo von Chartres und die Lösung des Investiturproblems, in: DA 15 (1959) 393—440, and in general R. SPRANDEL, Ivo von Chartres und seine Stellung in der Kirchengeschichte, in: Pariser Historische Studien 1, Stuttgart 1962.

[31] For a discussion of Placidus' thought see C. MIRBT, Die Publizistik im Zeitalter Gregors VII., Leipzig 1894, 524—530; A. SCHARNAGL, Der Begriff der Investitur in den Quellen und der Literatur des Investiturstreits, (= Kirchenrechtliche Abhandlungen 56) Stuttgart 1908, 103—110; BENSON, The Bishop-Elect, 247—250.

[32] Only one complete manuscript of Placidus' Liber de honore ecclesiae is known to have survived today (MGH Libelli de lite 2, 567—568). Placidus did, however, influence Gratian. S. Kuttner could show that Gratian included several texts of Placidus which Gratian derived from the Collection in Three Books. See S. KUTTNER, Urban II and Gratian, in: Traditio 24 (1968) 504—505 and idem, Urbano II, Placido da Nonantula e Graziano, in: Annali della Facoltà di Giurisprudenza 9 (1970). For the Collection in Three Books see J. ERICKSON, The Collection in Three Books and Gratian's Decretum, in: Bulletin of Medieval Canon Law n. s. 2 (1972) 67—75 with complete bibilography.

[33] Placidus, c. 2 = MGH Libelli de lite 2, 575, lines 34—35: Aecclesiam esse congregationem fidelium vel potius convocationem notissimum est...

council. Paschal's opponents overcame a second obstacle as well. Not only could a pope not be judged, but he had also the right to alter, renew or grant dispensation from old law 'because of the necessity of times,' or if need be create new law[34]. Seen in this light the agreement of Ponte Mammolo might appear unassailable. At this point Placidus came once again to the rescue of the critics of Paschal II. The canonical doctrine of dispensation was based on statements of Popes Innocent I (401?—417) and Leo the Great (440—461) which differed in precision[35]. In the Liber de honore ecclesiae Placidus explained: 'There are some who say that the Roman popes have always had the right to create new law; this we do not only not deny, but even strongly affirm'[36]. But instead of referring to the principles enunciated by Pope Innocent I who did not differentiate between types of law, Placidus stressed the limits of legal flexibility in the sense of Leo the Great who had distinguished unalterable law from laws that might be tempered if need arose. Placidus continued the passage just quoted with an argument 'ex ratione,' that is, based on his personal reasoning: '... But it should be most carefully noted that he can create new law where the holy fathers and especially the apostles and evangelists did not decree anything'[37]. Placidus

---

[34] On the meaning of 'new law' under the reform papacy see G. B. LADNER, Two Gregorian Letters: On the sources and Nature of Gregory VII' Reform Ideology, in: Studi Gregoriani 5 (1956) 221—242 with the references indicated; cf. S. KUTTNER, Urban II and the Doctrine of Interpretation: A Turning Point? in: Post Scripta, Essays on Medieval Law and the Emergence of the European State in Honor of Gaines Post, Studia Gratiana 15 (1972) 53—85.

[35] Ibid. 62—69. For Innocent I see JK 303, cap. 5—9 = Migne PL 20, 532: *Jam ergo quod pro remedio ac necessitate temporis statutum est, constat primitus non fuisse, ac fuisse regulas veteres, quas ab apostolicis vel apostolicis viris traditas ecclesia Romana custodit, custodiendasque mandat eis, qui eam audire consueverunt. Sed necessitas temporis id fieri magnopere postulabat. Ergo quod necessitas pro remedio invenit, cessante necessitate, debet utique cessare pariter quod urgebat: quia alius est ordo legitimus, alia usurpatio quam tempus fieri ad praesens impellit.* (Cf. GRATIAN, C. 1 q. 7 c. 7 and C. 1 q. 1 c. 41.) The relevant passage from Leo's letter, JK 544, is quoted by KUTTNER, Doctrine of Interpretation, 63: *Sicut quaedam sunt quae nulla possunt ratione convelli, ita multa sunt quae aut pro consideratione aetatum aut pro necessitate rerum oporteat temperari, illa semper conditione servata ut in his quae vel dubia fuerint aut obscura, id noverimus sequendum quod nec praeceptis evangelicis contrarium nec decretis sanctorum patrum inveniatur adversum.* (Cf. GRATIAN, D. 14 c. 2)

[36] Libelli de lite 2, 597, c. 70: *Sunt autem quidam dicentes Romano pontifici semper bene licuisse novas condere leges. Quod et nos non solum non negamus, sed etiam valde affirmamus...* See MCKEON, Lateran Council, 5—6.

[37] Libelli de lite 2, 597, c. 70: *... Sed sciendum summopere est, quia inde novas leges condere potest, unde sancti patres et praecipue apostoli vel evangelistae aliquid nequaquam dixerunt...* See CHODOROW, Ideology, 66—72 for a different interpretation of Placidus' text and his stimulating remarks on the origin of the texts in GRATIAN, C. 25 q. 1. The unfluence of JK 544 of Pope Leo the Great on Placidus is obvious: *... ita multa sunt quae ... oporteat temperari, illa semper conditione servata ut ... id noverimus sequendum quod nec praeceptis evangelicis contrarium nec decretis sanctorum patrum inveniatur adversum.* See n. 35 above for a fuller citation of this text.

experienced no difficulty in proving that the concession of Ponte Mammolo contradicted the decrees of the fathers; among other things he simply pointed to the prohibition of lay investiture that had been pronounced by Gregory VII, Urban II, and Paschal II himself[38]. In the case of lay investiture, therefore, the pontiff was not free to create new law. Since Placidus did not recognize papal judicial immunity there was consequently no reason why the question of the problematic papal privileges for Henry V should not be decided in a general synod[39].

It is ironical that by the Gregorian age a general synod in the Latin church was only considered legal and thus binding when summoned and supported by the pope. The corresponding canonical decree, derived from the Pseudo-Isidorian collections, is found with slight variations in the A n s e l m o d e d i c a t a (1.9 and 1.62), the D e c r e t u m of Burchard of Worms (1.42), the C o l l e c t i o c a n o n u m of Anselm of Lucca (1.52), the D e c r e t u m (5.153) and the P a n o r m i a (4.14) of Bishop Ivo of Chartres[40] as well as in the D i c t a t u s p a p a e of Pope Gregory VII[41]. It does not surprise, therefore, that Pope Paschal II presided at the 1112 synod. The only viable alternative for Paschal's opponents would have been the election of a new pope prior to the synod who might then have conducted the deposition proceedings against his predecessor at a council as so often in the past[42]. It seems likely that such a plan was discussed within the ranks of the opposition[43], but is was doomed to fail because papal elections lay essentially in the hands of the cardinalate since the election decree of 1059, although the consent of lower clergy and the laity was still required[44]. While we

---

[38] Libelli de lite 2, 624, c. 118, lines 26—30; for Paschal's earlier prohibitions see also ibid., 626, lines 11—20.

[39] Ibid., 629, c. 136: *Quid agendum sit, quando turbatur aecclesia. In causa fidei sacerdotum debet esse collatio, sicut factum est sub Constantino augusto piae memoriae, qui nullas leges ante praemisit, sed liberum dedit iudicium sacerdotibus.*

[40] The decree reads in the formulation of Anselm of Lucca as follows: *Quod auctoritas congregandarum synodorum generalium soli apostolicae sedi sit commissa, nec sine eius auctoritate rata esse potest. Gelasius papa. Sinodorum congregandarum auctoritas apostolicae sedi privata commissa est potestate nec ullam synodum generalem ratam esse legimus, quae eius non fuerit auctoritate congregata vel fulta. Haec auctoritas testatur canonica, haec historia ecclesiastica roborat, haec sancti patres confirmant.* See in general H. FUHRMANN, Das Ökumenische Konzil und seine historischen Grundlagen, in: Geschichte in Wissenschaft und Unterricht, 12 (1961) 672—695, especially pp. 680—686.

[41] Das Register Gregors VII., 2.55a, p. 205, c. 16.

[42] See ZIMMERMANN, Papstabsetzungen, especially 188—192.

[43] Bruno of Segni defended himself against such a charge in his letter to Pope Paschal II (MGH Libelli de lite 2.564, lines 11—13): *Ego enim sic te diligo, sicut patrum et dominum diligere debeo et nullum alium te vivente pontificem habere volo* ... See also the reference to the Chronica Casinensis in MCKEON, The Lateran Council, 5.

[44] MGH Const. 1, 538—541, no. 382. See H. G. KRAUSE, Das Papstwahldekret von 1059 und seine Rolle im Investiturstreit, Studi Gregoriani 7 (1960) and the recent study by D. HÄ-

often lack information on the activity of any but the most prominent cardinals, it is clear that many of them refused to turn against Paschal. Sixteen cardinals had been imprisoned together with the pontiff and had supported the agreement between Paschal and Henry V by an oath at Ponte Mammolo[45]. With a few exceptions like John of Tusculum, Bruno of Segni, Robert of S. Eusebio[46], Gregory of SS. Apostoli and at least temporarily also Leo of Ostia, the cardinals remained loyal to Paschal II[47]. The malcontents in the church, including the French around Josceran of Lyons and Guy of Vienne — an imperial ecclesiastic but with strong ties to France — were therefore unable to replace Paschal before the council convened, and the pontiff had perforce to preside. This paradoxical situation was not lost on contemporaries. Cardinal Hugh referred to the 1112 synod in a letter he addressed to Countess Mathilda of Tuscany saying that the 'Roman church . . . condemned his [Paschal's] heresies in the Lateran council at which he presided, being present bodily rather than spiritually . . .'[48].

Hugh's violent invectives against Paschal II to whom he referred as a 'new pharaoh,' who would not desist from oppressing the church unless the *romana ecclesia* would use the sword of the word of God[49], are echoed by the records of the 1112 synod. No information concerning the first three days of the meeting on 18, 19, and 20 March is preserved. On 21st March, the fourth day, the assem-

---

GERMANN, Untersuchungen zum Papstwahldekret von 1059, in: Zeitschrift der Savigny-Stiftung für Rechtsgeschichte, Kan. Abt. 56 (1970) 158—193 with an up-to-date bibliography.

[45] MGH Const. 1, 143, no. 93.

[46] He is also known as Robert of Paris but he should not be confused with Galo of St. Léon who was bishop of Paris at the time. For Robert of S. Eusebio see R. HÜLS, Kardinäle, Klerus und Kirchen Roms 1049—1130, (= Bibliothek des Deutschen Historischen Instituts in Rom 48) Tübingen 1977, 165. Cf. MCKEON, The Lateran Council, 4 n. 9.

[47] The best evidence for the cardinals' loyalty is the attack on them by Bruno of Segni. See B. GIGALSKI, Bruno, Bischof von Segni, Abt von Monte-Cassino (1049—1123), (= Kirchengeschichtliche Studien 3.4) Münster 1898, 88—91. Bruno's letters are edited by E. Sackur, MGH Libelli de lite 2.563—655.

[48] Benonis aliorumque cardinalium schismaticorum contra Gregorium VII. et Urbanum II. scripta, ed. K. Francke, MGH Libelli de lite 2 (1892) 366—422, epistle 10, 417—421, specifically p. 418, lines 7—10. The letter is usually dated ca. 1098 (see HÜLS, Kardinäle, 251), but it seems clear that epistle 10 at least was written after 1112. The editor, K. Francke, could not identify the Lateran synod to which this letter referred (p. 418 n. 3), presumably because the description fitted none of the synods which met in Rome during the pontificates of Gregory VII and Urban II. It fits precisely, however, the events at the Lateran synod of 1112. The extended passages referring indirectly to this assembly might be interpolations, but this is not obvious. The Latin is not always as clear as one might wish, and the combination of attacks on popes Gregory VII and Urban II with an attack on Paschal II appears inconsistent. However, Countess Mathilda did not die until 1115 and Hugh, whose date of death is unknown, might well have felt encouraged to write to her in the terms he did after her reconciliation with King Henry V in 1111. See also the references in Libelli de lite 2, 368 n. 8.

[49] Ibid., 418, lines 4—10.

bly was evidently preoccupied with the events of Ponte Mammolo [50]. Paschal rejected the accusation that he had granted wholesale absolution to Wibertist ecclesiastics, that is, prelates who had accepted investiture from the emperor [51]. The Wibertist problem was specifically discussed in two of the letters Bruno of Segni had written after April 1111. They illustrate the discussions of 1112, and when the fragmentary narrative for the fourth day of the council is read in conjunction with them it is seen that the real issue was not the imperialist clergy as one might assume, but rather the question of whether Paschal had gone over to the Wibertist party and thus had become a heretic himself. In his second letter addressed to the Roman cardinals, Bruno had explained in detail what he meant by *ad partem Guiberti transire:* to allow the emperor *investituram scilicet et aecclesiarum ordinationes,* since this according to Bruno constituted the only difference between Wibertists and catholics [52]. This was, of course, precisely what Paschal had done in the treaty of Ponte Mammolo. In Bruno's eyes, therefore, Paschal was a heretic and could no longer demand obedience as the bishop explained in his first letter to the cardinals: ... *Quicumque igitur catholicam aecclesiam relinquentes ad partem Guiberti transierunt, et eius impiam heresim defendunt et tenent, eos hereticos excommunicatos et apostolicis vinculis ligatos esse non dubium est. Qui vero excommunicati et ligati sunt neque se ipsos neque alios vel ligare vel solvere possunt* [53]. Paschal's statement at the Lateran synod on 21st March was in essence a denial of the accusation that he 'had left the catholic church,' and a repetition of his earlier declarations that he continued to uphold former prohibitions and decrees despite the privilege of Ponte Mammolo [54].

On the fifth day of the meeting, 22nd March, Paschal defended himself more formally. He admitted his guilt although he still refused to excommunicate Henry V [55]. Perhaps the most significant point in Paschal's declaration that he

---

[50] See LP 2, 370: ... *In qua nimirum synodo de Guibertinis die quarto questio facta est, eo quod referrentur quasi ex permissione pape interdicta officia celebrare. Tunc pontifex ait: 'Nec excommunicatos, sicut aiunt quidam, generaliter absolvi: constat enim neminem nisi penitentem et satisfacientem absolutionis gratiam consequi; nec Guibertinis officia interdicta restitui, immo Ecclesie sententiam in eos editam, iuxta predecessorum nostrorum deliberationem laudamus et confirmamus.* There is a single piece of evidence that business other than the privilege of Ponte Mammolo was discussed in 1112. It was a quarrel between Archbishop Landulf of Benevent and Bishop William of Troia. See F. KEHR, Papsturkunden in Benevent unter der Capitanata, Nachrichten der Gesellschaft der Wissenschaften zu Göttingen (1898) 45—97, 67. Italia Pontificia 10, ed. D. Girgensohn, Berlin 1975, was unvailable.

[51] Wibert of Ravenna, anti-pope Clement III, had died in 1100, but the adherents of imperialist popes and of Henry V continued to be called Wibertists.

[52] MGH Libelli de lite 2.565, ep. 4.

[53] Ibid., 563, ep. 1.

[54] See n. 50 above as well as Paschal's letter to Girard of Angoulême, ed. SCHUM, Kaiser Heinrich V., 279 and Ivo's reference to Paschal's attitude in his epistles no. 233 and 236 as noted above in n. 16.

[55] LP 2, 370, lines 7—20.

had done wrong when he concluded the agreement of Ponte Mammolo, is his statement that the privilege was invalid (prave factum) because it had been sealed under the force of circumstance without the advice or the subscriptions of his brethren. The term brethren was used by Paschal without qualification. A further reference to 'brethren' occurs in the subsequent sentence of the confession, where Paschal declared that he would determine the necessary corrective measures in accordance with the advice and judgment of his brethren who had gathered at the synod[56]. In response (tunc) the synod formed a committee of wiser and more knowledgeable members who were to present a resolution on the following day. This committee of six was numerically evenly divided between cardinals and bishops. It included the cardinals Leo of Ostia, Robert of S. Eusebio, Gregory of SS. Apostoli, and the bishops Gregory of Terracina, Galo of Paris, who was a friend and pupil of Ivo of Chartres[57], and Archbishop Girard of Angoulême. Unfortunately, the synodal documents contain no hint about the selection process for the committee, but it seems as if in March 1112 at least prerogatives of the cardinalate and the papal curia, an expression used in Rome since the pontificate of Urban II for the papal household and advisors[58], were still in a state of flux. In 1112 cardinals and other prominent prelates shared the honor of advising the pope. It is nevertheless true that Paschal's solemn declaration at the council that his 'brethren' had the legal right to share with the pontiff the leadership of the church, that they had to be consulted, and that their subscriptions were necessary to validate documents such as the privilege for Emperor Henry V, would particularly benefit the cardinals whom Peter Damian already had called senators of the pope[59]. Paschal in effect accepted in his confession the validity of the concept that the privilege of Christ for St. Peter was a privilege

---

[56] Ibid.: . . . Porro scriptum illud, quod magnis necessitatibus coactus, non pro vita mea, non pro salute aut gloria mea, set pro solis Ecclesie necessitatibus sine fratrum consilio aut subscriptionibus feci, super quo nulla conditione, nulla promissione constringimur, prave factum cognosco, prave factum confiteor, et omnino corrigi Domino prestante desidero. Cuius correctionis modum fratrum qui convenerunt consilio iudicioque constituo . . .

[57] Galo officially represented the archbishops of Vienne and Bordeaux. He had been sent to Paschal II by Ivo of Chartres on behalf of Gislebert, a canon of Tours. (Gallia Christiana 7, Paris 1744, col. 56—57). For Galo in General see SPRANDEL, Ivo von Chartres, 103, 143, 190 and 195; R. SOMERVILLE, Miscellany: Two Notes on Scotland and the Medieval Papacy, in: The Innes Review 23 (1972) 149—151 and FUHRMANN, Fälschungen, 3.777 n. 9. P. DAVID, Un disciple d'Yves de Chartres en Pologne, Galon de Paris, in: VIIe Congrès International des Sciences Historiques, Warsaw 1933, was not seen.

[58] See K. JORDAN, Die Entstehung der römischen Kurie: ein Versuch mit Nachtrag 1962, Darmstadt 1973, 36—41, and R. ELZE, Das „Sacrum Palatium Lateranense" im 10. und 11. Jahrhundert, in: Studi Gregoriani 4 (1952) 27—54.

[59] Contra philargyriam c. 7 (Migne PL 145, 540). See JORDAN, Die Entstehung der römischen Kurie, 32—35 and S. KUTTNER, Cardinalis: The History of a Canonical Concept, in: Traditio 3 (1945) 129—214, 174.

for the Roman see as a whole rather than the pope alone, an opinion expressed by Cardinal Hugh in support of the rights of the dissident cardinals of 1084[60]. Cardinal Hugh was not slow to react triumphantly to the news from the 1112 synod. In his letter to Countess Mathilda of Tuscany referred to earlier he boasted that the successor of Peter could only act through the intermediary of cardinal priests and cardinal deacons, 'through whom and with whom he confirms what is to be confirmed and disapproves what is to be disapproved, without whose subscriptions public statements of the highest pontiff are invalid'[61].

This fundamental concession of Pope Paschal II, accompanied as it was by his humble confession of guilt *(prave factum cognosco, prave factum confiteor),* must have satisfied many of his critics as his simple rejection of corresponding charges on the fourth day of the council apparently failed to do[62]. The confession together with Paschal's expressed willingness to correct his errors would make it difficult for anyone to uphold the accusation that he was heretical and thus remove the reason for conciliar proceedings against the pontiff. As the canonist Ivo of Chartres explained, a heretic was only someone who pertinaciously refused to admit his errors and refused to mend his ways[63]. This definition of heresy was well known and universally accepted[64]. Even Bruno of Segni, a bitter enemy of the pontiff after April 1111, had pointed out in one of his letters

---

[60] MGH Libelli de lite 2, 404, lines 14—18: *Ecce filii patrem ligaverunt, quorum sentenciam ipsi coeli firmaverunt iuxta verbum Domini, dicentis Petro et per Petrum Romanae sedi: Quodcumque ligaveris ... et in coelis, ut evidenter appareat, privilegium Petri tocius Romane sedis esse potius quam solius pontificis.* See also TIERNEY, Foundations 70.

[61] Ibid. 418, lines 14—18: *Est autem privilegium Romanae sedis semper assistere per cardinales presbiteros et diaconos ipsi summo pontifici vel vicario ipsius sedis, id est ei, quem ipsa sedes sacrosancta os suum facit, per quem et cum quo predicat, per quem sacramenta administrat, per quem et cum quo firmanda confirmat et improbanda improbat, qua non subscribente invalida est publica summi ponticis sententia.* Noteworthy is the omission of the cardinal bishops. The right of subscription to papal decrees was gradually acquired by the cardinals. See TIERNEY, Foundations, 71 and HÜLS, Kardinäle, 45 item b. It is interesting to note the different sequence of names in the lists of signatures in the acta of the 1112 council. Recension II (LP 2.371) listed the cardinal bishops present in the first place, whereas recension I (MGH Const. 1, 572) assigned this place of honor to the Patriarch of Venice and Italian archbishops. See in connection with Weiland's edition O. SCHUMANN, Zu den Teilnehmerlisten des Protokolls über den letzten Tag des Laterankonzils von 1112, in: Neues Archiv 35 (1910) 789—791. Cf. in general G. TANGL, Die Teilnehmer an den allgemeinen Konzilien des Mittelalters, Weimar 1932, reprinted Darmstadt 1969, 187—189.

[62] It is worth noting that four cardinals, including two of Paschal's severest critics, did not attend the final meeting of the synod: Bruno of Segni, John of Tusculum, Peter of S. Sisto and Alberic of S. Sabina. They did not sign the condemnation of the 1111 privilege until later. See MGH Const. 1, 572 with the article by Schumann cited in the preceding note.

[63] Ep. 236 to Josceran of Lyons = Libelli de lite 2, 653, lines 2—4.

[64] O. HAGENEDER, Der Häresiebegriff bei den Juristen des 12. und 13. Jahrhunderts, in: The Concept of Heresy in the Middle Ages, Proceedings of the International Conference Louvain, May 1973, 42—103, 51—54.

written before March 1112 that 'they are heretics who contradict faith and doctrine of the catholic church with an obstinate mind'[65]. Bruno's intention at the time was probably to split the cardinalate by encouraging individuals to reject the privilege of Ponte Mammolo as heretical, but under the circumstances of the 1112 synod an unprejudiced participant was presumably only too glad to exempt the pontiff from the charge of heresy on the basis of his confession which must have proven to all that Paschal was anything but obstinate[66].

Nevertheless, Paschal's confession had not yet completely won the day, and the final meeting of the council was to bring a further humiliation. The pontiff had to make a public profession of his catholic faith, *ne quis de fide ipsius dubitaret*[67]. The papal *professio fidei* has a long history[68]. It is one of the formulae incorporated into the L i b e r D i u r n u s, a formulary book of the Roman church, perhaps dating from the sixth century[69]. In the eleventh century the L i b e r D i u r n u s war excerpted by Cardinal Deusdedit who updated certain parts of the *professio* and included it in his canonical collection[70]. Briefer excerpts from the formula are found in Ivo's works and the S u m m a H a i m o n i s[71]. As the council of 1112 shows, the concept of the *professio* had not been forgotten or relegated to canon law books merely out of respect for the early church as is sometimes assumed[72]. The occasion for its twelfth-century use in greatly modified form was, however, not the pontifical consecration for which the formula was originally intended[73]. It was long customary for the church to require a special

---

[65] MGH Libelli de lite 2, 565, lines 36—38. On the probable date of the letter see GIGALSKI, Bruno von Segni, 82—83n.

[66] It is ironic that Bruno himself was far from satisfied as the events of the 1116 council show. See GIGALSKI, Bruno von Segni, 103—104.

[67] MGH Const. 1, 571.

[68] G. BUSCHBELL, Die professio fidei der Päpste, part 1, in: Römische Quartalschrift für christliche Alterthumskunde und für Kirchengeschichte 10 (1896) 251—297. H. HURKA, Die angebliche Professio fidei Papst Bonifaz VIII., diss. Freiburg 1954 (typewritten) was unavailable.

[69] See Liber diurnus, ed. H. Foerster (Bern 1958) 145—148 for the Indiculum pontificis = T. E. von Sickel, Liber diurnus romanorum pontificum (Vienna 1889, reprinted Aalen 1966) no. 83, 90—93. L. SANTIFALLER, Liber Diurnus: Studien und Forschungen, ed. H. Zimmermann (= Päpste und Papsttum 10) Stuttgart 1976 was not yet available.

[70] Die Kanonessammlung des Kardinals Deusdedit 2.110, pp. 235—236; cf. BUSCHBELL, 'Professio fidei,' 277—291.

[71] See Ivo's Panormia 2.103 (Migne PL 161, 1107) and his Decretum 5.23 (ibid. 329); for the Summa Haimonis, which is unpublished, see Paris, Bibliothèque Nationale, MS lat. 4377, fol. 22v (3.2).

[72] BUSCHBELL, 'Professio fidei,' 291.

[73] In Deusdedit's collection (2.110) it is inscribed: *Professio futuri pontificis, antequam consecretur*. No evidence for the use of the professio at papal consecrations has survived. See B. SCHIMMELPFENNIG, Die Zeremonienbücher der römischen Kurie im Mittelalter, Biblio-

profession of faith from schismatic or heretic bishops who were readmitted to the one catholic church[74], and one might conclude that Paschal was treated as a readmitted former heretic when he was obliged to recite the papal *professio*. It is more likely, however, although there is no proof, that Paschal's profession of faith should be interpreted as a declaration of innocence not unlike the statement given several centuries earlier by Pope Leo III[75]. But in either interpretation the report from the final meeting of the 1112 synod is once again evidence that the assembly must have charged Paschal with heresy and that his heresy was the main subject of discussion, day after day. It is clear that in contrast to Paschal II whose interepretation was supported by Ivo of Chartres, the assembly proceeded under the assumption that lay investiture was a heresy, for numerous manuscripts of recension I of the synodal minutes, presumably drafted by Girard of Angoulême and the conciliar committee, are inscribed *actio concilii contra heresim de investitura*[76]. As long as the pontiff permitted the use of lay investiture, as he had done in the privilege of Ponto Mammolo, he would actively support a heresy in the eyes of the council, and could be deposed without further ado. In the case of evident and active support for a heresy the one admissible exception to the canon 'the pope is to be judged by no one' would come into play: 'unless he errs from faith' as perhaps first phrased by Humbert of Silva Can-

---

thek des Deutschen Historischen Instituts in Rom 40 (Tübingen 1973) 13—14 where the oldest ordos are discussed. See also BUSCHBEIL, 'Professio fidei,' 266.

[74] See Th. GOTTLOB, Der kirchliche Amtseid der Bischöfe, (= Kanonistische Studien und Texte 9) Bonn 1936, 7—11.

[75] See ZIMMERMANN, Papstabsetzungen, 25—37 and especially L. WALLACH, The Genuine and the Forged Oath of Pope Leo III, in: Traditio 11 (1955) 37—63, 41.

[76] Recension I, MGH Const. 1, 571. The concept of lay investiture as a heresy was urged on the pontiff in particular by Bruno of Segni (Libelli de lite 2.565, line 11 and lines 27—37) and Placidus of Nonantola, Liber de honore ecclesiae (Libelli de lite 2.590, lines 21—22; 603, 3—6; 604, 26—31) as well as Geoffrey of Vendôme (Libellus I, ed. E. Sackur, ibid., 682, lines 24—31; Libellus IV, ibid. 690—693 in general). See in addition to this the references given by HAGENEDER, Der Häresiebegriff, especially 100—101, n. 189. It is sometimes said that Pope Paschal II used the council of 1102 to declare lay investiture a heresy, but this interpretation of the 1102 anathema formula is incorrect. *(Anathematizo omnem heresim et precipue eam, quae statum presentis aecclesiae perturbat, quae docet et astruit anathema contempnendum et aecclesiae ligamenta spernenda esse . . .* quoted from the chronicle of Ekkehard of Aura, ed. Schmale and Schmale-Ott, p. 180; see below n. 87.) Paschal's formula referred to the heresy of disobedience to the Roman see. This distinction should be carefully noted. Cf. HAGENEDER, 'Häresiebegriff', 58—65. Recension I of the acta of 1112 was widely distributed. Two manuscripts can now be added to the codices used by Weiland: MS Paris, BN lat. 10402, fol. 70v—72r and London, BL Royal XI D8, fol. 249r. Two fragments probably ought to be included here as well although they are so brief that it is impossible to say whether they are part of recension I or II: Rouen, Bibliothèque municipale, MS A 215, fol. 237v and Itier's chronicle of Saint-Martial at Limoges, ed. H. Duplès-Agier (Paris 1874) 51.

dida[77], notwithstanding the case of Marcellinus[78]. The opposition to Paschal, however, was unable to convict Paschal of heresy because of the pope's skilful manoeuvres. All of Paschal's actions served to remove any basis for such an accusation. From the rejection of the charge, Paschal moved to a confession, and finally to the *professio fidei* which served as a formal vindication of Paschal as the true pope and successor of Gregory VII and Urban II.

Through adaptation to the requirements of the 1112 synod the *professio* was used at the same time to lend expression to Paschal's statement that he 'continued to prohibit what he had always prohibited'[79]. The text of Paschal's profession of faith shows two singularities. After Paschal confirmed his acceptance of the canon of the Scripture, a brief reference to the sacred Canons of the Apostles was inserted before the pontiff continued with a confirmation of the first four ecumenical synods, Nicaea (325), Ephesus (431), Constantinople (381), and Chalcedon (451) which he compared in the manner of Pope Gregory the Great to the four Gospels[80]. At this point Paschal added a reference to a council of Antioch which like the reference to the Canons of the Apostles is puzzling at first sight[81]. The significance of the inserts becomes evident, however, in the light of the investiture controversy where both decrees played an important role because they provided the desirable ancient precedent for the prohibition of lay investiture. They were frequently quoted, especially by Pope Paschal II himself, and constitute the legal basis for his most familiar decree against lay investiture which was promulgated and re-promulgated at three of his synods:

---

[77] *[Papa] a nemine est iudicandus, nisi deprehendatur a fide devius;* see Deusdedit, Coll. can. 1.306; Ivo, Decretum 5.23; Gratian D. 40 c. 6 and the discussion in TIERNEY, Foundations, 57 ff., especially 57, n. 3. An extensive introductory discussion of this text is also found in ZIMMERMANN, Papstabsetzungen, 169—175.

[78] See the discussion of D. 40 c. 6 and D. 21 c. 7 in Gratian's Decretum by Huguccio of Pisa, ed. by B. TIERNEY, Foundations, Appendix 1, 248—250 und Tierney's discussion of Huguccio ibid. especially 58—64.

[79] Paschal as quoted by Ivo of Chartres, ep. 233. See above n. 16.

[80] See JE 1092 and the Collectio canonum of Anselm of Lucca, 6.50 (ed. Thaner, p. 239—294); Ivo, Decretum 4.117; Ivo, Panormia 2.104, derives a reference to the Gregory text from the Etymologies of Isidore of Seville. It is impossible to determine the direct source of Paschal's professio. In contrast to Paschal, the sources observe the chronological sequence of the councils. Gregory the Great continued the statement with a reference to the fifth ecumenical council, Constantinople II (553). This reference is dropped by Anselm of Lucca but included by Ivo of Chartres, Decretum 4.117. The last text is the only one which contains the verb 'amplector,' that was used in 1112.

[81] MGH Const. 1, 571: ... *Amplector omnem divinam scripturam, scilicet veteris et novi testamenti, legem a Moyse scriptam et a sanctis prophetis. Amplector IIII evangelia, VII canonicas epistolas, epistolas gloriosi doctoris beati Pauli apostoli, sanctos canones apostolorum, IIII universalia concilia sicut IIII evangelia, Nicenum, Ephesinum, Constantinopolitanum, Calcedonense, et Antiocenum concilium et decreta sanctorum patrum Romanorum pontificum ...*

Guastalla (1106), Troyes (1107), and at the Lateran council of 1110. The text of this canon itself is not very revealing:

Constitutiones sanctorum canonum sequentes statuimus ut quicumque clericorum ab hac hora in antea investituram ecclesiae vel ecclesiasticae dignitatis de manu laica acceperit, et qui ei manum imposuerit, gradus sui periculo subiaceat, et communione privetur [82]

but in a letter Paschal sent shortly after the synod of Troyes to Archbishop Rothard of Mainz (JL 6145) the pontiff indicated precisely to which *constitutiones sanctorum canonum* he referred. Among them are c. 31 of the Canons of the Apostles and a decree attributed in the Collectio canonum of Deusdedit to a council of Antioch [83]. Paschal's reference to these canons in the *professio fidei* of 1112, therefore, reaffirmed indirectly his old prohibition of lay investiture as demanded by his critics.

In this manner Paschal and his supporters appeased the opposition, and the synod ended with a compromise, possibly through the indirect influence of Ivo of Chartres. Ivo had sent his friend Galo, bishop of Paris, to the pontiff as his representative on behalf of a canon from Tours according to a note in the Gallia Christiana, but it is not very far-fetched to assume that Galo spoke in the conciliar committee, whose member he was, not only in his own name but also in that of his former teacher [84]. The assembly persisted in treating lay investiture as a heresy, but allowed Paschal to plead innocent to the corresponding charge. In return, however, Paschal had to accept a considerable strengthening of the corporate tendencies in the church.

The pontiff was, it seems, well aware of the threatening implications of the days in March 1112 for papal primacy as the concept had come to be understood during the Gregorian reform [85], and did his best in the remaining years of his pontificate to reverse the events as far as possible. The most telling example of these efforts is the Lateran synod of 1116. In August 1115 Paschal sent out invitations to a general synod which was to discuss the s c h i s m of lay investiture [86]. The council convened on March 6, 1116, but nobody seemed willing to discuss the thorny subject until an unnamed bishop asked that the pontiff should first of all discuss the business for which they had been primarily

---

[82] Cf. Gratian C. 16 q. 7 c. 17. The repromulgations of the decree is discussed in U.-R. BLUMENTHAL, The Early Councils of Pope Paschal II, Studies and Texts 43, Toronto 1978.

[83] Paschal quoted both texts from the Collectio canonum of Deusdedit (4.19 and 4.22) at the council of Troyes. See ibid. ch. 3.

[84] See the references above, n. 57.

[85] See Y. M.-J. CONGAR, Der Platz des Papsttums in der Kirchenfrömmigkeit der Reformer des 11. Jahrhunderts, in: Sentire Ecclesiam, Festschrift Hugo Rahner, Freiburg i. B. 1961, 196 bis 217.

[86] JL 64—62 = Migne PL 163, col. 385.

summoned to Rome[87]. Paschal thereupon repeated the 1112 confession. Inevitably he was once again accused of heresy for having permitted a heresy[88]. In 1116, however, the pontiff was well prepared to reject the accusation which he seems to have expected. He pointed out that the Roman church was never tainted by heresy but rather conquered all heresies threatening the faith because of Christ's prayer for Peter[89]. There is no doubt that Paschal identified himself with St. Peter and thus with the church to the exclusion of cardinals and curia, but the classical statement for the infallibility of the church represented by the pope was used four years too late. The twelfth century became a period of growth for conciliarist ideas for varied reasons, but the council of 1112 was not the least among them[90].

[87] Mansi 21, 145—151. The account of Ekkehard of Aura is critically edited by F.-J. Schmale and I. Schmale-Ott, Frutolfs und Ekkehards Chroniken und die Anonyme Kaiserchronik, Ausgewählte Quellen zur deutschen Geschichte des Mittelalters, (= Freiherr vom Stein-Gedächtnisausgabe 15) Darmstadt 1972, 318—324. See especially p. 320. A probably better account of the synod of 1116 is found in Gerhoch of Reichersberg, Opusculum de edificio dei, ed. E. Sackur, MGH Libelli de lite 3 (Hanover 1897) 190—191n., but Gerhoch's narrative is briefer than that of Ekkehard. The discussion of the synod in this present note is based on the chronicle of Ekkehard of Aura.

[88] Cf. GIGALSKI, Bruno von Segni, 103—104.

[89] According to Ekkehard of Aura, Paschal replied: *Fratres et domini mei, audite: ecclesia ista nunquam habuit heresim, immo hic omnes hereses conquassatae sunt ... destructi sunt. Pro hac ecclesia Filius Dei in passione sua oravit, cum dixit, Ego pro te rogavi, Petre, ut non deficiat fides tua ...* See the discussion of Luke 22.32 in TIERNEY, Foundations, especially 44 ff.

[90] See ibid., 55, where the distinction between incipient and fully grown conciliar theory is clarified.

XI

PASCHAL II AND THE ROMAN PRIMACY

Summarium. — In hoc commentario ostenditur Paschalem II (1099-1118) intellegentiam de primatu papali, paulo ante inter sic dictam reformationem gregorianam efformatam, efficaciter sustinuisse. Explicationem litterarum apostolicarum maioris momenti a Paschali II datarum consequitur disceptatio de synodo Lateranensi anno 1112 habita. Ex hac nempe synodo adversarii papae Paschalis, id est, ii qui rationi consiliorum in rebus Ecclesiae pariter capiendorum favebant, victores discesserunt. In synodo tamen anno 1116 celebrata contra evenit, cum Paschalis II auctoritatem suam et inde instituta primatialia redintegrare valuit. Demum res in synodo a. 1116 gestae enucleantur [1].

It is commonly accepted that the assertion of papal leadership within the church, or in other words the realization of papal primacy, was one of the aims of the ecclesiastical reformers of the eleventh century. The Pseudo-Isidorian Decretals often used to be held responsible for this emphasis among the Gregorians, but Y. Congar's, M. Maccarrone's and H. Fuhrmann's studies in particular have since corrected this erroneous impression [2]. In the memorable phrase of H. Fuhrmann the reformers rediscovered the church not Pseudo-Isidore, although Pseudo-Isidore became subsequently part and parcel of the new self-consciousness within the church [3]. The result was an ecclesiology that was Roman to the very core [4].

---

[1] Some of the research for this paper was done with the help of a Fellowship for Independent Study and Research by the American Council of Learned Societies. The author is very grateful to Professor R. Somerville with whom she discussed some sections of this paper.

[2] H. FUHRMANN, *Einfluß und Verbreitung der pseudoisidorischen Fälschungen von ihrem Auftauchen bis in die neuere Zeit* (MGH *Schriften* 24, 2-3), Stuttgart 1972, 1973 and 1974. Vol. 1. chapter 1, pp. 1-38 in particular reviews and analyzes in detail Pseudo-Isidorian historiography. (Fuhrmann's work will be cited below FUHRMANN, *Einfluß*). Y. M.-J. CONGAR, *Der Platz des Papsttums in der Kirchenfrömmigkeit der Reformer des 11. Jahrhunderts*, in *Sentire ecclesiam. Das Bewußtsein von der Kirche als gestaltende Kraft der Frömmigkeit* (Festschrift H. Rahner), ed. J. DANIÉLOU and H. VORGRIMLER, Freiburg 1961, 196-217 (this article is abbreviated below CONGAR, *Kirchenfrömmigkeit*). M. MACCARRONE, *La dottrina del primato papale dal IV all'VIII secolo nelle relazioni con le chiese occidentali* (Settimane di Studio del Centro Italiano di Studi sull'Alto Medioevo 7, 1959) Spoleto 1960, 633-742 (the article is abbreviated below MACCARRONE, *Dottrina*). For a brief introduction to the Pseudo-Isidorian Decretals in English see *New Catholic Encyclopedia* 5 (1967) 820-824 (H. FUHRMANN) s.v. *False Decretals (Pseudo-Isidorian Forgeries)*.

[3] FUHRMANN, *Einfluß*, chapter 8, pp. 346-353.

[4] CONGAR, *Kirchenfrömmigkeit*, 205s; FUHRMANN, *Einfluß*, index D, p. 1109s, s.v. *Papsttum, Primat.*

XXI

68

The idea of the primacy of Rome was not new, of course [5]. It held already a prominent place in several pre-Gregorian canonical collections as, for instance, the *Decretum* of Burchard of Worms and the *Pseudo-Isidorian Decretals* [6]. The eleventh century, however, saw a shift in emphasis as well as the expansion of the concept. The Petrine texts, *Matt.* 16,18.19; *Luke* 22,32 and *John* 21,15-17 were interpreted by the reformers in favor of the Roman see alone. In this new light the concept of primacy underwent a subtle change. It became part of the dogma of the church without losing its juridical characteristics. « Der päpstliche Primat wird auf diese Weise nicht nur als eine kirchenrechtliche Gegebenheit begründet, die von Bestimmungen herrührt, durch die die Kirche ihr eigenes Leben regelt, sondern als eine ihrer Natur und Tragweite nach dogmatische Gegebenheit: als eine Glaubenswahrheit, die die gottgewollte Struktur der Kirche beinhaltet » [7]. Put briefly, obedience to Rome became one aspect of faith [8].

---

5 It seems almost unnecessary to point out that the literature on the history of papal primacy is voluminous and that the following references indicate only those articles and monographs which were particularly useful in connection with the present study. MACCARRONE, *Dottrina*; CONGAR, *Kirchenfrömmigkei*, 201; W. ULLMANN, *Leo I and the Theme of Papal Primacy*: Journal of Theological Studies, n.s. 11 (1960) 25-51; R. BENSON, *Plenitudo potestatis: Evolution of a formula from Gregory IV to Gratian*, in *Studia Gratiana* XIV (Collectanea Stephan Kuttner, 4), Rome 1967, 195-217; E. HIRSCH, *Die rechtliche Stellung der römischen Kirche und des Papstes nach Kardinal Deusdedit*: Archiv für katholisches Kirchenrecht 88 (1908) 595-624; F. HEILER, *Altkirchliche Autonomie und päpstlicher Zentralismus*, Munich 1941, part 2: *Die Entstehung und Entwicklung des Papsttums*, pp. 186-261, with further references.

6 CONGAR, *Kirchenfrömmigkeit*, 196; an introduction to the *Decretum* of Burchard of Worms is found in P. FOURNIER and G. LE BRAS, *Histoire des collections canoniques en occident*, 2 vols., Paris 1931 and 1932 (reprinted Aalen 1972): I, 364-421; A. VAN HOVE, *Prolegomena ad Codicem iuris canonici*, Mechlin ²1945, 320s; A. M. STICKLER, *Historia iuris canonici latini* I, Turin 1950, 154-159.

7 CONGAR, *Kirchenfrömmigkeit*, 201s.

8 See *Das Register Gregors VII.*, ed. E. CASPAR (MGH *Epistolae Selectae* 2), in 2 vols., Berlin 1920 and 1923, reprinted 1967, 502-505, letter 7,24 (JL 5167) to Abbot William of Hirsau: « ... si aliquo tempore Constantiensi ecclesiae presidens ab apostolica sede discordaverit eique inoboediens fuerit, quod confirmante Samuhele peccatum ariolandi et idolatriae scelus est, dicente quoque beato Ambrosio: 'Ereticum esse constat, qui Romanae ecclesiae non concordat' liceat abbati sibi suisque a quocunque religioso episcopo placuerit ordinationes ... expetere ... » (504s). See also ibid. 2, 55a, pp. 201-208, no. 26: "Quod catholicus non habeatur, qui non concordat Romanae ecclesiae" (207). In connection with both JL 5167 and the *Dictatus papae* see particularly the following most recent studies with copious bibliographical annotations: H. MORDEK, *Proprie auctoritates apostolice sedis. Ein zweiter Dictatus papae Gregors VII.?*: Deutsches Archiv 28 (1972) 105-132, especially p. 115 '*Proprie auctoritates*' no. 6: "Qui decretis sedis apostolice non consenserit, hereticus habendus est"; the review of Mordek's article by F. F. KEMPF, *Ein zweiter Dictatus Papae? Ein Beitrag zum Depositionsanspruch Gregors VII*: Arch. Hist. Pont. 13 (1975) 119-139; O. HAGENEDER, *Der Häresiebegriff bei den Juristen des 12. und 13. Jahrhunderts*, in *The Concept of Heresy in the Middle Ages* [11th-13th C.] (Proceedings of the International Conference Louvain, May 13-16, 1973), Leuven and The Hague 1976, 42-103, especially pp. 58-71 and n. 67 p. 61; P. CLASSEN, *Der Häresie-Begriff bei Gerhoch von Reichersberg und in seinem Umkreis, ibid.* 27-41, 31s; H. FUHRMANN, *'Quod catholicus non habeatur, qui non concordat Romanae ecclesiae'. Randnotizen zum Dictatus Papae*, in *Fest-*

Among the first expressions of the new ecclesiology are the replies sent by Pope Leo IX in 1053 to the African church at Carthage which had sought papal support in defense of its primatial rights. Leo welcomed the inquiry:

... multum tamen gaudemus, quia sanctae Romanae ecclesiae matris vestrae sententiam requiritis et exspectatis super quaestionibus vestris; et quasi rivulis ab uno fonte erumpentibus, et in suo se cursu per diversa spargentibus ad ipsius fontis primam scaturiginem reverti debere optimum putatis, ut inde resumatis directionis vestigium, unde sumpsistis totius Christianae religionis exordium [9].

The Roman primacy is here asserted independently from its juridical characteristics and taken beyond the context of the *Pseudo-Isidorian Decretals*. The high esteem which has to be accorded to the Roman church is also due to its decrees. As the pontiff wrote, the preeminence of Carthage was confirmed through the council of Cyprian, the synods of Augustine, and all the African synods, and *quod maius est ex venerabilium praedecessorum nostrorum Romanorum praesulum decretis* [10]. It has been noted that Leo's African letters are also an exceptionally clear statement of papal claims to exclusive jurisdiction in *omnium ecclesiarum maiores et difficiliores causae* which is supported by a tightly interwoven web of Pseudo-Isidorian quotations [11], but for the purposes of this paper it suffices to point out the new ecclesiology which they reveal. The view of primacy expressed by Pope Leo IX was the common property of the reformers as shown in their writings. Rome is described as the center, the *caput* and *cardo*, the origin, the mother and teacher of all churches [12]. A most eloquent statement of these sentiments was the *Dictatus papae*

---

schrift für Helmut Beumann zum 65. Geburtstag, ed. K.-U. JÄSCHKE and R. WENSKUS, Sigmaringen 1977, 263-287. Pope Paschal II used the Ambrose quotation of Gregory VII directly in two of his letters, JL 5847 (« ... Beato quippe Ambrosio attestante dicimus quod hereticum esse constat, qui a Romana dissentit ecclesia; et Samuel quasi idololatrie, ait, scelus est nolle acquiescere » = MIGNE PL 163,55D) and JL 6392 (« ... Diu enim propter pertinacie sue nequitiam a sede apostolica excommunicati sunt, que caput et magistra omnium ecclesiarum ab ipso omnipotenti Domino constituta est. Cui profecto qui non concordat procul dubio, sicut beatus Ambrosius scribit, hereticus est » = MIGNE PL 163, 356 A).

[9] JL 4304 = MIGNE PL 143, 728 B; see FUHRMANN, *Einfluß*, 343-345 and 353 .
[10] JL 4305 = MIGNE PL 143, 729 D; see also the fragments *De sancta Romana Ecclesia* which are attributed to Cardinal Humbert of Silva Candida and published by P. E. SCHRAMM, in *Kaiser, Rom und Renovatio. Studien und Texte zur Geschichte des römischen Erneuerungsgedankens vom Ende des Karolingischen Reiches bis zum Investiturstreit*, 2 vols., Leipzig and Berlin 1929: II, 120-133. Fragment A is reprinted in CONGAR, *Kirchenfrömmigkeit*, 216s. See Congar's comments *ibid.* 197s and J. J. RYAN, *Cardinal Humbert 'De s. Romana ecclesia'. Relics of Roman-Byzantine Relations 1053-1054*: Mediaeval Studies 20 (1958) 206-238.
[11] JL 4304 = MIGNE PL 143, 728 D, and JL 4305 = MIGNE PL 143, 730 B; FUHRMANN, *Einfluß*, 343-345.
[12] CONGAR, *Kirchenfrömmigkeit*, especially pp. 199-200 and 202s.

as well as the canonical collections of Cardinal Deusdedit and Bishop Anselm of Lucca[13].

At a first glance the strife-torn pontificate of Paschal II (1099-1118) would appear to be a most unlikely time for a vigorous pursuit of papal primacy, for it is customary to attribute weakness and inconsistency to this pope. True, certain historians qualified Paschal in the past as a radical Gregorian, but their argument rested on the premise that Paschal's proposal of S. Maria in Turribus of February 4, 1111, implied 'apostolic poverty' for the church[14]. This premise is false. The momentous dissension in St. Peter's basilica on Sunday, February 12, which culminated in the imprisonment of Paschal and his entourage by Henry V of Germany, arose not over Paschal's proposal to request the clergy of the Empire to return *regalia* to the king, but rather over the interpretation of the term *regalia*. Henry's interpretation which corresponded to that of the *Tractatus de investitura*, and of Placidus of Nonantola, differed radically from that of Paschal. While Henry submitted that return of *regalia* meant the return of all possessions of the church, territorial and otherwise, which had been given to the church by the laity since the time of Charlemagne, Pope Paschal II and the curia maintained consistently that the church everywhere, including Germany, was to have forever the exclusive, outright ownership of all estates and gifts which were not of regalian character[15]. In other words, Paschal

---

[13] CONGAR, *ibid.* 204s; for Deusdedit see the article by E. HIRSCH cited in n. 5 above as well as FOURNIER-LE BRAS, *Histoire des collections canoniques* II, 37-53; VAN HOVE, *Prolegomena*, 324s; STICKLER, *Historia iuris canonici latini* I, 172-174; CONGAR, *Kirchenfrömmigkeit*, 208; FUHRMANN, *Einfluß*, 522-533; the collection was edited by V. W. VON GLANVELL, *Die Kanonessammlung des Kardinals Deusdedit*, Paderborn 1905, reprinted Aalen 1967. For the canonical collection of Anselm of Lucca (ed. F. THANER, Innsbruck 1906-15, reprinted Aalen 1965) see especially FUHRMANN, *Einfluß*, 509-522; FOURNIER-LE BRAS, *Histoire des collections canoniques* II, 25-37; VAN HOVE, *Prolegomena*, 323s; STICKLER, *Historia iuris canonici latini* I, 170-172. For the *Dictatus papae* see the references cited in n. 8 above and especially G. B. BORINO, *Un ipotesi sul 'Dictatus Papae' di Gregorio VII*: Archivio della R. Deputazione Romana di storia patria 67 (1944) 237ss, and S. KUTTNER, *Liber Canonicus. A Note on 'Dictatus Papae'* c. 17, in *Studi Gregoriani* II, Rome 1947, 387-401. The recent article by H. FUHRMANN, *Randnotizen* (cited above n. 8) notes once again the ambiguity which still surrounds the document known as *Dictatus papae*.

[14] P. ZERBI, *Pasquale II e l'ideale della povertà della Chiesa*, in *Annuario dell'Università Cattolica del Sacro Cuore*, Milan 1964-65, 207-229; N. H. CANTOR, *Church, Kingship, and Lay Investiture in England: 1089-1135*, Princeton 1958, especially pp. 122-124; cf. A. FLICHE, *La Réforme grégorienne et la Reconquête chrétienne (1057-1123)* (Histoire de l'Église depuis les origines jusqu'à nos jours, ed. A. Fliche and V. Martin, VIII), Paris 1950, 339. The relevant section from the proposal of February 4, 1111 was published by L. WEILAND with the inscription *Promissio papae per Petrum Leonis dicta* (MGH *Legum* sectio IV, 1, no. 85, pp. 138s [the volume is cited below *Const.* 11]). For the more formal version of this document see *ibid.* no. 90, pp. 140-142, *'Paschalis II. Privilegium primae conventionis'* (JL 6289).

[15] See my paper *Patrimonia and Regalia in 1111*, in *Law, Church, and Society: Essays in Honor of Stephan Kuttner*, ed. K. PENNINGTON and R. SOMERVILLE, Philadelphia 1977, 9-20. To the bibliography on the *Tractatus de investitura* should now be added J. KRIMM-BEUMANN, *Der Traktat « De investitura episcoporum » von 1109*: Deu-

never advocated poverty for the church. On the contrary, he attempted to increase the territorial holdings of the Roman church wherever possible as will be seen below.

Paschal proved himself a worthy heir of Gregory VII and Urban II through his struggle to secure the liberty of the church under a strong papacy. This paper will address itself to this question and show that Paschal persistently stressed papal primacy and furthered these claims throughout Christendom. Paschal perceived the primacy in the manner of Pope Leo IX, and maintained its Gregorian image. It may be well, however, to mention here in order to avoid new misconceptions about Paschal's pontificate, that Paschal's attitude to the *regnum* differed noticeably from the much debated view of the nature of the state as developed by Pope Gregory VII, for instance in his famous second letter to Bishop Hermann of Metz [16]. Paschal's perception of the dignity of the priesthood was very exalted [17], but there is no evidence either in his correspondence or among the fragmentary canons from his councils that Paschal ever juxtaposed the sacred and superior *sacerdotium* to an inferior and unsanctified *regnum*. In accordance with contemporary assumptions Paschal consistently described the task of the *regnum* as that of protecting and assisting the church [18], but he acknowledged with St. Paul that all power that it is from God: *Legimus in apostolo Paulo, non est potestas nisi a Deo. Tunc vero recte potestas agitur, cum ad deum respicitur, a quo datur* [19]. His letters repeatedly ex-

---

tsches Archiv 33 (1977) 37-83, with a critical edition of the treatise. Among Paschal's letters JL 6293, 6295 and 6299 are particularly relevant.

[16] *Das Register Gregors VII.*, letter 8, 21 (JL 5201), pp. 544-563.

[17] See JL 5909 to Anselm of Canterbury: «... Liberam esse ecclesiam Paulus dicit: indignum est igitur ut clericus qui iam in dei sortem est assumptus, et iam laicorum dignitatem excessit, pro terrenis lucris hominium faciat laico ... » (MIGNE PL 163, 93 A); see also c. 1 of the council of Benevento, held in 1108: « Et divine legis preceptis instruimur quod omnia tabernaculi utensilia a levitis custodiantur et tractentur. Et per Iezechielem prophetam dominus precipit ut terra circa templum sanctificata sit et solis sacerdotibus concedatur. Quamobrem laicis omnibus interdicimus ne aecclesias cum possessionibus suis teneant ... » (JL 6613). The text is critically edited in U.-R. BLUMENTHAL, *The Early Councils of Pope Paschal II, 1100-1110* (Pontifical Institute of Mediaeval Studies, Studies and Texts 43), Toronto 1978, chapter 4.

[18] JL 6557: « ... In his et aliis nequitiis cohercendis regni tui debes pontificibus adiutor et cooperator existere. Tunc enim bene mundus regitur, cum sacerdotali auctoritati potestas regia comitatur, sacerdotes enim in Christi ecclesia oculi sunt, quos sequi condecet populum quia et virtute domini corpus eius illuminatur ... » Cf. a similar passage in JL 4790 of Gregory VII addressed to Duke Rudolf of Swabia (*Das Register Gregors VII.*, letter no. 1, 19, p. 31). See also Paschal's letter JL 6562 to Count Roger of Sicily and the promises of Henry V of Germany given in 1111 (MGH *Const.* 1, no. 83, p. 137s and no. 87, p.139s). The references in the following note are also relevant.

[19] JL 6557; see also JL 6562 « ... Cognosce, fili carissime, modum tuum et datam tibi a domino potestatem, noli contra dominicam erigere potestatem. Sic enim a domino Romane ecclesie potestas concessa est, ut ab hominibus auferri non possit ... » and JL 6565: « Nosse debes, fili carissime, quia non est potestas nisi a Deo. Per ipsum igitur potestate accepta, noli adversus eum cervicem cordis erigere ... »; see further JL 6450 and JL 6554; cf. JL 5868 and JL 6453 (= MIGNE PL 163, 70s and 378s) The

pressed the conviction that the *regnum* had an appropriate and legitimate sphere of its own, and he was completely sincere when he assured Henry V of Germany through Archbishop Rothard of Mainz that he had no desire to abrogate the rights of the *regnum*: *Nos enim regibus que sui iuris sunt integra servare optamus, nec in aliquo minuimus, dummodo ipsi sponse sui Domini libertatem integram patiantur ... Habeant reges quod regum est; quod sacerdotum est, habeant sacerdotes; sic pacem invicem teneant, et se invicem in uno Christi corpore venerentur* [20]. The problem was unfortunately that pope and king could not agree on the nature of these rights as is well known, just as they could not agree on the meaning of *regalia*. It is debatable whether the attitude towards secular government expressed for example by Pope Gregory VII or the attitude of Paschal II is more characteristic of the Gregorian reform as a whole. It is certain, though, that the most characteristic aspect of the Reform, the new ecclesiology, is fully evident in the pontificate of Paschal II. The following pages will analyze Paschal's ecclesiology on the basis of his letters and selected synodal documents. They will also deal with the synod of 1112, a defeat for proponents of papal primacy, and the Lateran council of 1116, where Paschal fully reasserted his leadership of the church and with it the primacy.

The Primacy in Paschal's Letters.

The basic image employed by Paschal to describe the relationship between Rome and all other churches is the well-known simile of head and members which was liberated from its Pseudo-Isidorian context [21]. Congar noted that *caput* and similar titles for the Roman church such as *cardo, mater, fons,* and *fundamentum* as used by the eleventh-century reformers conveyed their Rome-centered eccle-

---

quotation in these letters « Pro patribus tuis nati sunt tibi filii: constitues eos principes super omnem terram » (*Ps.* 44,17) refers to the institution of ecclesiastical dignitaries as the context shows.

[20] JL 6050. The same principle lies behind the compromise between Pope Paschal and King Henry I of England and the dispensation for Archbishop Anselm of Canterbury which permitted homage to the king by ecclesiastics temporarily (JL 6073). See also Suger's account of the negotiations between Henry V of Germany and Paschal at Châlons-sur-Marne in 1107 (*Vita Ludovici grossi regis*, ed. and transl. H. WAQUET [Les Classiques de l'histoire de France au moyen âge, 11], Paris 1929, reprinted 1964, chapter 10, pp. 56-58.) On the difficulties of interpreting this passage see particularly R. L. BENSON, *The Bishop-Elect. A Study in Medieval Ecclesiastical Office*, Princeton 1968, 243s; see also A. BECKER, *Studien zum Investiturproblem in Frankreich*, Saarbrücken 1955, 121s and J. FRIED, *Der Regalienbegriff im 11. und 12. Jahrhundert*: Deutsches Archiv 29 (1973) 450-528, 468.

[21] This was already the case under Pope Leo IX. See JL 4305 = MIGNE PL 143, 729 C: « Hoc acceptabile est domino nostro Jesu Christo ut caput omnibus membris prospiciat et invigilet; membra vero sui capitis salutem sine intermissione quaerant et optent ».

XI

PASCHAL II AND THE ROMAN PRIMACY 73

siology [22]. This is indeed the case. A notable example for this ideology as well as terminology are the opening *capitula* of book 1, *De potestate et primatu apostolicae sedis*, of the *Collectio Canonum* of Anselm of Lucca [23]. Paschal's references to *caput* carry the same connotation. In his letter to Emperor Alexios of 1112 the pontiff declared that the subordination of the church of Constantinople to Rome was a precondition for a settling of all differences between Latin and Greek churches: *Ea enim que inter Latinos et Graecos fidei vel consuetudinem [diversitatem] faciunt non videntur aliter posse sedari nisi prius capiti membra coherent* [24]. Paschal pointed out elsewhere that it is the connection between *caput* and *membra* which provides unity despite geographical distance, and that affronts and injuries to members were suffered by the head as well [25] In a letter to St. Anselm of Canterbury Paschal implied a certain mutuality in this relationship: *De illata tibi iniuria membra ecclesie non modicum patiuntur, quia sicut dicit apostolus si compatitur unum membrum, compatiuntur et cetera membra. Licet enim corporali separemur presentia, unum tamen in capite sumus* [26]. Elsewhere, however, the image is used unaccompanied by the referenc to *I Cor.* 12,26,

---

[22] CONGAR, *Kirchenfrömmigkeit*, 202-205.

[23] For a discussion of the relationship between the Pseudo-Isidorian Decretals and the collection of Anselm of Lucca see especially FUHRMANN, *Einfluß*, 511-522, and CONGAR, *Kirchenfrömmigkeit*, 207. The contrast between the *Collection in 74 Titles*, also known as *Sentences* (*Diversorum patrum sententie sive Collectio in LXXIV titulos digesta*, ed. J. T. GILCHRIST [Monumenta iuris canonici, series B, vol. 1], Vatican City 1973) and the *Collectio canonum* of Anselm is emphasized by FUHRMANN: « Hatte der Sentenzenautor zum Ziel, den Papst als den Richter über die gesamte Kirche auftreten zu lassen, so hebräite Anselm den römischen Bischof aus dieser speziellen Funktion: Er zeigt die Besonderheit der römischen Kirche und die Vielfalt der Vorrechte ihres Vorstehers » (*Einfluß*, 514). A discussion of the *Sentences* is found *ibid.* 486-509; see also H. FUHRMANN, *Über den Reformgeist der 74-Titel-Sammlung* (*Diversorum patrum sententiae*), in *Festschrift für Hermann Heimpel zum 70. Geburtstag* II, Göttingen 1972, 1101-1120. The differences in the reception of Pseudo-Isidore between the *Collection in 74-Titles* and the *Collectio canonum* of Anselm of Lucca are exemplified by a comparison of Anselm 1.9 (« Quod ecclesia Romana omnibus preest ecclesiis, sicut beato Petro datum est preminere ceteris apostolis ») and c. 12 of *74-Titles* with a much longer excerpt from Pseudo-Vigilius, ep. 2 c. 7 (See *Decretales Pseudo-Isidorianae et capitula Angilramni*, ed. P. HINSCHIUS, Leipzig 1863 [reprinted Aalen 1963], p. 712).

[24] JL 6334. For the negotiations between Paschal and Constantinople in 1111-1114 see the basic narrative account in S. RUNCIMAN, *The Eastern Schism. A Study of the Papacy and the Eastern Churches during the Eleventh and Twelfth Centuries*, Oxford 1955, reprinted London 1970 (Panther Books), 122-127; R. HIESTAND, *Legat, Kaiser und Basileus. Bischof Kuno von Praeneste und die Krise des Papsttums von 1111/1112*, in *Aus Reichsgeschichte und Nordischer Geschichte. Festschrift Karl Jordan* (Kieler Historische Studien, 16), Stuttgart 1972, 141-152; J. G. ROWE, *Paschal II, Bohemund of Antioch and the Byzantine Empire*: Bulletin of the John Rylands Library 49 (1966) 165-202.

[25] See JL 6028, JL 6301 and JL 6293 = MIGNE PL 163,287B: « Non enim possunt sine detrimento capitis membra persequi et abscindi et filiorum contumelia ad patris spectat iniuriam ».

[26] JL 6028 = MIGNE PL 163, 154B.

presumably on the basis of canonical collections that incorporated Pseudo-Isidorian material, and stresses the preeminence of Rome. Immediately linked with the divinely founded primacy is the idea of obedience to Rome. Disobedience is heresy: ... *Diu enim propter pertinacie sue nequitiam a sede apostolica excommunicati sunt, que caput et magistra omnium ecclesiarum ab ipso omnipotente Domino constituta est. Cui profecto qui non concordat procul dubio sicut beatus Ambrosius scribit hereticus est* [27]. Because of the relationship between head and body disobedience to the Roman church is in a sense impossible. *Cum Romane ecclesie membra sitis, miramur quod vestro capiti scienter contraitis* wrote Paschal to Bishop Peter of Poitiers [28]. He who disobeys places himself outside the church. Excommunication simply acknowledges the fact. Disobedience is given as the reason for Paschal's solemn excommunication of Emperor Henry IV according to ancient custom on Maundy Thursday 1102 [29]. The excommunication concluded the Lateran council of 1102. Earlier, the synod had adopted a sworn and signed declaration of anathema and obedience which is further evidence for the emphasis on obedience as a consequence of the primacy among Paschal II and his advisors. The text is worth quoting because it is usually misinterpreted as a condemnation of lay investiture: *Anathematizo omnem heresim et precipue eam, quae statum presentis aecclesiae perturbat, quae docet et astruit anathema contempnendum et aecclesiae ligamenta spernenda esse. Promitto autem oboedientiam apostolicae sedis pontifici domno Paschali eiusque successoribus sub testimonio Christi et aecclesiae, affirmans quod affirmat, et dampnans quod dampnat sancta et universalis aecclesia* [30]. Disobedience to papal strictures is here formally declared a heresy, and this may or may not mean investiture. The papal primacy is a divine institution [31], and perfect obedience to papal decrees is therefore required of every member of the church. In a decretal letter which was probably addressed to Archbïhop Crescentius of Spalato, Paschal

---

[27] JL 6392 = Migne PL 163, 356A; see also JL 5847 and above n. 8 on the source of this quotation.

[28] JL 5884 = Migne PL 163, 81C.

[29] Ekkehard of Aura, ed. F.-J. Schmale and I. Schmale-Ott, *Frutolfs und Ekkehards Chroniken und die Anonyme Kaiserchronik* (Ausgewählte Quellen zur deutschen Geschichte des Mittelalters. Freiherr vom Stein-Gedächtnisausgabe, 15), Darmstadt 1972, 180: « Quia, inquit, tunicam Christi scindere, id est aecclesiam rapinis et incendiis devastare, luxuriis, periuriis atque homicidiis commaculare non cessavit, primo a beatae memoriae Gregorio papa, deinde a sanctissimo viro Urbano predecessore meo propter suam inoboedientiam excommunicatus est atque condempnatus, nos quoque in proxima synodo nostra iudicio totius aecclesiae perpetuo eum anathemati tradidimus ». See Gratian, *De cons.* D. 3 c. 17; R. Somerville, *Honorius II, Conrad and Lothar III*: Arch. Hist. Pont. 10 (1972) 341-346, 345s and n. 25; LThK 6 (1961) 197-199 s.v. *Kirchenbann* and *ibid.* 1 (1957) 484s, s.v. *Anathema*.

[30] Ekkehard of Aura, 180.

[31] JL 6392; JL 6453.

equated disobedience with a crime that justified papal demands for an oath of loyalty, or oath of office, which had to be given in exchange for the pallium [32]. On another occasion Paschal cited the response of Pope Gelasius I to eastern complaints about Roman highhandedness in the excommunication of Acatius as evidence for the nature of papal decrees in order to emphasize their inviolability [33]. The apostolic see is *caput et magistra*, and the members of the *ecclesia* are like branches which cannot green when they are cut off from the stem, or like streams which run dry when they are cut off from the source [34].

The privileges of the Roman church are those which were bestowed by Christ on the Apostle Peter, and thus on Peter's heir, the bishop of Rome. *Apostolorum principis vices in ecclesiae regimine teneamus*, wrote Paschal in identical arengas of two letters addressed to French bishops early in his pontificate [35]. Paschal continued the epistles with a description of Peter's singular position, quoting *Matt.* 16,18 *Tu es Petrus, et super hanc petram edificabo ecclesiam meam*, and verse 19 in a characteristic paraphrase: *cui etiam tantam potestatis prerogativam concessit, ut eius arbitrio in coelo et in terra vel liganda ligarentur vel solvenda solverentur.* Peter's preeminent authority and his prerogatives were subsequently

---

[32] JL 6570 = MIGNE PL 163,429 A-B: «... Nonne malum est ab ecclesiae unitate, a sedis apostolicae obedientia resilire? Nonne malum est contra sacrorum canonum statuta prorumpere? ... Hoc nimirum malo ac necessitate compellimur, iuramentum pro fide, pro obedientia, pro unitate requirere». On the oath see T. GOTTLOB, *Der kirchliche Amtseid der Bischöfe* (Kanonistische Studien und Texte, 9), Bonn 1936, 8s, 49ss.

[33] JL 5846 = MIGNE PL 163,54 A: «Quanta reverentia sedis apostolicae constitutionibus debeatur, fraternitatem vestram non ignorare credimus. Si qua vero vel minus dicta, vel aliter intellecta conspiciuntur, meminerint qui adversus sanctam Romanam ecclesiam conqueri consueverunt, quod pro Felicis papae scriptis adversus Acatium datis, orientalibus episcopis sanctae memoriae Gelasius papa responderit ... » Paschal did not indicate to which passage of the long and frequently quoted letter of Pope Gelasius I (*ep. 26, JK 664*) he referred. The most likely paragraph is *Cuncta per mundum* (*Decretales Pseudo-Isidorianae*, ed. HINSCHIUS, p. 643), a strong statement for the Roman primacy and in particular the absolute inviolability of papal decrees. This canon was incorporated into the collection of ANSELM OF LUCCA (2.16 and 1.47, 1.48 and 1.49), *74-Titles*, c. 10, the *Collection in Three Books* (MS Biblioteca Apostolica Vaticana, *Vat. lat. 3831*, fol. 4va), and the *Polycarpus* (MS Biblioteca Apostolica Vaticana, *Reg. lat. 987*, fol. 10r-10v). Cf. GRATIAN, C. 9 q. 3 c. 17 and c. 18. For brief introductions to the *Collection in Three Books* see FOURNIER-LE BRAS, *Histoire* II, 198-203; VAN HOVE, *Prolegomena*, 328; STICKLER, *Historia iuris canonici* I, 179, n. 2. For the canonical collection called *Polycarpus*, compiled between 1109 and 1113, see FOURNIER-LE BRAS, *Histoire* II, 169-180; VAN HOVE, *Prolegomena*, 327; STICKLER, *Historia* I, 178s.

[34] JL 6392 = MIGNE PL 163,356 A: «Non potest, beato attestante Cypriano, ramus fractus ab arbore germinare, et rivus a fonte praecisus arescit ...». Cf. JL 4304 of Pope Leo IX, above n. 9. On Cyprian cf. H. RAHNER, *Symbole der Kirche; die Ekklesiologie der Väter*, Salzburg 1964, 221s.

[35] JL 5831 and JL 5832 = MIGNE PL 163, 39 B and 40 D. See also JL 6088 and JL 6450; cf. JL 6558. For the historical development of the identification of the popes with Peter see the references in n. 5 above. MACCARRONE, *Dottrina*, and ULLMANN, *Leo I*, are particularly relevant.

granted to Clement and his legitimate successors: *Quam potestatis sue successionem ipse B. Clementi et per eum omnibus concessit, qui eius sedi iuste presidere, et ecclesiam dei canonica studuerint ordinatione disponere*[36]. Perhaps on account of the crusades as well as the long drawn-out negotiations with Byzantium[37] Paschal seems to have been more aware than his predecessors of certain difficulties which the Gregorian view of primacy might entail for the eastern patriarchs. He nonetheless upheld the claim to primacy, resorting in a communication to Patriarch Bernard of Antioch to the argument of Peter's martyrdom in Rome[38]. There is also one reference to c. 28 of the council of Chalcedon in support of Rome's primacy[39] which is used to strengthen the usual references to *Matt.* 16,18 and 19. Generally, Paschal considered it self-evident that the prerogatives of the church, that is the papacy, were directly instituted by God and that it was superfluous to stress the point: *Qualiter ecclesia dei fundata sit non est a nobis nunc temporis disserendum. Hoc enim plenius evangelii textus et apostolorum littere profitentur*[40].

This quote is found in a letter to King Henry I of England. The same letter contains the statement that Peter received the stewardship of the church jointly with the other apostles: *universum siquidem terrarum orbem dominus et magister noster suis discipulis dispertivit, sed Europae fines Petro singulariter commisit et Paulo*[41]. Ironically, though, the point was made in order to strengthen a reference to the Petrine texts *John* 21,15-17 and *Luke* 22,32 and with them the special relationship between England and the apostolic see. One would like to know what Paschal considered the frontiers of Europe, since the sphere of Peter and Paul certainly included Palestine with Jerusalem and Antioch. The enigmatic reference to the division of the world among all of the apostles, which is found nowhere else in Paschal's correspondence, is perhaps no more than a rhetorical device to emphasize the special authority of Peter, and therefore of Paschal, with regard to English ecclesiastical matters.

The Petrine passages, *Matt.* 16,18-19 and particularly *Luke* 22,32 and *John* 21,15-17 served often to emphasize papal orthodoxy and as a basis for the whole span of specifically papal activity in the church, that is papal jurisdiction as the universal ordinary. The

---

[36] JL 5831 and JL 5832.

[37] See above n. 24.

[38] JL 6334; JL 6088; JL 6328 to Bernard of Antioch = MIGNE PL 163, 303 D: « Quamvis inter caeteras sedes apostolica illa sedes emineat, quam Petri apostoli morte in corpore dignatio superna clarificavit, inter Romanum tamen et Antiochenum episcopos tanta quondam legitur caritas exstitisse, ut nulla inter eos diversitas videretur ... ». See MACCARRONE, *Dottrina*, 650ss.

[39] JL 6570 = MIGNE PL 163, 429 C. For c. 28 of the council of Chalcedon see *Conciliorum oecumenicorum decreta*, ed. J. ALBERIGO et al., Bologna ³1973, 99s.

[40] JL 6453 = MIGNE PL 163, 378 B.

[41] *Ibid.* 378s.

identical arengas of letters to Archbishop Peter of Acerenza and Archbishop Guy of Vienne are good evidence for this usage. The quote from *Matt.* 16,18-19 is continued with *Luke* 22,32:

Ipsi quoque et proprie firmitas et aliene fidei confirmatio eodem Deo auctore prestatur, cum ad eum dicitur, 'Rogavi pro te ut non deficiat fides tua, Petre, et tu aliquando conversus, confirma fratres tuos.' Oportet ergo nos qui licet indigni Petri residere in loco prava corrigere, recta firmare et in omni ecclesia ad interni arbitrium iudicis sic disponenda disponere, ut de vultu eius iudicium nostrum prodeat, et oculi nostri videant aequitatem [42].

Many of Paschal's judicial decisions, exceptions are the numerous exemptions of monasteries and the rarer grant of tithes to monks [43], corresponded to Pseudo-Isidorian decrees. Some examples are episcopal translations [44], the prohibition to establish new bishoprics in small towns [45], or cases concerning the division, creation, suppression or unification of existing bishoprics [46]. A letter of April 1115 to King Henry of England which Paschal sent through his legate, Anselm of S. Saba, is a very notable example for the assertion of papal primacy in conjunction with papal prerogatives [47]. A closer analysis of this letter is rewarding because it shows that Paschal did not derive papal claims to primacy from Pseudo-Isidore whom he cited either directly or indirectly in order to support his claims to specific rights, but rather that these specific rights were exclusively papal in nature because they were derived from the pontiff's fulness of power which he enjoyed as a successor of Peter by divine institution.

Paschal's letter was written in response to the uncanonical translation of Bishop Ralph d'Escures from Rochester to Canterbury without papal consent. It is a strong indictment of Henry's ecclesiastical policies which was read publicly by Anselm of S. Saba before king, clergy, and nobles at the Westerminster court of September 16, 1115. Paschal condemned not only the translation of bishops without his consent, but also royal judicial decisions in cases involving bishops, the royal custom to hold councils without papal knowledge and the

---

[42] JL 6088 to Peter of Acerenza = Migne PL 163, 194 B and JL 6596 to Guy of Vienne. See also JL 6575 = Migne PL 163, 431s.: «... Nescit enim beatus Petrus deficere, pro cuius fide ipse auctor fidei Christus oravit ...».
[43] See G. Constable, *Monastic Tithes from their Origins to the Twelfth Century* (Cambridge Studies in Medieval Life and Thought, 10), Cambridge/Engl. 1964, especially p. 95s. with further references.
[44] See JL 5912, JL 6222, JL 6285, JL 6298, JL 6449, JL 6450, JL 6453, JL 6570
[45] See JL 5872, JL 5912, JL 5931, JL 6210, JL 6212, JL 6285, JL 6329, JL 6358, JL 6417, JL 6490.
[46] See JL 6210, JL 6212, JL 6329, JL 6358, JL 6396, JL 6417, JL 6490.
[47] JL 6453 = Migne PL 163, 378s. The letter and its background are discussed by H. Böhmer, *Kirche und Staat in England und in der Normandie im XI. und XII. Jahrhundert*, Leipzig 1899 (reprinted Aalen 1968), 290-292; F. Barlow, *The Feudal Kingdom of England, 1042-1216*, London ²1961, 185s.; M. Brett, *The English Church Under Henry I*, Oxford 1975, especially p. 36s., all with further references.

ratification of their canons [48], and the prevention of appeals. With an impressive array of canonical and scriptural authorities Paschal vindicated these rights for the Roman church. There is no need, Paschal asserted, to discuss the divine origin of the church which is clearly set out in the Scriptures [49]. The letter continues immediately with the claim that bishops need papal confirmation. The claim is supported by a reference to *Ps.* 40,17 [50] which is amplified by a reference to Paul, *I Tim.* 5,22: *Manum cito nemini imposueris neque communicaveris peccatis alienis,* and the commentary on this Pauline passage by Pope Leo I: *Quid est cito manum imponere, nisi ante aetatem maturitatis, ante tempus examinis, ante meritum laboris, ante experientiam disciplinae, sacerdotalem honorem tribuere non probatis?* [51] Confirmation is a papal duty, for *Ipse caput ecclesiae Dominus Jesus Christus cum pastori primo apostolo Petro ecclesiam commendaret, dixit: Pasce oves meas, pasce agnos meos* [52]. *Oves quippe in ecclesia ecclesiarum prepositi sunt ... Quomodo ergo vel agnos vel oves pascere possumus quos neque novimus, neque vidimus?* As *vicarius* of Peter, Paul, and their successors the papacy is now entrusted with this task through its legates. Papal decretals, which were ultimately derived from the *Pseudo-Isidorian Decretals,* are cited in support of the papal right to decide all cases involving bishops and *causae maiores*:

Vos autem inconsultis nobis etiam episcoporum negotia definitis cum martyr Victor ecclesiae Romanae pontifex dicat: Quamquam comprovincialibus episcopis accusati causam pontificis scrutari liceat non tamen definire inconsulto Romano pontifice permissum est. Zephyrinus quoque martyr et pontifex: Iudicia, inquit, episcoporum, maioresque causae a sede apostolica et non ab alia sunt terminanda [53].

Both decrees are part of several reform collections including the *Collection in 74-Titles* and the *Collectio canonum* of Anselm of Lucca, but Paschal quoted them very likely from the canonical collection of Cardinal Deusdedit, the only collection in which the excerpts are found in the same sequence as in Paschal's letter [54]. Another Pseudo-

---

[48] It is uncertain what Paschal meant. See *ibid.,* 37.

[49] This passage from JL 6453 was quoted earlier. See above n. 40.

[50] « Pro patribus tuis nati sunt tibi filii, constitues eos principes super omnem terram ». The context shows that the reference is to ecclesiastics.

[51] JK 410 = *Decretales Pseudo-Isidorianae,* ed. HINSCHIUS, p. 622. The letter is very largely genuine although transmitted through Pseudo-Isidore. See FUHRMANN, *Einfluß,* 771.

[52] Cf. *John* 21,15-17.

[53] Ps. Victor, JK †74, c. 5 = *Decretales Pseudo-Isidorianae,* ed. HINSCHIUS, 128; Ps. Zepherinus, JK †80, c. 6, *ibid.* 132.

[54] For the transmission of these canons in several canonical collections see FUHRMANN, *Einfluß,* 798 no. 25 for Victor, and *ibid.* 914 no. 285 for Zephyrinus. DEUSDEDIT, *Collectio canonum* 1.69 and 1.70. Two variants are noticeable: 1) the addition of 'Martyr' in JL 6453, and 2) the expression *iudicia episcoporum* which is not found in Deusdedit's collection, but only in the *74-Titles* (c. 3) and the *Collectio canonum*

Isidorian text, Pseudo-Nicaea c. 2, also found in the collection of Deusdedit but apparently quoted from that of Anselm of Lucca, is cited by Paschal as a confirmation for the prohibition to celebrate councils without informing the Roman see [55]. In conclusion the letter refers once again to *I Tim.* 5,22 and the commentary of Leo I [56] and threatens the king with excommunication and with Christ's declaration: *Qui non colligit mecum, dispergit; et qui non est mecum, adversum me est (Luke* 11,23). The letter is indeed remarkable, and one has to agree with M. Brett who wrote: « Whatever the grounds of the Pope's indignation its intensity comes through in this bull very clearly, for even at the height of the dispute over investitures Paschal delivered no more sternly worded protest and deployed no more formidable battery of authorities in support of his claims » [57]. The letter was writen only two or three months before invitations to the Lateran synod of 1116 were dispatched in the summer of 1115 and is therefore particularly relevant to this study.

The Councils of 1112 and 1116.

Paschal's correspondence leaves no doubt that he and his advisors consistently emphasized papal primacy in the sense of earlier eleventh-century reformers and that Paschal was always ready to come to the defense of papal prerogatives. This has never been noted. Historians who have discussed Pope Paschal II in the past fixed their attention exclusively, one might say, on the spectacular events of 1111 and 1112, ' reproaching ' the pontiff in the first place for having given in to Henry's threats and to have permitted investiture with ring and staff in the agreement of Ponte Mammolo and then, in the second place, to have rescinded this agreement half-heartedly when he was put under pressure by the church, particularly on the occasion of the Lateran synod of 1112 [58]. Both charges are

---

of ANSELM OF LUCCA (2.6). It seems nevertheless unlikely that Paschal used either *74-Titles* or Anselm's collection because the Victor and Zepherinus texts are widely separated from each other (*74-Titles*: c. 3 and c. 83; ANSELM: 2.6 and 2.81). Conceivably Paschal did not use Deusdedit's collection directly but instead an intermediate collection which was used later by both Deusdedit an Anselm of Lucca. Such a collection was postulated in a different context by FUHRMANN, *Einfluß*, 519.

[55] « Vos praeter conscientiam vestram (*sic*) decreta synodalia celebratis, cum Athanasius Alexandricae Ecclesiae scribat: Scimus in Nicaea magna synodo trecentorum decem et octo episcoporum ab omnibus concorditer esse corroboratum non debere absque Romani pontificis scientia concilia celebrari » (JL 6453). See ANSELM OF LUCCA, *Collectio canonum* 2.50 (end); cf. DEUSDEDIT, *Kanonessammlung* 1.22 with two variants; see also *Decretales Pseudo-Isidorianae*, ed. HINSCHIUS, p. 479 c. 2, and FUHRMANN, *Einfluß*, 912 no. 284.

[56] See n. 51 above.

[57] M. BRETT, *The English Church Under Henry I*, Oxford 1975, 37.

[58] The most detailed bibliography for Pope Paschal II with older literature is found in *Realenzyklopädie für protestantische Theologie und Kirche*, XIV, 717-724 (C. MIRBT); see also CARL-JOSEPH VON HEFELE and H. LECLERCQ, *Histoire des Conciles*,

XI

undeniably correct although the agreement of Ponte Mammolo (April 11/12, 1111) was not without its redeeming features at least in the eyes of Paschal and the curia, even though it prohibited in flat contradiction to previous papal policy that anyone should be consecrated unless he had first been invested by the emperor in whose presence the elections were to take place [59]. In return for this concession the emperor promised 1) to release the pontiff and his entourage from captivity; 2) to cease to support the antipope; and 3) to return and aid in regaining *patrimonia et possessiones Romane ecclesiae que abstuli ... et cetera que iure habere debet more antecessorum meorum* [60]. Just as in the February negotiations at S. Maria in Turribus, a church flanking the entrance to the atrium of the old basilica of St. Peter in Rome, Paschal insisted in his discussions with Henry in April 1111 on the full restitution of the patrimony of St. Peter to the papacy, that is towns and territories in Italy which had been granted to the papacy in the donations of Pepin, Charlemagne and their imperial successors of the east Frankish kingdom [61]. Paschal seems to have thought that this return of the patrimony would almost render even the investiture grant defensible. The solemn charters of the emperors which assured these possessions to the papacy had been incorporated into canon law for the first time by Cardinal Deusdedit (d. 1098/99) [62], and it is evident in general that the reform papacy was profoundly concerned about the sometimes abject poverty of the Roman church. The reformers recognized the need to strengthen its material resources if they wished to assure independence. The imperial donations had usually remained a dead letter, and it is in retrospect difficult to see what may have induced Paschal to take Henry's promises of 1111 seriously. That he did so cannot be doubted. [63].

V/1, Paris 1912, 465 n. 3; recent bibliographies are given by T. Schieffer: LThK 8 (1963) 128s; J. Gilchrist: *New Catholic Encyclopedia* 10 (1967) 1049, and H. Jedin and J. Dolan, eds., *Handbook of Church History*, vol. III: F. Kempf et al., *The Church in the Age of Feudalism*, transl. A. Biggs, New York 1969, 392-398 and esp. p. 542. Particularly useful are A. Fliche, *La Réforme grégorienne et la Reconquête chrétienne (1057-1123)* (Histoire de l'Église depuis les origines jusqu'à nos jours, VIII), Paris 1950, 340ss.; H. Guleke, *Deutschlands innere Kirchenpolitik von 1105 bis 1111*, Dorpat 1882; G. Peiser, *Der deutsche Investiturstreit unter König Heinrich V. bis zum päpstlichen Privileg vom 3. April 1111*, Berlin 1883; W. Schum, *Kaiser Heinrich V. und Papst Paschalis II. im Jahre 1112*, in *Jahrbücher der Akademie zu Erfurt*, n.s. 8 (1877) 191-318; see also N. F. Cantor, *Church, Kingship, and Lay Investiture in England: 1089-1135*, Princeton 1958, and U.-R. Blumenthal, *The Early Councils of Pope Paschal II*, Toronto 1978, with further references.
  [59] MGH *Const.* 1 (see n. 14 above), 144s., no. 96.
  [60] *Ibid.*, 143s., no. 94.
  [61] See in general P. Partner, *The Lands of St. Peter*, Berkeley and Los Angeles 1972, especially pp. 6-9; 46-48; 139-154 on Paschal's pontificate. Blumenthal, *Patrimonia and Regalia in 1111* (as in n. 15 above), 10 and the collection of sources and bibliography by H. Fuhrmann, *Quellen zur Entstehung des Kirchenstaates* (Historische Texte, Mittelalter, 7), Göttingen 1968.
  [62] Deusdedit, *Collectio canonum* (ed. W. V. von Glanvell) 3.280, 3.281; 3.282.
  [63] See Paschal's letters JL 6289, 6293, 6295, and 6299.

Henry, however, did not keep his oath[64]; if he had restored the papal states the 1112 synod would probably never have met, or at least under very different circumstances. As it was, the council of 1112 represents the most concentrated expression of ecclesiastical opposition to Pope Paschal II and thus indirectly to papal primacy. Paschal needed all his diplomatic skill to prevent his deposition by the synod on the charge of heresy. The synod of 1112 is discussed more fully elsewhere[65]. It is therefore possible to disregard in the context of the present paper the question of whether or not investiture was a heresy and to focus instead on the outcome of the discussions in the Lateran in the spring of 1112, that is the strengthening of collective tendencies in the church.

Two recensions of the *acta* as well as a *breviarium* of the synodal proceedings are preserved[66]. They all record the revocation of the agreement of Ponte Mammolo, which was condemned by the synod as *pravilegium*, a term that has been used ever since to describe the agreement. Recensions I and II announce the revocation in identical terms: *Privilegium illud quod non est privilegium sed vere debet dici pravilegium ... nos omnes in hoc sancto concilio cum domno papa congregati canonica censura et ecclesiastica auctoritate iudicio sancti Spiritus dampnamus et irritum esse iudicamus atque omnino cassamus*[67]. It is seen even here that it is in the first place the council which withdraws the papal privilege, but the full extent of the role of the synod becomes clearer yet in recension II of the *acta* which is preserved in Cardinal Boso's Life of Paschal II[68]. According to Boso the pontiff formally described to the assembly his treatment at the hands of Henry V and confessed that he had done wrong when he conceded the Ponte Mammolo privilege: *sine fratrum consilio aut subscriptionibus feci, ... prave factum cognosco, prave factum confiteor, et omnino corrigi Domino prestante desidero. Cuius correctionis modum fratrum qui convenerunt consilio iudicioque constituo ...*[69] This is a remarkable confession. Paschal conceded that the privilege for Henry V was at least in part *prave factum* because it had been granted « without the advice of the brethren or their subscription. »

---

[64] He did, however, call off a campaign against the Normans in southern Italy who were vassals of the papacy. See W. HOLTZMANN, *England, Unteritalien und der Vertrag von Ponte Mammolo*: Neues Archiv 50 (1935) 282-301.

[65] U. R. BLUMENTHAL, *Opposition to Pope Paschal II: Some Comments on the Lateran Council of 1112*: Annuarium Historiae Conciliorum (1978), in press.

[66] See the partial publication by L. WEILAND, MGH *Const.* 1 (as above n. 14), 570-574, nn. 399 and 400.

[67] *Ibid.*, 572, lines 3-5. See B. TIERNEY, *Foundations of the Conciliar Theory*, Cambridge/Engl. 1955, 55, for the distinction between incipient and fully grown conciliar theory.

[68] *Liber pontificalis*, ed. L. DUCHESNE (Bibliothèque des Écoles françaises d'Athènes et de Rome), II (reprinted Paris 1955), 369-371.

[69] *Ibid.*, 370.

In other words the pontiff recognized in his statement what one may perhaps call constitutional limitations on papal powers, although the technical term is anachronistic for the early twelfth century. Paschal's obvious departure from the concept of primacy contrasts strongly with the tenor of his correspondence[70]. The concession of 1112 must have been a very difficult decision to make despite the frequent use of the curia in advisory capacity under his administration which is also well-known for the expansion of the cardinalate[71].

Direct evidence for papal reluctance to recognize the right of a synod to revoke papal decrees is probably provided by the *Breviarium*, a brief summary of the activity of the synod that seems to have originated with the curia. In this document the revocation of the *pravilegium* is exclusively attributed to papal authority: *Hocque factum est auctoritate beati Innocenti pape, qui quod necessitate imminente male factum est, cessante necessitate mutandum precipit, et decretis felicis memorie Gregorii VII. atque Urbani Romanorum pontificum observatis*[72]. There is always some danger that the scarce evidence in a period of historical fluidity is overinterpreted by historians who have the advantage of hindsight. It is, therefore, fortunate that there is evidence that contemporaries, too, regarded the 1112 synod as a victory for collective tendencies in the church as opposed to the prevalent emphasis on papal primacy which was represented by the reform papacy. Cardinal Hugh, who had supported the rights of dissident cardinals in 1084 against Gregory VII with his interpretation of the privilege of Christ for St. Peter as a privilege for the Roman see as a whole rather than the pope alone, boasted in a letter written to Countess Mathilda of Tuscany after the council of 1112, that now the successor of Peter could only act through the intermediary of cardinal priests and cardinal deacons, « through whom and with whom he confirms what is to be confirmed and disapproves what is to be disapproved, without whose subscriptions public statements of the highest pontiff are invalid »[73]. Paschal's readi-

---

[70] Cf. CONGAR, *Kirchenfrömmigkeit*, 204s.

[71] See R. HÜLS, *Kardinäle, Klerus und Kirchen Roms 1049-1130* (Bibliothek des Deutschen Historischen Instituts in Rom, 48), Tübingen 1977, *passim*; H.-W. KLEWITZ, *Die Entstehung des Kardinalkollegiums*, originally published in Zeitschrift der Savigny-Stiftung für Rechtsgeschichte, Kan. Abt. 25 (1936) 115-221, reprinted in: KLEWITZ, *Reformpapsttum und Kardinalkolleg*, Darmstadt 1957, 11-134, especially pp. 98-111.

[72] MGH *Const.* 1, 573 no. 400; see also S. KUTTNER, *Urban II and the Doctrine of Interpretation: A Turning Point?*, in *Post Scripta. Essays on Medieval Law and the Emergence of the European State in Honor of Gaines Post* (Studia Gratiana, 15), Rome 1972, 53-85, especially pp. 62-69.

[73] *Benonis aliorumque cardinalium schismaticorum contra Gregorium VII. et Urbanum II. scripta*, ed. K. FRANCKE, MGH *Libelli de lite* II (1892) 366-422, epistle 10, pp. 417-421, here p. 418, lines 14-18: « Est autem privilegium Romanae sedis semper assistere per cardinales presbiteros et diaconos ipsi summo pontifici vel vicario ipsius sedis, id est ei, quem ipsa sedes sacrosancta os suum facit, per quem et cum quo predicat, per quem sacramenta administrat, per quem et cum quo firmanda confirmat

ness to admit to errors, his humble profession of faith before the synod, and his concession to the cardinals [74] brought the synod to a close on a conciliatory note and prevented Paschal's deposition. That the synod presented a threat to papal primacy was obvious to the pope and to the curia. Paschal used the remaining years of his pontificate to reverse the events of 1112 as far as possible.

The Lateran council of 6 March - 11 March, 1116 particularly served this purpose [75]. It was the last of the great general councils held by Pope Paschal II. Patterned on the councils of the ancient church [76] it was carefully prepared. Already in August 1115 a formal invitation, which has only survived for the church of Spain but was probably also sent to other churches, requested ecclesiastics to come to Rome for a council to be held on 4 March, 1116:

Ab ecclesiae patribus... praecepta suscepimus, ut quoties in ecclesia graviores emerserint quaestiones, frequentior fratrum numerus convocetur. Sane pro investituris episcopatuum, vel abbatiarum, quas sibi iam dudum assumpserunt laici, tantum in ecclesia scandalum est exortum, ut ad schisma processerit: unde opportunum et valde necessarium duximus, tam pro investituris ipsis, quam pro ecclesiarum occupationibus fraternitatem vestram ad agendum generale concilium excitare ... [77]

The revocation of 1112 had returned the relationship between the empire and the papacy to a state of affairs that differed little from that prevailing in 1110/111. Henry's position in Germany was so weakened through both revocation and excommunications by papal legates that he descended once again into Italy where he could

---

et improbanda improbat, qua non subscribente invalida est publica summi pontificis sententia ». The Latin is not very clear; noteworthy is the omission of the cardinal bishops. The letter is usually dated ca. 1098 (see HÜLS, Kardinäle [as in n. 71 above], 251), but it seems clear that epistle 10 at least was written after 1112. The editor, K. Francke, could not identify the Lateran synod to which this letter referred (p. 418 n. 3), but unless the extended passages which refer indirectly to this assembly are interpolations, the council in question is the Lateran council of 1112. Countess Mathilda did not die until 1115 and Hugh, whose date of death is unknown, might well have felt encouraged to write to her in the terms he did after her reconciliation with King Henry V in 1111. See also the references in Libelli de lite II, 368 n. 8.

[74] The word fratres in Paschal's declaration did not only refer to cardinals, but to advisors in general; it is clear, however, that the cardinals were in fact the chief beneficiaries.

[75] The basic sources for the synod can be consulted in J. D. MANSI, Sacrorum Conciliorum nova et amplissima collectio XXI, Venice 1776, reprinted Graz 1961, col. 145-152; see also C.-J. VON HEFELE and H. LECLERCQ, Histoire des conciles V/1, Paris 1912, 553-559; G. MEYER VON KNONAU, Jahrbücher des Deutschen Reiches unter Heinrich IV. und Heinrich V., VII (Jahrbücher der Deutschen Geschichte, 17), Leipzig 1909 (reprinted Berlin 1965), 1-8 and especially, VI, Leipzig 1907 (reprinted Berlin 1965), 350-356 with further references.

[76] G. TANGL, Die Teilnehmer an den allgemeinen Konzilien des Mittelalters, Weimar 1932 (reprinted Darmstadt 1969), 190-192, here: p. 191.

[77] JL 6462 = MIGNE PL 163, 385 A-B; cf. JL 6503, an invitation sent to Bishop Wido of Chur. It was published by P. EWALD, Churer Briefsammlung: Neues Archiv 3 (1878) 169 no. 2; the date should be 1110. See A. BRACKMANN, Germania Pontificia II/2, Berlin 1925, 88 n. 6.

establish himself as heir to the Mathildine lands early in 1116 [78].
The aim of the Gregorian reformers, *libertas ecclesiae*, remained as
elusive as ever. The synod was to find a remedy, but at the same
time it was to reassert Paschal's leadership in the church which had
suffered badly through the debacle of 1112. This explains the particularly careful preparation for the meeting and the considerable
efforts which were undertaken to make the assembly in a geographical sense representative of all of Latin Christendom [79] as a symbol
of papal authority and power.

Some information about the participants has survived, indicating
the wide-spread interest the synod aroused. The papal letter which
confirmed the council's judicial decision of the quarrel between the
cathedrals of St. John and St. Stephen at Besançon over the possession of the episcopal cathedra in favor of St. Stephen [80], was
signed by the cardinal bishops of Porto, Palestrina, and Sabina; the
cardinal priests of the title churches of S. Clemente, SS. Martino e
Silvestro, and S. Anastasia; the cardinal deacons of SS. Vito e Mo-
desto, S. Maria in Via Lata, SS. Sergio e Bacco, SS. Cosma e Damiano, S. Lucia in Septisolio [81], and S. Maria in Cosmedin. Other
signatories were the archbishops Arnald of Bordeaux, and Baldric
of Dol (Brittany), and the bishops John of S. Brieux (diocese Tours),
Beltran of Bazas (diocese Auch) as well as Hugo of Porto. It is
likely that a delegation from St. Stephen at Besançon was among
those present at the council and defended its position in the law suit.

The final session of the synod took place on Saturday, 11 March.
The signatories of the judicial decision preserved in JL 6517, which
was signed on 24 March, had evidently stayed on in Rome. Had
other members of the French and Spanish churches also stayed,
perhaps in order to celebrate Holy Week, Easter Sunday was 2 April,
in Rome? It does seem likely that the bishops and abbots sought
safety in numbers and returned jointly to the north, in particular
since Henry V, who cannot have been pleased by the outcome of
the synod, was stationed with his army in Tuscany. If these assumptions are correct, then the recipients of privileges granted by
Pope Paschal II to French and Spanish churches and monasteries
between 11 March and 5 April also attended the council. They are
Bishop Stephen of Autun, Archbishop Josseran of Lyons, Bishop
Reinhard of Halberstadt who obtained a privilege for his foundation
St. Pancrace and its prior Thietmar, Abbot Dominic of Sahagun,

---

[78] KNONAU, *Jahrbücher* (see n. 75 above) VII, 1-8.
[79] *Ibid.* VI, 351 n., where the theory of a possible participation of Byzantine emissaries is rejected.
[80] JL 6517 = MIGNE PL 163, 402-404.
[81] It is difficult to determine whether Cardinal John was deacon of S. Lucia in
Septisolio or S. Lucia in Orfea (in capite). See HÜLS, *Kardinäle*, 230 no. 2. I follow Hüls.

and Abbot Arnald of Saint-Thibéry (diocese Montpellier, formerly Agde) [82]. It seems certain that two letters dated 5 April 1116 which commended Bishop Gaufred of Chartres, whom Paschal had consecrated, to the clergy and people of Chartres and Archbishop Daimbert of Sens respectively, were carried back by Bishop Gaufred himself [83].

Ekkehard of Aura, the chronicler, noted that Archbishop Guy of Vienne did not attend the council but had sent messengers, unfortunately unnamed, to whom he entrusted letters. His chronicle also indicates that Abbot Pontius of Cluny had come as emissary of Emperor Henry V, mentions two prominent Roman nobles, Peter Pierleone and the Prefect Peter, as well as several Italian participants in addition to the signatories of the bull for St. Stephen at Besançon: Bishop Bruno of Segni (1079-1123), Bishop Rudolf of Lucca (1112-1118), Archbishop Peter of Pisa (1104-1119), and the contenders for the diocese of Milan, Jordan and Grossolan [84]. The chronicle of Montecassino contributes the name of Abbot Girard of Montecassino to the list of participants [85], and Landulf's *Historia Mediolanensis* is the source for the names of a group of north Italians who had come in support of either Grossolan or Jordan, including himself, Bishop Landulf of Asti (1103-1134), Anselm della Pusterla, and an unidentifiable suffragan of Milan, *Villanus Brisiensis*, who as Landulf wrote was consecrated *in quadam ecclesia Lateranensi* by Jordan with the assistance of himself [86]. Gerhoch of Reichersberg mentioned in his *Opusculum de edificio dei* the *Vulturnensis episcopus* as among the participants, possibly referring to the abbot of the Abbey of St. Vin-

---

[82] The letters are listed by Jaffé as JL 6509, 6510, 6512, 6513 and 6515, and 6514.
[83] JL 6518 and 6519.
[84] See Ekkehard of Aura, *Chronica* = *Frutolfs und Ekkehards Chroniken und die Anonyme Kaiserchronik*, ed. and transl. by F.-J. Schmale and I. Schmale-Ott (Ausgewählte Quellen zur deutschen Geschichte des Mittelalters. Freiherr vom Stein-Gedächtnisausgabe, 15), Darmstadt 1972, 318-324. For Bruno of Segni see H. Hoffmann's biography, in *Dizionario Biografico degli Italiani* XIV, Roma 1972, 644-647; basic is the monograph by B. Gigalski, *Bruno, Bischof von Segni, Abt von Montecassino. Sein Leben und seine Schriften* (Kirchengeschichtliche Studien, III/4), Münster 1898. For Grossolan and Jordan see E. Cazzani, *Vescovi e Arcivescovi di Milano*, Milan 1955, 133ss. Ekkehard's chronicle will be abbreviated Ekkehard below.
[85] *Chronica monasterii Casinensis*, ed. W. Wattenbach (MGH, *Scriptores* 7), Hannover 1846, 551-844, here: p. 790 = 4, cap. 60. The chronicle states that Abbot Girard accompanied Paschal to the synod since he wanted to present his claims to a cell of St. Sophia, Benevento, but it is not known whether the abbot had a chance to actually plead his case. For the chronicle see H. Hoffmann, *Studien zur Chronik von Montecassino*: Deutsches Archiv 29 (1973) 59-162.
[86] *Landulphi Junioris sive de Sancto Paulo Historia Mediolanensis ab anno MXCV usque ad annum MCXXXVII* (Rerum Italicarum Scriptores, V/3), ed. C. Castiglioni, Bologna 2[1934], cap. 41s., pp. 26s.; for a biography of Landulf see *ibid.*, pp. vii-x; for Landulf of Asti see A. Bellini, *Il beato Landolfo da Vergiate*: Archivio Storico Lombardo 49 (1922) 332-349; for Anselm della Pusterla see M. Marzoratti in *Dizionario Biogr. degli Italiani* III, Roma 1961, 415-417; for Grossolan see the previous note and the references given by Castiglioni in *Historia*, 26, n. 3.

cent, located at the source of the river Volturno in Campania, since the ancient Volturnum on the coast west of Capua was not the seat of a bishopric [87].

The Histoire de Béarn by Peter de Marca contains a passage, based by de Marca on the cartulary of the abbey of Lescar, which appears to indicate that the assembly at the Lateran in 1116 was also the forum for the quarrel between Guido, bishop of Lescar (1115-1141) and thus suffragan of Auch, and the contemporary bishop of Tarbes whose name is uncertain [88], over the monastery Saint-Pé-de-Générez:

Gui adjouste qu'il avoit succédé à Sance et renouvelé cette plainte en présence de l'évesque de Bigorre Grégoire, par devant le pape Paschal second, au concile de Latran (qui est à mon advis celuy qui fut tenu l'an 1110) et ensuite par devant les papes Gelase second et Calliste second au Consile de Tolose, tenu l'an 1124 [89].

De Marca was in error when he suggested the date 1110 for the Lateran synod at which Guido confronted his colleague from Tarbes, for Sance was bishop of Lescar from 1095-1115 when Guido succeeded him. It seems likely that the bishops of Lescar and Tarbes met at the council of 1116. As we have seen the region of the Pyrénées was represented at the council by another suffragan of Auch, the bishop of Bazas as well as Abbot Arnald of Saint-Thibéry [90]. The new bishop of Lescar might have accompanied them to Rome, and it is conceivable that both Guido of Lescar and the bishop of Tarbes should be added to the list of participants.

The response to his invitation must have pleased Pascal and the curia. The proceedings at the impressive assembly are fairly well documented, in particular through Landulf's *Historia Mediolanensis* [91], the *Chronicon Casinense* [92], recension III of Ekkehard of Aura's chronicle, and last not least Gerhoch's *Opusculum de edificio dei* [93]. The official protocol of the synod has to be considered lost, but is seems certain that both Ekkehard and Gerhoch used it in their accounts which are particularly valuable in the context of this

---

[87] GERHOCH OF REICHERSBERG, *Opusculum de edificio dei*, ed. E. SACKUR (MGH Libelli de lite 3), Hannover 1897, reprinted 1956, 136-202, here: pp. 190-191 n. On Gerhoch see P. CLASSEN, *Gerhoch von Reichersberg. Eine Biographie*, Wiesbaden 1960.

[88] The bishops of Tarbes listed by Gams are Pontius (ad a. 1103), Heraclius? (sic) and Guilielmus, 1120-1141. The seat of the bishop of the county of Bigorre (independent from 819 to 1607 when it became part of France, and today co-extensive with the Départment des Hautes-Pyrénées) was at Tarbes, also known by the Latin names *Tarba, Tarba Bigerriorum*, and *Castrum Bigorrae* (GAMS, Series episcoporum, 634).

[89] P. DE MARCA, *Histoire de Béarn*, ed. V. DUBARAT, II, Pau ²1912, 157-161 (book 5, ch. 31), here: p. 159; see also *Gallia Christiana* I, Paris 1715, 1289-1291.

[90] See JL 6517 and 6514.

[91] See n. 86 above.

[92] See n. 85 above.

[93] See n. 87 above.

paper because they focus on papal activity and central events. The other chronicles view the assembly from a strictly local perspective. The *Chronicon Casinense*, for instance, recorded only the quarrel between the abbots of Cluny and Montecassino over the use of the title *abbas abbatum* which was decided by the chancellor, Cardinal John of Gaeta, in favor of Montecassino. Landulf was a very observant eye-witness, but he too recorded only information that pertained to Milanese affairs.

This certainly kept him busy, for the case of the contending archbishops of Milan, « one of whom had deserted his church, and the other of whom had invaded the see, » as Ekkehard remarked [94], was discussed at the synod during the first session on Monday, 6 March, then entrusted by the pontiff to a committee of cardinal bishops, again discussed in the full council on Tuesday, and finally concluded during the last session of the synod on Saturday 11 March. Jordan was confirmed as archbishop of Milan and Grossolan was transferred back to his original see, Savona, despite his very moving protests [95]. During the third session of the council on Wednesday, 8 March, two other Italians, the bishops of Lucca and Pisa inflicted their territorial dispute on the assembly [96]. The suit between the bishops of Lescar and Tarbes is not mentioned by the sources, and no wonder, for few if any from among the participants can have known the litigants from the Pyrenées. The conciliar records leave no doubt, however, that the patience of the assembly was sorely tried when one local dispute after another was aired before the synod in which the assembly as a whole could have but scant interest even when the issue was as important as the title to the archbishopric of Milan. During the third session, on Wednesday, 8 March, an unnamed bishop rose during the litigation between Lucca and Pisa and complained that it behooved the pontiff to recall the purpose of the council:

Domnum patrem papam recordari decet, quare illius presentis et generalis concilii multitudo sancta per omnia periculorum genera mari terreque convenerit invitata; ibi non de spiritalibus vel aecclesiasticis, sed de secularibus ordine preposatero tractaturi negociis. Expediendum prius, propter quod principaliter convenerint, ut evidentius pernoscatur, quid domnus apostolicus sentiat, quidque in aecclesiis suis reversi predicare debeant [97].

This outburst finally provided Paschal with the opportunity to raise the chief issue which was scheduled for debate at the council: the controversy between Henry V of Germany and the papacy over investiture.

---

[94] EKKEHARD, 318, lines 10-12.
[95] See especially LANDULF, *Historia*, 26, lines 20-25.
[96] EKKEHARD, 318, lines 16-19.
[97] *Ibid.*, lines 20-27.

Paschal introduced the subject with a speech which is reported by both Ekkehard and Gerhoch [98]. As the full accounts indicate both authors seem to have used an official protocol although some differences, especially a greater spontaneity in Gerhoch's report, can be noted. Paschal's speech caused an uproar and an acrimonious argument between Bishop Bruno of Segni [99] and Paschal's supporters. Paschal had in essence repeated his admission of guilt of 1112. As soon as the speech was concluded Bruno of Segni exclaimed that God should be given thanks *quod dominum nostrum et caput nostrum illam heresim dedisse penitet* [100]. An irate John of Gaeta immediately responded threateningly, *Dicis nos heresim dedisse? Nullus amodo te debet audire* [101]. Bruno offered to prove the charge, but is contradicted by the *Vulturnensis episcopus,* who pointed out that since the pope was under duress when he granted the *pravilegium* his action could not be called heresy, which it would be if he had acted voluntarily. This reply was recorded by Gerhoch whose excerpts break off at this point. Ekkehard [102] preserved a stronger defense of the pontiff: *alter quidam adiecit, 'Immo nec malum dici debet, quia, si liberare populum Dei bonum est, quod domnus papa fecit, bonum fuit. Sed liberare populum Dei bonum est auctoritate evangelii, qua precipimur animas quoque pro fratribus ponere.'* At this point of the debate Paschal himself commanded silence and refuted the charge of heresy concluding his remarks with the classical statement for the infallibility of the Roman see:

Fratres et domini mei, audite. Aecclesia ista nunquam habuit heresim, immo hic omnes hereses conquassate sunt. Hic Arriana heresis... Fotinus ceterique heretici destructi sunt. Pro hac aecclesia filius Dei in passione sua oravit, cum dixit: Ego pro te rogavi, Petre, ut non deficiat fides tua (*Luke* 22,32).

As this paper has shown Paschal identified himself with Peter and thus with the church. It is certainly not by accident that Paschal's

---

98 *Ibid.,* lines 28-line 5, p. 320, and GERHOCH, *Opusculum,* 190-191 n.

99 See the references given above, n. 84.

100 This version is reported by GERHOCH, *Opusculum,* 191 n. Ekkehard reported formally, exonerating Bruno of Segni: « Bruno autem Signinus episcopus altius exorsus ait: Gratias agimus omnipotenti Deo, quod domnum Paschalem papam, qui presenti concilio presidet, audivimus proprio ore damnantem illud pravilegium, quod pravitatem et heresim continebat. Ad haec quidam cavillatorie subiunxit: Si privilegium illud heresim continebat, qui illud fecit, hereticus fuit » (p. 320).

101 GERHOCH, *Opusculum,* 191 n. EKKEHARD, p. 320: « Iohannes autem Caietanus ad hoc commotus Signino respondit: Tunc hic et in concilio nobis audientibus Romanum pontificem appellas hereticum? Scriptum, quod fecit domnus papa, malum quidem fuit, sed heresis non fuit ». This passage shows that Gerhoch's account is more direct and correct, for the reply of John of Gaeta to Bruno of Segni would not make sense unless Ekkehard's *quidam* referred to Bruno. See the text given in the preceding note.

102 All subsequent quotations from the Latin source refer to EKKEHARD's chronicle, 320-322, unless otherwise indicated.

admission of guilt stressed his human and fallible nature which he held responsible for the *pravilegium*: *feci autem ut homo, quia sum pulvis et cinis* [103]. A distinction between person and office enabled Paschal to condemn the agreement of Ponte Mammolo which he concluded as an individual while maintaining at the same time his orthodoxy as head of the church [104].

Paschal's statement seems to have ended the session of 8 March. When the debate was resumed on Friday, 10 March [105], it was hardly less animated than on Wednesday. In the general discussion of the state of the church the subject of the February 1111 negotiations apparently came up, for Paschal clarified his understanding of ecclesiastical possessions and, therefore, of the term *regalia* [106]. Against the advice of John of Gaeta and Peter Pierleone he then upheld the excommunications of Emperor Henry V by Cardinal Cono of Palestrina in his capacity as legate a latere at several synods [107]. Perhaps the solemn form of address which Cono used on this occasion should be pointed out because it reflects very well the different attitude towards the pope at the synod of 1116 when compared to the assembly of 1112: *Domine pater, si tuae placet maiestati, si vere tuus fui legatus et, quae feci, tibi placent esse rata ... legationem meam tua auctoritate corrobora.* Paschal acceded to this request which was supported by the emissaries and letters of Archbishop Guido of Vienne with the approval of bishops and abbots despite some dissension among the assembly [108]. The solemn final session on Saturday reveals the pontiff in full control of the proceedings. He decided the case of the archbishopric of Milan, consecrating Jordan, and pronounced a forty-day indulgence for penitents who had come to

---

[103] EKKEHARD, 318, line 33. See also GERHOCH, *Opusculum*, 190-191 n., where the same sentiment is expressed less dramatically.

[104] Cf. C. MIRBT, *Die Publizistik im Zeitalter Gregors VII*, Leipzig 1894 (reprinted 1965), 569s.

[105] It is possible that the council did not assemble on Thurday, 9 March, or if it met, it did so without Paschal, Pontius, John of Gaeta, Peter Pierleone and the Prefect Peter: « Quinta feria papa in concilio non sedit multis et maxime regis negotiis per domnum Cluniacensem, Iohannem Caitanum et Petrum Leonis et Urbis prefectum caeterosque illius partis fautores impeditus » (EKKEHARD, 320, lines 26-29). Ekkehard's references to an imperial party at the council are puzzling, since he included among them John of Gaeta and Peter Pierleone, two of Paschal's most faithful supporters.

[106] This important passage needs to be taken into consideration when the 1111 negotiations are discussed. See EKKEHARD, 320-322, line 8.

[107] See R. HIESTAND, *Legat, Kaiser und Basileus*, 141-152. The full reference is found above, n. 24.

[108] « Dum tali ratione et ordine tam variae et dissonae multitudinis assensus exquiritur, a saniori parte veritati et apertae rationi nichil contradictum, a paucis submurmuratum est, ab episcopis et abbatis nullo modo reclamatum » (EKKEHARD, 324).

the council and *ad apostolorum limina*. He concluded the proceedings with his apostolic blessing [109].

Most striking about the Lateran council of 1116, apart from the wide-spread participation, is the fact that its most crucial sessions were a re-play of the Lateran council of 1112, but under drastically different auspices. Paschal II, who barely escaped deposition in 1112 at the price of what amounted to a legal recognition of an increased role of papal advisors, was able to overcome precisely this concession in 1116 and to reassert papal primacy. Because he refuted the charge of heresy with the classical statement for the infallibility of the church he had no need to rely on supporters in the assembly in order to uphold his orthodoxy. The question why Paschal had no done so in 1112 cannot be answered satisfactorily because the sources are too scanty. It is a plausible conjecture, but no more, that Paschal was either unable or unwilling to use the concept of differentiation between person and office at the earlier meeting, which was far less diverse than the 1116 synod and almost entirely dominated by Paschal's critics. Only in the light of this concept was it possible for Paschal to admit his personal responsibility for the uncanonical agreement of Ponte Mammolo, uncanonical because it went against the decrees of his predecessors, and to claim orthodoxy at the same time. Paschal never accepted the definition of investiture as heresy, a label applied to it by the council of 1112 [110], as his invitation to the 1116 synod makes very clear [111], but he did not debate the point at the public sessions preferring instead to rely on scriptural support for his orthodoxy.

Paschal reasserted the papal primacy not only on the basis of his claim to orthodoxy as successor to Peter but also by reversing the role of council and pope. In 1112 the council prevailed, in 1116 the pontiff. Papal independence which is evident in the various accounts from the 1116 synod is forcefully underlined by Paschal's use of the first person singular instead of the majestic plural, not only in his confession where it would be expected but also in the condemnation of the *pravilegium*: *Illud autem malum scriptum, quod in tentoriis factum est, quod pro pravitate sui pravilegium dicitur, condempno sub perpetuo anathemate, ut nullius umquam sit bonae memoriae, et rogo vos omnes ut idem faciatis* [112]. The contrast with

---

[109] See *ibid.* and LANDULF's *Historia*, 26s.
[110] Recension I of the *acta* carries the inscription « actio concilii contra heresim de investitura » (MGH *Const.* 1, 571 no. 399).
[111] JL 6462 = MIGNE PL 163, 385: « ... tantum in ecclesia scandalum est exortum, ut ad schisma processerit ».
[112] EKKEHARD, 320, lines 2-5.

the condemnation of 1112, which was prepared by a committee and read by Girard of Angoulême [113], could not be more marked.

The same emphasis on the condemnation of the *pravilegium* on papal authority alone is also found in one of Paschal's letters to Archbishop Guy of Vienne, later Pope Calixtus II [114]. The letter is preserved without dating formula, and until now the debate focused on the years 1111 and 1112 as date of origin [115]. On the basis of content, however, it seems permissible to argue that JL 6325 should be dated 1116. The epistle constitutes probably Paschal's reply to the letters which emissaries of Guy of Vienne had brought to the synod in support of demands of Cardinal Cono of Palestrina for the recognition of legatine excommunications of Henry V [116]. Paschal's reply contains a more formal condemnation of the *pravilegium* and reiterates the terms of the 1111 document, but the letter also stresses papal action to the exclusion of all references to conciliar participation in terms which are very similar to those used by Ekkehard and in Gerhoch's *Opusculum* [117] for 1116: *Scripta qua in tentoriis ... facta sunt ... ego canonica censura cassa omnino et irrita iudico et sub damnatione perpetua permanere decerno, ut nullius unquam auctoritatis sint, et nullius bonae memoriae* [118].

It is not necessary, however, to rely on Paschal's letter to Guy of Vienne [119] in order to recognize the strength of Paschal's position at the synod of 1116. Other securely dated records are proof enough that his solemn, public affirmation of the primacy closed the gap that had been created in 1112 between the early and late phases of his pontificate [120]. Paschal was forced to leave Rome immediately after the Easter celebrations in the face of a rebellion in the city [121], but this did not derogate from the complete success of the 1116 council which effectively silenced his critics. Paschal's personality and his policies continued to influence the papacy after his death. Contemporaries evidently did not share the historical conception of Paschal as an otherworldly but negligible pope. His closest collaborator,

---

[113] MGH *Const.* 1, 571s., and especially Boso, *Liber Pontificalis*, ed. L. DUCHESNE, II, 370s.

[114] JL 6325 = MIGNE PL 163, 292.

[115] See JAFFÉ, *Regesta pontificum Romanorum*, under JL 6325 and particular W. VON GIESEBRECHT, *Geschichte der deutschen Kaiserzeit*, III, Braunschweig 1879, 1201.

[116] EKKEHARD, 324, lines 3-4: « Ad eundem modum legati et literae domni Viennensis postulabant ». See JL 6325: « ... Quae cognoscere postulasti haec sunt ... ».

[117] See p. 190 n.: « Confiteor ... quod penitet illud privilegium, potius pravilegium in tentoriis a nobis extortum ... » The quotation from Ekkehard is found above in the text of the paper.

[118] JL 6325.

[119] JL 6325.

[120] See here in general G. MEYER VON KNONAU, *Jahrbücher* (see n. 75 above) VII, 53-56.

[121] *Ibid.*, 6-8, 16, 30-33.

Cardinal John of Gaeta, was elected as his successor under the name Gelasius II, and his erstwhile opponent, Archbishop Guy of Vienne, willingly or unwillingly had to follow in Paschal's footsteps in order to find acceptance when he in turn had been elected to the papacy [122].

---

[122] Pope Calixtus II (1119-1124). The beginnings of his pontificate are still imperfectly understood despite the important studies by U. Robert, H.-W. Klewitz, F.-J. Schmale and the most recent contributions by S. CHODOROW, *Ecclesiastical Politics and the Ending of the Investiture Contest. The Papal Election of 1119 and the Negotiations of Mouzon*: Speculum 46 (1971) 613-640, and IDEM, *Christian Political Theory and Church Politics in the Mid-Twelfth Century*, Berkeley 1972. Chodorow critically analyzed earlier studies and provides an up-to-date bibliography. My remark is based on the evidence provided by the Lateran council of 1123 (see J. ALBERIGO et al., *Conciliorum Oecumenicorum Decreta*, Bologna ³1973, 187-194) and the negotiations leading to the so-called Concordat of Worms. See for this E. BERNHEIM, *Das Wormser Konkordat und seine Vorurkunden* (Untersuchungen zur deutschen Staats- und Rechtsgeschichte. Alte Folge, 81), Breslau 1906, reprinted Aalen 1970.

Decrees and decretals of Pope Paschal II in twelfth-century canonical collections*

The present article on texts of Pope Paschal II (1099-1118) which were transmitted in canonical and decretal collections to *Compilatio prima* (*ca.* 1191) is intended as a companion piece to similar studies for Pope Gregory VII (1073-1085) and Pope Urban II (1088-1099).[1] Twelfth-century legal changes dictated a different approach, and it was necessary to use a different format. My study focuses on Paschal's decrees and decretals themselves rather than on the collections in which they were transmitted and includes decretal collections in the analysis.

Whenever possible, texts attributable to Pope Paschal II are presented in the numerical sequence in which they were registered in the second edition of Jaffé's *Regesta*. The unregistered texts follow, listed by incipits in alphabetical order. Decrees and decretal letters are not differentiated from each other as such, because Jaffé and his successors sometimes assigned numbers to fragments which are now identifiable as conciliar canons.[2] The term decree is used in this paper

---

* This study was begun with the help of a Fellowship from the American Council of Learned Societies and was for the most part completed at the Institute of Medieval Canon Law, Berkeley. I am very grateful to Professor Stephan Kuttner and the Institute for their support and kind permission to use the papers of the late Professor Walther Holtzmann as well as an advance copy of Holtzmann-Cheney, *Studies in the collections of twelfth-century decretals* (MIC Corpus Coll. 3; Vatican City 1979). (Already before my stay at the Institute I had received, thanks to the kindness of Professors S. Chodorow and R. Somerville, copies of Holtzmann's notes for JE 2557, JL 6427, JL 6443, JL 6447, JL 6570, JL 6598, JL 6604, JL 6605, and JL 6611.) I owe special thanks to the editors of this journal for their help in giving this paper its final shape. In order not to overburden the footnotes, collections are cited in the conventional abbreviated form. Except where indicated otherwise, I have used MS Paris B.N. lat. 10743 for the Coll. 10P and MS Vat. lat. 1346 for the Coll. 7L, Vat. lat. 3831 for the Coll. 3L. H. Fuhrmann, *Einfluss und Verbreitung der pseudoisidorischen Fälschungen* (MGH Schriften 24/1-3; Stuttgart 1972-1974) and Holtzmann-Cheney, *Studies*, provide up-to-date bibliographies for the collections and should be consulted together with the standard reference works.

[1] F. Gossman, *Pope Urban II and canon law* (The Catholic University of America Canon Law Studies 403; Washington 1960); J. Gilchrist, 'The reception of Pope Gregory VII into the canon law (1073-1141)', ZRG Kan. Abt. 59 (1973) 35-82.

[2] The first canon of a series of decrees from the council of Guastalla (1106) was erroneously attributed to Paschal I and identified in the second ed. of the *Regesta* as JE 2556. In this present study, conciliar decrees from a particular synod will be treated as a single item and all references to this particular recension of the Guastalla legislation will therefore be found under this number. For a general discussion of conciliar texts in canonical collections see Fransen, *Les collections canoniques* (Typologie des sources du moyen âge occidental 10; Turnhout 1973) 17.

as synonym for conciliar canon, the word decretal is used in the broad sense of the word 'epistola decretalis', meaning excerpts from, or complete texts of Paschal's letters which were of interest to canon lawyers regardless of the type of letter involved.[3]

Paschal material which is preserved in canonical manuscripts has been excluded from the analysis below when the manuscripts did not contain evidence that the added fragments or letters were intended to supplement the canonical collection found in the respective codex. One example is Paschal's letter JL 5835, celebrating the success of the first crusade, which is preserved as the final item of the *Collection in Two Books* in MS Vat. lat. 3832.[4] Another example of omitted additions is provided by Paschal's letters JL 6158 and JL 6157, found in a manuscript of the Dionysio-Hadriana in Berlin (Staatsbibl. MS Phillipps 1744, fol. 1r).[5] In both instances the papal letters appear to have simply been added out of general historical interest.

A further type of texts which I did not include are *capitula incerta* when the inscription 'idem' or 'item', following upon a text of Paschal II, was the only evidence linking them to his pontificate. Included, however, are texts attributed to Paschal II in the inscription, unless available evidence indicated a different source. One illustration is the text of *Collectio Dunelmensis* 1.42.[6] This piece has the inscription 'Paschalis secundus' but its first sentence is taken from a section of Urban II's letter JL 5743 as it appears in the Dictum Gratiani after C.32 c.6.[7] Another part of this long letter, in C.1 q.3 c.8, includes a reference to 'Paschalis' (actually, the *Epistola Widonis*). This might explain how the ex-

---

[3] For the definition of and differentiation between types of decretals see S. Kuttner, 'Notes on a projected corpus of twelfth-century decretal letters', *Traditio* 6 (1948) 345-51, 345 and n.3; C. R. Cheney and M. G. Cheney, *The letters of Pope Innocent III (1198-1216) concerning England and Wales* (Oxford 1967) xiii-xvii; G. Fransen, *Les décrétales et les collections de décrétales* (Typologie des sources 2; Turnhout 1972), esp. 12-15; O. Hageneder, 'Papstregister und Dekretalenrecht', *Recht und Schrift im Mittelalter*, ed. P. Classen (Vorträge und Forschungen 23; Sigmaringen 1977) 319-47, esp. 320, 327f.

[4] The collection has been edited in part by J. Bernhard, *La Collection en deux livres* I (Strasbourg 1962); see also J. Gilchrist, 'The Collection of Cod. Vat. lat. 3832, a source of the Collection in seventy-four titles?', *Études Le Bras* (Paris 1965) I 141-56.

[5] For a description of the codex see H. Mordek, *Kirchenrecht und Reform im Frankenreich: Die Collectio Vetus Gallica* (Beiträge zur Geschichte und Quellenkunde des Mittelalters 1; Berlin-New York 1975) 243 and 248.

[6] 'Paschalis secundus. Officium simoniachorum—prohibeas. Item initiatus Israel—dispergentur in plures.' See Holtzmann-Cheney 84.

[7] Besides the Dict. Grat., Holtzmann-Cheney cite *Coll. Francofortana* 37.2, but, as Professor Kuttner informs me, this should be referred only to the second part of 1 Dun. 1.42 'Item initiatus' etc. which does not come from Urban's letter, while other occurrences of 'Officium simoniacorum' — variously inscribed 'Gregorius' or 'Augustinus' — in decretal collections should have been listed.

cerpt in Dun. 1.42 came by its inscription. Since it is demonstrably wrong, the text was omitted. In case of doubt, however, or if a text could have been intentionally ascribed to Paschal II, I have included it.[8]

As is customary, only texts which are not found anywhere in print are given in full below. Ordinarily, only inscription, incipit, and explicit are indicated and variants are omitted unless they were particularly relevant to this study of the transmission of canonical texts of Pope Paschal II. Occurrence in Gratian or Comp. I is always indicated first; then canonical collections and decretal collections are cited, usually in chronological order, except that here the collection which supplied the inscription will be given first place.

JE 2556 (JL 6608, 6609, 6610)
Ex concilio Pascalis pape.[9]
[i] Episcopi lectioni — inreprehensibiles inueniri. [ii] Nullus espiscopus — ordinis subiacebit. [iii] Nullus laicorum ecclesias — ecclesiae liminibus arceatur. [iv] Sicut domini uestimentum — destituantur officiis. [v] Abbatibus qui — exteris largiatur. [vi] Si quis clericus — subiaceat.[10]

[i] C.2 q.7 c.60 [iii] C.16 q.7 c.18 [iv] C.16 q.7 c.19 [v] C.18 q.2 c.18
[i-vi] Ans. Luc. bk 6 (addition); [ii-iv] Coll. 13L (fol. 147r).

JE 2557
Pascalis secundus.[a]
Nulli episcoporum liceat eos — neglexerint separare.

      [a] secundus 1 Dun: om. cett.

C.3 q.5 c.14 (palea); 1 Comp. 5.1.3 (X 5.1.5)
Coll. 9L 6.1.118 (Vatican, Arch. S. Pietro C. 118, fol. 76r; Berlin, Staatsbibl. Stift. Preuss. Kulturbes. lat. fol. 552, fol. 39v); 1 Dun. 1.26; 2 Par. 27.4; Erl. 58.3; Lips. 42.4; Tann. 3.3.10; Sang. 3.16.14; 1 Abr. 3.12.7; 2 Dun. 85. Tann. and Sang. (which derived the text from Tann. according to Holtzmann's notes) continue the text after the explicit 'separare' with the passage: 'Item. Liberam ecclesiam esse Paulus dicit — secularibus negotiis.' Holtzmann concluded that the segments which he labelled [a] 'Nulli — separare', and [b] 'Item. Liberam — negotiis', were part of a single decretal of Pope Paschal II which was dissected in decretal collections. The passage 'Liberam ecclesiam' can now be indentified as a brief excerpt from Paschal's letter JL 5909 to St. Anselm of Canterbury (see below).

------

[8] For example two decrees from councils held by Paschal's legates, Guy of Vienne and Cono of Palestrina. See below, under 'Inuestituram' and 'Nullus abbas'.
[9] The texts could be identified as part of the legislation of Paschal's council of Guastalla held in 1106. See Blumenthal, *The early councils of Pope Paschal II, 1100-1110* (Studies and texts 43; Toronto 1978) 57-71.
[10] Not all of the decrees occur in all of the MSS involved. See the app. crit. *ibid.* 68-71.

18

JL 5908 (excerpt)
Paschalis episcopus seruus seruorum dei uenerabili fratri et coepiscopo Anselmo Cantuariorum.
Nuper in synodo — procuretur eternam.[11]
    Panormia (appendix) Paris, B.N. lat. 4284, fol. 164r;[12] Coll. 10P 4.24.7;[13]
    Panormia (appendix) Saint-Omer, Bibl. mun. 364, fol. 152v.[14]

JL 5909 (excerpt)
Item.
Liberam esse ecclesiam Paulus dicit — secularibus negotiis.[15]
    Tann. 3.3.11; Sang. 3.16.15; 1 Abr. 3.12.8

JL 5928 (excerpt)
Item eidem in alia epistola.[a]
Dolemus autem — gladio feriuntur.[16]

    [a] Paschalis .II. Anselmo Cantuariensi archiepiscopo] *Coll. 10P*

    Panormia (appendix) Paris, B.N. lat. 4284, fol. 164r;[17] Coll. 10P 4.29.6.[18]

JL 5995
Paschalis episcopus seruus seruorum dei ad Manassem Remensem archiepiscopum.
Significauerat nobis — testes emerserint.
    Coll. in Four Books (appendix) Milan, Bibl. Ambros., C.51 sup., fol. 158v;
    Coll. 10P (addition to part 5).[19]

---

[11] Ep. 222 ed. F.S. Schmitt, *S. Anselmi Cantuariensis archiepiscopi opera omnia* (6 vols. Edinburgh 1938-1961) 4.125 lines 19-29 with slight variants in the beginning.

[12] An identical appendix is found in Vatican, Reg. lat. 972, with JL 5908 on fol. 103v. See S. Kuttner and R. Somerville, 'The so-called canons of Nîmes (1096)', TRG 38 (1970) 175-89, at 178 n. 18.

[13] The excerpt is very brief: 'In synodo nuper — hominium laico faciat' = ep. 222 ed. Schmitt 4.125 lines 19-21 (MS Paris, B.N. lat. 10743, p. 227.)

[14] This appendix is perhaps derived from 10P. See G. Fransen, 'Collections canoniques oubliées', *Traditio* 26 (1970) 446 no. 4 and R. Somerville, *Decreta Claromontensia* (AHC Supplementum 1; Amsterdam 1972) 68f.

[15] Cf. JE 2557 above. For the text see ep. 223 ed. Schmitt 4.128 lines 49-53.

[16] Ep. 281 ed. Schmidt 4.196-98, lines 8-40 and in addition the references given above under JL 5908.

[17] Vatican, Reg. lat. 972, fol. 103v-104r.

[18] The excerpt is briefer: 'Si uirgam — adulterio maculare.' = ep. 281 ed. Schmitt 4.197 lines 23-28.

[19] The excerpt is briefer: 'Licet ad simoniaci — omne uerbum'. —It is only found in MS Paris, B.N. lat. 10743, p. 296.

JL 6426

IP 3.284 no. 15

Paschalis[a] episcopus seruus seruorum dei militibus de Sancto Geminiano aliisque oppidis iuxta positis salutem et apostolicam benedictionem.[b] Unam esse — perducat eternam.

[a] Paschalis — benedictionem] Paschalis .II. militatibus *Dun.*   [b] iuxta positis]
** atat *Vat. lat. 1346*

Coll. 7L.[20] — 1 Dun. 1.24.

In Dun. only an excerpt, 'Qui fidem — perfidus comprobatur', is found (= Mansi 20.1097 B3-6).[21]

JL 6427

Pascalis .II.[a] dilecte filie comitisse Matilde.
Peruenit ad nos quod Fraxinorensis abbas — inquietare permittas.

[a] Pascalis .II. *om. Sang.*

1 Comp. 34.5 (X 3.39.5)
Sang. 2.7.5.[22]

JL 6436

IP 5.367 no. 7

Pascalis episcopus seruus seruorum dei uenerabili fratri et consacerdoti Bonoseniori salutem et apostolicam benedictionem.
[i] Questiunculas quas — respondere. [ii] Post uxoris obitum — spiritus pertransitur. [iii] Post susceptum — prohibent. [iv] Porro duorum — abstinendum est. [v] Illud sane — sententias commutamus. Data .VI. kalendas maii.
[ii] C.30 q.4 c.5 [iii] C.30 q.3 c.5 [iv] C.35 q.2 et 3 c.22
Mantua, Bibl. Com. MS 461 (D IV 15) fol. 2r (complete);[23] [ii-v] Ans. Luc. 10.33 (recension C, MS Vat. lat. 4983, fol. 456v-457r); [ii-iii] Coll. 13L 9.143-144 (MS Vat. lat. 1361, fol. 186v), Liber sententiarum, MS Novara, Bibl. cap. XXXIX (no. 126) fol. 190va-b; [ii] Coll. 74T (appendix, MS Vat. lat. 4977, fol. 3r), Coll. 7L 6.24.6b, Coll. 3L (MS Pistoia, Arch. cap 135, fol. 203v; [iv] add. in marg.),[24] Polycarpus 6.4.4,[24a] Coll. Caes.10.130 (recension

---

[20] The text is an addition in MS Vat. lat. 1346, fol. 12r of 7L. It was incorporated in the MSS Cortona 43, fol. 230v and MS Vienna Ö.N.B. 2186, fol. 259r of the collection.
[21] For the text see Holtzmann-Cheney, *Studies* 82.
[22] Cf. IP 5,392, n. 26.
[23] The letter was published from this codex by P. Torelli, 'Un' epistola di Pasquale II "de illicitis coniugiis",' *Scritti vari dedicati al Prof. Carlo Arnò nel XXX° anno di insegnamento del diritto romano nella R. Univerità di Modena (1898-1927)* (Modena 1928) 59-66; reprinted in his *Scritti di storia del diritto italiano* (Milan 1959) 651-61.
[24] Only fragm. [ii] is found in the Vatican codex of 3L (Vat. lat. 3831, fol. 119r = 3.11.128) with the incorrect inscr. 'Urbanus episcopus in sancta sinodo Placentie.' For 3L see J. Erickson, 'The Collection in Three Books and Gratian's Decretum', BMCL 2 (1972) 67-75, esp. 68 n.12.
[24a] Codex Vat. lat. 1354 continues after 'prohibent copulari' with an incomplete sentence: 'uxoris defuncte commatrem antequam se faceret istius coniugem.'

2, Paris B.N. lat. 3876, fol. 74r), Sententiae Magistri A (Florence, Med.-Laur. MS Santa Croce plut. 5 sin. 7, fol. 104r); [iii] Coll. 7L 6.24.6a, Panormia (appendix, MS Vat. lat. 1359, fol. 116v); [iv] Coll. 7L 6.41.7,[25] Coll. in Eight Books 8.12.2 (Wolfenbüttel, Herzog-August-Bibl., cod. Guelf. Helmstedt 308, fol. 130r [Heinemann 342]); [iv, iii, ii] Coll. Ans. ded. (addition, Vercelli, Bibl. cap. XV, fol. 1v).

JL 6437

Ex decretis Paschalis pape.

Paschalis episcopus seruus seruorum dei Taruensis parochie clericis salutem et apostolicam benedictionem.

Grauem ualde — priuatione plectantur.

Coll. 10P 3.30.2

JL 6443

Paschalis .II.

Decimas a populo — munda sunt uobis.

C.16 q.1 c.47

Ans. Luc. (addition, MS Pisa, Bibl. Caterin. 59, fol. 63v); Coll. 9L 3.4.14 (Vatican, Arch. S. Pietro C. 118, fol. 30r); Coll. in Eight Books 8.5.3 (Wolfenbüttel, Cod. Guelf. Helmstedt 308, fol. 127r); Sententiae Magistri A (addition, Florence, Med.-Laur. Santa Croce plut. 5 sin. 7, fol. 113v);[26] Panormia (addition, Vat. lat. 5002, fol. 83r.)[27] — Oriel. 13.21; 1 Abr. App. 5.[28]

---

25 This fragment [iv] alone is found among the additions in Vat. lat. 1346, fol. 169v.

26 The text in this transmission is garbled. The same version of JL 6443 is found in MS Paris B.N. lat. 13368. See K. Hampe, 'Reise nach Frankreich und Belgien im Frühjahr 1897', NA 23 (1898) 642.

27 This codex contains only the first section, 'Decimas a populo—extorquere debeant', JL 6443 and MS Vat. lat. 5002 are discussed, together with another of Paschal's decretals on tithes (JL 6605, see below), by G. Constable, *Monastic tithes from their origin to the twelfth century* (Cambridge studies in medieval life and thought n.s. 10; Cambridge 1964) 229-33 with further references. See also idem, 'The treatise "Hortatur nos" and accompanying canonical texts on the performance of pastoral work by monks', *Speculum historiale: Festschrift J. Spörl* (Freiburg and Munich 1965) 567-77, at 570f.

28 See H. Singer, 'Neue Beiträge', *Sb. Akad. Vienna* 171.1 (1913) 392 for Abr. App. 5. In many other early decretal collections the fragment appears among a small group of texts on tithes which became an appendix to JL 13873 of Alexander III. It will be discussed in that context in the forthcoming *Regesta decretalium saec. XII* prepared by S. Chodorow and C. Duggan on the basis of the papers of the late Walther Holtzmann. In the meantime see Singer, 'Neue Beiträge' 203f. = Coll. Sang. 4.10.19 for further references, as well as J. Juncker, 'Die Collectio Berolinensis: Ein Beitrag zur Geschichte des kanonischen Rechts im ausgehenden zwölften Jahrhundert', ZRG Kan. Abt. 13 (1924) 284-426 at 296f.; W. Holtzmann, 'Beiträge zu den Dekretalensammlungen des 12. Jahrhunderts', *ibid.* 16 (1927) 37-115 at 42. Paschal's decretal JL 6605 (see below) is also part of this little appendix on tithes.

JL 6456

Paschasius[a] .II. Guidoni Viennensi archiepiscopo apostolice sedis legato.
Controuersiam quam — testimonium proferant.

    [a] Pascalis Ans. Luc. (app.)

    Coll. 10P 5.14.18 (MS Paris B.N. lat. 10743, p. 282) Ans. Luc. (addition,
following bk 13, Vat. lat. 1363, fol. 245r).

JL 6467

Paschasius[a] .II. Guidoni Viennensi archiepiscopo apostolice sedis legato.[b]
Super prudentia — plenius decidatur.

    [a] Pasch' 10P, Paschalis 9L Grat.   [b] [I]dem papa eidem archiepiscopo Ans.
    Luc. (app.)[29]

    C.14 q.2 c.1
    Coll. 10P 5.14.19; Ans. Luc. (addition to bk 13 MS Vat. lat. 1363, fol. 245r-
245v); Coll. 9L 6.1.117 (Vatican Arch. S. Pietro C.118, fol. 76rb; Berlin,
Staatsbibl. Stift. Preuss. Kulturbes. lat. fol. 552, fol. 39r-39v);[30] Summa
Haimonis (MS Paris B.N. lat. 4286, fol. 47r-47v).[31]
    The decretal JL 6467[32] is also found in the Pistoia codex of the Coll. in Three
Books, and as a later marginal addition to Ivo's Panormia 5.22-24 in MS Vat.
lat. 1362, but in both cases the piece was derived from Gratian, C.14 q.2 c.1.
The same is true for the text of JL 6467 as found in a canonical collection at
Prague.[33]

---

[29] The preceding inscription is that just given under JL 6456.

[30] 9L 6.1.117 here does not depend on 3L; see Erickson, 'Three Books' 68 with n. 12.

[31] The Summa Haimonis depends on 10P. The excerpt from JL 6467 in the Summa is
briefer: 'Paschalis .II. In criminalibus — esse non debeat'.

[32] The following paragraphs are based on research notes which Professor Kuttner most
kindly put at my disposal.

[33] The text in MS Vat. lat. 1362 was published by Pflugk-Harttung, Acta Rom. Pont.
2.210f. no. 254 without any indication that it is an addition to Ivo derived from Gratian.
Therefore J. Fried, 'Die römische Kurie und die Anfänge der Prozessliteratur', ZRG Kan.
Abt. 59 (1973) 151-74, at 162 n. 31, citing Pflugk-Harttung, did not realize that this text
is nothing but C.14 q.2 c.1. — For the Prague collection of Univ. MS VIII.H.7 see Schulte,
'Über drei in Prager Handschriften enthaltene Canonen-Sammlungen', Sb. Akad. Vienna
57 (1867) 171-232, at p. 212 with n.35, where he argues that its c. 288 is independent of the
Decretum, C.14 q.2 pr.-c.1, perhaps even a source of Gratian. His main argument is the use
of the word 'districtio' in the Prague codex, where the dict. Grat. normally has 'distinctio';
but this proves nothing since the variant 'districtio' is well attested (see Friedberg's app.
crit. n. 3 ad loc,), and a collection which omits Gratian's 'apostolice sedis legato' in the address
of c.1 cannot have been his source. (Professor Kuttner's observations have in the meantime

Since JL 6467 'Super prudentia' was included in Gratian, it does not appear in the decretal collections from the second half of the twelfth century, although two closely connected collections at the end of the century refer to 'Super prudentia' as a continuation of JL 6604 'In omni negotio' and give Archbishop Guy of Vienne as addressee (see below, JL 6604). Walther Holtzmann therefore considered the possibility that the two were part of the same letter. But against this isolated and late testimony we must weigh the silence of the canonical tradition of JL 6467 and of all early texts of JL 6604. Above all, the complete, dated text of JL 6467, twice preserved in archival tradition and published in the seventeenth century independently by Pierre Chifflet and Luc d'Achery, begins after the formal papal greeting to Guy of Vienne with the words 'Super prudentia'.[34] Thus the fragment JL 6604 can not have been part of the original letter.

JL 6491a

Epistola Pascalis pape .II. de incestis Placentinis directa.

Pascalis episcopus seruus seruorum dei clero et populo Placentine urbis salutem et apostolicam benedictionem.

Quanto uero in fide catholica — et confirmamus.

Ans. Luc. (addition to bk 13 c. penult.)[35]

JL 6492

Paschalis papa .II. Rothoni praeposito et ceteris fratribus S. Fridiani.

Vite regularis propositum — regno dei. Data Lateranis .II. nonas martii.

Ivo, Decretum (addition, Cambridge CCC 19, fol. 33v); Ans. Luc. (MS Barb. lat. 535, fol. 206r-206v, bk 7, c. ult.).

---

been accepted by A. Gouron, 'Sur la collection en 294 chapitres [ms. Prague Univ. VIII.H.7]', *Annales de la Faculté de Droit...* Univ. de Bordeaux I, Centre d'Études et de Recherches d'histoire institutionelle et régionale 2 [1978] 95-106, at p. 12.)

[34] P. Chifflet, *Histoire de l'Abbaye royale et ville de Tournais* (Douai 1664) 372 (= Mansi 21.142-44 *ex* Labbe, *Sacrosancta concilia* 10.805); Luc d'Achery, *Spicilegium* 3 (1659) 132 (= 3 [1723] 459). D'Achery published the letter from a manuscript of St.-Florent-lès-Saumur (Marne-et-Loire). His text found its way into Labbe 10.691 and from there into Mansi 20.1047. The words 'apostolice sedis legato' in the inscription of most canonical collections correspond to d'Achery's text (Sed. ap. vicario' in Chifflet), but none of these canonical MSS includes the final clauses of the full letter. For the incipit of the abbreviated fragment in the *Summa Haimonis* see note 31.

[35] The text was edited by P. Kehr from the Anselm MS Graz, Univ. 351, fol. 195r in 'Nachträge zu den Papsturkunden Italiens', *Nachrichten Akad. Göttingen* (1911) no. 2, 274-77. See also IP 5, 510 n. 3. The addition is also found in Florence, Med.-Laur. S. Marco 499, fol. 184v-185v and in Naples, Bibl. Naz. XII A.39, fol. 96r-98v.

JL 6543

Paschalis papa .II. Johanni Teruannensi episcopo.

Latore presentium — hereditate repellunt.

Appendix to Decretales Ps.-Is. in MS Avranches, Bibl. mun. 146 [109] fol. 166r;[36] Coll. 10P 8.16.6.[37]

JL 6570

Paschalis Poloniensi archiepiscopo.[38]

Significasti, frater karissime, regem et regni maiores admiratione permotos — oriatur occasio.[39]

    1 Comp. 1.4.21 (X 1.6.4)

    App. Ln 47.21; Bamb. 31.9; Cass. 40.9; Erl. 31.9; Lips. 31.9; Chelt. 5.5; Frcf. App. 8; 1 Rot. 4.5 and 22.17; Tann. 4.1.13; Sang. 5.1.19.

Traditionally it has been assumed that Paschal's decretal was addressed to Archbishop Crescentius of Spalato and that the inscription as preserved in the *Vita Paschalis* by Cardinal Boso is a corruption.[40] The most thorough investigation of the question whether the recalcitrant archbishop of the decretal was installed at Palermo, in Poland, or in Hungary-Dalmatia at Spalato, is found in an article of 1937 by M. Gębarowicz, who concluded that the archbishop of Gniezno (Gnesen) was its recipient. His chief argument is a phrase in Paschal's decretal letter which, Gębarowicz argued, could only refer to the events preceding the murder of St. Stanislas, bishop of Cracow, by King Boleslav II the Bold in 1079. The archbishop of Gniezno at that time, together with his suffragans,

---

[36] The excerpt, here preceded by JL 6570, is abbreviated, 'Latore presentium — coniugium soluatur'. See S. Williams, *Codices Pseudo-Isidoriani* (MIC ser. C 3; New York 1971) 6-7; R. Somerville, 'The Council of Beauvais, 1114', *Traditio* 24 (1968) 494-503; H. Mordek, 'Proprie auctoritates apostolice sedis: Ein zweiter dictatus papae Gregors VII.?', DA 28 (1972) 105-32, and F. Kempf, 'Ein zweiter Dictatus papae Gregors VII.?: Ein Beitrag zum Depositionsanspruch Gregors VII.', AHP 13 (1975) 119-39.

[37] Only found in the Paris MS.

[38] The address shows numerous variants most of which are listed by M. Gębarowicz, 'Polska, Węgry czy Sycylia adbiorcą listu Paschalisa II J.L. nr. 6570 [Poland, Hungary, or Sicily, recipient of Paschal II's letter JL 6570]?', *Kwartalnik Historyczny* 51 (1937) 513-53, pp. 525f. and W. Deeters, *Die Bambergensisgruppe der Dekretalensammlungen des 12. Jhdts.* (Bonn 1956) 157. Inscription, incipit, and explicit given above correspond to the complete text of the letter in Boso's *Vita Paschalis*, ed. Duchesne, LP 2.374f. I am very grateful to Professor Irena Sławinska, Kat. Universytet Lublin, who translated Gębarowicz's article for me.

[39] The decretal collections abbreviated the text in varying degrees. Cf. the hypothetical stemma given by Gębarowicz 524.

[40] In addition to Duchesne, LP 2.374n and Jaffé's *Regesta* under JL 6570, see also the remarks on the decretal by T. Gottlob, *Der kirchliche Amtseid der Bischöfe* (Kanonistische Studien und Texte 9; Bonn 1936) 8f. and 49ff.; P. Hinschius, *System des katholischen Kirchenrechts* 3 (1883) 203 n. 6, and further references in Blumenthal, *Early councils* 12.

XII

24

had remained loyal to the king and refused to support Bishop Stanislas, who was accused of treason.[41] In an article of 1959 on twelfth-century decretals concerning Hungary (published only in Hungarian), Walther Holtzmann eventually came to the same conclusion: the address 'to the archbishop of Poland' is the only one that permits a fairly certain attribution.[42] Whatever one may think about the continuity of the first foundation of a metropolitan see at Gniezno in the year 1000,[43] its existence by the time of Paschal II cannot be in doubt, and its incumbent should be accepted as the addressee of JL 6570.[44]

JL 6598   IP 3, 401 no. 19

Paschalis .II. canonicis Sancti Martini.[45]

Causa Carpensis plebis, et infra. Ceterum primitie — sacrilegus.

1 Comp. 5.36.13 (X 5.40.13)
Sang. 10.36 2 Rot. 5.36.16

JL 6602

Paschalis papa .II. Lamberto abbati S. Bertini.

Postquam ab — non tenetur.

Appendix to Decretales Ps.-Is. in MS Avranches, Bibl. mun. 146 [109] fol. 166r.); Coll. 10P 4.3.4

---

41 Gębarowicz (n. 38 above), esp. 551-53. The sentence is '. . . Nonne predecessor tuus preter Romani pontificis conscientiam dampnavit episcopum? . . .' (Boso, ed. Duchesne, LP 2.375, line 1). It will always be impossible to reconstruct the precise events of 1079, but it is clear that the Polish ecclesiastical hierarchy sided with the king against bishop Stanislas at the time. See in general V. Meysztowicz, La Pologne dans la Chrétienté (Paris 1966) 21f.; O. Halecki, A history of Poland (New York 1943) 18-20; H. Holzapfel, Tausend Jahre Kirche Polens (Würzburg 1966) 29f.

42 W. Holtzmann, 'XII. Századi pápai levelek kánoni guyűjteményekből', Szdzadok 93 (1959) 404-17, at p. 407. I should like to thank Dr. Elemá Bakó of the Library of Congress for his help with the translation of this article, which was unknown to me at the time when I reported, and supported (Early councils 12f.) Holtzmann as favoring Spalato in his unpublished notes of an earlier date. (Only after the present article was written, did I learn from Professor Kuttner that the German original of Holtzmann's Hungarian paper exists in a carbon copy of the author's typescript at the Institute of Medieval Canon Law.)

43 See the material and bibliography collected for the events of 999-1000 A.D. in H. Zimmermann, Papstregesten 911-1024 (J. F. Böhmer, Regesta imperii, Neubearb. 2.5; Wien-Köln-Graz 1969) nos. 894-902. But there exists very little reliable information on the early eleventh century; see P. David, Les sources de l'histoire de Pologne à l'époque des Piasts (963-1386) (Paris 1934), especially at 176-79. In 1076 Gregory VII requested the (re-)establishment of a metropolitan see: Reg. 2.73, ed. Caspar, Das Register Gregors VII. (MGH Epp. sel. 2) I 233-45 = JL 4958.

44 As is done, e.g., in Diplomatarium Danicum (ser. 1) 2, edd. L. Weibull and N. Skyum-Nielsen (Copenhagen 1963) no. 33, pp. 77-78; D. Girgensohn, Miscellanea Italiae pontificiae 1 (Nachr. Akad. Göttingen 1974 No. 4) 178 n. 185.

45 On the uncertain location of the addressees see W. Holtzmann, Kanonistische Ergänzungen zur Italia pontificia (Tübingen 1959) no. 42, p. 39 (= QF 37 [1957] p. 93)

JL 6604

Paschalis .II.ª

In omni negotio — Ego[b] sum qui testimonium perhibeo de me ipso et testimonium perhibet de me pater. Nam in lege uestra scriptum est quod duorum hominum testimonium uerum est.[c]

> ª Item extrauag. Ex decreto Siluestri pape *Ambr.*, Paschalis papa .II. Widoni archiepiscopo Viennensi apostolice sedis legato *Lips, Erl.*   [b] Ego — uerum est] ego sum qui testimonio (*sic*) perhibeo etc. *Lips. with gloss (hand 2)* Nam in lege uestra scriptum est quia testimonium duorum uerum est. Super prudentia tua etc.   [c] uerum est super prudentia tua etc. *Erl.* (*without punctuation*)

1 Comp. 2.13.5 (X 2.20.4)
Ambr. 57; Flor. 140; Cus. 156; Frag. Trecense (E) 8 (Troyes MS 103, fol. 268vb); 1 Dun 1.29; 2 Par. 29.2; Erl. 39.16; Lips. 43.16; Frcf. 22.3; Tann. 5.4.32; Sang. 6.6.23.

The gloss of Lips. — a late decretal collection, after 1185 — links JL 6604 with JL 6467 'Super prudentia'; its close relative Erl. adds the words 'super prudentia etc.' to the text. For an evaluation of this testimony see above, under JL 6467. All earlier collections as well as the quotation from 'Paschalis' in the *Summa Elegantius in iure diuino* (*ca.* 1169)[46] end with the scriptural pericope (Jo. 8.18, 17).[47]

JL 6605

Paschalis .II.

[i] Nouum genus exactionis[b] — labores accipiunt. [ii] Conqueruntur siquidem clerici sancti Mathei[48] aduersus uos — molestiam ulterius inferatis.

> ª exactionis genus *transp. Ambr. Cott. App. Bamb. Erl. Lips. 23.7, Cass. Tann. Sang. Frcf.*

1 Comp. 3.26.7 (X 3.20.2) [i]
[Complete] Panormia (addition, MS Vat. lat. 5002, fol. 83rb);[49] 2 Par. 56.7; [i] Ambr. 49; Cott. 4.16a; App. 13.16; Bamb. 25.3; Erl. 25.3; Cass. 35.3; Tann. 3.14.2; Sang. 4.10.2; Frcf. 20.13;[50] [ii, i] Lips. 23.6, 7.

---

[46] *Summa Elegantius* 5.44, edd. G. Fransen and S. Kuttner II (MIC ser. A 1.2; Città del Vaticano 1978) p. 74.

[47] Information in this paragraph is based on the notes of Professor Kuttner; cf. note 32 above.

[48] Holtzmann, *Kanonistische Ergänzungen* no. 179, p. 119 (= QF 38 [1958] 137) suggests the cathedral clergy of Salerno as probable plaintiffs.

[49] Rubr.: 'Ne clerici qui sibi ministrant decimas dare cogantur'.

[50] Fragm. [i] occurs also elsewhere, like JL 6443, as part of the appendix on tithes to JL 13873 (Alexander III); for references see note 28 above.

JL 6606

Paschalis .II.

Sunt quidam — sacrilegos iudicandos.[51]

C.1 q.1 c.125
Coll. 9L 3.1.24 (Vatican, Arch. S. Pietro C.118, fol. 25v).

JL 6607

Item Paschalis .II.

Altare namque et decimas — nullus fidelium ignorat.

C.1 q.3 c.14
Coll. 3L 2.8.21 (Vat. lat. 3831, fol. 43r); Polycarpus 3.11.6 (Madrid, Bibl. Nac. 7127 fol. 339v);[52] Coll. 9L 3.5.8 (Vatican, Arch. S. Pietro C.118 fol. 31r); Coll. of Milan, Arch. cap. S. Ambrogio 145 inf., fol. 53r (inscr. Ex concilio Toletano);[53] Graz. Univers. 1242, fol. 131r (inscr. Augustinus de fide et operibus).

With the exception of Gratian, C.1 q.3 c.14, this brief fragment is nowhere attributed to Pope Paschal II. A partly similar text, also with an uncertain attribution, is found in C.1 q.1 c.3. In Coll. 3L the cap. follows upon two decrees from Paschal's council held at the Lateran in 1110.

[JL 6608, 6609, 6610: see above JE 2556]

JL 6611

Ex decreto Paschalis pape.[54]

Volumus ac iuxta — religiosis locis.

1 Comp. 3.24.2
Coll. S. Maria Novella 10.10;[55] 74T (app. Florence, Medic.-Laur. Conv. soppr. 91, fol. 17r); Ans. Luc. (addition, Pisa Bibl. Caterin. 59, fol. 15r;[56] Mantua Bibl. com. 318 (C.II 23), fol. 317v); Chronological coll. of MS vat. lat. 3829,

---

[51] JL 6606 is an abbreviation of c.6 of the Lateran council of 1110. See Blumenthal, *Early councils* 120.

[52] The text is here inserted into an unidentified decree attributed to a council of Toledo. See the notes of the *Correctores Romani* at C.1 q.3 c.14.

[53] See G. Picasso, *Collezioni canoniche milanesi del secolo XII* (Milan 1963) no. 192, p. 114. MS not seen.

[54] Thus the canonical collections and Ambr. The other decretal collections read 'Paschalis papa .II.'

[55] I have used MS Florence, Bibl. Naz., Conv. Soppr. A 4.269, fol. 54v. The most recent discussion of the collection is G. Motta, 'I rapporti tra la Collezione canonica di S. Maria Novella e quella in Cinque Libri', BMCL 7 (1977) 89-94. The tentative date (1070-1080) which Motta suggests, p. 92 n.17, needs however to be revised, for JL 6611 is an integral part of the collection, whereas the canons from Paschal's 1110 Lateran council form an addition.

[56] See G. Miccoli, 'Un florilegio sulla dignità e i diritti del monachesimo', *Bolletino storico pisano* 33-35 (1964-66) 117-29; cf. J. Gilchrist, *Diuersorum patrum sentenptie siue Collectio in LXXIV titulos digesta* (MIC ser. B 1; Vatican City 1973) xl-xli.

fol. 281v.[57] — Ambr. 56; Cus. 201; 1 Dun. 1.43; Chelt. 14.12; Cott. 4.63; Pet. 3.66; 2 Par. 52.1; App. Lp. 43.1; Bamb. 27.3; Erl. 23.3; Lips. 23.26; Cass. 36.3; Tann. 3.16.3; Sang. 4.12.3; Brug. 46.1; Frcf. 26.5.

JL 6612

Pascalis .II.

Testimonium est sermo — noui testamenti.

Coll. Taur. (MS Turin, Bibl. Naz. E V 44, fol. 57v).[58]

JL 6613

Ex decretis Paschalis pape .II. apud Beneuentum.

Et diuine legis — destituantur officiis.[59]

Ans. Luc. (addition, Naples, Bibl. Naz. XII A.39, fol. 109v-110r); Coll. 7L (addition, MS Vat. lat. 1346, fol. 183r); Coll. Caes. 7.115; Coll. S. Germain-des-Prés (app. Wolfenbüttel, Gud. 212, fol. 59r); Corpus decretalium 3.169 (Naples, Bibl. Naz XII A.27, fol. 90r); Coll. of Paris B.N. lat. 4283, fol. 9r.[61]

JL 6616

Pascalis episcopus seruus seruorum dei uenerabili fratri Victori Bononiensi episcopo salutem et apostolicam benedictionem.

Peruenit ad nos — omnino prohibeas. Data Lateranis .XI. kalendas maii.

C.16 q.1 c.9

Ans. Luc. (addition bk 5, rec. A and C).[62]

***

[57] Fol. 281v of the codex is so badly damaged that only part of JL 6611 remains.

[58] The codex, written in the late twelfth century, is partly burnt. Fournier, *Histoire* II 218-22 suggested that it might be a copy of an earlier manuscript. The text was published by Pflugk-Harttung, *Iter Italicum* (Stuttgart 1883) 216.

[59] Synod of Benevento held by Paschal in 1108, c.1. See Blumenthal, *Early councils* 103-06 with further references. Three additional manuscripts were recently brought to my attention. Professor R. Somerville referred me to Rome, Bibl. Naz. Centrale MS 529, where the text is found on fol. 14r. Professor R. Weigand kindly provided a transcription of the same text from the appendix to Gratian in MS Heiligenkreuz 44, fol. 300rb (inscr.: 'Decretum Pascasii. II. factum Beneuenti'). Professor G. Fransen found it in Paris, B.N. lat. 4283, fol. 9r, on which see his 'Collections canoniques dans le manuscrit 4283 de la Bibliothèque nationale de Paris', *Liber Amicorum Monseigneur Onclin* (Bibl. Ephemeridum theol. Lovan. 42; Gembloux 1976) 169-97, 172f. I am very grateful for all this information.

[60] The canon is abbreviated: 'Laicos in ecclesiis nil habere. Pascalis pape. Laici qui — destituantur officiis'.

[61] See G. Fransen (note 59 above) 172f.

[62] Friedberg's note accompanying C.16 q.1 c.9 should be emended accordingly. See also Constable, *Monastic tithes* (note 27 above) 92.

The following items were not included in Jaffé's *Regesta* and are therefore listed in alphabetical order by incipit.

Anno dominice incarnationis .m.c.xiii. — quam laicorum.
Lateran council of 1112.[63]
Chronological coll. of MS Vat. lat. 3829, fol. 282r-283r. (rubr.: Vt iniusta et exacta priuilegia dampnentur.)

Apostolica auctoritate — fidelium careat. Item. Quicumque ab — diaconibus statuimus.
Council of Troyes, 1107.[64]
Coll. can. of MS Göttweig, Stiftsbibl. 53 (56) fol. 86r-86v.

Apostolorum canonibus — patrum sequentes: see 'Constitutiones sanctorum.'

Constitutiones sanctorum — communione priuetur. Apostolorum canonibus — excommunitioni subiciantur. Quicumque res naufragorum — excludantur.
Lateran council of 1110.
Canonical collections containing the decrees are described in the introduction of my edition.[65]
Ex rescripto[a] Pascalis pape.
De negotiis super quibus mecum estis locutus cum episcopis et cardinalibus contuli et ex eorum consilio hoc uobis rescribo. Si duo fratres sine tenore iurauerint quod in simul habitare debeant, nisi cohabitatio et iuramenti obseruatio uergat eos in peiorem exitum aut adulterium aut aliquid simile, obseruare debent quod iurauerunt. Si autem pro iuramenti obseruantia patiuntur damnum in temporalibus, absit ut iuramentum propterea frangere debeant.

    a *uel* responso: R. *cod.*

Coll. 3L (addition in Pistoia, Arch. capit. 135, fol. 224rb).
The Latinity of this unidentified fragment is poor ('estis locutus', 'sine tenore iurare'), and especially the awkward use of 'nisi . . . uergat' with a direct object ('eos') distorts the implicit quotation from Bede.[66]

---

63 The best text is found in Cardinal Boso's *Vita Paschalis*, ed. Duchesne, LP 2.369-71.
64 See MGH Const. 1.566-67, no. 396; Blumenthal, *Early councils* 90-97.
65 *Early councils* 109-22. Cf. JL 6606 above.
66 Bede, *Homil.* 44.6: 'Si aliquid forte nos incautius iurare contigerit quod obseruatum peiorem uergat in exitum . . .' (Burch. 12.18; Ivo, Decr. 12.13, Panorm. 8.94; Grat. C.22 q.4 c.6). On this doctrine concerning illicit oaths see S. Kuttner, *Kanonistische Schuldlehre* (Studi e testi 64; Città del Vaticano 1935) 276, 320ff.

Paschalis episcopus .II. uenerabili fratri Gal. ecclesie Magalonensi episcopo eiusque successoribus canonice promouendis in perpetuum.
Et predecessoris nostri — fratrum regulariter.[67]
  Polycarpus 6.9.18.

Pascalis papa.
Illitterati et nonnulla parte corporis inminuti et penitentes sacris non possunt apti esse officiis.
  Coll. can. Wolfenbüttel, Guelf. 9.4. Aug. 4, fol. 67rb. Unidentified.

Paschalis .II. Guidoni Viennensi archiepiscopo.
Inuestituram episcopatuum, abbatiarum et omnium rerum ecclesiasticarum de manu laica sancte Romane ecclesie auctoritatem sequentes heresim esse iudicamus.
  Council of Vienne, September 1112, c.1.[68]
  Coll. 10P 3.7.7.

Pascalis episcopus seruus seruorum dei dilectis in Christo filiis clericis sancti Alexandri salutem et apostolicam benedictionem.
Litterarum uestrarum — habere debetis. Data Rome nonis octobris.[69]
  Coll. 13Lf13.45 (MS Vat. Lat. 1361, fol. 246r).

Paschalis papa.
Nullus abbas, nullus prior — conducente uel annuente.
  Synod of Beauvais [1114] c.5.[70]
  Panormia (addition, Paris B.N. lat. 10742, fol. 109v)

Decretum domni Paschalis pape quod decreuerat in sinodo que celebrata est apud Uuaristallam — conuenerunt.
Per multos iam — scientiaque commendat. Amen.
  Council of Guastalla [1106] c.4.
  Burch. (addition, Frankfurt, Stadt- und Universtätsbibl. MS Barth. 50, fol. 5v.);[71] Ivo, Decretum (addition, Vatican, Palat. lat. 587, fol. 108v).

Quicumque res naufragorum — excludantur: see 'Constitutiones sanctorum'.

---

[67] The letter to Bishop Walter of Maguelonne was published by H. Fuhrmann, 'Zwei Papstbriefe aus der Überlieferung der Rechtssammlung "Polycarpus",' *Aus Reichsgeschichte und Nordischer Geschichte* (Kieler Historische Studien 16; Stuttgart 1972) 131-40, at p. 140.

[68] The council was held by Archbishop Guy of Vienne, see Mansi 21.74-76. The incorrect attribution to Pope Paschal II reflects the wishes of his opponents during these years. Paschal was obliged to confirm the decrees of this French synod, but did so in very general terms. See JL 6330.

[69] The letter to the clergy of St. Alexander's at Bergamo was edited by S. Kuttner, 'Some Roman Manuscripts of Canonical Collections', BMCL 1 (1971) 7-29, at p. 28f.

[70] The synod was held by Cardinal Cono of Palestrina. See Mansi 21.124 and Somerville, 'Council of Beauvais' 493-503.

[71] G. Powitz and H. Buck, *Die Handschriften des Bartholomaeusstifts und des Karmeliterklosters in Frankfurt am Main* (Die Handschriften der Stadt- und Universitätsbibliothek... 2; Frankfurt a. M. 1974) 104ff.

Ex epistola Paschalis pape.
Sanctimonialis uirgo cum ad consecrationem suo episcopo offertur in talibus uestibus semper usura est professione et sanctimonie aptis.

    Coll. can. Leiden, Rijksuniv. B.P.L. 184, fol. 25r. Unidentified.

Pascalis .II.ᵃ
Si dominus et magister — precibus exorandus.

    ᵃ Item Pascalis secundus *Erl.* Adeodatus *vel* Deusdedit *pleraeque coll.*

1 Comp. 5.2.3 (X 5.3.3)
Lips. 1.11; Erl. 1.11; Harv. 25; Darmst. 4; Frag. Trec. (E) 7; 1 Dun. 3.28; Chelt. 2.11; Cott. 5.8b; Pet. 4.18; 2 Par. 26.1; Bamb. 1.10; Cass. 13.11; Tann. 2.1.9; Sang. 2.1.11; Frcf. 22.2.

With the exception of Lips. and Erl. this text of uncertain origin is nowhere attributed to Paschal II. It appears sometimes without inscription (Chelt. Cott. Pet. Sang.) but is mostly ascribed to the little-known Pope Deusdedit or Adeodatus (615-618). Under this name it occurs also as *palea* before or after C.2 q.4 c.1.[72]

Ex epistola Paschalis pape cap. xi.
Si qui igitur sanctimonialibus feminis in matrimonio sibi ad iniuriam Christi copulati, iuxta censuram christiani zeli separentur et nunquam eis concedatur iugali uinculo religari, sed in penitentie se lamentis uehementer dum uiuunt afficiant.

    Coll. 7L 5.68.3 (Vienna, Ö.N.B. 2186, fol. 213v) Unidentified.

[Si quis clericus — subiaceat: see JE 2556]

Eiusdem.
Sicuti non est ab oratione cessandum pro eis quos corrigi uolumus, etiamsi nullo hominum orante pro Petro Dominus respexit eum et fecit eum suum flere peccatum, ita non est neglegenda correctio, quamuis Deus quos uoluerit non tunc faciat esse correctos. Tunc autem correctione proficit homo cum miseretur atque adiuuat qui facit quos uoluerit etiam sine correctione proficere.

    Ans. Luc. (addition following JL 6491a in Florence, Med.-Laur. S. Marco 499, fol. 185v; Naples, Bibl. Naz. XII A.39, fol. 98v). Unidentified.

P[aschalis] seruus seruorum dei uenerabilibus fratribus R. Remensi archiepiscopo eiusque suffraganeis salutem et apostolicam benedictionem.
Tribulationibus et calamitatibus — operiis in eo adimpleatis.

    Letter to Archbishop Raoul of Reims.[73]
    Paris B.N. lat. 4283, fol. 93r.

---

[72] See H. Zapp, 'Paleae-Listen des 14. und 15. Jahrhunderts', ZRG Kan. Abt. 59 (1973) 83-111, at 101ff. no. 58,
[73] The letter was identified and edited by G. Fransen, 'Collections . . . dans le manuscrit 4283 . . .' (note 59 above) 173.

BEMERKUNGEN ZUM REGISTER PAPST PASCHALIS II.*

Zusammen mit anderen, jetzt verlorenen, Registern des 11. und 12. Jahrhunderts wurde das Register Paschalis' II. (1099–1118) in der zweiten Hälfte des 12. und zu Anfang des 13. Jahrhunderts häufig zitiert und durchgesehen, denn es war spätestens zur Zeit Innocenz' III. zur Regel geworden, daß in Streitsachen Registereinträge das beste Beweismittel darstellten[1]). Trotzdem weiß man nur wenig über das Paschalis-Register. Durch Johannes von Gaeta, der seit 1088 Leiter der Kanzlei war, bis er 1118 als Gelasius II. († 1119) Nachfolger Paschalis' II. wurde, war sicherlich eine gewisse Kontinuität mit dem Register Urbans II. gegeben[2]). Man darf außerdem

*) Anläßlich des Seventh International Congress of Medieval Canon Law in Cambridge (23.–27. 7. 1984) habe ich in einem Vortrag einige der hier besprochenen Punkte kurz gestreift. Der Vortrag wird in den von P. Linehan herausgegebenen Proceedings der Konferenz erscheinen. Ich möchte auch hier noch einmal Herrn O. Hageneder und Herrn D. Lohrmann für ihr wohlwollendes Interesse an dieser Arbeit vielmals danken.

[1]) Mehrere Beispiele werden in Papal registers in the twelfth century, Proceedings (s. Anm. *) gegeben. S. a. J. F. v. Schulte (Hg.), Die Summa d. Stephanus Tornacensis, Giessen 1891, zu D. 81 c. 3, S. 104: *Consuetudo est romanae ecclesiae quod, cum alicui de magno negotio mittit epistolam, apud se retinet eius exemplum. Quae omnia exempla in unum librum conficit, quem vocat registrum, ut, si quaestio postea super eodem mergat, proferatur exemplum et quieti detur negotium.* Die Stelle ist bereits zitiert bei H. Bresslau, Handbuch d. Urkundenlehre 1, Leipzig ²1912 (= Berlin ³1958), S. 121, Anm. 2.
[2]) D. Lohrmann, Das Register Papst Johannes' VIII. (872–882), Bibl. d. DHI Rom 30, Tübingen 1968, S. 55f., 80ff., 97ff., mit Literatur. P. Kehr, Scrinium und Palatium. Zur Geschichte des päpstlichen Kanzleiwesens im XI. Jh., Mitteilungen d. Inst. f. Österreichische Geschichtsforschung, Ergänzungsbd. 6, 1901,

voraussetzen, daß Johannes aufgrund seiner Ausbildung in Montecassino besonderes Interesse an päpstlichen Registern hatte[3]). Was
Einzelheiten angeht, so steht man heute jedoch im großen und ganzen noch auf dem Stand, der von Harry Bresslau und Ludwig Weiland repräsentiert wird[4]). Dazu kommen noch die vor allem von Carl
Erdmann veröffentlichten Texte, die im Zusammenhang mit den großen Prozessen der iberischen Halbinsel des späten 12. und frühen 13.
Jahrhunderts stehen[5]). In einem Plädoyer Bragas wird anhand eines
Briefes Paschalis' II. die Anordnung und der Umfang seines Registers sowie der Register des 12. Jahrhunderts allgemein beschrieben: *Dicta epistula „Experientiam" inuenitur circa principium in*

S. 106ff. P. R a b i k a u s k a s, Die römische Kuriale in der päpstlichen Kanzlei,
Misc. Hist. Pontificiae 20, Rom 1958, S. 127ff. C. S e r v a t i u s, Paschalis II.
1099−1118, Päpste u. Papsttum 14, Stuttgart 1979, S. 59f.
[3]) Zu Montecassino und den päpstlichen Registern zuletzt H. H o f f m a n n, Zum
Register und zu den Briefen Papst Gregors VII., DA 32 (1976), S. 86ff., hier
S. 101ff.
[4]) B r e s s l a u, Urkundenlehre 1, bes. S. 105−108; L. W e i l a n d (Hg.), Constitutiones et acta publica 1, MGH Legum sectio 4, Hannover 1893, Nr. 99, S. 147ff.
[5]) C. E r d m a n n, Papsturkunden in Portugal, Abhandlungen d. Ges. f. Wissenschaften, Göttingen 20 (1927), S. 104ff. u. bes. Nr. 160, S. 381ff. (Die moderne
Signatur der Madrider Abschrift ist B. N. 13042.) Darstellung aus portugiesi-
scher Sicht bei P. F e i g e, Anfänge des portugiesischen Königtums und seiner
Landeskirche, in: Spanische Forschungen der Görresgesellschaft (Hg. O. E n-
g e l s), 1. Reihe 29 (1978), S. 85−436, ein Hinweis, für den ich Herrn R. Elze
herzlich danke. Feige veröffentlicht mehrere der von Erdmann nur erwähnten
Dokumente mit vollem Wortlaut. Die Texte der großen Toledaner Kartularien
sowie des Archivs der Kathedrale von Toledo für den hier besprochenen Zeitraum sind endlich in einem einzigen Band herausgegeben: F. J. H e r n á n d e z,
Los cartularios de Toledo: Catálogo Documental, Madrid 1985. Unter den Nummern 545, 547, 549, 550−553 und 555−556 stehen dort mit speziellen Hinweisen
auf das Register Paschalis' II.: *Experienciam uestram* [JL −], JL 5934, JL 6222,
Et fratrum relatione [JL −], JL 6490, JL 6396, JL 6465 und JL 6475. (JL = Ph.
J a f f é, Regesta pontificum Romanorum [Hg. W. W a t t e n b a c h, S. L o e w e n-
f e l d, F. K a l t e n b r u n n e r u. P. E w a l d], Leipzig, [2]1885−1888.) Das Trans-
sumt Honorius' III. (P r e s s u t t i Nr. 977; Original Toledo, ACT X.7 X.3.4b) aus
dem Register Paschalis' II. enthält die Briefe JL 6316, JL 6455, JL 6490 und JL
6561. Zu den zahlreichen Abschriften der Toledaner Kartularien steht auch Hs.
Rom. Bibl. Vallic. C. 23 in Beziehung, die häufig unzuverlässig ist. S. u. Anm. 7.
Für Paschalis' Briefe JL 6414 und JL 6474 s. E r d m a n n, Papsturkunden in
Portugal, S. 105.

XIII

tercio libro; et quod primus liber contineat acta primi anni, secundus secundi, tercius tercii, et sic de aliis, probatur euidenter, nam Paschalis sedit XVIII annis et V mensibus et fecit decem et octo libros et incepit nonumdecimum, et ita de omnibus apostolicis, secundum quod dicent uobis qui regesta scribunt, et probatur manifeste per ipsa regesta inspecto libro et anno pape et anno dominico et indictione[6]). Im übrigen zeigen aber auch diese Texte nur, daß unter Paschalis II. Briefauslauf registriert wurde, chronologisch geordnet innerhalb der einzelnen Bücher, von denen es jeweils eins für ein Pontifikatsjahr gegeben hat[7]).
Es läßt sich jetzt etwas mehr über das Register Paschalis' II. sagen. In einer beiläufigen Bemerkung zum Register Gregors VII. wies Erich Caspar darauf hin, daß Benutzerspuren, Rubriken und Marginalien aus dem späten 11. und 12. Jahrhundert im Register Gregors VII. in Zusammenhang mit den „kompilatorischen Arbeiten des 12. Jahrhunderts, dem Liber Censuum und seinen Vorläufern" stehen[8]). Es war aber nicht nur das Register Gregors VII., das damals mehrfach „mit der Feder in der Hand durchforscht wurde", wie Caspar sich ausdrückte, sondern unter anderem auch das heute nicht mehr erhaltene Register Paschalis' II., wie in diesem Zusammen-

---

[6]) Erdmann, Papsturkunden in Portugal, Nr. 160, S. 382.
[7]) Es finden sich Hinweise auf folgende Bücher des Registers: 3, 4, 10, 12, 13, 14, 15, 16, 17, 18 und 19. Die Handschrift Rom, Bibl. Vallic. C. 23, fol. 86v., enthält den abgekürzten Text des Privilegs JL 6245 (*Egregias quondam*) für Burgos mit dem Hinweis: *in registro dni. Paschalis pape libro II°* (Ewald, NA 6, S. 295). Er muß aber falsch sein, wie die Datierung des Originals zeigt, veröffentlicht von D. Mansilla, Hispania Sacra 1 (1948), S. 50, Nr. 12 = Mansilla, La documentación pontificia hasta Inocencio III (965–1216), Rom 1955, Nr. 47, S. 66f. Es läßt sich bisher noch nicht nachweisen, daß Privilegien in das Register Paschalis' II. eingetragen wurden. Zur problematischen Frage der Privilegienregistrierung s. zuletzt Hoffmann, Zum Register (wie Anm. 3), S. 98ff. und S. 100.
[8]) E. Caspar, Studien zum Register Gregors VII., Neues Archiv 38 (1913), S. 145ff., hier S. 168f. S. a. R. Schieffer, Tomus Gregorii papae, Bemerkungen zur Diskussion um das Register Gregors VII., Arch. f. Diplomatik 17 (1971), S. 169ff., hier S. 183, sowie allgemein H.-E. Hilpert, Zu den Rubriken im Register Gregors VII. (Reg. Vat. 2), DA 40 (1984), S. 606ff., mit Literatur. Auf Marginalien und den Liber Censuum ist Hilpert nicht eingegangen.

4

hang vor allen Dingen die vatikanische Hs. Ottob. lat. 3057 zeigt[9]).
Dieser Codex mit den Digesta pauperis scolaris des Kardinals Albi-
nus enthält in den beiden letzten Büchern der Digesta (10 und 11)
Texte mit Verweisen auf die Register Paschalis' II. und Gregors
VII., die nur hier überliefert werden oder zumindest deren älteste
und beste Überlieferung heute in Ottob. lat. 3057 greifbar wird, vom
Register Gregors VII. selbst einmal abgesehen.

Die bisher im Zusammenhang mit den Papstregistern des 12.
Jahrhunderts nicht beachteten Texte aus dem Register Paschalis II.
in dieser Hs. ordnen sich größtenteils wie von selbst in die Serie ein,
die innerhalb der wenig systematisierten Sammlung des Kardinals
Deusdedit (3.184−289) und verwandten Handschriften eine deutlich
erkennbare Gruppe bildet und von Sickel treffend als Privilegiensammlung beschrieben wurde[10]). Die ursprüngliche Privilegiensammlung, sehr wahrscheinlich aus den Jahren 1083−1086, hat
Deusdedit bei der Abfassung seiner Kanonessammlung wohl schon
vorgelegen. Sie enthält Auszüge aus Registern und anderen päpstlichen Archivalien, die im großen und ganzen in eine der folgenden
drei Gruppen fallen: päpstliche Briefe an weltliche Fürsten und die
Kaiserpakten, Anmerkungen über Pachtverträge, über Besitz und
Einkommen der römischen Kirche; Eide[11]).

[9]) Zu dieser Hs. zuletzt T. Montecchi Palazzi, Cencius Camerarius et la
formation du ‚Liber Censuum' de 1192, Mélanges de l'École Française de Rome
96 (1984), S. 49 ff., hier S. 53 ff., mit Literatur.
[10]) Th. Sickel, Das Privilegium Otto I. für die Römische Kirche vom Jahre 962,
Innsbruck 1883, S. 69 ff. und S. 77 ff. Der Umfang der Zwischensammlung PS (=
Privilegiensammlung) ist unbekannt. E. Perels hielt sie für eine große kanonistische Sammlung und sie hat sicherlich Kapitel 184−289 des 3. Buchs der Kanonessammlung des Kardinals Deusdedit in der Ausgabe V. Wolf von Glanvells
(Paderborn 1905, Neudr. Aalen 1967) enthalten. S. dazu H. Fuhrmann, Einfluß und Verbreitung der pseudoisidorischen Fälschungen 2, MGH Schriften 24,
Stuttgart 1973, S. 517 ff., R. Schieffer, Tomus (wie Anm. 8), und T.
Schmidt, Alexander II. und die römische Reform-Gruppe seiner Zeit, Päpste
und Papsttum 11, Stuttgart 1977, S. 220 ff.
[11]) Die Überlieferung von Eiden und Eidformeln ist noch sehr unklar. E. Caspar (Hg.), Das Register Gregors VII., MGH Epistolae selectae 2, Berlin ³1967,
S. XI, und Schmidt, Alexander II., S. 222 f., mit Literatur. Eide werden hier
nicht gesondert behandelt, da sie aus dem Register Paschalis' nur im Zusammenhang mit den Verträgen des Jahres 1111 bekannt sind.

Zur ersten Gruppe gehören drei Briefe Paschalis' II., die schon Giesebrecht aus der Hs. Ottob. lat. 3057 veröffentlicht hat[12]): JL[13]) 6334, JL 6557 und JL 6562. Ihre Texte sind wahrscheinlich etwas gekürzt. Gewiß scheint dies für das Eingangsprotokoll, doch ist die Datierung am Schluß vollständiger überliefert, als es in der Privilegiensammlung bei den Briefen Gregors VII. der Fall ist. Die drei Briefe stehen zwar zusammen in Buch 11 der Digesta[14]), sind aber nicht chronologisch geordnet, obwohl sie eine Gruppe mit einer gemeinsamen Titelrubrik bilden: *Excertum ex registro Paschalis pp. libro xix, cap. iii Rogerio Sicilie comiti.* Die anschließende Inskription wiederholt die Rubrik zum Teil: *Paschalis papa II Rogerio comiti Sicilie* (JL 6562 vom 1.10.1117). An diesen Brief schließt ein Schreiben vom November 1112 an: *Idem, libro xiiii cap. vi, Alexio Constantinopolitano imperatori* (JL 6334). Als letztes folgt der Brief an König Nils von Dänemark vom 23. April 1117 (JL 6557): *Idem in libro xviii, cap. xxi Danorum regi*[15]).

Deutliche Parallelen zu dieser Briefgruppe Paschalis' II. finden sich in dem Teil der Privilegiensammlung, der Auszüge aus der Korrespondenz Alexanders II. und Gregors VII. mit weltlichen Fürsten enthält (Deusd. 3.268−277). Die Digesta sowie der Liber Censuum enthalten außerdem eine zweite Gruppe von drei Texten aus dem Register Paschalis' II., die sich inhaltlich eng an die Reihe von Besitztiteln in der Privilegiensammlung anlehnen[16]). Es handelt sich um folgende Auszüge:

---

[12]) W. v. Giesebrecht, Geschichte der deutschen Kaiserzeit 3, Braunschweig ⁴1876−1877, S. 1201.

[13]) JL = Jaffé, Regesta pontificum Romanorum, ²1885−1888 (wie Anm. 5).

[14]) Hs. Ottob. lat. 3057, fol. 151r−151v = Le Liber Censuum de l'Église Romaine (Hg. P. Fabre u. L. Duchesne) 2, Bibl. des Écoles franç. d'Athènes et de Rome 2e sér., Paris 1910, S. 125ff. = XI.18−20. Die Numerierung der Kapitel ist eine Zutat der Herausgeber des Liber Censuum, zitiert unten LC.

[15]) Zur Sache zuletzt mit älterer Literatur Servatius, Paschalis II. (wie Anm. 2), S. 93f., mit Literatur zu JL 6552, und S. 166, mit Literatur zu JL 6557. Auf JL 6334 wird nicht speziell eingegangen.

[16]) Dazu bes. Schieffer, Tomus (wie Anm. 8), mit L. Santifaller, Beiträge zur Gesch. d. Beschreibstoffe im MA, Mitt. d. Inst. f. Österr. Geschichtsforschung, Ergänzungsbd. 16,1, Graz−Köln 1953, S. 35ff.

6

1) *Excerptum ex registro Paschalis libro xiii, cap. xxii. Hec sunt que facient Ninphesini...*[17]).
2) *Et infra cap. iiii Proprietas que remansit curie de regalibus Beneuenti. Hec sunt que in dominicatu...*[18]).
3) *Excerptum ex registro Paschalis pp., libro xii, cap. iii. Septimo kalendas septembri...*[19]).

Die drei Texte stehen im Zusammenhang mit Paschalis' im großen und ganzen erfolgreichen Bemühungen, die legitimen Ansprüche des Papsttums gegenüber der aristokratischen Opposition in der Umgebung Roms sowie gegenüber den Unabhängigkeitsbestrebungen Benevents durchzusetzen. Namentlich genannte Zeugen verbürgen in dem Exzerpt des 13. Registerbuches die Unterwerfung Ninfas unter den Papst und die Bedingungen, unter denen der Frieden geschlossen wurde. Obwohl wir leider nicht wissen, ob der Registereintrag bei dem neuerlichen Abfall Ninfas in 1116 irgendwie von Nutzen war[20]), lassen schon allein die aufgeführten Namen der Zeugen vermuten, daß der Eintrag etwas anderes darstellt, als die historischen Notizen, die aus den Registern Gregors VII. und Urbans II. bekannt sind. Im dritten der genannten Auszüge meint man die Formen einer Urkunde in Datierung, Actum Zeile und Zeugenliste *(qui affuerunt)* zu erkennen. Trotzdem zeigen sowohl der Inhalt als auch die Form, daß es sich nicht um die unvollständige Abschrift einer offiziellen Urkunde über die Investitur des Abts Johannes von Subiaco mit Ponza und Affile handeln kann. Der Eintrag stellt technisch gesehen

---

[17]) Ottob. lat. 3057, fol. 137v = LC 2, S. 95, X.54; LC 1, S. 407f., Nr. 132. P. Kehr, Italia Pontificia 2: Latium, Berlin 1907, S. 109, 1. Das *castrum Ninfa* (Diöz. Velletri) wurde von Papst Eugen III. an die Frangipani verpfändet, doch 1204 von Innocenz III. zurückerworben. Servatius, Paschalis II., S. 73f.

[18]) Ottob. lat. 3057, fol. 137v = LC 2, S. 95, X.55; LC 1, S. 408, Nr. 133. W. Holtzmann (Hg.), Italia Pontificia 9: Samnium, Apulia, Lucania, Berlin 1962, S. 25ff., *29−51 zu Konflikten in und um Benevent zur Zeit Paschalis' II. Auf die Aufstellung in den Digesta des Albinus und im LC wird kein Bezug genommen. Servatius, Paschalis II., S. 87ff., zum allgemeinen Hintergrund.

[19]) Ottob. lat. 3057, fol. 139r = LC 2, S. 96, X.66; LC 1, S. 407, Nr. 131. P. Kehr, Italia Pontificia 2, S. 51f., mit Hinweis auf Paschalis' bestätigendes Privileg vom 24. August 1117 (JL 6560), sowie Servatius, Paschalis II., S. 77.

[20]) S. Anm. 17.

weder Einlauf noch Auslauf dar, sondern eine *Notitia*, nach Redlich eine „schlichte Beweisurkunde, die für eine schon rechtsgültig vollzogene Handlung ein schriftliches . . . Beweismittel zu schaffen hat"[21]). Der zweite Auszug aus dem Register Paschalis II., der zu den Besitzvermerken gehört, ist am deutlichsten als solcher zu erkennen. In dürren Worten wird in der Bestandsaufnahme der päpstlichen Regalien in Benevent aufgezählt, „was der Kurie an Eigentum verblieben ist"[22]). Das Registerbuch ist in der Inskription wohl aus Versehen nicht angegeben worden; falls das Kapitel in der chronologisch richtigen Reihenfolge erscheint und die Kapitelnummer stimmt, müßte sich die Überschrift auf ein jüngeres Registerbuch als 13 (1112/1113) beziehen[23]), aber Hypothesen scheinen wenig lohnend, zumal auch die Frage, aus welchem Anlaß die Aufstellung über päpstlichen Besitz in Benevent entstand, nicht sehr weit führt. Verhandlungen vor dem Papst über Beneventaner Streitfälle waren verhältnismäßig häufig[24]). Der Eintrag, der zwischen Einlauf und Auslauf steht, könnte aufgrund schriftlicher Aufzeichnungen über Beneventaner Besitz und Verleihungen zustande gekommen sein; man vergleiche etwa den Eintrag über Ninfa. Für das frühe 12. Jahrhundert liegt es jedoch näher, an eine Aufstellung aufgrund von Zeugenaussagen zu denken, die dann von einem Beauftragten der Kurie zusammengestellt und schließlich entweder ganz oder in einem Auszug ins Register eingetragen worden sein müßte. In jedem Falle ist es bemerkenswert, daß die Beneventaner Besitzliste ebenso wie die beiden *Notitiae* unter eigenen Kapitelnummern in das Register Paschalis' II. eingetragen wurden, wie dies vielleicht auch im 7. und 8. Jahrhundert üblich war und unter Umständen ebenfalls zur Zeit seines Vorgängers Urban II.[25]). Abgesehen von dem annalistischen Be-

---

[21]) O. Redlich, Die Privaturkunden des MA, München–Berlin 1911, S. 27ff.
[22]) S. Anm. 18. Vgl. J. Fried, Der Regalienbegriff im 11. und 12. Jh., DA 24 (1973), S. 450ff.
[23]) Hierzu schon E. Stevenson, Osservazioni sulla Collectio Canonum di Deusdedit, Arch. della R. Società Romana di Storia Patria 8 (1885), S. 373 n. 2, der für das 14. Registerbuch plädiert.
[24]) Servatius, Paschalis II., S. 86ff., und besonders Holtzmann wie Anm. 18.
[25]) Deusdedit (wie Anm. 10), 3.185 sowie 3.208–267. S. a. die folgenden Anm. 26f.

richt, der zu Urbans erstem Pontifikatsjahr gehört und aus der Collectio Britannica und spanischen Prozeßakten bekannt ist[26]), finden sich nämlich im Kartular von San Cugat Einträge, die auf Gerichtsnotitiae hinzuweisen scheinen, die aufgrund gerichtlicher Urkunden nachträglich in das Register Urbans aufgenommen wurden[27]). Paschalis und vielleicht auch Urban unterscheiden sich in dieser Beziehung von ihren unmittelbaren Vorgängern Leo IX. (Deusd. 3.202, 3.204; s. aber 3.197), Alexander II. (Deusd. 3.203) und Gregor VII. (Deusd. 3.201). Für Gregor VII. gibt es allerdings auch im Register eine Notiz über eine eventuelle Schenkung an St. Peter, die einen Übergang andeuten könnte[28]).

Das Register Paschalis' II. muß ein recht buntes Bild geboten haben. Außer Briefauslauf enthielt es auch *Notitiae* und eine inhaltlich zu den *Notitiae* in Beziehung stehende Besitzliste, beides Material, von dem bisher nicht bekannt war, daß es damals in den Registern gestanden hätte[29]). Im Gegenteil, Rudolf Schieffer zeigte überzeugend, daß die *tomi* im päpstlichen Archiv, auf die sich die Privilegiensammlung/Deusdedit bei derartigen Vermerken öfter berief, keine Register waren[30]). Die voneinander sehr verschiedenen Stücke wurden unter Paschalis alle in den Band eingetragen, dessen Beschreibung im Jahre 1199 durch den Prokurator der Erzdiözese Braga oben zitiert wurde. Nicht nur für Paschalis II., sondern auch für die anderen Päpste der Zeit bis auf Innocenz III., dessen Registrum super negotio imperii die berühmte Ausnahme darstellt[31]), fehlt in den noch vorhandenen Quellen jeder Hinweis auf ein zweites amtli-

---

[26]) P. Ewald, Neues Archiv 5 (1880), S. 357, Urb. ep. no. 17, sowie P. Pressutti, Regesta Honorii Papae III, 1 (Rom 1888), Nr. 980, S. 167. Zu den Registern Honorius' jetzt J. Sayers, Papal Government and England during the Pontificate of Honorius III (1216–1227), Cambridge 1984.

[27]) P. Kehr, Papsturkunden in Spanien 1: Katalanien, Abh. d. Ges. d. Wiss. Göttingen, N. F. 18/2 (1926), S. 277 ff., Nr. 17–20.

[28]) Caspar (Hg.), Register (wie Anm. 11), VI, 5a; LC 1, S. 385, und LC 2, S. 125 = XI. 12 (Ottob. lat. 3057, fol. 150v), aber ohne Hinweis auf das Register.

[29]) S. u. Anm. 51.

[30]) Schieffer, Tomus (wie Anm. 8).

[31]) F. Kempf, Die Register Innocenz III., Misc. Hist. Pontificiae 9, Rom 1945, bes. S. 45 ff., und ders., (Hg.), Regestum Innocentii III papae super negotio Romani imperii, Misc. Hist. Pontificiae 12, Rom 1947.

ches Register für einen Papst, anhand dessen Briefe, Privilegien und Prozeßentscheidungen überprüft wurden[32]). Wie bekannt, gab es außer Registern auch andere Aufzeichnungen, die im päpstlichen Archiv ihren Platz fanden, doch ist es sehr unwahrscheinlich, daß sich unter diesen Archivalien den amtlichen Briefregistern genau vergleichbare Unterlagen befunden haben[33]). Hoffmann hat unlängst im Zusammenhang mit dem Register Gregors VII. gezeigt, daß das Banzi-Privileg vermutlich aus einem Heft stammt, das dem Register Gregors einmal vorgebunden war und am ehesten als Formularbuch der päpstlichen Kanzlei zu betrachten sein dürfte[34]).

Trotzdem muß die scheinbar überflüssige Frage nach einem eventuellen zweiten Register für Paschalis II. noch einmal gestellt werden. Der bekannteste Auszug aus seinem Register ist der Bericht über die Ereignisse vom 4. Februar bis 13. April 1111[35]). Die wahrscheinlich älteste Textüberlieferung steht in der vatikanischen Hs. Vat. lat. 1984 mit der Rubrik: *Incipit registrum Pascali* [sic] *pape secundi*[36]). Der Schlußsatz gibt den Bericht als Einheit und sehr

---

[32]) S. o. Anm. 1 sowie z. B. M. Spaethen, Giraldus Cambrensis und Thomas von Evesham über die von ihnen an der Kurie geführten Prozesse, Neues Archiv 31 (1906), S. 612 f., Anm. 1 mit zwei Zitaten aus Schriften des Giraldus Cambrensis.

[33]) Cencius Savelli spricht in seinem Vorwort zum Liber Censuum (LC 1, S. 2 ff.; s. o. Anm. 14) von Anmerkungen *in thomis charticiniis et voluminibus regestorum antiquorum pontificum Romane ecclesie et modernorum, et aliorum librorum quorumdam, seu memorialium veratium*, die er in seinem Zinsbuch zusammengestellt habe. S. a. Die Register Innocenz' III. 1 (Hg. O. Hageneder u. A. Haidacher), Graz—Köln 1964, Brief I/537, S. 776 f., und die Bemerkungen in B. Schimmelpfennig, Die Zeremonienbücher der römischen Kurie im MA, Bibl. d. DHI Rom 40, Tübingen 1973, bes. S. 9 ff.

[34]) Hoffmann, Zum Register Gregors VII. (wie Anm. 3), S. 98 ff. und 100 f.

[35]) Die Texte wurden zuletzt von L. Weiland herausgegeben, MGH Const. 1, Nr. 99, S. 147 ff. (s. o. Anm. 4), wo auf die übrigen Nummern verwiesen wird. Der Text erscheint als einheitliches Ganzes in L. Duchesne (Hg.), Le Liber Pontificalis 2, Paris 1892, S. 338 ff. Der Einfachheit halber werde ich die von Weiland eingeführte Numerierung übernehmen, obwohl sie in den Hss. fehlt. Zur Sache s. Servatius, Paschalis II., 223 ff., 225 m. Anm. 75.

[36]) D. Whitton, The Annales Romani and Codex Vaticanus Latinus 1984, Bull. dell'Ist. Stor. Ital. per il Medio Evo 84 (1972—1973), S. 125 ff., mit älterer Literatur. Die übersichtlichste Beschreibung der Hs. findet man bei Duchesne,

10

persönliches Zeugnis zu erkennen: *Hec sicut passi sumus et oculis nostris vidimus et auribus nostris audivimus mera veritatę perscripsimus.* Der Codex enthält noch vier weitere Einzeltexte aus dem gleichen Zeitraum, von denen mindestens zwei, aber wahrscheinlich drei, von dem unbekannten Exzerptoren als dem Register Paschalis' entnommen beschrieben werden. Die gleiche Hand, die den 1111 Bericht *Incipit Registrum*... (Weiland 99) ausschrieb, trug auf fol. 193v zunächst das *priuilegium ... prime conuentionis* für Heinrich V. ein, das bei den Verhandlungen zwischen Papst und König im Februar 1111 für die ursprüngliche Krönung vorgeschlagen und beeidet, aber niemals verliehen wurde[37]). Im Anschluß daran steht in Vat. lat. 1984 eine kurze historische Notiz:

Postea rex cum omnibus suis consiliariis diabolico spiritu plenus his omnibus pactionibus et sacramentis ad nichilum deductis, post processionem pridie Idus Februar. anno duodecimo pontificatus eius in ecclesia beati Petri, sicut indutus erat ut missam celebraret et eum coronaret, cum episcopis cardinalibus, diaconibus, archipresbyteris, presbyteris et omni clero, iudices ac notarii, nobilibus etiam civitatis et suburbanis, cepit eum ac in custodia abuit per duos menses[38]).

Die Notiz geht in der gleichen Zeile direkt über in die Rubrik *Conuentio secunda ui extorta.* Was folgt, ist die kurze Abmachung aus der Nacht vom 11. April 1111 auf den Wiesen bei Ponte Mammolo, die also als *conuentio secunda* bezeichnet wird (Weiland 91). Dieser Eintrag schließt mit *Et hoc sacramentum* [= conuentio secunda] *ex parte pontificis sicut in registro residet. Eiusdem pape priuilegium secundo* [sic] *etiam.* Dieses *priuilegium secundo* ist das berüchtigte Investiturprivileg vom 13. April 1111, das im Vat. lat. 1984 in der

Liber Pontificalis 2, S. XXIIf.; auch G. Meyer v. Knonau, Jahrbücher des Deutschen Reiches unter Heinrich IV. und Heinrich V., 6, Leipzig 1907, Excurs I, S. 369ff., ist nach wie vor wichtig.
[37]) Weiland, MGH Const. 1, Nr. 90, S. 140ff., Incipit: *Et diuine legis...*
[38]) Weiland, Nr. 90, S. 142, in Petitdruck.

BEMERKUNGEN ZUM REGISTER PASCHALIS' II. 11

gleichen Zeile sofort anschließt[39]). Auf den Schluß des Privilegs folgt
wieder eine kurze historische Notiz über die Unterzeichnung und
Beeidigung dieser Urkunde durch den Papst und seine Begleitung
quamvis invitus[40]). In der Handschrift beginnt dieselbe Hand dann
in einer neuen Zeile mit Absatzzeichen und der Inskription *Actio
concilii contra heresim de inuestituris* mit der Abschrift des Schluß-
dokuments der Synode vom 18.–23. März 1112[41]). Aus diesem Text
geht hervor, daß es sich bei dieser *Actio concilii* um eine *carta*, also
eine Einzelurkunde handelt, die Paschalis z. B. einem Brief an Guido
von Vienne beifügen konnte[42]).

Codex Vat. lat. 1984 beweist also, daß zwei Texte, erstens die
Conuentio secunda ui extorta, die auch *sacramentum* genannt wird,
und zweitens das *priuilegium secundo* [sic] im Register Paschalis
gestanden haben. Sie sind auf den 11. und 12. April 1111 zu datieren
und gingen der Krönung vom 13. April voran. Der 13. April ist der
letzte Tag, dessen Ereignisse im langen Bericht *Incipit registrum...*
(Weiland 99) beschrieben werden. Die Urkunden vom 11. und 12.
April müßten also eigentlich dort stehen, da das Register Paschalis',
wie wir wissen, chronologisch angeordnet war: Weil es gerade das
Investiturprivileg vom 12. April war, das dem Papst schwere Vor-
würfe einbringen sollte, nahm man an, daß es samt seiner Vorurkunden eben absichtlich im Register ausgelassen worden wäre[43]). Wie
sich jetzt zeigt, stimmt das nicht. Das Register Paschalis' II. enthielt

---

[39]) Das eröffnende *P[aschalis]* des Privilegs (Weiland, MGH Const. 1, Nr. 96,
S. 144f.) ist in rot nachgezogen, doch sind Zwischenbemerkung und Text in der
gleichen kleinen, schwer zu lesenden Hand geschrieben und so wahrscheinlich
den Herausgebern entgangen.
[40]) Weiland, MGH Const. 1, Nr. 96, S. 145, Petitdruck.
[41]) Weiland, MGH Const. 1, Nr. 399, S. 570 ff.
[42]) JL 6313. W. Schum, Kaiser Heinrich V. und Papst Paschalis II. im Jahre
1112, Jahrbücher d. Kgl. Ak. gemeinnütziger Wissenschaften zu Erfurt, n. s. 8
(1877), S. 278f. Die Frage, ob die *carta* in das Register aufgenommen wurde,
kann hier nicht weiter verfolgt werden, da Vat. lat. 1984 sich dazu nicht äußert.
S. a. H. Hoffmann, Zur ma. Brieftechnik, Spiegel der Geschichte: Festgabe f.
Max Braubach, (Hg. K. Repgen u. S. Skalweit), Münster 1964, S. 141 ff.,
hier S. 145f., sowie für *carta* im Sinne von Brief G. Constable, Letters and
Letter-Collections, Typologie des Sources (fasc. 17, A-II, 1976), S. 25.
[43]) Meyer v. Knonau, Jahrbücher 6, S. 183, als Beispiel.

12

vermutlich alle Dokumente, die im Frühjahr 1111 entstanden sind, und über die wir überhaupt etwas wissen, sowohl die Texte des Berichts *Incipit registrum...* (Weiland 99) in Hs. Vat. lat. 1984, fol. 194r—195v, als auch wenigstens zwei der vier Texte, die in derselben Handschrift, die als sehr zuverlässig und in diesem Teil fast gleichzeitig erachtet wird, auf fol. 193v und 194r stehen. Aus diesem Blickwinkel heraus fällt die Unstimmigkeit auf, die zwischen der Rubrik und dem Datum der Einträge im Bericht *Incipit registrum...* besteht. Ganz gleich, ob man das Wort *registrum* dem mittelalterlichen Sprachgebrauch entsprechend als Nominativ oder als Akkusativ übersetzt, bedeutet die Rubrik, daß die Texte des Frühjahrs 1111, dem 12. Pontifikatsjahr Paschalis' II., das Register eröffnen. Dies steht im Widerspruch zu allem, was sonst aus und über das Register dieses Papstes bekannt ist. Als Ausweg bietet sich scheinbar die Möglichkeit an, den Wortlaut der Titelrubrik auf eine Sonderlage zu beziehen, die dem Gesamtregister vorgebunden gewesen sein könnte, etwa analog dem Banzi-Privileg im Register Gregors VII. Doch die Analyse der historischen Notiz *Postea rex*, die oben im Wortlaut zitiert wurde, zeigt, daß ein solches Verständnis den Texten nicht gerecht wird.

Die wenigen Zeilen *Postea rex ... per duos menses*[44]) sind nicht einfach, wie man denken könnte, eine Zusammenfassung des langen Berichts *Incipit registrum...*, obwohl sie ebenfalls die Ereignisse am 12. Februar 1111 betreffen. Der Absatz *Postea rex...* schließt auf fol. 193v sofort an das erste Einzelstück (Weiland 90) an, spricht aber gleich im ersten Satz von all den Abkommen und Eiden, die der König mit den Seinen gebrochen hätte, *...his omnibus pactionibus et sacramentis ad nichilum deductis...* Von diesen Pakten und Eiden gibt es jedoch unter den Einzelstücken auf fol. 193v und 194r keine Spur. Die Bemerkung in der Notiz kann sich daher logischerweise nur auf die verschiedenen Vereinbarungen und Eide beziehen, die wir lediglich aus dem Bericht *Incipit registrum...* kennen. Offensichtlich waren sie aber auch in der Vorlage vorhanden, aus der das *priuilegium primae conuentionis* (Weiland 90) zusammen mit der kurzen Notiz *Postea rex...* abgeschrieben wurde, denn im Anschluß

---

[44]) Weiland, MGH Const. 1, Nr. 90, S. 142, Petitdruck.

an das erste *priuilegium* ist die prägnant formulierte Zeile, so wie sie jetzt erscheint, sinnlos. Die sinnlos gewordene Bemerkung über die vielen gebrochenen Vereinbarungen in der Notiz *Postea rex* kann also keine Zutat des Abschreibers sein, wie es die nicht rubrizierte Versicherung am Schluß des zweiten Einzelstücks, der Promissio papae auf fol. 193v (Weiland 91), sicherlich ist: *Et hoc sacramentum ex parte pontificis sicut in registro residet; eiusdem pape priuilegium secundo* [sic] *etiam*[45]).

Aufgrund der Notiz *Postea rex...* darf man mit großer Wahrscheinlichkeit schließen, daß alle Dokumente, die in die Hs. Vat. lat. 1984 übernommen wurden, im amtlichen Register Paschalis' II. ihren Platz hatten, sowohl die Einzelstücke auf fol. 193v als auch die Abkommen und Eide, die im Bericht *Incipit registrum* (fol. 194r−195v) enthalten sind. Andererseits dürfte die lange Erzählung, die die letzteren umkleidet, dort gefehlt haben, da sie sich mit den historischen Notizen *Postea rex*[46]) und *Cui nimirum*[47]) überschneidet. In ihrer prägnanten Kürze entsprechen diese beiden Notizen der Form nach den aus den Registern Gregors VII. und Urbans II. bekannten Notizen genau[48]), was bei dem Bericht *Incipit registrum...* absolut nicht der Fall ist. Einen Beweis für diese Hypothese gibt es bisher nicht, doch würden bei der vorgeschlagenen Interpretation die Probleme, die der Text aufwirft: Rubrik, Auslassung von Urkunden, breit angelegte, im persönlichen Stil gehaltene Rahmenerzählung, eine einfache Erklärung finden. *Registrum* in der Rubrik *Incipit registrum...* (Weiland 99) ist dann eben nicht das Register, das ja nicht erst im

---

[45]) Weiland, Nr. 96, wo die Rubrik der Hs. Vat. lat. 1984 *Conuentio secunda ui extorta* und die zitierte Zwischenbemerkung aber fehlen. S. dazu U.-R. Blumenthal, Patrimonia und Regalia in 1111, in: Law, Church, and Society, Essays in Honor of Stephan Kuttner (Hg. K. Pennington u. R. Somerville), Philadelphia 1977, S. 9ff., hier S. 14f. Die Rubrik *Conuentio secunda* schafft eine Parallele zum ersten Einzelstück, dem *priuilegium primae conuentionis* (Weiland 90). Vielleicht darf man deswegen den Hinweis des Schreibers der Einzelstücke auf das Register Paschalis auch auf das *Priuilegium primae conuentionis* vom 12.2. ausdehnen, obwohl dies nicht ausdrücklich gesagt wird.
[46]) Weiland, MGH Const. 1, Nr. 90, S. 142, Petitdruck, Sigle V.
[47]) Weiland 96, S. 145, Sigle V.
[48]) Das Register Gregors VII. (wie Anm. 11). Zu Urban II. s. Anm. 26 sowie Duchesne, Liber Pontificalis 2, S. 293.

14

Jahre 1111 angefangen wurde, sondern ein Register[49]) im Sinne von Sonderlage oder Weißbuch[50]) über die Ereignisse des Frühjahrs 1111, das nachträglich aus dem Register zusammengestellt wurde, vielleicht für die Lateransynode von 1112. Die Annahme liegt deswegen nahe, weil auch die *carta* von 1112 abgeschrieben wurde (fol. 194r), aber jeder ausdrückliche Hinweis über den Zweck des Berichts fehlt. Sein Charakter würde der gleiche bleiben, ob er nun dem Register vorgebunden war oder als Einzelheft existierte.

Zusammenfassend läßt sich vielleicht sagen, daß die Texte in der Handschrift Vat. lat. 1984 wohl dahingehend auszulegen sein dürften, daß es für Paschalis II. neben dem amtlichen Register, dessen Gestalt wir kennen, ein Sonderheft oder Weißbuch über seine Gefangenschaft gegeben hat, für das Urkunden dem amtlichen Register entnommen wurden. Auch für seinen Pontifikat gab es also nur ein amtliches Register. Neben Briefauslauf fand man dort Notitiae verschiedenen Inhalts und Form unter eigenen Kapitelnummern, die um die Mitte des 12. Jahrhunderts von Notariatsinstrumenten verdrängt werden sollten, die nicht mehr in den Registern standen. Die Veränderung ist zur Zeit des Kämmerers Boso bereits deutlich zu erkennen[51]). Der wertvolle Codex Vat. lat. 1984 zeigt außerdem, daß

---

[49]) Die Vieldeutigkeit des Wortes *registrum* ist bekannt. Die vatikanische Hs. Barb. lat. 535, enthält auf fol. 212v den folgenden Nachtrag aus dem 12. Jh.: *Quidam dicunt regestum quod est liber continens memorias aliorum librorum et epistolas in unum collectas. Et dicuntur regestum quasi iterum gestum. Alii dicunt regestron cui plus conuenit noster usus. Liber uero Prudentii uult regestum dici in quo scriptum reperitur: In regestis caelestibus,* Vgl. Du Cange, Glossarium s. v. *regestum.*

[50]) S. die Definition von Kempf, Die Register Innocenz' III. (wie Anm. 31), S. 106.

[51]) Es ist noch nie beachtet worden, daß Boso merkwürdigerweise niemals von Registern spricht, obwohl er Urkunden häufig zitiert. (Duchesne, Liber Pontificalis 2, S. XXXVII, Absatz 28ff., hier S. XLII mit Anmerkungen. Zu Kardinal Boso und dem Liber Censuum zuletzt Montecchi, Cencius Camerarius, S. 59ff., mit Anm. 44 [wie Anm. 9].) Hier möchte ich nur kurz auf zwei Beispiele hinweisen, die Vita Paschalis (LP 2, S. XLI u. 369ff.) und den Bericht über das Treffen Friedrich Barbarossas und Papst Hadrians IV. bei Sutri 1155 (LP 2, S. 391f.). In beiden Fällen wird allgemein angenommen, daß Boso die Register benutzt hätte, aber nur, weil er im ersten Fall den Bericht aus Vat. lat. 1984

auch Vertragsurkunden, Eide und kurze historische Notizen im Register Paschalis' ihren Platz hatten. Dieses war offensichtlich eine sehr individuelle Sammlung, ganz gleich ob es seine Gestalt nun dem Papst selber oder, was wahrscheinlicher ist, seinem Kanzler und engen Berater Johannes von Gaeta verdankte. Wenn Friedrich Kempf den ausgesprochen persönlichen Charakter des Registers Innocenz' III. betonte, aus einer Zeit, als die Register bereits einen festen Platz im Rechts- und Verwaltungsleben der Kurie hatten[52]), so überrascht ein solcher Befund für die Zeit von rund hundert Jahren früher nicht, obwohl er deutlich macht, mit welcher Vorsicht Fragmente in die Registertradition eingeordnet werden müssen.

Abschließend möchte ich nur noch kurz auf die Frage eingehen, wann und durch wen das Register Paschalis' II. für die Auszüge im Codex Ottob. lat. 3057 benutzt worden sein könnte. Bei den drei oben besprochenen Briefen und den *Notitiae* handelt es sich um Auszüge, die irgendwann im Laufe des 12. Jahrhunderts zusammen mit der Privilegiensammlung und ähnlichem Material in die Zinsbücher der römischen Kirche aufgenommen wurden[53]). Im Gegensatz zu den Briefen JL 6334, JL 6557 und JL 6562, die nur bei Albinus überliefert werden, stehen die Notitiae auch im offiziellen Liber Censuum des Kämmerers und späteren Papstes Cencius von 1192, das über weite Strecken mit den beiden letzten Büchern der Digesta des Albinus, die, wie man bisher annahm, kurz vorher entstanden sein sollen, eng verwandt ist. Sowohl Albinus als auch Cencius weisen in ihren Vor-

---

ausschrieb (Weiland, MGH Const. 1, Nr. 99) und im zweiten Fall, weil Hs. Ottob. lat. 3057 einen sehr ähnlichen Bericht über das Treffen von 1155 mit der Rubrik *De receptione pape Adriani a Frederico imperatore, ex registro ipsius pape, cap. LXXXIII* enthält (LP 2,95, Nr. 53 mit Anm.). R. Holtzmann, Der Kaiser als Marschall des Papstes, Schriften der Straßburger Wissenschaftlichen Ges. in Heidelberg, N.F. 8 (1928), S. 44ff., hat gezeigt, daß die Berichte bei Boso und bei Albinus nicht aus einer gemeinsamen Quelle geflossen sein können. F. Kempf nennt die „Materialsammlung zum Pontifikat Paschalis' II." des Kardinals Boso ein „Sammelsurium", für das es „keine Parallele im päpstlichen Registerwesen" gibt. (Rezension Blumenthal, The Early Councils of Pope Paschal II, Arch. Hist. pont. 17 [1979], S. 458ff., hier S. 458f.)
[52]) Kempf, Die Register Innocenz' III., S. 117ff.
[53]) Zum Inhalt des LC s. jetzt die übersichtliche Zusammenstellung bei Montecchi, Cencius Camerarius, S. 51f.

worten darauf hin, daß sie älteres Material aufgenommen haben[54]). Cencius erwähnt Zinsverzeichnisse aus den Pontifikaten Eugens III. und Hadrians IV., die ihm zusammen mit *libri* und *memorialia* vorgelegen hätten. Wie er angibt, hat er all dies Material überarbeitet, übersichtlicher angeordnet und nicht nur mit neuen Zinsverpflichtungen vervollständigt, sondern auch mit älteren Anmerkungen, die er unter anderem den alten Registern der Päpste entnommen haben will[55]). War das Register Paschalis' darunter? Die Herausgeber des Liber Censuum, Paul Fabre und Louis Duchesne, haben versucht, so gut wie möglich Neues von Übernommenem zu trennen, doch ist insbesondere die Abhängigkeit der Arbeiten des Cencius und des Albinus voneinander in vielem noch unklar[56]). Es gilt jedoch allgemein als sicher, daß Albinus die Arbeiten der Vorgänger lediglich abgeschrieben habe und diese Vorgänger unverändert repräsentiert[57]), obwohl neuerdings zugegeben wird, daß Albinus unter Umständen die Briefe, die er wie gesagt allein überliefert, selbst dem Register Paschalis' entnommen haben könnte[58]). Beweisen läßt sich die Behauptung nicht, genausowenig wie sich sagen läßt, wer die *Notitiae* aus dem Paschalis-Register ausgeschrieben hat, die nach wie vor Boso zugewiesen werden[59]).

Die Zinsaufzeichnungen sowohl bei Albinus als auch bei Cencius enthalten jedoch noch einen Auszug aus dem Register Paschalis' II., einen Brief an die dänischen Bischöfe (JL 6335). Er ist die einzige Spur, die sich etwas weiter verfolgen läßt. Unter der Rubrik *In Dania* findet man in Hs. Ottob. lat. 3057 auf fol. 145r die Inskription *Excerptum ex registro Paschalis pape II, libro quinto, cap. xv circa finem. Episcopis per Daniam constitutis. Inter cetera...*[60]). Bei Cen-

---

[54]) LC 2, S. 88 (Albinus), und LC 1, S. 2ff. (Cencius).

[55]) S. das Zitat in Anm. 33.

[56]) Fabre, Étude (wie Anm. 62), S. 12; Montecchi, Cencius Camerarius, S. 54 u. S. 65.

[57]) Aufschlußreich sind die Konkordanztafeln, LC 1, S. 8ff., in denen Albinus nicht ein einziges Mal als Quelle des LC erscheint.

[58]) Montecchi, Cencius Camerarius, S. 64, die den auf S. 61 gemachten Bemerkungen hier widerspricht.

[59]) Montecchi, Cencius Camerarius, S. 61f.

[60]) Ottob. lat. 3057 ist die einzige Hs. der Digesta; die Buchminuskel wird allgemein auf Ende des 12. Jh.s, Rom und Umgebung, datiert. Vgl. Blumenthal,

cius erscheint der gleiche Text in der Zinsliste, doch zeigt Codex Vat. lat. 8486, die Originalhandschrift des Liber Censuum, daß JL 6335 auf fol. 56r im linken Innenrand von einer etwas jüngeren Hand nachgetragen wurde[61]). Zumindest bei diesem Text lag also das Zinsverzeichnis des Albinus (oder die Vorlage des Albinus, die heute einzig und allein aus seinen Digesta bekannt ist) Cencius vor, und zwar erst nach 1192.

Daß JL 6335 bei Cencius ein Nachtrag ist, wird nicht nur durch den paläographischen Befund, sondern auch durch den Inhalt bewiesen. Innerhalb der Zinsliste, die nach Diözesen, Provinzen und Ländern so gut wie möglich geordnet ist, nimmt sich der Brief sehr eigenartig aus. Nicht wegen seines Inhalts, er spricht von einem Zins, den die dänische Kirche Rom schulde, sondern wegen seiner Form. Im ganzen Verzeichnis, das nur Namen von Kirchen und Klöstern zusammen mit dem geschuldeten Zinsbetrag enthält, ist er der einzige Brieftext und noch dazu die einzige Stelle, wo auf ein päpstliches Register verwiesen wird. Der Papstbrief, so muß man daraufhin annehmen, war ein verhältnismäßig junger Nachtrag in ein schon bestehendes Zinsverzeichnis, der dem übrigen Text noch nicht angeglichen wurde – eben von Cencius Savelli noch nicht in die Zinsliste eingeordnet worden ist, der sein Augenmerk 1192 hauptsächlich galt, wie er in seinem Vorwort angibt. Im Gegensatz dazu wurde der Brief von der gleichen Hand und gleichzeitig mit den übrigen Texten dieses Teils der Handschrift in Codex Ottob. lat. 3057 eingetragen. Die Benutzung des Registers Paschalis' II. muß daher wenigstens in diesem Fall nicht Cencius, sondern Albinus zugeschrieben werden.

Es läßt sich zeigen, daß Albinus auch das Register Gregors VII. benutzt hat. Hs. Ottob. lat. 3057, fol. 137v, ist die einzige noch vorhandene Handschrift der Privilegiensammlung[62]), in der unter

---

Cardinal Albinus of Albano and the Digesta pauperis scolaris Albini. Ms. Ottob. lat. 3057, Arch. Historiae Pontificiae 20 (1982), S. 7ff.

[61]) Ich bin Herrn R. Elze sehr zu Dank verpflichtet, der meine Ansicht bestätigen konnte. S. den Text des Briefes LC 1, S. 227 mit Anm., sowie Stevenson, Deusdedit (wie Anm. 23), S. 374. Zu Cencius und der Zinsliste s. Montecchi, Cencius Camerarius, S. 72ff.

[62]) S. Anm. 10. Der Herausgeber der Kanonessammlung Deusdedits, V. Wolf von Glanvell, vertritt S. XXXVII die Ansicht, daß Albinus die Deusdedit-

dem Lemma *Ex registro Gregorii VII pape, libro iii, cap. xxi* der Eid Berengars von Tours erscheint, den dieser auf dem Fastenkonzil des Jahres 1079 leisten mußte. Wie bekannt, steht der Eid in verschiedener Form zweimal in Gregors Register, einmal an der chronologisch richtigen Stelle im 6. Buch (VI.17a) und dann im 3. Buch wie von Albinus angegeben (III.17a)[63]. Aber bei Albinus wird die Überschrift von Buch 3 mit dem Text aus Buch 6 verbunden. Daß es sich bei allem nicht einfach um einen Irrtum handelt, bei dem ein Schreiber die Zahlen III und VI in der Vorlage nicht sorgfältig las und verwechselte, wird durch den anschließenden Text in den Digesta bewiesen. Abgesehen vom Register Gregors VII. ist Codex Ottob. lat. 3057 die einzige Handschrift, die anschließend an Reg. III.17a den Eid des Bischofs Robert von Chartres in Übereinstimmung mit dem Register Gregors VII. bringt. Die Inskription auf fol. 138r lautet: *Idem in eodem. Juramentum R. dicti Carnotensis episcopi*[64]). Zwei weitere Texte aus dem Register Gregors VII., VIII, 23, und vielleicht VI, 5a, lassen ebenfalls vermuten, daß Albinus auf Papstregister zurückgegriffen, diese mit den in Sammlungen überlieferten Texten verglichen und gegebenenfalls vervollständigt hat. Die Papstregister waren ihm jedenfalls nicht fremd, und es ist nicht ausgeschlossen, daß er Ende des 12. Jahrhunderts das Register Paschalis' II. benutzt und zum Teil abgeschrieben hat.

Kapitel aus dem Liber politicus des Kanonikers Benedikt in der Hs. Cambrai, Bibl. mun. 554, übernommen haben könnte. Vgl. aber S. XL u. bes. Schimmelpfennig, Zeremonienbücher (wie Anm. 33), S. 6ff. u. 9f. Die Ansicht von P. Fabre, Étude sur le Liber Censuum de l'Église Romaine, Bibl. des Écoles franç. d'Athènes et de Rome 62, Paris 1892, S. 13ff., wird vertreten von Montecchi, Cencius Camerarius, S. 57ff. Ich bin Herrn D. Lohrmann für Hilfe bei der Beschaffung eines Mikrofilms der Hs. Cambrai sehr dankbar.
[63]) Ottob. lat. 3057, fol. 137v−138r (LC 2,95 = X.59). Der Text steht nicht im Liber Censuum des Cencius. Caspar (Hg.), Register, III, 17a und VI, 17a, S. 426f., mit Anm. Vgl. a. E. Caspar, Studien zum Register Gregors' VII., Neues Archiv 38 (1913), S. 145ff., hier S. 156, S. 178 und S. 185, mit Literatur.
[64]) Caspar (Hg.), Register, III. 17a, S. 282f., mit Anm. 1. Zum angeblichen Eid Wiberts von Ravenna, den Albinus sowie Cencius in Übereinstimmung mit Deusd. 4.424 (S. 600) bringen, s. a. die Literaturangaben bei J. Ziese, Wibert von Ravenna, der Gegenpapst Clemens III. (1084−1100), Päpste u. Papsttum 20, Stuttgart 1982, S. 36, Anm. 24. LC 2, S. 95f., X.59 und X.60.

XIV

THE CORRESPONDENCE OF
POPE PASCHAL II
AND GUIDO OF VIENNE
1111–1116

THE LETTERS EXCHANGED between Pope Paschal II and his legate, Guido, archbishop of Vienne, which are the subject of this paper, survive without any, or with only incomplete, dating formulae.[1] This is a serious lacuna because these letters are important evidence for the opposition within the church to Paschal's policies with regard to investiture and regalia. These connected issues arose during the Gregorian reform in the second half of the eleventh century, when the papacy began first to limit and then to abolish the customary investiture of bishops and abbots with the temporalities of their sees by kings and other lay nobles.[2] Pope Urban II, Paschal's predecessor, couched the prohibition for laymen to invest clergy in particularly strong terms at the council of Clermont in 1095, forbidding not only investiture but also homage.[3] Paschal II (1099–1118) reaf-

---

1. P. Jaffé, *Regesta pontificum romanorum*, 2nd rev. ed., 2 vols. (Leipzig, 1885 and 1888; repr. Graz, 1956). The letters under discussion are catalogued as JL 6313 ("Actionem concilii"), JL 6330 ("Cum alicuius"), and JL 6325 ("Si constantiam").

2. For the process see now R. Schieffer, *Die Entstehung des päpstlichen Investiturverbots für den deutschen König. MGH Schriften*, 28 (Stuttgart, 1981). The book contains a full bibliography. A brief and excellent introduction are the relevant chapters by F. Kempf in *Handbook of Church History*, ed. H. Jedin and J. Dolan, 3: *The Church in the Age of Feudalism*, tr. A. Biggs (New York and London, 1969) part 2, chapters 42–45, with outstanding bibliographies.

3. C.14: "Interdictum est ne reges vel aliqui principes aliquam investituram de honoribus ec-

2

firmed both these prohibitions at the Lateran council of 1102.[4] In April 1111, however, Paschal, who had been captured and imprisoned with his entourage by Henry V of Germany, turned around and granted Henry the right of investiture with ring and staff, the customary symbols, in return for his own liberty and that of the curia.[5] This privilege proved unacceptable to the church as a whole and after bitter struggles was revoked by the Lateran council of 1112. In the final analysis the authority of the council overrode that of the pope, who merely consented.[6] In brief, this is the context for the letters under discussion. Fixing their date, however, not only will reveal how the line of argument developed, but also will provide a more accurate date for the anonymous *Disputatio vel defensio Paschalis papae,* one of the few theoretical discussions of the investiture problem, and the only one from the later years of Paschal's pontificate.[7]

The treatise was discovered together with two letters of Paschal II in a twelfth-century manuscript, Naples, BN, MS V. C. 46, by Wilhelm Schum, who published his findings in 1877.[8] Because of the poor condition of the last folio, Schum (who, as he noted apologetically, was pressed for time when he copied the texts) remained uncertain about some of his

clesiasticis faciant"; c.15: "Ne episcopus vel sacerdos regi vel alicui laico in manibus ligiam fidelitatem faciat." The texts are quoted from the critical edition by R. Somerville, *The Councils of Urban II*, 1: *Decreta Claromontensia* (Amsterdam, 1972), 77, 78. See also *ibid.*, 145, nos. 18 and 19 for related transmissions.

4. See JL 5908: "Qua de re in synodo nuper apud Lateranense consistorium celebrata patrum nostrorum decreta renovavimus, sancientes et interdicentes, ne quisquam omnino clericus hominium faciat laico aut de manu laici ecclesias vel ecclesiastica dona suscipiat." A discussion is found in my *The Early Councils of Pope Paschal II, 1100–1110* (Toronto, 1978), 17–20.

5. *MGH Constitutiones et acta publica (Legum sectio IV)*, 1, ed. L. Weiland, 144ff., no. 96 (cited below as *MGH Const.* 1).

6. The best partial edition of the 1112 council is that by Weiland, *ibid.*, 570–74, nos. 399 and 400. The long version of the minutes has to be read in *Le Liber Pontificalis*, ed. L. Duchesne, 2 (Paris, 1892; repr. 1955), 369–371. For the discussion of some of the problems see my "Opposition to Pope Paschal II," *Annuarium Historiae Conciliorum*, 10 (1978):82–98.

7. *Disputatio vel defensio Paschalis papae*, ed. E. Sackur, *MGH, Libelli de lite*, 2 (1892):658–666, on the basis of Schum's publication. (See the following note.)

8. W. Schum, "Kaiser Heinrich V. und Papst Paschalis II. im Jahre 1112," *Jahrbücher der Königlichen Akademie gemeinnütziger Wissenschaften zu Erfurt*, n.s., 8 (1877): 189–318. Cf. the remarks by G. Meyer von Knonau, *Jahrbücher des deutschen Reiches unter Heinrich IV. und Heinrich V.*, 6 (Leipzig, 1907), Exkurs I, 387 with note 58. See in general the penetrating discussion by R. L. Benson, *The Bishop-Elect. A Study in Medieval Ecclesiastical Office* (Princeton, 1968), esp. 203–250; and M. J. Wilks, "Ecclesiastica and Regalia: Papal Investiture Policy from the Council of Guastalla to the First Lateran Council, 1106–1123," *Studies in Church History*, 7 (Cambridge, 1971): 69–85.

readings in the treatise and the letters to Guido of Vienne and Girard, archbishop of Angoulême. Sackur, with the help of Bethmann and Waitz, emended the treatise, but paid no attention to the letters. A visit to Naples showed that the letters are still sufficiently legible to permit a check of Schum's readings and a confirmation of most of his suggestions.[9] Of particular interest in the present context is Paschal's letter to Guido. The body of the texts reads as follows:

> Actionem concilii quod nuper Laterani domino presente egimus ab eis qui interfuerunt scire plenius poteris. Nos autem predecessorum nostrorum statuta sequentes precipue domni Gregorii VII et Urbani secundi quod dampnaverunt dampnavimus, quod firmaverunt firmavimus, quod statuerunt statuimus. Comisse tibi legationis officium vivaciter exequaris et ad amorem Dei et ecclesie periclitantis quorum poteris corda solicites.[10]

The textual correspondences between the letter (JL 6313) and the extant *acta* from the council held in the Lateran from March 18 to 23, 1112, leave no doubt that it is this synod to which the text specifically refers. The *actio* of the council also mentioned in JL 6313 is a reference to the formal document (*carta*) solemnly ratified by this assembly.[11] Under the circumstances, it is difficult to explain why the letter which was published and dated by Schum more than a hundred years ago is so often disregarded, Meyer von Knonau being the exception that confirms the rule.[12] The reason, perhaps, is the uncertainty regarding the text as well as a certain confusion caused by the manuscript transmission of the document known as *Actio concilii*. As it happens, it is often accompanied by a different letter of Paschal to Guido of Vienne as well as by a letter of Guido and the council of Vienne to the pontiff.[13] JL 6313 is not a part of this group of material.

---

9. I am indebted to Mr. Rolf Krause, Rome, who confirmed my readings of the manuscript.

10. Cf. Schum, "Kaiser Heinrich V," 278f.

11. See *ibid.*, 279 note 1 and compare the complete text of the letter as given here with *MGH Const.* 1, no. 399, 571ff. A relevant portion of the text is cited below, note 26.

12. Knonau, *Jahrbücher*, 6:235.

13. Manuscripts with the combination of *Actio concilii* and the letters are Paris, BN, MS lat. 10402, ff. 70v–72v; Boso's *Vita Paschalis* (ed. Duchesne, *Liber Pontificalis* 2:369–376) and the numerous MSS of the *Liber Censuum* which incorporate Boso's compilation. The original manuscript of the *Liber Censuum*, BAV, MS Vat. lat. 8486, does not contain the *Vita*; see the *Le Liber Censu-*

Paschal II had particular difficulties in reasserting his authority in France and imperial Burgundy during the years 1111 to 1116. Guido of Vienne coordinated and perhaps stirred up opposition to the pontiff, even after the Lateran council of 1112. The revocation of the April 1111 privilege in the *Actio concilii* was the result of a compromise by the assembly. In exchange for Paschal's reconfirmation of the validity of the prohibitions of his predecessors Gregory VII and Urban II, Paschal was permitted to refrain from personally excommunicating Henry V. Paschal thus did not violate the oath which he had sworn in the camp of the king just outside of Rome on April 11, 1111.[14] Archbishop Guido of Vienne, however, and his supporters were not satisfied with this outcome of the Lateran council of March 1112, of which they had been informed by Paschal's letter "Actionem concilii" (JL 6313) quoted earlier, as well as by participants. The pontiff therefore instructed Guido to hold a council at Vienne to discuss the problems.[15] Whatever Guido's motives, whether he was animated by reforming zeal or dynastic ambitions as has recently been suggested,[16] the council's discussions concluded on September 16, 1112, with the signing of a solemn letter to the pontiff threatening him with the withdrawal of obedience by the French, unless he sent an open letter con-

um de l'Eglise Romaine, ed. P. Fabre and L. Duchesne, "Introduction" [Paris, 1910], 32 with a stemma codicum. Fabre and Duchesne prove that not Vat. lat. 8486 but Florence, Bibl. Riccardiana, MS 228, where the Vitae were first added, was the source for all other extant copies. This codex is described ibid., 18–24 and 28f. The texts are also found in BAV, MS Ottob. lat. 3057 (Liber Censuum, 2:135–137), and in a "vetus liber" which was edited by François Juret (1553–1626) in his edition of the works of Ivo of Chartres, reprinted by J. P. Migne, PL, vols. 161–162. I have consulted the 1647 edition of Juret's work in the Biblioteca Apostolica Vaticana (signature: R. I. I 307: D. Ivonis Carnotensis episcopi opera omnia in duas partes distributa, . . . Parisiis, apud Laurentium Cottereau, Via Iacobaea sub signo Montis Carmeli. 1647). The text of the Actio concilii and the letters is found in vol. 2:194–196, as part of the commentary for Ivo's epistle no. 238. It has not been possible to identify Juret's manuscript. I suspect that my present list of manuscripts is still incomplete.

14. MGH Const. 1, 142f., nos. 91 and esp. 92: ". . . et penitus in personam regis Heinrici nunquam anathema ponet. . . ."

15. We do not know how Paschal made this request. No such letter from 1112 has survived. That the synod at Vienne was convened by Guido in accordance with the wishes of Paschal is made clear by the synod's letter to the pontiff. It begins: "Sancte pietatis vestre mandata sequentes apud Viennam convenimus. . . ." The letter is quoted on the basis of Duchesne's edition, Liber Pontificalis 2:373f. The material for the synod of Vienne is collected in Mansi, Amplissima collectio, 21:cols. 73–78. For a full citation see note 17 below.

16. See the astute article by M. Stroll, "New Perspectives on the Struggle between Guy of Vienne and Henry V," Archivum Historiae Pontificiae, 18 (1980):97–115, with further bibliographical references for Guido-Calixtus II.

firming the excommunication of Henry V by name. Such an excommunication had been pronounced by the assembled fathers at Vienne on their own initiative. Paschal's expected letter was to be circulated, the pope was informed, in order to rally forces in opposition to Henry V. Since Paschal was to promise all involved *remissio peccatorum suorum*, Guido seems to have thought in military terms.[17] Paschal sent the requested confirmation immediately, JL 6330, a sure sign of the vulnerability[18] under which he seems to have labored into the winter.[19] The letter, however, probably pleased Guido and his supporters very little, for it certainly did not urge a crusade against Henry by promising a *remissio peccatorum* to Guido's supporters, nor did Paschal repeat the excommunication of Henry V. He merely confirmed the decisions of the synod of Vienne in very general terms: ". . . Deo gratias referimus, et quae statuta sunt ibi rata suscipimus et confirmamus, et cooperante Domino Deo illibata permanere censemus." Guido and his circle did not circulate Paschal's reply. Instead, they apparently circulated the decisions of the council they had held at Vienne with an inscription which attributed these to the pontiff himself.[20]

17. See G. D. Mansi, *Sacrorum conciliorum nova et amplissima collectio* . . . , 21 (Venice, 1775), coll. 75f. for the text of the letter from the synod of Vienne with dating clause. After requesting papal confirmation for the decisions and excommunication at Vienne, the council added: ". . . Cuius confirmationis argumentum per apertas nobis litteras significare dignemini; quas etiam, ut gaudium nostrum sit plenum, alter alteri destinare possimus. Et quoniam principum terrae pars maxima, et universi fere populi multitudo in hac re nobiscum sentit: in remissionem peccatorum suorum omnibus iniungatis ut, si necesse fuerit, auxilium nobis et patriae unanimiter ferant. . . . Si vero . . . assertiones praedictas roborare nolueritis: propitius sit nobis Deus, quia nos a vestra subiectione et obedientia repelletis." See also note 15 above.

18. JL 6330. The short letter is found *ibid.*, col. 76, with the date: "Data Laterani XIII. Kal. Novembris." Since the text refers explicitly to the council of Vienne, the date is Oct. 20, 1112. The letter from Vienne (see note 17 above) accordingly took about four weeks to reach the pontiff in Rome. See R. Elze, "Über die Leistungsfähigkeit von Gesandtschaften und Boten im 11. Jahrhundert" in: *Histoire comparée de l'administration. Francia*, Beihefte, 9 (Munich, 1980):3-10.

19. A further letter of the pontiff from the same period, November 1, 1112, looks suspiciously like another effort to conciliate Guido. It is addressed to Archbishop William of Besançon and confirms Guido's decision in favor of the clergy of St. Jean in Besançon. Paschal gave the opponent of St. Jean, St. Etienne of Besançon, only five days to present its case—in the event they should appear in Rome—before he confirmed Guido's decision. Paschal did eventually revise his decision when St. Etienne was able to prove its case and requested Guido to hold a council to review his earlier decision. The letter to William of Besançon is published by W. Wiederhold, *Papsturkunden in Frankreich*. Gesellschaft der Wissenschaften Göttingen, Nachrichten (Göttingen, 1906), 1:26f., no. 6. Paschal's relevant letters from 1115 are JL 6456, JL 6467 and JL 6365. Further bibliography is found in the article by Stroll; see note 16 above.

20. This seems indicated by the canonical *Collection in Ten Parts* which contains as 3.7.7. the following text: "Paschalis .II. Guidoni Viennensi archiepiscopo. Investituram episcopatuum, ab-

The sequence of events so far appears unassailable. The confirmation of Schum's readings in the Naples codex provided a starting point for the chronological arrangement of the texts surrounding the councils of Vienne and of the Lateran in 1112, and especially for the papal letters JL 6313 ("Actionem concilii") and JL 6330 ("Cum alicuius"). All of the material is linked by dates as well as cross-references and fits in smoothly with the political circumstances prevalent in Rome as well as in Burgundy.[21] The only item not preserved as far as we know — perhaps it was an oral message delivered by the returning participants from the Lateran council — is Paschal's request to Guido to hold a council at Vienne.[22] Problems are created, however, by another letter of Paschal II, JL 6325 ("Si constantiam"), which is also addressed to Guido of Vienne and also refers to the events of the spring of 1111. Furthermore, "Si constantiam" happens to be frequently transmitted in the manuscripts together with the letter to Paschal II from the synod of Vienne requesting his confirmation of the decrees.[23] JL 6325 is undated and transmitted with few exceptions in a collection of various unrelated items from the pontificate of Paschal II that are also largely undated and undatable. They were probably collected by Cardinal Boso and are euphemistically called the *Vita Paschalis*.[24] It is easy, therefore, to connect the letter JL 6325 with the synod of Vienne of 1112 and to attribute it to that year as well. The letter exhorts Guido to stand fast in the face of adversity and reminds him that he, Guido, a member of the Church, could hardly expect a better fate,

batiarum et omnium rerum ecclesiasticarum de manu laica sancte Romane ecclesie auctoritatem sequentes heresim esse iudicamus." It corresponds to c.1 from the council of Vienne (= Mansi, *Amplissima collectio*, 21:col. 74). For the *Collection in Ten Parts* see P. Fournier and G. LeBras, *Histoire des collections canoniques en occident*, 2 (Paris, 1932; repr. Aalen, 1972), 296–306. See also my "Decrees and Decretals of Paschal II," *Bulletin of Medieval Canon Law*, n.s. 10 (1980):15–30, at 29.

21. For Burgundy see Stroll, "New Perspectives," (note 16 above); for Rome see Knonau, *Jahrbücher* 6:231–248 and C. Servatius, *Paschalis II. (1099–1118)*. Päpste und Papsttum, 9 (Stuttgart, 1982), 309–325, all with further references. The article by P. R. McKeon, "The Lateran Council of 1112, the Heresy of Lay Investiture, and the Excommunication of Henry V," *Medievalia et Humanistica*, 17 (1966):3–12, is somewhat misleading because of some misunderstandings.

22. JL 6456 (= Migne *PL* 163, col. 334f.), probably from 1115, also instructs Guido to hold a council, but its purpose is to review the case of the Besançon churches St. Jean and St. Etienne. It should not be confused with the council at Vienne in 1112. See also the references given in note 19 above.

23. This is the letter discussed and quoted in notes 15 and 17 above.

24. The text of JL 6325 is found in Migne, *PL* 163, col. 292 and *Liber Pontificalis* 2:373 and elsewhere as indicated by Jaffé-Loewenfeld. For the manuscripts see above note 13.

considering what had happened to its head.[25] In conclusion Paschal adds
a ringing denunciation of his agreements with Henry V at Ponte Mammolo in 1111 and reaffirms the decisions of his predecessors, especially
of Gregory VII and Urban II, as well as of conciliar decrees:

> ... Que cognoscere postulasti sunt hec: Scripta que in tentoriis, in
> quibus cum multitudine clericorum et civium Urbis et totius provincie
> custodiebamur, pro libertate Ecclesie, pro absolutione captivorum
> omnium et pro excidio quod Ecclesie, Urbi et universe provincie
> superincubante undique gladio imminere videbatur, de electione seu
> de investituris personarum facta sunt, ... ego canonica censura cassa
> omnino et irrita iudico, et anathemate et sub dampnatione perpetuo
> permanere decerno, ut nullius umquam auctoritatis sint et nullius
> bone memorie. Ea vero que ... predecessores nostri et precipue felicis
> memorie dompnus Gregorius et Urbanus de hiis prohibuerunt,
> dampnaverunt, statuerunt et firmaverunt, ego prohibeo, dampno,
> constituo et confirmo...." (*Liber Pontificalis* 2, 373, lines 14–23)

Despite similarities to the papal profession of faith of March 1112, the
differences are noticeable.[26] Nevertheless, scholars, including Jaffé and Loe-
wenfeld, never hesitated to follow the arguments of Wilhelm von
Giesebrecht, who suggested in 1877 that JL 6325 had been written several months after the Lateran synod of 1112. Giesebrecht clinched the argument with a reference to the letter dispatched to Paschal from the synod
of Vienne: "Es [JL 6325] ist dasselbe, welches Guido in seinem Bericht
über die Synode von Vienne an den Papst erwähnt."[27] Guido indeed referred to a letter from Paschal which he had received, but this letter is

25. JL 6325: "... Si enim in viridi ligno sic factum est quid fiet in aliis? Si in capite sic perpetra-
tum est, quid fiet in membris? ..." These references to the suffering of Christ refer by implica-
tion to Paschal's capture by Henry V and his troops in February 1111.
26. In addition to the text quoted above see especially *MGH Const.* 1, 571: "Actio concilii contra heresim de investitura. ... Amplector omnem divinam scripturam, scilicet ... et decreta sanctorum patrum Romanorum pontificum, et precipue decreta domni mei pape Gregorii et beate
memorie pape Urbani. Que ipsi laudaverunt, laudo; que ipsi tenuerunt, teneo; que confirmaver-
unt, confirmo; que dampnaverunt, dampno; que reppulerunt, repello; que interdixerunt, interdi-
co; que prohibuerunt, prohibeo in omnibus et per omnia, et in his semper perseverabo...."
27. W. von Giesebrecht, *Geschichte der deutschen Kaiserzeit,* 4th rev. ed., 3/2 (Anmerkungen),
(Braunschweig, 1877), 1201; for pp. 830–833 cited in the text see vol. 3/1.

the letter which was published by Schum from the Naples codex in 1877 and was, one assumes, still unknown to Giesebrecht.[28] It is, of course, impossible to exclude entirely the possibility that Paschal wrote twice to Guido confirming the decisions of the Lateran synod, provided that all else were equal.[29]

But this is not the case. In March 1116 Paschal held another council at the Lateran.[30] Among the extant sources are two chronicle accounts. The fuller account is found in the chronicle of Ekkehard of Aura, a very reliable source which covers the entire six days of the synod, March 6 to March 11, and is presumably based on a synodal protocol which is no longer extant.[31] Ekkehard included speeches by the pontiff as well as excerpts from the sometimes acrimonious discussions among the participants, sometimes verbatim and sometimes only in paraphrase. The textual correspondences between Paschal's letter JL 6325 ("Si constantiam") and Ekkehard's account from the council are so close that the question of its date has to be settled in favor of 1116:

> ... Postquam Dominus ... me [Paschal] populumque Romanum tradidit in manus regis ... huiusmodi mala cupiebam avertere ... et quod feci, pro liberatione populi Dei feci. ... Illud autem malum scriptum, quod in tentoriis factum est, quod pro pravitate sui Pravilegium dicitur, condempno sub perpetuo anathemate, ut nullius umquam sit bone memorie. ... (Ekkehard, pp. 318, 320)

The concluding statement of Paschal's letter to Guido that repeats the 1112 references to Gregory VII and Urban II is only indirectly reflected in Ekkehard's account, but we have at least proof that this repetition oc-

---

28. Schum's article (see note 8 above) appeared in the same year as Giesebrecht's revised edition (see the preceding note).

29. It should be noted that neither JL 6313 (the text is quoted above) nor JL 6325 (see note 24 above) instruct Guido to assemble what was to become the council of Vienne.

30. For the Lateran council of 1116 see Mansi, *Amplissima collectio,* 21 (Venice, 1776), col. 145–152, for the basic sources, as well as C.-J. von Hefele and H. LeClercq, *Histoire des conciles,* 5/1 (Paris, 1912), 553–559; Knonau, *Jahrbücher,* 6:350–356 with further references; Servatius, *Paschalis II.,* 330–332 and my "Paschal II and the Roman Primacy," *Archivum Historiae Pontificiae,* 16 (1978):67–92, esp. 83ff.

31. The chronicle of Ekkehard of Aura is critically edited by F.-J. Schmale and I. Schmale-Ott, *Frutolfs und Ekkehards Chroniken und die Anonyme Kaiserchronik.* Freiherr vom Stein-Gedächtnisausgabe, 15 (Darmstadt, 1972), 318–324, and 319 note 8.

curred.[32] The chronicle also mentions that Guido of Vienne had once again avoided the journey to Rome, and that he had sent emissaries with a letter supporting Cardinal Cono's request for a formal recognition by Paschal of the various legatine excommunications of Henry V, thus providing an explanation for the phrase: "Que cognoscere postulasti sunt hec . . ." in JL 6325.[33] Finally, even the second independent chronicle account of the 1116 council, although incomplete, shows obvious connections between the discussions of 1116 and Paschal's letter "Si constantiam" to Guido of Vienne.[34] The conclusion that this epistle belongs to the year 1116 and is a report from the second of Paschal's major councils which dealt with the problem of the privilege of 1111 seems indeed appropriate.

It is certainly helpful to be able to read the extant letters exchanged between Pope Paschal II and his legate, Archbishop Guido of Vienne, in the correct chronological sequence: JL 6313 ("Actionem concilii") sent after the Lateran synod of 1112, JL 6330 ("Cum alicuius") confirming the decisions of the council of Vienne of September 16, 1112, and JL 6325 ("Si constantiam") reporting from the Lateran council of March 1116. The sequence mirrors the tensions within the church with regard to lay investiture and shows how the pontiff reasserted his authority by 1116.[35] But the significance of the established chronology extends further than that. An anonymous treatise, *Disputatio vel defensio Paschalis papae*, has been dated by both its editors to 1112, either before or after the September synod of Vienne.[36] The more recent editor, Ernst Sackur, argued for a date just prior to this synod, a suggestion tentatively approved by Carl Mirbt in his standard work.[37] The disagreement reflects the uncertain nature of this text which scholars have been unable to explain.[38] The *Defen-*

---

32. ". . . Pravilegium investiture, quod in tentoriis concessisse videbatur, obliterare volens, iterans sententiam pape Gregorii VII. investituram ecclesiasticarum rerum a laica manu rursus excommunicavit. . . ." (Ekkehard, *ibid.*, 322).

33. *Ibid.*, 323–324, line 4.

34. Gerhoch of Reichersberg, *Opusculum de edificio dei*, ed. E. Sackur. MGH Libelli de lite, 3 (Hanover, 1897), at 190–191n.

35. Blumenthal, "Paschal II and the Roman Primacy," as in note 30 above. See in general G. M. Cantarella, *Ecclesiologia e politica nel papato di Pasquale II* (Rome, 1982).

36. *Disputatio vel defensio Paschalis papae*, ed. by W. Schum (see note 8 above) and by E. Sackur, MGH Libelli de lite, 2 (Hanover, 1892), 658–666. See esp. the introduction, 658 and note 5.

37. *Die Publizistik im Zeitalter Gregors VII* (Leipzig, 1894), 78.

38. The best discussion of the tract is found in A. Becker, *Studien zum Investiturproblem in Frankreich*

sio appears to reply to complaints raised in a lost letter or tract— presumably of French origin—against the perceived intention of Paschal to excommunicate Henry V. Such an excommunication is said to be unacceptable because it would force the pontiff to break his solemn oath of 1111 never to excommunicate the emperor.[39] The *Defensio* argues the contrary, somewhat speciously perhaps, but the main thrust of the reply is to show beyond a shadow of a doubt that kings had no right to lay investiture and that the 1111 privilege, known since the 1112 synod as "pravilegium," had no validity because it was extorted by force. It is particularly worth noting that the author relies on canon law as well as Roman law for support. The *Defensio*, as transmitted in the only extant manuscript, Naples, BN, MS V. C. 46, which also contains Paschal's letter JL 6313, makes yet a third point, probably in order to keep the doors open for further negotiations. After reasserting his opposition to lay investiture as currently practiced because of the use of ring and staff as symbols in the ceremony, the author continues:

> . . . Sicut enim in aecclesia pastoralis virga est necessaria . . . sic in domibus regum et imperatorum illud insigne sceptrum, quod est imperialis vel regalis virga, qua regitur patria, ducatus, comitatus, et cetera regalia distribuuntur iura. Si ergo dixerit [imperator] quod per virgam pontificalem et anulum sua tantum regalia velit conferre, aut sceptrum regale deserat, aut per illud regalia sua conferat. . . .
> (*MGH Lib. lit.* 2, 666)

This argument is striking. First of all it is close to the position of the canonist Ivo of Chartres. Secondly, the eventual settlement of the quarrel over investitures under Calixtus II, who was none other than Guido of Vienne, by the agreements of Worms in 1122/1123 was accomplished precisely because of the adoption of the royal scepter as investiture symbol.[40] It is well known that the negotiations between pope and king dur-

---

(Saarbrücken, 1955), 158f. Servatius, *Paschalis II,* refers only once to the *Disputatio* without discussing the work (at 289).

39. ". . . Nunc transeamus ad ea que nobis proposuistis: Paschalem nec dici nec haberi posse apostolicum, si excommunicaverit regem Henricum. . . ." (*Disputatio,* 663, lines 38f.)

40. See *MGH Const.* l, 159ff., no. 107f., to be supplemented with the edition of the papal documents in A. Hofmeister, *Das Wormser Konkordat,* ed. with a new preface by R. Schmidt (Darmstadt, 1962), 84, paragraph 3: "Electus autem regalia per sceptrum a te recipiat et, quae ex his iure tibi debet, faciat." For a discussion see P. Classen, "Das Wormser Konkordat in der deut-

ing the pontificate of Paschal II largely prepared the way for the concordat of Worms,[41] but there is no other witness apart from the *Defensio Paschalis* that Paschal's advisers, if not he himself, actually had come to accept the idea of investiture with regalia through the royal scepter by the end of the reign. The account of the Lateran council of 1116 by Ekkehard includes references to negotiations with an embassy sent by Emperor Henry V.[42] They have always been a puzzle and nothing is known about their substance.[43] Could it be that the statement quoted from the *Defensio* is an indication of the tendencies during these negotiations? I think that the answer is a qualified yes. The reason is that the treatise includes a long excerpt from Paschal's letter JL 6325 ("Si constantiam").[44] Barring interpolation which can be neither proven nor disproven, the *Disputatio vel defensio Paschalis papae* will have to be dated 1116 to 1118 instead of 1112. The treatise contains no hint that Paschal's death (January 21, 1118) had already occurred. Rather, the author defends this pontiff's policies and identifies himself fully with him. Further evidence would be desirable, but as long as there is no proof to the contrary the *Disputatio* may be considered a most welcome addition to the very meagre information that has been preserved for the last two years of Paschal's pontificate.

---

schen Verfassungsgeschichte," *Investiturstreit und Reichsverfassung*. Vorträge und Forschungen, 17 (Sigmaringen, 1973), 411–460.

41. See esp. E. Bernheim, *Das Wormser Konkordat und seine Vorurkunden*. Untersuchungen zur deutschen Staats- und Rechtsgeschichte, Alte Folge, 81 (Breslau, 1906) and the material cited in the preceding note.

42. Ekkehard, 320: "... Quinta feria papa in concilio non sedit multis et maxime regis negotiis per domnum Cluniacensem, Iohannem Caitanum et Petrum Leonis et Urbis prefectum ceterosque illius partis fautores impeditus. . . ."

43. See recently Servatius, *Paschalis II*, 331–335.

44. *Disputatio*, ed. Sackur, 661, lines 2–10. The derivation of the text from JL 6325 is indicated by the editor.

XV

Papal registers in the twelfth century *

Many years ago Harry Bresslau and Erich Caspar summarized in a few impressive pages the fragmentary evidence then available for papal registers of the twelfth century.[1] Since then work has continued, especially for the register of Gregory VII, and not long ago the original character of Reg. Vat. 2 as record book of official character was re-confirmed. Other papers have elucidated the close relationship between papal registers from the late-twelfth century and decretal collections in connection with the growth of scientific jurisprudence in both civil and canon law.[2] It should surely no longer be necessary to argue for the existence of some type of register for Gregory's predecessor, Pope Alexander II, and for his successors up to and including Pope Alexander III, even though their registers no longer exist.[3] It is, for example, impossible to disregard the sol-

* I gratefully acknowledge travel aid from the American Council of Learned Societies and the Catholic University of America. Thanks are due especially to Prof. Dr D. Lohrmann, Paris, for his encouragement and to Dr J.E. Sayers, London, for her kind advice and permission to see the relevant chapter of her recent book in typescript (n. 4 infra). Most of all, however, I would like to thank Prof. Dr O. Hageneder, Vienna, for generous advice and numerous references. Needless to say, all shortcomings are my own. Footnotes here are kept to a minimum; articles cited provide further bibliography.

[1] H. Bresslau, *Handbuch der Urkundehlehre*, 1 (2nd ed.; Leipzig 1912) 101-24; E. Caspar, 'Studien zum Register Gregors VII.', NA 38 (1913) 143-226 at pp. 214-26.

[2] R. Schieffer, 'Tomus Gregorii papae', *Archiv f. Diplomatik* 17 (1971) 169-84; H. Hoffmann, 'Zum Register und zu den Briefen Papst Gregors VII.', DA 32 (1976) 86-130; H.-E. Hilpert, 'Zu den Rubriken im Register Gregors VII. (Reg. Vat. 2)', DA 40 (1984) 606-11; A. Becker, *Papst Urban II. (1088-1099)*, (MGH Schriften 19/I; Stuttgart 1964) espec. p. 19 n. 57; D. Lohrmann, *Das Register Papst Johannes' VIII. (872-882)*, (Bibl. DHI Rom 30; Tübingen 1968); T. Schmidt, *Alexander II. und die römische Reformgruppe seiner Zeit* (Päpste und Papsttum 11; Stuttgart 1977) 220-35. W. Holtzmann, 'Die Register Alexanders III. in den Händen der Kanonisten', QF 30 (1940) 13-87; L.E. Boyle, 'The Compilatio quinta and the registers of Honorius III', BMCL 8 (1978) 9-19; O. Hageneder, 'Papstregister und Dekretalenrecht', *Recht und Schrift im Mittelalter*, ed. P. Classen (Vorträge und Forschungen, Konstanzer Arbeitskreis 23; Sigmaringen 1977) 319-47; S. Kuttner, 'The revival of jurisprudence', *Renaissance and renewal in the twelfth century*, ed. R.L. Benson and G. Constable with C.D. Lanham (Oxford 1982) 299-323.

[3] They are last referred to under Honorius III. F. Ehrle, 'Die Frangipani und der Untergang des Archivs und der Bibliothek der Päpste am Anfang des 13. Jahrhunderts',

XV

136

emn and explicit declaration of Pope Honorius III accompanying the various sets of transcripts from the registers of Gelasius II and Lucius II; Hadrian IV, Anastasius IV, and Alexander III; Paschal II, Eugene III, and Urban II, which were sent to Toledo prefaced by the words: 'Nos igitur ...presentium significatione testamur quod in regestis felicis recordationis [papal name] predecessoris nostri continentur littere in hec uerba...'.[4]

However, the transcripts tell us little besides the fact that the registers existed and were still accessible at the time of Honorius III and, furthermore, that they contained the letters transcribed.[5] The continuing discussion of the character of so unique, precious and carefully analyzed a document as the register of Gregory VII illustrates the obstacles in the way of an accurate evaluation of isolated medieval documents from a period which is famous for numerous new developments. Granted that registers for the later eleventh and the twelfth century did exist, what did 'registrum' mean at the time?[6] What was their structure and purpose? Are analogies with the ancient *commentarii* appropriate, as Rudolf von Heckel maintained, or should we look instead to the years after 1216,

---

Mélanges offerts à M. Emile Châtelain (Paris 1910) 448-83, and idem, 'Nachträge zur Geschichte der drei ältesten päpstlichen Bibliotheken', RQ Supplement 20 (1913) 337-69. The thesis of F. Bock, summarized in his article 'Bemerkungen zu den ältesten Papstregistern', *Archiv. Zeitschrift* 57 (1961) 11-51, has been evaluated most recently by Lohrmann, *Johannes VIII.* 160-63.

[4] The transcriptions were forwarded in this sequence. See P. Pressutti, *Regesta Honorii papae* III, 1 (Rome 1888) nos. 972, 976, 977, 979, 980. The text of the letters has also been published under the respective pontificates by D. Mansilla, *La documentación pontificia hasta Inocencio III (965-1216)*, (Rome 1955); see also idem, *La documentación pontificia de Honorio III (1216-1227)* (Rome 1965) (hereafter Mansilla, *Documentación* I and II respectively). This paper will only refer to Pressutti numbers. For the registers of Honorius III see now J.E. Sayers, *Papal government and England during the pontificate of Honorius III (1216-1227)* (Cambridge Studies in Medieval Life and Thought, 3rd ser. 21; Cambridge 1984), espec. 65-93.

[5] In addition to n. 3 supra see Bresslau, *Urkundenlehre* 1, 109. The copy of the register of John VIII disappeared at the latest at the same time as the 12th-century registers. (Lohrmann, *Johannes VIII.* 136, n. 80).

[6] 'The word register could be used for any authoritative book' (Sayers, *Honorius III* 75). An addition on fol. 212v (s. 12, second half) of MS Vat. Barb. lat. 535 shows the uncertainties of the 12th century: 'Quidam dicunt regestum quod est liber continens memorias aliorum librorum et epistolas in unum collectas. Et dicuntur regestum quasi iterum gestum. Alii dicunt regestron cui plus conuenit noster usus. Liber uero Prudentii uult regestum dici in quo scriptum reperitur: In regestis caelestibus.' The first definition fits in rather well with H. Steinacker's characterization of the medieval papal registers, and notably with his conclusion 'dass das Wesen der Registerführung des ausgehenden Altherthums und des beginnenden Mittelalters in der Mischung von Register und Copialbuch liegt.' ('Über das älteste päpstliche Registerwesen'. MIÖG 23 [1902] 1-49 at p. 6). The present paper comes to a similar conclusion.

when the extant series of complete papal registers begins? Heckel considered narratives and synodal protocols from eleventh- and twelfth-century papal registers explicit evidence for the link between these medieval books and the corporate *acta, gesta* or *commentarii* of late imperial Rome.[7]

These diaries of magistrates or ecclesiastical officials came to include 'everything that would serve to document and justify the magistrates' actions as Roman officials', minutes and documents from legal proceedings, letters received and despatched, edicts, regulations and narrative explanations connecting them.[8] When officially deposited, they were considered authentic texts — originals — and constituted legal proof.[9] The value of such a type of record for medieval history is at once apparent, even given the fact that the registers of Gregory I and John VIII already illustrate shifts in form and content that also mark the register of Gregory VII.[10]

The following observations, of necessity brief, will try to indicate some preliminary answers to the questions raised. They will be based primarily on Spanish and Portuguese records from several law suits that pitted Iberian ecclesiastics against one another at the turn of the twelfth and thirteenth century as well as related papal letters. Although Carl Erdmann published the records in part as early as 1927, they were ignored until recently and have never been considered in connection with the discussion of papal registers.[11]

The eleventh-century Reconquista provided fertile grounds for ecclesiastical litigation. With the support of popes and their legates, Spanish

---

[7] R. von Heckel, 'Das päpstliche und sicilische Registerwesen in vergleichender Darstellung mit besonderer Berücksichtigung der Ursprünge', *Archiv f. Urkundenforschung* 1 (1908) 371-501 at p. 428f.

[8] Ibid. 409.

[9] Ibid. 422-23. For the medieval concept of an 'authentic text' see H. Fuhrmann, 'Das Papsttum und das kirchliche Leben im Frankenreich', in: *Nascita dell'Europa ed Europa Carolingia* (Settimane di studio del Centro italiano di studi sull'Alto Medioevo 27; Spoleto 1981) 439f. An example of medieval understandings of 'original' is discussed by M. Bertram, 'Angebliche Originale des Dekretalenapparats Innocenz' IV.', *Proceedings of the Sixth International Congress of Medieval Canon Law*, ed. S. Kuttner and K. Pennington (MIC C/7; Città del Vaticano 1985) 41-47.

[10] Heckel, 'Registerwesen' 424-30.

[11] C. Erdmann, *Papsturkunden in Portugal* (Abh. Ges. Göttingen, N.F. 20,3; Berlin 1927) 105-09 and no. 160, pp. 381-384; P. Feige, *Die Anfänge des portugiesischen Königtums und seiner Landeskirche* (Spanische Forschungen der Görresgesellschaft, 1. Reihe: Gesammelte Aufsätze zur Kulturgeschichte Spaniens 29 [1978] 85-436). I am much obliged to Prof. Dr. R. Elze, Rome, for this reference.

rulers and their leading ecclesiastics had anticipated battlefield successes by drawing up blueprints for future diocesan organisation. Their effectiveness, however, depended not only on military but also on political circumstances, and original arrangements, either temporary or permanent by intent, were frequently challenged as the Reconquista proceeded.[12] In 1085 Toledo became once again a Christian city and Castilian efforts to re-establish the ancient ecclesiastical structure of Visigothic Spain were thus given a natural focus. Archbishop Bernard of Toledo, a monk from Cluny, obtained the pallium in 1088 from Urban II together with a privilege declaring him 'in totis Hispaniarum regnis primatem'.[13] The see of Toledo fought intrepidly for the effective recognition of this position but with scant success, numerous papal privileges which reconfirmed the primacy of Toledo notwithstanding.[14] Don Rodrigo Jiménez de Rada (1209-1247), the aristocratic and learned archbishop of Toledo,[15] tried to obtain more than the usual papal bull of confirmation: Innocent III and the Fourth Lateran Council of 1215 were to enforce the subjection of the archdioceses of Braga, Compostela, Tarragona and Narbonne to the primate of Toledo. Don Rodrigo's efforts failed. The council, however, marks the formal opening of a law suit between Toledo and Braga.[16] In January 1218 Honorius III broke off the ensuing hearings, declaring that further investigations were necessary.[17] The arguments and documents

---

[12] For background see art. 'Reconquista', LThK 8. 1060f. (O. Engels). Feige, *Königtum*, also provides background information and a detailed bibliography. The best introduction to the ecclesiastical aspects of the Reconquista during the pontificate of Urban II (1088-1099) is Becker, *Urban II.* 227-54, espec. p. 239 and n. 898. For the 13th century see P. Linehan, *The Spanish Church and the papacy in the 13th century* (Cambridge Studies in Medieval Life and Thought, 3rd ser. 4; Cambridge 1971).

[13] Becker, *Urban II.* 239 and n. 897; Feige, *Königtum* 104-10. Brief remarks are also found in H. Fuhrmann, 'Zur Geschichte mittelalterlicher Patriarchate, III', ZRG Kan. Abt. 41 (1955) 95-183 at p. 133f. Urban's privilege 'Cunctis sanctorum' (JL 5366) is preserved in Toledo, Archivo de la Catedral, X.7. A.1.1. See now F.J. Hernández, *Los cartularios de Toledo: Catálogo documental* (Monvmenta Ecclesiae Toletanae Historica I 1; Madrid 1985) 480, no. 538. For the Visigothic background of Toledo's claims see Feige, *Königtum* 357, n. 45.

[14] Ibid. 345 and 349f. n. 16 with a convenient list of the 12th-century privileges for the see of Toledo.

[15] For bibliographic references and a critical evaluation of Don Rodrigo see Linehan, *Spanish Church* 4, 8, 9, 10-16; D.W. Lomax, 'El arzobispo Don Rodrigo Jiménez de Rada y la Orden de Santiago', *Hispania* 19 (1959) 323-65.

[16] Feige, *Königtum* 345-58 with a detailed discussion also of the 'pars concilii Lateranii' (348f. n. 14b with a description of the codex); S. Kuttner and A. García y García, 'A new eyewitness account of the Fourth Lateran Council', *Traditio* 30 (1964) 115-78, espec. pp. 136-38.

[17] Pressutti 1012; Mansilla, *Documentación* II no. 137 and nos. 139 and 140 (Pressutti 1022); Feige, *Königtum*, p. 353.

used by both sides in the elaborate preparations for the hearings (Braga prepared two different sets of arguments) have been preserved in the archives at Lisbon and Braga on *rotuli*, that are sometimes no more than small strips of parchment,[18] and at Toledo, less directly, in the *Liber priuilegiorum de primatu Toletane ecclesie* as well.[19]

The *rotuli* contain *instrumenta*, *attestationes*, *acta* and *allegationes* of both parties. *Rotulus* 2 at Lisbon with the inscription 'Ista sunt pontificum instrumenta, quibus usa est Toletana ecclesia contra ecclesiam bracarensem in facto primacie' shows that Toledo supported its claim to primacy by papal privileges as well as letters and a narrative passage, generally copied from papal registers.[20] Braga also must have been well represented in Rome.[21] Her responses to Toledo's *instrumenta* included such precise and detailed references to the papal registers and archives that they must have been based on a thorough search of the registers in Rome.

Braga did its best to demolish the credibility of all the Toledan material that had been so carefully collected. Urban's privilege of 1088 'Cun-

---

[18] Erdmann, *Papsturkunden* 106. A detailed description is provided by Feige, *Königtum*, Appendix 8a, 400-23, espec. p. 401.

[19] Hernández, *Cartularios*, p. xvii, BCT, MS 42-21: 'Escrito por manos españoles en los primeros años del pontificado del arzobispo don Rodrigo Jiménez de Rada, tal vez en Roma, dado que muchas bulas papales se dicen sacadas directamente de los registros vaticanos de cada uno de los papas que se citan...'. See also Feige, *Königtum* 348 (n. 14b). Feige points out that it is unlikely that Don Rodrigo used this particular manuscript in 1217 at the hearings in Rome.

[20] Erdmann, *Papsturkunden* no. 160, pp. 381-384, §§ 1, 2, 3, 5, 6, 8, 12 and Feige, *Königtum*, Appendix 8a, pp. 400-23.

[21] Cf. R. von Heckel, 'Das Aufkommen der ständigen Prokuratoren an der päpstlichen Kurie im 13. Jahrhundert', *Studi e testi* 38 (1924) 290-321; M. Spaethen, 'Giraldus Cambrensis und Thomas von Evesham über die von ihnen an der Kurie geführten Prozesse', NA 31 (1906) 596-649. The register references in the records of the case Tours vs. Dôle under Innocent II do not permit definite conclusions (E. Caspar, 'Studien zum Register Johannes' VIII.', NA 36 [1910] 106 n. 1 and idem, NA 38 [1913], 217 with n. 2). Cf. also E. Müller, 'Der Bericht des Abtes Hariulf von Oudenburg über seine Prozessverhandlungen an der römischen Kurie im Jahre 1141', NA 48 (1930) 97-115, without reference to the use of registers at the curia, but one of several accounts which document how 'originals' might be taken to Rome. Letter JL 7268 of Pope Honorius II (1124-1130) to Peter the Venerable illustrates legal proceedings before that pontiff. Honorius explains how the claims of Pontius and his supporters were immediately proven false: 'statim productis apostolici uiri regestrorum papae Calisti uoluminibus et assertione testium qui presentes fuerant.' For *uolumina* as part of a larger work ('libri tres in sex uolumina') see Georges, *Ausführliches Lateinisch-Deutsches Handwörterbuch* (1962); for the specifically medieval meaning of charter or letter see Niermeyer. See also the study of L. Santifaller, 'Beiträge zur Geschichte der Beschreibstoffe im Mittelalter mit besonderer Berücksichtigung der päpstlichen Kanzlei', MIÖG, Ergänzungsband 16 (1953), Heft 1, 175-78.

ctis sanctorum' (JL 5366), for example, was not to be found anywhere in his register, a difficulty which had already hampered Archbishop Rodrigo at the Lateran council. To deal with this difficulty, one assumes, Toledo therefore opened its series of *instrumenta* with a narrative passage, which reads like an annalistic summary:[22]

> In registro domni Urbani II pape primo libro.
> Hoc tempore Toletanus archiepiscopus Bernardus Romam ad domnum Urbanum papam uenit, eique pro episcoporum more iurauit, palleum et priuilegium accepit regnisque Hyspaniarum primas institutus est. Tunc etiam in Gallicia omnis diocesis sancti Jacobi ab omni est officio excommunicata diuino, quia sancti Jacobi episcopus in regis carcere depositus fuerat.

The same text, also with attribution to the register of Urban II, is found in Urban's biography and in one of the intermediate canonical collections from the late eleventh — early twelfth century.[23] The excerpt from the first book of the register is not unlike the 'year-end reports' in the register of Gregory VII.[24] Toledan representatives copied it possibly from a collection such as the *Collectio Britannica*, but more likely directly from the register together with others of Toledo's *instrumenta* adduced in 1217.

The hearings took place in 1217 in Rome, where each reference to a register could be checked.[25] If the inscription for the excerpt 'Hoc tempore' had been incorrect, Braga's *allegationes*, preserved on a *rotulus* at Braga, would certainly have referred to that fact, as we may confidently assert considering the extant evidence as a whole. As it is, Braga rejected

---

[22] *Rotulus* 2, no. 1. See Feige, *Königtum* 402 n. 3 and n. 6. Bishop Diego Peláez of Iria-Compostela (1069-1088) had been imprisoned in chains by King Alfonso VI of León and Castile (1065-1109), and Urban's protest was immediate (JL 5367). See Becker, *Urban II.* 227 and 234-39 and Feige, *Königtum* 100-01.

[23] *Liber Pontificalis*, ed. L. Duchesne, II 293 and the *Collectio Britannica*, Urb. ep. no. 17: P. Ewald, 'Die Papstbriefe der Brittischen Sammlung', NA 5 (1880) 357.

[24] Caspar, 'Studien zum Register Gregors VII.' 204, 207. The *Jahresschlussbericht* for the first pontifical year is found in: *Das Register Gregors VII.*, ed. E. Caspar (MGH Epp. sel. 2; Berlin 1920-1923) no. I 85a, p. 123.

[25] For the date of the hearings see the invitation of Honorius III, Pressutti no. 1012. The archbishop of Braga was to be at the curia on 21 May 1217. In 1199 Braga obtained the re-opening of a law suit which judges delegate had decided in part on the basis of a transcription from, as they claimed, 'ultimo libro registrorum domni Calixti' (Calixtus II). Braga could point out in 1199 that the pretended transcription was false and should not have been admitted as evidence, 'nam in toto ultimo libro registrorum domni Calixti nullum rescriptum inuenitur, in quo de Salamantina ecclesia uel instrumentis eius mencio fiat, ned(um)...ibi inueniretur' (Erdmann, *Papsturkunden* 289, no. 99).

the excerpt 'Hoc tempore' with the argument that its form did not agree with the formulae of authentic papal privileges; that it lacked the signatures of the cardinals and that it was undated.[26] The response does not mention the register derivation of the excerpt. It does imply, however, that only formally correct documents — in other words, original privileges, but not their minutes or copies in the registers — were to have legal validity. As will be seen, this point of view was at variance with papal practice.

We do not know what Honorius III thought of Braga's argument. Braga, however, must have been aware of its weakness, for Braga also claimed at the very same hearings that the privilege 'Cunctis sanctorum' (JL 5366) was illusory because it had not been registered.[27] Advocates of the archdiocese also used the location of letters within a particular papal register with great skill and sophistication to make a point. Toledo's second and third documents submitted in 1217 were two letters of Urban sent in October 1088 enjoining obedience to Toledo upon other Spanish ecclesiastics (JL 5370, 5371). JL 5370, 'Quisquis', was addressed 'Tarragonensibus et ceteris Hispaniarum archiepiscopis'. The epistle and its companion, 'Venerabilem fratrem' (JL 5371), which announced to Abbot Hugh of Cluny Bernard's elevation to the primacy, were at the very least defective, Braga argued, for at the time of writing no Spanish archbishops existed as yet, not even at Tarragona, 'si enim ibi esset archiepiscopus, «Tarragonensi» diceret, non «Tarragonensibus»'.[28] Historically Braga's argument was correct, for the bishop of Ausona-Vich did not obtain the rank of archbishop as representative of Tarragona until 1091.[29] What is of interest here is Braga's method of dating the letters which were found in the register without a date: 'reperiuntur in primo libro..., et constat quod primus liber Urbani fuit in primo anno, nedum quia iste epistule inueniuntur statim circa principium libri'.[30] In other words, the letters, Braga argued, were sent at the beginning of Urban's pontificate and therefore in 1088. Braga further supported its contention that Tarragona was still without an archbishop in 1088 with a reference to a letter of Urban to Bernard of Toledo (JL 5406), where Urban inquir-

---

[26] Feige, *Königtum* 402, text no. 2.
[27] Erdmann, *Papsturkunden* 381, no. 160 § 2.
[28] Feige, *Königtum* 403, text no. 3 and pp. 405-06, texts nos. 8 and 9.
[29] Article 'Tarragona', LThK 9. 1301f. (O. Engels). Fuhrmann, 'Mittelalterliche Patriarchate III', 95-99, espec. p. 96, n. 4, points out that the letter expressed future intent.
[30] See n. 27 supra.

ed whether Tarragona was part of the province of Narbonne. Braga's representatives pointed out that this letter, JL 5406, was found in the second book of the register, i.e., that it was dated 1089 and sent out later than the epistles JL 5370 and JL 5371 in the first book.[31] They enunciated the accepted rules for the structure of the papal registers more explicitly during the same hearings in respect of a letter of Paschal II:

> Dicta epistula 'Experientiam' inuenitur circa principium in tercio libro; et quod primus liber contineat acta primi anni, secundus secundi, tercius tercii, et sic de aliis, probatur euidenter...et probatur manifeste per ipsa regesta, inspecto libro et anno pape, et anno dominico et indictione.

The remarks proceed to point out that all registers were organized in this manner 'secundum quod dicent uobis qui regesta scribunt'.[32] It is obvious, then, that Braga accepted registered privileges and letters as legally valid *instrumenta*, its arguments concerning 'Hoc tempore' notwithstanding. As we know from the largely extant registers of Pope Innocent III, however, 'year-end reports' familiar a century earlier were no longer customary, and Braga might have gotten away with its arguments unchallenged.[33]

References to the register of Urban II during the hearings of 1217, therefore, indicate that the volume was divided into books, each book encompassing one pontifical year as under Gregory VII;[34] and, furthermore, that the register contained not only letters but also at least one narrative passage. What about privileges? It did not include the 1088 privilege for Archbishop Bernard of Toledo. The reason for this is unclear, for the elevation of a prelate to the rank of primate was sufficiently exceptional to have found a place in the registers of both John VIII and Gregory VII.[35] Under Urban II, however, the annalistic note 'Hoc tempore' apparently sufficed as a reminder of Toledo's rank as primatial see. Privileges granted by this pontiff could be registered, as other evidence

[31] Feige, *Königtum* 403, text no. 3.

[32] Erdmann, *Papsturkunden* 382, no. 160 § 5.

[33] See the edition of the registers (in progress): *Die Register Innocenz' III.*, I, 1. Pontifikatsjahr, 1198/99, ed. O. Hageneder and A. Haidacher; II, 2. Pontifikatsjahr, 1199/1200, ed. O. Hageneder, W. Maleczek and A.A. Strnad (Publikationen des Österreichischen Kulturinstituts in Rom; Graz-Cologne 1964, Rome-Vienna 1979).

[34] Cf. Santifaller, 'Geschichte der Beschreibstoffe' 172f. n. 118 with a brief discussion of 'liber' as *gegenständliches Buch* in contrast with *Sinnabschnitt*, another meaning of 'liber'.

[35] Lohrmann, *Johannes VIII.* 168f. espec. with n. 45.

indicates. In a dispute between the sees of Lérida and Huesca over the churches of Barbastro, Bielsa and Gestau as well as over Alquézar, for instance, Pope Innocent III eventually decided to review an original decision of Eugene III in favor of Huesca, reasoning that both civil and canon law permitted under circumstances the review of decisions even in the case of *res bis iudicata*.[36] The circumstances here were the following: Eugene III had rejected as forgeries both a privilege of Urban II and a letter of Paschal II in support of Lérida. His decision was subsequently confirmed by Alexander III on the basis of Eugene's register where Alexander found a record of the *sententia*. Lérida nevertheless continued to pursue its cause, and Celestine III re-opened the investigation although he considered such action both new and inconvenient, because he had found in the 'archiuis Apostolice sedis' in the registers of his predecessors both the privilege of Urban II and the letter of Paschal II. These documents were definite proof for the claims of Lérida, Celestine argued, and named three bishops as delegate judges, sending them 'transcripta igitur priuilegii ipsius [Urbani] et litterarum, sicut sunt in regestis inuenta, de uerbo ad uerbum...sub bulla nostra'. The delegate judges were requested to review Eugene's decision which, Celestine wrote, would never have come about if Eugene 'regesta ipsa tempore sententie sic diligenter et sollicite reuoluisset, sicut nos modo reuoluimus'. Eugene could not have then declared the privilege of Urban II a forgery, 'cuius nos ipsi ueritatem inspeximus'.[37] Celestine's mandate clearly criticizes Eugene's failure to consult the registers of Urban and Paschal. It is equally clear that Urban's privilege was registered. Innocent III, who eventually decided in favor of Lérida, followed the precedent set by Celestine and inspected both the register of Eugene III and the privilege in the register of Urban II. He gives three reasons 'ex data sententia in registro...Eugenii' for re-committing the case: 1) the *sententia* was given in the first month of Eugene's pontificate, when he was, as it appears, not fully informed about the respective merits; 2) the privilege of Urban II (JL 5703) was mistakenly described as forgery 'cuius tenorem nos in registro ipsius subtiliter intuendo integrum inuenimus et penitus incorruptum'; 3) the

---

[36] 'Nam et per statuta canonica sententia Romane sedis non negatur posse in melius commutari, cum aut surreptum aliquid fuerit, aut ipsa pro consideratione etatum et temporum seu gravium necessitatum dispensative quicquam ordinare decrevit, et secundum iura civilia principes etiam contra res bis iudicatas in auditorio suo examinari restitutionem in integrum permiserunt': Mansilla, *Documentación* I 257-59, no. 224 (here p. 258; April 1200).

[37] P. Kehr, *Papsturkunden in Spanien. Vorarbeiten zur Hispania pontificia* I: Katalanien (Abh. Ges. Göttingen, N.F. 18.2; Berlin 1926) 551-54, no. 246 (pp. 553f.).

rights of the church of Lérida should be preserved.[38] It should be noted that Innocent, like Celestine before him, was persuaded of the authenticity of Urban's privilege because he found it in its entirety 'penitus incorruptum' in the register of this pontiff — not because he was presented with the formally perfect original. Consultation of older registers was evidently an essential part of the judicial review process. Failure to do so was negligence, and if the registers contained the letters and privileges as claimed, these would normally be accepted as authentic. The registers served as means of authentication, and thus had in fact the greater legal value.

The registration of *sententiae* just noted for Pope Eugene III (1145-1153) can be observed for the pontificate of Gregory VII [39] and Urban II as well. The relevant information about Urban's register is contained on a twelfth-century parchment leaf inserted into the thirteenth-century cartulary of San Cugat. That abbey as well as San Llorens del Munt had been forcefully reformed by Abbot Frotard of Saint-Pons de Thomières [40] and taken over by his monks. The complaints and intervention of Archbishop Dalmatius of Narbonne and the bishops of Barcelona and Carcassonne on behalf of the expelled monks of San Cugat were examined by Urban's legate, Cardinal Rainerius of San Clemente, at Narbonne in February 1090, and by archbishops Amatus of Bordeaux and Hugh of Grenoble at St.-Gilles in June 1091, when the decision of Rainerius was confirmed that San Cugat was subject only to Rome. Kehr found several items in connection with these events in the cartulary of San Cugat on a twelfth-century parchment insert: letters to Frotard and one letter to Amatus of Bordeaux as well as two notes which accompany the texts and are written in the same hand as the letters. The content of the notes suggested to Kehr that the material had been copied from Urban's register.[41]

---

[38] Mansilla, *Documentación* I 257-59, no. 224.

[39] There are many instances, but see especially Register VII 15. The synodal decision in the case Tours vs. Dôle is mentioned by Urban II in JL 5519 as follows: 'Quaesita est in registro beati Gregorii papae VII sententia et ita omnino, sicut audieramus inuenta'. See Caspar, 'Studien zum Register Gregors VII.' 170 n. 4, whose text I quote.

[40] For Frotard see P. Kehr, *Das Papsttum und der katalanische Prinzipat bis zur Vereinigung mit Aragon* (Abh. preuss. Akad.; Berlin 1926) 33ff., as well as idem, *Das Papsttum und die Königreiche Navarra und Aragon bis zur Mitte des 12. Jahrhunderts* (Abh. preuss. Akad.; Berlin 1928) 24ff.

[41] Kehr, *Papsturkunden in Spanien* 1 nos. 17, 18, 19, 20, pp. 277-83. The legation of Cardinal Rainerius, later Pope Paschal II, is discussed by C. Servatius, *Paschalis II., 1099-1118* (Stuttgart 1979) 20-23. In this context see, however, the important remarks

The first note, following directly upon the text of Urban's letter 'Venientes nuper' (JL 5419), begins:[42]

> 'Hoc est in quadam cedula consuta in regestro Urbani secundi. Anno dominice incarnationis...penitus et refutatum. Scriptum apud Narbon(am) per manum kamerarii domini legati et mandato suo. Acta sunt mense febroarii'.

The second note follows the letter to Amatus ('Inter uenerabiles', JL—), beginning with the rubric: 'Urbanus II. Iuditium Romane ecclesie cenobii sancti Cucuphatis. Tunc etiam adiudicatum est...penitus renuntiatum'.[43] The notes reflect the legatine decisions of 1090 and 1091, and at least the first note maintains that the *sententia* of Rainerius given at Narbonne and there, at Narbonne, recorded by his secretary (*kamerarius*) in a formal document, had been inserted into the register of Urban II — or, more precisely, sewn into the register. This probably means that it was attached to one of the folios of what must have been a book at that time and no longer merely a loose set of unconnected quires.[44]

The selected references to the register of Urban II find their natural explanation in the ever increasing importance of papal registers in judicial proceedings in the course of the twelfth century.[45] This was in part at least a response to frequent forgeries of papal documents. Beginning with Alexander III the papacy issued specific legislation to prevent them,

---

by Hoffmann, 'Zum Register Gregors VII.' 100. It could have been difficult to locate or reconstitute the text of the privilege of Gregory VII for San Cugat. The delay in Urban's reconfirmation would thus find a natural explanation.

[42] Kehr, *Papsturkunden in Spanien* 1 no. 18, p. 279f. L. Santifaller, 'Saggio di un Elenco dei funzionari, impiegati e scrittori della Cancelleria Pontificia dall'inizio all'anno 1099', BISM 56 (1940) 405f, recorded only a single use of the title 'kamerarius' (7 March 1068) in a document of dubious authenticity, J.L. + 4644a.

[43] Kehr, *Papsturkunden in Spanien* 1 no. 20, p. 283.

[44] The evidence is not as clear as one would like. Kehr apparently interpreted the note beginning 'Hoc est in quadam cedula consuta...' as pertaining to the entire set of documents which he discovered on this particular insert into the cartulary of San Cugat (cf. ibid. no. 31, p. 298: 'Ex regesto domini pape Urbani II, libro XII'). It should be pointed out that the note 'Hoc est...', dated Narbonne, 1090, contains already a reference to the later confirmation of St.-Gilles (p. 280). This type of material is further discussed in Blumenthal, 'Bemerkungen zum Register Papst Paschalis II.', QF 66 (1986) 1-19. Caspar has shown that the register of Gregory VII consisted 'aus einer Reihe von ursprünglich wohl lose zusammengelegten Pergamentlagen verschiedenen Umfangs...': 'Studien zum Register Gregors VII.' 161.

[45] Cf. P. Herde, *Beiträge zum Päpstlichen Kanzlei- und Urkundenwesen im 13. Jahrhundert*, 2nd rev. ed. (Kallmünz 1967) 83 with n. 23 for the consultation of older registers. See also ibid. 84.

legislation that reached its highpoint under Innocent III.[46] Since many
privileges seem not to have been registered, they could not be checked
against the registers, as could letters. Instead, the authenticity of the attached seal became an important criterion. The emphasis on seals in the
constitution of Innocent III (X 5.20.4) reflects not only tradition generally,[47] but presumably especially a decretal of Alexander III, X 2.22.2,
which attributes to an authentically sealed papal document the legal
standing of an *instrumentum publicum*,[48] simultaneously depriving
other documents of any validity altogether. The decretal of Alexander (X
2.22.2) does not mention papal registers, but as a spot check of his *sententiae* quickly reveals, registers did not lose their importance. On the
contrary, an attitude of almost rigid adherence to texts found in the registers emerges. The dispute between the abbeys of Prémontré and Ham
is a case in point. Alexander had entrusted its settlement to the bishop of
Amiens, the abbot of Saint-Rémi, and the deacon Fulco of Reims, or to
two of the group. Since the bishop of Amiens died, the remaining two delegates decided the case without explaining their procedure. Alexander
III to whom the sentence was submitted for confirmation refused to go
along because he found in his register that the decision had not been
entrusted to two delegates only. In this instance Alexander issued a revised commission.[49] But when the chapter of Saint-Jean at Valenciennes
requested the re-opening of their case against the prior and the convent
of Saint-Saulve (also at Valenciennes), Alexander refused the request because the agreement brought about by the archbishop of Reims had been
confirmed by Eugene III and because this confirmation had been recorded as final in the register.[50] As a last example of the important role of the
registers under Alexander III as well as under Innocent III the case of
the stolen folios from the register of Alexander III may be mentioned.[51]
Innocent was particularly incensed over the theft of a leaf

> cum pro litteris, de quibus dubium est, an a sede apostolica emana-

---

[46] Ibid. 98-103 with further references.

[47] A critical examination of papal documents in 1100 was recorded by Hugo of Fla-
vigny, MGH Scriptores 8.493, beginning line 44.

[48] Bresslau, *Urkundenlehre* I 656-63; Herde, *Beiträge*, espec. 94f. and n. 104.

[49] J. Ramackers, *Papsturkunden in Frankreich, N.F.* IV: Picardie (Abh. Akad. Göttingen, D.F. 27; Berlin 1942) nos. 120, 132, 139.

[50] J. Ramackers, *Papsturkunden in den Niederlanden* I (Abh. Ges. Göttingen, D.F. 8;
Berlin 1933-34) no. 172: '...nos in registro eiusdem patris nostri Eugenii pape diligentius
inquiri fecimus, in quo eum prescriptam concordiam inuenimus confirmasse' (p. 313).

[51] *Die Register Innocenz' III.*, I letter 537, pp. 776f.

rint, ad regestum de consuetudine recurratur, cum etiam vix posset
aliquis amplius Romanam ecclesiam offendere, quam si ei regesta et
alios libros subriperet, in quibus tam ipsius quam aliarum ecclesiarum privilegia continentur.

Innocent's mandate to the patriarch of Grado and two Hungarian
ecclesiastics to investigate the theft by *magister* L. of Treviso explains in
the narrative how the culprit was discovered, although he had removed
an entire leaf from the middle of a quire of the register of Alexander III,
thus leaving the thread undamaged. This leaf, however, contained more
than the letter in question. Three other letters, in part incomplete, were
found to fit in precisely with text remnants still evident in Alexander's
register when the stolen leaf was presented as proof before the pope.

As we have seen, the importance of seals was emphasized when the
authenticity of a papal document was questionable and it was unregistered. Innocent III himself seems to have relied exclusively on this criterion
when the seal of an alleged bull of Pope Constantine I († 715) for the monastery of Evesham was declared authentic.[52] Ordinarily, not only pope
and cardinals but also legates and judges delegate were far less willing to
pronounce on the authenticity of documents submitted if these were
unregistered. And wisely so, for ecclesiastics left no stone unturned to assert the rights of their churches and patron saints. Innocent's decision in
favor of Evesham is one example of the lack of historical knowledge at
his curia, although it should be noted that Innocent seems to have known
that a register for Pope Constantine I did not exist. Legates and judges
delegate away from Rome would find it impossible by recourse to the
registers to verify privileges and letters even from more recent pontificates.[53] One of the *rotuli* now preserved at the district archives at Braga
contains a very telling example of how the strict rules for authentication
could have the opposite effect to what was intended: the older an unregistered privilege, the less familiar, and therefore the more suspect,
would formulae and seal appear. In the course of the lengthy proceedings Braga vs. Compostela repeated hearings were held to decide the

---

[52] Spaethen, 'Giraldus Cambrensis und Thomas von Evesham', 638-42, and Herde,
Beiträge 84 n. 28, as well as C.R. Cheney, *Pope Innocent III and England* (Päpste und
Papsttum 9; Stuttgart 1976) 196ff. Cf. Erdmann, *Papsturkunden in Portugal* no. 37, p.
196, Erdmann's comments.
[53] One example is provided by the 1184 hearings at Coria, where judges delegate
found in favor of Compostela's claims that the see of Zamora was subject to the archbishop
of Compostela because of a transcript from the register of Calixtus II. This judgment is
mentioned n. 25 supra.

quarrel over the subjection (ownership and possession) of Coimbra, Viseu, Lamego and Idanha.[54] These hearings are extensively reported. In the present context it is of particular interest to note the contention between the two archbishops as well as the position taken by Innocent III himself in his decision of July 1199 with respect to old privileges, registered and unregistered. During the first hearings at Tuy in 1182 both Braga and Compostela brought forward their privileges together with much other evidence. Compostela showed two privileges of Calixtus II, one with 'signatures of cardinals and subdeacons'; Braga presented nine (ten at later hearings) from the pontificates of Paschal II, Calixtus II, Innocent II, Lucius II, Eugene III, Hadrian IV and Alexander III. Compostela immediately rejected Braga's Paschal privileges because, as Archbishop Pedro said, they differed from each other. Despite the historically accurate rejoinder of Archbishop Godinus of Braga that Paschal's pontificate had been a very long one and that he might well have changed his seal, especially since the privileges were obtained at different times, Compostela expanded his argument at the hearings in 1187, giving a detailed description of the objectionable Paschal privileges:[55]

> Compostellanus...primo obicit de bulla, quod dissimilis sit aliis bullis Romanorum pontificum. Nam capita habet cum humeris et brachio et manu crucem tenente, et littere quoque apparent contuse et uix legi possunt, et ante litteras crux premittitur...In secundi et tercii bullis eiusdem Pascalis sunt capita sine humeris, et iste due bulle in hoc sunt dissimiles a prima. Inter se uero hanc habent dissimilitudinem quod una habet circulos circa capita cum punctis, altera uero non...

During Paschal's pontificate papal seals eventually achieved their permanent basic form, but for Paschal himself at least two types of seals are known, just as described in the hearings of 1187.[56] Eventually, Braga

---

[54] The final decision of Innocent III with a review of the different stages of the proceedings has been edited and carefully annotated by Hageneder, Maleczek and Strnad, *Die Register Innocenz' III.*, II letter 124, pp. 246-59. See also Erdmann, *Papsturkunden in Portugal*, espec. no. 91 (pp. 266-82) and no. 110 (pp. 303-24) with further references; Feige, *Königtum* 313-44 with references.

[55] *Papsturkunden in Portugal* no. 110, p. 322, § 25: 'Littere quoque apparent contuse et uix legi possunt' seems to indicate that the privilege was written in a curial hand. See P. Rabikauskas, *Die römische Kuriale in der päpstlichen Kanzlei* (Miscellanea historiae pontificiae 20; Rome 1958) espec. pp. 236-41 with a list of Paschal's still extant privileges written in curial script.

[56] W. Ewald, *Siegelkunde* (Munich and Vienna 1975), table 35, 17 and 18, showing both sides of an early seal of Paschal II. Illustrations 19 and 20 show the sides of the later seal of Paschal which set the basic pattern for the remainder of the Middle Ages. The

was to maintain that Compostela's privileges had been obtained fraudu-
lently from Calixtus II, 'per suppressionem ueritatis et falsitatis' and that
Braga had the upper hand if it were a question of numbers, since it had
more privileges than Compostela.[57] In his decision, however, Innocent
did not specifically address the question either of numbers of privileges,
or of antiquity or fraud. Nor did he discuss registration where Compostela had the advantage, for its privileges of Calixtus II were said to be
above suspicion since their 'ueritas constat ex apostolice sedis archiuis,
in cuius regestis fideliter continentur'.[58] Conciliar records and considerations of equity were given a more important role than privileges when
Innocent divided the four dioceses between the contenders. Viseu and
Coimbra became part of the archdiocese of Braga; Lamego and Idanha
of that of Compostela. However, Compostela's claim to be the successor of
the ancient Mérida as confirmed in the registered privileges of Calixtus II
was clearly recognized.[59] Braga's privileges, rejected in earlier decisions of
the case, were once again at least implicitly relegated to an insignificant
place, very likely because they were not registered and because their
diplomatic form appeared unfamiliar and therefore unconvincing.

It has been seen throughout this paper that registration of letters and
privileges added significantly to their value in the case of litigation, and
that popes relied on the contents of registers as a guide to decisions of
their predecessors or even their own. Examples have been given from the
pontificate of Urban II up to that of Innocent III. These could be multiplied. However, the use of earlier papal registers in ecclesiastical litigation
was hardly new, although the extent of this use and the importance of
register entry are not generally known. Of greater interest is the emerging
picture of some external and internal characteristics of the registers: they
are among the books, *libri*, of the Roman church which are kept in the
archives of the Holy See. A separate register existed for each pontificate,
even for one as brief as that of Gelasius II, and it was subdivided by pontifical years. The entries were in roughly chronological order, and were
on occasion prepared from minutes or abbreviated drafts. This was perhaps the case for Gelasius II.[60] Letters and sometimes privileges as well as

---

originals of the seals are preserved in the Staatsarchiv, Düsseldorf. Ewald refers to relevant
literature.

[57] *Die Register Innocenz' III.*, II letter 124, at p. 250, line 20 and p. 252, lines 25-28.
[58] Ibid. 255, line 5.
[59] Ibid. 258.
[60] This is perhaps suggested by the different textual transmissions of the letter JL
6658 which can be compared to the formerly still extant original as published by M. Féro-

narratives were recorded. The practice with regard to privileges was very inconsistent. However, there is no evidence at all that *several* registers were kept side by side during a pontificate. As far as one can see, references always pertain to *the* 'regesta' of a particular pontiff, a term which is consistently used without qualifiers. It was undoubtedly in this one register of Urban II that Celestine and Innocent searched for and found Urban's privilege for Lérida fully written out, although the same register contained no record of Urban's privilege for Toledo except for an annalistic note which alluded to it. The inclusion in the registers of judicial decisions could be noted even when the *sententia* was given abroad by legates or judges delegate. At least under Pope Lucius II, as perhaps under Alexander II and certainly under Innocent III, letters received might be registered.[61] This was probably rare, however, and does not appear to have been the rule. Last but not least, the registers, which were so open for consultation that visitors could even steal a leaf, seem not to have changed very much, for they were perfectly familiar to scribes and ecclesiastics from the late twelfth century. With regard finally to the question

---

tin, *Recueil des chartes de l'abbaye de Silos* (Paris 1897) no. 29, p. 39f. For other transmissions see P. Kehr, 'Ältere Papsturkunden in den päpstlichen Registern von Innocenz III. bis Paul III.', *Nachrichten Ges. Göttingen* (1902) no. 5, p. 425 with further references; Mansilla, *Documentación* I no. 54, p. 73. Kehr noted (p. 428) that the excerpts in MS Rome, Bibl. Vallicelliana C.23, are often unreliable. In this case the excerpt is merely abbreviated, and preserves the inscription intact: 'In registro domini Gelasii pp. .ii. libro .i. pro Abbati Sancti Dominice' (fol. 82r). Reg. Vat. 9, fol. 196r, contains indeed the abbreviated text as published by Mansilla. This is exceptional in the case of letters which Honorius III had transcribed for Toledo from the registers of his predecessors although the method corresponds to that used under Honorius III himself. Did the copyist merely get tired of transcribing the text from the register of Gelasius II in full? Was he perhaps in a hurry to finish? Or was the text with abbreviations faithfully copied from the register of Gelasius II?

[61] For the letter 'Claves regni' of 13 December 1143, sent by Afonso I of Portugal to Pope Lucius II and recorded in the latter's register, see Feige, *Königtum* 278, and C. Erdmann, *Das Papsttum und Portugal im ersten Jahrhundert der portugiesischen Geschichte* (Abh. preuss. Akad; Berlin 1928/V) 30 n. 1. For Alexander II see Santifaller, *Beschreibstoffe* (n. 21 supra) 106. For references to the register of Alexander II in the *Vita* of Gregory VII by Paul of Bernried see Spaethen, 'Giraldus' 613n. That the miracle of Petrus Igneus was reported in a letter sent to Alexander is perhaps suggested by the content of Grenoble, Bibl. de la Ville, MS 473; see P. Fournier, *Une forme particulière des Fausses Décrétale d'après un manuscrit de la Grande-Chartreuse* (Nogent-le-Rotrou 1888) 1 and n. 3 with further references. As H. Fuhrmann has shown ('Zur Benutzung des Registers Gregors VII. durch Paul von Bernried', *Studi Gregoriani* 5 [1956] 299-312), it is unlikely that Paul used the registers of Gregory VII for the pontiff's letters which he included in the *Vita*. This does not mean, however, that Paul had *no* access to either the registers of Gregory VII or of Alexander II and did not consult them at all.

raised at the beginning of this paper, whether the role of the registers in the twelfth century corresponded more to the role of the ancient magistrates' diaries or to that of the thirteenth-century registers, the slender evidence would appear rather to indicate the first, for registers of the late-eleventh and earlier-twelfth centuries represented a combination of both register and memorial book.[62]

---

[62] Superficially this assessment resembles Kempf's outstanding analysis of the register of Innocent III, but I do not wish to disguise in any way the differences between the register of Gregory VII and that of Innocent III. For Innocent III see F. Kempf, *Die Register Innocenz' III.: Eine paläographisch-diplomatische Untersuchung* (Miscellanea historiae pontificiae 9; Rome 1945), espec. pp. 104-19.

XVI

The Text of a Lost Letter of Pope Honorius II[1]

In the first half of the twelfth century, the essentially commercial rivalries between Genoa and Pisa[2] developed into war over the question of Corsica.[3] Pisan domination of the island was juridically based on papal privileges.[4] In 1077, when the Saracens had been pushed back from the Tyrrhenian coast and islands thanks largely to the efforts of Pisa and Genoa,[5] Pope Gregory VII[6]

---

[1] The author would like to thank Professor Kuttner for this identification.

[2] G. Volpe, *Studi sulle istituzioni comunali a Pisa: Città e contado. consoli e podestà: Secoli XII-XIII*, ed. C. Violante (Biblioteca Storica Sansoni, n.s. 48; Florence 1970) 40n. and 126 f.; E. Cristiani, *Nobiltà e popolo nel comune di Pisa: dalle origini del podestariato alla signoria dei Donoratico* (Naples 1962) 18 with n. 7; O. Langer, *Politische Geschichte Genuas und Pisas im XII. Jahrhundert* (Historische Studien 7; Leipzig 1882) especially 1-5. G. Rossi-Sabatini, *L'espansione di Pisa nel Mediterraneo* (1935) could not be consulted.

[3] Primary sources for these events are chiefly Caffaro's *Annales Ianuenses*, ed. L. Tommaso Belgrano (Fonti per la Storia d'Italia 11; Genoa 1890) 16ff. and the *Annales Pisani di Bernardo Maragone*, ed. M. Lupo Gentile (RIS² 6/2; Bologna 1930) 9. The contradictory entries have probably been correctly interpreted by W. Heywood, *A History of Pisa, Eleventh and Twelfth Centuries* (Cambridge 1921) ch. 6. pp. 71ff. C. de Cesari-Rocca, *Origine de la rivalité des Pisans et des Génois en Corse, 1014-1174* (Genoa 1901) was unavailable; cf. in general *idem*, *Histoire de Corse* (Les vieilles provinces de France; Paris s.d.).

[4] Cf. F. Ughelli, *Italia Sacra*, 3 (2nd ed. Venice 1718) col. 368-385.

[5] See S. B. Casanova, *Histoire de l'église corse* 1 (Ajaccio 1931) 27ff. for a summary of the effects of the Saracen invasions; their expulsion by Pisans, Genoese, and last but not least Normans has been conveniently summarized by Langer, *Politische Geschichte* 3; cf. also P. Tronci, *Memorie istoriche della città di Pisa* (Livorno 1682) 30.

[6] As R. W. Dove has shown Gregory could base his claims on the donation of Charlemagne ('Corsica und Sardinien in den Schenkungen der Päpste', Sb. Akad. Munich 1894, 183-238, especially 214 and 221ff).

had sent Bishop Landulf of Pisa (1077-1079) to Corsica as his legate.[7] Pope Urban
II elevated Pisa in 1092 into an archbishopric with metropolitan rights over the
island,[8] a privilege that was confirmed in 1118 by Pope Gelasius II[9] and in May
1120 by Calixtus II.[10] Genoa resented the firm establishment of the Pisans on an
island that was at the same time a base for merchant fleets and an important
supplier of ship-building materials as well as slaves,[11] and they eventually obtained at the Lateran Council of 1123 a revocation of Pisan privileges.[12] Although
Pope Calixtus II had enjoined at that time perpetual silence touching the question
of Corsica upon the Pisans,[13] the revocation of 1123 did nothing to end the war
between Pisa and Genoa raging since 1119.[14] On the contrary, the war gained in
bitterness, and in 1126 Pope Honorius II decided to reconfirm once again the
metropolitan rights of Pisa.[15] Peace, however, was not achieved until the island
was partitioned between Genoa and Pisa by Innocent II in 1138.[16]

Pope Honorius' decision of 1126 in favor of the Pisans was the outcome of
protracted negotiations between the papacy on the one hand and the Genoese
and Pisans on the other. The pontiff's privilege, JL 7266, outlines efforts that
were made by the curia to end the war that threatened to cut off what little
aid the hard-pressed crusader states were receiving between 1101 and 1147.[17]
Amongst other stages of the negotiations, JL 7266 recorded that Honorius had
sent a legate to both Genoa and Pisa:

> . . . Legatum ergo nostrum comitem tunc diaconum cardinalem cum scriptis nostris
> Januam et Pisas misimus, praecipientes ut in manu ejus juramento firmarent, et de
> sacra Corsicae et guerra usque ad tunc proximum sancti Michaelis festum nostris jus-
> sionibus obedire.[18]

This embassy is not documented in either the *Annales Pisani* or *Annales
Ianuenses*. It is of interest, therefore, that a copy of the letter which Honorius
entrusted to his legate, the cardinal deacon and (since 1126) cardinal presbyter
Comes of S. Maria in Aquiro or S. Sabina,[19] has been preserved. It is found,

---

[7] Kehr, *Italia Pontificia* 3.319 nos. *2, 3, and 4 (JL 5046 and 5048). Casanova, *Histoire*
50 refers erroneously to 'Rodolphe' as legate in 1077. The same author (85) correctly speaks
of the legate as Landulf, but places Gregory's nomination into the year 1073.

[8] Kehr, IP 3.321 nos. 9 (JL 5464) and *10.

[9] *ibid.* *12.   [10] *ibid.* *13.

[11] Volpe, *Istituzioni* 127 n.1.

[12] Kehr. IP 3.323 no. 18 (JL 7056). For the events at the council itself see also the famous
story reported by Caffaro, *Annales Ianuenses* 18-20.

[13] JL 7056.   [14] See n. 2 above; cf. Volpe, *Istituzioni* 87.

[15] Kehr, IP 3.323-4 no. 22 (JL 7266).   [16] *ibid.* 325 no. 26 (JL 7890).

[17] J. Prawer, *The Crusaders' Kingdom: European Colonialism in the Middle Ages* (New
York and Washington 1972) passim and especially pp. 19 and 482ff. See also A. Waas,
Geschichte der Kreuzzüge 1 (Freiburg 1956) 165, where the importance of Italian help, es-
pecially of Genoa, Pisa and Venice, is stressed, as well as *A History of the Crusades*, ed. K. M.
Setton, 1: *The First Hundred Years*, ed. M. W. Baldwin (Philadelphia 1958) especially 368-
428.

[18] PL 166.1262.

[19] For Comes see H.-W. Klewitz, 'Die Entstehung des Kardinalkollegiums', ZRG Kan.
Abt. 25 (1936) 221 no. 17 with further references. See also *idem*, 'Das Ende des Reformpapsttums', DA 3 (1939) 371ff., especially 375 and 405 (both articles are reprinted in Klewitz,

66

without any inscription or date, on fol. 154v of MS 203 of the Biblioteca Civica Guarneriana at San Daniele del Friuli.[20] The letter, published below, was evidently addressed to the commune of Pisa. The erasure in the next to last sentence of the missive, where only the letters 'p' and 'i' are barely discernible, can probably be explained as a mistake by a Pisan scribe. As already pointed out by Kehr,[21] the embassy of Cardinal Comes must have taken place before September 29, 1125, since the privilege of Honorius II, JL 7266, is dated July 21, 1126.

* * *

Kehr, IP 3.323, no. *19
c.1125

San Daniele del Friuli, MS Guarn. 203, fol. 154v.

Calamitates et miserias que pro uestra et Ianuensium discordia uobis et habitanti in maritimis christiano populo contigerunt et temeritatem ac presumptionem quam sarraceni ad opressiones fidelium asumpsserunt non solum occidentales uerum etiam orientales dolere non est ambiguum. Quia igitur ex iniuncto nobis officio ad reformandam pacem et concordiam nos conuenit modis omnibus laborare, deliberato fratrum nostrorum episcoporum cardinalium et aliorum religiosorum iustorum consilio, dilectum filium nostrum C.(omitem) diaconem cardinalem ad uos delegamus per quem uniuersitati uestre mandamus atque precipimus quatinus in eius presentia iuramento firmetis uos de guerra ista usque ad proximam[a] beati Michaelis festiuitatem quod romana ecclesia iusserit adimplere. Nos enim honorem et prosperitatem terre uestre diligimus et ut firmam interim inter uos treuguam habeatis precipiendo mandamus; et ut idem / / /[b] observent similiter per litteras nostras mandauimus. Si qua vero pars mandatis nostris obedire contempserit, apostolice animaduersionis sentiat ultionem, obedientes autem manutenere et tutiare curauimus.

a proximum MS   b lege Ianuenses

Reformpapsttum und Kardinalkolleg, Darmstadt 1957); also J. Bachmann, *Die päpstlichen Legaten in Deutschland und Skandinavien (1125-1159)* (Historische Studien 115; Berlin 1913) 19-20; F.-J. Schmale, *Studien zum Schisma des Jahres 1130* (Köln-Graz 1961) 59. J. M. Brixius, *Die Mitglieder des Kardinalkollegiums von* 1130-1181 (Diss. Strasbourg; Berlin 1912) could not be consulted.

[20] The codex, containing *inter al.* a hitherto unknown copy of the Collection in 74 Titles, will be described and partially edited in the 1975 BMCL.

[21] Kehr, IP 3.323 no. *19.

XVII

CARDINAL ALBINUS OF ALBANO AND THE
DIGESTA PAUPERIS SCOLARIS ALBINI
MS. OTTOB. LAT. 3057

Summarium. — Cardinalis Albinus, episcopus Albanensis († 1196/97), codicem manuscriptum collectaneum variorum argumentorum reliquit, qui hodie in Bibliotheca Apostolica Vaticana (*Ottob. lat.* 3057) asservatur, quique hucusque, excepto *Libro Censuum* Albini, fere inexploratus remansit. In hoc articulo et vita card. Albini exponitur, et ea quae in codice continentur singula explicantur. Ex tali explicatione — ad eam quoque Appendix de scriptis Gaufridi de Claravalle (Geoffroy d'Auxerre) contra Gilbertum Porretanum (Gilbert de la Porrée) pertinet — necnon ex investigatione palaeographica et codicologica ipsius manuscripti ostenditur *Digesta* Albini alio tempore orta esse debere, quam hucusque credebatur, undeque rationem inter *Librum Censuum* Albini et similem librum Cencii Savelli novam inquisitionem requirere *.

Among the Ottoboni manuscripts in the Biblioteca Apostolica Vaticana is the unique codex which preserves the writings of Cardinal

---

* I would like to thank Professor R. Somerville who first interested me in codex *Ottob. lat.* 3057, and Professor Leonard E. Boyle, O.P., who first taught me to consider the task of analyzing the manuscript not an impossible one. Work was begun thanks to an ACLS research fellowship, and could not have continued without the hospitality of the German Historical Institute in Rome. I am also most grateful to Dr. M. Bertram, Professor D. Lohrmann, and Professor B. Schimmelpfennig for their assistance and advice. Last not least I owe thanks to the Biblioteca Apostolica Vaticana and the Archivio Segreto Vaticano, the Institut de Recherche et d'Histoire de Texte in Paris, and the editor of the Arch. Hist. Pontificiae, Professor P. Rabikauskas, S.J.

The abbreviations used in the notes:

BRIXIUS, *Kardinalskollegium* J. M. BRIXIUS, *Die Mitglieder des Kardinalskollegiums von 1130-1181*, Diss. Berlin 1913;

LC . . . . *Le Liber Censum de l'Eglise Romaine*, edd. P. FABRE and L. DUCHESNE (Bibliothèque des Ecoles Françaises d'Athènes et de Rome, 2e série), I-II, Paris 1889-1910; III: *Tables de matières*, edd. L. DUCHESNE, P. FABRE, and G. MOLLAT, Paris 1952;

SCHALLER, *Kanzlei* . . . . H. M. SCHALLER, *Die Kanzlei Kaiser Friedrichs II.: Ihr Personal und ihr Sprachstil*. Zweiter Teil: *Der Sprachstil der Kanzlei*: Archiv für Diplomatik 4 (1958) 264-327;

Series episcoporum. . . . *Series episcoporum Ecclesiae Catholicae occidentalis*, edd. O. ENGELS and S. WEINFURTHER, I/1: *Italia*, ed. G. Melville [a specimen], Stuttgart 1978.

8

Bishop Albinus of Albano († 1196/97), entitled *Eglogar(um) digesta pauperis scolaris Albini* [1]. This codex, *Ottob. lat.* 3057, from the late twelfth or, more likely, the early thirteenth century, has already attracted the attention of historians, not so much because it is evidence for the life and thought of Albinus, but rather because scholars noted close correspondences between the final books ten and eleven of Albinus' miscellaneous collection and the *Liber Censuum*, the census book of the Roman Church which was compiled in 1192 under the direction of Cencius Savelli, later Pope Honorius III (1216-1227), who was at the time *camerarius* of Pope Celestine III (1191-1198) [2]. The editors of the *Liber Censuum*, Paul Fabre and Msgr. Louis Duchesne, documented these correspondences in detailed tables and concluded (despite some hesitation, especially on the part of Duchesne) that the collection of Albinus served as inspiration for the work of Cencius [3]. They therefore published parts of Albinus' *Digesta* which they

---

[1] Basic bibliographies for Albinus and MS *Ottob. lat.* 3057 are given in the *Dictionnaire d'histoire et de géographie ecclésiastiques*, I, Paris 1912, 1700 (J. Fraikin); *Diz. Biografico degli Italiani*, II, Roma 1960, 11f (V. Fenicchia); *Repertorium fontium medii aevi*, II, Rome 1967, 177. Albinus' miscellaneous collection is usually known as « Gesta pauperis scholaris Albini », because it was long impossible to decipher the inscription. The correct reading was first provided by M. Andrieu with the help of Msgr. G. Mercati. See M. Andrieu, *Les Ordines Romani du Haut Moyen Age*, I: *Les Manuscrits* (Spicilegium Sacrum Lovaniense, Etudes et Documents, II), Louvain 1931, 317f, n. 1. The most recent biographical note regarding Albinus is found in the *Series episcoporum*, p. 20f. (G. Melville).

[2] For Cencius Savelli, see E. Kartusch, *Das Kardinalskollegium in der Zeit von 1181-1227*, typewritten diss., Vienna 1948, 109-112; H. Tillmann, *Ricerche sull'origine dei membri del collegio cardinalizio nel XII secolo*, II/2: Rivista di storia della Chiesa in Italia 29 (1975) 391-393; P. Fabre, *Etude sur le Liber Censuum de l'Eglise Romaine* (Bibl. des Ecoles françaises d'Athènes et de Rome, 62), Paris 1892, esp. pp. 1-10; and *LC* (= *Liber Censuum* ...). See also V. Pfaff, in *Diz. Biografico degli Italiani*, XXIII, Rome 1979, 392-398, s.v. ' Celestino III. ' Most notable among recent contributions to the study of the Liber Censuum are R. Elze, *Der Liber Censuum des Cencius* (*Cod. Vat. lat. 8486) von 1192 bis 1228. Zur Überlieferung des Kaiserkrönungsordo Cencius II*: Bullettino dell'« Archivio paleografico italiano », n.s. 2-3 (1956-1957) 251-270, and T. Schmidt, *Die älteste Überlieferung von Cencius' Ordo Romanus*: Quellen u. Forschungen aus italienischen Arch. u. Bibliotheken 60 (1980) 511f.; see also G. Fedalto, *Appunti al Liber Censuum Romanae ecclesiae*, in: *Atti del Convegno internazionale di Studi Muratoriani, Modena 1972*, II (Antiquitates Italicae medii aevi, vol. V), Florence 1975, 117-138. E. Stevenson, *Osservazioni sulla Collectio Canonum di Deusdedit*: Arch. della R. Società Romana di Storia Patria 8 (1885) 305-398, p. 357, examines the relationship between the work of Deusdedit, Albinus, and Cencius, noting with regard to MS Vat. *Ottob. lat.* 3057 that the codex has never been studied in its entirety, a statement which is still valid. Stevenson's article remains the most detailed and careful analysis of the work of Albinus, even though Stevenson focused only on the final two books of Albinus' compilation. The editor of Deusdedit's collection, V. Wolf von Glanvell (*Die Kanonessammlung des Kardinals Deusdedit*, I [no more appeared], Paderborn 1905, pp. xxxvii-xl), added desirable precision at certain points, but the more complete discussion of Albinus remains that by Stevenson. Glanvell's parenthetical criticism of Stevenson's description of the quaternions which make up the codex (p. xxxviii) is mistaken and was caused by his erroneous translation of the Italian ' fogli ' (Stevenson, p. 357) as ' Blätter ' = ' pages,' instead of ' folio ' (' Doppelblätter '). The literature generally ignored both Stevenson and Glanvell. See also the following note.

[3] Fabre, *Etude*, esp. pp. 10-12: « Albinus a plutôt inspiré Cencius qu'il ne lui a

considered relevant, as well as the preface to his digest, together with the *Liber Censuum* [4]. The personality of Albinus, however, and the major portion of the writings which he left behind in MS *Ottob. lat.* 3057, remained practically unknown. Fabre and Duchesne had focused their attention exclusively on the two final books of *Ottob. lat.* 3057. Scholars who investigated the history of the cardinalate were usually content to repeat for Cardinal Albinus entries found in older bio-

---

fourni les matériaux eux-mêmes » (p. 12). See also the remarks by FABRE-DUCHESNE, *LC* I, pp. 2 and 7f. The concordance tables are found *ibid.*, p. 8-12. The debate about the relationship between the compilations of Albinus and Cencius dates back to C. CENNI, *Monumenta dominationis pontificiae sive codex Carolinus*, I, Rome 1760, p. XXVIIIf., and II, Rome 1761, pp. IV, VIII-XII. Cenni first asserted Albinus' claim to priority over Cencius: « Ut autem paucis multa complectar, quae Cencius anno 1192 se collegisse ait, ante annos minimum octo, aut decem Albinus collegerat, et decimum in librum sui Codicis retulerat » (II, p. X = MIGNE, *PL* 98, col. 455D); « Tanti enim non erat Cencius, ut cum Albino eruditione ac diligentia comparari valeat » (II, p. XII = MIGNE, *PL* 98, col. 458A). See also STEVENSON, *Osservazioni*, p. 356; TH. SICKEL, *Das Privilegium Otto I. für die römische Kirche vom Jahre 962*, Innsbruck 1883, esp. pp. 55-58, 66-69; and GLANVELL, *Kanonessammlung*, p. XXXVIII, n. 98; all with further bibliography. In his own analysis of the texts which Deusdedit, Albinus, and Cencius have in common, STEVENSON (*Osservazioni*, esp. pp. 332, 356, 363-377) reached the same conclusion as Fabre, with whom he shares several arguments. Like Fabre, STEVENSON is aware that problems remain (*Osservazioni*, p. 379, n. 1), but he is nevertheless convinced of « una intimissima relazione fra Cencio ed Albino » (*Osservazioni*, p. 372). See further, R. L. POOLE, *Lectures on the History of the Papal Chancery*, Cambridge/Engl. 1915, Appendix VI: *The Roman Provinciale*, pp. 193-192, with the conclusion (p. 194) that Cencius used the source of Albinus, presumably Boso's *Provinciale*, directly.

[4] *LC* II, 86-137. It should be noted that the impression of a more or less complete publication of books 10 and 11 of the compilation of Albinus is rather misleading. Apart from the *Provinciale* and the census lists (10, nos. 68-74 = *LC* II, 96-122), Fabre and Duchesne were content to provide cross-references to the work of Cencius, usually without noting variants in Albinus' text (*e.g.*, book 10, nos. 5-28, 30, 32-41, 43-49, etc.; book 11, nos. 1-2, 4-17, 22, 27-40, 43-54, etc.). Variants are given when Fabre assumed direct dependence of Cencius on Albinus. See *LC* I, pp. 345-357, nos. 71-73; cf. p. 345, n. 2. Fabre and Duchesne were not the first to publish excerpts from codex *Ottob. lat.* 3057. C. BARONIUS, *Annales ecclesiastici*, XII (Cologne, sumptibus Ioannis Gymnici et Antonii Hierati, sub Monocerote, 1609, with the note « Editio novissima ab ipsomet ante obitum [1607] aucta et recognita »), col. 439-445 ad a. 1148, and col. 1003-1005, ad a. 1188, most likely used a different manuscript for his publication of two letters to Albinus (see the Appendix below), but C. CENNI, *Monumenta dominationis pontificiae*, II, pp. XIV-LIV, published the *Provinciale* and the census lists of Albinus' *Digesta* (= MIGNE, *PL* 98, 457C-476 and 476C-488B = *LC* II, 96-106, nos. 67-71 and pp. 107-122, nos. 72-74) as well as excerpts from Albinus' preface (*ibid.*, I, p. XXVIIIf.). Additional excerpts from the preface were published a year later by P. L. GALLETTI, *Memorie per servire alla Storia della vita del Cardinale Domenico Passionei*, Rome 1762, 233-235. A. MAI, *Spicilegium Romanum*, VI, Rome 1841, 277-280, edited from the codex its fragment of BONIZO OF SUTRI's *Liber de vita christiana*. More recently, J. VON PFLUGK-HARTTUNG published a letter of Pope Alexander II from the *Digesta* (*Acta pontificum romanorum inedita*, II, Stuttgart 1884, 110, no. 145 = JL 4683; cf. PFLUGK-HARTTUNG, *Iter Italicum*, Stuttgart 1883, 139-141). His edition of a privilege of Pope Clement III (JL 16340) was not based on this codex (*Acta inedita*, III, Stuttgart 1886, 367f.; cf. GLANVELL, *Kanonessammlung*, p. XXXVIII, p. 98). MS *Ottob. lat.* 3057 was also used by L. WEILAND, MGH *Const.* I, Hanover 1893, 134ff., for nos. 83-87, 92, 94, and 95, as well as for the edition of no. 399, pp. 570-573. Sickel and Glanvell used the manuscript in their editions as well. See GLANVELL, *Kanonessammlung* (see n. 2 above), book 3, cc. 184-186, 188-289 and book 4.1, cc. 246-266, 420-427 (pp. 348-401; 532-541; 596-602) and SICKEL, *Privilegium* (see n. 3 above), pp. 178-182.

graphical dictionaries, adding references to the work of Fabre and Duchesne in the twentieth century. The exception, E. Kartusch's dissertation, confirms the rule [5]. Since the publication of the *Liber Censuum* in 1905 and 1910, only one of the liturgical segments of Albinus' text has received further scholarly attention [6].

It is the primary purpose of this paper to present a description and analysis of the content of MS *Ottob. lat.* 3057, but a codicological and palaeographical examination of the manuscript has proven to be necessary as well, for it is still not always accepted that codex *Ottob. lat.* 3057 is not an autograph. Furthermore, even when the manuscript is not considered an autograph, it is implicitly assumed that the history of the composition of the codex — that is, its date — mirrors the history of Albinus' compilation of the texts. As will be seen, the generally accepted date 'ante quem' for the *Digesta pauperis scolaris Albini* (May, 1189) will have to be revised. As a consequence, the relationship between books ten and eleven of the Digest and the *Liber Censuum* of Cencius Savelli will have to be reconsidered in the light of their sources [7].

---

[5] In addition to the literature of n. 1 above, see: O. PANVINI, *De episcopatibus, titulis et diaconiis cardinalium liber*, in *Romani Pontifices et Cardinales S.R.E. ab eisdem ... creati*, Venice 1557, 123; A. AUBERY, *Histoire generalle* [sic] *des cardinaux*, I, Paris 1642, 206f.; F. UGHELLI, *Italia sacra sive de episcopis Italiae*, I, Rome 1644, col. 296, no. 36; A. CIACONIUS (Alonso Chacon)-A. OLDOINUS, *Vitae et res gestae summorum pontificum Romanorum et S.R.E. cardinalium*, I, Rome 1677, col. 1117, no. 7; C. OUDIN, *Commentarius de scriptoribus ecclesiae antiquis*, II, Leipzig 1722, col. 1581; L. CARDELLA, *Memorie storiche de' cardinali della Santa Romana Chiesa*, I/2, Rome 1792, 149f. [an embroidered translation of OUDIN]; G. MORONI, *Dizionario di erudizione storico-ecclesastica*, I, Venice 1840, 205; E. KARTUSCH, *Das Kardinalskollegium in der Zeit von 1181-1227*, Vienna 1948 (diss. typewritten), no. 5, pp. 79-82; H. MÜLLER, *Die Mitglieder des Kardinalkollegiums von 1181-1216*, Göttingen 1950 (diss. typewritten), 15; V. PFAFF, *Die Kardinäle unter Papst Coelestin III*. (*1191-1198*); Zeitschrift der Savigny-Stiftung für Rechtsgeschichte, Kan. Abt. 41 (1955) 58-94 (here no. 1, p. 84); V. PFAFF, *Die Kardinäle unter Papst Coelestin III*. (*1191-1198*). Zweiter Teil: *Beurkundungslisten, Nachträge und Berichtigungen*: Zeitschrift d. Savigny-Stiftung f. Rechtsgesch., Kan. Abt. 52 (1966) 332-369; *Series episcoporum*, pp. 20f.

[6] It is the brief *Ordo ad benedicendum imperatorem, quando coronam accipit* (*Ottob. lat.* 3057, fol. 150vb). See the critical edition by R. ELZE, *Die Ordines für die Weihe und Krönung des Kaisers und der Kaiserin* (MGH, Fontes iuris germanici antiqui, IX), Hanover 1960, 22-25, no. x, with further bibliography (for this, see also ibid., pp. XLIV-XLVII); ANDRIEU, *Les Ordines Romani* I (see n. 1 above), pp. 24, 317f., and IV: *Les Textes* (*Ordines XXXV-XLIX*) (Spicil. sacrum Lovaniense, 28), Louvain 1956, 459-462. Cf. S.J.P. VAN DIJK, J. HAZELDEN WALKER, *The Ordinal of the Papal Court from Innocent III to Boniface VIII and Related Documents* (Spicilegium Friburgense, 22), Fribourg 1975, pp. xxxIIff., with references to Albinus' transmission in the annotations to the edition, pp. 90-483, passim. Cf. also P. SALMON, *Les manuscrits liturgiques latins de la Bibliothèque Vaticane*, III: *Ordines romani pontificaux rituels cérémoniaux*, Vatican City 1970, p. 4, no. 3, and p. 117, no. 395. The folio numbers have to be corrected.

[7] This will be done in a future, second article.

THE BIOGRAPHY OF ALBINUS

To begin with, however, a biographical note on Albinus [8]. It is well known that the cardinal described his youth in part himself in the preface to the *Digesta*. Very briefly, Albinus tells us the following: While still fairly young, he was left an orphan, but an uncle of his, a monk, provided a home for the destitute boy as well as the rudiments of his education until, after the death of this uncle, Albinus began more formal studies together with a brother (or close relative) of his, named Richard, who later became bishop of Orvieto (1177-1201). Albinus taught to make a living and, at some point of his career, changed 'faculties'. Eventually, he was called to Rome and became cardinal. Throughout his career, he collected notes because, as he says, he was too poor to afford books. He continued note-taking in Rome, but now with the intention of furthering the interests of the papacy which he served, rather than his own studies. All of these notes he transcribed into a (manuscript) book, because he wanted to preserve the fruits of his labor for other students who were just as poor and diligent as he himself had been [9]. It is this digest which has come down to us in codex *Ottob. lat.* 3057, the 'codex unicus'.

It is not easy to go beyond these statements in the interpretation of the preface, for meaning is often obscured by an elaborate style. Only the passages which explain the content and purpose of his collection, and therefore constitute the heart of the preface, are relatively clear [10]. The lengthy introductory sections, in twelfth-century

---

[8] See, in addition to the bibliography given in notes 1 and 5 above, for the cardinalate of the period, K. WENCK, *Die römischen Päpste zwischen Alexander III. und Innozenz III. und der Designations-Versuch Weihnachten 1197*, in *Papsttum und Kaisertum. Forschungen zur politischen Geschichte und Geisteskultur des Mittelalters, Paul Kehr zum 65. Geburtstag dargebracht*, ed. A. BRACKMANN, Munich 1926, 415-474; B. KATTERBACH-W. M. PEITZ, *Die Unterschriften der Päpste und Kardinäle in den 'Bullae Maiores' vom 11. bis 14. Jhdt.*, in *Miscellanea Francesco Ehrle*, IV (Studi e Testi, 40), Rome 1924; for Albinus, see pp. 234, 236, 241f. In general, see also the surveys in H. E. FEINE, *Kirchliche Rechtsgeschichte*, I: *Die katholische Kirche*, Weimar 1954, no. 28, pp. 277-280, with further bibliography; J. B. SÄGMÜLLER, *Die Tätigkeit und Stellung der Kardinäle bis Papst Bonifaz VIII.*, Freiburg/Breisgau 1896; P. HINSCHIUS, *System des Katholischen Kirchenrechts mit besonderer Rücksicht auf Deutschland*, I, Berlin 1969, 309-373, is also still useful, although superseded in part by S. KUTTNER, *Cardinalis. The History of a Canonical Concept*: Traditio 3 (1945) 129-214, with a detailed bibliography for older literature. H.-W. KLEWITZ, *Die Entstehung des Kardinalkollegiums*: Zeitschrift der Savigny-Stiftung für Rechtsgeschichte, Kan. Abt. 25 (1936) 115-221 (repr. in KLEWITZ, *Reformpapsttum und Kardinalkolleg*, Darmstadt 1957, 11-134), and R. HÜLS, *Kardinäle, Klerus und Kirchen Roms, 1049-1130* (Bibliothek des Deutschen Historischen Instituts in Rom, 38), Tübingen 1977, as well as C. G. FÜRST, *Cardinalis. Prolegomena zu einer Rechtsgeschichte des römischen Kardinalskollegiums*, Munich 1967, deal exclusively with an earlier period.

[9] The preface was published by FABRE-DUCHESNE, *LC* II, 87-89. E. KARTUSCH, *Das Kardinalskollegium* (see n. 5 above), p. 79, assumed that the *Gesta pauperis scholaris* were an autobiography and the *Collectio Canonum* a second, separate work.

[10] *LC* II, 88 a-b: « Factus tandem imitator Crisippi ... anno sui pontificatus », and

12

terminology the 'exordium' or 'captatio benevolentiae', are a different matter. Unusual expressions almost overwhelm the reader — in keeping with the stylistic fashions of the second half of the twelfth century, when rhetorical training both north and south of the Alps came under the influence of the schools at Tours and Orléans, and the 'stilus supremus' of Orléans was dominant [11]. The extraordinary flowering of the medieval Latin language in this period still escapes adequate analysis [12], and on the basis of the relatively short prologue [13], only a few, tentative remarks regarding the style of Albinus can be ventured here. Nevertheless, they will be helpful, for they will place Albinus into the scholarly traditions of his age and facilitate the use of the preface for his biography.

It is apparent that Albinus used the 'cursus planus', 'tardus', and 'velox' in accordance with the *Forma dictandi* which is usually attributed to Albert of Morra (the future Pope Gregory VIII), and the *Introductiones de arte dictandi* of Transmundus, although other endings occur as well [14]. Transmundus was a student of Albert, and,

---

LC II, 89b: « Auctoritatibus autem quas ... id decernat ». The intervening moral exhortation, « Diversarum igitur rerum diversas sententias colligentes ... putavit aut finxit », is largely a paraphrase of Peter Lombard, Sent. 1, d. 1, c. 2, which follows the original closely (see n. 116). Albinus did not want to make matters too easy for his readers. Discussing his quires, he wrote: « Non enim in eis ordo servatus aut continuatio lectionis, ut capax ingenium et sensus exercitatus in illis refici possit; sed si quis est lactis egens et paupertine intelligentie vel memorie tenuis, inveniet qualemcumque sorbitiunculam ... » *LC* II, 88a. The annotations of the editors, FABRE and DUCHERNE, *LC* II, 87-89, reveal their impatience with Albinus' ornate rhetoric.

[11] C. H. HASKINS, *The Renaissance of the Twelfth Century*, Cambridge/Mass. 1927, chapters 5 and 6, pp. 127-192 (in the Meridian Books reprint of 1957), gives an introduction to the over-all theme. The recent analysis of the developments in the medieval Latin language during the twelfth century by SCHALLER, *Kanzlei*, especially pp. 268-283, is excellent. Also useful is S. J. HEATHCOTE, *The Letter Collections Attributed to Master Transmundus*: Analecta Cisterciensia 21 (1965) 35-109, 167-238. For more complete bibliographical information, see the articles by SCHALLER and HEATHCOTE, as well as the following notes.

[12] Cf. SCHALLER, *Kanzlei*, pp. 264f.

[13] Up till now, this is the only known piece of continuous writing by Albinus himself. M. Bertram kindly brought MS 90 of the library of Kranj/Zupnisce (Yugoslavia) to my attention, which contains on fol. 40r-59v, according to the catalogue, an *Epistola Albini magistri ad Singulfum presbiterum*: « Dilectissimo in Christo fratri ... suspensi simus ad solum Jesum Christum qui ... » (incomplete). (M. Kos, *Codices aetatis mediae manuscripti qui in Slovenia reperiuntur*, Ljubljana 1931, 158, 160; cf. P. O. KRISTELLER, *Latin Manuscript Books Before 1600*, New York 1960, 39). I have not yet seen the manuscript.

[14] For the cursus, see K. STRECKER, *Introduction to Medieval Latin*, Engl. trans. and rev. R. B. PALMER, Dublin and Zurich 1957, 86-90, and H. BRESSLAU, *Handbuch der Urkundenlehre für Deutschland und Italien*, II, Leipzig 1931, 247-263, and the bibliographies given by both authors. A very valuable recent contribution is A. DALZELL, *The « Forma Dictandi » attributed to Albert of Morra and related texts*: Mediaeval Studies 39 (1977) 440-465. A. MARIGO, *Il « cursus » nella prosa latina dalle origini cristiane ai tempi di Dante*: Atti e memorie della R. Accademia di scienze, lettere ed arti in Padova 47 (1931) 321-356, was unavailable. See SCHALLER, *Kanzlei*, pp. 270-273, here p. 271, n. 28. The difficult question of what constituted dactyls and spondees in the eyes of the dictatores of Orléans is most fully discussed by N. VALOIS, *Etude sur le rythme des bulles pontificales*: Bibl. de l'Ecole des Chartes 42 (1881) 161-198 and

in 1185-86, when the papal curia was at Verona, Transmundus substituted for the chancellor. Transmundus may have written the first recension of his *Introductiones* while he was still in papal service [15]. As will be seen, Albinus, too, was a member of the pontifical entourage at Verona at the time, and while this fact is probably not very significant in itself, it does show how useful Albinus' familiarity with the latest requirements for elegant prose must have been, exemplified, for instance, by the prologue:

Cum ante meam infantiam paulo minus utriusque cura parentis orbatus essem, rebus alendo mihi deficientibus quia parentum suppellex curta fuerat, ad colligendum puerum de plateis, ad eripiendum eum fame, frigore, calcibus bestiarum, nulla carnalium fratrum subveniebat affectio, nulla propinquorum miserabatur dilectio ... [16]

The 'cursus' is not the only means on which the prologue relies for effectiveness. Rhetorical devices (*colores rhetorici*) that were taught in the schools of the time are liberally employed to make a point. They are, besides the 'climax', which was just illustrated together with the 'cursus', primarily alliteration, parallelisms, antithesis, repetition of similar sounding words or words with the same root, wordplay, and assonance. Biblical imagery and direct quotations from the Vulgate abound in the text, at times interwoven with mythological allegories. Albinus' pronounced preference for unusual and obscure words is also evident throughout. These characteristics of the prologue accord very well with what is known about the 'stilus supremus' of Orléans [17]. Some of its excesses provoked a

---

257-272, here pp. 174-196, and particularly clearly by BRESSLAU, *Urkundenlehre* II, pp. 361-371. The explanation by Valois is based on the *Forma dictandi* of Albert de Morra which he cites from the only extant MS, Paris, *BN lat.* 2820 (not seen); see the texts *ibid.*, pp. 181-182 and 188-189 and in DALZELL, *The « Forma Dictandi » attributed to Albert of Morra*, pp. 442f. The same MS contains the *dictamen* by Transmundus (See HEATHCOTE, *Transmundus*, esp. pp. 67-68 and 82-86 and now particularly DALZELL, *The « Forma Dictandi » attributed to Albert of Morra*, passim). See also E. HELLER, *Die Ars dictandi des Thomas von Capua*: Sitzungsberichte, Heidelberger Akademie d. Wissenschaften 29 (1928/29), 4. Abh. Transmundus († after 1216), pupil of Albert of Morra, who was chancellor of the Roman curia (1178-1187) and subsequently pope as Gregory VIII (Oct.-Dec. 1187), was himself a papal notary (1185-1186), and later probably became a monk at Clairvaux. In the *Introductiones de arte dictandi*, which are otherwise closely related to the *Forma dictandi* attributed to Albert of Morra, Transmundus added to Albert's description of the *cursus velox* and *planus* the description of the *cursus tardus*. The first few sentences of Albinus' prologue (LC II, 87a) end as follows: « ... miserabatur dilectio » (*c. tardus*); « ... indesinenter ostendit » (*c. planus*); « ... matris pietatem exhibuit » (*c. tardus*); « ... pullis corvorum sperare » (*c. planus*); « ... in gente alia factus essem » (*c. velox*). Cf. BRESSLAU, *Urkundenlehre* II, 367, no. 3 regarding the ending « nimis dure » in Albert's *Forma dictandi*, and now DALZELL, *The « Forma Dictandi » attributed to Albert of Morra*, pp. 451 f.

[15] HEATHCOTE, *Transmundus*, p. 86 and p. 89, but see the important qualifications by DALZELL, *The « Forma Dictandi » attributed to Albert of Morra*, esp. p. 456.

[16] LC II, 87a.

[17] See the analysis by SCHALLER, *Kanzlei*, pp. 274-275. HEATHCOTE, *Transmundus*,

reaction around the turn of the thirteenth century, especially at Bologna, but the 'stilus supremus' continued to be influential, particularly at the curia [18]. Albinus' prologue also reflects the influence of the Cistercian preaching tradition and of the crusading appeals. Long, sonorous phrases, later to become typical of some of the 'exordia' in the letters of Pope Innocent III, alternate with brief sequences of colons that would be most effective when spoken aloud [19]. Albinus' interest in preaching as an art is clearly reflected in his digest as well as in the prologue. Furthermore, his office of *vicarius pape* may imply that preaching was one of his special tasks at the Roman curia [20].

pp. 59f., follows Schaller closely. A well-known representative of the Orléans school is Alain de Lille. See E. R. CURTIUS, *Europäische Literatur und Lateinisches Mittelalter*, Bern 1948 (the rev. ed., Bern 1954, was unavailable), 125-129; J. DE GHELLINCK, *L'Essor de la littérature latine au XIIe siècle*, 2 vols., Brussels and Paris 1946: I, p. 82, no. 15 and II, pp. 240-243; SCHALLER, *Kanzlei*, p. 276, n. 50. Alain's preface to the Anticlaudianus (MIGNE, *PL* 210, cols. 485-488) shows definite differences and the stronger influence of the preaching tradition on the prologue of Albinus manifests itself. Another famous writer and orator of the French tradition is Stephen of Tournai, a correspondent of Albert of Morra. (See SCHALLER, *Kanzlei*, p. 277, n. 54, and J. DESILVE, ed., *Lettres d'Etienne de Tournai*, Valenciennes 1893, nos. 63, 71, 80, 99, 127, 146, 148, 160, 166, and 210.) See also H. KANTOROWICZ, *The Poetical Sermon of a Mediaeval Jurist: Placentinus and his « Sermo de Legibus »*: Journal of the Warburg Institute 2 (1938) 22-41. Among the literature dealing with the schools of Orléans in the twelfth and early thirteenth century, I found the following particularly helpful: L. DELISLE, *Les écoles d'Orléans au douzième et au treizième siècle*: Annuaire-Bulletin de la Société de l'histoire de France 7 (1869) 139-154; L. DELISLE, *Notice sur une « Summa dictaminis » jadis conservée à Beauvais*, in *Notices et extraits des manuscrits*, XXXVI/1, Paris 1899, 171-205; L. AUVRAY, *Documents Orléanais du XIIe et du XIIIe siècle*: Société archéologique et historique de l'Orléanais, Mémoires 23 (1892) 393-413; L. J. PAETOW, *The Arts Course at Mediaeval Universities with Special Reference to Grammar and Rhetoric* (The University of Illinois Studies 3, no. 7), Urbana 1910, here pp. 87-90; L. ROCKINGER, *Die Briefsteller und Formelbücher des 11. bis 14. Jahrhunderts*, I (Quellen und Erörterungen z. bayerischen u. deutschen Geschichte, IX/1), Munich 1863 (repr. New York 1961), pp. 95-114, and in general C. H. HASKINS, *The Early Artes Dictandi in Italy. Studies in Mediaeval Culture*, Oxford 1929, 170-192, here pp. 190-192. Among the many texts published by CH.-V. LANGLOIS the following are the most relevant: *Formulaires de lettres du XIIe, du XIIIe et du XIVe siècle*, part 3: *Notices et extraits de trois formulaires Orléanais*, in *Notices et extraits des manuscrits*, XXXIV/2, Paris 1895, 1-18. See also CH.-V. LANGLOIS, *Maître Bernard*: Bibliothèque de l'Ecole de Chartes 54 (1893) 225-250 and 792-795, here esp. pp. 225-237; cf. F.-J. SCHMALE, *Die Bologneser Schule der Ars dictandi*: Deutsches Archiv 13 (1957) 16-34, here pp. 33f. See also G. VECCHI, *Il magistero delle « artes » latine a Bologna nel medioevo* (Pubblicazioni della Facoltà di Magistero, Univ. di Bologna, 2), Bologna 1961 [?].

[18] See the discussion and bibliography given by SCHALLER, *Kanzlei*, pp. 276-283 and the evidence presented by A. DALZELL, *The « Forma Dictandi » attributed to Albert of Morra*: Mediaeval Studies 39 (1977), esp. pp. 456f., for the mixture of the French and Italian styles in the later twelfth century, and esp. P. CLASSEN, *La curia romana e le scuole di Francia nel secolo XII*, in *Le istituzioni ecclesiastiche della « Societas christiana » dei secoli XI-XII*, I (Miscellanea del Centro di Studi Medioevali, 7), Milan 1974, 432-436.

[19] C. R. CHENEY, *The Letters of Pope Innocent III*: Bulletin of The John Rylands Library 35 (1953) 23-43, esp. pp. 33-37. Cf. SCHALLER, *Kanzlei*, pp. 280-283.

[20] Both the office of *vicarius pape* and the books of sermons will be discussed below. J. J. MURPHY, *Medieval Rhetoric. A Select Bibliography*, Toronto 1971, ch. 6, provides an introductory bibliography for sermon literature.

A few examples will suffice as an illustration of the preceding remarks, for Albinus often managed to combine more or less successfully several of the 'colores rhetorici' in a single sentence, not to mention the 'cursus'. Perhaps the most successful passage in the preface is the following:

Liber igitur rerum, libros in artibus sine omni libro, quia secus non poteram, legebam. Liberum patrem et matrem Cererem inveniendi crepusculo valde sollicitus, stringebam siliquas in villa civium regionis illius; simul cum aliis coaxabant et rane una mecum iuxta Nilum telluris Memphitice (*LC* II, 87b).

In a remarkable display of both classical and biblical learning in combination with a play on the word 'liber', Albinus describes here his life as a typical student before his conversion to the 'scola divinitatis', that is, before he took up what later would be called theology. A direct quotation from the parable of the Prodigal Son[21] is combined with a double mythological allusion that may be derived in part from Martianus Capella for the reference to Ceres and Tellurus[22], and in part from Graeco-Roman mythology in general for the pairing of Liber and Ceres as personifications for wine and bread[23]. To some extent the learned passage remains obscure. Contemporaries may have known which river Albinus wished to compare to the Nile, whether his 'croaking with the frogs' is a description of humble efforts as a poet, and whether the reference to the earth of Memphis (i.e. Egypt)[24] means in analogy to the Exile of the Israelites that Albinus studied 'abroad,' and/or whether Albinus takes up the earlier desert image which he used to describe his youthful experiences; historians, unfortunately, do not, primarily because neither the pro-

---

[21] *Luc 15*, 15-16: « Et abiit, et adhaesit uni civium regionis illius. Et misit illum in villam suam ut pasceret porcos. Et cupiebat implere ventrem suum de siliquis, quas porci manducabant: et nemo illi dabat ». (For the use of 'siliquae' = 'silver deniers', see J. M. WALLACE-HADRILL, *The Long-Haired Kings*, London 1962, p. 112, n., and *Cod. Just.* 4, 32, 26 fin). A further citation from the same parable follows upon the excerpt from Albinus' preface which I quoted in the text: « ... Sero tandem ad me reversus; videre cepi quanti mercennarii in domo patris pane divini verbi affluerent » (*LC* II, 87b; *Luc 15*, 17), and the « de domo patris longius me iam recedente » (cf. *Luc 15*, 13) used earlier in the preface (*LC* II, 87a), ties together the experiences of Albinus' youth under the single image of the Prodigal Son. The editors of the preface, FABRE and DUCHESNE, suggest that Albinus probably referred to Hagar in the allegory of which the reference to *Luc 15*, 13 is a part (*LC* II, 87a, n. 2). It does nevertheless seem more likely that 'mater' ought to be interpreted as 'Church.' Cf. *Thomas of Capua*, ed. E. HELLER (as in n. 14 above), p. 11: « ... Celebris est et gloriosa Romana ecclesia, de sub cuius pedibus defluunt aque vive ... '

[22] *De nuptiis Mercurii et philologiae*, l. 49; PAULY-WISSOWA, Zweite Reihe IX (1934), col. 408f. (MIELENTZ), s.v. Tellurus.

[23] For Liber = Dionysos, and Ceres = Demeter (= Libera), see *Ausführliches Lexikon d. griech. u. röm. Mythologie*, ed. W. H. ROSCHER, II, Leipzig 1890-1897, article Liber (WISSOWA), col. 2021-2029, esp. 2024-2025 and article Libera (WISSOWA), col. 2029-2030.

[24] PAULY-WISSOWA, XV/1 (1931), s.v. Memphis, cols. 660-688, here col. 675 for the use of 'memphiticus' as a synonym for 'Egyptian' by the Roman poets.

16

logue nor the digest as a whole give more intelligible evidence elsewhere [25]. But obscurity was a hallmark of the ' stilus supremus ' and
therefore probably delighted its practitioners, criticism by contemporaries notwithstanding [26].

Passages in the prologue that illustrate repetitions, climax, antithesis, inversion, and, as a natural concomitant, alliteration, are easily
recognizable [27]. The predilection for unusual words — in the case of
Albinus these are sometimes of Greek origin [28] — is hardly less evident [29], and it seems natural that references to the Old Testament take
their place alongside more familiar allusions to the New Testament.
More often than not they exemplify another characteristic of the
' stilus supremus ': display of learning for unusual ends. Albinus
himself felt the need for a direct explanation of his play on the word
' penna '. Following a reference to his lack of books, Albinus explains:

Deficiebant mihi *penne columbe deargentate* (*Ps* 67,14), quia ingenium fecu-
lentum deficiebant *penne ventorum* (*Ps* 17,11); virtutes scilicet meritorum quibus ad discendum me de terra suspenderem. Deficiebant etiam mosayce *pen-
nule ad* quas *capud detorqueri* valeret, ne *collum* prorsus *abrumperetur*. ... (*Lev*
5,8); (*LC* II, 87b).

The preface as a whole leaves no doubt of Albinus' mastery of
rhetoric. He seems to tell us this much directly, when he declares
that he took Chrysippos, presumably the fifth-century presbyter of
of Jerusalem who was famous for his ornate writings, for his model [30].

---

[25] A case in point is Albinus' reference to his first school as « gignasium Ariopagi » (*LC* II, 87a). According to Du Cange, ' gignasium ' was occasionally used as
the equivalent of ' schola. '. The term was apparently not restricted to any particular
school. Eventually, the University of Bologna became known as ' Archiginnasio ',
but this term cannot be traced back to the eighties of the twelfth century. (Cf. M.
SARTI and M. FATTORINI, *De claris Archigymnasii Bononiensis professoribus*, I, Bologna
1896 [repr. Turin 1962], 33, for the forged coin showing on the face an effigy of
Irnerius with the inscription « Irnerius Glossator » and on the reverse the inscription
« Instauratio Archigymnasii », the earliest documented use of the name ' Archiginnasio' that I could find). ' Areopagus' perhaps describes an independent municipal
government, but no such use elsewhere at the time of Albinus can be demonstrated.
In short, ' gignasium Ariopagi ' does not tell us where Albinus went to school.

[26] See the prologue by Gunther of Pairis, who explains that he is going to write
« ... humili stylo ac sermone pedestri: tum quia nec aliter possumus propter ingenii
crassitudinem, tum ne quosdam maxime superstitiosos videamus imitari, qui nil se
dixisse arbitrantur, nisi tam egregie dixerint, ut nec ipsi intelligant. Habeant sibi
tales odiosam suam obscuramque subtilitatem. ... » (MIGNE, *PL* 212, col. 164).

[27] See, for instance; « Veni ergo mendicus atque mendicans, pauper et nudus,
egenus et egens ... veni inquam in gignasium Ariopagi » (*LC* II, 87a); « ... [vixi] indoctus docens et inexpertus expertos presumptuose facere gliscens ... » (87b); « ... Va-
cavi et vidi, vidi et gavisus sum ... » (87b).

[28] Examples are the inscription of the work, « Eglogarum digesta pauperis scolaris Albini », the use of « gignasium Ariopagi », as well as « apophoreta » (MS *Ottob.
lat.* 3057, fol. 2v), used in Latin as the title of the fourteenth book of the epigrams
of Martial.

[29] ' Menia ' (moenia), for example, is employed in the sense of ' mansion ', ' dwelling '
(*LC* II, 88a) as in VIRGIL (*Aeneid* 6.541).

[30] *LC* II, 88a: « Factus tandem imitator Crisippi, sed non in omnibus, de auditis

Numerous statements to the contrary in the text do not invalidate this observation. The references to his inability, his apology for his weak intellect, and the remark that he wrote in his youth — to name but a few examples — are familiar expressions of the humility topos[31]. More unusual, even for the twelfth century, is Albinus' declaration: ... *Que autem deinceps secuntur sentecata sunt et apophoreta blacterantis et luscitantis adunatoris huius fasciculi* (MS *Ottob. lat.* 3057, fol. 2va). Part of the same topos is the cardinal's habit to refer to himself in the third person as in the preceding quote and elsewhere. And, finally, when Albinus emphasized in the preface that he bequeathed the material which he had collected not to the learned but rather to poor, beginning students as *sorbitiunculam*[32], he again presented a variation of the humility topos, for there is little likelihood that poor students who could not afford the acquisition of manuscripts would have been able to obtain the digest of Albinus, supposedly a textbook for them[33]. Although the use of a topos does not necessarily mean that a particular theme is factually inaccurate[34], it has to be admitted that in many cases expressions of humility can indicate no more and no less than that the author was familiar with the literary conventions of the time, given the

---

multa collegi ... » For Chrysippos see A. SIGALAS, *Des Chrysippos von Jerusalem Enkomion auf den hl. Johannes den Täufer* (Texte u. Forschungen zur byzantinisch-neugriechischen Philologie, 20), Athens 1937, esp. p. 61 with a biography, and pp. 63-72 for a discussion of Chrysippos' rhetorical training and style. Further literature is found ibid., pp. 114f.; see also PAULY-WISSOWA III (1899), cols. 2498ff., here no. 12, cols. 2501-2502. The speeches of Chrysippos are not mentioned among the authors who were ordinarily used in twelfth-century schools of rhetoric (cf. C. H. HASKINS, *The Twelfth-Century Renaissance*, Cambridge/Mass. 1927 [repr. Cleveland 1957 is cited here], 113-116, and SCHALLER, *Kanzlei*, p. 275, with further references), but then, Albinus was never content with the familiar and ordinary.

[31] *LC* II, 88b: « Quos cum componerem, quia pauper erat intelligentia, securius peto super his et aliis inepte prolatis ab ea legentibus veniam. Omnia supradicta facta fuerunt inconstantis etatis et infirme scientie ». Topoi are the main theme of CURTIUS, *Europäische Literatur* (see n. 17 above); see pp. 91-93 for humility, as well as L. ARBUSOW, *Colores rhetorici*, Göttingen 1948, 105-106; G. SIMON, *Untersuchungen zur Topik der Widmungsbriefe mittelalterlicher Geschichtsschreiber bis zum Ende des 12. Jahrhunderts*: Archiv für Diplomatik 4 (1958) 52-119 and 5 (1959) 73-153, gives numerous examples for the overwhelming importance of this particular topos during the period of the Middle Ages which she covers and which she attributes to the combination of ancient and Christian tradition; see esp. part 1, pp. 61ff. and p. 119.

[32] *LC* II, 88a.

[33] The statement that the *digesta* would be of no interest to the learned would of course also go far to disarm possible critics. Cf. SIMON, *Topik der Widmungsbriefe*, part 1, pp. 91 and 116, 84ff.

[34] Other topoi of the preface are the ' gathering of flowers ' image (*LC* II, 88b: « Diversarum igitur rerum diversas sententias colligentes et in fasciculum quosdam flosculos de multis pratis et fenis montium ad utilitatem legentium combinantes ... quasdam auctoritates premittere dignum duximus ») and the use of ' aemulus ' to describe the relationship with his brother (?) Richard (*LC* II, 87a: « Veni inquam in gignasium Ariopagi, factus emulus et adiutus Riccardo ... »). See ARBUSOW, *Colores rhetorici*, p. 107 for florilegia, and *ibid.*, p. 108 as well as SIMON, *Topik der Widmungsbriefe*, part 1, p. 94 for ' aemulus '.

exaggerated and frequent use of the humility topos in the prefaces and dedicatory letters in medieval works.

It is generally assumed that Albinus was a Milanese by birth[35]. The information on which these statements are based originated in the sixteenth century. Giovanni de Filippi (ca. 1480-ca. 1535) — perhaps the same person as Giovanni de Gozano —, at first a regular canon at S. Spirito in Novara, then transferred to S. Maria de Crescenzago (Crescentiaco) at Milan, and eventually provost of the canons at Tortona, devoted a good part of his life to a history of the canons regular. It is said that he visited all houses of regular canons in France on foot, and in 1528 he completed a *Chronica Canonici Ordinis* which was published at Cremona in 1535[36]. De Filippi claimed in this chronicle that Cardinal Albinus had been a member of the congregation of canons at S. Maria de Crescenzago. Gabriele Pennotto referred to de Filippi's chronicle in not very flattering terms, but nevertheless relied heavily on the information which he provided. This includes the reference to Cardinal Albinus as a member of the congregation of canons at Milan [37]. S. Maria de Crescenzago was founded in 1140, but almost all documents pertaining to its early history have been destroyed, and it is therefore impossible to check de Filippi's assertions as Pennotto already noted[38]. Pennotto was the first scholar who used de Filippi's work. Onofrio Panvini (1529-1568) and Alfonso Chacón (1540-1599) referred to Albinus only very briefly without indicating a source[39]. Ferdinand Ughelli[40] and the

---

[35] This opinion is held unanimously, *e. g.* G. MELVILLE, in *Series episcoporum*, p. 20; V. FENICCHIA, in *Dizionario Biografico degli Italiani*, II (1960), 11, and the *Repertorium fontium* (see n. 1 above), II, 177.

[36] LAZARO AGOSTINO COTTA, *Museo Novarese*, Milan 1701, 142f., no. 341. At the time of Cotta, GIOVANNI DE FILIPPI's *Chronica* was preserved « nella Bibl. Ambrosiana, V. Novaria Miscell. Novarese 5 ». My search for the volume proved so far unavailing. I would like to thank Don P. F. Fumagalli of the Biblioteca Ambrosiana for his kind help.

[37] G. PENNOTTO, *Generalis totius sacri ordinis clericorum canonicorum historia tripartita*, Rome 1624, 461ff., esp. pp. 463 and 710. The characterization of de Filippi's work is found *ibid.*, p. 696: « ... Habuit etiam hoc monasterium [S. Maria Gratiarum of Novara] Ioannem Philippum Novariensem, qui Chronicam canonici ordinis septem libris distinctam collegit, stylo quidem satis demisso, et diminutam, utpote in qua maxima pars eorum, quae de ordine canonicorum regularium in illa scribit, est minima pars eorum, quae merito desiderari possunt; in qua nonnullos historicos secutus ignaros, et illorum autoritate deceptus, quaedam falsa, et apocrypha notavit, cui tamen omnes canonici regulares pro labore, et solicitudine in antiquis monumentis pervestigandis, et conquirendis, et ex tenebris oblivionis ad lucem eruendis multas gratias habere debent ».

[38] A privilege for the congregation by Pope Urban III, the descendant of a noble Milanese family, exists (JL 15700), but there is no indication that this pontiff particularly furthered the career of Albinus who owed his appointments to Popes Lucius III and Clement III. Cf. PENNOTTO, part 2, pp. 461ff.

[39] O. PANVINI, *De episcopatibus, titulis et diaconiis cardinalium liber*, in *Romani Pontifices et Cardinales S.R.E. ab eisdem ... creati*, Venice, apud Michaelem Tramezinum, 1557, p. 123: « Magister Domnus Albinus Mediolanensis canonicus regularis monasterii S. Mariae de Erescentiaco [*sic*] Mediolanen. Dioecesis, S. Mariae novae ». CIACONIUS, *Vitae et gesta summorum pontificum necnon ... cardinalium ...*, Rome, apud

Ciaconius-Oldoini edition of 1677, which incorporates Pennotto's information, are the standard references in modern biographical notes [41]. Albinus may well have been a member of the canons regular at S. Maria de Crescenzago [42], but this need not imply that he was also born in that northern city [43]. Indeed, an inquiry into the background of Bishop Richard of Orvieto (1177-1201) to whom Albinus referred in his preface in unusual form as his brother, tends to strengthen the impression that Albinus may not have come from a poverty-stricken Milanese family after all [44]. Several authorities on the history of Orvieto were convinced that Richard was a member of the influential Pisan branch of the Gaetani family, an origin that would apply equally to his brother, or « stretto parente » [45]. However,

---

Stephanum Paulinum, 1601, p. 507: « M. Dominus Albinus Mediolanensis canonicus regularis et presbyter S. Crucis in Hierusalem, Lucii III. Episcopus Cardinalis Albanus ».

[40] F. UGHELLI, *Italia sacra*, I, Rome 1644, col. 296, no. 36 = Venice ²1717, col. 256, no. 37. See n. 5 above. Ughelli, who does not quote any source, was one of the editors of the 1630 edition of the work of Ciaconius. For CIACONIUS-OLDOINUS see above n. 5.

[41] See above n. 35.

[42] Cf. SCHALLER, *Kanzlei*, pp. 276f. and n. 52, and p. 281 with references to the place of Augustinian canons in the twelfth-century literary movement as well as HEATHCOTE, *Transmundus* (see n. 11 above), p. 88 n. 1.

[43] UGHELLI's text (« Albinus Mediolanensis canonicus Regularis monasterii sanctae Mariae de Crescentiaco, diaconus cardinalis ... », see n. 40 above), and perhaps the references in PANVINIUS and CIACONIUS as well (n. 39 above) can probably be interpreted as a mere statement to the effect that Albinus had been a canon at Milan. Neither Cenni nor Pennotto considered Albinus as of Milanese descent. Cf. the critical remarks on the methodology of Ciaconius by H. TILLMANN, *Ricerche sull'origine dei membri del collegio cardinalizio nel XII secolo*, part I: Rivista di storia della Chiesa in Italia 24 (1970) 441-464, here pp. 453-454.

[44] *LC* II, 87 a-b: « ... Veni inquam in gignasium Ariopagi, factus emulus et adiutus Riccardo, Urbevetano longo tempore post episcopo, pauperrimo tunc et uterino eodem patre germano ... ». Historians hesitate to translate « uterino eodem patre germano » as brother (see *ibid.*, n. 1: « Parenté bien peu clairement définie »), but no other translation would seem accurate. The exceptions are CAJETANUS CENNI, *Monumenta dominationis pontificiae*, II, Rome 1761, p. VIII, and V. FENICCHIA, in *Diz. Biogr. Ital.* II, p. 12, col. a: « Albino riuscì ... a continuare gli studi in una scuola superiore, dove ebbe per compagno un suo stretto parente (forse fratello) Riccardo ... ». The complicated expression « brother of the same mother and the same father » is not the only puzzling rhetorical flourish as was seen above.

[45] See F. UGHELLI, *Italia sacra*, vol. I, 2nd ed. by N. COLETI, Venice 1717, col. 1468: « Richardus quem nos e familia Cajetana Pisana ex monumentis eiusdem nobilissimae familiae asseruimus, juxta seriem in hoc throno collocandus videtur an. 1177. Revera tamen in monumentis Saxi vivi [Sassovivo] vetusti apud Fulgitanenses coenobii an. 1169 [*lege* 1179] videtur jam eo tempore fuisse Urbevetanus Episcopus, de quo series illa haec habet: Richardus Patria, non cognomento Caietanus, eadem die S. Benedicti, quo antecessor obierat, biennio transacto Urbevetanae Ecclesiae est ascitus anno 1177, ita ut, cum primo ad aras mitra redimitus accessit, mortuale sacrum anniversario ritu pro Rustico celebraverit ... et paulo post obiit anno 1201. Episcopali palatio prius restaurato, et sepultus est apud S. Severum ». This information is not yet found in the first edition of vol. I of *Italia sacra*, Rome 1644. UGHELLI first mentioned his researches in the Gaetani archives in *Italia sacra*, V, Rome 1653, col. 1549. Bibliography for the see of Orvieto will be given in n. 47 below. See esp. G. BUCCOLINI, *Serie critica dei vescovi di Bolsena e di Orvieto*: Bollettino della R. Deputaz. di Storia Patria per l'Umbria 38 (1941) 31-32.

the genealogy of the Pisan Caetani or Gaetani family is still rather obscure and poorly documented[46], and the argument of other scholars like Cenni that the reference to *Riccardus Caietanus* in documents of the cathedral of Orvieto indicated only that Richard was a native of Gaeta, cannot be refuted[47]. One may perhaps cautiously conclude that at the very least the surname ' Gajetanus ' of Bishop Richard of Orvieto indicates that he and Albinus had family ties to the city of Gaeta rather than to Milan. The slender evidence can perhaps be further supported. In a privilege for the city of Gaeta, King Tancred of Sicily referred to the intervention by Cardinal Albinus on behalf of the city[48].

Whatever the origins of Albinus, a contemporary document, the notarial registration of an eight-day indulgence for visitors and bene-factors of the church of S. Pietro in Castello at Verona by Pope

---

[46] GELASIO CAETANI, *Caietanorum Genealogia* (Documenti dell'Archivio Caetani), Perugia 1920, relied for information about the Pisan branch of the family on the researches by Abbot GAETANI COSTANTINO, preserved in manuscript: *De Familia Caietana, 1620-1650*, Rome, Bibl. Alessandrina, MS N. 184, vol. 3 (see CAETANI, *Genealogia*, table LIX: « Gaetani di Pisa », note). Richard, bishop of Orvieto, is listed by G. CAETANI on table LVIII: « Cronologia dei primi Gaetani di Pisa. Notizie varie riguardanti gli antichi Gaetani di Pisa non ancora controllate dall'A[utore] », with the dates 1180-1206, on the authority of COSTANTINO, vol. 3, c. 384 (I have not seen the MS). UGHELLI, *Italia sacra*, V, Rome 1653, col. 1549 is probably an independent authority for this information.

[47] The best bibliography for the bishopric of Orvieto is still P. F. KEHR, *Italia Pontificia*, II, Berlin 1907, 221; G. BUCCOLINI, *Serie critica dei vescovi* (see n. 45 above) should now be added. A brief recent history of medieval Orvieto is D. WALEY, *Mediaeval Orvieto. The Political History of an Italian City-State, 1157-1334*, Cambridge/ Engl. 1952. For the episcopate of Richard see BUCCOLINI, *Serie critica*, pp. 31-33 (with older bibliography) and pp. 75f. in addition to UGHELLI (see n. 45 above) and C. CENNI, *Monumenta dominationis pont.*, II, p. VIII. BUCCOLINI, *art. cit.*, pp. 75f. notes that there is no documentary evidence for the traditional Orvietan assumption that Pope Celestine III visited Orvieto during Richard's episcopate in 1193 and founded there « lo studio ' Bonarum Artium ' ». — The most important collection of documents for Richard's episcopate was published by L. FUMI, *Codice diplomatico della città d'Orvieto. Documenti e regesti dal secolo XI al XV*, Florence 1884, 32-46; there are no references under Richard's origin or to his brother Albinus. The declaration that Richard was « patria Cajetanus, non cognomento » was traced back by BUCCOLINI, *art. cit.*, p. 31, to « Marabottini, e [dice] così la Serie V.to. » See F. MARABOTTINUS, *Catalogus Episcoporum Urbisveteris ex antiquis et publicis autographis fere totus excerptus*, pp. 5-6 under Riccardus. (The excerpt here corresponds almost verbatim to the text which was published by UGHELLI, see n. 45 above.) MARABOTTINI's catalogue was published as appendix to F. POLI, *Constitutiones et decreta*, Rome 1650; see the second ed. of this work by I. DELLA CORGNA, with the title *Constitutiones*, Orvieto 1667, 10. The copy of POLI-MARABOTTINI-DELLA CORGNA in the Biblioteca Apostolica Vaticana contains carefully added handwritten cross-references to the original documents in the archives of the cathedral of Orvieto. For « Riccardus Patria Caietanus non cognomento ut alii asseruerunt ... » this reference reads « in praecit. Libr. fol. 81 col. 2 scribitur Gajetanus » [i.e. instead of the Caietanus of the print]. The « Liber » is a parchment manuscript with the signature B (not seen). Cf. FUMI, *Codice diplomatico della città d'Orvieto*, p. XIII: « ... si riposero in Archivio vesc. i copiarii A e B che contengono documenti e regesti dal secolo XI ». It should be noted that Marabottini did not give any reasons for his statement that Gajetanus designated origin rather than family. Buccolini leaves the question open.

[48] See below n. 93. The document does not give any reasons for the intercession.

Urban III, is evidence that Albinus was known as 'magister'. In the recorded indulgence, which was granted on June 29, 1186, in connection with a solemn mass at the church, numerous cardinals are mentioned by name as present during the celebration, many of them with the title 'magister', among them Albinus [49]. The use of the title 'magister' in the last decades of the twelfth century was still fluid and varied from place to place [50]. It is therefore difficult to interpret the term correctly, especially when the title 'magister' precedes the name of a cleric [51]. However, Albinus, who referred in the inscription to the prologue to himself as 'pauper scolaris', clearly had a more than passing acquaintance with the schools of his time. While we cannot say where he and Richard of Orvieto studied, Albinus states that he not only studied but also taught [52]. Not a great deal is known about requirements for the 'licentia docendi' at the nascent universities of the later twelfth century [53], but Abelard already provoked negative comments when he set up a lecture course on his own in competition with Anselm of Laon, not all of whose courses

---

[49] The instrument was published from the original by W. HOLTZMANN, *Anecdota Veronensia*, in *Papsttum und Kaisertum* (see n. 8 above), pp. 369-375, here pp. 372-373, no. 2. Cf. O. PANVINIUS, *Antiquitates Veronenses*, Pavia 1648, 186; KEHR, *Italia Pontificia*, VII/1, p. 250, no. 5; JAFFÉ-LOEWENFELD, *Regesta pontificum romanorum* (abbreviated below JL) II, p. 503.

[50] See the discussion by J. FRIED, *Die Entstehung des Juristenstandes im 12. Jahrhundert*, Cologne and Vienna 1974, 9-24 with relevant literature.

[51] *Ibid.*, p. 10: « Von der ' magister '-Bezeichnung voreilig auf ein Studium an einer Hochschule zu schließen, ist in jedem Falle verkehrt ». See now also R. M. HERKENRATH, *Studien zum Magistertitel in der frühen Stauferzeit*: Mitteilungen des Inst. für österreichische Geschichtsforschung 88 (1980) 3-35.

[52] *LC* II, 87b: « Gessi mores illis cum quibus vixi; indoctus docens et inexpertus expertos presumptuose facere gliscens ».

[53] Little is known about late 11th- and 12th-century schools with the exception of Paris and Bologna which evolved into universities and are therefore included in the literature dealing with the rise of this medieval institution. H. RASHDALL, *The Universities of Europe in the Middle Ages*, 2nd ed. by F. M. Powicke and A. B. Emden, 3 vol., Oxford 1936; H. DENIFLE, *Die Entstehung der Universitäten des Mittelalters*, vol. I (no more issued), Berlin 1885; P. KIBRE, *Scholarly Privileges in the Middle Ages*, London 1961, and A. B. COBBAN, *The Medieval Universities: Their Development and Organization*, London 1975, are basic. For schools in the twelfth century the most essential and comprehensive work is P. CLASSEN, *Die Hohen Schulen und die Gesellschaft im 12. Jahrhundert*: Archiv für Kulturgeschichte 48 (1966) 155-180 with further bibliography, esp. for French schools; see also IDEM, *Die Renaissance der Wissenschaften im 12. Jahrhundert*, in *Zürcher Hochschulforum*, II, Zurich and Munich 1981, 11-32; J. FRIED, *Die Entstehung des Juristenstandes im 12 Jht.*, Cologne 1974; D. A. BULLOUGH, *Le scuole cattedrali e la cultura dell'Italia settentrionale prima dei comuni*, in *Vescovi e diocesi in Italia nel medioevo (sec. IX-XIII)* ‹Atti del II° Convegno di Storia della Chiesa in Italia, Roma 1961 = Italia Sacra, 5), Padua 1964, 211-243; G. CENCETTI, *Studium fuit Bononie. Note sulla storia dell'Università di Bologna nel primo mezzo secolo della sua esistenza*: Studi medievali 7 (1966) 781-833; N. G. SIRASSI, *Arts and Sciences at Padua. The Studium at Padua before 1350*, Toronto 1973; *La scuola nell'occidente latino dell'alto medioevo*, 2 vols. (Settimane di studio del Centro italiano di Studi sull'Alto Medioevo, 19), Spoleto 1972, is less helpful for the early period than expected. The 'licentia docendi' is regulated in c. 18 of the Third Lateran Council (1179) (= *Conciliorum oecumenicorum decreta*, ed. J. ALBERIGO *et al.*, Bologna ³1973, 220).

he had heard [54]. Albinus was certainly more conventional in his methods, and when he refers to a change of faculties as well as to his teaching activity, we can probably assume that he had pursued his studies long enough to satisfy the requirements for a license to teach, and would therefore qualify for the designation ' magister ' in a more than honorary sense. The style of the preface indicates that he had emphasized rhetoric during the first phase of his scholarly life [55], the content that he later changed to the field of philosophy/ theology, where he heard lectures on several books of Peter Lombard's Sentences [56]. Albinus disparaged some of his old learning in favor of the new — that is, theology — that helped him escape the wrath of God: *didiceram in aliis facultatibus que me lex Domini inreprehensibilis ... dediscere suadebat ...* [57]. What Albinus rejected was perhaps the emphasis on classical pagan authors in schools of rhetoric. The reliance on classical readings was one of the chief objections by contemporaries against the French schools [58]. There is no evidence that Albinus had studied law, another area of study that had come under criticism [59]. On the contrary, at Bologna in the second half of the

---

[54] ABELARD, *Historia calamitatum*, ed. J. MONFRIN, Paris 1967, 68-70.

[55] Rhetoric was taught in schools of the liberal arts as well as in the faculties of theology/philosophy, medicine, and law. See the literature given in n. 17 above.

[56] See the following references in the preface: *LC* II, 87b (comparison of the ' scola divinitatis ' with the Father's house); *LC* II, 88a (reflections on the exposition of *Prov 30*,38 by an unnamed ' magister '); *LC* II, 89b (explanation of the origin of his sentence collection). His collection is based on authorities, « quas a magistris in scolis audivi de cultu et adoratione Dei et hominis Filii » (*LC* II, 89b). The first passage is largely dependent on P. LOMBARD, *Libri quatuor sententiarum*, book 1, d. 1, c. 2; a second passage which follows immediately, but has not been included by FABRE and DUCHESNE, depends on LOMBARD's *Sentences*, book 3, d. 9, cap. unicum. (See below n. 116). The recent edition of the *Sentences* argues that they were composed between the years 1155 and 1158 (*Magistri Petri Lombardi Sententiae in IV libris distinctae*, editio tertia [Spicil. Bonav., IV], vol. I, part 1 and 2, Grottaferrata 1971, 32). Albinus, therefore, did not belong to the generation of Pope Lucius III or Celestine III. He must have attended courses on theology in the late fifties or later. Albinus may have attended lectures at several schools as was frequently done. For examples see *The Letters of John of Salisbury*, I: *The Early Letters (1153-1161)*, ed. by W. J. MILLOR and H. E. BUTLER, rev. by C. N. L. BROOKE, London 1955, introduction by Professor Brooke, p. XXVIII, n. 2.

[57] *LC* II, 87b. Albinus' use of ' facultates ' with the meaning of a field of study or perhaps even in the modern sense of faculties at universities is noteworthy. A. LANDGRAF, *Philologisches zur Frühscholastik*: Mediaeval Studies 8 (1946) 53-67, here pp. 56-59, traced such use to the school of Gilbert de la Porrée. Landgraf also documented this use in the writings of Alain de Lille. Cf. n. 17 above.

[58] See E. NORDEN, *Die antike Kunstprosa*, II, Leipzig 1909, 724-731; SCHALLER, *Kanzlei*, p. 278; DELISLE, *Les écoles d'Orléans* (see n. 17 above), pp. 139ff., with Boncompagno's commentary on the Orléans tradition *ibid.*, p. 152. Alexandre of Villedieu is quoted *ibid.*, p. 145: « Aurelianiste via non patet ad paradisum // Ni prius os mutet ».

[59] Albinus' reference to Gratian in the preface is frequently misinterpreted in this sense: « Adiuncxi quosdam necessarios canones quos de diversis Patrum opusculis non omnibus perviis, nec in editione Gratiani redactis cum labore collegi » (*LC* II, 88a-b). He excerpted writings of the Church Fathers rather than pre-Gratian canonical collections as will be seen below (cf. n. 113). The majority of the biographical notices of Albinus repeat an assertion by CIACONIUS, derived from DE FILIPPI: « ... [Albinus] librum edidit praenotatum *Collectio Canonum*, qui manu scriptum asser-

twelth century, the title 'magister' was generally reserved for non-jurists, that is, those who were learned in the arts like rhetoric, philosophy/theology, and medicine, as a letter of Pope Alexander III to the Bolognese community shows [60].

It would be rather unusual if the highly successful career of Albinus at the papal curia had come about without the help of family connections and were solely due to his learning [61]. Three notaries from Orléans who were employed by the papal curia at the time of Chancellor Albert of Morra presumably did reasonably well and were reasonably proficient, but none of them became even a cardinal deacon, let alone cardinal bishop of Albano [62]. Learning was indeed an esteemed qualification for future cardinals, but a majority of them combined scholarly achievements with the solid backing of family connections [63]. Wealth and poverty are relative terms, and at least a suspicion is justified that the abject poverty of which Albinus complains in his prologue was to some extent an image that was chosen because of its rhetorical effectiveness as 'captatio benevolentiae'. Albinus reports himself that his uncle was a monk who was able to support an orphaned nephew (*LC* II, 87a), and also that his brother Richard became bishop of Orvieto. Last but not least, Albinus himself was probably a canon at S. Maria de Crescenzago at Milan. To find these positions in a single family in the second half of the twelth century does imply that this family was at least a member of the middle class.

Poor scholars are a familiar picture in association with life in

vatur in Bibliotheca Vaticana, ex Chronico Canonicorum Regularium D. Ioannis Philippi Novarnensis » (see n. 5 above). E. KARTUSCH, *Das Kardinalskollegium* (see n. 5 above), pp. 56 and 79, listed for Albinus the *Gesta pauperis scholaris* and a *Collectio canonum* as separate writings. She concluded, *ibid.*, that he must have possessed legal training.

[60] JL 10587 of 1159. See FRIED, *Entstehung des Juristenstandes* (see n. 50 above), p. 21 and H. RASHDALL, *The Universities of Europe* (see n. 53 above), I, pp. 19-20. Rashdall shows that this usage was later transferred to Paris.

[61] Cf. n. 13 above.

[62] See SCHALLER, *Kanzlei*, p. 277 and n. 54 with further references.

[63] See J.M. BRIXIUS, *Die Mitglieder des Kardinalskollegiums von 1130-1181*, Diss. Berlin 1912, 130-133; B. ZENKER, *Die Mitglieder des Kardinalskollegiums von 1130 bis 1159*, Diss. Würzburg 1964. 201-203, 210-216, is also relevant; E. KARTUSCH, *Das Kardinalskollegium in der Zeit von 1191-1227*, Diss. Vienna 1948, continued the work of Brixius and also emphasized the geographical, educational, and family background of cardinals. She tabularized the results (pp. 50-55), and also listed extant writings (pp. 56-57); out of a total of 73 cardinals for whom such information is available, 29 completed a full course of study and held the title of 'magister' before they were elevated to the cardinalate. Well-known examples for noble descent as well as learning are Pope Celestine III, the former Cardinal Hyacinth (KARTUSCH, no. 46), Pope Gregory VIII, the former Cardinal Albertus de Morra (*ibid.*, no. 4), and Pope Honorius III, the former Cardinal Cencius Savelli (*ibid.*, no. 19); cf. *ibid.*, no. 101 for the career of Soffredus (Gaetani?) and *ibid.*, no. 6 for Aldebrandinus Gaetani. Cf. D. GIRGENSOHN, *Wie wird man Kardinal? Kuriale und ausserkuriale Karrieren an der Wende des 14. zum 15. Jahrhundert*: Quellen und Forschungen aus ital. Archiven u. Bibliotheken 57 (1977) 138-162.

twelfth-century schools as reflected in the poetry of the time and especially in epistolary formularies. The letter asking parents or relatives for money because their diligent off-spring had fallen into dire straits is one of their standard components [64]. The 'poor' at the schools were numerous, apparently. Well-known from the second half of the twelfth century is the Liber pauperum of Vacarius, a text-book for poor students of the law [65] Recently, an attempt has been made to define the 'pauper scolaris' of a century or two later, but for the twelfth century no more can be said than that Albinus was not alone. His complaint seems to have been fairly general, even down to the topic of the missing books [66].

Uncertainty surrounds the background of Albinus, but it is incontestable that he eventually became an eminent cardinal and vicarius pape. At long last we are on somewhat firmer ground, for the remarks of Albinus in the prologue can be supported and expanded by external evidence, at least occasionally. In the preface, Albinus, explaining the changing character of his collection, pointed out that:

Cum autem factus sum vir, meritis peccatorum vocatus sum ad Romanam ecclesiam, et ex tunc sollicitus fui quando et ubi potui in hoc eodem fasciculo annectere que cognoveram vel inveniebam iuris esse beati Petri, per libros antiquitatum vel ea que per me ipsum audivi et vidi, a tempore Lucii III qui me indignum diaconum ordinavit anno II° et sacerdotem quarto anno sui pontificatus (LC II, 88b).

Cardinal Bishop Hubald of Ostia, a Cistercian and an influential member of the college of cardinals since 1138, was elected Pope Lucius III (1181-1185) in the early fall of 1181, entering Rome in November [67]. Albinus placed his elevation to cardinal deacon of S. Maria

---

[64] See especially C. H. HASKINS, The Life of Mediaeval Students as Illustrated by Their Letters, in Studies in Mediaeval Culture, Oxford 1929, 1-35.

[65] F. DE ZULUETA, ed., Publications of the Selden Society, XLIV, London 1927. See ibid., p. XIV, for the account of Robert de Monte: «...Magister Vacarius ... in Anglia discipulos doceret, et multi tam divites quam pauperes ad eum causa discendi confluerunt, suggestione pauperum, de Codice et Digesta excerptos novem libros composuit, qui sufficiunt ad omnes legum lites ... decidendas ».

[66] See DELISLE, Les écoles d'Orléans (see n. 17 above), pp. 142 and 150, no. IV. See further c. 18 of the Third Lateran Council (see n. 53 above) which stipulates that cathedrals are to provide a benefice for teachers at their schools so that the poor can be educated free of charge. The remarks by P. CLASSEN, Die Hohen Schulen und die Gesellschaft (see n. 53 above), pp. 160-162, are particularly illuminating. A later time was to provide more precise definitions of the 'pauper scolaris'. See M. DITSCHE, Zur Studienförderung im Mittelalter: Rheinische Vierteljahrsblätter 41 (1977) 53-62. This article was kindly brought to my attention by Professor R. Elze. See in general the description and analysis of poverty in M. MOLLAT, Les pauvres au moyen-âge, Paris 1978, esp. pp. 77-142 with further references and K. BOSL, Das Problem der Armut in der hochmittelalterlichen Gesellschaft: Sitzungsberichte der Österreichischen Akademie der Wissenschaften, Philos.-hist. Kl. 294/5 (Vienna 1974).

[67] A brief biographical note for Hubald as cardinal is given by BRIXIUS, Kardinalskollegium, p. 43 and n. 111, p. 103 with the statement that Hubald was probably a regular canon from either Bologna or Lucca. For his pontificate see especially K. WENCK, Die römischen Päpste zwischen Alexander III. und Innozenz III. (as in

Nuova into the second year of the pontificate of Lucius, and in accordance with this statement his first signature is found under a privilege of Thursday, December 23, 1182, shortly after his ordination had taken place [68]. Albinus signed for the last time as cardinal deacon on Ember Friday, March 15, 1185 [69]. On Tuesday of the following week, March 19, 1185, he subscribed already as cardinal presbyter of S. Croce in Gerusalemme, and one may assume that his elevation to the new title occurred in the course of these days [70].

n. 8 above), which is most helpful, notwithstanding the fact that Wenck's interpretation is rather one-sided, as pointed out P. ZERBI, *Papato, Impero e « Respublica Christiana » dal 1187 al 1198*, Milan [s.d.], here pp. 2f. with notes. The essay by H. HALLER, *Heinrich VI. und die römische Kirche:* Mitteilungen des Instituts für österreichische Geschichtsforschung 34 (1914) 385-454, 545-669, is in most respects a brilliant contribution (cf. ZERBI, *Papato, Impero e « Respublica Christiana »*, pp. 1-8) with important corrections to T. TOECHE, *Kaiser Heinrich VI.,* in *Jahrbücher der deutschen Geschichte,* Leipzig 1867, which, despite its age, still has its uses and is often cited; see also W. LENEL, *Der Konstanzer Frieden von 1183 und die italienische Politik Friedrichs I.:* Historische Zeitschrift 128 (1923) 189-261, here esp. pp. 209-216 and 245 ff. with criticism of HALLER. All materials contain bibliographies. The bibliography by J. PETERSOHN, *Der Vertrag des Römischen Senats mit Papst Clemens III. (1188) und das Pactum Friedrich Barbarossas mit den Römern (1167):* Mitt. des Instituts für österreichische Geschichtsforschung 82 (1974) 289-337, is a valuable bibliographical up-date, although the paper is not pertinent in the present context.

[68] JL 14716. The Ember days of December 1182 were used by Lucius for his first creation of cardinals. See O. PANVINI, *De episcopatibus* (see n. 5 above), p. 122; cf. BRIXIUS, *Kardinalskollegium,* pp. 7-15, on the dates for the creation of cardinals. — H. MÜLLER, *Die Mitglieder des Kardinalskollegiums von 1181-1216,* Diss. Göttingen 1950, 15, gives May 18, 1182 as the date of the first signature of Albinus as cardinal deacon, following W. WIEDERHOLD (*Papsturkunden in Frankreich,* IV [Nachrichten der Ges. d. Wissenschaften zu Göttingen, 1907, Beiheft], p. 147, no. 66). KARTUSCH, *Das Kardinalskollegium,* p. 440, rightly noted several discrepancies between that date, May 18, 1182, and the signatures found under the privilege. MELVILLE (*Series episcoporum,* p. 20) nevertheless followed Müller uncritically. The difficulties which Kartusch noticed can be resolved easily. Wiederhold accidentally failed to observe that under the *calculus Florentinus,* which was exclusively in use at the curia between 1143 and 1216 (H. GROTEFEND, *Taschenbuch der Zeitrechnung,* Hanover ⁷1935, 37f.), the year of the *datum* line as transmitted in the document giving 1183 as year did not require any change. — V. PFAFF, *Die Kardinäle unter Papst Coelestin III.:* Zeitschr. d. Savigny-Stiftung, Kan. Abt. 41 (1955) 84, referred to JL II, p. 432, where the cardinalate of Albinus is dated « c. Aug. 1182 »; this date is derived from JL 14686, a privilege that is either incorrectly transmitted or of a later date. See BRIXIUS, *Kardinalskollegium,* pp. 124 and 125f. JL 14711, dated December 4, 1182 (F. UGHELLI, *Italia sacra,* I, Venice ²1717, cols. 1185f. and MIGNE *PL* 201, cols. 1160f.), includes a signature of Albinus as cardinal presbyter of S. Croce in Gerusalemme. He did not attain this dignity until 1185; the signatures of the cardinals are found in the proper sequence, and it seems, therefore, that Ughelli's date has to be corrected.

[69] W. HOLTZMANN, *Papsturkunden in England,* I (Abhandlungen ... Göttingen, Neue Folge 25/1-2, 1930-31), pp. 512ff., no. 231.

[70] JL 15390. Older biographies of Albinus should be corrected. The Ember days began Wednesday, March 13. Cf. BRIXIUS, *Kardinalskollegium,* here pp. 10-11, now to be corrected. The ember days extended from Wednesday to Saturday, so that he could have signed with his old title just prior to his ordination. Occasionally, privileges could be post-dated (BRIXIUS, *Kardinalskollegium,* p. 15). PANVINI, *De episcopatibus* (see n. 5 above), p. 123, erroneously placed the second cardinals' creation of the pontificate of Lucius III into December 1184. — JL 15396, dated by JAFFÉ-LOEWENFELD March 29, 1185, seems to present a problem because Albinus here signed as cardinal deacon of S. Maria Nuova. But the date of this privilege has to be considered uncertain, for both editions to which JAFFÉ-LOEWENFELD refer (J. B. MITTARELLI, *Annales*

26

Pope Lucius III died in November, 1185. Albinus' signatures under the pontiff's successor, Urban III (1185-1187), continued until October 24, 1186 (JL 15684), when he seems to have left the curia at Verona for unknown reasons. No signatures of the cardinal of S. Croce are known from the brief pontificate of Pope Gregory VIII (Oct.-Dec. 1187). Under Pope Clement III (1187-1191)[71], his signatures as cardinal priest of S. Croce extend with some interruptions from February 18, 1188[72] to May 18, 1189 (JL 16414). On Ember Wednesday, May 31, 1189, Albinus signed for the first time as cardinal bishop of Albano[73]. Albinus' last signature is dated July 9, 1196[74]. Until that date his signature had been a regular feature of the great privileges with one exception (JL 17408), and in May he had participated in the solemn consecration of the church of S. Lorenzo in Lucina[75]. His disappearance from the signature lists seems sudden, therefore. The date of his death is unknown. His successor as cardinal bishop of Albano was not appointed until early 1199[76], but already in March 1198 Pope Innocent III (1198-1216) referred to Albinus as having died[77]. The year 1197 was a difficult one at the curia, and Albinus,

---

Camaldulenses O.S.B., IV, Venice 1759, appendix, cols. 126-128 and G. LAMI, *Sanctae ecclesiae Florentinae monumenta*, II, Florence 1758, 1185n) leave the exact date in March 1185 open, replacing it by dots (reproduced in MIGNE *PL* 201, col. 1345). The original was apparently illegible in several places. JAFFÉ-LOEWENFELD'S source for ' 29 March' is unknown, and it could therefore well be that the document belongs to the first half of March 1185 when Albinus indeed still was cardinal deacon.

[71] For Pope Clement III see (in addition to the general bibliography of n. 67 above) ZERBI, *Papato, Impero*, pp. 11-62; V. PFAFF, *Papst Clemens III. (1187-1191)*: Zeitschrift der Savigny-Stiftung f. Rechtsgesch., Kan. Abt. 97 (1980) 261-316; PETERSOHN, *Der Vertrag des Römischen Senats mit Papst Clemens III. (1188)* (as in n. 67). For the presence of cardinals at the election of Clement see PFAFF, *Clemens III.*, pp. 262f. and 263 n. 12: « ... So muß man annehmen, daß die zur Kurie gehörenden Pandulf, Albinus, Johann S. Marci, Adelhard erst in Rom zur Kurie stießen ... », with further references.

[72] PFAFF, *Clemens III.*, no. 25, p. 287.

[73] W. WIEDERHOLD, *Papsturkunden in Frankreich*, IV (as in n. 68 above), no. 81, pp. 160f. MÜLLER, *Kardinalskollegium*, p. 15, mistakenly indicates that Albinus signed as ' electus '. The ' electus ' only accompanies the signature of Cardinal Bishop Octavian of Ostia and Velletri according to Wiederhold. C. ERDMANN, *Papsturkunden in Portugal* (Abhandlungen d. Ges. d. Wissenschaften zu Göttingen, Neue Folge, vol. XX/3), Berlin 1927, no. 119, pp. 335ff., published a privilege for the monastery of S. Maria de Alcobaça which is dated June 26, 1189. It is signed by Albinus as cardinal priest of S. Croce. A reason for this cannot be given, but it should be noted that the privileges PFAFF, *Clemens III.*, no. 158, p. 305 (June 5), JL 16419 (PFAFF, no. 159), and PFAFF, no. 160, both of June 6, as well as JL 16420 of June 12 (PFAFF, no. 161, p. 306) were all signed by Albinus as cardinal of Albano in addition to the privilege of May 31, 1189 (PFAFF, no. 157, p. 305).

[74] V. PFAFF, *Die Kardinäle unter Papst Coelestin III. (1191-1198)*, Zweiter Teil: Zeitschrift der Savigny-Stiftung f. Rechtsgesch., Kan. Abt. 52 (1966) 332-369, p. 364, no. 211 of July 9, 1196, correcting PFAFF I (1955), p. 84, with a reference to JL 17416 of July 12.

[75] V. FORCELLA, *Iscrizioni delle Chiese e d'altri edificii di Roma dal secolo XI fino ai giorni nostri*, V, Rome 1874, no. 344, p. 119.

[76] KARTUSCH, *Kardinalskollegium*, no. 48, pp. 229-232.

[77] *Die Register Innocenz' III.*, I: *1. Pontifikatsjahr 1198/99*; Texte, ed. O. HAGENEDER, A. HAIDACHER, Graz and Cologne 1964, no. 37, pp. 52f. (early March 1198) and no. 364, pp. 548f. of Sept. 16, 1198. See also KARTUSCH, *Kardinalskollegium*, p. 82, n. 28 and MELVILLE, in *Series episcoporum* (as in n. 1 above), p. 20 and n. 297.

the senior member of the highest ordo among the cardinals, would surely have been heard from unless he was either gravely ill or had died already late in 1196 or early 1197. There is no indication that he participated in the election of Innocent III. His date of death may therefore be given as 1196/97.

Ordinary, the signatures of cardinals under the solemn privileges of the period indicate little more than the approximate date of a cardinal's elevation, and his presence or absence from the curia at certain times. The signatures of Albinus are different only insofar as they show once again how fond he was of the ornate and the unusual. He was one of the very few cardinals, Lothar of Segni was another, who varied signature cross and signature [78]. Fortunately, there is some other evidence for the cardinalate of Albinus. The census lists and the *Provinciale* in the *Digesta pauperis scolaris* show that he had access to these documents, and reveal his concern for the prerogatives of the Roman See as well as for the financial affairs of the curia [79]. But none of this is reflected in the offices with which he was entrusted: auditor, legate and *vicarius pape*.

Only one instance of Albinus' function as auditor is now known. The bishop and the chapter of Narni had become involved in litigation, and Albinus and Cardinal Deacon Gregory of S. Maria in Porticu were sent together as auditors to the city of Narni by Pope Celestine III (1191-1198). The pontiff eventually decided the case on the basis of their report in December 1194 [80].

It has long been recognized that Albinus was particularly active in Sicilian affairs [81]. In 1188, under Pope Clement III, Albinus, who

---

[78] B. KATTERBACH, W. PEITZ, *Die Unterschriften der Päpste und Kardinäle* (see n. 8 above), esp. pp. 241f.

[79] Cf. PFAFF, *Clemens III.*, p. 267.

[80] KEHR, *Italia Pontificia*, IV, Berlin 1909, 32, nos. *7 and 8, Dec. 17, 1194.

[81] I. FRIEDLÄNDER, *Die päpstlichen Legaten in Deutschland und Italien am Ende des XII. Jahrhunderts (1181-1198)* (Historische Studien, 177), Berlin 1928, 56-58, 78f., 122f. WENCK, *Die römischen Päpste* (see n. 8 above), esp. p. 441, suggested that Albinus' elevation to the bishopric of Albano occurred in connection with his Sicilian negotiations. There is no evidence to support this assumption. His negative interpretation of the whole of the pontificate of Clement III, and implicitly of the elevation of Albinus, presents a one-sided view, based as it is on the *Epistolae Cantuarienses* (ed. W. STUBBS, *Chronicles and Memorials of the Reign of Richard I*, vol. II: *Epistolae Cantuarienses; The Letters of the Prior and Convent of Christ Church Canterbury, from A.D. 1187-A.D. 1199* [Rerum Brit. medii aevi scriptores = Rolls Series, vol. XXXVIII/2], London 1865, here p. 196 no. 211), and the satirical gospel of marks and silver, or Albinus and Rufinus. Cf. P. LEHMANN, *Die Parodie im Mittelalter*, Stuttgart ²1963, 44-57, esp. p. 48, and the text of the satire *ibid.*, pp. 184-188. The *Epistolae Cantuarienses* are responsible for Albinus' 'bad press'. Their description of Albinus as 'homo convertibilis' taken out of context (see *Ep. Cant.* no. 315, p. 301), translated as 'Blatt im Wind' in connection with 'Emporkömmling' (WENCK, *Die römischen Päpste*, p. 440 and p. 441), is found in most modern biographical notes. In the context of the Canterbury quarrel it merely meant that Albinus could not be considered a devoted partisan of either one side or the other, i.e. either convent or archbishop. The remark in the *Epistolae* (no. 315, p. 301) that the Cardinals Gratian and Soffred left the curia protesting the creation of Cardinals Octavian, Bobo,

was at the time cardinal priest of S. Croce, was sent as legate to the court of King William II at Palermo. He was accompanied by Cardinal Priest Peter of S. Lorenzo in Damaso. The legates were to obtain from the king the observation of the royal obligations which were stipulated by the 1156 Treaty of Benevento. The treaty, which had been arranged by Cardinal Hubald, afterwards Pope Lucius III, among other things recognized the hereditary succession of the Norman rulers in return for their oath of fidelity and homage to the canonically elected reigning pontiff [82]. William II, who was sole ruler since 1171, still had not performed either one or the other. The date of the embassy cannot be fixed precisely [83], although two documents pertain to it: 1) an oath of fidelity of King William II of Sicily for Pope Clement III [84], and 2) a decretal letter of Pope Clement III addressed to the king, and dated 15 July 1188. Both the oath of fidelity given into the hands of the legates, and the decretal are fully discussed elsewhere [85]. It suffices here, therefore, to point

and Albinus would be curious if both Soffred and Albinus had belonged to the Gaetani clan.

[82] H. ENZENSBERGER, Der ' böse ' und der ' gute ' Wilhelm. Zur Kirchenpolitik der normannischen Könige von Sizilien nach dem Vertrag von Benevent (1156): Deutsches Archiv 36 (1980) 385-432, here pp. 396-401; J. DEÉR, Papsttum und Normannen. Untersuchungen zu ihren lehnsrechtlichen und kirchenpolitischen Beziehungen (Studien und Quellen zur Welt Kaiser Friedrichs II., vol. 1), Cologne and Vienna 1972, esp. pp. 247-251. See the texts of the bilateral treaty in MGH Const. I, no. 413 (p. 588f.) and no. 414 (p. 590f.) as well as the critical edition of the papal privilege by H. HOFFMANN, Langobarden, Normannen, Päpste. Zum Legitimitätsproblem in Unteritalien: Quellen u. Forschungen aus ital. Archiven u. Bibliotheken 58 (1978) 137-180, pp. 178-180, no. 3.

[83] FRIEDLÄNDER, Legaten, pp. 56-58, esp. p. 56 n. 44 and p. 57 n. 46, already noted a discrepancy between the date which was given by L. WEILAND, MGH Const. I, p. 592, no. 415, and the dates which fit in with Albinus' absence from the curia. See also P. KEHR, Die Belehnungen der süditalienischen Normannenfürsten durch die Päpste (1059-1192) (Abhandlungen d. Akademie der Wissenschaften Berlin, 1934, no. 1), 49f.

[84] MGH Const. I, pp. 591f., no. 415. Cf. KEHR, Italia Pontificia VIII, Berlin 1935, 55, no. 218. For the Rotuli of Cluny see now in addition to J. HUILLARD-BRÉHOLLES, Examen des chartes de l'Eglise romaine contenues dans les rouleaux dits Rouleaux de Cluny, in Notices et extraits des manuscrits, XXI, Paris 1865, 267-363; G. BATTELLI, I transunti di Lione del 1245: Mitteilungen des Instituts f. österreichische Geschichtsforschung 62 (1954) 336-364, reprinted in G. BATTELLI, Scritti scelti. Codici, Documenti, Archivi, Rome 1975, 173-201, here p. 187, Transunto III (15), no. 5. As KEHR noted, William's oath is transmitted without a date (Belehnungen, p. 49). See also DEÉR, Papsttum und Normannen, pp. 253f.

[85] JL 16375: KEHR, Italia Pontificia VIII, no. 222 (1188), p. 56; W. HOLTZMANN, Kanonistische Ergänzungen zu Italia Pontificia: Quellen und Forschungen aus italien. Archiven und Bibliotheken 38 (1958) 67-175, here p. 123 no. 159. An abbreviated text of the letter became part of the Decretals of Pope Gregory IX, 2.24.14. In his edition of the Decretals, AE. FRIEDBERG reconstituted a fuller text on the basis of the Collectio Lucensis. See S. KUTTNER, Repertorium der Kanonistik (Studi e Testi, 71), Vatican City 1937, 306, and the full description and analysis in C. R. CHENEY and MARY G. CHENEY, Studies in the collections of twelfth-century decretals: From the papers of the late Walther Holtzmann (Monumenta Iuris Canonici, series B, vol. 3), Vatican City 1979, 243-271, here p. 256 no. 2. For other twelfth-century decretal collections with the letter JL 16375 see the index ibid., p. 328. The date for the letter is found in the Collectio Remensis, c. 14 (ibid., pp. 279-283, p. 281, c. 14) as pointed out by KUTTNER, Repertorium, p. 307. See also the over-all discussions of the legation in FRIEDLÄNDER, Legaten, pp. 56-58; KEHR, Belehnungen, pp. 49-50; DEÉR, Papsttum und Normannen,

out that the efforts of the cardinals were successful, some concessions to the king notwithstanding. What was achieved was a reconfirmation of the Treaty of Benevento, that is, the papal feudal suzerainty over the Norman Kingdom was once again effectively recognized [86].

Secondary literature usually cites as a further instance for the activity of Albinus as papal legate his participation in the papal adjudication of litigation that had arisen between the bishop and the chapter of the cathedral of Spoleto [87]. The only source for such a mission is the document in which Pope Clement III confirmed the decision of the judges delegate, bishops Gentilis of Osimo and Boniface of Narni, whom Albinus had entrusted with the settlement of the quarrel [88]. Albinus had done so, according to Pope Clement III, *cum esset uicarius* [89]. He was not a legate, therefore, when he intervened in Spoleto. We do not even know whether he visited Spoleto at that time, for the meaning of *vicarius pape* is poorly understood [90].

A further reference to Albinus as *vicarius pape* dates from what was possibly his second embassy to the Norman Kingdom of Sicily. At the unexpected death of King William II without direct heirs on November 18, 1189, several candidates pursued their claims to

pp. 253-255 and pp. 267-275 with the appendix referring to n. 1150. Some disagreements with Deér's conclusions were registered by H. HOFFMANN, *Langobarden* (see n. 32 above). The dissertation by VERHEIN, *Lehen und Feudalemphyteuse*, which is quoted by Deér was unavailable.

[86] See also FRIEDLÄNDER, *Legaten*, pp. 122f. The privilege of 1156, but not a copy of the oath of William II of 1188 is found among the series of documents which constitute books 10 and 11 of codex *Ottob. lat.* 3057 = 10.62, in the analysis of FABRE-DUCHESNE (*LC* II, p. 96).

[87] Recently, for instance, V. PFAFF, *Die Kardinäle unter Papst Coelestin III.*: Zeitschrift der Savigny-Stiftung f. Rechtsgesch., Kan. Abt. 41 (1955) 84 and MELVILLE, in *Series episcoporum* (as in n. 1 above), p. 20: « ... Inter a. 1187 exeuntem et a. 1188 ineuntem Clementis (III) Spoletium ivit ... »

[88] KEHR, *Italia Pontificia* IV, p. 10, no. *5 and no. 6 (cf. also p. 8, nos. *13 and 14) as well as P. KEHR, *Nachträge zu den Papsturkunden Italiens*, I: Nachrichten der Ges. d. Wissenschaften zu Göttingen (1905) 371f., no 41: « ... Eapropter ... sententiam, quam uenerabiles fratres nostri G. Auximanus et B. Narniensis episcopi super controuersia ... de auctoritate dilecti filii nostri Al. tit. sancte Crucis in Iherusalem presbiteri cardinalis, qui eis commisit negotium decidendum cum esset uicarius, promulgarunt ... auctoritate apostolica confirmamus ». The decision of the bishops is still preserved in the archives of the cathedral chapter of Spoleto, but I was unable to locate the document during a brief visit to the Arch. Capitolare despite the gracious assistance of Don Falcinelli. The confirmation of Pope Clement III (no. 6) is dated March 7, 1189. Under no. *5 the approximate date 1187/88 is given.

[89] See the preceding note.

[90] In the later thirteenth century the office of papal vicar evolved into the office that was eventually defined in the sixteenth century as that of the *Cardinalis Vicarius Urbis*, who represented a pontiff in the city. No such general definition can be attempted for the earlier period. See K. EUBEL, *Series vicariorum Urbis a. 1200-1558*: Römische Quartalschrift 8 (1894) 485-491, esp. p. 486, where the distinction between a legate *a latere* and the *vicarius pape* is emphasized; W. M. PLÖCHL, *Geschichte des Kirchenrechts*, II, Vienne and Munich 1955, 75. As will be seen, we possess additional references to Albinus as *vicarius pape*. Three references to the office under Pope Alexander III (1159-1181) have come to my attention. See BRIXIUS, *Kardinalskollegium*, pp. 55 (no. 13), 60 (no. 12), and 57 (no. VI/1) with further references. Cf. also PFAFF, *Clemens III.* (as in n. 71 above), p. 262 n. 9 and p. 263 n. 12.

the crown of Sicily, among them Constance of Sicily, daughter of Roger II and aunt of William II as well as wife of King Henry VI, Count Roger of Andria, and Count Tancred of Lecce[91]. In the end it was Tancred who was crowned by Archbishop Walter of Palermo in January 1190 as successor to William II. In the mid-nineteenth century Toeche, who assumed that Pope Clement III had actively furthered the candidacy of Tancred, suggested that Albinus may have served as legate late in 1189/90, a statement which is usually repeated without Toeche's qualifiers[92]. But no evidence for such an embassy exists until perhaps the summer of 1191 when Albinus is mentioned in a privilege of King Tancred of Sicily for the city of Gaeta. The king referred to the intercession of « Albinus, venerable bishop of Albano, vicar of the Lord Pope, and his [Tancred's] dearest friend », when he remitted the delivery of one of the two armed galleons which the city of Gaeta customarily owed to its lord[93]. It would appear that direct negotiations between the curia and Tancred were perhaps not taken up until after the death of Pope Clement III[94], under his successor Celestine III (1191-1198). Albinus is a very likely intermediary, and his intercession on behalf of Gaeta probably implies his presence in July 1191 at Messina. At the very least the privilege for the city of Gaeta is definite evidence for contact between Albinus, *vicarius pape*, and King Tancred in the summer of 1191. Since the signature of the cardinal of Albano is not found on two privileges which were issued between July 6 and July 26, 1191, both dated July 24, a brief visit to Messina, where the privilege of Tancred was issued, is a distinct possibility[95].

In the privilege for Gaeta King Tancred had referred to Albinus

---

[91] HALLER, *Heinrich VI. und die römische Kirche* (as in n. 67 above), pp. 545ff.; ZERBI, *Papato, Impero* (see n. 67 above), pp. 53-62; PFAFF, *Clemens III.*, pp. 277f.

[92] TOECHE, *Kaiser Heinrich VI.* (see n. 67 above), pp. 144f., n. 3; MELVILLE, in *Series episcoporum*, p. 20 and n. 288 is the most recent author to mention an embassy for 1190.

[93] KEHR, *Italia Pontificia* VIII, p. 57 no. *230 and *ibid.*, p. 84 no. 19. The text is most accessible in TOECHE, *Kaiser Heinrich VI.*, pp. 608ff., esp. p. 610: « Concedimus quoque ad preces et intuitum Albini, venerabilis Albanensis episcopi, domini pape vicarii, karissimi amici nostri, civitati Gaiete, ut de duabus galeis, quas soliti estis armare non cogamini armare nisi unam galeam tantum ad mittendum eam in servitium nostrum ... » For the possibility that Albinus was a native of Gaeta see above p. 20. In the forthcoming edition of the records of King Tancred and William III of Sicily by H. Zielinski the privilege for Gaeta will be found under no. 18. See ZIELINSKI, *Zu den Urkunden der beiden letzten Normannenkönige Siziliens, Tankreds und Wilhelms III. (1190-1194)*: Deutsches Archiv 36 (1980) 433-486, with a detailed bibliography. Here relevant is table 1, p. 478, with references to P. F. PALUMBO, *Gli atti di Tancredi e di Guglielmo III di Sicilia*: Rivista Storica del Mezzogiorno 2 (1967) 104-152, p. 128f. no. 16.

[94] After March 20, 1191, perhaps on April 10, 1191. See PFAFF, *Clemens III.*, p. 278.

[95] PFAFF, *Die Kardinäle unter Papst Coelestin III.* (see n. 87 above), pp. 338-339, nos. 19 and 20. Cf. also V. PFAFF, *Der Liber Censuum von 1192*: Vierteljahrschrift f. Sozial- und Wirtschaftsgeschichte 44 (1957) 78-96; 105-120; 220-242; 325-351, here p. 328, no. 556. The privilege for Grandmont is missing in Albinus' *Liber Censuum*.

as *vicarius pape* although, unfortunately, the title is unaccompanied by any explanation. No such explicit reference to the title of Albinus is found during the subsequent negotiations between Pope Celestine III and Tancred in the early summer of the following year. They were conducted jointly by Albinus and Cardinal Deacon Gregory of S. Maria in Aquiro, and it seems appropriate to describe both of them as legates. On April 15, 1191, Henry VI had been crowned emperor[96], but his attempts to conquer the Kingdom of Sicily failed. Worse, his empress, Constance of Sicily, was captured by Tancred of Lecce, and illness forced Henry VI to withdraw to Germany. Under these circumstances, Pope Celestine III finally recognized Tancred as the legitimate heir of William II in return for considerable concessions. This was the setting for the legation of Albinus and Gregory in 1192. The result of what was for Albinus either the second or the third visit to Sicily as papal representative, was the privilege of Gravina, dated June 1192[97].

In addition to the privilege for Celestine III, the formula of Tancred's oath of fealty has been preserved, together with a written promise of King Tancred concerning future homage by himself and his heirs to the pontiff and his canonical successors[98]. These connected documents are now dated July 1192 at Alba Fucente, where Cardinals Albinus and Gregory met King Tancred and accepted his homage in the place of Pope Celestine who had been prevented from coming[99]. It is usually assumed, based on the text of Tancred's promise of fidelity[100], that Albinus and Gregory of Aquiro had returned to the curia in Rome between June and July 1192 after they had obtained the privilege of Gravina, but no real evidence exists for such an assumption, and it has to remain uncertain, therefore, whether the meetings at Gravina and Alba Fucente occurred during a single or during two separate legations[101].

---

[96] HALLER, *Heinrich VI. und die römische Kirche* (see n. 67 above), esp. 552-564.
[97] MGH *Const.* I, no. 417, pp. 593f., and no. 25 of H. ZIELINSKI's edition (see n. 93 above); KEHR, *Italia Pontificia* VIII, no. 235, p. 58; BATTELLI, *Transunti di Lione* (see n. 84 above), p. 187, Transunto IIII (15), no. 2. The significance and the resulting gains for the papacy, for which Albinus certainly deserves at least partial credit, are fully discussed by DEÉR, *Papsttum und Normannen* (see n. 82 above), pp. 260f.; see also KEHR, *Belehnungen* (as in n. 83 above), pp. 51f. and FRIEDLÄNDER, *Die päpstlichen Legaten* (see n. 81 above), pp. 78f.
[98] For the oath see MGH *Const.* I, no. 416, pp. 592f.; BATTELLI, *I transunti di Lione*, p. 187, Transunto III (15) no. 4; KEHR, *Italia Pontificia* VIII, no. 234, p. 58. For the promise, MGH *Const.* I, no. 418, pp. 594f.; BATTELLI, Transunto III (15) no. 3; KEHR, *Italia Pontificia* VIII, no. 236, p. 59.
[99] H. ZIELINSKI, *Zu den Urkunden der beiden letzten Normannenkönige* (see n. 93 above), p. 480 under no. 26. See also the two preceding notes.
[100] 'Fidelity' is used in this document as a synonym for homage.
[101] The last privilege from before their embassy with the signatures of Albinus and Gregory of Aquiro is JL 17619, dated May 23, 1192; their first signatures upon their return to Rome are found under JL 16920 of August 3, 1192. See PFAFF, *Die Kardinäle unter Coelestin III.*, p. 344 no. 65, and p. 346 no. 81.

32

At Alba Fucente Albinus and Gregory as legates stood in for an absent pontiff, a feature that eventually was to characterize the office of *vicarius urbis* during papal absences from Rome. Before the time of Innocent III (1198-1216) the duties of the *vicarius* apparently were not limited to the city[102]. The career of Albinus seems to illustrate that a *vicarius* could stand in for the pope whenever and wherever the pontiff asked him to take his place. As mentioned earlier, Albinus was given the title on two occasions, once in connection with Spoleto, and once by King Tancred. There are three additional references to Albinus as papal vicar. The first two are connected. Geoffrey of Auxerre, the secretary of Bernard of Clairvaux[103], sent two letters to Albinus with the address: *Amantissimo patri et domino .A., dei gratia Albanensi episcopo, domini pape uicario.* Both are found in codex *Ottob. lat.* 3057[104]. The third piece of evidence is a dedicatory preface to a short treatise, *Liber de dulia et latria*, which is addressed by its author, Master Michael, to Albinus as cardinal of Albano and *vicarius pape*, because — Magister Michael wrote — Albinus had been charged with the office of preaching, and he might on occasion consider it useful to pass on to the Romans some of the sentences which he had collected[105].

It is not clear, of course, whether the office of preaching to the Romans had anything to do with the title *vicarius pape*. But Master Michael was a papal notary, at least for a time, and was thus familiar with the curia. A connection between the title and the office which are both mentioned is, therefore, at least conceivable. The remark by Master Michael, at any rate, helps to explain Albinus' interest in sermons and proverbs, or clever sayings, which take up

---

[102] Cf. n. 90 above.

[103] For Geoffrey see N. M. HÄRING, *The Writings Against Gilbert of Poitiers by Geoffrey of Auxerre*: Analecta Cisterciensia 22 (1966) 1-83; J. LECLERCQ, *Les écrits de Geoffrey d'Auxerre*: Revue Bénédictine 62 (1952) 274-291; IDEM, *Saint Bernard et ses sécrétaires*: Revue Bénédictine 61 (1951) 208-229.

[104] Together with the *Libellus* of Geoffrey. Fols. 34vb-37va and fols. 37va-42vb. See the appendix for a further discussion.

[105] N. M. HÄRING, «*Liber de dulia et latria*» *of Master Michael, Papal Notary*: Mediaeval Studies 33 (1971) 188-200, p. 196: «Incipit prologus libri Magistri Michaelis, notarii domini pape, de dulia et latria. Reuerendo patri et domino Albino, Albanensi episcopo, domini pape uicario ... Nuper ab officio notandi uacans in Sacro Triduo Septimane penose quedam de latria et dulia que tempori et loco necessaria occurrunt (et) in locis multis legi possunt que respersa sub quodam compendio colligere studui et uobis quibus datum est offitium predicandi si qua hic utilia uideritis ea tempore opportuno Romanis ciuibus et aliis intimetis ...» Master Michael's brief collection is closely related to parts of the sentence collection of Albinus, so closely, in fact, that it is difficult to believe that. as Master Michael claims, he collected the material himself — presumably meaning that he himself made the excerpts from the works of the Fathers. Albinus claims in the preface only that he reproduces in part what he has heard in the schools, and in part what he had collected himself for the purposes of emendation. HÄRING, p. 194, points out that «the texts are quoted much more accurately by Albinus», although he is willing to take Master Michael's word for the originality of the little work. Hopefully, the analysis of the sentence collection of Albinus which I plan will set the record straight.

so much space in his digest [106]. In its preface Albinus included the sermons among the material of which he says that he collected it in his youth. The sermon collection, therefore, predates his stay in Rome, but it would be unreasonable to suppose that he did not make use of the relevant material in the scholarly notes which he had taken with him to Rome, and to which he continued to add [107].

Yet a little more light is shed on Cardinal Albinus in two letters of Pope Innocent III. As this pontiff noted in a letter of perhaps 1194, the cardinal had decided an appeal by the archbishop of Milan against a decision by a judge delegate (the bishop of Verona) in favor of the judge delegate. In the second epistle, Pope Innocent III mentioned that Albinus consecrated Bishop Daniel of Ross (ca. 1195/ 96) in the stead of Pope Celestine III [108].

When everything is considered, the few facts which have emerged regarding the career of Albinus at the curia can be summarized very briefly. He served as legate and *vicarius pape*, was particularly charged with preaching duties in Rome, and if one may speak of a Sicilian party among the college of cardinals, he would be found among its members. Albinus certainly spared no effort to serve the interests of the papacy, witness the Sicilian negotiations both with King William II and King Tancred as well as the collection of documents in books ten and eleven of his digest [109]. He was anxious to uphold and strengthen the dignity of the papacy as well as of the Roman Church in general. The following dates could be obtained, omitting references to his signatures:

1182 (Dec.)	Cardinal deacon of S. Maria Nuova
1185 (March)	Cardinal priest of S. Croce in Gerusalemme
1186 (June)	at Verona
1188 (June/July)	Legate at Palermo
1187/1188	*vicarius pape*, entrusted with the Spoleto quarrel
1189 (May)	Cardinal bishop of Albano
between 1191 and 1194	Auditor in the Narni quarrel
1191 (July)	*vicarius pape*; embassy to Messina?
1192 (June)	Legate at Gravina
(July)	Legate at Alba Fucente
1194 *ca.*	decides appeal by the archbishop of Milan
1196 *ca.*	consecration of Bishop Daniel of Ross
1196 (May)	present at the consecration of S. Lorenzo in Lucina
1196 (July 9)	last signature

---

[106] MS *Ottob. lat.* 3057, fols. 82ra-122va.

[107] See the preface LC II, 88a-b.

[108] O. HAGENEDER et al. edd., *Die Register Innocenz' III.*, I: *1. Pontifikatsjahr*, Graz 1964, no. 37, pp. 51-61, here pp. 52f., and no. 364, pp. 548-551, here pp. 548f. Cf. P. J. DUNNING, *Pope Innocent III and the Ross Election Controversy*: The Irish Theological Quarterly 26 (1959) 346-359.

[109] See R. HOLTZMANN, *Der Kaiser als Marschall der Papstes* (Schriften der Strassburger Wissenschaftl. Gesellschaft in Heidelberg, Neue Folge 8), Berlin-Leipzig 1928, p. 38 n. 1 and Exkurs, pp. 44-49. I am grateful to M. Bertram for this reference.

CONTENT AND DESCRIPTION OF MS OTTOB. LAT. 3057

The *Digesta pauperis scolaris Albini* are the cardinal's most enduring and today also his most interesting legacy, whether we may regard the manuscript as a textbook, as Albinus seems to indicate at one time in his preface, or whether it is more properly called a florilegium reflecting his scholarly, professional, and religious interests. A fuller discussion of the content of codex *Ottob. lat.* 3057 and an analysis of the sources of Albinus will be given in a future paper, but the following brief indications of the content and the codicological and palaeographical analysis will provide the framework for the discussion of the date of the miscellaneous collection.

As mentioned in passing earlier, Albinus himself provided a guide to the content of his digest of « little flowers from many meadows » [110]. Originally Albinus began with many notes on « what he had heard, of what had been compiled by others, and with excerpts from various books which are also not easily distinguished in schools » [111]. He kept these notes on loose, 'sybilline' leaves, but for fear that they might be lost, he transcribed them eventually into quaternions so that his collection might serve as aid and inspiration to poor scholars, whose paths *vel ad proverbium, vel ad sententiam, vel ad proloquium, vel ad dictamen* [112] the collection was to prepare.

---

[110] The different senses of the word 'flosculus' are all applicable, yet another proof for the care and skill with which the preface was written. Cf. n. 34 above for the flower topos. The use of the diminutive enables Albinus to combine it with the humility topos.

[111] *LC* II, 88a.

[112] *LC* II, 88a. Despite its multiple connotations, the word 'sententia' here seems to be a clear reference to the *lectura divina* in the schools and the attendant compilation of sentence collections. See, in general, M. PH. HUBERT, *Einige Aspekte des philosophischen Lateins im 12. und 13. Jahrhundert*, transl. into German in *Mittellateinische Philologie*, ed. A. ÖNNERFORS (Wege der Forschung, 292), Darmstadt 1975, 283-312, from the original: Revue des études latines 27 (1949) 211-233; for 'sententia' see *ibid.*, p. 303; G. PARÉ, A. BRUNET, P. TREMBLAY, *La renaissance du XIIe siècle. Les écoles et l'enseignement*, Paris and Ottawa 1933, 8, n. 1; B. SMALLEY, *The Study of the Bible in the Middle Ages*, Notre Dame, Indiana 1964, an invaluable introduction; V. I. J. FLINT, *The « School of Laon » — A Reconsideration*: Recherches de théologie ancienne et médiévale 43 (1976) 89-100, here esp. 93-97 with bibliography; F. STEGMÜLLER, *Repertorium Commentariorum in Sententias Petri Lombardi*, I, Würzburg 1947, p. IX; P. FOURNIER, G. LE BRAS, *Histoire des collections canoniques en Occident*, II, Paris 1932 (repr. Aalen 1972), 326-352; CURTIUS, *Europäische Literatur* (see n. 17 above), pp. 65ff. Although the theological sentence literature originated in France, it immediately influenced Italy. See HASKINS, *Early Artes dictandi* (see n. 17 above), pp. 177, 191f. Like 'sententia', 'proloquium' can be used in a juridical sense in both classical and medieval Latin, as a synonym for prologue, or more generally as meaning 'statement'. Niermeyer's definition, 'charge d'avoué', attorneyship, approaches more closely 'public speaking'. Albinus seems to have used 'proloquium' to describe the rhetorical components of his manuscript other than the sections pertaining to 'dictamen' (the art of prose writing), referring perhaps to the preface and the sermons. For 'proverbium' see H. LAUSBERG, *Handbuch der literarischen Rhetorik (nebst) Registerband*, II, München 1960, pp. 789 and 652: « auf konkrete Fälle anwendbarer

Albinus added to this compilation with much labor « some necessary canons which I gathered from the works of various Church Fathers which are not accessible to all and which are not included in Gratian's edition », and « some little sermons, some exordia, which I invented from all of these and which are not stolen ... »[113]. This, Albinus explains further, occurred during his youth. Later he was called to Rome and from that time on, that is, from the time of Lucius III, « who ordained me, unworthy though I am, deacon in the second and priest in the fourth year of his pontificate, I took care to add to the very same book whenever and wherever I could what I knew or discovered to belong to the rights of St. Peter, either from books of antiquities or from what I myself heard and saw »[114]. He concludes this description of the content with a two-part exhortation that was to strengthen the readers' faith and to protect them from errors. The *Digesta* of Albinus are divided into eleven books, but this division does not always coincide with the content of a particular section. The books carry no titles, and the chapters found in each are unnumbered[115].

Biblioteca Apostolica Vaticana, codex Ottob. lat. 3057, content:

fol. 1ra: « Incipiunt eglogar(um) digesta pauperis scolaris Albini »,
                   inscr.

fol. 1ra-2va   *Inc.*: « Cum ante meam ... »   Preface
                   expl.: « ... propter quem adorat »[116].

Weisheitsspruch », a particularly apt description, for what Albinus apparently meant by it are the short sayings with which he interspersed his ' sententia ' (e.g. *Ottob. lat.* 3057, fol. 14v, 17r, 20, 22v). According to LANGLOIS, *Maître Bernard* (as in n. 17 above), p. 227, Bernard de Meung used the word in the sense of ' exordium '. This may also apply to Albinus, who mentions ' proverbia ' as well as ' initia ' (*LC* II, 88b).

[113] *LC* II, 88a: « Adiuncxi quosdam necessarios canones quos de diversis Patrum opusculis non omnibus perviis [MS preuiis, *fol. 1va*], nec in editione Gratiani redactis cum labore collegi. Quosdam quoque sermunculos et sermones, quedam initia de invento non de furto compositos ex cunctis istis compegi ... » Cf. above, n. 59. The close connection between canon law and theology is well known. See J. DE GHEL-LINCK, *Le mouvement théologique du XIIe siècle*, Paris 1914, 277ff.; FOURNIER, LE BRAS, *Histoire des collections canoniques* II, pp. 314-333; S. KUTTNER, *Zur Frage der theologischen Vorlagen Gratians*: Zeitschrift der Savigny-Stiftung f. Rechtsgeschichte, Kan. Abteilung 23 (1943) 243-268; C. MUNIER, *Les sources patristiques du droit de l'Eglise du VIIIe au XIIIe siècle*, Mulhouse 1957; A. M. LANDGRAF, *Diritto canonico e teologia nel secolo XII*: Studia Gratiana 1 (1953) 371-413.

[114] See pp. 24-25 above. V. PFAFF, *Die Kardinäle unter Papst Coelestin III.*: Zeitschrift d. Savigny-Stiftung, Kan. Abt. 41 (1955) 84, wrote: « Vor seiner Erhebung in das Kardinalat schon in päpstl. Diensten », without indicating a source. The preface is the only evidence for Albinus' coming to Rome, and all that can be said, therefore, is that Albinus was made a cardinal deacon by Lucius III at the first opportunity.

[115] FABRE and DUCHESNE added chapter number in their edition of books 10 and 11.

[116] Published by FABRE-DUCHESNE, *LC* II, 87-89 in part. The preface strictly speaking ends already with: « ... qui me indignum diaconum ordinavit anno IIo et sacerdotem quarto anno sui pontificatus » = *LC* II, 88b. The following passage: « Diversarum igitur rerum ... studium id decernat » (*LC* II, 88b-89b end) is largely an exhortation to the reader for his spiritual benefit, which Albinus based on PETER LOMBARD,

36

fol. 2va 34vb (books 1, 2, and 3 *partim*)	*Inc.*: « His auctoritatibus premisse inuestigationis absolutio explicatur. Que autem deinceps secuntur sentecata sunt et apophoreta blacterantis et luscitantis adunatoris huius fasciculi. Augustinus de ciuitate dei libro VIII. Illud quod ab hominibus ... » *expl.*: « ... et tamen ut aliquid exinde exeat non optinetur » [117].	Collection of *sententia* and *prouerbia*
fol. 34vb-36vb (book 3)	*Inscr.*: « Amantissimo patri et domino .A. dei gratia Albanensi episcopo, domini pape uicario, frater Gaufridus de Claraualle minimum [*cod.* miniṁ] id quod est ». *inc.*: « Iniunxerat uestra paternitas ... » *expl.*: « ... quare sint condempnata ».	Letter I of Geoffrey of Auxerre to Albinus (see Appendix)
fol. 36vb-37va (book 3)	*Inscr.*: « Amantissimo domino et patri .A. dei gratia Albanensi episcopo et domini pape uicario, frater Gaufridus de Claraualle minimum id quod est ». *inc.*: « Quia semel cepi ... » *expl.*: « ... credi debeat uel doceri ».	Letter II of Geoffrey of Auxerre to Albinus (see Appendix)
fol. 37va-42vb (book 4)	*Inc.*: « Quatuor in his scedulis capitula ... » *expl.*: « ... sed in filio ».	Geoffrey of Auxerre, treatise against Gilbert of Porrée [118]
fol. 43ra-43va (book 5)	*Inc.*: « Hec sunt nomina septuaginta duorum discipulorum ... » *expl.*: « ... .LXXII. et alibi. .LXX. solummodo ».	
fol. 43va-60rb (book 5)	*Inscr.*: « Hec sunt excerpta de Ambrosio super beati inmaculati de illuminatione mentis ». *inc.*: « Osculatur nos uerbum dei ... » *expl.*: « ... postquam mortis passus est Christus ».	Ambrose, *Expositio de psalmo 118* [119], excerpts

Libri quatuor sententiarum, book 1, d. 1, c. 2. Albinus referred to his source in the sentence which follows immediately upon the section which was published by Fabre-Duchesne. The editors probably considered it the inscription for the following, second exhortation: « Hec sunt scripta magistri Petri usque ad primum capitulum. Preterea inuestigari oportet ... cuius scabellum est propter quem adorat » (fol. 2ra-2va). Some variants apart, this text corresponds to Peter Lombard, *Libri quatuor sententiarum: Liber III et IV*, Quaracchi ²1916, book 3, d. 9, *cap. unicum* (pp. 591-593). This passage should have been included by the editors as part of the exhortatory conclusion of the preface.

[117] Comments by the author cease with the end of book 2 (fol. 28vb). However, the first folios of book 3, fol. 28vb-34vb, otherwise do not differ in content from books 1 and 2, although the excerpts from the Fathers tend to be lengthier, and although on fol. 34r-v room is given to some explanations of the extraordinary and of relics. No *explicit* marks the end of the sentence collection.

[118] See n. 103 and the Appendix below.

[119] E. Dekkers, *Clavis Patrum Latinorum*, Bruges [1955], no. 141.

fol. 60rb-64va (book 6)	*Inscr.*: « Excerpta de doctrina sancti Basilii ». *inc.*: « Siquid unusquisque deesse sibi ad scientiam putat ... » *expl.*: « ... siue in cogitatione ».	Basil the Great, excerpts from the Rule, translation Rufinus [120]
fol. 64va-69va (book 6)	*Inscr.*: « De doctrina patrum » *inc.*: « Sicut auis cubans ... » *expl.*: « ... sibi nichil reseruauit ».	
fol. 69va-81vb (book 6)	*Inscr.*: « Liber de collatione patrum ad theoriam ». *inc.*: « Omnes artes ac discipline ... » *expl.*: « ... uitam possidebit eter- nam ».	Johan Cassian, *Conlationes*, excerpts [121]
fol. 82ra-122va (books 7, 8)	*Inc.*: « Vincenti dabo edere ... » *expl.*: « ... spiritus sanctus ut non di-| » [123]	Anonymous sermons [122]
fol. 123ra-126vb (book 9)	*Inc.*: « Domine, quinque talenta ... » *expl.*: « ... naturam intelligimus. Ex- plicit ».	Theobald of Langres, *De quatuor modis qui- bus significationes nu- merorum aperiuntur* [124]

---

[120] J. QUASTEN, *Patrology*, III, Utrecht and Westminster 1960, 212-214; for Rufinus see B. ALTANER, *Patrologie*, 5th rev. ed., Freiburg 1958, 353f.

[121] DEKKERS, *Clavis*, no. 512.

[122] Less than half the sermons could be identified so far, and only thanks to the *Incipit* collection of HAUREAU and the files at the Institut de Recherche et d'Histoire de Texte, Paris. I am grateful for the assistance by the members of the Institut. All of the identified sermons are of French origin. Because of the relatively early date of the sermons, J. B. SCHNEYER's *Repertorium der lateinischen Sermones des Mittelalters* has not proven helpful.

[123] The last (?) sermon ends incomplete at the foot of col. a of fol. 122v. Fol. 122vb has been left blank to accommodate the remaining text.

[124] See H. MEYER, *Die Zahlenallegorese im Mittelalter. Methode und Gebrauch* (Münstersche Mittelalter-Schriften, 25), Munich 1975, 49-50 and 52-53; *Histoire littéraire de la France*, XIV, Paris 1817, 200-205, s.v. ' Guillaume, abbé d'Auberive '; J. LECLERCQ, *L'arithmétique de Guillaume d'Auberive*, in IDEM, *Analecta Monastica*, Première série (Studia Anselmiana, 20), Vatican City 1948, 181-204; G. BEAUJOUAN, *Le symbolisme des nombres à l'époque romane*: Cahiers de civilisation médiévale 4 (1961) 159-169, here pp. 166-168. Meyer characterized the sophisticated, rare treatise as « Mischform zwischen einer Anleitung zur Bibelexegese und einer Abhandlung über arithmetische Fragen ». Theobald's treatise is without attribution in MS *Ottob. lat.* 3057. Two other MSS of the work are known: Paris, *BN lat.* 2583, fol. 25r-35v, and Luxembourg MS 60, both younger than *Ottob.* G. Beaujouan and H. Meyer analyzed the work on the basis of the Paris MS, the Luxembourg copy was used by J. Leclercq. The comparison between the Vatican and the Paris MS revealed only minor variants. The writings of Theobald and William of Auberive are closely related. William was abbot of Auberive from 1165 to 1186. Nothing is known about the life of Theobald, but on the basis of *Ottob. lat.* 3057 we have to assume that they were contemporaries of each other as well as of Albinus. The question of dependence of William on Theobald or vice versa has to remain open for the time being. Both their works are still unedited. It is unfortunately impossible to date their treatises more accurately than s. 12, second half. William may have been at work before he became abbot.

fol. 127ra-160vb   *Inscr.*: « Incipiunt excerta politici
(books 10, 11)   a presbitero Benedicto compositi
                    de ordinibus Romanis et dignitati-
                    bus urbis et sacri palatii ».
                    Inc.: [H]ec sunt festiuitates ... »
                    expl.: « ... esse digesta » [125].

To summarize, books 1 - 3 (fols. 2va-34vb) contain a collection of sentences and *prouerbia*; the remainder of book 3 two letters by Geoffrey of Auxerre to Albinus, book 4 is entirely taken up by the treatise of Geoffrey against Gilbert of Porrée; book 5 contains excerpts from St. Ambrose; book 6 excepts from St. Basil and John Cassian; books 7 and 8 sermons; book 9 a mathematical treatise by Theobald of Langres; books 10 and 11 materials from the papal archives.

In the discussion of the date of the collection scholars have always insisted upon a definite distinction between books 1 through 9, and books 10 and 11. Codicology and palaeography were used to support this argument [126]. It is certainly correct that the content of books 10 and 11 differs from that of the preceding books, but as the following description will show, the assumed codicological and palaeographical differentiation can no longer be maintained. The final books 10 and 11 contain what is known as the *Liber Censuum* of Albinus, and new criteria which would assist to establish its date are desirable, especially since its relationship to the *Liber Censuum* of Cencius Savelli — known to have been compiled in 1192 — is not very clear [127].

Codex Ottob. lat. 3057, description [128]:

Little is known about the history of the manuscript, except that it was acquired by Cardinal Domenico Passionei (1682-1761) for 80 Lira in 1759 from the collection of Philipp Baron von Stosch (1691-1757), a German collector of coins and bibliophile who had made his home in Florence since 1731. Through Passionei, *bibliothecarius* of the Biblioteca Apostolica Vaticana since 1755, the codex came to the Biblioteca Ottoboniana and from there to the Vatican Library [129].

---

[125] For the composition of these final books see *LC* II, 90-137.

[126] GLANVELL, *Die Kanonessammlung des Kardinals Deusdedit* (see n. 2 above), p. XXXIX.

[127] See the bibliography for the *Liber Censuum* of Cencius in n. 2 above and esp. n. 3.

[128] Cf. the bibliography in nn. 2-4 above. For earlier descriptions of the codex see GLANVELL, *Kanonessammlung*, pp. XXXVII-XL; ANDRIEU, *Les Ordines romani* (as in n. 1 above), I, pp. 317-318; FABRE, *Etude sur le Liber Censuum* (as in n. 2 above), pp. 10-13, esp. p. 10, n. 2 with further bibliography; *LC* I (Introduction), p. 32; GALLETTI, *Memorie* (see n. 4 above), pp. 232-235.

[129] GALLETTI, *Memorie*, p. 232; GLANVELL, *Kanonessammlung*, p. XXXVII; see also G. MERCATI, *Note per la storia di alcune biblioteche Romane nei secoli XVI-XIX*

The usual identification of *Ottob. lat.* 3057 with the « liber qui dicitur Albinus » or « Cronica Albini » of the inventories of the papal archive of 1327 and 1339 is probably incorrect [130].

Parchment, modern white parchment binding with the arms of Pope Pius IX and underneath the arms of Cardinal Tosti, who became *bibliothecarius* in 1857, 160 folios, consisting of 19 quaternions of 8 fols. or 4 leaves each, and a final quinternion of 5 leaves or 10 fols. (fol. 151-160). One quaternion is incomplete (fol. 121r-126v). Two folios were cut out after fol. 122, what is now fol. 123 contains the beginning of book 9 with the treatise of Theobald of Langres [131]. The foliation is modern and therefore continues without interruption. Originally, the correct sequence of the quires was maintained through running titles at the top of the folios which indicate the number of the respective book. On the final folio of several quires traces of the number of a particular quire are still recognizable, or at least of the frame which surrounded them in the lower right corner [132].

The folios measure *ca.* 335 × 245 mm, and the text is written in 2 cols., measuring *ca.* 285 × 75 mm of written space each. Fols. 1-8 are ruled for 39 horizontal lines, the remainder of the codex for 51, rarely 50, lines. Three pairs of vertical lines are drawn to indicate the columns and to provide space for the initials. The verticals go across the whole length of the folio, the horizontals end irregularly

---

(Studi e Testi, 164), Vatican City 1952, 89-113:Sulla fine della Biblioteca e delle carte del Cardinale Passionei.

[130] F. EHRLE, *Historia Bibliothecae Romanorum Pontificum tum Bonifatianae tum Avenionensis*, I, Rome 1890, 23 (no. 2), and p. 105, no. 223, and n. 398; H. DENIFLE, *Inventar der Regesten und Archivalien vom Jahre 1339*: Archiv für Litteratur- u. Kirchengeschichte 2 (1886, facsimile repr. Graz s.d.), 1-105, here p. 102, and FABRE, *Etude sur le Liber Censuum*, p. 10 n. 2 with further references. Denifle is erroneously quoted for the *incipit* ' onum ' on fol. 2r. The *incipit* of *Ottob. lat.* 3057, fol. 2ra is indeed ' onum ', but according to both Ehrle and Denifle the 1339 inventory indicated ' omni ' as *incipit* for the second fol. of the codex which was taken from Assisi to Avignon and described in the inventories of 1327 and 1339. No other *incipit* or *explicit* given in the 1339 inventory (EHRLE, p. 23, and DENIFLE, p. 102) agrees with the corresponding words and syllables in MS *Ottob. lat.* 3057 either, and the tempting identification of the « liber qui dicitur Albinus » (1339 inventory) or « Cronica Albini » (1327 inventory) with the *Digesta* of Albinus in *Ottob. lat.* 3057 has to be rejected. The unlikely alternative would be to argue that the notaries faultily transcribed each of the four words from their codex, or to assume with F. Ehrle that the codex was defective. It is just possible that the *Cronica Albini* in the papal treasury corresponds to a Carolingian *Abbreviatio chronicae*, known as *Liber Albini magistri*, which by its name suggests some connection with Alcuin († 804), although the chronicle contained materials for the year 809. See B. BISCHOFF, *Eine Sammelhandschrift Walahfrid Strabos (Cod. Sangall. 878)*, repr. in: IDEM, *Mittelalterliche Studien* II, Stuttgart 1967, 34-51, here p. 43 with further references, and p. 47 n. 38 (MS not seen).

[131] The inner margin of fol. 124r still shows a small strip of parchment, the remnant of the other half of the original leaf that was cut out. It seems unlikely that any text was lost, for the text on fol. 122v ends in the middle of a word in col. a; fol. 122v, col. b, is left blank.

[132] The first quaternion ends on fol. 8v with the still clearly visible indication ' Q. 1 ' surrounded by a frame drawn with red ink. The remaining traces at the end of other quaternions show that these were executed in brown ink. See fols. 56v, 64v, 72v, 88v, 96v, 104v, 112v and 120v.

in the outer margins with the exception of the first and the last pair which were drawn across the margin like the verticals. In the first two quaternions (fol. 1 - 16) and on fols. 127-160 the leaves were ruled across the whole width, and prickings appear therefore only in the outer margins. From fol. 17 to fol. 126 each folio was ruled separately and prickings are found in both the inner and outer margins of each.

The carefully executed codex has red inscriptions on fols. 1r-16v, 43v, 44r, and 48r, as well as 127r-160v. Elsewhere inscriptions are lacking or were written with the brown/black ink of the text hand. Sometimes they were written in as indications for the rubricator, who did not complete his task. The red inscriptions on fols. 43v, 44r and 48r are written over erasures. Red initials are found throughout the codex. They are sometimes slightly flourished: on fol. 10v they are decorated with yellow. In general, all initials are simple, with relatively elaborate text initials only in the first and second quires (fols. 1-16) and in the invocations of the notarial instruments which are transcribed in books 10 and 11.

The text is divided into books, which do not always correspond to the division of the subject matter. From book 3 (fol. 28v) to book 8 (fol. 112r), the first initial of each book is executed in red with black decoration. The style of these initials is the same. Book 9 (fol. 123r) as we have it now, begins with an ordinary red text-initial, and only the running title indicates that book 9 has been reached. The initial beginning book 10 (fol. 127r) has not been executed, although space has been provided for it. The red inscription of the text begins with a flourished initial by the rubricator, in this case also the scribe of the text. The ascenders of *l, b, d,* and long *s* of the first line are elongated in the notarial style [133]. The first text-initial at the beginning of book 11 (fol. 146r) is red and slightly decorated, also in red. The initials of books 9, 10, and 11, therefore, differ from each other as well as from the more elaborate initials of the earlier books.

The color of the ink in the manuscript varies from light to dark brown, to black; the changes occur irregularly and do not coincide with the changes of hands. Marginal notes are found throughout the codex, ranging from entries by the text-hand or contemporary scribes to nineteenth-century annotations. The most frequent entries are cross-references to similar texts found in the first eight books of the compilation. It should be noted that these references do not include the material of books 9, 10, and 11, which is natural, considering the different nature of these texts. The red marginalia of books 10 and 11 often are brief regesta of the documents in the text.

---

[133] Elongated descenders are found earlier in the codex on fols. 10v, 21v, 22r, 36r, and on 71v in the last line.

TABLE I

1. MS *Ottob. lat.* 3057, fol. 11ra (ll. 7-17)
Hand C

2. MS *Ottob. lat.* 3057, fol. 129vb (ll. 19-28)
Hand C

TABLE II

1. MS *Ottob. lat.* 3057, fol. 72vb (ll. 32-42)
Hand D

2. MS *Ottob. lat.* 3057, fol. 15va (ll. 26-36)
Hand E

1. MS *Ottob. lat.* 3057, fol. 23ra (ll. 20-29)
Hand G

2. MS *Ottob. lat.* 3057, fol. 23rb (ll. 20-29)
Hand H

TABLE IV

1. MS *Ottob. lat.* 3057, fol. 120ra (ll. 41-50)
Hand D

2. MS *Ottob. lat.* 3057, fol. 120rb (ll. 41-50)
Hand I

The codex is well preserved, apart from wormholes in the first few and the final folios. Fols. 1 and 2 and the final folio have been repaired. The original red inscription of the codex (fol. 1ra) is now almost illegible. A nineteenth-century hand supplied in black ink: *Incipiunt gesta pauperis scolaris Albini* [134]. Beginning with fol. 146, the folios are scorched and some of them were considerably darkened, although the text remains legible. The manuscript is carefully written in book hand, a minuscule familiar from the late twelfth and early thirteenth century from Rome and southern Italy [135]. One or two of the hands with long and curved ascenders and descenders approach the notarial script found in the privileges. Fol. 2ra begins « onum », ends « etiam »; the penultimate fol. (159r) begins « nostro », ends « Gallicano viris clarissimis consulibus ».

It is difficult to differentiate book-hands of this period. In the following analysis the criteria which were established by F. Kempf proved most useful [136]. Accordingly, the hands are primarily distinguished on the basis of their technical aspects (minuscules, majuscules, capitals, abbrevations), and the over-all appearance of a script was used in second place. For each hand only those features will be mentioned which differentiate it from the other hands in the codex.

Hand A: 1ra - 10rb. A careful, neat hand; noticeable are the use of capitals and majuscules in the proper names of the preface, capital *L* and *S*, superscript *a* which looks like a small *u*, the flat ascender of uncial *d*, the abbreviation *-que*; there is a preference for long *s* [137].

---

[134] See ANDRIEU, *Les Ordines Romani* (as in n. 1 above), I, pp. 317f., n. for the correct inscription: « Incipit eglogar[um] digesta pauperis scolaris Albini ».

[135] The similarity of the hands found in MS *Ottob. lat.* 3057 to some of the hands of the scribes of the registers of Pope Innocent III is particularly noticeable. They are not identical, however. See the facsimile edition of the RNI by W. M. PEITZ, *Regestum domni Innocentii papae super negotio Romani Imperii* (Reg. Vat. 6), Riprodotto in fototipia a cura della Biblioteca Vaticana (Codices e Vaticanis selecti, vol. 16), Rome 1928, and the relevant tables in: *Specimina palaeographica ex Vaticani tabularii Romanorum Pontificum registris selecta*, introduction by H. DENIFLE with G. PALMIERI, Rome 1888. They should be consulted with F. KEMPF, *Die Register Innocenz III. Eine paläographisch-diplomatische Untersuchung* (Miscellanea Historiae Pontificiae, 9), Rome 1945. See further the facsimiles in S. H. THOMSON, *Latin Bookhands of the later middle Ages 1100-1500*, Cambridge 1969, table no. 61 (MS Cambridge, Fitzwilliam Museum, *McClean* 24), « early Italian Gothic », 1204, and table no. 60 (MS Paris, *BN lat.* 16528), Italy (Apulia), 1188. Instructive in the *Catalogo dei Manoscritti in scrittura latina datati o databili*, 1: *Bibl. Nazionale Centrale di Roma*, Tavole I, Turin 1971, are tables XXXVI, MS *Sess.* 51 (2079) fol. 202r, and XXXVII from the same codex, dated 1216-1226.

[136] KEMPF, *Die Register Innocenz III*, especially p. 24: « ... Daß wir uns für eine einzige Hand entschieden, dazu bestimmte uns der methodische Grundsatz, daß das allgemeine Schriftbild vor der tiefer eindringenden Analyse des Alphabetes und der Abkürzungen zurückzutreten hat ... »

[137] The decision, whether Hand A continued on fol. 9r, the new quire, or not, has been so difficult that I am still not entirely certain that Hand B does not begin

Hand B: 10rb - 10vb. Narrower and smaller, writing directly on the line, permitting descenders to protrude below; *-rum* abbreviation: both elements have the round neck of the numeral two; all capitals are quite distinct from those of hand A.

Hand C: 10vb - 11ra, 127ra - 139rb, 139va - 160vb (with the exception of fol. 132vb, fol. 139rb lower part, and the last lines on fol. 142vb). Superficially hardly distinguishable from B, but with definite characteristics of its own, *e.g.* the abbreviation for *enim*, *-bus* = *b* with a long open loop, like an elongated letter-height comma, attached at the top of the loop of the letter *b*; superscript *a* is a carefully written curial *a*; the use of uncial and minuscule *d*; the use of long *i* without dot at the end of words even if it is not double-*i*; in the case of double-*i* the second *i* may be long in the middle of words; especially characteristic is the lower loop of the letter *g*, showing at the left side a more or less pronounced angle, and the beautiful *-ur* abbreviation which is also used for *-er*; at times the letter *x* can be written like a left inclined *r*, the descender is added afterwards like a loop; majuscules and capitals in the text are fracefully decorated; the neck of majuscule *F* is curved upward to the right, the descender of majuscule *P* is curved to the left; Hand C is responsible for the red inscriptions and the marginal notes which are part of the text of the census book (see Table I, 1 and 2).

Hand D: 11rb - 15rb, 15vb - 22rb, 23v - 120rb (upper section). This beautiful and even hand transcribed the major part of the text although, at first sight, the hand seems to change; especially noticeable are the letter *g* and the relative absence of abbreviations; = above the word as abbreviation sign is not used; the abbreviation *con*, a curled numeral 9, has a very brief descender and is written on the line and has the same height as letters; the abbreviation *et* descends below the line and is most often initiated with a small dot on the line with a hairline leading to the wavy horizontal of the ' 7 '; the same abbreviation is used for *etiam*; quia-*r* [2] is not found; *-bus* = the letter *b* with superscript curl; the majuscules and capitals are often decorated with a wavy line; the capitals *B* and *P* are open at the top; capital *I* is decorated with a dot in the middle of the

---

until fol. 10rb. Careful weighing of the evidence eventually led me to the conclusion that the differences between fols. 8v and 9r are the result of the narrower ruling of the folio (for 51 lines instead of for 39 as on fols. 1-8v) and the tighter script. It did not only become shorter in order to fit the lines, but also narrower.

shaft which ends in a curve to the left below the line (see Tables II, 1 and IV, 1).

Hand E: fol. 15va [138]. A very curvaceous script with strongly clubbed ascenders turning to the right: *l, d, b*; the bottom loop of the letter *g* appears open, often with a long descender to the left, but it is actually closed with a hardly visible hairline; final *s*: the bottom loop is treated like a descender; the over-all impression is untidy (see Table II, 2).

Hand F: fol. 22rb. Unpractised impression, especially in the beginning; special features: the final *m* and short ascenders and descenders.

Hand G: fol. 22rb bottom - 22vb middle, 23ra. Most noticeable are the superscript *a*, the open lower loop of the letter *g*, and the opening of the *pro* abbreviation loop to the left (see Table III, 1).

Hand H: fol. 22vb lower part, fol. 23rb. Special features are the curved and relatively long descender of *et* and *etiam*; the abbreviation -*ur* = superscript 2, and the paragraph sign (see Table III, 2).

Hand I: 120rb - 126v. Most characteristic of the script is the shortening of ascenders and descenders which are not clubbed, resulting in a very square script (see Table IV, 2).

Hand J: fol. 139rb beginning a few lines from the top and in the margin, fol. 142vb at the end of the column. The script is so curved and elaborate that it is almost closer to a notarial than a book-hand; the outer margin is uneven, an extra line has been added at the foot of the column in order to fit in the text which is perhaps an addition.

The preceding description leads to the conclusion that not only books 10, 11, and to some extent book 9 do have features in common which they do not share with the major portion of the codex [139], but that the first quire differs from the remainder of the codex as well. It became clear at the same time that other characteristics such as the quality of the parchment, the running title (the indication of the number of a book at the top of the folios) and the change of hands are common to all 11 books. Scribe C, who transcribed most of books 10 and 11, also wrote a brief section of book 1. Leaving aside the argument that codex *Ottob. lat.* 3057 need not have been the only manuscript of the *Digesta* nor the first transcription of the notes of Albinus into a single codex — two possibilities that one cannot either

---

[138] The same hand is probably responsible for the red inscriptions on fol. 43v and 44r.

[139] Examples are the initials at the beginning of books, the marginalia, and the rubrics or inscriptions.

prove or disprove at the moment — one has to admit that codicological and palaeographical evidence no longer supports the thesis
that books 1 through 9 have nothing in common with books 10 and
11, that the former were transcribed in Albinus' youth, and the latter
after he had come to Rome, but before he became cardinal bishop
of Albano in May 1189. It is true, of course, that Albinus does not
refer to his elevation to the cardinal bishopric of Albano, but taken
by itself this omission does not suffice as dating criterion. It has
been seen earlier that Albinus referred to his elevation to the cardinalate without any particular emphasis almost in passing, in order
to explain to future generations the change in the nature of his collection. He tells us nothing about his career in Rome, or about the
pontiffs under whom he served: Lucius III (1181-1185), Urban III
(1185-1187), Gregory VIII (Oct.-Dec. 1187), Clement III (1187-1191), and
Celestine III (1191-1198). Only Lucius III is briefly mentioned in
connection with his offices of cardinal deacon and cardinal priest.
The preface leaves no doubt that Albinus wrote it after all of his
materials had been transcribed [140]. Among these texts are two letters
which were addressed to Albinus as cardinal bishop of Albano [141], and
since they as well as the accompanying treatise of Geoffrey of Auxerre
against Gilbert of Porrée are an integral part of the codex as well
as a major component, the codex must have been transcribed in its
present form after and not before May 1189.

---

[140] See the preface, *LC* II, 88b: « ... ex tunc sollicitus fui quando et ubi potui in
hoc eodem fasciculo annectere que cognoveram vel inveniebam iuris esse beati Petri ... »
[141] See the Appendix.

APPENDIX

Writings of Geoffrey of Auxerre against Gilbert of Porrée

Albinus' *Digesta* provide valuable manuscript evidence for the proceedings against Gilbert of Porrée at Reims in 1148. Pope Eugene III (1145-1153) presided at a consistory held in the palace of the archbishop of Reims, which debated the case after the conclusion of the general council which the pontiff had celebrated in that French city [142]. At the time, Bernard of Clairvaux was Bishop Gilbert's most determined opponent. One of St. Bernard's secretaries, Geoffrey of Auxerre, is among the chief witnesses whose accounts of these post-conciliar proceedings have been preserved to this day [143]. In the early seventeenth century, Cardinal Cesare Baronio published two letters of Geoffrey to Cardinal Albinus, one of which concerns the events at Reims in 1148 [144], and later Jean Mabillon included this particular letter as well as a more formal treatise by Geoffrey against Gilbert in his edition of the works of Bernard of Clairvaux [145]. According to John of Salisbury this treatise, usually known as *Libellus*, was written by Geoffrey while he was abbot of Igny (1157 - ca. 1162). after the death of Gilbert of Porrée in 1154 [146]. As for Geoffrey's second letter to Albinus, Mabillon merely referred his readers to its publication by Baronius, still the only place where it can be found in print. The manuscripts of Baronius and Mabillon have to be considered lost [147].

Recently, N. M. Häring gathered the available evidence in several distinguished papers [148]. Except for the summary of the errors of which Gilbert was

---

[142] See J. D. Mansi, *Sacrorum conciliorum amplissima collectio*, XXI, Venice 1776, 711-736; N. M. Häring, *Die spanischen Teilnehmer am Konzil von Reims im März 1148*: Mediaeval Studies 32 (1970) 159-171 with further bibliography; C. N. R. Brooke, *Canons of English Church Councils*: Traditio 13 (1957) 471-480; cf. R. Somerville, *The Canons of Reims (1131)*: Bulletin of Medieval Canon Law 5 (1975) 122-130.

[143] Among the writings of Geoffrey of Auxerre relevant are the *Epistola ad Albinum cardinalem* (Migne *PL* 185, 587-596) and the *Libellus* (*PL* 185, 595-618) which are discussed in this appendix with further bibliography; John of Salisbury, *Historia pontificalis*, ed. and transl. M. Chibnall, London etc. 1956, chapters 8-14, pp. 15-41; Otto of Freising, *Ottonis et Rahewini Gesta Friderici I imperatoris*, ed. G. Waitz (MGH, *Scriptores rerum germanicarum in usum scholarum*), Hanover-Leipzig 1912, 74-88.

[144] *Annales ecclesiastici*, XII, Cologne 1609, cols. 439-445 [the letter *Iniunxerat*], and *ibid.*, cols. 1003-1005, ad a. 1188 [the letter *Quia semel*] with a cross-reference to the letter *Iniunxerat* which was published ad a. 1148, in connection with the Reims proceedings.

[145] *S. Bernardi Opera omnia* II/6, Paris 1690, 1319-1339, reprinted in Migne *PL* 185, 587-618.

[146] John of Salisbury, *Historia pontificalis*, ed. Chibnall, p. 25.

[147] Mabillon's reference to Geoffrey's second letter (*inc.* « Quia semel ») is found in *S. Bernardi Opera omnia* II/6, p. 1342. Baronius, *Annales* XII, Cologne 1609, as in n. 144, gives no hint as to the manuscript he used for the letters. Mabillon, as in n. 145, used a transcript from the abbey of Longpont. A full discussion of the manuscripts is found in N. M. Häring, *Das sogenannte Glaubensbekenntnis des Reimser Konsistoriums von 1148*: Scholastik, Vierteljahresschrift für Theologie und Philosophie 40 (1965) 55-90; see also idem, *Texts Concerning Gilbert of Poitiers*: Archives d'histoire doctrinale et littéraire du moyen âge 45 (1970) 169-203 and n. 148.

[148] N. M. Häring, *The Case of Gilbert de la Porrée, Bishop of Poitiers (1142-1154)*: Mediaeval Studies 13 (1951) 1-140; idem, *Das sogenannte Glaubensbekenntnis* (see the preceding note); idem, *The Writings Against Gilbert of Poitiers by Geoffrey of Auxerre*: Analecta Cisterciensia, 22 (1966) 1-83; see also n. 159 below. For Geoffrey of Auxerre's

accused at the time (*capitula*), and the corresponding statement of faith by the ecclesiastics who were assembled at St. Bernard's hospice (*symbolum*), Professor Häring's investigations uncovered originally only two manuscripts for Geoffrey's *Libellus*, and none at all for Geoffrey's letters to Albinus [149]. Codex *Ottob. lat.* 3057 is a third manuscript for the *Libellus*, called here *Tractatus de capitulis magistri Gisleberti Porrate*, and the only currently known copy of Geoffrey's letters to *Amantissimo patri et domino .A. dei gratia Albanensi episcopo, domini pape uicario*, or, as in the second letter, *Amantissimo domino et patri .A. dei gratia Albanensi episcopo et domini pape uicario* [150]. While some of the variants in the generally excellent text of the *Libellus* found in MS *Ottob. lat.* 3057 would be of interest to Gilbert scholars, the slight variants in the letters are relatively insignificant [151].

Geoffrey's first letter to Albinus (*inc.* « Iniunxerat ») explains the circumstances which had given rise to the correspondence. Albinus had sent the cleric or monk Augustine (*specialis filius*) to Geoffrey, who by then lived at Clairvaux, with the request that Geoffrey inform Albinus by letter about the discussions under Pope Eugene III at Reims in connection with Gilbert's

---

works in general see also J. LECLERCQ, *Les écrits de Geoffroy d'Auxerre*: Revue Bénédictine 62 (1952) 274-291.

[149] HÄRING, *The Writings Against Gilbert*, esp. pp. 20-29; cf. n. 159 below. HÄRING, *The Writings*, reprinted Geoffrey's letter *Iniunxerat* from the edition by Baronius, and omitted the second letter which deals with different subject matter.

[150] See above, pp. 32 and 36. It has occasionally been argued that the initial '.A.' in the address of Geoffrey's letters, is a mistake and that the letters had in reality been sent to Cardinal Henry of Albano, Albinus' famous predecessor (*e.g.* LECLERCQ, *Les écrits de Geoffroy d'Auxerre*, p. 276; HÄRING, *The Case of Gilbert de la Porrée*, p. 1, n. 3 and p. 14; IDEM, *Das sogenannte Glaubensbekenntnis*, pp. 56 and 83; for Henry of Albano see Y. CONGAR, *Henri de Marcy, abbé de Clairvaux, cardinal-évêque d'Albano et légat pontifical*, in *Analecta Monastica* [Studia Anselmiana, 43], Vatican City 1958, 1-90). This erroneous emendation can be traced back to the *Histoire littéraire de la France*, XIV (see n. 124 above), pp. 430-451, here p. 439 n. 1, misprint for p. 449 n. 1. The learned editors noted that « Dans toutes les éditions, le nom de ce cardinal évêque d'Albano est désigné par la lettre A..... » but concluded that Albinus had not been « vicaire du pape », a title which they interpret as meaning legate, and that, therefore, « Il est donc vraisemblable qu'on aura lu A au lieu de H... » Since Albinus was indeed *vicarius pape*, whatsoever this office may have encompassed in the late twelfth century, there is absolutely no reason to change the initial '.A.' of the manuscript and of the editions of Baronius and Mabillon to the letter H. HÄRING has reached the same conclusion, see *The Writings Against Gilbert of Poitiers*, pp. 13-15.

[151] In the present context it is only of interest that the text of the *Libellus* contains at least five brief contributions to the debate or inscriptions which read ' Fr. G. ', for instance on fol. 38va, where we read: « Fr. G.: Sed quid pretergredimur viam, ad Boetium reuertamur ». These references to ' Fr. G. ' are not found either in the MABILLON (see the repr., *PL* 185, here col. 599, paragraph 14) or HÄRING editions (*Writings Against Gilbert*, here p. 41; the divisions as well as the Roman and Arabic enumerations were introduced by the editors and are not found in MS *Ottob. lat.* 3057). Both editions, however, contain the text of the remark, which is followed, as in codex *Ottob. lat.* 3057, by the inscription to the subsequent text: « Boetius de trinitate. Catholicis ... ». While definite proof is lacking, one may perhaps assume that ' Fr. G. ' stands for « Frater Gaufridus », whether he added these references to himself at the time when the *Libellus* was copied for Cardinal Albinus, or whether the inscriptions to the usually not very weighty interjections were already found in the original composition and omitted by other scribes. The characteristics of these interjections by ' Fr. G. ' are perhaps even more clearly marked in the passage which follows the Boetius text, once again with the inscr. ' Fr. G. ' in codex *Ottob. lat.* 3057 only (fol. 38va): « Fr. G.: Vides certe non esse catholicum qui in deo aliud quidem esse formam qua est, aliud uero quod est opinatur ».

teachings [152]. The letter *Iniunxerat* was Geoffrey's reply. Towards the end of the epistle Geoffrey exclaimed that just as the letter had been readied by a scribe, one of the monks at Clairvaux had unexpectedly and suddenly re-discovered *scriptura alia diu quesita iam penitus desperanti mihi exhibita est, quam super eisdem capitulis ante annos pene quadraginta edideram cum ipso symbolo ...* [153]. A clearly delighted Geoffrey thereupon dispatched to Cardinal Albinus both the letter and the treatise, as well as some materials regarding the proceedings against Abelard [154]. N. M. Häring assumed that the writings (*scriptura*) which are mentioned by Geoffrey corresponded to a text which was first published by Dom J. Leclercq from MS *Regin. lat.* 278, fols. 72-73, a codex which was written *ca.* 1200 in northern France according to A. Wilmart [155]. On the basis of Geoffrey's letter *Iniunxerat*, he therefore classified the material in the *Reginensis* as a distinct work of Geoffrey, named it *Scriptura*, and reprinted it among Geoffrey's writings [156].

Earlier, the *scriptura* had been identified tentatively with the treatise of Geoffrey known as *Libellus*, although MS *Ottob. lat.* 3057 was still unknown [157]. This manuscript, which contains the *Libellus* with the letters from Geoffrey to Albinus [158], would seem to be a welcome proof for what earlier had been a hypothetical deduction. However, the misconception « that the author of the *Liber censuum* compiled by the papal chamberlain Cencius in 1192 used the *Gesta pauperis scolaris Albini* as ' one of his major sources ' » prevented Professor Häring from accepting this conclusion in his most recent article on the subject, the first which he wrote on the basis of codex *Ottob. lat.* 3057 [159]. He concluded:

---

[152] Epistle *Iniunxerat*, ed. HÄRING, *Writings Against Gilbert*, p. 70, § 2: « Iniunxerat uestra paternitas uenerabilis [uenerabili *codex Ottob. lat. 3057*] fratri nostro et uestro speciali filio Augustino ut de mandato uestro mihi imponeret uobis per epistolam diligenter notum facere qualiter in Remensi concilio quod dominus Papa beate memorie Eugenius tercius celebrauit super quibusdam capitulis ... fuerit iudicatum » (= *PL* 185, 587).

[153] HÄRING, *Writings Against Gilbert*, p. 80 § 68.

[154] *Ibid.*, § 69: « ,Unde satis exultans illam quoque scripturam adiciens huic epistole tamquam charissimo domino meo uobis utramque filiali deuotione transmitto »; see also pp. 80-81 for the Abelard material. The second letter (*inc.* « Quia semel »), an inquiry concerning a new French Eucharistic custom about which Geoffrey had his doubts, may, I think, have been sent at the same time. The letter begins, « Quia semel cepi, loquar ad dominum meum, super uerbo etiam altero, cum uobis oportunum fuerit, uestram desiderans obtinere responsum ... » (fol. 36vb = BARONIUS, *Annales eccl.* XII, 1003). This would appear to be a reference to earlier correspondence, perhaps to the letter *Iniunxerat*. The similarity in the proceedings against Abelard and Gilbert of Porrée has often been noted. See especially J. MIETHKE, *Theologenprozesse in der ersten Phase ihrer institutionellen Ausbildung: Die Verfahren gegen Peter Abaelard und Gilbert von Poitiers*: Viator 6 (1975) 87-116.

[155] J. LECLERCQ, *Textes sur Saint Bernard et Gilbert de la Porrée*: Mediaeval Studies 14 (1952) 107-128, here pp. 108-111. See also the detailed analysis by F. PELSTER, *Petrus Lombardus und die Verhandlungen über die Streitfrage des Gilbertus Porreta in Paris (1147) und Reims (1148)*, in *Miscellanea Lombardiana*, Novara 1957, 65-73, and the references there to MABILLON who had discovered the text in a codex *Ottobonus* (pp. 68f. and n. 40, p. 73).

[156] HÄRING, *Writings Against Gilbert*, pp. 18-20 and 31-35.

[157] See LECLERCQ, *Textes sur Saint Bernard et Gilbert de la Porrée*, p. 108; HÄRING, *Das sogenannte Glaubensbekenntnis*, p. 84: « In seinem Brief an Albinus [letter *Iniunxerat*] sagt Gottfried, er habe im *Libellus* die *capitula* besprochen und das *symbolum* beigefügt. Er sagt nicht, er habe die *capitula* beigefügt ». Cf. IDEM, *Writings against Gilbert*, pp. 18-20, with further bibliography.

[158] See above, p. 36, and the text quoted at the beginning of n. 154 above.

[159] HÄRING, *Texts Concerning Gilbert of Poitiers* (see n. 147 above), pp. 169-203, here esp. pp. 176-178.

If the *Libellus* is considered identical with the *scriptura* the date of the *Libellus* would move the date of the letter to Albinus to approximately 1195, a date which conflicts with the previously established date of the *Gesta pauperis scolaris Albini* [160].

Häring arrived at the date of 1195 on the basis of the report by John of Salisbury that Geoffrey composed the treatise after the death of Gilbert while abbot of Igny, that is, in 1157 at the earliest [161], in conjunction with Geoffrey's own statement in the epistle *Iniunxerat*, that he had written the re-discovered *scriptura alia ... ante annos pene quadraginta ...* [162], while keeping in mind that Albinus died 1196/97, and that both John of Salisbury's statement and Geoffrey's 'pene' imply a certain imprecision. The argument that the *scriptura* corresponded to a certain *Reginensis* text (see n. 165), seemed a solution to this assumed chronological dilemma. According to this theory Albinus omitted the *scriptura* in his digest, and added the *Libellus* which he obtained on some other, unspecified occasion.

With the exception of Cenni, however, the texts which are common to Albinus and Cencius, but cannot always be derived from each other, have never been accepted as evidence for a direct dependence of Cencius on Albinus [163]. The only reason for the assumption that Albinus' *Digesta* slightly preceded the compilation of Cencius has so far been the fact that Albinus did not refer to his elevation to the cardinal bishopric of Albano in his preface. Since he became cardinal bishop of this see in May 1189, he must have completed the *digesta* before May 1189, the argument goes. As I have shown earlier, this argument is untenable, primarily because the codex contains Geoffrey's letters addressed to Albinus as cardinal of Albano, which, therefore, were written after May 1189 [164]. As a result, the chief argument for the identification of the *Tractatus de capitulis magistri Gisleberti Porrate* in MS *Ottob. lat.* 3057 with the text found in MS *Reg. lat.* 278, collapses [165].

Without his support it becomes exceedingly difficult to accept a secondary contention. On its own merits, the argument that the *scriptura* mentioned in Geoffrey's letter *Iniunxerat* could not be the treatise known as *Libellus*, because « ... there is no evidence in the cardinal's copy of any archbishops, bishops, abbots, and scholars whose names were, according to Geoffrey, attached to the creed », is not convincing [166]. Indeed, MS *Ottob. lat.* 3057 does not include signatures, but Geoffrey does not say unambiguously that he sends the profession of faith with the signatures. His clause [167] can be translated as

---

160 *Ibid.*, p. 178.

161 See n. 146 above.

162 See n. 153 above.

163 See n. 3 above.

164 Häring's discussion presupposes this assumption, but because this scholar's attention was focused on Gilbert of Porrée he was not familiar with the reasoning behind the argument for the priority of Albinus versus Cencius and its complications. (*Writings Against Gilbert of Poitiers*, pp. 177-178). See n. 3 above.

165 The author or authors of this text with the inscription « Error Gilleberti Pictaviensis episcopi » (LECLERCQ, *Textes sur Saint Bernard*, p. 108) or a very similar one (see HÄRING, *Texts Concerning Gilbert*, pp. 170-176, for 3 additional MSS which he has discovered) has to be considered anonymous.

166 HÄRING, *Texts Concerning Gilbert*, p. 178.

167 HÄRING, *Writings Against Gilbert*, p. 80, § 68: « ... Ab altero siquidem fratre priusquam mihi presens epistola redderetur, scriptura alia diu quesita iam penitus desperanti mihi exhibita est quam super eisdem capitulis ante annos pene quadraginta edideram cum ipso symbolo *quod domino Pape et Romane ecclesie ex parte decem archiepiscoporum et omnium episcoporum pene qui in illa adhuc die Remis inuenti sunt cum abbatibus maximis atque plurimis et magistris scolarum, et sub-*

a historical footnote, alerting the cardinal of Albano to the fact that the *symbolum* which he added to the *scriptura* had been presented with signatures (*nominibus subscriptis*) to Pope Eugene III by Hugh of Auxerre, Milo of Thérouanne, and Abbot Suger of St. Denis on behalf of St. Bernard and the ecclesiastics and scholars who were present at the meeting at St. Bernard's hospice in 1148 at Reims [168]. After all, Albinus did not join the curia until about 30 years after these events had taken place. In short, there is no convincing evidence that the *Libellus* which is now found in codex *Ottob. lat.* 3057 was not also the *scriptura* which Geoffrey said he would send together with his letter *Iniunxerat*, and the very arguments which have shown that the date of the *Libellus* falls into the nineties rather than the end of the 1180's now provide additional evidence that the date of the compilation of Albinus cannot be regarded as set by the omission of any reference to Albano in the preface [169].

---

scriptis nominibus singulorum per superius memoratas personas fuerat presentatum » (italics mine).

[168] See the preceding note for Geoffrey's text and for the events HÄRING, *Writings Against Gilbert*, p. 11.

[169] The description of the Libellus by John of Salisbury fits the *tractatus* which is found in MS *Ottob. lat.* 3057: « [Gaufridus] qui postea abbas Igniacensis contra eundem episcopum, sed iam defunctum, scripsit librum eleganti quidem stilo, recte gratus uniuersis, nisi uideretur inuehentis habere speciem, et ... amaritudinem continere » (*Historia pontificalis*, ed. CHIBNALL, p. 25). Cf. n. 157 above and Geoffrey's description, above n. 167: :« ... *super eisdem capitulis.* ... »

XVIII

AN EPISCOPAL HANDBOOK
FROM TWELFTH-CENTURY SOUTHERN ITALY:
CODEX ROME, BIBL. VALLICELLIANA F. 54/III

Some years ago Professor Stephan Kuttner drew attention to several Roman manuscripts, among them codex Vallicellianus F. 54.[1] Parts I and II of the codex are relatively well known, containing the *Diuersorum patrum sententie* or *Collection in 74-Titles* with an appendix (fol. 1r-130v) and a Penitential (fol. 131r-169v), respectively.[2] The same cannot be said for part III of the codex which is the subject of this paper, for as Kuttner pointed out, fol. 170r-226r of Vallicellianus F. 54 (= Vall. III below) deserve a full analysis. They reflect the influence of the great Roman reform collection of Cardinal Deusdedit[3] in combination with the *Collectio Tripartita* of Ivo of Chartres.[4] In light of the overwhelming importance of Gratian's *Decretum* as basis for the evolution of scientific canonistic jurisprudence, part III of Vall. F. 54 is a salutary reminder

---

[1] S. KUTTNER, *Some Roman Manuscripts of Canonical Collections, Bulletin of Medieval Canon Law*, n.s. 1 (1971) 7-29, here pp. 23-25. I would like to thank Dr. Martin Bertram, Rome, who kindly helped me to obtain a microfilm of the manuscript.

[2] See the bibliography cited by KUTTNER and J.T.GILCHRIST, ed., *Diuersorum Patrum sententie siue Collectio in LXXIV titulos digesta*, Monumenta iuris canonici series B, vol. 1 (Vatican City 1973) pp. xlvii-xlix.

[3] KUTTNER, *Some Roman Manuscripts*, p. 25. For the Collection of Deusdedit see A. STICKLER, *Historia iuris canonici* I (Turin 1950) pp. 172-174; P. FOURNIER · G. LE BRAS, *Histoire des collections canoniques* 2 (Paris 1932; reprint Aalen 1972) pp. 37-54 and H. FUHRMANN, *Einfluss and Verbreitung der pseudoisidorischen Fälschungen*, MGH Schriften 24,II (Stuttgart 1973) pp. 522-533 with an extensive bibliography. In this paper the collection has been used in the critical edition, V. W. VON GLANVELL, ed., *Die Kanonessammlung des Kardinals Deusdedit* (Paderborn 1905; reprint Aalen 1967).

[4] For Ivo's collections see STICKLER, *Historia*, pp.179-184; FOURNIER-LE BRAS, *Histoire* 2,55-114 and FUHRMANN, *Einfluss* 2,542-562. Side by side with the unreliable edition of Ivo's *Decretum* in Migne PL 161 I have used a microfilm of Ms Paris, BN lat. 14,315; two microfilms of Ivo's unpublished *Tripartita* have been consulted: Berkeley, Robbins Ms 102 (for *Trip. A* part I) and Paris, BN lat. 3858 B (for *Trip. A* part II and *Trip. B*). See also below n. 31.

of the scope offered for different types of private collections during the formative earlier twelfth century in Italy.

1. Description

Vallicellianus F. 54 Part III = fol. 170r-226r (Vall. III) originally constituted a separate codex. Clear evidence are the darkening of the first and final folios and in particular the foxing of fol. 170r in the upper left corner. In contrast to Parts I and II of Ms F. 54 in Beneventan script, Part III is written in minuscule by several scribes in long lines. The only exception is a brief text in Beneventan on fol. 219r-219v, *Cauendum summopere prepositis*.[5] On the same line as the explicit of the canon, the same hand continues in minuscule, giving the rubric of the following text. Throughout Vall. III the twelfth-century Caroline script shows strong Beneventan influence. Typical are the final *nt* ligature and the letter *i/j* in combination with the vowels *i* and *u* written like the letter *l*.[6] The neat appearance of much of the codex is deceptive. Errors are encountered frequently and only rarely corrected. Up to fol. 211r rubrics are given in most cases, but inscriptions are usually omitted. Towards the end of the codex initials have not been executed although spaces have been left for them. The various hands that transcribed the codex appear to be contemporary and date from the later twelfth century. The leaf 118r-v is missing and fol. 172v, fols. 219v, 223r, 224r-v, and 226r are only partially legible because the script has been almost obliterated, the folios have been damaged or are extremely dark.

---

[5] The text on fol. 219r-v reads: *Cauendum summopere prepositis ecclesiarum est ut in ecclesiis sibi commissis non plus ammittant clericos quam ratio sinit et facultas ecclesie [e caudata] suppetat. Ne si indiscrete et extra ordinare plures adgregauerent; nec ipsos gubernare nec ceteris ecclesie necessitatibus ut oportet ualeant adminiculare. Sunt namque nonnulli uanagloriam ab hominibus captantes qui numerosas clericorum congregationes uolunt habere, cui nec anime nec corporis curant solacia exhibere. Hi namque taliter adgregati dum a prelatis stipendia necessaria non accipiunt neque canonicum seruant ordinem nec diuinis officiis insistunt, claustra societatemque [e caudata] ceterorum relinquentes, efficiuntur uagi et lasciui gule et ebrietati et ceteris suis uoluptatibus dediti, quicquid sibi libitum est licitum faciunt. Proinde prepositis sollerter prouidendum est ut in hoc negotio modum discretionis teneant; scilicet ut nec plus quam oportet et possibilitas ecclesie suppetit in congregatione admittant, nec eos quos rationabiliter gubernare possunt causa auaritie habitant [!]. In the right margin the indication «Aug.» for the rubricator is found in Caroline minuscule.*

[6] It should be noted that Part II of Ms Vall. F. 54 also shows a shift between minuscule and Beneventan. Part II throughout is in Beneventan hands, but a partial text from Paschal II's Lateran Council of 1110 on fol. 169v was written in minuscule to be followed by c.9 of Calixtus II's Lateran Council of 1123 once again written in Beneventan. For Paschal's council see U.-R. BLUMENTHAL, *The Early Councils of Pope Paschal II, 1100-1110* (Toronto 1978), especially p. 117.

2. Place of Origin

Vall. III unfortunately does not contain any item like letters, charters, obituary notices or list of relics that might indicate the origin of the thematically arranged collection of canocical texts. The script and in particular the short passage in Beneventan are the only indications that we are dealing with a compilation from southern Italy. The texts clearly reflect episcopal interests and those of a chapter of cathedral canons. The topics addressed, beginning with the elaborate justification for the collection of tithes and not excluding an unidentified anathema, all concern issues of daily concern to a bishop supervising the laity, the monks, and the canons of a diocese. One of the decrees on monastic life taken over from book 8 of Burchard's *Decretum* and found on fol. 206r of Vall. III (= Burch. 8.80 *Abbatissa nequaquam...*) adds *que in ciuitate monasterium habeat*. The addition is apparently unique to Vall. III and indicates perhaps an important convent in the vicinity of the anonymous south Italian episcopal city. The collection was compiled in a period when the interests of the chapter and of the bishop still largely coincided although the canons, who probably were responsible for transcribing the text, or having it transcribed, left their mark on it. On fol. 198v in the left margin *canonici* is written out in capitals to draw attention to a Carolingian capitulary requiring the common life for canons, *In omnibus igitur quantum*.[7] Earlier, on fol. 170v in the middle of a text derived from Burchard (3.133), the text hand inserted in red ink the reference *et clericis*, found neither in Burchard nor in Ivo's *Decretum* (3.199).

3. Date of Origin

The most recent texts with a clear attribution are letter fragments of Pope Urban II (1088-99). The compilers relied heavily on the *Decretum* of Burchard of Worms, updating this older material with canons drawn from the collections of Deusdedit (1087) and Ivo of Chartres (c. 1094). They also do not take us beyond the late eleventh century. Many of the texts found in Vall. III were also included by Gratian, but as a critical analysis of the texts (here omitted) has shown, his *Decretum* can always be excluded as a source.

There is, however, one possible exception. Four decrees added by a new hand at the end of the codex on fol. 225r-226r where only a few words can now be deciphered, might conceivably have been transcribed from a copy of Gra-

---

[7] The text corresponds to Ivo, *Decretum* 6.402 = *Tripartita B* (= 3).10.37. In Vall. III the text is based on *Trip.* as will be shown. See Gratian, *Decretum* c.34 D.5 *de cons.*

tian's *Decretum*, given the deficiencies of Friedberg's edition. The identifiable decrees in support of episcopal authority could correspond to C.22 q.4 c.22; C.16 q.2 c.6;[8] C.2 q.7 c.1 and C.11 q.1 c.22. But the variants between the text in Vall. F. 54 and Gratian are significant, especially for C.2 q.7 c.1. This canon composed of excerpts from Pseudo-Evaristus[9] cannot have been derived from the far briefer text in Friedberg's edition.[10] For C.22 q.4 c.22 the only recognized source is the *Collectio Caesaraugustana* 6.2 as indicated by Friedberg. Biblioteca Vaticana, Ms Barb. lat. 897, fol. 125r-v, agrees in its variants with the readings found in Vall. F. 54 against Gratian with a single exception.[11] The decree from Urban's council of Clermont (C.16 q.2 c.6) is only preserved in Gratian and the *Polycarpus;* once again, the text in Vall. F. 54 agrees with the *Polycarpus* as edited by Somerville and not with Gratian.[12] To sum up, as unlikely as it may seem because neither the *Caesaraugustana* nor the *Polycarpus,* not to mention the *Pseudo-Isidorian Decretals,* were used elsewhere in Vall. III, the compiler of these texts on episcopal rights and protection on the final folio of codex Vall. F. 54 Part III probably relied on Gratian's sources rather than on the *Decretum* itself. This means that the most recent texts in Vall. III date from the second decade of the twelfth century.[13] It is difficult to pursue the analysis further. No attempt has been made to treat the texts dialectically. Despite the later twelfth-century charateristics of the script and the Beneventan passage alluding to the overcrowding of chapters, circumstances more likely to be found in the mid-twelfth-century than in the early years of the century, it is possible that the text in Vall. F. 54 is the copy of an earlier twelfth-century exemplar.[14]

---

[8] For a critical edition of this decree *(Sane quia monachorum)* as transmitted among the material for Urban II's council of Clermont see R. SOMERVILLE, *The councils of Urban II, 1: Decreta Claromontensia, Annuarium Historiae Conciliorum Supplementum I* (Amsterdam 1972) p. 123 c.4 with note 12.

[9] The excerpts comprise HINSCHIUS, p. 91, line 31-33 (explicit: *rectorum)* and p. 92, line 5-9 (explicit: *presumpserint*).

[10] Compare FUHRMANN, *Einfluss,* Vol. 3, p. 890 no. 233 and p. 994 no. 435 under *Unde si qui sunt vituperatores.* The *Anselmo dedicata,* seen in a microfilm of Ms Vercelli, Biblioteca Capitolare XV, can be excluded as a source. The same is true for all other parallel texts listed by Fuhrmann.

[11] F. 54 reads ... *alimonie unquam inpendere* with Gratian against ... *unquam prebere* in the *Caesaraugustana.*

[12] See the references in n. 8 above.

[13] For the date of the *Polycarpus* and the *Caesaraugustana* see STICKLER, *Historia,* pp. 178f. and 184f., respectively. The most recent arguments for a date for the *Polycarpus post* 1111 are carefully summarized by HORST, *Polycarpus* (as in n. 21 below), pp. 3-6 and have been generally accepted.

[14] But see G. PICASSO, *Collezioni canoniche Milanesi del secolo XII* (Milan 1969) p. 167 for

4. The Sources

a) *Burchard of Worms*

The thematically arranged compilation Vall. III has no subdivision into books or titles. As mentioned earlier, rubrics are given but inscriptions are missing more often than not. The basic formal source[15] for the compilers of Vall. III was the *Decretum* of Burchard of Worms (died 1025).[16] All of the major topics of Vall. III are anchored firmly in Burchard's work: tithes and their administration, baptism, penance especially for homicides, monks, consanguinity and marriage. The following blocks can be noted:

fol. 170r-172v = Burch. 3.129-146

fol. 181r-192v = Burch. 4.1; 4.3-6; 4.8-10; 4.13; 4.16; 4.24-25; 4.27; 4.33; 4.37; 4.44; 4.47; 4.57; 4.59; 4.60; 4.61-65; 4.67-68; 4.70; 4.72-74; 4.76-80; 4.82; 4.92-93; 6.1-4; 6.8-10; 6.20; 6.32-33; 6.37-39; 6.41-43; 6.46-47; 7.1-29.

fol. 202r-211r = Burch. 8.1-2; 8.4-5: 8.7-10; 8.12-13; 8.15; 8.18-24; 8.30-31; 8.33-35; 8.37; 8.58-60; 8.64-68; 8.70; 8.73-82; 8.84-88; 8.92; 8.94; 8.95; 8.96; 8.98; 8.101; 9.1-21; 9.23-31; 9.33-35; 9.37-38; 9.40; 9.43-44.

---

the date of the coll. *Amb. I.* The collection was composed in Milan between 1130 and 1139 during the Anacletian schism although *«i testi più recenti recepiti nella collezione Amb. 1 appartengono al pontificato di Gregorio VII»* (p. 168).

[15] The attempt to determine material sources had to be abandoned. Only a single complete manuscript is known for Deusdedit's collection; Italian manuscripts for Ivo's still unedited *Tripartita* remain largely unknown. As for Burchard's *Decretum*, a major gap in the transcription of Book 8 in the Vallicellianus is the section Burch. 8.38-57 which has been omitted. According to G. FRANSEN, *Le Décret de Burchard de Worms. Valeur du texte de l'édition. Essai de classement des manuscrits*, in: *Zeitschrift der Savigny-Stiftung f. Rechtsgeschichte, Kan. Abt.* 63 (1977) 1-19, here p. 2 and pp. 8-10; the lacuna 8.38-49 is characteristic of the second manuscript group of Burchard's *Decretum*, the *deteriores*, particularly frequent in Italy. Cf. T. KOELZER, *Collectio canonum Regesto Farfensi inserta*, Monumenta iuris canonici Series B. vol. 5 (Vatican City 1982) pp. 59-61. For Italian manuscripts of Burchard see especially H. MORDEK, *Handschriftenforschungen in Italien I*, in: *Quellen und Forschungen in Italienischen Archiven und Bibliotheken* 51 (1972) 626-651 with further literature.

[16] FUHRMANN, *Einfluss* 24/II, pp. 442-485 provides a critical and detailed bibliography for Burchard's work. Brief introductions are given by STICKLER, *Historia*, pp. 154-159; FOURNIER-LE BRAS, *Histoire* 1, 364-421. I have relied on the text of the *Decretum* reprinted in MIGNE PL 140, 537ff.

Practically the entire *Decretum* of Burchard was taken over into the collections of Ivo of Chartres.[17] It has been thought that the rare *Decretum* of Ivo rather than the popular *Decretum* of Burchard was source for the excerpts in Vall. III.[18] Burchard, 3.129-146, for instance, appears to be almost identical with Ivo, D. 3.195-211. But there are a few significant variants, and since the excerpts on fol. 170r-172v of Ms F. 54 agree in practically every instance with Burchard against Ivo, we may conclude that Burchard's *Decretum* must have been the formal source.[19] The dependence of Vall. III on Burchard rather than Ivo can be illustrated unambiguously for the excerpts on fol. 181r-192v, placing Vall. III on the same footing as other approximately contemporary Italian collections, the *Liber canonum diuersorum sanctorum patrum siue Collectio in CLXXXIII titulos digesta*[20] and the *Polycarpus*.[21] Except for Burchard Book 4 c.1 *(Baptismus grece)* all of the canons on fol. 181-192v are also found in Ivo's *Decretum*. Still, there is no need in this instance to rely exclusively on textual variants to eliminate Ivo's *Decretum* from among the possible sources. On fol. 184v where the excerpts from Burchard's Book 6 begin and Burchard's c.1 of book 6 *(In primis ut licet)* has been copied, the scribe indicated the Roman numeral .i. in the left margin. The text continues with Burch. 6.2, and is again

---

[17] In addition to the references given in n. 4 above, see especially P. FOURNIER, *Les Collections canoniques attribuées à Yves de Chartres, Bibliothèque de l'Ecole des Chartes* 57 (1896) 645-698 and 58 (1897) 26-77.

[18] KUTTNER, *Some Roman Manuscripts*, p. 24.

[19] By way of example some of the variants for the passages on fol. 170r-172v are listed here. Vall. III always agrees with Burch. unless noted otherwise. Burchard D. 3,130: *modo multi*; Ivo D. 3,196: *multimodo*. Burchard D. 3,133: *nempe meus es, o homo*; Ivo D. 3,199: *nempe meus est homo*; Burchard D. 3,133: *quibusque holusculis, ruta videlicet, menta et cimino* [F. 54: *quibusque oculis ...*]; Ivo D. 3,199: *quibusque minimis rebus, ruta videlicet, imenta et cimino*; Burchard D. 3, 135: *et ideo*; Ivo D. 3,201 *et deo*; Burchard D. 3,136: *parochitanas*; Ivo D. 3,202: *ad ecclesiam a parochianis*; Burchard D. 3,137: *fabricis applicanda*; Ivo D. 3,203: *fabricis amplificandis ecclesie*; Burchard D. 3,137: *sic clerus*; Ivo D. 3,203: *sic clericus* [NB: both Ivo and F. 54 (fol. 171v), however, share *orationibus* in this canon against Burchard's *rationibus*]. Because of the poor condition of fol. 172v it was impossible to compare the texts for Burchard D. 3,143 (Ivo D. 3,208b) and Burchard D. 3,144 (Ivo D. 3,209). The readings for Ivo are those found in Paris Ms BN lat. 14315.

[20] Ed. J. MOTTA, *Monumenta iuris canonici Series B, 7* (Vatican City 1988); see the concordance for Burchard *ibid.*, pp. 350-357.

[21] U. HORST, *Die Kanonessammlung Polycarpus des Gregor von S. Grisogono: Quellen und Tendenzen, MGH Hilfsmittel* 5 (1980), concordance tables for Burchard of Worms and Ivo of Chartres beginning on p. 104.

accompanied by the marginal notation .ii. In Ivo's *Decretum* this series of Burchard excerpts begins with c.130 of part 10. The marginal references in Ms Vall. F. 54 by a contemporary hand, therefore, must refer to a codex of Burchard's work. Last not least, the excerpts from Burchard's Book 7 on fol. 188r under the rubric *De incesta copulatione consanguinitatis* begin with Burchard 7.1 *(Quod infames uocentur qui ex consanguineis nascuntur. Coniunctiones autem...).* The chapters from Burchard in Ivo's *Decretum* (9.39-66) omit Burchard 7.1-3, confirming the conclusion that Burchard was the formal source for these excerpts as well.

Not so clear- cut is the case for the final block of Burchard excerpts on fol. 202r-211r. As Fournier has noted, book 8 of Burchard finds exact equivalents in chapters 26-199 of part 7 of the *Decretum* of Ivo of Chartres.[22] The few variants once again point to Burchard as source.[23] However, a difficulty arises with the excerpts on fol. 207r-211r dealing with marriage and excerpted presumably from Burchard's *Decretum* book 9. The *praefatiunculum* preceding Burch. 9.1 and found on fol. 207r-v parallels Ivo's preface to part 8 rather than Burchard's preface.[24] Still, in the light of the remark of Gerard Fransen in his evaluation of the Burchard edition «les *praefatiunculae* au debut de chaque livre sont loin de correspondre au text des manuscrits...» and in the absence of any other indication in codex Vall. F. 54 that Ivo's *Decretum* was used, it would be hasty to assume the contrary alone on the basis of this *praefatiunculum*.[25] Moreover, it seems most unlikely that a compiler would have gone from the preface of Ivo to part 8 of the *Decretum* to Ivo D. 8.139 = Burch. 9.1. Burch. 9.1 is the text directly following the preface in Vall. III. In short, the deficiencies of the Burchard text in the Migne volume are the most likely explanation for the divergent reading just discussed.

---

[22] *Les Collections, Bibliothèque de l'Ecole des Chartes* 58, p. 32.

[23] It may be noted that the first decree transcribed in Vall. F. 54 (fol. 202r) corresponds to Burch. 8.1 in practically all respects. There is one minor variant: *sumere* (F. 54) as against *adsumere* in Burchard. In contrast, the text forms only the final segment of Ivo D. 7.27. The second text copied in F. 54 corresponds to Burch. 8.2 and Ivo D. 7.20. Lastly, an intercalation between Ivo D. 7.41 and 7.42 also points to Burchard as source for Ms Vall. F. 54/III, for the c. *Clerici qui monachorum* constitutes c. 371 of Ivo D. 6. In Burchard's *Decretum* as well as in F. 54 this text = Burch. 8.21 is found in the proper sequence.

[24] The text in Ms Vall. F. 54 *(De uirginibus et uiduis non uelatis; de raptoribus earum et de separatione eorum; de coniunctione legitimorum concubitorum; de concubinis et de transgressione et penitentia singulorum* [fol. 207r]) agrees with the preface to Ivo D. 8 (PL 161, col. 583; Ms Paris BN lat. 14315, fol. 171v omits *de coniunctione legitimorum concubitorum*) with the exception of the initial *De legitimis coniugiis* which has been omitted in F. 54. Cf. Burchard, PL 140, col. 815: *Libro hoc de uirginibus et uiduis Deo non sacratis... poenitentia tractatur.*

[25] FRANSEN, *Décret de Burchard* (as in n. 15 above), p. 3. Ivo's *Tripartita* does not contain the passage.

b) *The collection of Deusdedit*

On fol. 172v-176v the opening theme of Vall. III, tithes and ecclesiastical possessions in general, is further elaborated in a series of excerpts derived from the canonical collection of Cardinal Deusdedit.[26] Clear is the great care used by the compilers of Vall. III to integrate these relatively recent texts with the material derived from the more traditional *Decretum* of Burchard of Worms. It has been seen that the material on tithes in Burchard's work was transcribed as a block on fol. 170r-172v. In a completely different manner the texts with Deusdedit as a source[27] were selected and transcribed on fol. 172v-176v and on fol. 176v-179v after two brief canons from Burchard enjoining penance for the withholding of tithes (fol. 176v: Burch. 19.5, *De oblatione* and *De decimis*). Derived from Deusdedit's books 3, 2 and 4, they form the following sequence:

> 3.59; 3.61-65; 3.72-74; 3.25-29; 3.38-39; 3.12-14; 2.157; 2.159; 3.158-162; 3.179-183 [followed by the two Burchard texts] 3.176-178; 3.168; 4.56-71.

The canons inserted from Burchard conclude what could be called a treatise on tithes.[28] They are followed by four Justinian texts (Deusd. 3.176; 3.177-178 and 3.168) dealing with the administration of ecclesiastical property. The texts Deusd. 4.56-71 on fol. 177v-179v introduce a brief section on monks and penance with statements on the priestly duty to admonish those who have deviated from the straight and narrow path. During the eleventh-century reform the theme was important; the excerpts could well have served to rally supporters of the papal cause who might otherwise have been inclined to follow custom rather than a novel and strict interpretation of ancient canonical prescriptions. A series very similar to Deusd. 4.56-71 is found in the *Col-*

---

[26] See n. 3 above.

[27] See KUTTNER, *Some Roman Manuscripts*, p. 24f. Except for an easily explained switch of a rubric [*Ex concilio vii pape Gregorii episcoporum .1.* (p. 293)] which appears in Vall. F. 54 with Deusd. 3.59 instead of with Deusd. 3.58, the Deusdedit texts in Vall. F. 54 correspond entirely to the text found in Glanvell's critical edition. This agreement includes the segments marked by Glanvell as Deusdedit's variations from the source. Moreover, in several instances Vall. F. 54 gives Deusdedit's original chapter numbers as in the rubric for Deusd. 2.159 = *cxxviiii* (fol. 175r) and on fol. 173v with *lxvi, lxvii,* and *lxviii* for Deusd. 3.72, 3.73 and 3.74 in Glanvell's edition (p. 299). They are found in the right and left margins of Ms Vall. F. 54.

[28] In general see G. CONSTABLE, *Monastic Tithes from their Origins to the Twelfth Century, Cambridge Studies in Medieval Life and Thought* n.s. 10 (Cambridge 1964).

lectio Barberiniana (2.1-8).[29] The series is also parallelled, and this more close-ly, in Alger's *De misericordia et iustitia*.[30] But since the investiture controversy left hardly any trace among the texts of Vall. III, it seems probable that the compilers merely included them to emphasize the right and duty of clerical supervision. In general, Deusdedit's collection provided the compiler with ac-cess to relatively recent papal decretals and especially synodal decisions, repres-enting Popes Gregory VII (Deusd. 3.59 and 3.61), Alexander II (Deusd. 3.64), and Leo IX (Deusd. 3.65) as well as Roman law texts concerning ecclesi-astical temporalities. The authors clearly picked and chose what was of inter-est to them and their associates expanding the reach of Burchard's collection.

c) *The* Tripartita *of Ivo of Chartres*

As mentioned, Deusdedit's chapters 4.56-71 on fol. 179v-181r of the Vallicellianus form a transition to a series of canons dealing with monks and penance. The source for this group of texts was Ivo's *Tripartita*.[31] Excepting the first canon transcribed from *Trip.* (*De monasteriis uirginum. Undecima ac-tione... leuis omnino locutio*, Ms F. 54, fol. 179v-180r) the canons are derived from the second and final series of patristic excerpts concluding Ivo's *Triparti-ta A*.[32] The letter of Pope Urban II among them forms a transition to the Bur-

---

[29] M. FORNASARI, *Collectio canonum Barberiniana*, in *Apollinaris* 36 (1963) 127-141, 214-297, here p. 224f. FUHRMANN, *Einfluss* 2, p. 529 n. 281, argued that the textual parallels be-tween the *Collectio Barberiniana* and the collection of Deusdedit resulted from the use by both authors of a common intermediate source. *Barb.* 2.1-4 correspond to Deusd. 4.56-59; *Barb.* 2.5 = Deusd. 4.61; *Barb.* 2.6-8 = Deusd. 4.64-66. The source for the compiler of F. 54 was clearly Deusdedit. See also *Barb.* 12.4 second paragraph *Preter uictum*...). It should be compared with Deusd. 3.161 and Ms F. 54, fol. 175v-176r. Once more Deusdedit's text proves to be the source for the decree in Ms F. 54.

[30] All of the canons *Coll. Barb.* 2.1-8 have equivalents in Alger's treatise in this sequence: Alger II,5 can. e; Alger I,28 can. b; Alger II,5 can. f; Alger II,5 can. d; Alger II,6 can. b; Alger II,6 can. a; Alger II,6 can. c; Alger II,5 can. c. See R. KRETZSCHMAR, *Alger von Luettichs Traktat «De misericordia et iustitia»: Ein kanonistischer Konkordanzversuch aus der Zeit des Investitur-streits*, Quellen und Forschungen zum Recht im Mittelalter 2 (Sigmaringen 1985).

[31] The author of the *Collectio Tripartita* is still debated; see FUHRMANN, *Einfluss*, vol. 2, p. 543 n. 323 as well as p. 544 n. 325. Ms Paris, BN lat. 3858 B which I used for *Tripartita A*, part II and for *Tripartita B*, is closely related to Ms Berkeley, Robbins Collection 102 which I used for *Tripartita A*, part I. See M. BRETT, *The Berkeley Tripartita*, *Bulletin of Medieval Canon Law* n.s. 16 (1986) 89-91, here p. 90. I would like to thank Mr. Steve Horwitz for a microfilm of the Berkeley manuscript. See also n. 4 above.

[32] Especially helpful in working with the *Tripartita* is P. FOURNIER, *Les Collections Canoni-ques attribuées à Yves de Chartres*, *Bibliothèque de l'Ecole des Chartes* 57 (1896) 645-698. See *ibid.* p. 695f and 697 for the incipits and explicits of the texts found in Ms Vall. F. 54 where the

chard excerpts on baptism (Burch. 4.1 and following) and other sacraments discussed earlier, concluding with Burch. 7.29 in the upper third of fol. 192v. On the remainder of the folio a contemporary twelfth-century hand squeezed in three texts that could be either derived from Ivo's *Decretum* or his *Tripartita*, before regular spacing is resumed on fol. 193r, where a long sequence of excerpts from the *Tripartita* begins ending on fol. 201v.[33] For these canons the *Decretum* of Ivo can be excluded as a source both on account of the sequential nature of the texts and variants.[34] Moreover, on fol. 193r of the codex the c. *Mandastis ut scriberem* is found, one of the rare items specific to the *Tripartita B*.

It is impossible to decide whether the *Decretum* or the *Tripartita* furnished the texts entered on fol. 192v. This insert consists of 1) the letter fragment JL 5399 of Urban II;[35] 2) a *caput incertum* attributed to Jerome;[36] 3) the letter fragment JL 5382 of Pope Urban II.[37] The texts address questions arising in connection with the sacrament of marriage. More importantly, they highlight the fact that as in the case of the *Collectio canonum* of Cardinal Deusdedit the compilers used the *Tripartita A* and *B* to up-date Burchard's statements on the clerical life. The selection of relatively recent materials is conspicuous. Besides the decrees of Pope Urban II, found both earlier on fol. 180v,[38] in the insert on fol. 192v and among the excerpts on fols. 193r-201 = *Trip. B* 10.41, 10.42 (attributed to both Urban II and Gregory VII), 10.43 and 10.44 (all on fol. 199r-v), there is an excerpt from a letter of Pope Alexander II *(Trip. B* 10.40; fol. 199r).

---

rubrics are omitted. The decrees on fol. 180r-181r correspond to the following items listed by FOURNIER: 1 (*Quicumque a parentibus...*); 2 (*In lege quippe...*); 7 (*Ieiunia sane legitima...*); 8 (*Die autem dominico...*); 9 (*Quelibet causa...*); and 22,23,24 = a letter of Pope Urban II (1088-1099) to the priest Vitalis of Brescia. The single letter is calendared by Jaffe-Lowenfeld as JL 5741; JL 5742 and JL 5740. See FOURNIER, *ibid.*, p. 697 and 677 n. 3 and KUTTNER, *Some Roman Manuscripts*, p. 24f. with further references. It should be noted that in F. 54 items 2 and 7 are both found under the inscription *Ex dictis Sancti Apollonii* which precedes item 2. For the relationship between this *Tripartita* series and the *Quadripartitus* see FOURNIER, *ibid.*, pp. 670, 673f., and F. KERFF, *Der Quadripartitus* (Sigmaringen 1982) pp. 74, 102 and the table beginning on p. 105. The canons listed by FOURNIER as nos. 8 and 9 correspond to *Quadripartitus* IV,2 and IV,19.

[33] The *Tripartita B* sequence reads as follows: 10.7; 10.9-28; 10.30-51.

[34] The text sequence for Ivo's *Decretum* is as follows: 6.226; 6.229; --; 6.420; 6.230-232; 6.236; 5.367; 6.308; 6.383-393; 6.395-406; 6.410-412; 6.415-416; 6.413; 6.417-419; 6.427. Burchard's *Decretum* can be excluded for the same reasons.

[35] Cf. Gratian C.31 q.2 c.3 where the explicit differs from both Ivo and Ms F. 54.

[36] See Gratian C.36 q.2 c.8

[37] See Gratian C.31 q.2 c.1. Both JL 5399 and JL 5382 of Pope Urban II are found in the *Collectio Britannica*, not, however, the Jerome text. The *Coll. Brit.* can therefore be excluded as a source for the texts in Ms F. 54.

[38] JL 5741/5742/5740 = *Trip. A*. See n. 32

The third and final series of excerpts from the *Tripartita A* on fol. 211v-217r follow upon Burch. 9.1-44 after a brief insert on fol. 211r-211v. The insert, a solemn anathema against *potentes* who lay hands on clergy and three penitential canons against violators of churches, could reflect a local synod.[39] The*Trip.* texts open with *Trip. A*, part 1.55.45 = Ivo, *Decretum* 5.112, the only text in Val. III specifically relating to simony as a heresy.[40] The excerpts include passages on the characteristics of alms, the nature of priestly ordinations and the limitations on priestly functions. Their content varies, approaching the miscellaneous character of the addenda on the final folios.

Fol. 219r-226r have been filled haphazardly with a variety of texts whose origin could not always be determined.[41] Often they are barely legible as in the case of some fragments on fol. 220r-220v from a treatise on numerology. They are distinguished by an interest in theology and include two excerpts from Augustine's sermon 88 on fol. 221v as well as numerous sequential excerpts from Augustine's *Liber de perfectione iustitie hominis* that fill fol. 221v-224v.[42] The very different texts found on fol. 225r-226r have been discussed earlier.

* * *

In concluding I would like to stress the sophistication and elegance, especially in connection with the initial treatise on tithes and property, that are evident in the combination of Burchard's *Decretum* with Deusdedit's canonical collection and Ivo's *Tripartita*. The use of the *Tripartita* in Italy has never

---

[39] Regrettably the texts could not be further identified with the exception of one of the 3 penitential clauses, *Si quis ecclesiam igne...* = Burch. 3.204. The anathema (inc. *Quod si quis dei sancteque ecclesie extiterit contemptor et pro sue tiranidis potentia cuiuslibet gradus custodie deputauerit... sic de quibusdam gradibus*) reflects in content one of the decrees transmitted from the 1095 counciol of Clermont, celebrated by Pope Urban II. See SOMERVILLE, *Councils* (as in n. 8) p. 81, c. 30 as well as the text given in n. 119 on p. 81f. The texts are found without rubric or inscription.

[40] On fol. 221r under the inscription *De VIIa sinodo* Can. Apostolorum c. 30 against lay investiture is cited in part. The source for the mutilated quotation cannot be determined, but since it is found among the *Trip.* excerpts, Trip. A/part 2.14.6 (Ms Paris, BN lat. 3858 B, fol. 90rb) is one hypothetical possibility.

[41] Two excerpts, perhaps from sermons, on fol. 220v could not be identified. 1) inc. *Intelligat Iob qui debet equo animo... etiam stercora existimauit;* 2) *Habebat Dominus loculos... nichil pecunie seruetur.* The Beneventan text transcribed in n. 5 above belongs also to the odds and ends on these final folios.

[42] For *sermo* 88 see MIGNE PL 38, here cap. 18 (col. 549) *A malis corde semper... insultanter arguatis* and cap. 22 (col. 553) *Recedite, recedite... ore non parcere.* The *Liber de perfectione iustitie hominis* is edited in CSEL vol. 32. The excerpts in Ms Vall. F. 54 form a sequence beginning with 4.9 in its entirety (pp. 8f) and include 6.13 (p. 12), 7.16 (p. 14,3-20), 8.17-18 (p. 15,10 - p. 16,22), 8.19 (p. 18,1-19), 9.20 (p. 20, 13-23), 10.21 (p. 21,5 - p. 22,8), 11.23 (p. 24,9-12), 11.24-25 (p. 24,20 - 25,17) and, this is only partially legible, 11.28 (p. 26f.).

been investigated, but the *Coll. Ambrosiana 1*, analyzed by G. Picasso,[43] throws some light on the quite different approach to Deusdedit found in Vall. III. The Milanese compilers relied on the cardinal's collection to furnish a dossier on the primacy of the see of Rome in search for support of their position in the Anacletian schism. Val. III in contrast omitted all reference to the Patrimony of St. Peter, for instance the imperial donations (Deusd. 3.184), or to prerogatives that were only applicable to the Roman church and clergy. The orientation of Val. III is extremely practical, guided by the necessities of the administration of a diocese. Abstract discussions on the validity of sacraments bestowed by unworthy priests, for instance, are entirely lacking as are the theological passages that permeate the corpus of Ivo's writings. Nevertheless, the selection of excerpts indicated a strong sense of fairness and moral concern for pastoral obligations. Val. III seems an ideal handbook for a bishop or episcopal administrator who, it should be pointed out, was very well educated indeed.

---

[43] G. Picasso, *Collezioni canoniche Milanesi del secolo XII* (Milan 1969), here especially p. 171ff.

ADDENDA AND CORRIGENDA

Only references to particularly relevant recent literature will be given for each article.

I. EIN NEUER TEXT FÜR DAS REIMSER KONZIL

Jacques Hourlier, 'Anselme de Saint-Remy, Histoire de la dédicace de Saint-Remy', *La Champagne bénédictine* (Travaux de la Académie nationale de Reims 160; Reims 1981).

II. CODEX GUARNERIUS 203

p. 13, line one: replace *only three* by *none of the*
Robert Kretzschmar, *Alger von Lüttichs Traktat* De misericordia et iustitia: *Ein kanonistischer Konkordanzversuch aus der Zeit des Investiturstreits* (Quellen und Forschungen zum Recht im Mittelalter 2; Sigmaringen 1985), pp. 86–92.
Claudia Märtl, "Ein angeblicher Text zum Bußgang von Canossa 'De paenitentia regum'," *Deutsches Archiv* 38 (1982), pp. 555–63.
For the Lateran council of 1059 (p. 19) see: Rudolf Schieffer, *Die Entstehung des päpstlichen Investiturverbots für den deutschen König* (MGH Schriften 28; Stuttgart 1981).
Detlev Jasper, *Das Papstwahldekret von 1059: Überlieferung und Textgestalt* (Beiträge zur Geschichte und Quellenkunde des Mittelalters 12; Sigmaringen 1986).
Hans-Georg Krause, 'Die Bedeutung der neuentdeckten handschriftlichen Überlieferung des Papstwahldekrets von 1059,' *Zeitschrift der Savigny-Stiftung für Rechtsgeschichte, kan. Abt.* 76 (1990). pp. 89–134.
Linda Fowler-Magerl, 'Fine Distinctions and the Transmission of Texts,' *Zeitschrift der Savigny-Stiftung für Rechtsgeschichte. kan. Abt.* 83 (1997), pp. 146–186.

III. CANOSSA AND ROYAL IDEOLOGY

Claudia Märtl, "Ein angeblicher Text," (as chapter II) identified the text *de paenitentia regum* as excerpt from a theological sentence collection on the penance of Salomon, widely known and copied in the first half of the twelfth century but originating c. 400 A.D.

IV. FÄLSCHUNGEN BEI KANONISTEN

p. 255, line eleven from above: replace *auctritatis* by *auctoritatis*

Linda Fowler-Magerl, 'Fine Distinctions and the Transmission of Texts,' *Zeitschrift der Savigny-Stiftung für Rechtsgeschichte. kan. Abt.* 83 (1997), pp. 146–186.

Rudolf Schieffer, *Die Entstehung des päpstlichen Investiturverbots für den deutschen König* (MGH Schriften 28; Stuttgart 1981).

Claudia Märtl, ed., *Die falschen Investiturprivilegien* (MGH Fontes iuris germanici antiqui in usum scholarum 13; Hannover 1986).

V. ROM IN DER KANONISTIK

p. 39, line six from above: replace *Brief* by *Briefs*

Detlev Jasper, *Das Papstwahldekret von 1059* (Sigmaringen 1986) (as chapter II).

Linda Fowler-Magerl, "Fine Distinctions and the Transmission of Texts," (as chapter IV).

Peter Landau, "Erweiterte Fassungen der Kanonessammlung des Anselm von Lucca aus dem 12. Jahrhundert," in: *Sant'Anselmo, Mantova e la lotta per le investiture* (Atti del convegno internazionale di studi [Mantova 23–25 maggio 1986], ed. Paolo Golinelli; Bologna 1987), pp. 323–37. Other papers in the volume are also relevant.

Gérard Fransen, 'Anselme de Lucques canoniste?', in: *Sant'Anselmo vescovo di Lucca (1073–1086) nel quadro delle trasformazioni sociali e della riforma ecclesiastica*, ed. Cinzio Violante (Rome 1992), pp. 143–55 with other relevant papers in the conference proceedings.

VI. HISTORY AND TRADITION

J. Ruysschaert, 'Le tableau Mariotti de la mosaique absidale del'ancien s.-Pierre,' *Atti Pontif. Accademia Romana di Archeologia: Rendiconti* 40 (1968), pp. 295–317.

VII. CONCILIAR CANONS AND MANUSCRIPTS

p. 359, line four from below: replace *ecumenical* by *œcumenical*.

p. 368, line eight from below: replace in parenthesis *B N Nac* by *Bibl. Nac.*

Hans-Georg Krause, 'Die Bedeutung der neuentdeckten handschriftlichen Überlieferungen des Papstwahldekrets von 1059,' (as chapter II).

Linda Fowler-Magerl, 'Vier französische und spanische vorgratianische Kanonessammlungen,' in: *Ius commune* 21 (Festgabe Helmut Coing; Frankfurt am Main 1984), pp. 123–46.

Linda Fowler-Magerl, 'Fine Distinctions and the Transmission of Texts,' (as chapter IV).

Robert Somerville with the collaboration of Stephan Kuttner, *Pope Urban II, the Collectio Britannica and the Council of Melfi* (1089) (Oxford 1996).

VIII. SOME NOTES ON PAPAL POLICIES

Glauco Maria Cantarella, *Ecclesiologia e politica nel papato di Pasquale II* (Istituto Storico Italiano per il Medio Aevo, Studi storici 131; Rome 1982).
Glauco Maria Cantarella, *La costruzione della verità. Pasquale II. un papa alle strette* (Istituto Storico Italiano per il Medio Aevo, Studi storici 178–79; Rome 1987).
Carlo Servatius, *Paschalis II. (1099–1118)* (Päpste und Papsttum 14; Stuttgart 1979).
Stefan Beulertz, *Das Verbot der Laieninvestitur im Investiturstreit* (MGH Studien und Texte 2; Hannover 1991).
Claudia Märtl, ed. *Die falschen Investiturprivilegien* (Hannover 1986) (as chapter IV).
Peter Landau, Erweiterte Fassungen der Kanonessammlung des Anselm von Lucca aus dem 12. Jahrhundert, (as chapter V).

IX. PATRIMONIA AND REGALIA

David Whitton, "The *Annales Romani* and codex Vaticanus latinus 1984," *Bullettino dell'Istituto Storico Italiano* 84 (1972/73), pp. 125–44.
Paola Supino-Martini, *Roma e l'area grafica romanesca (secoli X–XII)* (Biblioteca di scrittura e civiltà 1; Alessandria 1987).
Claudia Märtl, ed. *Die falschen Investiturprivilegien* (Hanover 1986) (as chapter IV).

X. OPPOSITION TO POPE PASCHAL II

Rudolf Schieffer, *Die Entstehung des päpstlichen Investiturverbots* (Stuttgart 1981) (as chapter II).
Carlo Servatius, *Paschalis II.* (Stuttgart 1979) (as chapter VIII).
Stefan Beulertz, *Das Verbot der Laieninvestitur im Investiturstreit* (Hanover 1991) (as chapter VIII).
Giorgio Picasso, Testi canonistici nel Liber de honore ecclesiae di Placido di Nonantola,' *Studia Gratiana* 20 (Melanges G. Fransen 2; Rome 1976), pp. 289–308.
Jörg W. Busch, *Der Liber de Honore Ecclesiae des Placidus von Nonantola: Eine kanonistische Problemerörterung aus dem Jahre 1111* (Quellen und Forschungen zum Recht im Mittelalter 5, Sigmaringen 1990).

XI. PAPAL PRIMACY

p. 74, last line: replace *Archbihop* by *Archbishop*

Stefan Beulertz, *Das Verbot der Laieninvestitur im Investiturstreit* (Hanover 1991) (as chapter VIII).
Peter Landau, 'Erweiterte Fassungen der Kanonessammlung des Anselm von Lucca aus dem 12. Jahrhundert,' (as chapter V).

XII. DECREES AND DECRETALS

Liber canonum diuersorum sanctorum patrum siue Collectio in CLXXXIII titulos digesta, ed. Joseph Motta (Monumenta iuris canonici ser. B, 7; Vatican City 1988) should be added to the bibliography on p. 26, n. 55. Motta's date is correct for the Paschal materials are indeed additions made to the codex.

XIV. THE CORRESPONDENCE OF POPE PASCHAL II

Stefan Beulertz, *Das Verbot der Laieninvestitur im Investiturstreit* (Hanover 1991) (as chapter VIII).

XV. PAPAL REGISTERS

Robert Somerville with Stephan Kuttner, *Pope Urban II, the 'Collectio Britannica' and the Council of Melfi (1089)* (as chapter VII).
Michael Horn, *Studien zum Pontifikat Papst Eugens III. (1145–1153)*, Diss., Mainz 1987.

XVIII. AN EPISCOPAL HANDBOOK

Martin Brett, Urban II and the collections attributed to Ivo of Chartres, in S. Chodorow, ed., *Proceedings of the Eighth International Congress of Medieval Canon Law* (Monumenta iuris canonici, Subsidia 7; Vatican City 1985), pp. 1–21.
Linda Fowler-Magerl, 'Fine Distinctions', (as chapter II).
Robert Somerville with Stephan Kuttner, *Pope Urban II, the Collectio Britannica and the Council of Melfi (1089)* (as chapter VII).

INDEX

This index omits editions and their apparatus and item XII, 'Decrees and Decretals of Pope Paschal II in Twelfth-Century Canonical Collections,' entirely, since it is an index itself. Footnotes are not included with the exception of papal letters (in the case of item XI it is a selection) and manuscripts. The abbreviations JK, JE, and JL refer to the second edition of Ph. Jaffé's *Regesta pontificum romanorum* (Leipzig 1885 and 1888); abp = archbishop; pr.= priest; abt = abbot; bp = bishop; card = cardinal; k = king.